Monographs on oceanographic methodology 5

In this series:

Coral reefs: research methods

Edited by D. R. Stoddart and R. E. Johannes

The designations employed and the
presentation of the material in this
work do not imply the expression of any
opinion whatsoever on the part of Unesco
concerning the legal status of any country or
territory, or of its authorities, or concerning
the delimitations of the frontiers of any
country or territory.

Published in 1978 by the United Nations
Educational, Scientific and Cultural Organization,
7 Place de Fontenoy, 75700 Paris
Printed by Page Brothers (Norwich) Ltd.

ISBN 92-3-101491-9

Printed in the United Kingdom

Preface

The wealth and diversity of the fauna and flora found in and around coral reefs makes these areas a fascinating subject for research. However, the complex nature of the reef environment renders it particularly susceptible to external influence, which is often deleterious.

From the earliest times, atolls and other coastal coral reef formations have been used for recreation, as a source of food and of material for crafts. Man's curiosity has been stimulated by the beauty and mystery of coral reefs and, until quite recently, human activities have caused little damage as they have been, for the most part, in harmony with the reef ecosystem. This situation, however, is changing rapidly.

Protection of coral reefs is becoming increasingly difficult because the areas in which they are found, particularly near the coast, are used as sites for tourism, industry and resource exploitation. Already in the Red Sea area coral reefs have been threatened by oil spills; in the Caribbean, spear fishing has been so intensive that the larger reef fishes have almost disappeared; and in other areas, similar encroachments have been made by man. Despite the considerable research which has been carried out on coral reef communities, human influence on this environment is proceeding faster than our understanding of the ecological changes that are taking place.

To encourage the scientific community to accelerate research in this area, Unesco is developing a programme of international co-operation with the Scientific Committee on Oceanic Research and the International Association of Biological Oceanography. As a first step, the present volume, fifth in the series of Monographs on Oceanographic Methodology, has been published to assist scientists in their understanding of the basic techniques required for research on the quantitative ecology of coral reefs and to recommend those methods which have proven most effective.

Unesco expresses its thanks to the editors, D. R. Stoddart and R. E. Johannes, for their expertise and guidance in bringing this text to print.

The scientific opinions expressed in this work are those of the authors and are not necessarily those of Unesco. Equipment and materials noted in the text are given as examples of those most currently used during the experimental

v

phase of SCOR Working Group 35 and their inclusion does not imply that they should be considered as preferable to others available at that time or developed since.

Contents

Introduction

The preparation of this Monograph arose initially from the need for a revision of the *Handbook for Atoll Research,* issued in a preliminary trial edition in May 1951 and in a second preliminary edition in May 1953 (Fosberg and Sachet, 1953). This had developed from a Symposium on Coral Atoll Research organized by the Pacific Science Board of the National Academy of Sciences—National Research Council, held at the University of Hawaii, Honolulu, in February 1951, and it served as a basic statement of techniques for the highly successful series of coral atoll expeditions sponsored by the Pacific Science Board during the 1950's, to such sites as Arno, Onotoa, Kapingamarangi, Raroia and Ifaluk. Twenty-six authors contributed to the *Handbook,* which included sections on geography, meteorology, geology, hydrology, soils, botany, zoology, marine ecology, anthropology, and the organization of expeditions.

Interest in the study of coral reefs greatly expanded as a result of the impetus given by the Pacific Science Board expeditions and related investigations, and also changed in character. The initial period of largely reconnaissance investigations was followed by an increasing concern with quantitative methods of measuring and recording ecological data (Stoddart, 1969), and also, following the innovative study by Odum and Odum (1955), with studies of the functional ecology of reefs. These latter, in particular, led to increasing concern with analytical methods and the development of many new techniques (e.g. Johannes *et al., 1972*).

Several of these problems were discussed during the Symposium on Corals and Coral Reefs organized by the Marine Biological Association of India and held at Mandapam Camp in January 1969. Two papers at this meeting were concerned with field problems of quantitative recording of data (Stoddart, 1972; Scheer, 1972), and Johannes and others discussed functional aspects of reef ecosystems (e.g. Kinsey, 1972; Nair and Pillai, 1972). It became clear that some standardization of methods was required to ensure comparability of results between different reef areas. This need was informally discussed with officers of the International Association for Biological Oceanography (G. Hempel, R. I. Currie, and T. Wolff) during the Symposium on the Biology of the Indian Ocean at Kiel, Germany, in April 1971, when it was suggested that a working group might be set up to consider the problems and to make recommendations for standardized procedures in reef studies. This suggestion was adopted, and at an Executive Meeting in Madrid in May 1971 the Scientific Committee on Oceanic Research (SCOR) set up Working Group 35 for this purpose. The terms of reference of the Group were:

1. To identify the major scientific problems in the quantitative ecology of coral reefs;
2. To evaluate and test existing methods for the quantitative description of abundance, composition and distribution of benthic invertebrate communities on reefs;
3. To recommend standard field techniques suitable for the problems identified under (1) above; and
4. To consider the need for a future symposium on the quantitative ecology and productivity of coral reefs.

The members of the Working Group (with their affiliations at that time) were Dr. D. R. Stoddart, chairman (Department of Geography, Cambridge University); Dr. R. E. Johannes (Department of Zoology, University of Georgia); Prof. K. Konishi (Kanazawa University, Japan); Dr Y. Loya (State University of New York, Stony Brook, New York); Dr M. Pichon (Station marine d'Endoume, Marseille); Dr G. Scheer (Hessisches Landesmuseum, Darmstadt); and Dr. F. Talbot (The Australian Museum, Sydney).

The Group began work by correspondence, and in November 1971 three members (Stoddart, Johannes and Talbot) met during a meeting organized by the Smithsonian Institution on Glover's Reef, Belize (British Honduras), at which a number of other contributors to the present volume were also present. The formal terms of reference were broadened in several respects: to include benthic plants as well as invertebrates; to include the infauna as well as the surface biota of both hard and soft substrata in the reef environment; to include other groups of importance in the reef economy, most notably the fish; and, most important, to give greater emphasis to methods of studying the functioning of reefs as well as morphology and distributions. On this basis, the members of the Working Group prepared a series of position papers during 1972, with the intention of arranging a formal meeting at which they could be discussed. Progress was reported to the General Meeting of SCOR at Oban, Scotland, in September 1972, and SCOR then agreed to support a working meeting in Queensland at the time of the Second International Symposium on Coral Reefs.

This meeting was held at the Research Station on Heron Island during 2–10 July 1973, immediately following the Symposium. All the members of the Working Group were present, together with the following additional participants: Dr N. Gundermann (South Pacific Commission, Nouméa, New Caledonia); Dr P. Hutchings (The Australian Museum, Sydney); Dr D. W. Kinsey (Mauri Brothers and Thompson, Sydney); Dr D. H. H. Kühlmann (Humboldt Universität, Berlin, German Democratic Republic); Dr E. Lovell

(University of Queensland, Brisbane); Dr J. Marsh (The Marine Laboratory, University of Guam, Guam); Dr and Mrs J. Porter (University of Michigan, Ann Arbor, Michigan); Dr B. Russell (The Australian Museum, Sydney); Dr H. Schuhmacher (Ruhr Universität, Bochum, Germany); Dr B. Thomassin (Station marine d'Endoume, Marseille); Dr C. C. Wallace (The Queensland Museum, Brisbane); and Dr M. Wijsman-Best (Rijksmuseum, Leiden, Holland). The workshop was made possible by permission of the Heron Island Board and the Great Barrier Reef Committee. It received much help from the Director of the Heron Island Research Station, Dr Klaus Rohde; from Dr B. Russell, who acted as local organizer; and from the Secretary of the Great Barrier Reef Committee, Dr P. Mather. The purpose of the meeting was to plan the present handbook, to consider the responsibility for different sections, and to give members of the workshop an opportunity to test various methods on the reefs of Heron Island and adjacent islands, on the basis of the preliminary papers already circulated. Dr Talbot was able to arrange for most members to visit the Australian Museum Field Station on One Tree Island, and to make the Station's boat available in logistic support.

A provisional contents list for the present publication was drawn up during this meeting, and Dr Johannes assumed editorial responsibility for Part III of the volume. Most of the contributions were written during 1974 and 1975, and a final contents list was circulated in December 1975. The Working Group reported to the 12th General Meeting of SCOR, held in Guayaquil, Ecuador, in December 1974, where it was clear that the Group had fulfilled its commission. SCOR therefore terminated the Working Group, but requested the members to constitute an editorial committee to remain in being until the final results were published. It was also proposed at this meeting that the contributions be published in the series of UNESCO Monographs in Oceanographic Methodology.

The contents of this Monograph are both narrower and wider than those of the 1953 *Handbook for Atoll Research*. In the first place no attempt is made to include the terrestrial ecology of coral islands; on the other, the treatment of the functional ecology of coral reefs is vastly extended. There are gaps in the coverage, some resulting from the non-appearance of promised manuscripts, but others because it seemed unnecessary to duplicate here the kinds of technical advice readily available in other publications on collecting and preserving plants and animals (e.g. Knudsen, 1966), on the chemical analysis of sea-water (Strickland and Parsons, 1968), and on the study of the meiofauna (Hulings and Gray, 1971). At least two of the International Biological Programme Handbooks (Vollenweider, 1969; Holme and McIntyre, 1971) are of direct relevance to the study of reefs, and to some extent make it unnecessary to expand the coverage of this volume. Other technical manuals which supplement information contained herein include those of Forstner and Rützler (1970) and of High and Hanna (1970).

This Monograph on coral reefs has now been in active preparation for some time, and we are grateful to the earlier contributors for their patience in waiting for publication. Some of the ground covered here has also been covered in recently published work, for example by Laxton and Stablum (1974) and by Dart and Rainbow (1976).

The Editors wish to thank the members of Working Group 35 and all the other contributors for their assistance; SCOR for practical support, especially for the Heron Island meeting; and UNESCO for assuming responsibility for publication. We thank Dr Stevenson Buchan for major editorial assistance; Sir Eric Smith and Dr P. Spencer Davies for critical review; and Mr R. I. Currie, Mr G. E. Hemmen, Prof. G. Hempel, Prof. Warren Wooster, and Dr T. Wolff for their aid and encouragement. Lastly we thank Dr F. R. Fosberg and Dr M.-H. Sachet, the editors of the 1953 *Handbook,* whose contributions to coral reef studies on many levels have contributed much to the present state-of-the-art.

D. R. Stoddart

References

DART, J. K. G.; RAINBOW, P. S. 1976. Some underwater techniques for estimating echinoderm populations. In: E. A. Drew, J. N. Lythgoe and J. D. Woods (eds). *Underwater research.* London, Academic Press, p. 303–11.

FORSTNER, H.; RÜTZLER, K. 1970. Measurement of the micro-climate in littoral marine habitats. *Oceanogr. Mar. Biol. Ann. Rev.* vol. 8, p. 225–40.

FOSBERG, F. R.; SACHET, M.-H. (eds). 1953. Handbook for atoll research (2nd prelim. edit). *Atoll Res. Bull.,* vol. 17, p. 1–129.

HIGH, C.; HANNA, E. K. 1970. A method for the direct measurement of erosion of rock surfaces. *Br. geomorph. Res. Gp Tech. Bull.,* vol. 5.

HOLME, N. A.; MCINTYRE, A. D. (eds). 1971. *Methods for the study of marine benthos.* Oxford, Blackwell Scientific Publications. (IBP Handbook no. 16) (334 p.).

HULINGS, N. C.; GRAY, J. S. 1971. A manual for the study of meiofauna. *Smithsonian Contr. Zool.* vol. 78, i–xii, p. 1–84.

JOHANNES R. E.; ALBERTS, J.; D'ELIA, C.; KINZIE, R. A.; POMEROY, L. R.; SOTTILE, W.; WIEBE, W.; MARSH, J. A., Jr.; HELFRICH, P.; MARAGOS, J.; MEYER, J.; SMITH, S.; CRABTREE, D.; ROTH, A.; McCLOSKY, L. R.; BETZER, S.; MARSHALL, N.; PILSON, M. E. Q.; TELEK, G.; CLUTTER, R. I.; DU PAUL, W. D.; WEBB, K. L.; WELLS, J. M., Jr. 1972. The metabolism of some coral reef communities: a team study of nutrient and energy flux at Eniwetok. *BioScience,* vol. 22, p. 541–43.

KINSEY, D. W. 1972. Preliminary observations on community metabolism and primary productivity of the pseudo-atoll reef at One Tree Island, Great Barrier Reef. In: *Proc. Symp. Corals and Coral Reefs (1969).* Mar. Biol. Assoc. India, p. 13–32.

KNUDSEN, J. W. 1966. *Biological techniques: collecting, preserving, and illustrating plants and animals.* New York, Harper and Row (xi + 525 p.).

LAXTON, J. H.; STABLUM, W. J. 1974. Sample design for quantitative estimation of sedentary organisms of coral reefs. *Biol. J. Linn. Soc.,* vol. 6, p. 1–18.

NAIR, P. V. R.; PILLAI, C. S. G. 1972. Primary productivity of some coral reefs in the Indian seas. In: *Proc. Symp. corals and coral reefs (1969). Mar. Biol. Assoc. India,* p. 33–42.

ODUM, H. T.; ODUM, E. P. 1955. Trophic structure and productivity of a windward coral reef community at Eniwetok Atoll. *Ecol. Monogr.* vol. 25, p. 291–320.

SCHEER, G. 1972. Investigations of coral reefs in the Maldive Islands with notes on lagoon patch reefs and the method of coral scoiology. In: *Proc. Symp. Corals and Coral Reefs (1969).* Mar. Biol. Assoc. India, p. 87–120.

STODDART, D. R. 1969. Ecology and morphology of recent coral reefs. *Biol. Rev. Camb. Philos. Soc.* vol. 44, p. 433–98.

——1972. Field methods in the study of coral reefs. In *Proc. Symp. Corals and Coral Reefs* (*1969*). Mar. Biol. Assoc. India, p. 71–80.

STRICKLAND, J. D. H.; PARSONS, T. R. 1968. A practical handbook of seawater analysis. *Bull. Fish. Res. Bd Can.*, vol. 167, (311 p.).

VOLLENWEIDER, R. A. (ed). 1969. *A manual on methods for measuring primary production in aquatic environments*. Oxford, Blackwell Scientific Publications. (IBP Handbook no. 12) (224 p.).

Part I

Morphology and structure

Introduction

D. R. Stoddart

A basic concern in reef studies is to define the geometry of the reef, both externally (as a surface) and internally (as a complex three-dimensional geological structure). The methods used are heavily constrained by the nature of the reef environment, especially by wave energy and tidal range, but all are adaptations of standard techniques for mapping, drilling, dating, analysing sediments, and determining various physical parameters. Nevertheless many of the papers in this section contain substantial advances over the methods described in the *Handbook for Atoll Research* (Fosberg and Sachet 1953).

Aerial photographs have been much used at a reconnaissance level in reef studies since 1945. Satellite imagery and the use of colour and infra-red film have greatly extended the range of information which can be extracted from this source, as Hopley shows in chapter 3. Rützler (Chapter 4) also demonstrates how work on individual reefs can be greatly assisted by low-level large-scale air photography controlled from the ground.

The study of reef geology has been revolutionised in the last twenty years by the use of radiocarbon dating. However, few workers have fully appreciated the ambiguities of the method and the errors which can result from inadequate sampling. Chappell and Thom (Chapter 8) provide criteria which should be followed before any material from the reef is dated. Many samples for dating are obtained by drilling, and relatively inexpensive techniques both for surface and submarine drilling are described by Thom (Chapter 6) and Macintyre (Chapter 7). No special attention is given here to geophysical methods, because these are not specific to reef environments.

The chapter by Pugh (Chapter 9) describes a new and highly reliable method of obtaining accurate tidal information on atolls. There is certainly scope for more information on the measurement of other physical parameters on reefs. As this book was in preparation, such techniques began to be developed by S. P. Murray, H. H. Roberts and their colleagues at the Coastal Studies Institute, Louisiana State University (Roberts *et al.*, 1975), but again the technology is not specific to the reef environment and is therefore not considered here.

3

References

Fosberg, F. R.; Sachet, M.-H. 1953. Handbook for atoll research (2nd prelim. edit.) *Atoll Res. Bull.* vol. 17, p. 1–129.

Roberts, H. H.; Murray, S. P.; Suhayda, J. N. 1975. Physical processes in a fringing reef system. *J. mar. Res.* vol. 33, p. 233–60.

1

Descriptive reef terminology

D. R. Stoddart[1]

INTRODUCTION

The basis for existing descriptive reef terminology derives largely from the American studies in the Marshall Islands after the Second World War and the subsequent series of Pacific Science Board expeditions to atolls in the Gilberts, Carolines, and Tuamotus. Terms were codified and related to an idealized transect of an atoll by Ladd, Tracey, Wells and Emery (1950), and were defined both explicitly and implicitly in greater detail by Emery, Tracey and Ladd (1954) and by Wells (1957). These workers were concerned to provide physiographic, sedimentological and ecological categories which would be useful in the field recognition and description of similar units elsewhere; and the use of their terminology led, for example, to the widespread search for and discovery of such features as algal ridges and groove-and-spur.

Their scheme derived mainly from the Marshall Islands, and primarily from Bikini Atoll. It was also related to a particular scale of investigation (mainly features which could be mapped at scales of 1 : 1,000 to 1 : 50,000). Since the 1950's there has been a great expansion of reef studies, within the Pacific, the Indian Ocean and the Caribbean. It has become apparent that the Marshall Islands terminology does not apply equally well to all reef areas, and that the features recognized in the Marshall Islands do not necessarily have analogues elsewhere. As a result, many reef workers have felt compelled either to coin new terms, or to re-define old ones, and this has already led to considerable and avoidable confusion. Only one systematic attempt has been made (for the reefs of southwest Madagascar) to draw up a scheme of terminology comparable to that developed for the Marshall Islands (Clausade *et al.*, 1971).

There is no comprehensive glossary of reef terms generally available. One major effort (Fairbridge and Fosberg, *in litt.*), based on a retrospective analysis of usage in the reef literature, remains in manuscript and now needs revision. A recent work by Battistini *et al.* (1975) proposes a series of French terms, with English and German equivalents, for features encountered in

1. Department of Geography, Cambridge University, Cambridge CB2 3EN, United Kingdom.

Madagascar, New Caledonia, the Society Islands, and the Tuamotus, but does not relate these to terms already in common use. Because of the complexity and extent of the problem, it would not be a useful exercise to propose recommended standard terms here. Instead, this note considers and illustrates some of the problems inherent in the provision of an accepted terminology, and outlines criteria which terms need to meet before they are acceptable. The criteria were suggested at a discussion on reef terminology held during the Second International Symposium on Coral Reefs in June 1973, when contributions were also made by J. I. Tracey, Jr., M. Pichon, and L. S. Land, and at which A. Guilcher, G. Scheer and I. G. Macintyre participated.

PROBLEMS

Ambiguities

The fundamental problem in supplying a terminology for reefs is that it is, in effect, a taxonomy of reef forms, but a taxonomy derived from imperfect and perhaps biased knowledge of the range and complexity of reef phenomena. The difficulty is compounded by the fact that many workers seek to make their terms more powerful by making them genetic as well as generic, a habit which has a long history in the earth sciences (Davis, 1909). Not surprisingly, in the first case, it is frequently found that terms have either been too broadly defined, in the sense of including diverse forms within a single category, or too narrowly defined, in the sense of leaving intermediate forms unlabelled. In the second case it is frequently discovered that similar forms can have dissimilar origins, and that form alone is an ambiguous guide to genesis.

These two problems may be briefly illustrated. Darwin (1842) distinguished three main types of reefs: atolls, barrier reefs, and fringing reefs, linked together in a genetic sequence (though he did also recognize that his mechanism of subsidence of foundations was not the only means by which such reef forms could be generated). For many workers, however, terms such as *atoll* came to carry a heavy theoretical loading, implying a necessary history of Darwinian subsidence for the term to be validly used. This led many, recognizing such forms but disagreeing over origins, into terminological difficulties. The literature was thus invaded by a series of terms applicable to grossly similar forms but which aimed to be theory-free. *Pseudo-atoll* and *pseudo atoll* were used by Agassiz (1898, p. 105) and Forbes (1893, p. 545) for ring-shaped reefs not formed by subsidence. The same term was used by Newell and Rigby (1957, p. 25) for a ring-shaped 'reef' not of coral origin (originally termed a *pseudatoll* by Verrill (1900, p. 319), and further confusion was added by Mergner's (1971, p. 154) use of *pseudoatoll* for what is usually termed a microatoll. Similarly Molengraaff (1930, p. 56) used *pseudo-barrier-reef* for a barrier not formed by subsidence, and Fairbridge (1950, p. 337) the same term for such a reef not formed of coral. Such terms carried with them other usages, such as *pseudo-lagoon*, used either for the shallow lagoons of pseudo-atolls (Hedley and Taylor, 1908) or for

6

lagoons formed by barriers not composed of coral (Pichon, 1971, p. 187). Comparable terms in the reef literature which seek to avoid the apparent genetic implications of established terms include *pseudo-platform* (Steers, 1937, p. 8), *pseudo-beachrock* (Russell, 1971, p. 2345), *pseudo-pellet* (Fahraeus *et al.,* 1974, p. 27), *pseudo-oolite* (Carozzi, 1960), *pseudo-stalactite* and *pseudo-stalagmite* (Stoddart, 1969, p. 400), and *pseudo-reef* (McKee *et al.,* 1959, p. 556).

A comparable but more confused series is provided by the *almost*-terms Davis (1920, p. 292) introduced *almost-atoll* for atolls with small residual non-coral islands; the genetic implication was clearly that Darwinian subsidence had almost proceeded far enough to change a reef-encircled volcanic island into an atoll. Wiens (1962, p. 100) used the same term, however, for volcanoes which had subsided too rapidly for reefs to be maintained at the surface; his usage is thus technically counterfactual. Stearns (1946, p. 251) introduced *near-atoll* for Davis's original almost-atoll, but this same term was subsequently used with a quite different meaning (of reef bodies with incomplete sea-level rims) by Fairbridge (1950, p. 345) and MacNeil (1954, p. 395). MacNeil then introduced *semiatoll* as a synonym for Davis's almost-atoll (1954, p. 395), even though Fairbridge had already used this term as an equivalent to MacNeil's *table reef* and Agassiz (1894, p. 146) had pre-empted it as equivalent to pseudo atoll in the sense of an atoll not formed by Darwinian subsidence. Other *almost* terms include *almost barrier reef, almost platform reef* and *almost table reef* (Tayama, 1952, p. 221, p. 277), though these are less commonly used.

Descriptive measures

Few purely descriptive terms are in use in reef studies, and this lack corresponds with a poverty in development of quantitative morphometric indices. Tayama (1952) pioneered the measurement of components of entire reefs (e.g. length, width, circumference), Stoddart (1965) the use of shape indices such as form ratios, circularity and elongation measures, and an ellipticity index, all applied to atolls, and Maxwell (1968) orientation measures. Less work has been done on patterns within reefs, partly because of the limitations imposed by availability of data. Roy (1970) at Kaneohe Bay, Oahu, used measures of point density and orientation to describe patch-reef pattern, and these techniques were used in an heuristic context in different environmental conditions at Fanning Atoll by Roy and Smith (1971). Strahler's hypsometric integral has been used to describe the degree to which lagoon floors form basins in the Maldives and Chagos atolls (Stoddart, 1971), though no-one has so far applied to atolls the battery of techniques developed to describe the topography of lake floors (Håkanson, 1974). On a larger topographic scale several authors have developed essentially similar indices of topographic diversity based on the ratios of actual to projected areal or linear measures: these include the T index of Risk (1972), the SI index of Dahl (1973), and the 'hole count' and 'string measures' of Goldman (1973). Roberts (1974) has also used a variety of quantitative measures (spur frequency, percentage cover, orientation index, crenulation index) in studying and defining

7

the features of groove-and-spur systems on Grand Cayman. For a review of the field of available techniques which might be used to give definition to descriptive reef terms, see Mark (1975), Håkanson (1974), and Clark and Gaile (1973).

Meanwhile, most workers continue to use terms descriptive of distinctive pattern (e.g. *dispersed, anastomosing, cellular, reticulate, mesh*) but these are rarely defined except intuitively or by reference to air photographs.

Genetic indicators

Two main attempts have been made in recent years to develop and extend a middle-scale descriptive reef terminology with direct genetic implications. One is that of Maxwell (1968, 1970) for reefs of the Great Barrier system, the other is that of Garrett *et al.* (1971) for smaller patch reefs at Bermuda.

Maxwell's taxonomy (Fig. 1) was based on 'shape, morphological zonation and central structure' and provided a series of categories of reefs differentiated by surface form which could be arranged in a development sequence as a result of processes of either symmetrical or asymmetrical growth. His major classes included *wall reef* (previously usually called *ribbon reef*), *cuspate reef, prong reef, plug reef, resorbed reef, remnant reef, platform reef,* and *lagoon platform reef.* Some of these terms are overtly descriptive of form (cuspate, plug), others of origin (remnant, resorbed). In the absence of information on the internal structure of the reefs Maxwell's sequential order of development must be largely inferential, and in the absence of information on rates of growth and erosion and of the chronology of sea-level change can only be speculative. Insofar as some of his terms describe widespread reef forms hitherto un-named, and now defined with reference to type-examples on air photographs, his terms are likely to be widely used irrespective of the particular genetic connotation he gave them: they are in practice being used as generic rather than genetic terms.

Garrett *et al.* (1971) distinguish various types of patch reefs in terms of size, depth, planimetric shape, and profile. These include *knob reefs, pinnacle reefs, mesa reefs, cellular reefs,* and *microatoll reefs* (the last term introduced without regard to pre-existing usage: Stoddart and Scoffin, 1978). The terms are overtly descriptive, and are defined descriptively rather than morphometrically, but they are linked in a genetic sequence which generates characteristics which are diagnostic of each type. It is noticeable that the terms are applied *de novo,* without considering earlier usage; that the patch-reef classification so defined is based only on Bermuda examples; and that as the authors themselves state 'there are many intermediates between these types'. Clearly in these circumstances there is considerable scope for extension, modification and redefinition of the terms proposed.

CRITERIA FOR TERMINOLOGY

In our general state of ignorance of reef genesis and development, the absence

8

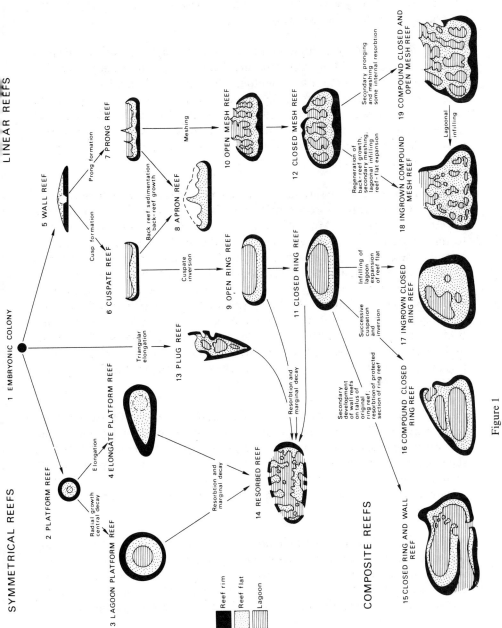

Figure 1
Taxonomy and terminology of reefs, after Maxwell (1970).

of any well-developed quantitative descriptive morphometry, and the clear inadequacy, arising from a variety of causes, of many existing descriptive terms, criteria are needed by which both existing and new terms can be judged. Such criteria might include the following points.

Explicit definition. Any term should be clearly, concisely, and explicitly defined on being introduced. Many reef terms are defined only contextually; some are defined only with reference to a photograph or figure. Examples of terms in common use for several years before being formally defined are *drop-off* and *sill reef* (see Goreau and Goreau, 1973, p. 415; and Goreau and Burke, 1966, for definitions). In some cases an undefined form is attributed by implication to an undefined process and becomes widely used in spite of this; an example is *resorbed reef.*

Singular definition. There should be a one-to-one correspondence between term and form. Often terms are proposed which apply to forms of different magnitudes, as with *groove-and-spur.* Much of the early controversy about the nature of this feature arose because a variety of forms (differing in topography as well as origin) were confused under a single label. As a result, terms such as *buttress* in the Tuamotus and Jamaica (Morrison, 1954, p. 18; 1959, p. 76) and *bastion* at Aldabra (Barnes *et al.,* 1971, p. 89) have been introduced to differentiate similar but distinct features. In the Persian Gulf groove-and-spur forms have been reported at three different scale intervals (Kendall and Skipwith, 1969, p. 882). Zankl and Schroeder (1972, p. 526) consider that problems of form, scale, and origin have now become so confused that groove-and-spur be dropped in favour of a purely descriptive term lacking any genetic implications, *bar and furrow.*

Internally correct. Terms should not be misleading, in terms of form, constitution, or origin. The best-known example of such confusion is the widespread use of *Lithothamnion ridge* for a feature which is generally composed, at least superficially, of species of *Porolithon*; it has now been generally replaced by the more inclusive term *algal ridge,* though in some areas it has been shown that calcareous algae do not constitute the topographic features so named but only veneer them.

Not redundant. There is no point in introducing new names for features already adequately named. The introduction of terms such as *near-atoll* for *almost-atoll* and of various synonyms for *micro-atoll* illustrates redundancy of this kind. The satisfaction of this criterion thus requires a knowledge of previous literature, and would be greatly aided by the existence of a comprehensive glossary.

No radical redefinition. Terms should not be re-introduced into the literature carrying a definition radically different from one already generally accepted. The use of almost-atoll in the sense of a guyot violates this principle as well as that of redundancy, since not only is almost-atoll well-established in quite a different sense, but an alternative term for the feature under discussion is readily available in the term guyot.

Explicit limitation. Once a term is introduced, there is a tendency to extend the range of its usage both descriptively and genetically outside the scope of its original application. This raises questions not only of spatial variations but also of actualistic extensions into the past of present observations. Thus there is a vast literature on the meaning of the term *reef* itself, much of which revolves round the extension of present-day concepts into the geological record (Braithwaite, 1973).

Innocuous. Few terms could be considered offensive; one such is *negro-head* or *nigger-head* (Flinders, 1814, II, p. 88), both much used in the older literature. (It is interesting that Dalrymple in 1782 used *cat's head* for the same feature, but his term was not generally accepted). Both Spender (1930, p. 203) and Stephenson *et al.* (1931, p. 66) suggested as alternatives *coral head* for submerged and *boulder* for emerged forms, both of which were unacceptably wide. Newell (1954, p. 6) robustly substituted *reef block*, a term already used in this sense by Davis (1928, p. 10).

Comparability between languages. Where possible new terms should be usable in a form close to the original in all the major languages of the reef literature (English, German, French), or they should at least be readily translatable. Scheer (1959) provided the first guide to German terms, and also contributed German equivalents to the Anglo-French synonymy provided by Battistini *et al.* (1975). That translation problems have not yet been overcome can be seen by the use of *couloir, glacis* and *banquette* in English equivalents by Clausade *et al.* (1971) and Battistini *et al.* (1975), none of which is in common usage.

ETYMOLOGY

New terms may be coined in a variety of ways, of which three are particularly important.

Vernacular terms. Many terms represent technical redefinitions of ordinary words in common use; examples include *blowhole, blue hole, boiler, ironshore.* Some may themselves have originated in native languages and have been incorporated into a European vernacular before being appropriated for scientific use; thus *bommie* is said to derive from the aboriginal *bombara* in Queensland usage (F. Talbot, pers. comm.).

Local terms. Many terms have been appropriated directly from non-European languages. Atoll itself derives from Maldivian *atolu* (Gardiner, 1931, p. 16,

11

though Hackett (1977) points out that this refers to a political rather than a physiographic unit), and other Maldivian words in common use include *faro, velu* and *kelu*. Danielsson (1954) gives a comprehensive catalogue of Polynesian (Tuamotuan) topographic terms, several of which have been widely adopted for features not otherwise named; these include *feo* (Agassiz, 1903, p. 45), *makatea, motu, kaoa,* and *hoa* (Chevalier, 1972). French Creole provides *barachois, champignon, platin* and *pavé* (Stoddart *et al.* 1971, p. 45), and Spanish *cay* or *key* (from cayo), and *boca*.

Fabricated terms. Increasingly, however, new terms are being composed from Greek or Latin roots, and with mixed success. Among the earliest were *bioherm* and *biostrome* (Cumings, 1930), followed by such simple formulations as *intraclast* and *allochem* (Folk, 1962, p. 63) and *rhodolith* (Barnes *et al.,* 1971, p. 88). *Cryptobion, epibion, hypobion* and *parabion* of Morton and Challis (1969, p. 469) were followed by the *epilithion, mesolithion* and *endolithion* of McLean (1972). More extensive polysyllabic enormities such as the *calcibiocavite* and *calcibiocavicole* of Carriker and Smith (1969, p. 1012) and the *hermatobiolith* of Bond (1950, p. 270) have not proved popular. Perhaps a principle of simplicity should operate in devising such forms, together with a principle of parsimony, in that large numbers of new terms suddenly released are less likely to be accepted than a single proposal judiciously introduced. Hence the attraction of *phytokarst* (Folk *et al.,* 1973, p. 2351), in spite of its dubious genetic loading. Few reef terms have been fabricated from personal names, with the conspicuous exception of *drewite*, or from proper names, with the exception of *bahamite*.

Metaphor and analogy. Much description in the reef literature is loosely based on metaphor and analogy rather than on precisely defined terminology. This is well seen in descriptions of atoll shape: 'Ebon in the Marshalls is shaped like a circle. Nukuoro in the Carolines is a slightly squeezed circle. Kapingamarangi is more oval. Nomwin is like a pear. Lukunor and Ngaruangl are ham-shaped; and Namonuito, Etal and Namoluk rather triangular. Ujae resembles a stretched out diamond, Taongi a crescent moon, Sorol looks like the outline of a heron, and West Fayu like a headless goose without legs' (Wiens, 1962, p. 25). Canton has been compared to a pork chop, and the literature is full of similar characterizations (Degener and Degener, 1959; Niering, 1956). This usage is at least graphic, but has no other advantage.

CONCLUSION

This note can only be suggestive, not definitive. It aims to encourage caution in the coining of new names, care in their definition, together with a proper regard for the accumulation of proposals made during the last century of reef study. Hopefully it will generate sufficient interest to stimulate the production of a proper reef glossary.

References

AGASSIZ, A. 1894. A reconnaissance of the Bahamas and of the elevated reefs of Cuba in the steam yacht 'Wild Duck', January to April, 1893. *Bull. Mus. comp. Zool. Harvard Coll.*, vol., 26, no. 1, p. 1–203.

——. 1898. A visit to the Great Barrier Reef of Australia in the steamer 'Croydon', during April and May, 1896. *Bull. Mus. comp. Zool. Harvard Coll.*, vol. 28, no. 4, p. 95–148.

——. 1903. The coral reefs of the tropical Pacific. *Mem. Mus. comp. Zool. Harvard Coll.* vol. 28. p. 1–410.

BARNES, J.; BELLAMY, D. J.; JONES, D. J.; WHITTON, B. A.; DREW, E. A.; KENYON, L.; LYTHGOE, J. N.; ROSEN, B. R. 1971. Morphology and ecology of the reef front of Aldabra. *Symp. zool. Soc. Lond.*, vol. 28, p. 87–114.

BATTISTINI, R.; BOURROUILH, F.; CHEVALIER, J.-P.; COUDRAY, J.; DENIZOT, M.; FAURE, G.; FISHER, J. C.; GUILCHER, A.; HARMELIN-VIVIEN, M.; JAUBERT, J.; LABOREL, J.; MASSE, J. P.; MAUGÉ, L. A.; MONTAGGIONI, L.; PEYROT-CLAUSADE, M.; PICHON, M.; PLANTE, R.; PLAZIAT, J. C.; PLESSIS, Y. B.; RICHARD, G.; SALVAT, B.; THOMASSIN, B. A.; VASSEUR, P.; WEYDERT, P. 1975. Eléments de terminologie récifale indopacifique. *Téthys*, vol. 7, p. 1–111.

BOND, G. 1950. The nomenclature of Lower Carboniferous 'reef' limestones in the north of England. *Geol. Mag.*, vol. 87, p. 267–78.

BRAITHWAITE, C. J. R. 1971. Reefs: just a problem of semantics? *Bull. Am. Assoc. petrol. Geol.*, vol. 57, p. 1100–16.

CAROZZI, A. V. 1960 *Microscopic sedimentary petrography*. New York, John Wiley (485 p.).

CARRIKER, M. R.; SMITH, E. H. 1969. Comparative calcibiocavitology: summary and conclusions. *Am. Zool.*, vol. 9, p. 1011–20.

CHEVALIER, J.-P. 1972. Observations sur les chenaux incomplets appelés hoa dans les atolls des Tuamotu. In: *Proc. Symp. Corals and Coral Reefs, 1969.* Mar. Biol. Assoc. India, p. 477–88.

CLARK, W. A. V.; GAILE, G. L. 1973. The analysis and recognition of shapes. *Geogr. Annlr.* vol. 55B, p. 153–63.

CLAUSADE, M.; GRAVIER, N.; PICARD, J.; PICHON, M.; ROMAN, M.-L.; THOMASSIN, B.; VASSEUR, P.; VIVIEN, M.; WEYDERT, P. 1971. Morphologie des récifs coralliens de la région de Tuléar (Madagascar): éléments de terminologie récifale. *Téthys.* Suppl. 2, 1–74.

CUMINGS, E. R. 1932. Reefs or bioherms? *Bull. geol. Soc. Am.*, vol. 43, p. 331–52.

DAHL, A. L. 1973. Surface area in ecological analysis: quantification of benthic coral-reef algae. *Mar. Biol., Berlin*, vol. 23, p. 239–49.

DALRYMPLE, A. 1782. *Plan of the Atoll Maldiva or King's Island Atoll*. London, The author.

DANIELSSON, B. 1954. Native topographic terms in Raroia, Tuamotus. *Atoll Res. Bull.*, vol. 32, p. 92–6.

DARWIN, C. R. 1842. *The structure and distribution of coral reefs*. London, Smith, Elder (214 p.).

DAVIS, W. M. 1909. The systematic description of land forms. *Geogr. J.*, vol. 34, p. 300–18.

——. 1920. The small islands of almost-atolls. *Nature* (Lond.), vol. 105, p. 292–3.

——. 1928. The coral reef problem. *Am. Geog. Soc. Spec. Publ.*, vol. 9, p. 1–596.

DEGENER, O.; DEGENER, I. 1959. Canton Island, South Pacific (resurvey of 1958). *Atoll Res. Bull.*, vol. 64, p. 1–24.

EMERY, K. O.; TRACEY, J. I.; LADD, H. S. 1954. *Geology of Bikini and nearby atolls*. Part 1. Geology. U.S. Geol. Surv. (Prof. Paper 260-A), p. 1–265.

FAHRAEUS, L. E.; SLATT, R. M.; NOWLAND, G. S. 1974. Origin of carbonate pseudopellets. *J. sedim. Petrol.*, vol. 44, p. 27–9.

FAIRBRIDGE, R. W. 1950. Recent and Pleistocene coral reefs of Australia. *J. Geol.*, vol. 58, p. 330–401.

——; FOSBERG, F. R. *In litt. The reef index: a terminology and gazetteer of organic reefs, recent and fossil.* Final report ONR N7-Onr-29165, Task order NR 388 037 (iii, 377+39 p.).

FLINDERS, M. 1814. *A voyage to Terra Australis . . . in the years 1801, 1802, and 1803*. London, G. and W. Nicol (2 vols.; 269 p. and 613 p.).

FOLK, R. L. 1962. Spectral subdivision of limestone types. *Mem. Am. Assoc. petrol. Geol.*, vol. 1, p. 62–84.

——; ROBERTS, H. H.; MOORE, C. H. 1973. Black phytokarst from Hell, Cayman Islands, British West Indies. *Bull. geol. Soc. Am.*, vol. 84, p. 2351–60.

FORBES, H. O. 1893. The Great Barrier Reef of Australia. *Georg. J.*, vol. 2, p. 540–6.

GARDINER, J. S. 1931. *Coral reefs and atolls*. London, Macmillan (181 p)

13

GARRETT, P.; SMITH, D. I.; WILSON, A. O.; PATRIQUIN, D. 1971. Physiography, ecology, and sediments of two Bermuda patch reefs, *J. Geol.*, vol. 79, p. 647–68.

GOLDMAN, B. 1973. *Aspects of the ecology of the coral reef fishes of One Tree Island.* Ph.D. thesis, Macquarie University.

GOREAU, T. F. 1959. The ecology of Jamaican coral reefs. 1. Species composition and zonation. *Ecology*, vol. 40, p. 67–90.

——; BURKE, K. 1966. Pleistocene and Holocene geology of the island shelf near Kingston, Jamaica. *Mar. Geol.*, vol. 4, p. 207–25.

——; GOREAU, N. I. 1973. The ecology of Jamaican coral reefs. II. Geomorphology, zonation, and sedimentary phases. *Bull. mar. Sci.*, vol. 23, p. 399–464.

HACKETT, H. E. 1977. Marine algae known from the Maldive Islands. *Atoll Res. Bull.*, vol. 210, p. 1–30.

HÅKANSON, L. 1974. A mathematical model for establishing numerical values of topographical roughness for lake bottoms. *Geogr. Annlr.*, vol. 46A, p. 183–200.

HEDLEY, C; TAYLOR, T. G. 1908. Coral reefs of the Great Barrier Reef, Queensland. *Rept. Australas. Assoc. Adv. Sci.*, 1907, p. 394–413.

KENDALL, C. G. St. C.; SKIPWITH, P. A. d'E. 1969. Geomorphology of a Recent shallow-water carbonate province: Khor al Bazam, Trucial Coast, southwest Persian Gulf. *Bull. geol. Soc. Am.*, vol. 80, p. 865–92.

LADD, H. S.; TRACEY, J. I., JR.; WELLS, J. W.; EMERY, K. O. 1950. Organic growth and sedimentation on an atoll. *J. Geol.*, vol. 58, p. 410–25.

MACNEIL, F. S. 1954. Organic reefs and banks and associated detrital sediments. *Am. J. Sci.*, vol. 252, p. 385–401.

MARK, D. M. 1975. Geomorphometric parameters: a review and evaluation. *Geogr. Annlr.*, vol. 57A, p. 165–77.

MAXWELL, W. C. H. 1968 *Atlas of the Great Barrier Reef.* Amsterdam, Elsevier (258 p.).

——. 1970. Deltaic patterns in reefs. *Deep-sea Res.*, vol. 17, p. 1005–18.

MCKEE, E. D.; CHRONIC, J.; LEOPOLD, E. B. 1959. Sedimentary belts in lagoon of Kapingamarangi Atoll. *Bull. Am. Assoc. petrol. Geol.*, vol. 43, p. 501–62.

MCLEAN, R. F. 1972. Nomenclature for rock-destroying organisms. *Nature* (Lond.), vol. 240, p. 490.

MERGNER, H. 1971. Structure, ecology and zonation of Red Sea reefs (in comparison with south Indian and Jamaican reefs). *Symp. zool. Soc. London.*, vol. 28, p. 141–61.

MOLENGRAAFF, G. A. F. 1930. The coral reefs in the East Indian archipelago, their distribution and mode of development. In: *Proc. 2th Pacific Sci. Congr.*, Batavia and Bandoeng, Java. vol. 2A, p. 55–89.

MORRISON, J. P. E. 1954, Animal ecology of Raroia Atoll, Tuamotus. I. Ecological notes on the mollusks and other animals of Raroia. II. Notes on the birds of Raroia. *Atoll Res. Bull.*, vol. 34, p. 1–26.

MORTON, J. E.; CHALLIS, D. A. 1969. The biomorphology of Solomon Islands shores with a discussion of zoning patterns and ecological terminology. *Phil. Trans. R. Soc., Lond.*, (B: *Biol. Sci.*), vol. 255, p. 459–516.

NEWELL, N. D. 1954. Expedition to Raroia, Tuamotus. *Atoll Res. Bull.*, vol. 31, p. 1–23.

——; RIGBY, J. K. 1957. Geological studies on the Great Bahama Bank. *Spec. Publs Soc. econ. Palaeont. Miner., Tulsa*, vol. 5, p. 15–72.

NIERING, W. A. 1956. Bioecology of Kapingamarangi Atoll, Caroline Islands: terrestrial aspects. *Atoll. Res., Bull.* vol. 49, p. 1–32.

PICHON, M. 1971. Comparative study of the main features of some coral reefs of Madagascar. La Réunion and Mauritius. *Symp. zool. Soc. Lond.*, vol. 28, p. 185–216.

RISK, M. J. 1972. Fish diversity on a coral reef in the Virgin Islands. *Atoll. Res. Bull.*, vol. 153, p. 1–6.

ROBERTS, H. H. 1974. Variability of reefs with regard to changes in wave power around an island. In: *Proc. Second Int. Coral Reef Symp.* Brisbane, Great Barrier Reef Committee, vol. 2, p. 497–512.

ROY, K. J. 1970. Change in bathymetric configuration, Kaneohe Bay, Oahu, 1882–1969. *Hawaii Inst. Geophys. Rept.*, HIG-70-15, p. 1–26.

——; SMITH, S. V. 1971. Sedimentation and coral reef development in turbid water: Fanning lagoon. *Pac. Sci.*, vol. 25, p. 234–48.

RUSSELL, R. J. 1971. Water-table effects on seacoasts. *Bull. geol. Soc. Am.*, vol. 82, p. 2343–48.

SCHEER, G. 1959. Contribution to a German reef-terminology. *Atoll Res. Bull.*, vol. 69, p. 1–4.

SPENDER, M. A. 1930. Island-reefs of the Queensland coast. *Geogr. J.*, vol. 76, p. 193–214, p. 273–93.

14

STEARNS, H. T. 1946. An integration of coral reef hypotheses. *Am. J. Sci.,* vol. 244, p. 245–62.

STEERS, J. A. 1937. The coral islands and associated features of the Great Barrier Reefs. *Geogr. J.,* vol. 89, p. 1–28, p. 119–39.

STEPHENSON, T. A.; STEPHENSON, A.; TANDY, G.; SPENDER, M. A. 1931. The structure and ecology of Low Isles and other reefs. *Sci. Repts. Gt Barrier Reef Exped. 1928–29,* vol. 3, p. 17–112.

STODDART, D. R. 1965. The shape of atolls. *Mar. Geol.,* vol. 3, p. 369–83.

——. 1969 Geomorphology of the Marovo elevated barrier reef, New Georgia. *Phil. Trans. R. Soc. Lond.,* (B: *Biol. Sci.*), vol. 255, p. 383–402.

——. 1971. Geomorphology of Diego Garcia Atoll. *Atoll Res. Bull.,* vol. 149, p. 7–26.

——; SCOFFIN, T. P. 1978. Microatolls: review of form, origin and terminology. *Atoll Res. Bull.,*

——; TAYLOR, J. D.; FOSBERG, F. R.; FARROW, G. E. 1971. Geomorphology of Aldabra Atoll. *Phil. Trans. R. Soc. Lond.,* (B: Biol. Sci.), vol. 260, p. 31–65.

TAYAMA, R. 1952. Coral reefs in the South Seas. *Bull. hydrograph. Off. (Japan),* vol. 11, p. 1–292.

VERRILL, A. E. 1900. Notes on the geology of the Bermudas. *Am. J. Sci.,* vol. 159, p. 313–140.

WELLS, J. W. 1957. Coral reefs. *Mem. geol. Soc. Am.,* vol. 67, no. 1, p. 609–31.

WIENS, H. J. 1962. *Atoll environment and ecology.* New Haven, Yale University Press (532 p.).

ZANKL, H.; SCHROEDER, J. H. 1972. Interaction of genetic processes in Holocene reefs off North Eleuthera Island, Bahamas. *Geoi. Rdsch.,* vol. 61, p. 520–41.

2

Mapping reefs and islands

D. R. Stoddart[1]

Few reef islands and fewer reefs have been mapped to standards commonly accepted in topographic surveys of continental areas, and even where good surveys have been carried out in the past, the processes of topographic change may be so rapid that revision of existing maps is usually necessary. The techniques of survey in reef areas do not differ from those in general use elsewhere, and this note is not intended to duplicate the treatment of such methods in standard surveying texts (e.g. Clendinning, 1960; Sandover, 1961; Hydrographer of the Navy, 1965). But the reef environment imposes many constraints, and some practical comments may be useful to expand the brief treatment by Wentworth (1953).

PLANIMETRIC MAPPING

The basic requirement of a land-based survey is a map showing major topographic features. The following methods have been used in reef areas.

Theodolite triangulation. This is a high-accuracy method which has rarely been employed, most notably by Spender (1930) in establishing a network of topographic control points on reefs about 1.5 km in longest axis, the detail being subsequently plotted by plane table. The method is time-consuming and requires additional personnel for flagging stations and erecting permanent markers. For most reef surveys it is unlikely that the degree of accuracy made possible by using theodolite triangulation will be required.

Plane-table survey. Standard plane-table surveying methods using a telescopic alidade have been used on reefs, but have two disadvantages. A staff man is required who must be able to reach the points to be plotted, and lines of sight can be substantially reduced, especially on the convex shores of vegetated

1. Department of Geography, Cambridge University, Cambridge CB2 3EN, United Kingdom.

islands. The method has the great advantage that the progress of the map can be seen in the field and errors and omissions rectified.

Compass traverse. This has been the standard method of survey for sand cays and for small reefs with substantial dry-land areas (Kemp, 1937; Lofthouse, 1940a, 1940b; Stoddart, 1962). Horizontal angles are measured with a prismatic surveying compass, preferably about 10 cm in diameter and either tripod-mounted or hand-held; angles should be read without difficulty to half a degree. The main problem in this kind of survey is in measuring distance. For detailed work a fibron tape should be used (sand and sea-water make metal chains useless), but for much work pacing is adequate. Paces should be frequently calibrated against a tape, and with practice the standard pace can be adjusted to take account of differences in terrain. Difficulties arise in pacing across boulders, and more especially in shallow water on soft bottoms round man-groves. Even so, closure errors using pacing should be well under one percent, and if a tape is used can be negligible. In pacing it is best to adopt an ordinary walking pace rather than try deliberately to use an artificial 1-yard or 1-metre stride which is difficult to maintain over long distances.

Usually a compass traverse forms a closed circuit, but on small islets offsets from a central traverse line will be sufficient to establish shape. Large and complex islands should be divided into sectors and a primary network established before detail is mapped within each sector.

Tacheometric methods. A variant of the compass traverse uses tacheometric methods of distance measurement. On small islands Domm (1971) recommends using binoculars fitted with stadia hairs, and a compass, sighting onto a staff set up vertically in the centre of the island. The method has limitations of accuracy and scale; it is of less value on larger islands, in surveys where greater precision is needed, and in areas where lines of sight are interrupted by vegetation. If the method is used to establish a closed traverse, a staff man is needed, in contrast to the compass and pacing method which requires only one man.

Optical rangefinder methods. A further method of distance measurement, using an optical rangefinder with a range of 5–300 m, is suggested by Nason (1975). Error increases with distance in the model he recommends from less than one per cent at 18 m to 4 per cent at 100 m. The rangefinder has the advantage that distances can be measured to points not directly accessible, but there is always the possibility of damage to the instrument in reef conditions. Nason's model has a vertical circle which can be used with the distance measurement to establish altitudes. The method is well-suited for rapid surveying to a rather low standard of accuracy.

Horizontal sextant methods. Horizontal sextant angles can be used to establish locations in areas where traversing is not possible, such as shorelines with man-groves and on extensive reef flats. The accuracy of the method depends largely on the accuracy of location of fixed reference points. Reliance should not be placed, for example, on the ends of islands as mapped on hydrographic charts: these features may have changed since the chart survey, and angles are usually taken with reference to the edge of vegetation rather than to the shoreline itself. If sights are taken on human constructions such as aerials, their positions on pre-existing maps should also be checked; even maps of military installations may be sufficiently inaccurate to introduce unacceptable errors into locations determined by horizontal-angle methods. These methods, of course, simply establish planimetric control, and detail must then be mapped by one of the other methods described.

PLOTTING DETAIL

The amount of detail to be plotted will depend on the purpose of the survey. In practice it is helpful in advance to have recognized 'ecologic field units' of the kind determined by Cloud (1952). On reef islands this is aided by the fact that many vegetation units consist of single-species stands. Geological detail should be similarly categorized in advance, as for example in the geological maps of Kapingamarangi islands by McKee (1956). Wherever possible, maps should include the locations of relatively permanent objects: houses, jetties, conspicuous trees, etc., so that even where topographic changes are rapid, maps made in subsequent years may be related to the original one.

DETERMINATION OF HEIGHTS

Accurate determination of elevations for the purpose of inter-island or inter-reef comparison depends in the first instance on the establishment of a reference datum, and this can pose major problems especially in macrotidal areas. Few reef surveys include the accurate determination of tidal components from long-term instrumental records, and in practice less rigorous methods of determining a sea-level datum are usually employed. A tide pole can be used to measure tidal range, preferably during a period of spring tides, and the levels thus determined then related to a local land benchmark from which further surveys can be carried. This local benchmark can then be related to a standard datum by comparing the local tide curve at a given time with published tide predictions for a nearby station. There are many sources of error in this procedure, however. First, in trade-wind and cyclone areas, sea level can be substantially affected by weather, giving considerable seasonal and also short-term variations. Second, tide poles are often erected in rather sheltered conditions, partly for physical reasons, partly because the pole itself is difficult to read with any accuracy where the water is rough; but sheltered situations especially on reef flats and on the lee sides of islands may be subject to ponding, and the tide curve measured is then lagged behind that of the open sea and in some cases may also be attenu-

19

ated or truncated. Third, local water levels can be affected by topographic features such as the presence of tidal channels. In extreme cases it is possible to measure tides which are completely out-of-phase with those of the open sea; it is unlikely that a tide pole would be erected in such a situation other than deliberately, but much less extreme distortions can nevertheless introduce considerable errors into the establishment of a datum. There is no easy and rapid way out of these difficulties, but repetitive determination of a datum from tide curves measured under different conditions and in different topographic situations is preferable to reliance on a single determination. In spite of the difficulties, a datum established in this way is, with care, much more reliable than one based on other less formal methods, such as the use of the general level of reef flats or of zone-forming organisms such as oysters.

Actual altitudes with reference to datum are best determined using a tripod-mounted level. Self-levelling levels with stadia hairs for distance-determination give very rapid results. Wooden tripods are heavy and warp in sea-water, and aluminium ones should be used. If a lower order of accuracy is required, e.g. in plotting in detail on a topographic map, a hand-held Abney level is sufficient. Wentworth (1953) suggested using a simple water level to determine datum levels in different situations on islands, and the method has been further outlined by Debenham (1964), but it is too cumbersome to be widely used in reef work.

Accurate levelling over long distances on reef islands introduces quite different problems; some of these are considered by Dale (1972). When detailed surveys are carried out, permanent benchmarks should be constructed, and records kept in sufficient detail to enable them to be relocated. Metal bolts set in concrete are satisfactory in protected situations, but where there is a lot of salt spray they can corrode very quickly; in such circumstances the bottom of a glass bottle set in concrete will have a longer life.

MARINE SURVEYING

Most reef expeditions require marine topographic information on two scales: either bathymetric maps of extensive areas such as lagoons, or more detailed maps at larger scales of small sectors of reefs.

The first of these is best achieved by echo-sounding along traverses. Note that it is not sufficient to set a course between two objects and assume that the path followed is a straight line. The actual course followed should be frequently checked by horizontal sextant fixes on known points, and the echotrace marked. Such relatively informal surveys cannot approach hydrographic survey standards: the topographic information derived, if presented as a bathymetric map, can only be generalized, because of the known irregularity of reef and lagoon floors and the probable wide spacing of the traverse lines. Saville and Caldwell (1953) discuss some of the constraints on accuracy in such situations.

Detailed mapping of underwater detail is usually carried out with specific requirements in mind. At its most simple it is designed as an extension of land surveying, with marker buoys being laid in the area to be surveyed and their positions determined by triangulation from shore stations. The points can then be transferred to plastic plane tables and detail plotted directly underwater, either by eye, in which case distortion can present difficulties (Ross, 1971), or by simple instrumental methods (Milne, 1972). More detailed methods, many devised in underwater archaeological work, are potentially available for reef use (e.g. Farrington-Wharton, 1970), but in practice reef workers either sketch in detail or use photographic methods supported by depth and inclination measurements (Drew, 1977). For a brief survey of underwater surveying methods, see Morrison (1971).

LOGISTICS

Problems of mapping in reef areas are such that logistics must be considered at an early stage, and could determine both the choice of a working area (if surveying is to be an important component of the work) and also the timing of the investigation. Very large atolls are very difficult to survey. The mapping of smaller atolls with either a continuous land rim or no land rim at all can also be difficult, since much effort must be devoted to building adequate markers, which are both expensive and in inhabited areas are readily stolen. Position-fixing becomes difficult in any lagoon wider than about 8 km, even where there are numbers of small islets on the reef rim.

Access to many areas on reefs is governed by tides. On the northern Great Barrier Reef, where the tidal range is considerable, low tides occur during daylight hours only in the winter months (May–August); during the summer, low tides are at night, when obviously survey is out of the question. Similar seasonal changes occur in other parts of the world.

References

CLENDINNING, J. 1960. *The principles of surveying*, 2nd edit. London, Blackie. (xiv + 376 p.).

CLOUD, P. E., JR. 1952. Preliminary report on geology and marine environments of Onotoa Atoll, Gilbert Islands. *Atoll Res. Bull.*, vol. 12, p. 1–73.

DALE, P. F. 1972. Levelling operations on Aldabra Atoll. *Geogr. J.*, vol. 138, p. 53–9.

DEBENHAM, F. 1964. A simple water level. *Geogr. J.*, vol. 130, p. 528–30.

DOMM, S. B. 1971. Mapping reefs and cays, a quick method for the scientist working alone. *Atoll Res. Bull.*, vol. 148, p. 15–7.

DREW, E. A. 1977. A photographic survey down the seaward reef-front of Aldabra Atoll. *Atoll Res. Bull.*, vol. 193, p. 1–7.

FARRINGTON-WHARTON, R. 1970. The development and use of a practical underwater theodolite. *Proc. Inst. civil Eng.*, vol. 45, p. 491–506.

Hydrographer of the Navy. 1965. *Admiralty manual of hydrographic surveying*, vol. 1. London, Hydrographer of the Navy. (xiv + 671 p.).

KEMP, F. E. 1937. Surveying. *Geogr. J.*, vol. 89, p. 139–40.

LOFTHOUSE, J. A. 1940a. The surveying methods employed on the cays. *Geogr. J.*, vol. 95, p. 41–2.

——. 1940b. Survey problems of sand cays and mangrove islands. *Geogr. J.*, vol. 96, p. 327–28.

MCKEE, E. D. 1956. Geology of Kapingamarangi Atoll, Caroline Islands. *Atoll Res. Bull.,* vol. 50, p. 1–38.

MILNE, P. H. 1972. In-situ underwater surveying by plane-table and alidade. *Underwater J. inform. Bull.,* vol. 4, p. 59–63.

MORRISON, I. A. 1971. Underwater surveying. In: J. D. Woods and J. N. Lythgoe (eds). *Underwater science.* Oxford, University Press, p. 23–8.

NASON, J. D. 1975. Reconnaissance and plot mapping of coral atolls: a simplified rangefinder method. *Atoll Res. Bull.,* vol. 185, p. 13–20.

ROSS, H. E. 1971. Spatial perception under water. In: J. D. Woods and J. N. Lythgoe (eds). *Underwater science.* Oxford. University Press, p. 69–101.

SANDOVER, J. A. 1961. *Plane surveying.* London, Arnold (viii + 424 p.).

SAVILLE, T., Jr.; CALDWELL, J. M. 1953. Accuracy of hydrographic surveying in and near the surf zone. *Tech. Mem. Beach Erosion Board,* vol. 32, p. 1–17, A1–A11.

SPENDER, M. A. 1930. Island-reefs of the Queensland coast. *Geogr. J.,* vol. 76, p. 194–214, p. 273–97.

STODDART, D. R. 1962. Surveying. *Atoll Res. Bull.,* vol. 87, p. 129.

WENTWORTH, C. K. 1953. Use of hand level and Brunton compass for determining and mapping minor topography. *Atoll. Res. Bull.* vol. 17, p. 22.

3

Aerial photography and other remote sensing techniques

D. Hopley[1]

The environmental complexity and intricate patterns of coral reefs combined with the paucity of relevant information on hydrographic charts and logistic difficulties of systematic ground survey, have meant that where possible a high proportion of coral reef studies involving areal definitions have utilized aerial photography. In Australia, vertical aerial photographs of the Great Barrier Reef were taken as early as 1925 and, in September 1928, the Royal Australian Air Force made a vertical coverage of the Low Isles at a scale of 1:2,400 which was used extensively as a ground check by the first Great Barrier Reef Expedition led by Yonge (Stephenson *et al.,* 1931). Elsewhere, Umbgrove (1928, 1929) was similarly discovering the advantages of such tools. However, only subsequent to the Second World War and the widespread photography of many Pacific islands and reefs for military purposes was the utilization of reef photography widely developed and it is in the years since 1945 that many reef papers are consciously based on air photography or have used aerial photographs for illustrative purposes (for example in the manner of Flood, 1974; Guilcher, *et al.,* 1969; Maxwell, 1968; Orme, *et al.,* 1974).

Systematic aerial surveys have been undertaken in many coral reef areas and combined with wartime coverage and special purpose photography for commercial or scientific survey, sequential photography is available for some reef areas. In addition to the 1925, 1928 and wartime photography of the Great Barrier Reef, the whole of this major reef province was photographed at scales of between 1:50,000 and 1:80,000 by the Australian Commonwealth Government between 1964 and 1972, selected sections by the Royal Australian Air Force (e.g. the Bunker–Capricorn Group at 1:48,000 in 1969) and other smaller areas for special purposes (e.g. a colour coverage of the Bunker–Capricorn Group at 1:12,000 with selected areas at 1:6,000 in 1972 by the Queensland Government).

In spite of the widespread availability and use of aerial photographs for reef studies, little systematic research appears to have been carried out on the recognition and differentiation of photo-patterns. Such approaches have been

---

1. Department of Geography, James Cook University, Townsville, Queensland, Australia 4811.

widespread in other fields and, although research papers have been published on the general fields within the many disciplines which have an interest in reef research, coral reefs themselves have received scant attention. Thus whilst numerous papers are available on the applications of aerial photography to geomorphology (e.g. Fezer, 1971), oceanography (e.g. Ewing (ed.), 1965; Badgley *et al.* (eds), 1969) and biological studies (e.g. Howard 1972) only a few papers deal with the systematic interpretation of coral reef features or use of aerial photographs in reef research, notably Steers (1946) and Teichert and Fairbridge (1948, 1950) on geomorphology and Kumpf and Randall (1961), Kelly (1969) and Kelly and Conrad (1969) on general ecology.

This paper attempts to provide guidelines for the general application of aerial photography to reef studies, not only in the traditional field of panchromatic photography but also extending into colour and false colour media and active scanning systems in which rapid advances have been made over the last ten years. Further, the use of manned and unmanned satellites as observational platforms over the same period has added a new dimension to remote sensing which may be of some value to the coral reef researcher.

PHOTOGRAMMETRIC PROBLEMS

Various types of aerial photography are available each with its own photogrammetric problems. Most commonly the reef researcher who attempts an aerial reconnaissance of his area will be able to obtain only oblique views which obviously suffer from scale distortion due to perspective, which increases with a decreasing depression angle of the camera. Whilst any oblique photograph may be used to plot detail on base maps, some obliques may be used to produce the base maps themselves by reconstructing the geometry of the principal plane of the photograph. A method of intersection is utilized based on the fundamental principle of perspective, that all parallel lines converge on the same point on the horizon, and on the photogrammetric principle that all bearings from the orthocentre (observer's position) are correct. High oblique photographs, in which the horizon is visible, taken with a camera which has an accurately calibrated lens are prerequisites for base mapping from oblique photographs (see for example Rich, 1947 or Lattman and Ray, 1965 for details). Photography of reef areas is particularly suited to this type of construction as most of the reef features visible are at, or very close to sea level, and the normal distortion produced by relief is minimal.

Although the hand-held oblique can be utilized in this way, in remote areas such as some of the Pacific Islands, the only photographs available may be from wartime multiple lens photography. Most commonly this will be trimetrogon photography whereby a three camera assembly comprising a central vertical camera flanked by two obliquely directed cameras at a high angle produce a photographic triplet from horizon to horizon. It is thus possible to extend the mapping beyond the areas immediately below the line of flight where overlapping vertical photographs are taken. The less common four-lens and nine-lens photography is not suited to this treatment as the horizon is not usually visible in such photography.

The vertical photograph, however, provides the most useful base for field work, although not a planimetrically accurate depiction of the ground surface, being subject to scale distortion as a result of any tilt in the aircraft at time of photography, or, more importantly, radial displacement due to relief. Thus radial line plotting techniques should be utilized for accurate base mapping (see for example, American Society of Photogrammetry, 1966 for details). However the general lack of relief on photographs of coral reefs reduces the amount of radial displacement.

With space photography, relief displacement is minimal due to the ratio of relief to height of photography. The greatest distorting element here is the curvature of the earth's surface which becomes important on photographs taken from high orbit.

The clarity of water in many coral reef areas allows the depiction of features many metres below the water surface. Stereoscopic imagery of these features is possible utilizing pairs of vertical photographs under a stereoscope. However, problems arise in calculating accurate heights or depths of such submarine features utilizing parallax displacement (as with subaerial imagery) due to the effect of refraction at the air–water interface. Accurate photogrammetric triangulation requires that the mathematical model be based on the actual underwater point rather than its refracted or apparent position. A correcting factor, based on the index of refraction of water, the angle of observation and the depth of water, has been calculated by Tewinkel (1963). The factor varies with the relative location of points in the stereoscopic model as well as with the separation, or air base, of the photographs. Calculations are also adversely affected by wave action, particularly from low level photographs. However, Harris and Umbach (1972) successfully undertook underwater mapping of a 20 square mile (50 sq.km.) reef area off the south coast of Puerto Rico. Peripheral vertical control in the off-shore side of this coastal area was provided by premarking underwater points. Compilation of depth curves and soundings was accomplished with conventional stereoplotters using datum correction curves to convert model readings from apparent to true depths. Whilst temperature and salinity variations affect the refractive index of water, within the accuracy of the method neither appear significant (Jerlov, 1968). More important may be the variation in water levels between individual photo-runs particularly in macrotidal reef waters.

WATER PENETRATION

The results of global mapping of coastal water clarity from GEMINI series space photographs show that about 35 per cent of the world's coastal sea floor can be mapped to 20 m depth by aerial photogrammetry (Lepley, 1968). Areas containing coral reefs generally have water not more turbid than 5 m Secchi. However, whilst the general advantages of colour photography have been outlined by the U.S. Coast and Geodetic Survey (Smith, 1963), it is clear that penetration can be optimised by sensing in the proper region of the spectrum and displaying the resulting record so as to make use of the dynamic density range of the presentation material (Helgeson, 1970). Special films have been prepared with the specific purpose of photographing through water. Specht, Needler and Fritz (1973) suggest that a film with two layers having peak sensitivities of about 480 and 550 nm will provide maximum penetration of water with various amounts of organic matter present, and will allow some estimate of such material. Where maximum penetration to show reef front or lagoonal features is required, careful selection of film is thus recommended.

INTERPRETATION OF CORAL REEF ENVIRONMENTS FROM AERIAL PHOTOGRAPHS—IMAGE INTERPRETATION TECHNIQUES

Although photometric spectral-photograph density and colour-measuring techniques show promise for objective mechanical separation of specific features (see below) the interpretation of aerial photographs and other remotely sensed images is still largely a matter of subjective assessment. As with all interpretation, the recognition and mapping of coral reef photopatterns requires a systematic approach (see for example, American Society of Photogrammetry, 1960). Interpretation should, where possible, go through the following procedure:

1. Preliminary scan of imagery to determine the tonal or colour structure and range of tones or colours. It is particularly important at this early stage to note variations due to isolated cloud patches, flaring from the sun's reflection, and contrasts between individual photographs or runs due to variations in the sun's angle, weather conditions or, occasionally, in the quality of processing.
2. Relate tonal or colour structure to specific coral reef features of biological and geomorphological significance, remembering the variations which may exist. Familiarity with coral areas in general and with the specific area under examination obviously enhances interpretation. Recognition of specific features is greatly aided by their pattern of location.
3. Confirm the tone or colour codes. Where possible, field checking should be made to confirm the photopatterns subsequent to the initial interpretation even when the observer is familiar with the area. Spot checks can indicate the consistency of the interpretation.
4. Final map preparation.

Accuracy and range of interpretation increases rapidly with experience. However, subjective judgment may be removed by utilizing mechanical aids to interpretation. These have been developed largely in conjunction with satellite sensing. The collection of data by satellite systems has become so rapid that it has been necessary to find such aids for the interpreter particularly as new sensing techniques have been introduced. Further, the satellite images cover many more times the area of normal aerial photograph thus reducing the pitfalls of mechanically comparing images on separate photographs, on which tonal variations of similar objects may exist due to exposure or processing contrasts, in order to obtain regional patterns.

Image processing may thus remove some of the tedium of interpretation but may also lead to the recognition of information in a picture which would otherwise remain hidden during visual inspection. For example, a 70 mm colour photograph taken from space contains approximately 16 million picture points, each of which may take on about 200 different hues of the three colour layers. The resulting information content is somewhere between 10^8 and 10^9 pieces per picture (Helbig, 1973). Processing may be by means of optical methods, including enlarging, colour filtering or contrast-enhancing development. Alternatively the information contained in the image may be converted into an electrical signal by scanning and subsequently picked up by a photo-electronic converter. Images stored on magnetic tape may be computer analysed. Colour-tone separation is a standard part of such processing in which only one part of the spectrum (blue, red, infra-red) is filtered out. The resulting pattern of a single colour may closely resemble a map of a particular feature or features. More advanced equidensity images extend this objective mapping technique. It is possible to split up the density range of a photographic original into a family of equidensities by use of a special film utilizing a series of exposures. Equidensities may then be reproduced in different colours to produce a strongly defined pattern greatly aiding the interpretation of the original (Zeiss, 1973).

Whilst these methods have yet to be applied to coral reef areas it is worthwhile considering the advantages of such approaches which may be readily quantified. Colour separation and equidensity patterns appear to have particular application to defining morphological zones and water depths.

SCALE VARIATION

The scale of an aerial photograph is determined from $f/(H - h)$, where f is the focal length of the camera; H is the height of the aircraft above sea level and h the height of the ground surface above sea level. Scale will be affected by any enlargement of the original negative. In general the scale of photography usually available ranges from approximately 1:5,000 to about 1:100,000. Teichert and Fairbridge (1950) suggested that for detailed mapping the scale should not be less than 1:5,000 and preferably 1:3,000. However, Kelly and Conrad (1969) found advantages from photography at a scale of 1:50,000 and Harris and Umbach (1972) suggest an optimum scale of 1:15,000 for stereomapping of the ocean bed in a reef area. Where choice of scale is possible, the intended use of the photography should be the deciding factor. Gross morphology can be quite easily mapped from 1:80,000 photographs, with an accuracy down to 10 m. However, if detailed site mapping is required, particularly where it is related to quadrat or linear transect studies of a particular zone, the larger scale photography may be most suitable. Whilst individual features, such as particular coral heads, may be more easily discerned, the larger scale sometimes makes it more difficult to define the larger zones. If the original negatives can be obtained, it is quite feasible to enlarge from recent high quality photographs by at least five times before loss of definition becomes a problem. From the author's experience a scale of about 1:25,000 has been found to have the most consistent advantages in mapping morphological features in the Great Barrier Reef province.

THE USE OF AERIAL PHOTOGRAPHY AND OTHER SENSORS IN CORAL REEF RESEARCH

All materials exhibit characteristics of reflecting, absorbing and emitting energy which give them unique spectral signatures. The human eye is sensitive to only a narrow part of this electro-magnetic spectrum between 0.4 and 0.7 microns and traditional aerial photography has a similar range. However, by utilizing sensors designed to detect radiation from less familiar wavelengths both shorter (ultraviolet and x-ray) and longer (infra-red and radar) than that of visible light, the range of qualities it is possible to determine by remote sensing is greatly increased (Fig. 1).

As this paper is aimed at utilizing remote sensing for coral reef research essentially from aircraft or orbiting satellites, it is necessary to be aware of the effects of both the atmosphere and water on the radiation signatures. Within the visible spectrum aerial haze produces more scattering of visible radiant energy at shorter rather than longer wavelengths, giving the familiar blueness to aerial views and necessitating the use of a minus-blue filter for most photography. However, other parts of the spectrum may be more seriously distorted. The ultraviolet region is inhibited by strong atmospheric attenuation at wavelengths shorter than 0.29 microns, though ultraviolet sensing is making possible elemental analyses of surface rocks and detection of certain pollution sources (Lancaster, 1968). Near infra-red radiation (0.7 to 0.86 microns) is freely transmitted through the atmosphere even where a visible haze is present. It is this part of the spectrum that infra-red aerial photography utilizes. However, larger wavelengths in the infra-red range (thermal radiation) are greatly distorted by the atmosphere except for two 'windows' around 4.3 microns and 8 to 14 microns. Through these windows it is possible to perceive variations in thermal radiation, both day and night and through haze and smoke. At larger wavelengths (>1 mm) there are several windows relatively free from atmospheric attenuation between 1 and 8 mm. This microwave radiation, and its active mode radar, can be detected by highly sensitive radio-metric techniques

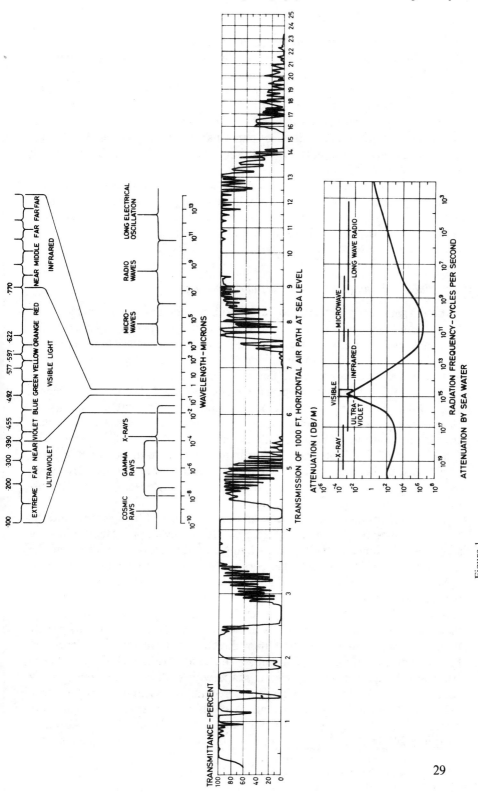

Figure 1
The electro-magnetic spectrum (upper figure) showing attenuation through the atmosphere (centre) and sea water (bottom) (after Szekielda, 1971).

29

even through considerable thickness of solid and unconsolidated materials.

Unfortunately, strong attenuation of electromagnetic radiation by water further limits the parts of the spectrum available for remote sensing of the ocean (Fig. 1). Direct detection is limited to the narrow visible portion of the spectrum. Transmission of radiation, in clearest oceanic water, peaks at approximately 0.47 microns with a shift to longer wavelengths in coastal waters which have greater concentrations of particular matter. Nevertheless infra-red and radar imagery has application to studies of exposed surface characteristics of reefs and related features.

The following sections examine the variation in appearance of some coral reef features utilizing different types of remote sensing, and attempts to compare the suitability of each medium. The features described are characteristic of the patch reefs of the Great Barrier Reef Province and are diagrammatically illustrated in Figure 2.

Black and white (panchromatic) aerial photography

Although some early aerial photography utilized orthochromatic film (sensitive to green and blue light) most ordinary black and white photographs are taken on panchromatic film sensitive to green, blue and red light. This is the most available form of aerial photography and the easiest for the non-professional to use. Table 1 summarizes the key tones and textures for identification of common coral reef features. In general, black and white photography is highly successful in defining most reef flat features and cheapest to purchase. Occasionally problems may arise from exposure of the film. Reef flats strongly reflect visible light and over-exposure, with too light a tone and lack of detail, may result especially on photographs of fringing reefs where the lower reflectance of the adjacent land may necessitate over exposure for reef features. However, where correctly exposed, tonal and textural characteristics give strong definition to the morphological zones of the reef flat.

Greatest contrast appears between the dark tones of living corals and the very light tones of sandy areas. Dead coral has a greyer appearance indicating a greater reflectance to light than its living counterpart. On the reef edge, the dark tones of the living reef-edge corals may merge into a uniform textural lighter-toned zone of algal rim which, particularly on the windward side of the reefs, gives way to a narrow zone of even lighter tone and coarser photo-texture which is the rubble zone. Reef flat corals are prominent not only for their stark tonal contrast with the white sand of the flat but also for a strongly linear pattern, normal to the dominant direction of refracted wave approach. Lagoon corals in the form of 'bombies' are easily distinguished by the steep rise from the lagoon floor, irregular shape with dark marginal tones (living coral) and central grey areas where the percentage cover of living coral is less. Where scale is sufficiently large, micro atolls have a similar though more regularly shaped image. Thin dark lines near the reef flat margins are normally indicative of algal terraces, the lines being the rim of each terrace, lighter areas

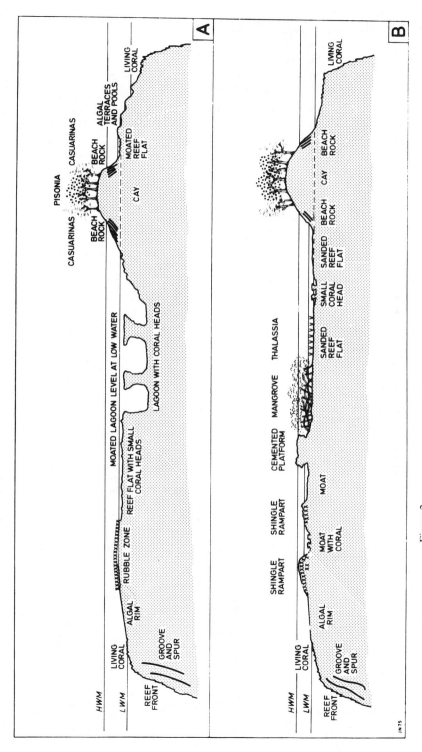

Figure 2
Diagrammatic cross-section of lagoon and low-wooded island reefs of the Great Barrier Reef showing spatial relationships of morphological and ecological zones described in text.

TABLE 1. Identification criteria for coral reef features—panchromatic aerial photographs

	Feature	Location key (where applicable)	Tonal key	Texture-Pattern
ISLAND	Cay		Very light tones if un-vegetated	—even texture, some linear pattern
			Grey tones if low vegetation	—fine texture, some linear pattern
			Dark tones if forested	—mottled texture, irregular pattern
	Beachrock	Cay beaches, sandy areas of reef (former cay areas)	Light to dark grey, contrasting with light beaches. May be confused with tree shadows	Parallel or sub parallel to beach. Strong lineation
	Raised reef		Depends on vegetation	Irregular karstified surface. No surface drainage. Fringing reefs parallel to main physiographic trends
	Mangroves	Lee-side, sheltered behind cays or ramparts	Variety of dark tones, often with sharp junctions where different species or ages of mangrove are adjacent	Coarse to mottled texture
MOAT AND RAMPART	Shingle ramparts	Reef flat margins, particularly weather side	Light tones, sharply defined towards reef flat, grading into darker tones towards reef edge.	Fine even texture. Spurs normal to reef edge
	Basset edges and cemented reef rubble	Reef flat margins, particularly weather side	Medium tones which may be difficult to distinguish from other reef flat environments	Strong but irregular lineation with pattern similar to shingle ramparts
	Moats	Adjacent to shingle ramparts	Tones vary according to water depth but generally darkest (deepest) immediately behind ramparts	Mottled if containing moated corals, otherwise fine, even texture
REEF FLAT	Lagoon	Central reef area	Darker tones associated with depth of water	Smooth texture of sanded floor broken by many irregular dark coral patches
	Lagoon corals		Light patches within lagoon (with sharply defined dark edges (the living corals)	Irregular shapes rising from lagoon floor
	Reef flat corals	Behind algal rim	Dark tones but generally diagnosed by texture pattern	Fine 'micro-dot' pattern often with strong lineation determined by wave passage over the reef flat
	Sandy reef flat	Lee side	Very light tones, brilliant white on areas of major accumulation	Smooth texture, pattern again following wave refraction

TABLE 1 *(continued)*

Feature	Location key (where applicable)	Tonal key	Texture-Pattern
Sea grass beds	Sheltered reef flat	Dark patches standing out sharply against lighter tones of reef flat	Fluffy 'cotton-wool' appearance especially around edges

REEF EDGE

Feature	Location key (where applicable)	Tonal key	Texture-Pattern
Algal terraces	Reef edge, particularly where tidal range is high	Dark lines, very dark on reef edge side	Linear pattern
Algal rim	Reef edge, especially weather side	Uniform light grey tones	Even texture, broad band with serrated lagoonward edge
Sand chute	Especially leeward side	Light tones, becoming darker at depth	Delta-like wedges but may form a channel labrynth amongst coral heads
Spurs and grooves including living coral	Especially weather side	Very dark. Very dark, black around margins	Strong notched pattern normal or near normal to reef edge. Irregular pattern

the sandy pools. On the Great Barrier Reef these are prominent only in areas of higher tidal range (in excess of 4 m).

Reef islands are easily distinguished. Brilliant white sand or shingle beaches merge into slightly darker reef flat sands with spits or drift areas sharply defined. Beach rock has a much darker appearance, with supplementary keying from its position closely parallel to the beach and a linear pattern. Vegetated areas have variable appearance. Low herbaceous vegetation, or areas of dune creepers, have light tones with fine texture and some linear pattern representing the beach ridge structure of the cay. Forested areas are darker and coarser textured, generally coarsest and most open in pattern on younger sand bodies, darker and finer on the older interior portions of cays where *Pisonia* sp. or even rainforest may be found. *Casuarinas* immediately behind the beach may stand out in darker tones if sufficiently dense and the photo-scale is suitable. Mangrove areas provide the darkest tones of the reef flat and together with a mottled texture and a sheltered location are readily identified. On large scale photographs variable dark tones, often with sharp boundaries, generally indicate species changes. However, in cyclone prone areas, such as north Queensland, these photo patterns of mangroves may be misleading and erosion into the mangroves during cyclones may be followed by recolonization by the same species. The sharp tonal contrast may thus be one of age of the stands, not species.

Raised reef is very variable in its photo patterns, depending to a large extent on its age and degree of karstification, and on the vegetation it bears. Older reef limestones may have distinct solution hollows, enclosed depressions

D

and lack surface drainage. Younger emerged reefs may still retain much of the original morphology though in their raised state the morphological zones are all darker in tone than the active features. Raised fringing reefs will be parallel to the major high island physiography and the fringing nature of the terrace sequences is normally easily distinguished.

Although penetration through the water allows some interpretation of deeper lagoon and reef margin features, the dark tones of both living coral and deeper waters combine to handicap panchromatic photography in this respect.

Colour aerial photography

The range of tonal contrasts seen in black and white photographs is greatly increased by the introduction of colour. Theoretically at least this should aid in the range and accuracy of interpretation. This is certainly true of most features seen on photography of coral reefs. However, the introduction of colour may lead to a decrease in tonal contrast and on some photographs the differentiation between algal rim and reef rubble may not be so marked in colour. Table 2 summarizes the advantages and disadvantages of colour photography for reef work. Greatest advantage probably lies in greater water depth penetration and more precise definition of subsurface features which leads to a better stereoscopic image of the reef. Living coral shows blue-black coloration, dead coral is browner in colour. The tonal variation in single colours is most enhanced in the darker tones and in particular vegetation contrasts, both on cays and in mangroves, are greater. However, the light tones of sandy areas also have a greater range of recognizable photo images. Coral sand above water level appears in very light tones, almost white, whilst shingle frequently has a buff coloration. Sandy areas below water are much darker (buff grading to green and turquoise) a contrast which does not always occur on panchromatic film.

Although these colour patterns were noted on three different types of colour film, it is worth remembering that variations (of film type, exposure and lighting conditions) in the exact appearance of reef features are greater on colour than on panchromatic film (for general application and interpretation of colour aerial photography, see Am. Soc. Photogram. and Soc. Photo. Sci. and Eng., 1969; and Am. Soc. Photogram., 1969).

Colour infra-red photography

Colour infra-red film as used in aerial survey is sensitive to the complete light spectrum from blue to near infra-red, but blue light is prevented from reaching the film by using a yellow filter. The result is that colours of blue, green and red result from exposure to green, red and infra-red radiation respectively. Hence this is false colour photography, with the advantage that near infra-red radiation is now visibly recorded.

34

TABLE 2. Identification criteria for coral reef features—colour aerial photographs compared with panchromatic.

	Feature	Colour-tone
ISLAND	Cay	Sand (buff) and coral shingle (white) better differentiated than on panchromatic. Greater tonal variation in vegetation, e.g. dark greens of *Casuarina* v lighter *Pisonia*.
	Beach rock	Dark brown, grey: stands out sharply, but no great advantage over panchromatic imagery of same scale.
	Raised reef	Colour and tone vary according to vegetation cover. Karst features are easily identified.
	Mangroves	Tonal variation in greens greatly enhanced. Bare areas—mud flats (grey-black) easily identified.
MOAT AND RAMPART	Shingle ramparts	Grey to grey-brown in colour (depending on film type). The junction with the algal rim is poorly differentiated. Strong definition of higher lagoonward margins.
	Moats	Where water is less than 15 cm deep the definition of moated areas is no better in colour than on panchromatic. Deeper areas (light blues) are better defined.
	Basset and cemented edges of reef rubble	Grey, light to medium in tone. Greater contrast with buff colours of reef flat.
REEF FLAT	Lagoon	Penetration of water depths by colour film is greatly superior. Allowance has to be made for variation in bottom sediments, but the range of colours in the blue-green area provides a good guide to morphology.
	Lagoon corals	These stand out more clearly being black to dark grey in colour against a blue-green background.
	Reef flat corals	These do not gain as much from colour photography, particularly where substratum is very sandy.
	Sandy reef flat	Clearly defined in light buff but no great advantage over panchromatic.
	Sea grass beds	Blue-green of light tone. The 'cotton-wool' texture slightly enhanced by greater contrast.
REEF EDGE	Algal terraces	Dark brown tones, no significant gain from colour.
	Algal rim	Medium tone brown to buff. Tonal contrast with rubble area not as great as on panchromatic.
	Sand chute	Light turquoise from buff coloured sandy reef flat areas. Depth penetration by colour film allows for identification of mega ripples and other submarine features.
	Spurs and grooves	Although dark in tone (blue-black) reef front morphology is enhanced on colour photographs.
	Living coral	Again the dark blue-black colours may be traced more evenly and to greater depths than on panchromatic film.

There are both advantages and disadvantages in using infra-red imagery of coral reef areas (see Table 3). Water is almost transparent to near infra-red radiation and dark tones are recorded, sharply defining any areas above water level but lacking penetration beyond depths of 3 to 4 m. However, whilst deeper reef edge and lagoon features are obscured the full range of these tones, which water areas produce, are limited to a range of approximately 3 m water depth. Tonal differentiation of differences in water depths of a few centimetres is thus possible. Reef-flat morphology in particular is sharply defined. Emerged

TABLE 3. Identification criteria for coral reef features—colour infra-red aerial photographs compared with panchromatic and colour.

	Feature	Colour-tone and comparative value
ISLAND	Cay	Unvegetated areas—white. Vegetation in various tones of magenta, with deepest colours on oldest sand/shingle components. Structure of cay via vegetation already indicated.
	Beach rock	Light blue-grey colour clearly defined from unconsolidated beach, but inferior image compared with true colour photography.
	Raised reef	Karst surface, where delineated by vegetation, is clearly depicted. Colour depends on local vegetation.
	Mangroves	Bright magenta with a greater tonal variation related to species than in panchromatic or colour.
MOAT AND RAMPART	Shingle ramparts	White. Very clearly defined.
	Basset edges and other cemented reef flat shingle.	Blue-grey, light tone. Difficult to distinguish from uncemented areas.
	Moats	Clearly picked out in blue with tonal variations related to depth as in the lagoon system.
REEF FLAT	Lagoon	Shallow areas and margins explicitly defined. Shallow water depths differentiated but not depths greater than 3 m—deep blue.
	Lagoon corals	Emerged heads at low water red to pink, blue tones where submerged. Deeper corals below 3 m not visible.
	Reef flat corals	As above.
	Sandy reef flat	Well defined in light blue tones varying according to depth of water.
	Sea grass beds	Reds and pinks when occasionally emerged, otherwise dark blue tones and 'cloudy' texture.
REEF EDGE	Algal terraces	Anastomosing pattern defined in greater detail as a result of range of water depth tones.
	Algal rim	Blue colour with spotty distribution of very light pinks if exposed at low tide. Much darker tones than adjacent shingle ramparts and thus, more easily defined.
	Sand chute	Upper areas only visible to about 3 m depth. Light blues near surface. deep indigo at depth.
	Spurs and grooves	Surface pattern visible, but no penetration. Dark blue.
	Living coral	Pink tones when exposed, light blues when just submerged, dark blues deeper than 1 m. Not visible at depths greater than 3 m.

features or coral-sand shingle or rubble are shown in very light tones and shingle ramparts become sharply defined, particularly where they drop into moats. Even minor areas of sand or shingle are defined with great clarity.

Infra-red photography has had wide use in vegetation studies as healthy foliage reflects radiation across a relatively narrow band of the visible spectrum (0.54 to 0.56 microns) but across almost the entire band of the near infra-red area utilized in photography (0.7 to 0.9 microns). Thus the reds which record this radiation have a much greater tonal range than the greens recorded in normal colour photography. Cay and mangrove vegetation is thus differentiated most clearly. For example, on photography of the Howick group of islands on the Great Barrier Reef north of Cooktown, the following species could be identified:

Rhizophora: deep red, fine, even texture;
Avicennia: lighter tone, spotty texture;
Suriana: very light tones, poorest infra-red reflection, even texture.

Other species (incl. *Excoecaria, Bruguiera, Ceriops, Aegialitis*) have uneven mottled texture but generally bright red tones lying between *Rhizophora* and *Avicennia*. Rollet (1973) has described the use of colour infra-red photography in differentiating *Rhizophora, Laguncularia, Avicennia* and *Conocarpus* in coastal lagoon environments in Mexico. He also emphasizes the importance of age of the mangrove stands in influencing their false colour image, together with the time of photography and conditions of developing the film. Nevertheless he also concludes that the infra-red film is superior for species determination.

Unfortunately under even five centimetres of water, all infra-red radiation is not recorded. Thus sea-grass beds such as *Thalassia* or *Zostera* while having strong infra-red reflectance, rarely show this on aerial photography as their location is normally one in which water does not entirely drain, even at low tide. Emerged beds turn brown rapidly and in doing so lose their ability to reflect in the infra-red range. However, the increased range of tones within shallow waters emphasizes the cloudy, cotton-wool texture of sea-grass beds thus enhancing their recognition.

Little is known about the images produced by living coral and other marine organisms on infra-red film. On photographs taken at extreme low tides of fringing reefs around islands in the Townsville area, and on reefs north of Cooktown on the Great Barrier Reef, some areas of pink and red are shown on reef edges, associated with emerged coral heads. In an effort to determine the origin of this reflection close up colour infra-red photographs were taken of a number of organisms which could normally be expected in these locations. Results are summarized in Table 4. Clearly infra-red radiation is being reflected by both encrusting algae and living coral (though the symbiotic algae may be contributing). However, from aerial photography of areas examined on the ground, it is also clear that the brightest reds and pinks are associated with the living coral heads, lighter tones with encrusting algae. Under certain lighting and exposure conditions, the exposed algal rim may also show as slightly pink in

TABLE 4. Results of infra-red photography of coral reef organisms.

1.	Dead coral, no algal encrustation (*Pocillopora* sp)	White
2.	Dead clam shell (*Tridacna*) with algal encrustation, and boring organisms	Clam-blue-grey. Encrusting organisms purple to dark red
3.	Living staghorn coral (*Acropora* sp.)	Bright red
4.	Living coral (*Pocillopora* sp)	Deep red
5.	Living coral (*Moselyea* sp) under stress, some corallites dead	Red only in areas of living tissue
6.	Dead coral, heavy algal encrustation (including *Lithothamnion*)	Light purple colours of encrusting organisms
7.	Chlorophyta	Bright red

colour infra-red, though this is minimal. Further work is required although the technique is limited in its application by the very few tides in the year which are low enough to expose living coral.

Other remote sensors

Remote sensing in other wave lengths may have application to reef research. Of particular relevance are infra-red thermal sensors utilizing the two windows of 4.3 and 8 to 14 microns. Imagery is generated not by a frame format of a camera system but by a continuous raster scan system similar to television (Colwell and Olson, 1964; Estes, 1966; Van Lopick, 1968). Small thermal variations can be perceived which may be influenced by moisture content, density changes or by subsurface features. Thermal scanning has particular significance to oceanographic studies (see below).

Within the microwave region, little work has been carried out with passive systems by environmental scientists. However, the active mode, radar, has been utilized though not in coral reef environments. The amount of reflected return from a surface illuminated by a polarized radar beam is partially determined by size, shape, texture, attitude, density and moisture content. Shorter wave lengths detect surface detail while longer wave lengths have the property of surface penetrability. The value of this system for mapping an area too consistently cloud-covered for normal photography is indicated by Lewis and Macdonald (1972). They mapped an area of mangrove and shell reefs in southeastern Panama with side-scanning radar. Although difficulties in interpretation exist in discriminating between changes due to surface roughness or vegetation cover and those attributable to surface composition, Lewis and Macdonald were able to identify mangrove, separating *Rhizophora* from *Avicennia,* and three other vegetation zones, *Mora,* freshwater swamp and selva (see their interpretative keys, p. 193). In addition, vegetation-free zones within the mangrove were distinguished due to smooth texture and low radar return. Shell reefs, near low tide, 100 m wide and 1 km in length were also detectable on radar imagery.

CORAL REEF IMAGERY FROM SPACE

A large proportion of the rapid advances made in remote sensing over the last 10 years must be attributable to the use of satellites as sensing platforms and their ability to provide data rapidly and extensively. The image processing procedures already mentioned are one result. The gathering of oceanographic data (see below) is another. Yet again, however, little use appears to have been made of satellite imagery in coral reef research. Possibly a basic reason is the small scale of such imagery which means that small features, often the ones on which the coral reef researcher is requiring information, are below the ground resolution of the space photography. Nevertheless, space photography has been successfully used in geomorphological and geological mapping (Bannert, 1970; Bodechtel and Gierloff-Emden, 1969; Cavelier *et al.*, 1973; Gedney and Van Wormer, 1973; Lyon, 1970; Pouquet and Rashke, 1968; Verstappen and Von Zudiam, 1970) and procedures for interpretation utilizing these new dimensions of colour, texture and pattern appear to have relevance to reef research.

The colour photographs from a hand-held camera during the 1965 GEMINI flights were amongst the earliest available which showed coral reef areas including Pacific atolls (Marshall Islands) parts of the Great Barrier Reef and the Bahamas (NASA, 1967). Details of shallow bottom topography were revealed particularly around the Bahamas, and the possibility of correcting existing charts of complex reef areas was realized. The ERTS programme of 1972–3 has greatly extended the coverage of coral reef areas and has made generally available multiband imagery including three images (0.475–0.575 microns, 0.58–0.68, 0.69–0.83) from Return Beam Vidicon and four images (0.5–0.6 microns, 0.6–0.7, 0.7–0.8, 0.8–1.1) from the Multispectral Scanner. Each scene, thus recorded seven times, covers an area of 10,000 square nautical miles (185 × 185 km).[2]

Large areas of the Great Barrier Reef are covered by ERTS imagery. Clearest depiction of the reef areas is in the green wavelengths (0.5 to 0.6 microns) although the area of reef, from just below the surface to about 10 m, is also seen in the red wavelengths (0.6 to 0.7 microns). The reefs do not show at all on the infra-red images though these are useful for delineating mainland coastal areas and islands within the reef complexes. A surprising amount of detail is visible in these photographs. Small islands no longer than 200 m can be detected. Lagoons, and sometimes the complex of coral heads within them, are clearly seen and on larger reefs more than 5 km in length differentiation between algal rim (light tones) and reef flat corals (darker tones) can be made. Mangrove areas on reef islands stand out as relatively light tones but with uneven texture.

The greatest value of these photographs, however, lies in the fact that they supplement existing hydrographic charts, many of which date back to the last century with only minor subsequent corrections. Large areas of the Great Barrier Reef are simply marked 'numerous reefs' or 'discoloured water' and are based on surveys of HMS *Fly* between 1843 and 1845. Although normal panchromatic aerial photography is now available, there are photogrammetric problems in establishing accurately the locations of isolated reefs up to 150 km from land with many frames of uninterrupted sea between individual reefs. The satellite photographs overcome this problem by providing an overall synoptic view in which the photogrammetric problems resulting from curvature of the earth are relatively minor.

2. ERTS imagery is available in a number of forms from EROS Data Centre, Data Management Centre, Sioux Falls, South Dakota, 57198, U.S.A.

OCEANOGRAPHIC DATA FROM REMOTE SENSING

So far this review has been limited to the environments provided on and within coral reefs. Many biological and physical studies however, require information on the larger environment in which the reefs themselves are located. Normal black and white and even colour photography is limited in providing oceanographic data, though short term sequential photography of drogues, dyes or colour markers has been advocated. Smith (1963) describes a method of obtaining tidal current measurements at various depths from sequential photography of the positions of floats moved by under water drogues travelling at different depths. Symbol marking of such floats, would appear to overcome the higher costs of colour compared to panchromatic photography. However, by combining some of the advanced and experimental techniques of sensing and image processing described earlier it is clear that it is now possible for detailed information on the physical and biological characteristics of the water bodies around the reefs to be collected.

This type of approach to oceanographic studies is epitomized by a paper by Szekielda and Mitchell (1972) on the oceanographic applications of colour-enhanced satellite imageries. Densities of black and white infra-red space imagery were transformed into colour presentations by way of a precision monochrome television camera which converts the transmitted light to an electrical video signal, an analyser that separates the shades of grey, or voltage levels in the video signal, into 12 colours and converts the levels into colour television signals, and a colour television monitor for reproduction of the original or colour separated image. The grey scale of satellite infra-red imagery is thus transformed into colours from white (cold) to black (warm) with increasing temperatures indicated by 12 colour steps (white, dark blue, light blue, dark green, light green, olive, brown, gold, red, magenta, violet and black). Temperature differences of 2° Celsius can be easily recognized and significant temperature structures can be obtained if the skies are cloud free. Areas of upwelling may be recognized and actual synoptic situations mapped.

This ability to produce real time images of thermal anomalies is also stressed by Adams et al. (1970). They describe the results of a study of coastal Hawaii utilizing the 3 to 5.5 micrometer band of infra-red imagery from a plane flying at 11,000 feet. It was found that temperature differences as small as 0.2° Celsius could be detected. Again the great advantage of infra-red thermo-vision was its ability to provide a real time display of the thermal dynamics of a coastal area in a matter of hours. The application to reef studies in terms of planulae dispersal and nutrient status of water bodies appears to be warranted, particularly where thermal scanning can be linked to current movements (see for example Maul and Hansen, 1972; Maul, 1973) or areas of upwelling (as in Szekielda and Mitchell, 1972 or Szekielda, 1971).

Turbidity may be determined more directly. Several studies have been made of the relationship between light attenuation and water colour (e.g. Jerlov, 1964a, b; Moore, 1947; Kinney et al., 1967; Clarke and James, 1939;

and Lepley, 1968). Figure 3 shows these general relationships which may be applied to photography from aeroplanes. Lepley (1968) extended the work to a global scale by analysing GEMINI space photography. In spite of an increase in atmospheric colour distortion observed from space, data from the satellite photographs correlated closely with *in situ* observations. Lepley recommends the use of metric cameras in multispectral array, or with colour film with strong

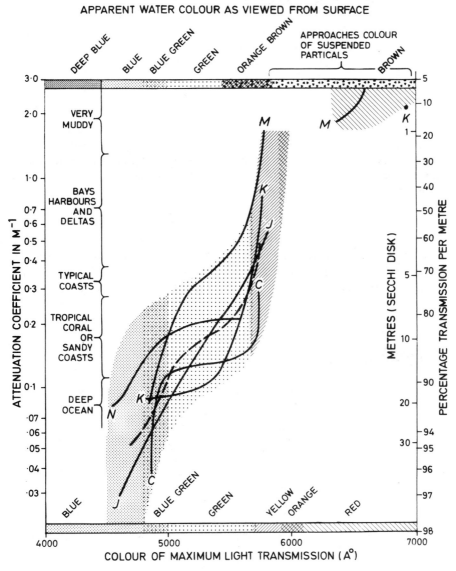

Figure 3
Light attenuation as a function of water colour (after Lepley, 1968).

minus-blue (dark yellow) filters, or film without the blue emulsion layer to prevent the unwanted blue fogging that degraded the GEMINI imagery.

Aspects of biological oceanography also may be monitored by remote sensing (see for example Ewing, 1965; Texas A and M Univ, Remote Sensing Centre, 1971). As light penetrates the sea, it is altered not only by the water but also by absorption and scattering due to the particulate and dissolved materials present. Phytoplankton and especially the chlorophyll and other pigments which it contains are especially important. These changes in the spectrum can be measured from the air and the shape of the spectrum can be used to measure the kinds and amounts of substances present (Clarke, 1969; Ewing, 1971). The procedures described suggest a method for the rapid delineation of water masses from the air which may have application to coral studies.

CONCLUSIONS

Although coral reef researchers have been foremost in utilizing traditional forms of aerial photography, comparatively little use appears to have been made of newer forms of remote sensing. There is little doubt that panchromatic and colour aerial photography can provide both base maps, and, with a systematic approach to interpretation, a great deal of basic data. However, experiments in the use of near infra-red and sensing in other wavelengths would appear warranted. Satellite photography may be limited in providing reef detail, but its use is recommended in areas which are poorly charted. The utilization of thermal scanning in particular appears to have value in oceanographic studies of coral reef waters. More experimentation and testing are needed in both data gathering and processing within the field of coral reef research.

References

ADAMS, W.; LEPLEY, L.; WARREN, C.; CHANG, S. 1970. Coastal and urban surveys with I.R. *Photogramm. Eng.*, vol. 36, p. 173–180.

AMERICAN SOCIETY OF PHOTOGRAMMETRY, 1960. *Manual of photographic interpretation*, (868 p.)
——. 1966. *Manual of photogrammetry*, 3rd edit., (1199 p.).
——. 1969. *Manual of color aerial photography*.
—— and SOCIETY OF PHOTOGRAPHIC SCIENTISTS AND ENGINEERS. 1969. *New horizons in color aerial photography*, Seminar Proc.

BADGELEY, P. C.; MILOY, L.; CHILDS, L. (eds). 1969. *Oceans from space*, Houston, Gulf Pub.

BANNERT, D. 1969. Geologie auf Satellitenbildern, *Naturwissenschaftliche Rundschau*, vol. 22, p. 517–24.

BODECHTEL, J.; GIERLOFF-EMDEN, H. G. 1969. *Weltraumbilder der Erde*, München, (176 p.).

CAVELIER, C.; SCANVIC, J. Y.; WEEKSTEEN, G.; ZISSERMANN, A. 1973. Apport des images orbitales (ERTS 1) à la connaissance géologique et structurale d'un bassin sedimentaire: le bassin Parisien (France). *Photo Interpretation*, vol. 73–2, p. 1–11.

CLARKE, G. L. 1969. The significance of spectral changes in light scattered by the sea. In P. L. Johnson (ed.). *Remote sensing in ecology*, p. 164–72.
——; JAMES, H. R. 1939. Laboratory analysis of the selective absorption of light by sea water. *J. Opt. Soc. Am.*, vol. 29, no. 10, p. 43–55.

COLWELL, R.; OLSON, D. L. 1964. Thermal infra-red imagery and its use in vegetation analysis by remote aerial reconnaissance. In: *Proc. Third Symp. on remote sensing of environment,* p. 607–21.

ESTES, J. E. 1966. Some applications of aerial infra-red imagery. *Annals Assoc. Am. Geog.,* vol. 56, p. 673–82.

EWING, G. C. (ed.). 1965. *Oceanography from space.* Proc. Conf. Woods Hole Oceanographic Inst., August 1964.

——. 1971. Remote spectrography of ocean colour as an index of biological activity. In: *Proc. Symp. on remote sensing in marine geology and fishery resources.* Texas A and M University, Remote Sensing Center.

FEZER, F. 1971. Photo interpretation applied to geomorphology. *Photogrammetria,* vol. 27, p. 7–53.

FLOOD, P. G. 1974. Sand movements on Heron Island—a vegetated sand cay, Great Barrier Reef Province, Australia. In: *Proc. Second Int. Coral Reef Symp.* Brisbane, Great Barrier Reef Committee, vol. 2, p. 387–94.

GEDNEY, L.; VAN VORMER, J. 1973. Tectonic mapping in Alaska with ERTS-1 imagery. *Photo. Interpretation,* vol. 73-1, p. 23–7.

GUILCHER, A.; BERTHOIS, L.; DOUMENGE, F.; MICHEL, A.; SAINT-REQUIER, A.; ARNOLD, R. 1969. *Les récifs et lagons coralliens de Mopelia et de Bora-Bora.* ORSTOM, Memoires.

HARRIS, W. D.; UMBACH, M. J. 1972. Underwater mapping. *Photogram. Eng.,* vol. 38, p. 765–72.

HELBIG, H. 1973. NASA false colour photograph. In: 1973 *Space Calendar, Zeiss.*

HELGESON, G. A. 1970. Water depth and distance penetration. *Photogram. Eng.,* vol. 36, p. 164–72.

HOWARD, J. A. 1972. *Aerial photo-ecology.*

JERLOV, N. G. 1964a. Optical classification of ocean water. In: *Physical aspects of light in the sea.* University of Hawaii.

——. 1964b. Factors influencing the color of the sea. In: M. SEARS (ed.). *Studies in oceanography.*

——. 1968. *Optical oceanography.* Elsevier, (194 p.)

JOHNSON, P. L. (ed.). 1969. *Remote sensing in ecology.* University of Georgia.

KELLY, M. G. 1969. Aerial photography for the study of nearshore ocean biology. In: Am. Soc. Photogram. and Soc. Phot. Sci. and Eng. *New horizons in colour aerial photography,* p. 347–56.

——; CONRAD, A. 1969. Aerial photographic studies of shallow water benthic ecology. In: P. L. Johnson (ed.). *Remote sensing in ecology.* University of Georgia, p. 173–84.

KINNEY, J. S.; LURIA, S. M.; WERTZMAN, D. O. 1967. Visibility of colors underwater. *J. Opt. Soc. Am.,* vol. 57, p. 806–9.

KUMPF, H. E.; RANDALL, H. A. 1961. Charting the marine environments of St. John, U.S. Virgin Islands. *Bull. mar. Sci.,* vol. 11, p. 543–51.

LANCASTER, J. 1968. Geographers and remote sensing. *J. Geog.,* 67, 301–10.

LATTMAN, L. H.; RAY, R. G. 1965. *Aerial photographs in field geology.* New York, Holt, Rinehart and Wilson.

LEPLEY, L. K. 1968. Coastal water clarity from space photographs. *Photogram. Eng.,* vol. 34, p. 667–74.

LEWIS, A. J.; MACDONALD, H. C. 1972. Mapping of mangrove and perpendicular-oriented shell reefs in southeastern Panama with side looking radar. *Photogrammetria,* vol. 28, p. 187–200.

LYON, R. J. P. 1970. Multiband approach to geological mapping from orbiting satellites. *Remote Sens. of Envir.,* vol. 1, p. 237–44.

MAUL, G. A. 1973. Remote sensing of ocean currents using ERTS imagery. *Photo-Interpretation Rev. 1973–4,* p. 48–65.

——; HANSEN, D. V. 1972. An observation of the Gulf Stream surface front structure by ship, aircraft and satellite. *Remote Sens. of Envir.,* vol. 2, p. 109–16.

MAXWELL, W. G. H. 1968. *Atlas of the Great Barrier Reef.* Amsterdam, Elsevier.

MOORE, J. G. 1947. The determination of the depths and extinction coefficients of shallow water by air photography using colour filters. *Phil. Trans R. Soc. Lond.* (A: *Phys. Sci.*), vol. 240, p. 163–217.

NASA. 1967. *Earth photographs from GEMINI III, IV and V.* NASA-SP-129.

ORME, G. R.; FLOOD, P. G.; EWART, A. 1974. An investigation of the sediments and physiography of Lady Musgrave reef—a preliminary account. In: *Proc. Second Int. Coral Reef Symp.* Brisbane, Great Barrier Reef Committee, vol. 2, p. 371–86.

POUQUET, J.; RASHKE, E. 1968. Geomorphological aspects of the northeast Sahara after a comparative study of surface temperatures and reflectance from Nimbus II measurements. *Trans. Am. geophys. Union,* vol. 74, no. 5.

RICH, J. L. 1947. Reconnaissance mapping from oblique aerial photographs without ground control. *Photogram. Eng.*, vol. 13, p. 600–9.

ROLLET, B. 1973. Comparaison de photographies aériennes panchromatiques et fausse couleur pour l'interprétation des mangroves des États de Oaxaca et de Chiapas, Mexique. *Photo-Interpretation Rev.*, 1973–4, p. 28–47.

SMITH, J. T. 1963. Color a new dimension in photogrammetry. *Photogram. Eng.*, vol. 29, p. 999–1013.

SPECHT, M. R.; NEEDLER, D.; FRITZ, N. L. 1973. New color film for water penetration. *Photogram. Eng.*, vol. 39, p. 359–69.

STEERS, J. A. 1945. Coral reefs and air photography. *Geog. J.*, vol. 106, p. 232–5.

STEPHENSON, T. A.; TANDY, G.; SPENDER, M. 1931. The structure and ecology of Low Islands and other reefs. *Sci. Repts. Gt Barrier Reef Exped., 1928–29*, vol. 3, no 2, p. 17–112.

SZEKIELDA, K-H. 1971. Upwelling studies with satellites. In: *Proc. Symp. on Remote Sensing in Marine Biology and Fishery Resources*. Texas A and M University, Remote Sensing Center, p. 271–93.

——; MITCHELL, W. F. 1972. Oceanographic applications of color-enhanced satellite imageries. *Remote Sens. of Envir.*, vol. 2, p. 71–6.

TEICHERT, C.; FAIRBRIDGE, R. W. 1948. The Low Isles of the Great Barrier Reef: a new analysis. *Geogr. J.*, vol. 111, p. 67–88.

——, 1950. Photointerpretation of coral reefs. *Photogram. Eng.*, vol. 16, p. 744–55.

TEWINKEL, G. C. 1963. Water depths from aerial photographs. *Photogram. Eng.*, vol. 29, p. 1037–42.

TEXAS A and M UNIVERSITY, Remote Sensing Center. 1971. In: *Proc. Symp. on Remote Sensing in Marine Biology and Fishery Resources*. College Station, Texas, (299 p.).

UMBGROVE, J. H. F. 1928. De Korallriffen in de Baai van Batavia, *Wet. Med. Dienst. v.d. Mijnbouw in Ned-Indie*, vol. 7, 68 p.

——. 1929. De Korallriffen der Duizend-Eilanden (Java Zee). *Wet. Med. Dienst v.d. Mijnbouw in Ned-Indie*, vol. 12, 47 p.

VAN LOPIK, J. 1968. Infrared mapping: basic technology and geoscience applications. *Geo. Science News*, vol. 1, p. 3.

VERSTAPPEN, H. T.; VAN ZUDIAN, R. A. 1970. Orbital photography and the geosciences—a geomorphological example from the Central Sahara. *Geoforum*, vol. 1, p. 33–47.

ZEISS, C. OPTICAL COMPANY. 1973. *Space calendar*.

4

Photogrammetry of reef environments by helium balloon

K. Rützler[1]

Present findings show that aerial photography by balloon-suspended camera is an inexpensive and easy-to-use technique with a good potential for hitherto unexplored applications. At remote locations where airplanes or helicopters with sophisticated photogrammetric equipment are not available, the balloon method may be the only means for producing accurate maps with substantial area coverage.

When undertaking an ecological study the initial step is to survey the region to determine the kinds of habitats present, their extent and their location. A coral reef comprises a number of geomorphic and biogenous features, such as the actual reef framework, rock, sand patches, sea grass areas, mangroves, lagoons and islands. An accurate knowledge of this topography and of the water depth distribution enables one to pinpoint localities for collecting and subsequent floristic and faunistic inventory. More imporant, a careful reconnaissance provides the basis for understanding the impact of physical, chemical and biological processes that are connected with water currents, waves and tides, as well as with meteorological and other parameters. Habitat maps are valuable tools for the selection of significant sampling locations and experimental sites and, finally, they serve as a reference for future topographical changes caused by constructive processes or destructive forces.

Ground-level mapping of cays and shallow reefs is routine (Stoddart, 1962; Domm, 1971; Stoddart, Chapter 2) and will continue to produce records of unequalled resolution. The same techniques can also be used by divers underwater where they are aided by the possibility of taking vertical photographs (Johnston et al., 1969; Rützler, 1976). This touches one of the weaknesses of ground-level mapping, the difficulty of copying complex shapes and maintaining correct proportions. The procedures are tedious and frequently subject to error.

Aerial photography has long been used for large-scale mapping and for creating matrices where details can be filled in by other surveying methods

1. Department of Invertebrate Zoology, National Museum of Natural History, Smithsonian Institution, Washington, D.C. 20560, U.S.A.

(Kumpf and Randall, 1961; Macintyre, 1968; Smith and Anson, 1968; Adey, 1975; Hopley, Chapter 3). The problem of speed, inherent in low-flying airplanes, has been overcome by the use of helicopters, which have been successfully employed for survey of marine habitats (Ellis, 1966; Burton and Buhaut, 1975).

Many ecological studies, on coral reefs in particular, are conducted in remote areas where logistical support in the form of airplanes or helicopters are difficult and expensive to obtain. Although small private airplanes can be chartered at many locations, they usually do not permit good vertical photography at low altitude. Discouraged by similar problems, archaeologists developed a camera system which was suspended from a hydrogen-inflated balloon and which could be used to detect and map Greek temple sites in the Mediterranean (Whittlesey, 1967). This technique was applied with equal success to terrestrial and submarine excavations (Jameson, 1974).

During the Smithsonian Reef Project at Carrie Bow Cay, Belize, the cay and reef flat, including principal community components, were mapped from the ground. A 600 m main transect crossing the barrier reef, from the lagoon to and down the fore-reef slope was the focal point for many efforts to determine

Figure 1
Balloon-supported camera over the barrier reef of Belize. South Water Cay is in the background. The front tether-trigger cable is operated from the small raft. A transect marker is visible in the centre. (photo: E. Kirsteuer).

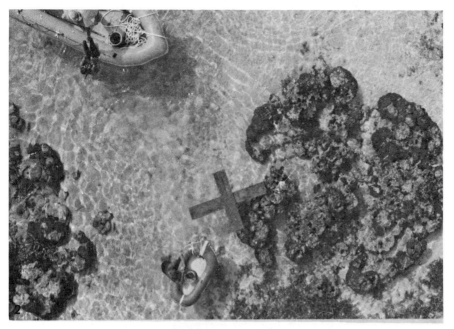

Figure 2
The location of Fig. 1, as it is seen by the balloon camera. The same
transect marker is visible to the right of the longer bar of the cross. The
cross measures 2 × 1.5 metres.

the distribution pattern of bottom types, framework constituents and associated biota. No great problems were encountered when recording changes
along the transect line proper. It is almost impossible, however, to map complicated structures in the right proportions within a 5 m belt on either side of the
transect line, covering 6000 m². The same is true with areas surveyed outside
the transect. These had to be localized in relation to the cay and to the main
transect with the help of compass bearings and range-finder measurements.
Since only oblique photographs could be obtained from the locally available
low-winged aircraft, the balloon technique was used for much of the photogrammetric work (Figs. 1–5).

EQUIPMENT AND SURVEYING METHODS

A standard 35 mm Nikon F Camera was chosen because it was available and
could easily be equipped with an electrical motor drive (Nikon F-36). Unnecessary accessories, like viewfinder and exposure meter, were removed to
reduce weight, and the mirror locked in the up position to avoid vibrations.
The camera was mounted, lens down, on the bottom plane of the tetrahedron
built from 1/2 inch (13 mm) angular aluminum moulding, with 50 cm side

47

length (Fig. 3). It was balanced and positioned so that the longer axis of the picture frame would be parallel to one side of the tetrahedron. To the centre of this side, a plastic-coated fishing leader wire (35 kg test strength) was fastened to serve as the rear tether. The opposite corner supported the trigger cable, a two-stranded size 22 (0.6 mm diameter) conductor, which was also used as front tether and to guide the balloon. Maximum tether length used during the tests was 40 m. A manual switch at the end of the conductor cable was used to trigger exposures and subsequent film advance.

The camera, complete with film, motor drive and batteries, weighs 1600 g, the tetrahedron frame, with two 40 m tether lines, weighs 800 g. A balloon had

Figure 3
Tetrahedron frame with camera ready for use. A bucket holds the trigger cable and keeps the contact switch dry (photo: E. Kirsteuer).

to be chosen that could lift this weight, with some allowance for extra tether length, but with minimum size to save helium gas and offer small resistance to air currents. The selected 1450 g meteorological balloon (Weathermeasure Corporation, Sacramento, California) has 2665 g free lift. It uses 4 m³ of helium gas for this performance and inflates to 2 m in diameter. Helium has less lifting capacity (93 per cent) and is not as easily obtained as hydrogen, but it is much safer to use and does not require expensive non-static balloons. Helium is stored in standard 240 cu ft. (6.8 m³) cylinders. Sixty per cent of this volume is needed to fill one balloon. The rest can be used to compensate for gas losses during storage. Filling is effected through a two-stage helium regulator and a filling adaptor that fits the 32 mm diameter balloon neck and has a 2665 g weight built-in. The neck is tied off after the balloon has lifted its filling device off the ground. The balloon with camera frame attached can easily be handled by one person and can be carried to the survey area on foot, by swimming or by slow-moving boat.

The field to be covered by each exposure is a function of camera height and focal length of the lens used. For 36 × 24 mm film size, lenses with no less than 24 mm focal length should be used to avoid glare and distortion problems. These, however, depend also on water depth and sun angle. Balloon height above 50 m is impractical because camera orientation and movement cannot be seen clearly and handling becomes difficult, particularly for overlapping picture series. Our experience indicates that routine surveys of a given area should be conducted at two levels. For coarse structure and general proportions a 24 mm lens at 50 m altitude covers a field of 75 × 50 m. For high resolution mapping a 50 mm lens at 35 m altitude covers a 24 × 16 m area. On a calm day, however, the only limitation to camera altitude is the resistance of the trigger wire which should not exceed 100 ohms. Trigger control by radio was found to be impractical because of the additional expense and because tether lines have also to be used.

Some variation of balloon height will always occur because of air turbulence and changing angle and pull on the tether lines which are handled by two persons. It is therefore important to have a scale on each picture. A brightly painted wooden cross, 2 × 1.5 m, is used. The longer axis is kept in line with the transect by a swimmer (Fig. 4). The image of the cross permits subsequent corrections of scale and picture orientation and provides a control of the vertical viewing angle (Figs. 3 and 5). In deep water (below 1 m), the scale must be placed on the bottom or a correction factor based on the water depth must be applied.

A negative colour film (Kodak Vericolor II) has been used exclusively to date. Colour or black-and-white prints and transparencies can be produced from this material, it has a greater exposure latitude than reversal colour films, and colour balance and density can be controlled during printing. At a film speed of ASA 100 (20 DIN) common exposure values were 1/1000 sec at f4 for 11.00–14.00 hours time, cloudless sky, 1–2 m water depth off Carrie Bow Cay (16°48′N latitude) in December.

Figure 4
Ground crew during mapping procedure. Two persons are aligning the
balloon with its tether lines, a third one is positioning the cross for later
orientation and scale reference (photo: E. Kirsteuer).

Figure 5
Vertical view of Carrie Bow Cay reef flat showing sand areas, live *Acropora,
Diploria* and *Montastrea,* and coral rubble. The area covered by this
photograph is 18 × 12 metres.

DISCUSSION

Experiments with remote aerial photogrammetry by helium balloon show that this method combines many advantages of ground-level mapping with those of higher altitude aerial photography. Calm weather conditions are required but will usually be encountered during studies of some duration. A zeppelin-shaped balloon could operate even in moderate winds.

The altitude of the camera can be readily varied to combine general views and close-ups of the same location. On a 12 × 8 m area with 1–2 m water depth, covered by a 36 × 24 mm negative frame, prominent coral species, live versus dead coral, coralline algae coverage, sand, sea grass and even a 6 mm diameter nylon rope that served as transect line could be distinguished. Use of a camera with larger negative format would increase this resolution.

Penetration of water depth by means of the balloon camera equals, in the author's experience, that of a diver's eye swimming at the surface. Noon time with steepest sun angle will ensure optimal results. The condition of the water surface is of course critical. Even small ripples should be avoided as they cause distortions during close-up exposures. High altitude photographs are less affected as long as the ripples or waves are small, compared with the structures be be recorded.

Camera oscillations can occur after positioning the balloon at a new location. These and the horizontal orientation of the camera can both be controlled with the two tether lines. Just before each exposure the tethers should be relaxed to ensure vertical position of the lens axis. Suspension of the camera in gimbals might be an improvement.

When mapping a reef, cay or similar structure, it is important to allow for a generous overlap of exposures in a particular transect series. With a rect-angular camera format, especially, even small horizontal deviations can cause undesirable gaps. Some of these can be compensated for by a duplicate picture series on a smaller scale. Clearly visible reference markers installed for the entire survey area ensure proper localization of each exposure. These can be anchored to the bottom and serve as scale reference at the same time.

Experience is restricted to the use of standard colour negative film. The applications of infrared sensitive materials and other remote sensing tech-niques have not yet been explored. Particularly, films and filters allowing maximum penetration in deep water should be tested.

Although the present arrangement is designed for vertical photogram-metric recording using still pictures, the camera angle could be adjusted for oblique exposures, and motion picture sequences could be produced in a similar manner.

ACKNOWLEDGMENTS

The author thanks E. Kirsteuer, H. Pulpan, C. Ruetzler and K. Sandved for enthusiastic cooperation in the field, as well as I. G. Macintyre and D. L. Pawson for reviewing the manuscript.

This work was supported by the Smithsonian Research Foundation and by a grant from the Exxon Corporation, Contribution no. 29. Investigations of Marine Shallow Water Ecosystems Project, Smithsonian Institution.

References

ADEY, W. H. 1975. The algal ridges and coral reefs of St. Croix: Their structure and holocene development. *Atoll. Res. Bull.,* vol. 187, p. 1–67.

BURTON, B. W.; BUHAUT, J. 1975. Progrès en photographie aérienne à partir d'hélicoptères pour les travaux hydrographiques. *Rev. Hydrog. Int.,* vol. 52, no. 2, p. 39–56.

DOMM, S. B. 1971. Mapping reefs and cays, a quick method for the scientist working alone. *Atoll Res. Bull.,* vol. 148, p. 15–7.

ELLIS, D. V. 1966. Aerial photography from helicopter as a technique for intertidal surveys. *Limnol. Oceanogr.,* vol. 11, p. 299–301.

JAMESON, M. H. 1974. The excavation of a drowned Greek temple. *Sci. Am.,* vol. 231, no. 4: p. 111–9.

JOHNSTON, C. S.; MORRISON, I. A.; MACLACHLAN, K. 1969. A photographic method for recording the underwater distribution of marine benthic organisms. *J. Ecol.,* vol. 57, p. 453–9.

KUMPF, H. E.; RANDALL, H. A. 1961. Charting the marine environments, St. John, U.S. Virgin Islands. *Bull. mar. Sci. Gulf Caribb.,* vol. 11, no. 4, p. 543–51.

MACINTYRE, I. G. 1968. Preliminary mapping of the insular shelf off the west coast of Barbados, W.I. *Caribb. J. Sci.,* vol. 8, p. 95–8.

RÜTZLER, K. 1976. Ecology of Tunisian commercial sponges. *Téthys,* vol. 7, no. 2, p. 249–64.

SMITH, J. T.; ANSON, A. (eds.). 1968. *Manual of color aerial photography.* Falls Church, Virginia, (American Society of Photogrammetry) (500 p.).

STODDART, D. R. 1962. Three Caribbean Atolls: Turneffe Islands, Lighthouse Reef and Glover's Reef, British Honduras. *Atoll Res. Bull .,* vol. 87, p. 1–151.

WHITTLESEY, J. 1967. Balloon over Sardis, *Archaeology,* vol. 20, p. 67–8.

5

Mechanical analysis of reef sediments

D. R. Stoddart[1]

There is a large literature on methods of mechanical analysis of sediments (Krumbein and Pettijohn, 1938; Müller, 1967; Griffiths, 1967; Carver, 1971), but much of it refers specifically to clastic non-carbonate materials, which differ in important respects from the largely skeletal sediments of coral reefs. These are derived either directly from the release of skeletal materials following the death of living organisms, or from the transport, breakdown and deposition of such material. The relative importance of skeletal origin and mode of transportation in controlling the character of reef sediments also varies greatly with depositional environment, from high-energy highly-winnowed beaches on the one hand to low-energy tidal flats or lagoon floors on the other. Because the properties of constituent particles reflect the geometric and structural characters of the skeletons from which they are derived, some of the descriptive measures and analytical techniques developed to describe clastic sediments have been found to be less appropriate. This contribution briefly reviews the sedimentological methods applicable to reef materials, and considers some problems in interpreting the results. The re-appraisal of mechanical analysis of carbonate sediments was initiated by R. L. Folk (1962; 1964; 1966; Folk and Cotera, 1971; Folk, Hayes and Shoji, 1962; Folk and Robles, 1964; Folk and Ward, 1957), and his methods with some modification are followed here. This review is confined to mechanical analysis because other sedimentary attributes have been well dealt with in standard texts by Bathurst (1971) and Milliman (1974).

SAMPLING

Most sediment studies in reef areas employ sampling on line transects along environmental gradients, usually transverse to the reef edge (Illing, 1954; Ginsburg, 1956), or purposive areal sampling designed to give adequate cover of main reef environments (McKee et al., 1959; Hoskin, 1963; Maiklem, 1968).

1. Department of Geography, Cambridge University, Cambridge, CB2 3EN, United Kingdom.

Other studies have sampled within intuitively perceived sedimentary units in order to categorize adequately the main sediment types present (Folk and Robles, 1964; Folk and Cotera, 1971; Fosberg and Carroll, 1965). The frequency of sampling in these studies varies widely with the magnitude of area studied and the heterogeneity of the sedimentary patterns; in beach studies the spacing of samples may be only a few metres whereas in Purdy's (1963) work on the Andros shelf the spacing reached 9 km.

Reef sediments are generally stratified or zoned, and samples are best taken within such already-recognized zones. Topographic, tidal and safety factors introduce major constraints on sampling design, and it is usually found impracticable to attempt random or other such designs over large areas. In smaller areas, such as beaches, the boundaries of zones may change quite rapidly, and this introduces problems in sequential sampling to determine sediment change over time. Krumbein (1954) has shown that purposive sampling gives a reasonable indication of many sediment properties, and this is probably adequate for non-specialist sediment studies in reef areas.

Little attention has been given to the actual collection of samples in the reef environment. Samples are generally taken by scoop or by grab; the former is the more controllable and more readily standardized, and is to be preferred for underwater as well as subaerial sampling. Since sediments often accumulate in discrete layers of restricted thickness, the depth penetrated by the sampling instrument is of critical importance: deep samples may penetrate more than one such sedimentary unit. The process of formation of such units has been demonstrated in the Bahamas by Boon (1968). Large samples should therefore be obtained by increased area of sampling rather than by increased depth (Krumbein and Slack, 1956). Small samples (100 g) are usually sufficient for mechanical analysis. Unless required for specific analyses, over-large samples should be avoided. They pose considerable problems of storage and transportation, and considerable sorting can take place within the sample container during long voyages, making thorough mixing necessary before the sample can be split.

Sand-sized sediments may be stored in polythene bags or screw-top jars, dried as collected, wet with the addition of an agent such as mercuric chloride, or in alcohol. However, even with mixing, alcohol will not penetrate muddy sediments, and some discoloration will occur. Adequate labelling is of great importance: numbers marked with felt pens on the outsides of bags or jars can be erased by sea-water, alcohol or friction, and a further identification tag within the container (e.g. pencil on rough-surfaced plastic tags) is essential.

SEDIMENT MEASUREMENT

As a first approximation, sediments may be described using terms defined in the 'Wentworth scale' (Table 1), which implicitly recognizes the sharp discontinuities which exist in nature between sediment populations in the gravel,

TABLE 1. Grain size scales

Millimetres	Microns	Phi (ϕ)	Wentworth class
4096		−12	
1024		−10	Boulder
—— 256		−8	
			Cobble
—— 64		−6	
16		−4	Pebble
—— 4		−2	
3.36		−1.75	
2.83		−1.5	Granule
2.38		−1.25	
—— 2.00		−1.00	
1.68		−0.75	
1.41		−0.50	Very coarse sand
1.19		−0.25	
—— 1.00		0.0	
0.84		0.25	
0.71		0.50	Coarse sand
0.59		0.75	
—— 0.50	500	1.00	
0.42	420	1.25	
0.35	350	1.50	Medium sand
0.30	300	1.75	
—— 0.25	250	2.00	
0.210	210	2.25	
0.177	177	2.50	Fine sand
0.149	149	2.75	
—— 0.125	125	3.00	
0.105	105	3.25	
0.088	88	3.50	Very fine sand
0.074	74	3.75	
—— 0.0625	62.5	4.00	
0.053	53	4.25	
0.044	44	4.50	Coarse silt
0.037	37	4.75	
—— 0.031	31	5.0	
0.0156	15.6	6.0	Medium silt
0.0078	7.8	7.0	Fine silt
0.0039	3.9	8.0	Very fine silt

sand, silt and clay ranges, and also the geometric relationships. Note that the term 'shingle', not employed by Wentworth (1922, 1953), is in rather common use in the reef literature to denote well-sorted gravel-sized sediment consisting of irregular and often interlocking skeletal fragments, forming a sediment of high permeability characteristic of medium to high energy beaches (Hedley, 1925). The Wentworth scale remains useful in reconnaissance description, and terms such as sand and gravel should only be used as defined therein.

For more accurate characterization of sediments, measurement techniques depend on the size range present.

(a) For gravel or coarser material, direct measurement of individual particles is used. This involves substantial problems of sample selection and sample size, which are frequently ignored in practice; and in the case of reef materials it is often necessary to measure three axes of individual particles, especially in the gravel range (boulders are usually more equidimensional). Descriptive statistics are then derived from counts of individual grains.

(b) Bulk measures are derived for sand-size material by sieving through a nest of standard sieves; general statistics are then obtained from cumulative curves based on the weight retained by inidvidual sieves. This is the standard method of mechanical analysis for sand-size clastic sediments, but it has the disadvantage that in reef areas sand-size particles are often discoid (*Halimeda* plates, many Foraminifera) or rodlike (echinoderm spines), and the ability of a particle to pass a sieve may give a misleading indication of its physical behaviour.

(c) Pipette or hydrometer methods are used for finer materials; these are not considered here.

Most sediment analyses reported in the reef literature have been carried out on sand-size material using sieve methods. Before sieving, samples should be dried at 80°C. If necessary, organic matter should be removed by soaking in 5 per cent hydrogen peroxide or sodium hypochlorite for 48 hours (greater concentrations may destroy some particles) and then washed in distilled water and dried. Muddy sediments should be wet-sieved through a 62-micron mesh to remove silt and clay prior to mechanical analysis; the washed sediment should then be dried at 80°C. Large samples should be thoroughly mixed and then split before analysis: it is very important not to use too large a sample and thus overload the sieve. Ingram (1971) tabulates maximum sieve load in terms of mesh interval. Sieves should be mechanically shaken on a Ro-tap or similar machine for a standard time interval (10 min). Brushing is not recommended because of the fragility of some carbonate particles.

SEDIMENT DESCRIPTION

Because of the lognormal nature of many grain-size distributions, sediments are commonly described by a transformation of the millimetre diameter to the ϕ (phi) scale proposed by Krumbein, such that $\phi = -\log_2 D$ (mm). Thus $0\phi = 1$ mm, $-1\phi = 2$ mm, $-2\phi = 4$ mm, and $+1\phi = 0.5$ mm, $+2\phi = 0.25$ mm, and so on. Tables of mm/ϕ equivalents are given by Page (1955).

Cumulative percentage frequency curves can be drawn from the data of weight retained in each sieve, and used to read off standard percentiles used in subsequent analysis. Older studies often used curves drawn with a logarithmic abscissa and an arithmetic percentage ordinate, but more accurate readings at the tails of the distribution can be obtained by constructing cumulative percentage probability plots on probability paper (logarithmic abscissa, cumulative probability ordinate). The accuracy of the curve so constructed depends on the number of data points available and hence on the sieve interval used. Folk (1966) states bluntly that 1ϕ interval sieves are useless if the curves are to be used for deriving subsequent descriptive statistics, and he recommends 0.25ϕ interval sieves with the analysis carried to 0.1 and 99.9 per cent of the total distribution. Further problems arise when different parts of the distribution have been measured by different methods, e.g. direct grain measurement, sieving, and pipette analysis, since these can yield incommensurate results. Reef sediments if not carefully sampled may also yield 'open-ended' curves, by the inclusion of a coarse particle or of a fine tail. Methods exist to extrapolate curves in such situations, but the possibilities of error are considerable. Clearly a decision must be made at an early stage about the purpose of the analysis: whether it is to give some further precision to a Wentworth-type description, in which case less rigorous analytical methods are called for, or if it is intended to use derived statistics to make inferences about sedimentary processes and environments of deposition, in which case greater care and adherence to Folk's prescription will be required.

A cumulative frequency curve can be described either by the calculation of moment measures, or by their graphical approximation. Several methods exist for the interpolation of a curve between data points automatically, using either linear (Seward-Thompson and Hails, 1973) or lognormal interpolation (Burger, 1976). Descriptive statistics can then be calculated from interpolated values, without necessarily constructing a curve, a practice strongly deplored by Folk (1966), who feels that a curve is essential to give the 'feel' of a sediment. Most of the machine methods of calculation have been devised to derive moment measures, either from a histogram (Schlee and Webster, 1967) or from automatically constructed cumulative curves (Seward-Thompson and Hails, 1973; Burger, 1976). Kane and Hubert (1963) also give a computational programme for moment measures. However, most sedimentologists now usually use Folk's graphic approximations because of the ease with which they are calculated by hand, and these are well established in the literature. Scatt and Press (1976) give a programme for calculating Folk graphic measures using a desk calculator and plotter. In this, the data points are linked by straightline segments, which strengthens the argument for a narrow sieve interval, though unfortunately the curve is plotted with an arithmetic ordinate and thus sensitivity is lost. Folk (1966, p. 77) has stated that 'values of skewness and kurtosis obtained from curves drawn on arithmetic ordinates are utterly worthless because of the uncertainty of interpolating an S-shaped curve between data points'.

The following are the graphical measures usually derived, mainly from the work of Inman (1962) and Folk (1964, 1966); the latter are now in more common use.

Central tendency

ϕ median diameter (Md_ϕ) is given by the 50th percentile (ϕ_{50}) of the distribution. ϕ mean diameter may be calculated by $M_\phi = 0.5(\phi_{16} + \phi_{84})$. These measures are useful in assigning sediments to major classes, but otherwise have restricted meaning; this is especially so of the median measure.

57

Sorting

Sorting is a measure of the spread of the grain-size distribution, and is roughly indicated by the slope of the cumulative curve. Earlier sorting measures, such as Trask's Sorting Coefficient S_0, were based on millimetre measures and included only the central part of the distribution:

$$S_0 = \sqrt{(Q_3/Q_1)}$$

Trask values are used in some of the older literature, but the measure is now obsolete.

Inman's ϕ deviation (σ_ϕ) approximates the standard deviation, is based on a greater proportion of the curve, and is rapid to calculate:

$$\sigma_\phi = 0.5\,(\phi_{84} - \phi_{16})$$

It has, however, been largely superseded by the Inclusive Graphic Standard Deviation, ϕ_1, of Folk and Ward (1957), which is based on 90 per cent of the distribution:

$$\sigma_1 = 0.25\,(\phi_{84} - \phi_{16}) + 0.1515\,(\phi_{95} - \phi_5)$$

It does, however, imply that the 5th and 95th percentiles are known, i.e. that the distribution is not open-ended.

Folk (1964) recommends the following scale of sorting values, measured in ϕ units:

0.35	very well sorted
0.35–0.5	well sorted
0.5–0.71	moderately well sorted
0.71–1.00	moderately sorted
1.0–2.0	poorly sorted
2.0–4.0	very poorly sorted
4.0	extremely poorly sorted

Skewness

Skewness measures the asymmetry of the distribution compared with a normal distribution: a positively skewed sediment (right-tailed in the histogram) has a relative excess of fines, and a negatively skewed (left-tailed) sediment has an excess of coarse material. Earlier measures of skewness are now replaced by either the Inman ϕ skewness, which covers 68 per cent of the distribution:

$$\phi = (\phi_{16} + \phi_{84} - 2\phi_{50})/(\phi_{84} - \phi_{16})$$

or by the more efficient Inclusive Graphic Skewness Sk_1 of Folk and Ward, which covers 90 per cent of the curve:

$$Sk_1 = \frac{\phi_{16} + \phi_{84} - 2\phi_{50}}{2(\phi_{84} - \phi_{16})} + \frac{\phi_5 + \phi_{95} - 2\phi_{50}}{2(\phi_{95} - \phi_5)}$$

This rather cumbersome expression has been simplified by Warren (1974) to

$$Sk_1 = \frac{\phi_{84} - \phi_{50}}{\phi_{84} - \phi_{16}} - \frac{\phi_{50} - \phi_5}{\phi_{95} - \phi_5}$$

Sk_1 is a pure number and is not quoted in ϕ units. A symmetric sediment has $Sk_1 = 0$, and the measure varies between limits of $+1$ and -1. Folk recommends the descriptors

$+0.1$ to -0.1	near-symmetrical
0.1 to 0.3	skewed
0.3 to 1.0	strongly skewed.

Kurtosis

Kurtosis measures the peakedness of the distribution; it has not been greatly used in reef studies. Inman's ϕ kurtosis is given by

$$\frac{\phi_{95} - \phi_5 - \phi_{84} + \phi_{16}}{\phi_{84} - \phi_{16}}$$

and Folk and Ward's Graphic Kurtosis by

$$K_G = \frac{\phi_{95} - \phi_5}{2.44 \, (\phi_{75} - \phi_{25})}$$

Since it is based on a ratio of spreads this is also a pure number. Absolute limits of K_G vary from 0.41 to infinity, but most values cluster in the range 0.85--1.4. Folk recommends as descriptors

0.67	very platykurtic
0.67–0.9	platykurtic
0.9–1.11	mesokurtic
1.11–1.5	leptokurtic
1.5–3.0	very leptokurtic
3.0	extremely leptokurtic.

It is very important to realize that the measures of sorting, skewness and kurtosis are highly dependent on the accuracy of the percentiles used, which are in their turn dependent on the spacing of the data points or the sieve intervals used. These must be standardized if comparability of results is required. Hails et al. (1973), using data derived from sieving at intervals of 0.25, 0.5 and 1.0ϕ, showed that sorting became poorer and skewness and kurtosis both decreased with increasing sieve interval. Care must obviously be exercised in comparing computed sediment parameters derived from different studies or using different methods.

For further details on textural parameters and their relative advantages, see Folk (1966) and McCammon (1962).

SEDIMENT BEHAVIOUR

With grains of similar shapes and specific gravity, it is reasonable to suppose that grain diameter as determined by sieving will bear a direct relationship to hydraulic behaviour, as indicated by Stokes Law and Rubey's Impact Law for the settling velocities of small and large particles respectively. Because of the skeletal origins of many carbonate particles, however, shapes depart considerable from spherical, specific gravities are variable, and some particles (notably molluscs and forams) are chambered with air pockets. Terminal fall velocities of carbonate grains can therefore depart markedly from those of non-carbonate grains of equivalent nominal diameter as determined by sieving (Maiklem, 1968; Braithwaite, 1973). It follows that grain size information derived from sieving may be misleading in terms of physical behaviour, and that data derived from sieving and from settling-column studies may not be directly comparable.

Braithwaite (1973) has shown that there are four basic modes of fall of particles in a settling column, with abrupt transitions between modes. These are (a) straight fall, with no oscillation or rotation; (b) spinning, in which a particle rotates about a vertical axis internal to the grain; (c) spiralling, in which the rotation axis is external to the grain; and (d) tumbling, at higher fall velocities. Grains move through these modes as their size increases; within a mode the velocity of fall is a function of shape and density. The modes apply to individual particles, but velocities may be affected by interference between grains in mixtures of grains, especially when fall is by spiralling or tumbling. Figure 1 illustrates these effects on the settling velocities of a variety of reef organisms of different sizes and shapes, and Figure 2 generalizes these results with reference to general fall-velocity curves (Maiklem, 1968). It is clear that fall velocities progressively diverge from the general curves as particles move from blocks through rods to plates in their external form.

These results cast doubt on the physical interpretation of sieve data for carbonate sediments, and suggest that frequency curves derived from settling tube analysis (e.g. the Woods Hole Rapid Sediment Analyzer: Ziegler et al., 1960; Schlee, 1966) should give a more realistic guide to grain behaviour. However, settling velocity is only one component of grain behaviour, and while much effort has been given to the hydraulic interpretation of frequency curves, e.g. in terms of transportation thresholds (Middleton, 1976) it is doubtful whether the use of settling tube rather than sieve data lessens the difficulties involved.

INTERPRETATION OF TEXTURAL PARAMETERS

Once grain-size curves have been constructed and descriptive parameters calculated, various interpretations of the results are possible.

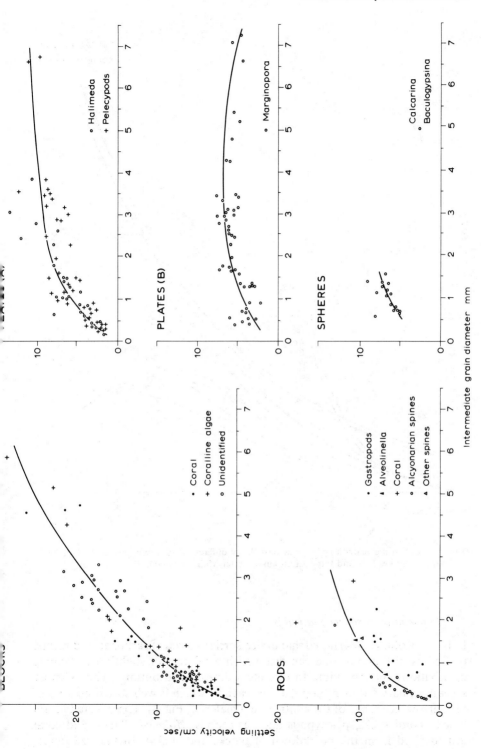

Figure 1
Settling velocities of organic particles of different shapes, sizes and origins
(from Maiklem 1968).

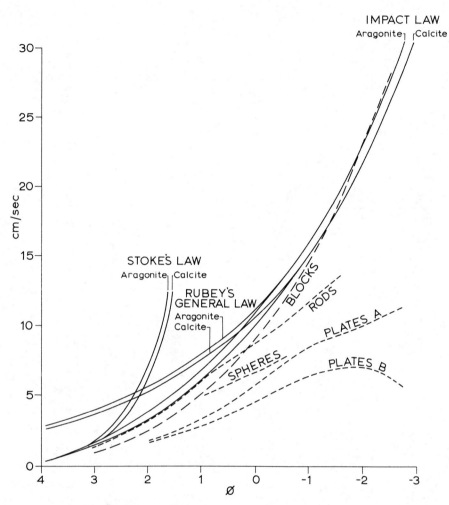

Figure 2
Settling velocities of organic particles of different shapes compared with
Stokes Law and Impact Law curves (after Maiklem, 1968).

Importance of source materials

Folk and Robles (1964) noted that in size-sorting curves of carbonate sediments,
plotted as histograms, one can distinguish a number of slightly overlapping
distributions corresponding to discrete sediment distributions. They identify
several primary sediment populations, each of which is well sorted because of
the narrow size range of the contributing material (Fig. 3). These include coral
blocks, coral sticks, pelecypods and gastropods, *Halimeda* flakes, and coral
grit (derived from the breakdown of blocks and sticks). In the size ranges

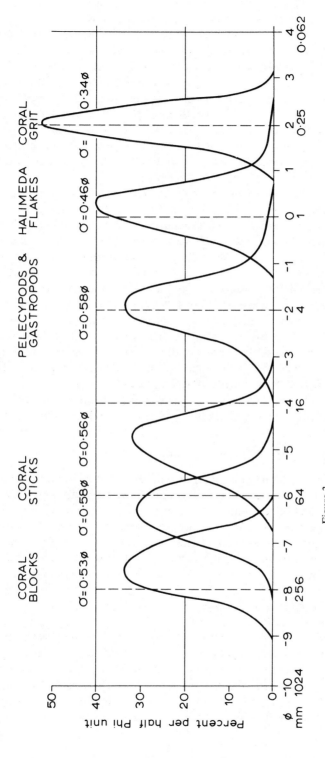

Figure 3
Frequency curves of bench sediments from Isla Perez, Alacran, showing
discrete sediment populations (from Folk and Robles, 1964).

between the modes for each of these materials, natural sediments are less common and where they do occur they consist of mixtures of the primary populations; they are hence less well sorted and show more pronounced skewness and kurtosis. Thus, well-sorted sediments include fine sands (2ϕ, $\sigma = 0.34\phi$), coarse sands (0ϕ, $\sigma = 0.46\phi$), mollusc shells (-2ϕ, $\sigma = 0.58\phi$), and coral-stick gravel (-5ϕ, $\sigma = 0.56\phi$); the intermediate sizes, notably at -1ϕ and -3ϕ, are less well sorted. Some sediment sizes, notably $0--2\phi$ and $6-8\phi$, are scarce in nature because of the absence of contributing organisms in these size ranges or of skeletal structures which yield clastic particles in these ranges. Folk has termed this control of sediment characteristics by the nature of the source materials the 'Sorby Principle'.

Note that this operates not only through the primary skeletal characteristics of the organisms themselves, but also by the ways in which particles disintegrate under stress, which is controlled by internal skeletal structure. Thus Folk has shown how *Acropora cervicornis,* for example, yields first a population of sticks when the colony fragments, and then a coral grit by disintegration of the sticks, and *Halimeda* a coarse sand of flakes and then a silt. Such breakdown patterns have been experimentally demonstrated in tumbling-mill experiments by Chave (1960) and Force (1969). This process of discontinuous breakdown, and the size-sorting relationships which follow from it, holds only in moderate to high wave energy environments, however. In low energy environments where transportation is reduced, poorly sorted sediments accumulate. Swinchatt (1965) found sediments comprised of skeletal grains, mainly molluscan, mixed with 10–55 per cent silt and clay under marine angiosperms in the Florida Keys; in these circumstances the evaluation of textural parameters as a guide to hydraulic process is somewhat meaningless.

Importance of depositional environment

There is a large literature suggesting that depositional environments can be inferred from textural characteristics. Thus dune sands are better sorted than beach sands, and beach sands than river sands. A further differentiation may arise from skewness: beach sands are symmetrical or negatively skewed, and dune sands positively skewed. These properties are explained in terms of depositional processes, though in some cases the rate of sediment supply can mask expected values. The sensitivity of textural parameters to environment of deposition appears to be variable, and many studies have been made with not always consistent results (Friedman, 1961, 1967; Moiola and Weiser, 1968).

Recently it has been argued that sediment frequency curves are better characterized and differentiated by being plotted as successive straightline segments on probability paper (Visher, 1969; Middleton, 1976). The segments then define sedimentary components attributable to different transportation processes, e.g. traction, saltation, and suspension. Because of problems with sieve data, Reed *et al.* (1975) have refined this method by using settling-column data. These methods have not yet been applied to reef sediments, though Flood

(1978) has reached similar conclusions though by different methods. These interpretations apply mainly to mobile sand-size material.

CONCLUSION

It will be apparent that once sediment analysis aims at more than a quantitative characterization of the main properties of a sediment, severe problems arise on both the technical and the conceptual levels. Before embarking on a programme of sediment collection and analysis, the investigator should be quite clear about the aims of the exercise, and he should ensure that the methods adopted are not too elaborate to yield the results required. As Milliman (1974, p. 16) noted: 'Many investigators have found that a complete size analysis of a carbonate sediment may require more time and effort than the results warrant'.

References

BATHURST, R. G. C. 1971. *Carbonate sediments and their diagenesis.* Amsterdam, Elsevier (xix +620 p.).

BOON, J. D., III. 1968. Trend surface analysis of sand tracer distributions on a carbonate beach, Bimini, B.W.I. *J. Geol.,* vol. 76, p. 71–87.

BRAITHWAITE, C. J. R. 1973. Settling behaviour related to sieve analysis of skeletal sands. *Sedimentology,* vol. 20, p. 251–62.

BURGER, H. 1976. Log-normal interpretation in grain size analysis. *Sedimentology,* vol. 23, p. 395–405.

CARVER, R. E. (ed.). 1971. *Procedures in sedimentary petrology.* New York, Wiley–Interscience (xiii, +653 p.).

CHAVE, K. E. 1960. Carbonate sediments to limestones: problems. *Trans. N.Y. Acad. Sci.,* (2) vol. 23, p. 14–24.

FLOOD, P. 1978. Reef flat sediments from the northern region of the Great Barrier Reef Province. *Phil. Trans. R. Soc.,* (in press).

FOLK, R. L. 1962. Sorting in some carbonate beaches of Mexico. *Trans. N.Y. Acad. Sci.,* (2) vol. 25, p. 222–44.

——. 1964. *Petrology of sedimentary rocks.* Austin, Hemphill's (154 p.).

——. 1966. A review of grain-size parameters. *Sedimentology,* vol. 6, p. 73–93.

——; Cotera, A. S. 1971. Carbonate sand cays of Alacran Reef, Yucatan, Mexico; sediments. *Atoll Res. Bull.,* vol. 137, p. 1–16.

——; HAYES, M. O.; SHOJI, R. 1962. Carbonate sediments of Isla Mujeres, Quintana Roo, Mexico, and vicinity. *Yucatan Peninsula Field Trip Guidebook.* New Orleans, New Orleans Geological Society, p. 85–100.

——; ROBLES, R. 1964. Carbonate sands of Isla Perez, Alacran Reef complex, Yucatan. *J. Geol.,* vol. 72, p. 255–92.

——; WARD, W. C. 1957. Brazos River bar: a study in the significance of grain size parameters. *J. sedim. Petrol.,* vol. 27, p. 3–26.

FORCE, L. M. 1969. Calcium carbonate size distribution on the west Florida shelf and experimental studies on the microarchitectural control of skeletal breakdown. *J. sedim. Petrol.,* vol. 39, p. 902–34.

FOSBERG, F. R.; CARROLL, D. 1965. Terrestrial sediments and soils of the northern Marshall Islands, *Atoll Res. Bull.,* 115, p. 1–156.

FRIEDMAN, G. M. 1961. Distinction between dune, beach, and river sands from their textural characteristics. *J. sedim. Petrol.,* vol. 31, p. 514–29.

——. 1967. Dynamic processes and statistical parameters compared for size frequency distribution of beach and river sands. *J. sedim. Petrol.,* vol. 37, p. 327–54.

F

GINSBURG, R. N. 1956. Environmental relationship of grain size and constituent particles in some south Florida carbonate sediments. *Bull. Am. Assoc. petrol. Geol.*, 40, p. 2384–427.

GRIFFITH, J. C. 1967. *Scientific method in analysis of sediments.* New York, McGraw–Hill, (508 p.).

HAILS, J. R.; SEWARD-THOMPSON, B.; CUMMINGS, L. 1973. An appraisal of the significance of sieve intervals in grain size analysis for environmental interpretation. *J. sedim. Petrol.*, vol. 43, p. 889–93.

HEDLEY, C. 1925. Coral shingle as a beach formation. *Rept. Gt Barrier Reef Comm.*, vol. 1, p. 66.

HOSKIN, C. M. 1963. Recent carbonate sedimentation on Alacran Reef, Yucatan, Mexico. National Academy of Sciences–National Research Council., Publ. 1089, p. 1–160.

ILLING, L. V. 1954. Bahamian calcareous sands. *Bull. Am. Assoc. petrol. Geol.*, vol. 38, p. 1–94.

INGRAM, R. L. 1971. Sieve analysis. In: R. E. Carver (ed.). *Procedures in sedimentary petrology.* New York, Wiley–Interscience, chap. 3, p. 49–67.

INMAN, D. L. 1962. Measures for describing the size distribution of sediments. *J. sedim. Petrol.*, vol. 22, p. 125–45.

KANE, W. T.; HUBERT, J. F. 1963. Fortran program for calculation of grain-size textural parameters on the IBM 1620 computer. *Sedimentology*, vol. 2, p. 54–86.

KRUMBEIN, W. C. 1954. Statistical significance of beach sampling methods. *Tech. Mem. Beach Erosion Board*, vol. 50, p. 1–33.

——; PETTIJOHN, F. J. 1938. *Manual of sedimentary petrography.* New York, Appleton–Century–Crofts (xiv + 549 p.).

——; SLACK, H. A. 1956. Relative efficiency of beach sampling methods. *Tech. Mem. Beach Erosion Board*, vol. 90, p. 1–43, Al–A9.

MAIKLEM, W. R. 1968. Some hydraulic properties of bioclastic carbonate grains. *Sedimentology*, vol. 10, p. 101–09.

McCAMMON, R. B. 1962. Efficiencies of percentile measures for describing the mean size and sorting of sedimentary particles. *J. Geol.*, vol. 70, p. 453–65.

McKEE, E. D.; CHRONIC, J.; LEOPOLD, E. B. 1959. Sedimentary belts in lagoon of Kapingamarangi Atoll. *Bull. Am. Assoc. petrol. Geol.*, vol. 43, p. 501–62.

MIDDLETON, G. V. 1976. Hydraulic interpretation of sand size distributions. *J. Geol.*, vol. 84, p. 405–26.

MILLIMAN, J. D. 1974. *Marine carbonates.* Berlin, Springer-Verlag (xv + 375 p.).

MOIOLA, R. J.; WESIER, D. 1968. Textural parameters: an evaluation. *J. sedim. Petrol.*, vol. 38, p. 45–53.

MÜLLER, G. 1967. *Methods in sedimentary petrology.* Stuttgart, Schweizerbart Verlag (283 p.).

PAGE, H. G. 1955. Phi-millimeter conversion table. *J. sedim. Petrol.*, vol. 25, p. 285–92.

PURDY, E. G. 1963. Recent calcium carbonate facies of the Great Bahama Bank. *J. Geol.*, vol. 71, p. 334–55, p. 472–97.

REED, W. E.; LE FEVER, R.; MOIR, G. J. 1975. Depositional environment interpretation from settling-velocity (psi) distributions. *Geol. Soc. Am. Bull.*, vol. 86, p. 1321–28.

SCATT, R. M.; PRESS, D. E. 1976. Computer program for presentation of grain-size data by the graphic method. *Sedimentology*, vol. 23, p. 121–31.

SCHLEE, J. 1966. A modified Woods Hole rapid sediment analyzer. *J. sedim. Petrol.*, vol. 36, p. 403–13.

——; WEBSTER, J. 1967. A computer program for grain-size data. *Sedimentology*, vol. 8, p. 45–54.

SEWARD-THOMPSON, B. L.; HAILS, J. 1973. An appraisal of the computation of statistical parameters in grain size analysis. *Sedimentology*, vol. 20, p. 161–70.

SWINCHATT, J. 1965. Significance of constituent composition, texture, and skeletal breakdown in some recent carbonate skeletons. *J. sedim. Petrol.*, vol. 35, p. 71–90.

VISHER, G. S. 1969. Grain size distribution and depositional processes. *J. sedim. Petrol.*, vol. 39, p. 1074–106.

WARREN, G. 1974. Simplified form of the Folk-Ward skewness parameter. *J. sedim. Petrol.*, vol. 44, p. 259.

WENTWORTH, C. K. 1922. A scale of grade and class terms for clastic sediments. *J. Geol.*, vol. 30, p. 377–92.

——. 1953. Describing size grades of beach and other sedimentary materials. *Atoll. Res. Bull.*, vol. 17, p. 23.

ZEIGLER, J. M.; WHITNEY, G. G., Jr.; HAYES, C. R. 1960. Woods Hole rapid sediment analyzer. *J. sedim. Petrol.*, vol. 30, p. 490–95.

6

Shallow core drilling

B. G. Thom[1]

As demonstrated at Bikini, Mururoa, and the Great Barrier Reef, the thickness of Holocene reef sediments may be as small as 10 to 65 ft. (3 to 20 m). This makes it possible to investigate the Holocene-Late Pleistocene stratigraphy of reef complexes economically by using a lightweight drilling machine. During the 1973 Royal Society–Universities of Queensland Expedition to the Great Barrier Reef, such an operation was undertaken. This report outlines techniques used on the Expedition which may be adapted by others in studies of coral reef problems.

THE DRILLING UNIT

The Expedition used a Gemco model 210B drilling unit owned by the Australian National University. The unit is a multipurpose, lightweight, vertical drilling machine suitable for auger drilling, diamond core drilling, vacuum sampling, rotary drilling using air or water flush techniques, and for use with down-the-hole hammers. As shown in Figure 1, it is supplied with a two wheeled trailer, but it can be mounted on a four-wheel tandem axle trailer, or on a suitable light truck.

The drilling unit is powered by a four stroke, petrol, air cooled, 1600 cm³ capacity Volkswagen engine (Model 126A). Transmission from the engine is through a dry plate single disc clutch coupled with a four speed and one reverse heavy-duty gearbox. The engine and drill head are mounted on a frame which is arranged to travel vertically on grease lubricated rollers in channels attached to the inner section of the mast. The frame is operated by means of hydraulic rams. The drill head assembly can be swivelled to one side to give easy access over the hole (e.g. allow use of the winch). A hydraulically operated winch is built into the crown of an extension type mast. The capacity of the winch, single line pull, is 800 lb (363 kg). A hydraulic system provides power for ram and winch

---

1. Department of Geography, Faculty of Military Studies, University of New South Wales, Duntroon A.C.T., Australia 2600.

Figure 1
Gemco model 210B drilling unit in operation on Bewick Island, northern region, Great Barrier Reef. Drill rods, 10 feet (3 m) in length, are shown drilling into cay beachrock which overlies coral-algal calcarenite.

operation at an operating pressure of 1000 psi (70·3 kg/cm²) from a pump which is driven from the engine crank shaft.

The drill chassis is equipped with two jacks built into the mast frame to ensure stability when drilling. The mast is hinged and can be raised or lowered by means of a linkage to the main hydraulic cylinders. The dimensions of the drilling unit are as follows:

Working height	19 ft 6 in	(5 m)
Working width	6 ft 0 in.	(1·8 m)
Working length	11 ft 0 in	(3·3 m)
Folded height	11 ft 0 in	(3·3 m)
Weight	37 cwt	(1880 kg)

DRILLING EQUIPMENT

In drilling unconsolidated sediment, such as cay sand, 'solid' augers can be used. Standard augers are six feet (1·8 m) long with a single spiral. Male and female hexagon ends ensure rapid coupling secured by spring steel dee clips. Augers range in size, but a diameter of three to five inches is usually adequate, the larger size producing bulkier samples.

Sampling below the water table is possible in spite of collapse of hole on withdrawal. If the augers are spun slowly into the sediment and withdrawn without rotation, the lower 1 or 2 feet (0·3–0·6 m) of auger will contain a disturbed but in-place sample. The contaminating material from higher up the hole can be readily scraped off the outer part of the spiral. If the augers are advanced in increments of six feet (1·8 m) or less and withdrawn without rotation after each advance, then more-or-less continuous samples can be obtained. Using five-inch augers, up to 150 feet (45·7 m) of sand-sized material can be drilled using this technique.

In drilling consolidated sediments (e.g. beachrock, aeolianite or reef-rock) diamond-drilling techniques have to be employed. This involves the use of a water pump to maintain circulation at the drill bit. On the 1973 Expedition, a Mindrill 750–1200 water pump 400 psi (28.12 kg/cm²) was employed along with about 50 feet (15.2 m) of high pressure suction hose and 200 feet (61 m) of delivery hose.

The Gemco drill is capable of diamond drilling to 750 feet (45.7 m) according to the manufacturers. Depth of drilling is limited by type of material being drilled, capacity of water pump, size of drill rods and capacity of the winch. In 1973, drilling to 100 feet (30.5 m) was easily accomplished.

Selection of drilling rods is largely determined by the type of core barrel used. BQ rods 2.187 inches (5.56 cm) outside diameter were used on the Expedition, and although successful, they were regarded by the operator as being too light when recovery problems were encountered. N 2.375 inches (6.03 cm) outside diameter or NW 2.625 inches (6.67 cm) outside diameter rods were preferred with an NMLC barrel 2.045 inches (5.2 cm) core diameter as this type of rod can be more readily recovered with a recovery hammer. Alternatively, HQ rods, 3.5 inches (8.89 cm) outside diameter could be used with HQ barrels 2.5 inches (6.4 cm) core diameter. Barrel length may be in either five feet (1.5 m) or 10 feet (3 m) lengths.

The BQ rods were coupled with a BMLC barrel 1.386 inches (3.5 cm) core diameter in the 1973 operation. This barrel was of the retractable type, 2 ft 6 in (76 cm) long. The diameter is not large enough for coral reef drilling, as it is susceptible to jamming with small hard pieces of coral. NMLC or HQ barrels are recommended, preferably five feet in length. These barrels should contain split inner tubes with a 'blow out' adaptor. A 'soft formation' core catcher may be useful on occasions. Figure 2 illustrates the type of barrel used in 1973 and an example of core recovered. The success of the rubber-sleeve core barrel in drilling below 70 feet (21 m) on Midway Atoll (Ladd *et al.*, 1970) suggests a technique which, although expensive, should be considered by all planning to drill reef limestone.

Both diamond and tungsten–carbide drill bits were used on the 1973 Expedition. However, problems were encountered with diamond bits. When insufficient water reached the drill bit, the diamond cutting surface was smoothed, and the water ways became restricted causing high-water pressure problems. Drilltech tungsten–carbide-faced bits were not affected in this way especially when drilling limestone containing micrite. It is suggested that in reef drilling both diamond stepface bits and tungsten–carbide-faced bits should be used. Reamers should be of both types.

The use of casing in drilling reef limestone depends on the type of material. If drilling begins in unconsolidated sediment, casing has to be sunk to the indurated material. The possibility of encountering uncemented layers within the reef rock dictates the need to install casing. On the 1973 Expedition, an attempt was made to overcome hole collapse by using BQ Wireline Equipment. This technique involves the drill rods remaining in the hole, and a recovery tool on a cable being sent down the hole to recover the core barrel. However, there were problems in isolating the core from the action of water which tended to wash the core from the barrel. Core loss was so great using Wireline that the retractable barrel had to be used almost exclusively. Fortunately, the hole remained open permitting easy extraction and installation of drill rods. It is recommended that casing should be available in the event of hole collapse. Although not tried, it is possible that a BQ retractable barrel could be used with Wireline Equipment. This may prevent core washing, but a pump which could operate at a higher pressure (up to 800 psi, 56.24 kg/cm^2) would be needed.

DRILL OPERATION

The Gemco drill mounted on a trailer can be transported by barge to the drill site. The trailer can be off-loaded to a site above high-water springs using a winch, or tractor or suitable manpower. This operation can be difficult if the barge

Figure 2
BMLC core barrel, two feet six inches (76 cm) long 1.386 inches (3.5 cm)
core diameter, with tungsten-carbide drill bit and a sample of core
recovered on Bewick Island, August, 1973.

is being buffetted by waves. Alternatively, in shallow water, the barge could be of a type which is capable of being positioned over the drill site and pumped full of sea water so that it settles firmly on the sand or reef surface (see Ladd *et al.* 1970). The drill plant is stable if supported by its jacks but when drilling from a barge in shallow water, it may be necessary to have the drill mast secured by guylines to nearby coral heads or other objects.

The 1973 Expedition operation found that drilling was most successful when second gear was used, because first gear was too slow and resulted in increased water pressure and core loss. Third gear also resulted in washing away of core. Speed of penetration has to be controlled by the operator depending on nature of material and type of drill bit. If penetration is too fast, fine-grained material (micrite or ground limestone) can plug the bit and cut off the water supply. On the other hand, if penetration is too slow core recovery is reduced by washing away of the core. The operator should try to maintain minimum waterflow to the drill bit to minimize loss of core.

Hard coral or well-indurated limestone rich in micrite may cause temporary jamming of the core barrel and force the drilling rig to jack up. When this happens operations should be stopped and the barrel recovered and cleared. Inevitably, when a hard formation is entered, a cutting vibration can be felt on the clutch. When the barrel is reinserted in the hole it usually does not reach the depth at which drilling finished on the previous run because of material falling from the wall of the hole. Second gear with minimum revolutions and maximum water pressure should be used to clear the hole until starting depth is reached.

The water pump may have to be located close to the water source because of suction limitations. Sea water is used in drilling. The pump can be situated near the water line, but may have to be moved as the tide rises or falls. It is preferable either to float the pump, or pump into a storage tank when drilling on a cay, or Pleistocene coral outcrop. A plastic swimming pool is suitable for this purpose. When using the Gemco drill for diamond drilling the Kelly hose may tangle around the operator or the controls. The hose could be channelled through a pipe up the mast, then led to the drill rod and water swivel by a flexible rubber hose.

CORE RECOVERY

The retractable barrel may achieve 70–90 per cent core recovery in well-indurated coral–algal limestone. Less recovery must be expected when there are cavities and variations in the hardness of layers. Unless control of revolutions, drilling pressure and water supply is carefully maintained, high core recoveries in alternately hard–soft bedded materials may be difficult to obtain. Core loss can occur when a contact is encountered involving a change in drilling technique. The operator must be highly skilled in order to obtain maximum recovery.

The use of pressure to extract the core from the barrel must be undertaken with great care. It is easy to wash away loose friable core and destroy the sequence. Invariably, in the author's experience, the core is composed of fragmented material ranging in length from six inches to sand size. The frustrations of recovering no sample, or just a few pieces, on some runs must be balanced against the exhilaration experienced when a full barrel is collected (Fig. 2). The upper part of a sample from a core must be examined for contamination as it may contain material which has fallen from a higher level in the hole.

References

LADD, H. S.; TRACEY, J. I.; GROSS, H. G. 1970. *Deep drilling on Midway Atoll.* U.S. Geol. Surv. (Prof. Paper 680-A) (22 p.).

7

A hand-operated submersible drill for coring reef substrata

I. G. Macintyre[1]

The need for an effective method of collecting subsurface samples from the sub-littoral zones of modern coral reefs has led to the development of a portable submersible drill (Macintyre, 1975) that enables diver scientists to obtain cores measuring $2\frac{1}{8}$ inches (54 mm) in diameter (Fig. 1) from penetration depths of

Figure 1
Core measuring $2\frac{1}{8}$ inches (54 mm) in diameter from the base of Galeta Reef, Panama. Contact between Holocene corals, *Acropora palmata* and *Diploria* sp., and calcareous argillaceous siltstone of the Middle Miocene Gatun Formation. Scale in centimetres.

50 feet (15 m) or more. Other submersible drills already in use have demonstrated a more limited capability; for example, Land's electric submersible drill produced a short, one-inch-diameter (25.4 mm) core (pers. comm., 1970) and the U.S. Navy's hydraulic drill (see Anon., 1973) obtained cores slightly smaller than Land's. Penetration depths were also limited when either a pneumatic drill (Scoffin, 1972) or blasting (Shinn, 1963; Ginsburg and Schroeder, 1969;

1. Division of Sedimentology, National Museum of Natural History, Smithsonian Institution, Washington, D.C. 20560, U.S.A.

Goreau and Land, 1974; Glynn, pers. comm., 1972) was used to expose sections of submerged substrata. In addition, blasting may severely alter local environments, while the removal of rubble resulting from underwater quarrying may require long hours of diving time. To date, no diver-operated drill has been available to marine scientists comparable in penetration capabilities and core size to the unit described below whose efficiency has been tested during two successful years of active field use in the study of fringe reefs off the Pacific and Caribbean coasts of Panama.

The basic concept used in designing this drill was to convert an underwater hydraulic wrench to a coring tool. This was done by fitting an Ackley hydraulic impact wrench with core pipe and NWM double-tube core barrels ($2\frac{1}{8}$ inches (54 mm) in diameter), which are standard drilling equipment. A ring inserted in the wrench by Ackley permits lock-out of the impact mechanism, which would otherwise shatter and displace the carbide teeth in the drill bit. During operation, a locked reverse control knob on the drill prevents the reverse assembly from becoming engaged accidentally and releasing the drill pipe. The power unit driving the wrench consists of a dual-drive Webster hydraulic pump, which is powered by a Triumph 4-cylinder industrial gasoline motor.

A manifold attachment on the hydraulic unit allows both sides (i.e., pressure systems) to be operated on one pair of hydraulic lines. This attachment also permits a fluid flow of 16 gal/min (73 cu dm/min), which is required to drive the drill at optimum efficiency. The maximum rpm for this drill is 600, which so far has proved more than adequate for drilling operations.

The hydraulic power unit is connected to the drill by $\frac{3}{4}$ inch (19 mm) hydraulic hose, except for the last 10 feet (3 m) where $\frac{1}{2}$ inch (13 mm) hose is used to ensure greater flexibility in the working area. Although the submerged operational limits of hose-line length have not yet been established, experience has shown that drill efficiency is not reduced over distances up to 300 feet (91 m) from the hydraulic power unit on surface. Hose problems in submerged drilling operations are not foreseen to depths of at least 150 feet (45 m) (Black and Quirk, 1970). Present equipment operated successfully at a depth of 35 feet (11 m), from which a 40-foot (12 m) hole was drilled.

The size of the hydraulic power unit (Table 1) introduces logistical problems in offshore drilling operations, but these can be overcome by building the compressor unit into a boat in which the motor is used to drive the hydraulic pump (adaptation recommended by E. A. Shinn, pers. comm., 1974). A 21-oil-barrel raft adequately supported all the necessary drilling equipment offshore; its draft clearance of about 1 foot (0.3 m) ensured navigability in broad areas of irregular bathymetry in shallow water.

Carbide drill bits were found to be more effective for drilling into coral-reef substrata than diamond bits, and they are an order of magnitude less expensive. Together with the 2-foot (0.6 m) long core barrel, the drilling unit weighs approximately 150 lb (68 kg) and can be handled comfortably by two divers (e.g. for shallow penetration into a large coral head as in Fig. 2). The addition of drill pipe or a 5-foot (1.5 m) long core barrel, however, necessitates the use

TABLE 1. Specifications of hydraulic submersible drill (Macintyre, 1974)

Components	Specifications
Hydraulic wrench	Ackley impact wrench and drill, model 23HS-OC Weight: 80 lb Overall length: $21\frac{1}{2}$ in Chuck rpm: 600 Torque rating: 6,000–9,000 ft/lb[a]
Hydraulic power unit	Ackley hydraulic power unit PU 2-10-2000 and manifold system Weight: 1,800 lb operating wt Size: $50 \times 37 \times 76$ in
Water pump	Acker model APS-7 pumping station 7.6 gal/min at 75 psi Weight: 230 lb Size: $36 \times 24 \times 17$ in
Other equipment	Core barrels, reamers, core catchers, core bits, drill extension rods, water swivel, water hose, custom-made spindle to attach drill pipe to chuck, hydraulic hose and fittings.

a. This rating is with impact mechanism in operation; with lockout ring, it is 159.25 ft/lb at 16 gal/min and 2,000 psi.

Figure 2
Two divers coring a large head of *Pavona* sp. with a 2-foot (0.6 m) long core barrel. Depth 15 feet (4.5 m). Pearl Islands, Gulf of Panama, Pacific coast of Panama.

of a tripod-winch assembly for retrieving the cores (Fig. 3). Torque effects were experienced by the diver only when the pipe was pulled from holes greater than 5 or 10 feet (1.5 or 3 m). This situation was corrected by the addition of a short length of pipe (3 or 4 feet) (1 or 1.2 m) to the drill handle which could then be braced against one of the tripod legs to take up any torque otherwise experienced by the diver (Fig. 3). Although the drill is easily hand-operated by one diver, an efficient drilling operation requires a three-man team: one to operate the

Figure 3
Three-man drilling crew in mangroves at shoreward edge of Galeta Reef,
Caribbean coast of Panama. Note pipe on wrench handle braced against one
of the tripod legs.

drill, a second to operate the winch on the tripod, and a third to assist in adding and removing drill pipe or operating the power-unit and water-pump.

The noise level of this drill in operation is not troublesome to the operator since the hydraulic motor emits a medium-high frequency whine which generally goes unnoticed. Another advantage of the Ackley wrench is its 'dead-man' trigger, which provides sensitive control of the speed of drill-bit rotation and automatically stops the drill the instant that the trigger is released.

Under ideal weather conditions a 40-foot (12 m) deep hole was completed in two days—a time factor which did not vary in either above- or below-water operations. The factor most critical to the success of underwater operations is an experienced drill crew because communication has to be minimal during drilling. A well-documented drilling record is also essential, and an example of the type of data sheet established for work in Panama is given below (Table 2).

The most detailed project in which this submersible drill has been used to date has been a study of the internal structure of a Caribbean fringe reef off Galeta Point, Panama. Thirteen holes were drilled over an area extending from mangroves at the shoreward edge of the reef to the fore-reef at depths of 35 feet (11 m). This series of closely-spaced cored holes produced data on reef community succession, rate of framework construction and post-depositional processes (Macintyre and Glynn, 1974; Macintyre, 1977). The maximum depth

TABLE 2. Galeta Core Hole No. 5[a]

Core No.	Drill procedure[b]	Length of core barrel[c]	Surface to top of core barrel[d]	Length drill-rod assembly[e]	Surface to top of rod assembly[f]	Depth of bit[g]	Core interval	Recovery[h]	Comments[i]
1	5 ft core barrel	81	6			75	0–75	14	
2	"	"	—	1 × 5 ft ⟍ 60	60	81	75–81	6	
3	"	"	—	3 × 2 ft ⟍ 72	33	120	81–120	16	
4	"	"	—	4 × 2 ft / 1 × 5 ft ⟍ 156	20	217	120–217	55	
5	"	"	—	1 × 2 ft / 3 × 5 ft ⟍ 204	11	274	217–274	30	
6	"	"	—	2 × 2 ft / 4 × 5 ft ⟍ 288	6	363	274–363	50	
7	"	"	—	3 × 2 ft / 5 × 5 ft ⟍ 372	7	446	363–446	45	

a. All measurements in inches unless otherwise stated.
b. Type of core barrel or drill bit.
c. Length of core barrel. This is the measured distance between the drill bit and the top of the core barrel assembly (i.e. top of pin).
d. Measured distance between substrata surface and the top of the core barrel assembly.
e. Length of the drill-rod assembly. Convert 2 and 5-foot barrel lengths into a total measurement in inches.
f. Measured distance between substrata surface and the top of the drill-rod assembly.
g. Calculated depth of core bit.
h. Measured length of core recovery.
i. Comments on rate of drilling, characteristics of washout material, etc.

of core penetration so far has been 52 feet (15.8 m) and recovery has been almost 100 per cent from solid substrata such as a coral head, the Miocene siltstone foundation of the Panama Caribbean fringe reef (Fig. 1), and the volcanic tuff at the base of some reefs off the Pacific coast of Panama. Low recoveries of 50 per cent or less from the reef framework, resulted from the difficulty in recovering loose material and the extensive void space within some of the reef framework.

ACKNOWLEDGEMENTS

Special thanks are extended to Jeff King (Ackley Manufacturing Co.) and Ed Wesolowski (Acker Drill Co. Inc.) for their assistance in assembling the drilling equipment. Help given by J. G. Babb, P. W. Glynn, B. Hitchko, G. B. McLeod, R. H. Stewart, B. Smith and A. Velarde during the drilling and their valuable suggestions for improving field operations are gratefully acknowledged.

References

ANON. 1973. U.S. Navy develops new underwater tools. *Ocean Industry* (Houston), vol. 8, p. 32–5.

BLACK, S. A.; QUIRK, J. T. 1970. Hydraulic tool systems for divers. In: *Symp. Proc.* 24–25 February, 1970, Columbus, Ohio, Marine Technology Society (478 p.).

GINSBURG, R. N.; SCHROEDER, J. H. 1973. Growth and submarine fossilization of algal cup reefs, Bermuda. *Sedimentology,* vol. 20, p. 575–614.

GOREAU, T. F.; LAND, L. S. 1974. Fore-reef morphology and depositional processes, North Jamaica. In: Laporte, L. F. (ed.). *Reefs in time and space.* Tulsa, Oklahoma, Soc. Econ. Paleontologists and Mineralogists Spec. Pub. 18, p. 77–89 (256 p.).

MACINTYRE, I. G. 1975. A diver-operated hydraulic drill for coring submerged strates. *Atoll Res. Bull.,* vol. 185, p. 21–6.

——; 1977. Distribution of submarine cements in a modern Caribbean fringing reef, Galeta Point, Panama. *J. sedim. Petrol.* vol. 47. p. 503–16.

——; GLYNN, P. W. 1976. Evolution of modern Caribbean fringing reefs, Galeta Point, Panama. *Bull. Am. Assoc. petrol. Geol.,* vol. 60, p. 1054–72.

SCOFFIN, T. P. 1972. Fossilization of Bermuda patch reefs. *Science,* vol. 178, p. 1280–82.

SHINN, E. A. 1963. Formation of spurs and grooves on the Florida reef tract. *J. sedim. Petrol.,* vol. 33, p. 291–303.

8

Radiometric dating of coral reefs

J. Chappell,[1] B. G. Thom[2] and
H. A. Polach[3]

INTRODUCTION

Ancient coral reefs may be dated directly by two radiometric methods, using either C^{14} or Th^{230}/U^{234}: the time-depth achievable with the former in principle is about 45,000 years before present (B.P.), and up to about 250,000 B.P. for the latter. This potential for dating, using two different radiometric methods, is uncommon amongst biogenic and sedimentary formations, and comparison of results from both methods has substantially improved the understanding of problems of age estimation of reefs.

The principal problem arises from violation of one of the assumptions of well-controlled radiometric dating, *viz.*, that the radioisotope content is fixed at death of the organism. After death, corals are prone to modification of their radio-isotope content by chemical exchange with their surroundings, because calcium carbonate (the skeletal substance) is more reactive than many materials used in radiometric dating (charcoal or cellulose, in the C^{14} method for example). Consequently, certain guidelines for sample collection, and for validation of age estimates, must be observed. These are set out in the final section of this article, following a review of both the dating methods and results obtained by them.

The basic assumption, that half-lives of the radio-isotopes themselves are known, is not questioned. Concerning half-lives, however, it must be pointed out that 2 different values for C^{14} are in use, the conventional being 5,560 years but 5,780 years are used by some laboratories. Clearly, before any correlations are made, the user of C^{14} data must know which value was employed in calculating sample ages at the laboratory. Other basic assumptions about constancy of the particular radio-isotope levels in living tissues in Upper Quaternary times, and about geographical variations of the isotope levels, are discussed below.

1. Department of Geography, Australian National University, A.C.T. Australia 2601.
2. Department of Geography, Faculty of Military Studies, University of New South Wales, Duntroon A.C.T., Australia 2600.
3. Prehistory Dept., Research School of Pacific Studies, Australian National University, A.C.T. Australia 2601.

81

G

C^{14} DATING OF REEF MATERIALS

In addition to the assumption that no chemical exchange has occurred between the fossil and its surroundings, it is assumed that the C^{14} content at time of death is known. This is limited by two factors. Firstly, the C^{14} content of the atmosphere is known to have varied throughout the last 7,000 years, and presumably varied before that. Secondly, natural C^{14} levels in the ocean and its organisms differ from the atmospheric level, and vary geographically, as a result of several processes:

Variations of atmospheric C^{14} levels through time have been proved by comparison of tree-ring chronologies, reckoned in sidereal years, with C^{14} ages determined from the tree-ring sequences. Results of primary studies are discussed by Ferguson (1970), Olsson (1970), Stuiver (1970), and Damon *et al.,* (1972), and range back to about 8,000 sidereal years B.P. The age difference generally is attributed to increased production of C^{14} in the upper atmosphere earlier than 5,000 B.P. There is no reason to believe that C^{14} production was constant before this (Stuiver, 1970; Wollin *et al.,* 1971). However, from the practical viewpoint of using radiometric dating for reef chronology and correlation, no problem arises as long as each research worker explicitly uses the C^{14} time scale.

Variations in C^{14} levels in living corals and reef organisms create more substantial problems for correlation of age estimates between different facies and regions. A recent comprehensive review for carbonate organisms in general is given by Mangerud (1972). The variations stem from *isotopic fractionation* at each chemical interface between the atmosphere and the living organism, and from the *reservoir effect,* reflecting mixing within the ocean of waters of different C^{14} content.

Isotopic fractionation varies with the biological pathway to skeleton or tissue, and C^{14} dates for different organic remains from the same environment are put on an equivalent footing by correcting for fractionation differences. Measurements of C^{13} content provide reliable indication of such fractionation differences (Rafter and O'Brien, 1954), and standard age correction procedures are set out by Polach (1969), and by Olsson and Osadebe (1974). When C^{14} dates from corals are being compared with one another, or with results from reef molluscs, this correction is not strictly necessary as C^{13} variations between and within reefs are small (Weber, 1974). The correction *must* be applied when coral ages are being compared with dates from plant materials. Practice regarding the use of fractionation correction varies between laboratories, and the user of C^{14} dates is strongly advised to make the following checks before comparing dates obtained from reef materials with dates from other stratigraphical situations and from other laboratories:

1. Does the laboratory concerned refer the date to modern wood standard?
2. Is the age estimate, relative to modern wood, corrected for fractionation by using the δC^{13} correction?

Only when both constraints apply is the C^{14} determination properly standard-ized. The date is still not on a common footing with terrestrial results, owing to the reservoir effect, discussed below. Pursuant to these considerations, the user of C^{14} results interested in precise chronology is advised to read Polach (1969), Mangerud (1972), and Olsson and Osadebe (1974).

Variations due to the reservoir effect must also be understood. Ocean C^{14} levels are lower than atmospheric levels mainly because the volume of dissolved CO_2 is about 60 times its volume in the atmosphere. Mean residence time of carbon atoms in the atmosphere is about 10 years (Rafter and O'Brien, 1970) and hence, if the oceans were perfectly mixed, the apparent C^{14} 'age' of their waters and of organisms at isotopic equilibrium therein would be around 600 years. The oceans are very imperfectly mixed, however, with deeper waters showing C^{14} levels substantially lower than surface waters (Broecker *et al.,* 1960; Bien *et al.,* 1963; Rafter and O'Brien, 1970). The apparent age of lower latitude surface waters is around 400 years (Bien and Suess, 1967; Rafter and O'Brien, 1970); and the effect will vary with the geography of vertical mixing and upwelling. In principle, corrections to C^{14} ages from reefs should be made in the light of modern variations of C^{14} levels between different marine regions. Application of this procedure is complicated by post-atomic bomb effects (increased C^{14} activity), and the simplest means for indexing a given modern reef environment is to measure C^{14} levels in a coral known to have lived before 1950. Furthermore, variations are likely to have changed in the past, as Late Pleistocene ocean circulation differed from present patterns (see Weyl, 1968, for example). However, as reefs occur mostly in lower latitude areas, remote from strong upwelling, the differences between past and present are probably relatively minor, and uncertainty about relationships between reef ages from different places, due to this factor, is likely to be less than 200 years.

A final complication by the reservoir effect may arise in estuarine or lagoonal situations when there is substantial admixture with waters of fluvial and groundwater drainage. Streams and surface runoff normally contain C^{14} close to atmospheric level, and by mixing can raise activity in nearshore waters above the common surface reservoir levels. The opposite effect can occur in runoff and in groundwater discharge from old limestone terrain, in which C^{14} activity is diluted by dissolved carbonate no longer containing C^{14}. Old carbonate derived from nearshore limestone sea floor may dilute C^{14} activity in burrowing and boring organisms (Mangerud, 1972), although this factor is unlikely to affect reefs. Of value, however, would be a systematic study of the effects of fluvial and groundwater discharge on C^{14} in fringing and lagoon reef environments. Such has yet to be reported. Again, measurement of modern (pre-1950) organisms from such environments provides corrective information.

Summarizing thus far, C^{14} results from reef corals may be compared for chronologic relationships, accepting uncertainties between regions which may amount to several hundred years stemming from reservoir effects. Uncertainty may be reduced by measuring pre-1950 C^{14} levels in the modern environments. The results may be compared with dates from terrestrial remains after due correction for ocean reservoir and isotopic factors. Overriding these considerations is the question of post-death contamination, which is a major problem in both C^{14} and Th^{230}/U^{234} dating, discussed in a later section.

URANIUM-SERIES DATING

This method has an advantage over C^{14} dating by having a much greater time-depth. With uncontaminated corals, sample ages up to 250,000 B.P. can be measured, thus enabling reef chronologies to be extended well beyond the last interglacial epoch. However, laboratories using the technique are few compared with the number of C^{14} laboratories, largely because the method is applicable only to corals and certain inorganic marine deposits, and hence is not in demand in archaeology and terrestrial stratigraphy. Methods of analysis and age calculation are set out by Thurber et al., (1965), Kaufman and Broecker (1965) and Veeh (1966); and a different laboratory approach is described by Moore and Somayajulu (1974).

The method as applied to reefs depends on the fact that living corals incorporate uranium into their skeletons at a level close to its concentration in sea water (about 3 parts per million), but contain no detectable amounts of the daughter radio-isotopes of thorium (reflecting the very low concentration of thorium in sea water: Moore and Sackett, 1964). The residence time of uranium in sea water is greater than several hundred thousand years (Broecker, 1971), hence there is no reservoir problem as there is for C^{14}. Isotopic fractionation between sea water and uranium deposition in coral is also negligible (Veeh, 1966). The method is much less useful for molluscs as these biologically exclude uranium from their shells while alive. Although after death such shells slowly acquire uranium from sea water (presumably by chemical diffusion), an unknown age error is implicit. Data described below show that uncontaminated molluscs sometimes yield age estimates very similar to corals from the same horizon, but in other case yield ages significantly too low.

As for the C^{14} method, uranium-series dating of corals is circumscribed by post-death contamination.

POST-DEATH CONTAMINATION

Contamination after death of reef-building skeletons can seriously falsify estimates of radiometric age. Contamination of corals occurs in four ways: mechanical entry of sediment washed into the corallites, accretions from boring organisms, chemical precipitation of calcium carbonate within the corallites, and chemical exchange between the fossil and surroundings during recrystallization. The last three processes also act on reef-dwelling molluscs. Amongst these, the chemical process of recrystallization and surface precipitation pose the greatest problems for sample selection, cleaning and dating. Effectiveness of both chemical processes increases with specific surface area, and corals therefore are much more susceptible to contamination than massive molluscs such as *Tridacna*. The expectation that tridacnids are intrinsically better than corals for reef dating C^{14} is borne out by results discussed later. Unfortunately, these molluscs are unsuitable for Th^{230}/U^{234} dating as they biologically exclude uranium while alive, and corals themselves must be used for dating by this method, as described in the previous section.

The contamination problem must be met by careful examination in the field of all potential samples, followed by laboratory examination and cleaning. Age estimates of even mildly contaminated samples can be erroneous (as data, presented later, indicate), and in principle no contaminated samples should be submitted for dating. Guidelines for sample examination and collection, and cleaning are as follows:

1. Field check for recrystallization. After breaking a specimen, rotate it to and fro in *direct sunlight*. Bright daylight beneath overcast sky is not adequate. Sparkles or flashes indicate recrystallization, as the aragonite fibres of the sclerodermites are too fine to produce the effect. This is the simplest and best test for initial selection. Field testing with staining solutions which react differently to aragonite and calcite, such as Fagel's solution, is less satisfactory, especially when the field specimen is saturated with rain or sea water. In the case of *Tridacna*, specimens should show the same light grey, somewhat translucent appearance across a broken face as is seen in modern shells. In all cases, specimens of white chalky appearance are rejected.

2. Laboratory check for recrystallization. X-ray diffraction analysis of carbonate types present in a sample is a good rapid technique, and suitable quantitative methods are indicated by Husseini and Mathews (1972), and Chappell and Polach (1972). Corals and tridacnids build aragonite skeletons, which mostly recrystallize to calcite—the low-Mg form being characteristic for sub-aerial recrystallization. An infra-red spectrophotometer can also be accurately used to determine calcite–aragonite ratio (Polach *et al.*, in press).

3. Microscopic examination. Contamination by sediment infill, infilled borings, and surface deposits of carbonate, can be readily seen with a low-power binocular microscope. Internal recrystallisation, or precipitation of secondary carbonate within solution cavities, requires thin section for identification. As surface precipitates and cavity fills may be aragonite, a zero-calcite assay by X-ray diffraction is no absolute guarantee of zero contamination. If surface coatings of aragonite needles or the occurrence of solution cavities are seen under the binocular microscopic, examination of a thin section is warranted. Processes of internal recrystallization, principally by an advancing front of sparry calcite accompanied by subjacent zones of aragonite leaching in Pleistocene corals from Barbados, are well described by James (1974). A second mode of recrystallization by

progressive coarsening of the aragonite fibres—particularly clear in *Tridacna,* is described by Chappell and Polach (1972), and Chappell *et al.,* (1974). Slow inversion to calcite appears to occur in this mode.

4. Cleaning. Cleaning of mildly contaminated samples is often possible. Samples should first be cut into slabs about 5 to 8 mm thick. Trapped sediment and light powdery surface deposits can often be shaken out in an ultrasonic water bath. However, tougher secondary rinds, infilled borings, and patches of discolouration require cutting out. Dentistry tools (drill and probes) may be used, and such cleaning is best done under a magnifying lens or plate, in a strong light with a fine jet of water. A diamond grinding lap is useful for large cuts, especially for tridacnids. Recrystallization can sometimes be cut out where it has progressed as a discrete front, but for widespread partial recrystallization or secondary void fillings there is no remedy. Chemical cleaning, e.g. by acid, should be avoided as the possible leaching effect on uranium-series isotopes is not known.

5. Preferred genera for dating. When samples for dating are being collected, in an area where recrystallization is widespread, types with large thick-walled corallites and negligible coenosteum, such as *Favites* or *Goniastrea,* are preferred. The more delicate the structural elements, the more difficult is cleaning. In simple thick-walled types, light deposits of secondary carbonate and sediment can be readily drilled out—an operation not possible in spongy types such as *Porites.*

The falsifying effects of contamination increase with age of sample, and towards the limit of a dating method large errors will result from only one per cent of contamination. It is clearly desirable to have means of assessing dating validity by analysing isotopes which are independent of the primary age calculation. For C^{14} dating, relying on a single radio-isotope, this is not possible. Nor can mild contamination be detected by measuring the stable C^{13} isotope, as recrystallization has little effect on the level of this isotope (Chappell and Polach, 1972). For uranium-series dating such cross-checking is possible, because ages may be estimated from 3 different isotope pairs in the series (Th^{230}/U^{234}, Pa^{231}/U^{235}, and U^{234}/U^{238}) (Thurber *et al.,* 1965; Broecker, 1965). Additionally, contamination by chemical exchange with groundwater (in uplifted reefs) is indicated by the presence of Th^{232}. As this isotope is not formed by uranium decay its presence indicates access of secondary thorium. Use of these cross-checks is illustrated by data discussed in the next section.

CONTAMINATION ERRORS, AND LIMITATIONS: ILLUSTRATIVE DATA

The effect of contamination errors in samples which pass the binocular micro-scope screening is illustrated by 10 samples in Table 1. These data, chosen from

TABLE 1. Effect of contamination errors in samples

Sample code	Genus	Alteration	Calcite %	C^{14} age, error	Total U, ppm	U^{234}/U^{238}	Th^{230}/U^{234} age, error
Group 1—Satisfactory C^{14} and Th^{230}/U^{234} results							
L1351H	Goniastrea	clean	0	$7,500 \pm 90$	2.51	1.12	$9,400 \pm 600$
L1351F	Favia	clean	0	$7,610 \pm 90$	2.89	1.12	$9,700 \pm 600$
L1347H	Leptoria	clean	1	$7,720 \pm 140$	2.47	1.12	$9,400 \pm 600$
Group 2—Unsatisfactory C^{14}, Satisfactory Th^{230}/U^{234} results							
L1353D	Hydnophora	clean	$\leqslant 3$	$29,000 \pm 1,000$	2.53	1.13	$42,000 \pm 3,000$
L1351E	Symphyllia	clean	$\leqslant 3$	$19,000 \pm 1,000$	3.03	1.10	$42,000 \pm 3,000$
Group 3—Unsatisfactory U-series results							
TM74-12	Leptastrea	s.r.[a]	3		3.99	1.10	$69,000 \pm 4,000$
TM74-9	Porites	s.r.[a]	10		2.70	1.39	$> 200,000$
Group 4—Tridacna: Satisfactory C^{14}, Unsatisfactory U-series results							
A116	Tridacna	clean	$\leqslant 5$	$35,770 \pm 1,500$	0.24	1.14	$34,000 \pm 4,000$[b]
A117	Tridacna	clean	$\leqslant 5$	$35,350 \pm 1,400$	0.13	1.13	$23,000 \pm 2,000$[b]
NG625	Tridacna	clean	$\leqslant 3$		0.36	1.10	$74,000 \pm 4,000$

s.r.—slight surface recrystallization
Th^{232} present

about 100 determinations from raised reefs in New Guinea and Timor, are from samples without secondary deposits or sediment, and which show zero or low levels of recrystallization to calcite.

The first group (3 coral samples from a raised Holocene reef in New Guinea: Chappell and Polach, 1975) appear unaltered, with only L1347H showing a trace (1 per cent) of calcite. Agreement among the C^{14} results is excellent, as it is among the Th^{230}/U^{234} results. There is no reason to fault any of these dates. The difference of about 1,800 years between C^{14} and Th^{230}/U^{234} sets is not fully understood, but appears larger than the C^{14}-sidereal time discrepancy. Clearly the C^{14} and uranium-series chronologies cannot be put on a common footing.

The second group (2 coral samples from the well-dated, 42,000 year old, reef IIIB in New Guinea: Bloom et al., 1974) shows the effect of contamination when samples are near the limit of a dating method. Both show C^{14} age markedly younger than their real age.

The third group (2 coral samples from adequately-dated, raised reefs in Timor: Chappell and Veeh, 1977) shows sample unreliability indicated by aberrant uranium values. The level of total uranium in TM74-12 is abnormally high (normal range 2.3 to 3.3 ppm.), suggesting accession of secondary uranium. Samples TM74-9 has very high U^{234}/U^{238} ratio, indicating secondary uranium exchange with groundwater (the ratio in unaltered coral initially is 1.15 and diminishes with time). The relatively high calcite content (10 per cent) also indicates an unreliable sample.

The last group contains 3 tridacnids from well-dated terraces in New Guinea (Veeh and Chappell, 1970; Bloom et al., 1974). Samples A116, A117 throw interesting light on limits of the C^{14} method. In thin section and in calcite levels these samples are indistinguishable from much older tridacnids from the same area. Three such older tridacnids show zero C^{14}, and 2 others have apparent C^{14} ages exceeding 40,000 B.P.[4] Hence there is nothing to suggest that the C^{14} results for A116, A117 are seriously in error (see Chappell and Polach, 1972). However, 5 Th^{230}/U^{234} determinations from clean corals from the same reef have ages around 42,000 B.P. (Bloom et al., 1974), and it is impossible to know the extent to which the difference reflects C^{14}-sidereal time difference and how much is due to minor C^{14} contamination. Because uncertainty is inevitable near the limit of C^{14} dating, it is recommended that U-series dating of corals be used for all reefs expected to be about, 30,000 years old or more.

The Th^{230}/U^{234} results for A116, A117 cannot be considered reliable, even though the results for A116 agrees with its C^{14} age, because Th^{232} in both shows post-death accession of thorium. On the other hand, NG625 which has zero Th^{232} shows a falsely young age, illustrating the uncertainty attached to U-series dating of molluscs, arising from the fact that they acquire most of their uranium after death. Results from molluscs are sometimes comparable with dates from adjacent corals, e.g. one tridacnid date from the 60,000 B.P. reef in New Guinea (Bloom et al., 1974) and 2 gastropod dates from the 60,000 B.P. reef in Barbados (James et al., 1971). However, the fact remains, that mollusc dates should not be accepted as definitive.

Attempts have been made to establish the age of ancient shorelines when uncontaminated samples could not be found. Suggested procedures for the use of the U-series are explained by Kaufman and Broecker (1965), Szabo and Rosholt (1969), and Osmund et al., (1970). The strategy is to take many samples from a given horizon and then to use Th^{232} levels as a guide to the degree of contamination. Results show large spreads around the mean values, and at best provide only a guide to possible correlations with reefs accurately dated elsewhere, for example, the Th^{230}/U^{234} age estimates of A116, A117 in Table 1, which contain Th^{232}, were obtained using the Kaufman and Broecker (1965) correction procedure (Veeh and Chappell, 1970). Such correction methods depend on untested assumptions about contamination rates. Cross-checking by C^{14} dating of partly recrystallized corals, taken from reefs where ages are well established from multiple reliable samples and using the percentage of calcite as a guide to level of contamination, shows that within a single locality the contamination history varies widely between specimens and that there is no evidence of uniform contamination rate within a single specimen (Chappell

---

4. It should be noted that these 3 tridacnids which are substantially older than 40,000 years and which show zero C^{14} activity also have up to 4 per cent low-Mg calcite present, apparently developed by inversion from aragonite during slow coarsening of the aragonite fibres. This suggests internal recrystallization in a system closed to carbon exchange (Chappell and Polach, 1972; Chappell et al., 1974).

and Polach, 1972; Chappell *et al.,* 1974). The conclusion is that age estimates based on patchworks of contaminated samples are not reliable.

CONCLUSIONS: SUMMARY GUIDE FOR REEF DATING

Great care must be exercised when ages of ancient coral reefs are being determined, because the chemically reactive nature of calcium carbonate makes the potential high for sample contamination.

In the ideal situation:

1. Samples must show no visible signs of contamination, by microscopic and X-ray examination;
2. C^{14} dating should be used only when the reefs are younger than about 20,000 years. If ages between 20,000 and about 30,000 B.P. are suspected, corals should not be used for the C^{14} determinations; interior cuts from massive molluscs such as *Tridacna* should be used.
3. U-series samples, in addition to meeting criterion (1), must show zero Th^{232} and have both the total U content and the U^{234}/U^{238} activity ratio consistent with zero contamination.
4. Direct comparison should not be made of C^{14} and Th^{230}/U^{234} age estimates, because the methods are not yet on a common chronological footing.
5. The age of a given reef crest can be established only with concordant results from at least two samples. Where samples are taken across an extended section of a given reef, at least three dates consistent with stratigraphy should be attained.

When dating Pleistocene reefs (as against Holocene), *the real situation* often falls short of the ideal when widespread recrystallization makes it impossible to collect samples which scrupulously meet ideal criteria. In these instances, samples with less than 10 per cent calcite may be submitted to the cleaning procedures described above, and the final age estimate based on concordant results between samples passing the zero-Th^{232} and the 2 uranium-level criteria. When a dating programme is undertaken, reference can be made to the baseline studies from Barbados (Broecker *et al.,* 1968), New Guinea (Chappell, 1974; Bloom *et al.,* 1974), Hawaii (Ku *et al.,* 1974), and Timor (Chappell and Veeh, 1977). Detailed dating of a Holocene reef in New Guinea, by C^{14} and Th^{230}/U^{234}, is described by Chappell and Polach (1975).

The most severely restricted situation is when reefs are being examined by means of drill holes. These not only provide limited samples, but also uncertainty arises about the true stratigraphical position of samples, due to processes of reworking and transport within the reef itself as well as accidental transport downwards by the drill (Thom, Chapter 6). When only recrystallized material is available from a drill run, radiometric determinations represent minimum age estimates and possible correlations must be interpreted in this light.

References

BIEN, G.; RAKESTRAW, N. W.; SUESS, H. 1963. Radiocarbon dating of deep water in the Pacific and Indian Oceans. *Bull. Inst. Oceanogr. Monaco*, vol. 61, p. 1–16.

——; SUESS, H. 1967. Transfer and exchange of C^{14} between the atmosphere and surface water of the Pacific Ocean. In: *Radioactive Dating and Low Level Counting*, Vienna, International Atomic Energy Agency, p. 105–15.

BLOOM, A. L.; BROECKER, W. S.; CHAPPELL, J.; MATTHEWS, R. K.; MESOLELLA, K. J. 1974. Quaternary sea level fluctuations on a tectonic coast: new $^{230}Th/^{234}U$ dates from Huon Peninsula, New Guinea. *Quaternary Research*, vol. 4, p. 185–205.

BROECKER, W. S. 1965. Isotope geochemistry and the Pleistocene climatic record. In: W. H. Wright and D. G. Frey (eds). *The Quaternary of the United States*. Princeton University Press, p. 737–53.

——. 1971. A kinetic model for the chemical composition of sea water. *Quaternary Research*, vol. 1, p. 188–207.

——; GERARD, R.; EWING, M.; HEEZEN, B. C. 1960. Natural radiocarbon in the Atlantic Ocean. *J. geophys. Res.*, vol. 65, p. 2903–31.

——; THURBER, D. L.; GODDARD, J.; KU, T-L.; MATTHEWS, R. K.; MESOLELLA, R. L. 1968. Milankovitch hypothesis supported by precise dating of coral reefs and deep sea sediments. *Science*, vol. 159, p. 297–300.

CHAPPELL, J. 1974. Geology of coral terraces, Huon Peninsula, New Guinea: a study of Quaternary sea level changes and tectonic movements. *Geol. Soc. Am. Bull.*, vol. 85, p. 553–70.

——; BROECKER, W. S.; POLACH, H. A.; THOM, B. G. 1974. Problem of dating Upper Pleistocene sea levels from coral reef areas. In: *Proc. Second Int. Coral Reef Symp*. Brisbane, Great Barrier Reef Committee, vol. 2, p. 563–71.

——; POLACH, H. A. 1972. Some effects of partial recrystallisation on ^{14}C dating of Late Pleistocene corals and molluscs. *Quaternary Research*, vol. 2, p. 244–52.

——; ——; 1975. Holocene sea level change and coral reef growth at Huon Peninsula, New Guinea. *Geol. Soc. Am. Bull.*, vol. 86.

——; VEEH, H. H. 1977. Quaternary uplift and sea level changes at Timor and Atauro Island. *Geol. Soc. Am. Bull.*, vol. 88.

DAMON, P. E.; LONG, A.; WALLICK, E. I. 1972. Dendro-chronologic calibration of the C^{14} timescale. In: *Proceedings of the International Conference on Radiocarbon Dating*. Lower Hutt, New Zealand, p. 44–59.

FERGUSON, C. W. 1970. Bristlecone pine chronology and calibration of the radiocarbon time scale. In: J. H. G. Smith and J. Worrall (eds). *Tree Ring Analysis with Special Reference to Northwest America, Forest Bull*. Vancouver, University of British Columbia, vol. 7, p. 88–91.

HUSSEINI, S. I.; MATTHEWS, R. K. 1972. Distribution of high-magnesium and calcite in lime muds of the Great Bahama Bank—diagenetic implications. *J. sedim. Petrol*. vol. 42, p. 179–82.

JAMES, N. P. 1974. Diagenesis of scleractinian corals in the subaerial vadose environments of Barbados. *Paleontol.*, vol. 48, p. 785–99.

——; MOUNTJOY, E. W.; ONURA, A. 1971. An Early Wisconsin reef terrace at Barbados, West Indies, and its climatic implications. *Geol. Soc. Am. Bull.*, vol. 82, p. 2011–18.

KAUFMAN, A.; BROECKER, W. S. 1965. Comparison of Th^{230} and C^{14} ages for carbonate materials from Lakes Tahoutan and Bonneville. *J. geophys. Res.*, vol. 70, p. 4039–54.

KU, T-L.; KIMMEL, M. A.; EASTON, W. H; O'NEILL, T. J. 1974. Eustatic sea level 120,000 years ago on Oahu, Hawaii. *Science*, vol. 183, p. 959–62.

MANGERUD, J. 1972. Radiocarbon dating of marine shells, including discussion of apparent age of Recent shells from Norway. *Boreas*, vol. 1, p. 143–72.

MOORE, W. S.; SOMAYAJULU, B. L. K. 1974. Age determinations of fossil corals using $^{230}Th/^{234}Th$ and $^{230}Th/^{227}Th$. *J. geophys. Res.*, vol. 79, p. 5065–68.

——; SACKETT, W. M. 1964. Uranium and thorium series inequilibria in sea water. *J. geophys. Res.*, vol. 69, p. 5401–05.

OLSSON, I. U. (ed.). 1970. *Radiocarbon variations and absolute chronology*. Stockholm, Almquist and Wiksell, p. 233–337.

90

——; OSADEBE, F. A. N. 1974. Carbon isotope variations and fractionation corrections in ^{14}C dating. *Boreas*, vol. 3, p. 139–46.

OSMUND, J. K.; CARPENTER, J. R.; WINDON, H. 1965. Th^{230}/U^{234} age of the Pleistocene corals and oolites of Florida. *J. geophys. Res.*, vol. 70, p. 1843–47.

POLACH, H. A. 1969. Optimisation of liquid scintillation radiocarbon age determinations and reporting of ages. *Atomic Energy in Australia*, vol. 12, p. 21–8.

——; MCLEAN, R. F.; CALDWELL, J.; THOM, B. G. (in press). Radiocarbon ages from the Northern Great Barrier Reef. *Phil. Trans. R. Soc. Lond.*

RAFTER, T. A.; O'BRIEN, B. J. 1970. Exchange rates between the atmosphere and the ocean as shown by recent C^{14} measurements in the South Pacific. In: I. U. Olsson (ed.). *Radiocarbon variations and absolute chronology*. Stockholm, Almquist and Wiksell. p. 355–78.

STUIVER, M. 1970. Long term C^{14} variations. In: U. Olsson (ed.). *Radiocarbon variations and absolute chronology*. Stockholm, Almquist and Wiksell, p. 197–213.

SZABO, B. J.; ROSHOLT, J. N. 1969. Uranium series dating of Pleistocene molluscan shells from Southern California—an open system model. *J. geophys. Res.*, vol. 74, p. 3253–60.

THURBER, D. L.; BROECKER, W. S.; BLANCHARD, R. L.; POTRATZ, H. A. 1965. Uranium series ages of Pacific Atoll coral. *Science*, vol. 149, p. 55–8.

VEEH, H. H. 1966. Th^{230}/U^{234} and U^{234}/U^{238} ages of Pleistocene high sea level stand. *J. geophys. Res.*, vol. 71, p. 3379–86.

——; CHAPPELL, J. 1970. Astronomic theory of climatic change: support from New Guinea. *Science*, vol. 167, p. 862–5.

WEBER, J. N. 1974. ^{13}C/^{12}C ratios as natural isotopic traces elucidating calcification processes in reef-building and non-reef-building corals. In: *Proc. Second Int. Coral Reef Symp.* Brisbane, Great Barrier Reef Committee, p. 289–98.

WEYL, P. K. 1968. The role of oceans in climatic change: a theory of the ice ages. *Meteorological Monographs*, vol. 8, p. 37–62.

WOLLIN, G.; ERICSON, D. B.; RYAN, W. B. J.; FOSTER, J. H. 1971. Magnetism of the earth and climatic changes. *Earth Planet Sci. Lett.*, vol. 12, p. 175–81.

9

Techniques for the measurement of sea level around atolls

D. T. Pugh[1]

INTRODUCTION

Measurements of sea level in the environs of atolls are usually required for one of two distinct purposes. On an oceanic scale they may be invaluable for the development of cotidal charts, giving information in a region where no other data exist. An example of this kind of application for the Central Pacific Ocean is given by Luther and Wunsch (1975). More locally, measurements are required for the generation of predictions of water level to assist in planning boating operations, and as input for biological and geological models of atoll processes. Farrow and Brander (1971) have described the measurement of sea level on Aldabra atoll in the Indian Ocean and show that considerable distortions of the ocean tide occur over short distances where a shallow lagoon is connected to the ocean by only a few narrow channels.

The instrumental problems are similar for both oceanic and local applications. Levels must be recorded at regular intervals, averaging out the short-period wind-wave fluctuations, for periods varying from 12 hours to in excess of a year. Instruments should be simple to operate and easy to repair as skilled technical assistance will generally be unavailable. Moreover, it is characteristic of coral islands that the water line at extreme low water is separated by a considerable distance from the extreme high water line, above which it is convenient to site a recorder. This separation eliminates the possibility of using the conventional stilling well and float gauge configuration, commonly operated by coastal authorities, as it requires the recorder to be mounted over deep water on a vertical structure such as a pier or harbour wall. The purpose of this account is to discuss the physical principles of simple instrumental techniques which may be used around atolls. A recent successful installation of a long term pneumatic gauge on Aldabra atoll is discussed in detail to illustrate the considerations and problems which may be encountered in a practical installation.

1. Institute of Oceanographic Sciences, Bidston Observatory, Birkenhead L43 7RA, Merseyside, United Kingdom.

TIDE POLES

The simple tide pole is often the most economical way of making water-level measurements over short periods of up to 24 hours. A series of poles sited at intervals down a beach, all levelled to the same datum, may be necessary where the foreshore slopes gently, if readings are to be made from above the water line. Poles should be firmly fixed, by guy lines if possible, and must, of course, be vertical. Figure 1 illustrates a simple device for increasing the accuracy of

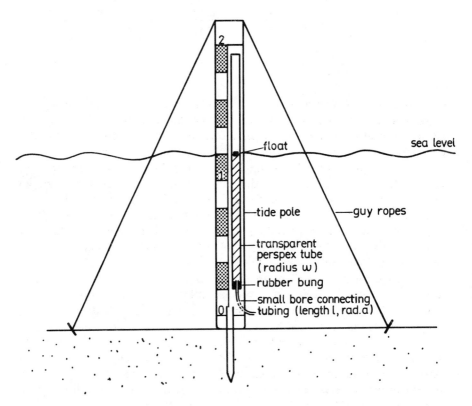

Figure 1
Schematic diagram of a stilling pole system. (for $w = 0.0125$, $l = 3.8$ m and $a = 0.002$ m, the time constant is 30 seconds).

reading in the presence of waves. A transparent (perspex) tube is strapped to a tide pole and connected to the sea through a narrow bore tube. The fluctuations of the level of the water within the tube are stilled relative to the external wave oscillations, making reading easier. The water in the tube may be coloured with a dye to make surface identification easier, or a float may be used—allowance being made for the height of the float surface above the water level. In an experiment to determine the errors introduced when reading an estimated average in the presence of waves, a standard deviation of 0.05 m was obtained with waves of 1.5 m peak to trough height.

SYPHON-STILLING WELL SYSTEMS

Traditional float and stilling well (or stand pipe) gauges may be used even over a broad drying reef, if a well is dug or blasted in a sheltered position ashore, and connected by a syphon pipe to a position beyond the low water line. Groves (1965) has used this technique successfully on Pacific atolls. Figure 2 shows the details of his installations. The hose was taped to a small multistrand steel cable which was stretched between the two points and fixed at intervals to spikes in the reef to prevent longshore motions by currents. A filter and sediment trap on the outer end of the syphon was used to keep out debris. Periodically air should be bled from the tube by opening the valve fitted at the highest level in the syphon pipe, near the time of high tide, when the whole pipe, including the valve, is below sea level.

Short period wave oscillations are damped out because of friction in the long connecting pipe. This damping may be expressed quantitatively in terms of a time constant, c, given by:

$$c = \frac{8vlw^2}{a^4g}$$

where v is the kinematic viscosity of sea water ($10^{-6} \text{ m}^2 \text{ s}^{-1}$),

a, l are the internal radius and the length of the syphon pipe,

w is the radius of the stilling well,

and g is gravitational acceleration.

In terms of this time constant a sinusoidal wave of period $2\pi/\sigma$ is attenuated by a factor

$$F(\sigma) = (1 + c^2\sigma^2)^{-\frac{1}{2}}$$

and the corresponding time lag is

$$T(\sigma) = \sigma^{-1} \arctan(\sigma c)$$

For a tube of 0.0125 m internal radius, and 200 m length, connecting to a well of 0.075 m radius the time constant is 38 seconds and the attenuation factor for a 15 second period wave is 0.06. Groves used a tube of only 0.006 m internal radius so that his time constant (17 minutes) was substantially longer. During the period of operation no increase in the time constant due to biological fouling of the inner surface of the syphon pipe was observed. More recently Bilham (1977) has used a similar system for tectonic studies in the Aleutians and in the Caribbean.

The formulae given above may also be used to calculate the response of the

95

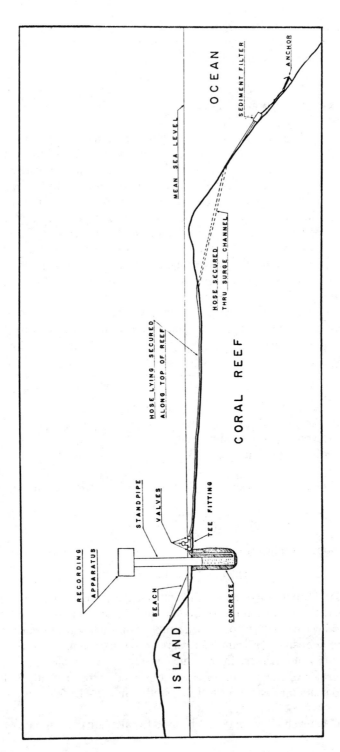

Figure 2
The syphon-stilling well system (after Groves, 1965).

stilling pole to waves. For a perspex tube of internal radius 0.0125 m connected through a tube of radius 0.002 m, 3.8 m long, the time constant (Fig. 1) is 30 seconds at 20°C. The time constant may be determined empirically by raising the water level in the stilling well or pole above the external level and then allowing the levels to equalize through the connecting tube by suddenly opening a tap (this test could be done before final installation). The time taken for the well or pole level to fall to 0.37 (e^{-1}) of the original difference is the time constant. To ensure that the flow in the pipe is laminar during this test the original water level difference should not exceed 0.10 m for the syphon dimensions described earlier, or 0.45 m for the stilling pole dimensions. A full theoretical discussion of stilling well characteristics is given by Noye (1974).

PNEUMATIC SYSTEMS

The principle of all pneumatic systems is to transfer a hydrostatic pressure, measured at a fixed point below the low water level, to a recorder sited above the high water level. One simple form consists of a partly inflated flexible container ('floppy bag') connected by an air tube to a pressure sensor and recorder. Farrow and Brander (1971) used the commercial Foxboro–Yoxall gauge which may be suitable for many applications. However, the accuracy is only about 0.10 m, and the circular recording paper introduces a time error which depends on the observed water level so that low water times are poorly determined, which is unsatisfactory for tidal analysis.

In the bubbling system compressed air (or other gas) from a cylinder is reduced in pressure through one or two valves so that there is a small steady flow down a connecting tube to escape through an orifice in an underwater canister or 'pressure point'. At this underwater outlet, for low rates of gas escape, the gas pressure is equal to the water pressure. The pressure of gas in the system is measured and recorded at the shore end so that, apart from small pressure gradient in the connecting tubing, the measured pressure P_m is related to the water level above the outlet by the elementary hydrostatic relationship: relationship:

$$P_m = \rho g h_m + P_A$$

where ρ is the water density,
   P_A is the atmospheric pressure,
and h_m is the water head above the pressure point orifice datum.
If the pressure P_m is measured using a differential transducer which responds to the difference between the system pressure and atmospheric pressure, then the recorded pressure is $\rho g h_m$.

The flow of gas along the tube will be driven by a pressure gradient so that the measured pressure is higher than the true water pressure by an amount which depends on the tube dimensions and the rate of gas flow. This flow rate, which is usually monitored through a liquid filled bubble counter, should therefore

H

be kept low to minimize the pressure gradient error and to conserve the supply of gas. However, if the rate of supply of gas is too low, the pressure in the system may be unable to increase as rapidly as pressure changes at the outlet due to increasing water depth. Consequently, water will be forced into the system until the pressures balance and the recorded pressure is not then related to the pressure point orifice datum. For a connecting tube of internal radius 0.002 m and lengths up to 200 m errors are small and the gas flow rate in ml per minute should be set slightly greater than:

$$\frac{V}{600}\alpha$$

where V is the total gas volume in the system, including the recorder, tube
             and pressure point, in ml,
and α is the maximum rate of tidal water level increase in metres per hour.

In the presence of waves of amplitude s expressed in metres, the measured water head is less than the true water head by :

$$\frac{V}{A}\left(\frac{s}{(h_0 + 10 - s)}\right)$$

where A is the cross sectional area of the pressure point, which should be as
             large as practicable
and h_0 is the mean water head above the outlet orifice in metres. (The 10
             represents the water head equivalent of atmospheric pressure in
             metres).

For general application a cylindrical pressure point, 0.05 m deep and 0.20 m diameter will suffice. However, for longer tube lengths and high accuracy more exact design specifications must be satisfied.

    The three principal design considerations for a pneumatic tube gauge system are (a) to have a pressure point buffer volume and cross-sectional area sufficient to damp out wave effects, (b) to have a flow of air into the system sufficient to prevent water entering due to tidal increases in water pressure, and (c) to have as small a pressure head drop in the connecting tube as possible. The constraints are the length of tubing required (l), the expected maximum wave amplitude, the range to be measured, the maximum rate of water level increase (α) and the accuracy required of the system (τ). Where the pressure point is mounted near the sea bed and for systems where the pressure point and tube volume are large compared with the air volume in the recording instrument, the optimum design parameters are given by the following formulae:

cylindrical pressure point radius $= 0.4a(l/\tau)^{\frac{1}{4}} \times 10^{-3}$ m
depth $= 1.6\tau$ m
minimum air flow rate $= 0.0065\,(\alpha a^2 l)$ ml per minute
maximum total head loss in tube $= 0.7\,\alpha(l/a)^2 \times 10^{-6}$ m

where a, the internal radius of the connecting tube is in mm, l and τ are in metres and α is in metres per hour. Full details of the physics of pneumatic systems are given by Pugh (1972) and Pugh and Waller (1975).

THE ALDABRA BUBBLER GAUGE INSTALLATION

The Royal Society of London which maintains a scientific Station on Aldabra atoll approached the Institute of Oceanographic Sciences in 1972 for advice on the technical feasibility of installing a recording tide-gauge at a site which would be little affected by the lagoon characteristics. The Passe du Bois site (Fig. 3) which had been used for earlier measurements by Farrow and Brander (1971) would not be suitable. A detailed survey of the reef to the west of the Station was made in April 1973. It showed that about 500 m of connecting tubing would be required. For this length of tubing the time constant for a system pipe would have been unacceptably long; however, a pneumatic bubbler system would be suitable. Installation of a pneumatic bubbler system was effected in May 1975.

Site selection

Following a further survey of the reef area between Station and Settlement, it was decided that the gauge should be sited approximately 1 km north of Passe Femme (Fig. 3) and not along the line already surveyed. The site chosen had several advantages.

1. The reef was sand covered for much of the tube length so that, with suitable ballast, the tube would settle into the sand; the original site consisted almost entirely of coral reef in which it would have been particularly difficult to bury tubing, particularly as water discharged from the lagoon over this reef, even at low water, at speeds in excess of $0.5\,\text{ms}^{-1}$.
2. The rock face below the laboratory block was undercut, and was reported to vary in height from 1 m to 3 m, according to the movement of sand. Below this was a channel used by boats moving into the lagoon, often when the water was shallow. The outboard motors of these might have reacted with a tube to their mutual disadvantage. Boats cross the line chosen much less frequently.
3. By siting the gauge further away from the lagoon entrance the shallow-water lagoon effects would be reduced.
4. The length of tubing required was less by at least 50 m, and a suitable, roofed, building existed for siting the recorder.
5. Wave action was observed to be less over the reef edge at the site selected than at that previously surveyed.

Pneumatic design considerations

The instrument selected for recording was the Neyrpic 'Telimnip' gauge operat-

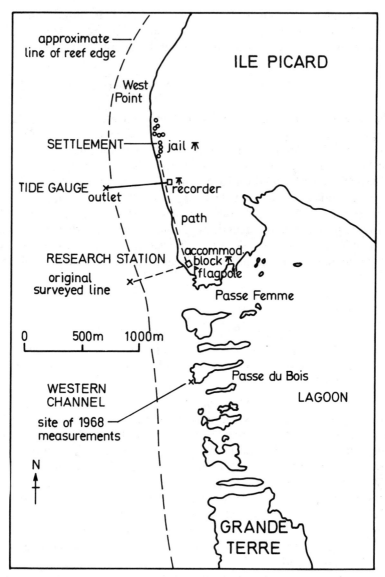

Figure 3
Detailed map of the Aldabra Station area showing tide gauge sites and
bench mark locations (🛪).

ing on a 5 m range, with a chart speed of 10 mm per hour. On this range the
instrument is potentially accurate to 0.01 m. Pressure in the pneumatic system is
balanced by a mercury manometer open to the atmosphere on the opposite
side, so that only water head pressures are measured—atmosphere pressure
variations are automatically eliminated.

For the Aldabra installation the design parameters were:

$$l = 455 \text{ m}$$
$$a = 1.9 \text{ mm}$$
$$\alpha = 0.75 \text{ m per hour}$$
$$\tau = 0.025 \text{ m}$$

which gave:

pressure point radius	= 0.105 m
depth	= 0.04 m
minimum flow rate	= 8.0 ml per minute
maximum total head loss	= 0.030 m

In practice, a lower pressure point radius of 0.075 m was used with a correspondingly increased depth. This was because of the difficulty of mounting a broad shallow pressure point truly horizontally in an environment of high wave activity. Theoretically, the maximum error due to the system's response to waves was therefore increased, but, because of the relatively large time constant of the extreme length of tubing, the effective volume for wave response was significantly less than the total system volume, and gave a lower error in practice. For the required gas supply rate, a normal SCUBA diving cylinder of capacity 1 m^3 had a lifetime of 90 days. The demands on the Aldabra stock of diving cylinders and on the air compressor were minimal. The pressure drop in the connecting tube depends on the gas viscosity which is temperature dependent; however, as the viscosity of air increases by only 13 per cent between 20°C and 75°C, the effect was negligible when making a total correction of 0.03 m.

The gauge was calibrated against a dead-weight pressure standard before shipment, and a small adjustment made for the density change of mercury to a mean operating temperature on Aldabra of 30°C. The gauge and tubing were assembled in the laboratory and the gauge inflated to 1.0 m pressure equivalent, with the pressure point end sealed. When this end was suddenly opened to the atmosphere, the recorded pressure fell at a rate proportional to the pressure head across the tube, showing that to a first approximation the system had a linear response. The time constant for this response was 45 seconds.

Installation details

The pressure point and associated equipment were designed to offer flexibility in the method of installation, the final decisions being made after a detailed site survey had been conducted.

The recorder, sited in a roofed building, was further housed in a wire mesh cage to protect it against rodent and crab bites. Double walled, 8 mm external diameter, nylon tubing, sheathed in 15 mm internal diameter, 22 mm external diameter, polypropylene tubing to provide protection against abrasion and fish bite, was used for the pressure transmission. The outer cover was drilled at intervals to allow for free flooding, so reducing buoyancy and affording some degree of thermal stability to the inner tube.

The inner tube was blanked off at the seaward end and the assembly laid along the beach to the selected underwater pressure point site (Fig. 4). Scrap chain (weighing approximately 2 kg per m) was fastened to the tubing using nylon 'one-way' Insuloid grips to give a uniformly distributed ballast. This method not only provides weight to sink the assembly into the sand but also offers a firm anchorage where rock outcrops are encountered.

The pressure point (Fig. 5) was constructed from rigid p.v.c. and heavy duty Insuloid grips were used for securing the equipment to the selected coral boss. Final air connection to the pressure point was made by a diver and compressed air was purged through the system. This prevented any ingress of water to the tubing and avoided the possibility of water being trapped in any local tube depressions, although normal flow of dry diving air clears a tube of water in a few days.

Over a period of several months after installation the tube gradually settled under the weight of chain into the sand.

Datum determinations

To give permanent value to any record of water levels. it is necessary to connect them to some permanent datum ashore. A primary bench mark was established on a substantial concrete pillar which was erected on bed rock near the tide gauge building, and marked with an identifying inscription on an aluminium plate set into the top. This bench mark was also connected to three secondary marks on other buildings, whose continuing existence seemed assured by their social functions, namely the jail, the tide gauge building and the accommodation block, as a precaution against accidental movement.

The level of the pressure point outlet, which is the tide gauge zero, was determined relative to the tide gauge benchmark by means of a series of simultaneous readings of the gauge and the tide pole (Fig. 4). These readings were made in groups of five, every fifteen minutes over a period of six hours spanning a high tide. By connecting the tide staff zero to the bench mark, gauge datum was established at 6.220 ± 0.010 m below the main bench mark. This exercise should be repeated once a year to check for movement of the pressure point.

Tidal analyses

Table 1 compares the results of the harmonic analysis of the first month of data from the new installation with the results obtained from the analysis of a month of data from Passe du Bois (Farrow and Brander, 1971) and with analyses of a year of data from Kilindini Harbour, Mombasa, and Port Victoria in the Seychelles. The very small amplitude of the shallow water constituents, M_4, MS_4 and M_6 fully justifies the decision to move the installation away from the channel region, and suggests that the oceanic tide at Aldabra is virtually free

102

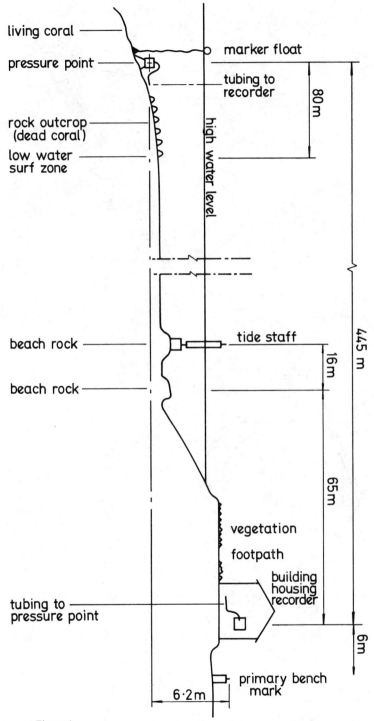

living coral

pressure point

rock outcrop
(dead coral)

low water
surf zone

marker float

tubing to
recorder

80 m

high water level

beach rock

tide staff

16 m

beach rock

65 m

445 m

vegetation

footpath

building
housing
recorder

tubing to
pressure point

6 m

primary bench
mark

6·2 m

Figure 4
Transverse section of the Aldabra pneumatic tide-gauge installation.

103

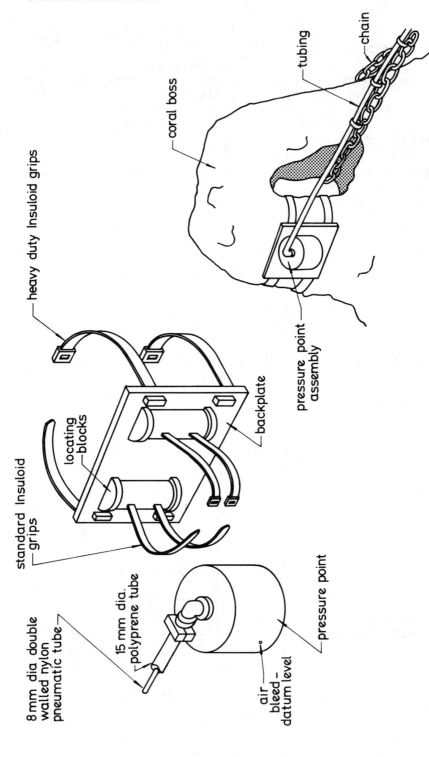

Figure 5
Details of the underwater pressure point for the Aldabra installation.

TABLE 1. Comparison of harmonic analyses from the new installation, the Passe du Bois data of Farrow and Brander (1971), Kilindini Harbour, Mombasa, and Port Victoria, Seychelles. All phases are in Seychelles time (GMT-0400).

		New installation (1 month—May/June 1975)		Passe du Bois (1 month—August/Sept 1968)		Kilindini (1 year 1933–34)		Port Victoria (1 year 1964)	
O_1	H	0.104 m		0.096		0.119		0.107	
	g		59.7°		67.1		50.2		60.9
K_1	H	0.156		0.154		0.187		0.183	
	g		64.6		67.1		48.9		60.3
N_2	H	0.170		0.129		0.197		0.084	
	g		111.6		125.5		107.5		103.1
M_2	H	0.927		0.854		1.060		0.404	
	g		139.5		147.4		129.2		129.4
S_2	H	0.466		0.415		0.514		0.182	
	g		185.9		193.1		172.3		172.7
M_3	H	0.007		not analysed		0.004		0.004	
	g		346.1				304.7		149.9
M_4	H	0.001		0.036		0.013		0.003	
	g		327.3		170.1		314.7		164.0
MS_4	H	0.003		0.049		0.008		0.002	
	g		149.2		221.1		2.4		204.5
$2MS_6$	H	0.001		0.029		0.005		0.002	
	g		108.0		210.9		111.2		31.0

of non-linear distortion. The Passe du Bois measurements are distorted by the channel: apart from the local shallow-water effects, the tidal amplitudes in the semi-diurnal band are reduced by around 9 per cent, while the phases are retarded by 15 minutes. The new values of phase are in better agreement with those obtained at Kilindini and Port Victoria. When studying tides in an oceanic region, where differences of amplitude and phase are small over hundreds of kilometres, then, as originally stated, measurements from islands are invaluable, but only if they are made after proper site selection.

The non-tidal residuals for the month of data analysed were extremely small, giving a standard deviation of only 0.028 m between the observed and the tidally computed levels.

NON-BUBBLING PNEUMATIC SYSTEMS

If a pneumatic bubbling system is inflated, so that air flows through the orifice in the underwater pressure point when the water head is h_i, and, if the water level then increases without a further supply of air, water gradually enters the system until the increase in system pressure, due to the reduction in system volume, balances the increased water head pressure. The datum level for the instrument is no longer at the orifice and to correct for this the recorded water head must be corrected by adding:

$$\frac{V}{A}\left(1 - \frac{h_i + 10}{h_m + 10}\right)$$

where all measurements are in metres. This correction is useful if the air supply cannot be maintained for some reason, although the bubbling mode is better for routine use. The water head pressure changes must not be so large as to force water beyond the pressure point into the connecting tube.

This non-bubbler mode of operation was used during the Aldabra survey to monitor water levels over high tide at sites around the island. Brief details of the system used are given here because they may be useful for similar surveys where, for example, the times of high water are required at a number of sites. One of the principal advantages of such a system over tide pole readings is that the observer may be comfortably housed in a tent or hut; for readings over a long period or during darkness the increased accuracy which results is not the only attraction.

Figure 6 shows the simple system used for transmitting and reading the water head. A water manometer was fitted with a perspex tube to which was attached a metre ruler. The use of local sea water in the manometer removes any need for density corrections. The time constant of the system, which depends on the length of tubing and the volume of the manometer, was measured by fitting a tap at the seaward end and measuring the time taken for the pressure in the manometer to fall to 0.37 of its initial value when the tap was opened. This time constant was adjusted to a suitable value by adjusting the amount of sea

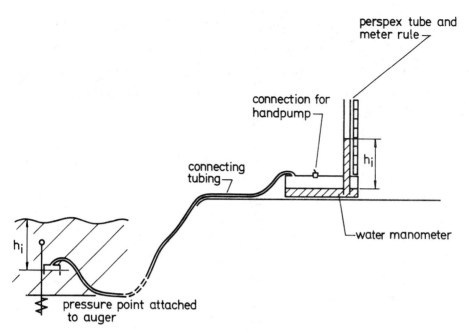

Figure 6
Schematic diagram of a simple non-bubbling pneumatic system.

water in the manometer. About an hour before high tide the system was inflated using a hand pump. Water levels in the perspex tube were then read at regular intervals through the time of high water so that a smooth curve could be drawn. To avoid water entering the connecting tubing the maximum level to be observed should not exceed:

$$\frac{V(h_i + 10)}{(V - Ad)} - 10 \text{ metres}$$

where d is the depth of the pressure point and Ad is its volume. In the Aldabra experiments the manometer drum and hand pump were taken from a discarded kerosene cooker; pneumatic systems present many opportunities for improvization and ingenuity, both valuable attributes for research workers on remote islands.

References

BILHAM, R. G. 1977. A sea-level recorder for tectonic studies, *Geophysical J. R. Astronom. Soc.* vol. 48, p. 307–14.
FARROW, G. E.; BRANDER, K. M. 1971. Tidal studies on Aldabra, *Phil. Trans. R. Soc. Lond.* (B: *Biol. Sci.*), vol. 260, p. 93–121.
GROVES, G. W. 1965. Observations of sea level at remote islands. In: *Proceedings of the Symposium on tidal instrumentation and prediction of tides.* Paris, IAPO–UNESCO, no. 27, p. 35–8.

LUTHER, D. S.; WUNSCH, C. 1975. Tidal charts of the Central Pacific Ocean, *J. Phys. Oceanogr.*, vol. 5, p. 222–30.

NOYE, B. J. 1974. Tide-well systems II: The frequency response of a linear tide-well system, *J. mar. Res.*, vol. 32, p. 155–81.

PUGH, D. T. 1972. The physics of pneumatic tide gauges, *Int. hydrogr. Rev.*, vol. 49, no. 2, p. 71–97.

——; WALLER, W. R. 1975. Sea-level measurements in the Wash Bay. In: *Proc. 14th Coastal Engineering Conference, Copenhagen, June 1964*. New York, American Society of Civil Engineers, p. 2519–38.

10

A platform as a base for coral reef studies

S. M. Head[1] and R. F. G. Ormond[2]

INTRODUCTION

The Cambridge Research Group at the Marine Biological Laboratories, Port Sudan, in 1972, constructed a simple platform, on top of a coral reef, for use as a temporary base by up to six research workers. In the two and one half years the platform has been in operation, its success and value as a tool in coral reef research have greatly exceeded expectations, and the Group feels that workers in other areas may benefit from the construction of similar structures. Indication is given below of the design of the platform, and of some of the advantages and problems associated with its use.

THE SUDANESE RED SEA AND THE VALUE OF A REEF PLATFORM

Since 1969, the major research activity of the Cambridge Research Group has been the study of the ecology of the Crown of Thorns starfish, *Acanthaster planci*. In the earlier stages of this project a large number of reef systems, spread over a large area, were surveyed and with the accent on mobility a semi-field base was unnecessary. With the discovery in 1971, of large aggregated populations of starfish on the Towartit complex (see Fig. 1), attention shifted to the detailed study of one related group of reefs, both by day and night. Daily visits to the same reef by one or more small boats were expensive in petrol and outboard engine wear, occupied too much time, and formed an inadequate diving base for night operations.

Various alternatives were considered to improve the efficiency of the operation. Unfortunately none of the Towartit reefs rises above sea level, so the easiest solution, that of an island camp, was impossible. Mooring a small research launch on the site was tried for a short period, but was expensive, and did not provide the stability required for aquarium experiments carried out in

1. Department of Zoology, Oxford University, Oxford 0X1 3PS, United Kingdom.
2. Department of Biology, York University, York YO1 5DD, United Kingdom.

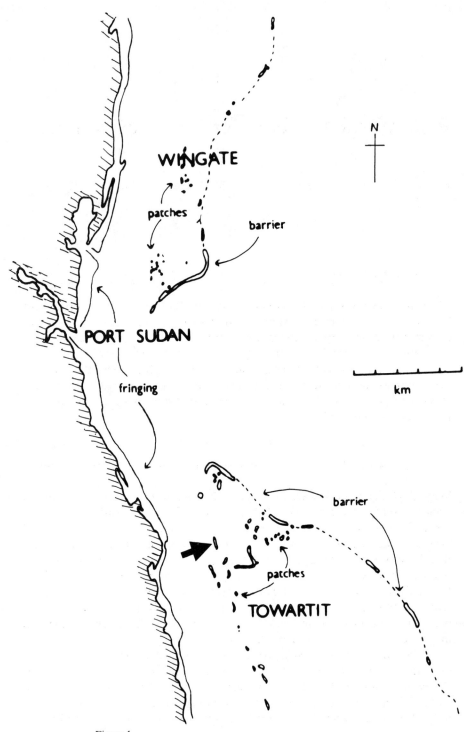

Figure 1
The Sudanese coast in the immediate region of Port Sudan. The arrow
indicates the reef on which the platform stands, shown in more detail in
Figure 3. Where the barrier reef fails to break the surface, and the reef top
lies at a depth of two to twenty metres, its position is indicated by a dotted
line.

110

conjunction with work underwater. Eventually, after consideration of the reef structure and physical conditions of the area, a two-storey, square platform was designed and installed on the main study reef.

It should be emphasized that the Sudanese Red Sea enjoys an ideal combination of physical conditions, which make it readily possible to build and use a simple platform on a reef, and enable maximum benefit to be obtained from the use of such a facility.

The more significant environmental variables are summarized in Table 1.

TABLE 1. Climatic conditions in the region of Port Sudan[a]

	February	May	August	November
Air temperature (°C):				
mean daily maximum	27	36	41	31
mean daily minimum	19	24	29	24
mean maximum in month	30	40	45	33
mean minimum in month	15	20	25	20
Surface water temperature (°C):				
mean during month	26	28	30	29
Wind (knots):				
mean wind speed 08.00 hr	3	2		3
14.00 hr	4	3		3
number of gales (force 7)	0	0		0
Tides (metres):				
mean seasonal change	0.1	0.2	−0.4	0.1
highest high water	0.3	0.4	−0.2	0.3
lowest low water	0.1	0.2	−0.3	0.1
largest diurnal range	0.2	0.2	0.1	0.2
lowest high water	0.3	0.4	−0.25	0.2
highest low water	0.2	0.4	−0.25	0.2
smallest diurnal range	0.1	0.0	0.0	0.0

a. Data for temperature and wind are taken from the Admiralty Pilot for the Red Sea and Gulf of Aden. Tide levels are calculated from data in the Admiralty Tide Tables, and are the predicted values for 1974. The mean seasonal levels are given with respect to the annual mean water level, other levels from an arbitrary datum line. It should be noted that storm surges can affect water level by about ∓0.1 m. Surface water temperature on the sheltered side of a patch reef can be one degree centigrade higher than on the exposed side, at noon on a calm day.

It will be noted that there is very little diurnal change in water level, Port Sudan lying close to the nodal point of the Red Sea tidal system. Greater level changes are associated with seasonal wind patterns, so that in late winter sea level is approximately 0.6 m higher than in midsummer. Allowing about 0.4 m for waves encountered occasionally on the reef top during the winter, the ground floor of the platform need be only 1.0 to 1.2 m above mean summer water level.

The central Red Sea is unusually calm; no tropical storm (force eight) has ever been definitely recorded in the area, and force seven gales are extremely rare. Winds of up to about six knots blow with great predictability from the north-east, and windbreaks can be constructed in the knowledge that abrupt changes of wind direction are most unusual. To the north and east, the Towartit patch reefs are well protected by a nearly continuous barrier structure, reducing considerably the wave action to which the platform reef is subjected.

Ambient air and water temperatures are high throughout the year, enabling a diver to spend six to eight hours in the water every day without discomfort. In the summer a wet suit is quite unnecessary for most diving. Arrangements which maximize the time available for underwater study are thus well worth while. The benign weather conditions mean that a platform does not have to withstand severe wind, wave or tide action, nor does it have to afford much protection from the elements for its inhabitants. Such favourable conditions will not prevail in all areas.

DESIGN, CONSTRUCTION AND LOCATION OF THE PLATFORM

Conventional steel scaffolding was chosen for the framework of the platform. In Britain scaffolding is supplied in standard lengths of 21 ft (6.4 m) and 11 ft (3.35 m). It is relatively cheap, easy to transport, and requires no great skill for assembly. Furthermore, it is easy to dismantle the structure should it be needed on another reef.

The design of the scaffolding framework is shown in Figure 2. It has two floors, each 20 ft square (6.1 m square) supported by nine vertical load-bearing poles, at the corners, centres of the sides and middle of the structure. The floors are supported on the lower and upper horizontal frameworks, which also serve to keep the load-bearing poles in proper alignment Further floor support is afforded by a series of 11 ft (3.35 m) poles, not shown in the diagram, set on the primary horizontal frames. The precise positioning of the short poles depends on the length of flooring planks used.

On each face of the platform are set two diagonal poles, which not only strengthen the structure by forming a rigid triangular lattice, but are set with their bases on the reef top, providing essential bracing against horizontal forces due to wind or movement of heavy articles on the platform itself.

The lower floor stands 1.35 m above the substratum and the upper floor 2.3 m above the lower. Excess lengths removed from the vertical poles were used to provide further supports for the lower floor (not shown in the figure), and in construction of a small landing stage set close to the water level.

Both upper and lower floors were made from uncut softwood planks, each 4 m by 0.21 m by 0.04 m. Approximately 80 planks were required, and represented the major part of the cost of the platform, which in total cost some £400 (pounds sterling) in 1972. In areas subject to splashing, the planks were treated with creosote as a preservative, but neither treated nor untreated planks have deteriorated very much, while the persistent aroma of creosote was not conducive to a comfortable working environment.

The site chosen for the platform is shown in Figure 3. The reef, which became the main *Acanthaster planci* study area, is about 800 m long by 100 m wide, and the long axis runs roughly north–south. The site is near the centre of

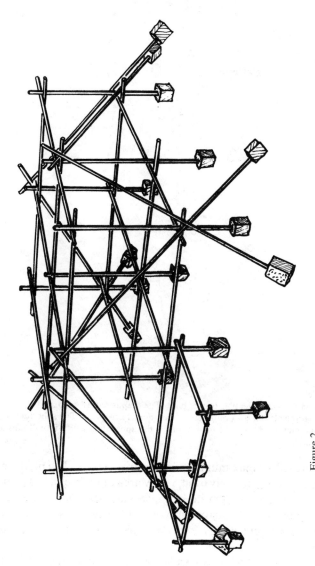

Figure 2
A scale drawing of the main platform framework. The small extension on the left foreground is the landing stage. For further details see the text.

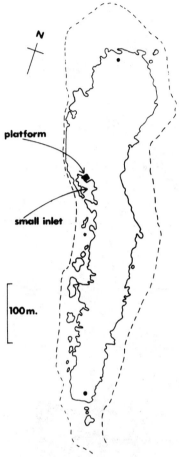

Figure 3.
The reef on which the platform is built. The map is redrawn from
photographs taken by a radio-controlled model aeroplane. The solid line is
the one-metre contour, the broken line is the approximate fifty-foot (15 m)
contour.

the west side, providing maximum protection from waves. The platform stands
on coral rock in a comparatively even, rocky area of the reef flat. It abuts on to
a small sandy inlet, about 1.5 m in depth, so that small boats can be moored
against the landing stage. A narrow arm of reef flat protects the inlet and platform from the west, light winds sometimes blow from that direction in the
early morning.

Construction presented no particular problems, and took five hours, with
six people involved. It is strongly recommended that a trial assembly be carried
out on land in order to familiarize all concerned with the sequence of assembly.
It proved useful initially to construct a square frame as a support and guide to
the placing of the corner uprights, when the first floor is in position this frame
can be removed. To protect the poles, and improve the overall platform

stability, each upright and each diagonal pole had a base of reinforced concrete cast around it, and the extra weight at the base of the upright poles made them much easier to keep in position during construction. The pole bases should be bedded on an absolutely firm base, this may involve a little judicious gardening of coral colonies. The laying of the planks must be considered when the floor supports are being placed, otherwise it may be difficult to keep the floor level. Safety helmets are strongly recommended since scaffolding clips are heavy, angular and easily dropped. In extreme tropical climates, the period around midday should be avoided for construction work, since the scaffolding poles may become too hot to handle.

To protect against corrosion, all poles and clips were coated before and after construction with three layers of epoxy coal-tar resin, after an initial sand-blasting to remove rust patches. It is advisable to plug the ends of poles to prevent sea water entry during construction. Subsequently the uprights could be filled with oil to prevent internal corrosion.

After two and one half years of continuous use the platform is still sturdy, and almost corrosion free. A recent survey revealed several small rust marks about the water line, but these were not extensive and did not penetrate deeply into the steel. Apparently corrosion proceeds very slowly under the epoxy coat, presumably since this form of paint does not flake off in the way that conventional single-part paints frequently do.

It is worth noting that coating with an epoxy-coal tar resin is one of the methods most frequently used to protect the above-water steel parts of offshore drilling platforms. Experience gained in the oil industry in protecting such structures has been recently summarized by Colegate (1972). Below water, cathodic protection by galvanic anodes, normally of mercury containing aluminium alloy, is commonly used without a protective coating. Unfortunately anodes were not available in Port Sudan, and considering the small part of our structure underwater it was decided that it was not worth the expense of importing them. Corrosion is usually most serious in the splash and intertidal zones of structures. In our case both of these zones were of minimal extent; in a less favourable situation, where corrosion may be a greater problem, some form of cathodic protection would be highly desirable.

PLATFORM FACILITIES AND EQUIPMENT

Within the basic frame of the platform, space can be utilized in a variety of ways, depending on the weather, number of prople resident, and the nature of the research in progress. In the summer, when the top floor can be used for sleeping accommodation, as many as eight people can use the platform at once. In the winter four is generally a more suitable number. Half of the lower area has been enclosed with wood and canvas walls, providing a sheltered space for cooking, paperwork and sleeping during poorer weather. It is also useful as a storage area for items that have to be kept out of the sun. The remainder of the lower floor is reserved for aquaria, compressor and diving gear. Drums of water and petrol are conveniently stored on the landing stage. Windbreaks and tenting are easily moved, allowing considerable flexibility in the accommodation arrangements. For example, during the summer a small laboratory is set up on the upper floor of the platform where it has the full benefit of cooling breezes. In the winter this is dismantled and re-erected as an extension of the living area on the lower floor.

Cooking is by gas supplied from large cylinders. Supplies of tinned food are kept on the platform, but it is found that most vegetables keep tolerably well for up to a week, as do dairy products if kept in an evaporative cooled refrigerator. Supplies of fresh food, water, petrol and minor equipment are sent out once a week, or whenever there is a change in personnel. A short wave radio link serves as contact with the main laboratories in Port Sudan, and is an essential safety factor, as well as allowing greater flexibility and efficiency in supplying the platform. Emergency food supplies and a comprehensive medical kit are kept and carefully maintained.

For lighting, a combination of paraffin pressure lamps and twelve volt headlamp bulbs are most convenient. The twelve volt supply comes from a bank of accumulators, which also supply the radio and sea water pumps for aquaria. Petrol driven generators are used to recharge the accumulators, and to provide a 250 volt 8 amp. circuit for power tools, extra lighting or special equipment. With normal (fairly heavy) use of the twelve volt supply, it was found that a daily battery charge of about three hours was sufficient to replace current losses.

In working out the details of the electrical and other fittings, there is a great deal to be said for simplicity, and the use of equipment that can be readily repaired without recourse to special tools or complex manuals. The salty air of tropical marine areas rapidly corrodes unprotected equipment, particularly electrical apparatus, in which a mixture of metals in electrical contact encourages electrolytic dissolution. To avoid rapid deterioration, equipment must be regularly stripped and cleaned, and where necessary, sprayed with silicon grease, a most valuable corrosion preventive.

All non bio-degradable waste must be taken back to land for disposal, plates and cooking equipment however, are conveniently 'washed-up' by dropping them into shallow water where they are most effectively cleaned by fish. This practice also economizes in the use of fresh water, and keeps detergent effluent to a minimum. It is of course important to prohibit collecting and spearfishing except for scientific purposes, and apart from the death of a few corals damaged during the assembly of the platform there has been no observable adverse effect on the local fauna.

ADVANTAGES OF THE REEF PLATFORM

As was mentioned above, the primary function of the platform is to allow workers to maximize the time available for study in the field, and this advantage does not require further elaboration. In addition, the platform removes the need to carry heavy equipment to boats, or down a beach, and long swims to the study area are not necessary. Facilities are available to the diver to which he may repeatedly return; to replace or exchange equipment, or for rest and refreshment between dives.

The platform has proved an excellent base for photography, for quantitative ecological investigations, for marking and tracking experiments, and for long-term behavioural work requiring daily monitoring. The situation allows sea water to be pumped directly from the reef top to supply aquaria and special experimental tanks, in which invertebrate behaviour can be studied in optimal conditions. Concrete and mesh livestock pens, through which the sea will circulate naturally, are planned for construction on the adjoining reef flat.

Many of the animals in the study area have after two years become completely accustomed to the presence of divers on the reef. As a result the group was able to make many observations on the natural behaviour of fish, which would be very difficult in the more usual situation when they are disturbed by the presence of a large, strange animal on the reef. Examples worth quoting concern fish predators of *Acanthaster planci* (Ormond *et al.,* 1973) reproductive behaviour in wrasse (Ormond, in preparation) and *Anthias squamipinnis* (Shapiro, 1977). Observations on the interaction of fish with other reef inhabitants can be found in Vine (1975) and Head (in preparation).

Perhaps the most important advantage of the platform has been the detailed and intimate knowledge that has accrued from continual study in one small area. The cross fertilization of ideas among the range of specialists who have participated has been a considerable stimulation to all concerned.

CONCLUSIONS

It is appreciated that in many situations the construction and operation of a reef platform may not be as easy as that of the Group. However, the return has been so great that a strong recommendation is made for consideration to be given to the construction of a platform whenever the long term study of a particular reef area is being planned. In deeper water, or a larger tidal range, there is no reason why there should not be an underwater horizontal frame linking and strengthening the legs. This part of the structure could be protected against corrosion by the use of sacrificial anodes. Even where the reef under consideration is adjacent to the mainland or an island, it may be worthwhile to construct a platform near the fore-reef if a large lagoon intervenes between land and the study area. Some workers may feel a more permanent structure, using concrete cast *in situ*, would offer advantages, others, like the Group may consider the mobile and economical structure described above better meets their requirements.

ACKNOWLEDGEMENTS

The authors are grateful for the full involvement of other members of the Cambridge Research Group in developing the use of the platform. They thank Dr C. H. Roads and Dr D. N. F. Hall for administrative assistance. The research group is funded by a grant from the Overseas Development Administration of the U.K. Government. During 1973 S. M. Head was in possession of a Royal Society Leverhulme Studentship, and the support of the Leverhulme Trust is gratefully acknowledged.

References

COLEGATE, G. T. 1972. The protection from corrosion of offshore drilling platforms and similar structures. *Underwater J. inform. Bull.* vol. 4, p. 127–29.

HEAD, S. M. (In preparation). Observations on the interactions of fish, filamentous algae and corals in the Red Sea.

ORMOND, R. F. G. (In preparation). On the reproductive, social and feeding behaviour of some coral reef wrasse and parrot fish.

——; CAMPBELL, A. C.; HEAD, S. M.; MOORE, R. J.; RAINBOW, P. R.; SANDERS, A. P. 1973. Formation and breakdown of aggregations of the Crown-of-Thorns Starfish, *Acanthaster planci* (L.) *Nature* (Lond.), vol. 246, p. 167–9.

SHAPIRO, D. Y. 1977. Social organisation and sex reversal in *Anthias squamipinnis.* Ph.D. Thes., University of Cambridge.

VINE, P. J. 1974. Effects of algal grazing and aggressive behaviour of the fishes *Pomacentrus lividus* and *Acanthurus sohal* on coral-reef ecology. *Mar. Biol.,* vol. 24, p. 131–6.

Part II

Biotic distribution

Introduction

D. R. Stoddart[1]

Detailed knowledge of the composition and structure of reef communities awaited the development of means of direct access to the submarine environment. Early workers such as Alexander Agissiz and J. Stanley Gardiner were limited to the use of the dredge and to collections by local divers, although the first sketches of reefs underwater, from a diving bell, had been made by Baron Eugène de Ransonnet (1867) in the 1860s. The first colour photographs of reefs were taken in the Dry Tortugas by Longley (1927) sixty years later. By this time several workers were starting to record the occurrence of organisms along transects and in quadrats, using cumbersome diving helmets (e.g. Manton and Stephenson 1935). But the major developments followed the perfection of scuba apparatus in the 1940s and 1950s, and it was not long before both technical and practical problems of recording biotic distributions on reefs became apparent.

Reefs are topographically highly irregular, with pinnacles, crevices, tunnels, and enclosed caverns. Organisms live in the surfaces of these forms, and within them; others live on the water column itself. Substrata are either of hard limestone or of loose or bound sediments. The organisms themselves vary in size over several orders of magnitude, and exhibit a diversity of growth form. Much attention has been given to the transference of techniques developed for the analysis of terrestrial vegetation to the study of coral distribution, building on such standard texts as those of Kershaw (1964) and Greig-Smith (1964). Thus Scheer (Chapter 15) has followed Braun-Blanquet's school of phytosociology in his work on reefs in the Maldive Islands, whereas Loya's quantitative transect studies (Chapter 16) draw on the Anglo-American school of quantitative ecology. Pichon (Chapter 17) considers some of the practical problems involved in carrying out such surveys, based on his work at Tuléar, Madagascar.

Much attention has been given in recent years, both at Tuléar and elsewhere, to problems of quantitative sampling of cryptofauna in both hard and soft

1. Department of Geography, Cambridge University, Cambridge, CB2 3EN, United Kingdom.

substrata, and of soft-bottom communities. Papers by Pichon (Chapter 14), Thomassin (Chapter 20) and Hutchings (Chapter 19) deal with this type of reef community, where much of the basic theory has been developed in northern temperate seas.

No attempt is made here to cover techniques applicable to individual plant and animal groups which comprise the reef community, since methods for collection and preservation are well described in many places, including the original *Handbook for Atoll Research* (Fosberg and Sachet 1953). Sponges and nemerteans, however, are of great importance in the reef economy and also present special problems; they are therefore treated here in Chapter 21 by Rützler and Chapter 22 by Kirsteuer. Fishes are likewise of great significance, and present problems quite different to those of the benthic biota: the treatment by Russell, Goldman and Talbot in Chapter 23 derives from their important work on the fish fauna of One Tree Reef in Queensland.

Biotic distributions can be studied at a variety of spatial scales, at various taxonomic levels, and for different purposes. Many of the technical problems involved, both in data collection and in data analysis, have only recently been seriously studied, and it is likely that many of the methods described here will be greatly extended and modified as they are tested more widely, and as our theoretical understanding of the reef community is extended.

References

Fosberg, F. R.; Sachet, M.-H. 1953. Handbook for atoll research (2nd prelim. edit) *Atoll Res. Bull.* vol. 17, p. 1–129.

Greig-Smith, P. 1964. *Quantitative plant ecology.* 2nd. edit. London, Butterworths (256 p).

Kershaw, K. A. 1964. *Quantitative and dynamic ecology.* London, Edward Arnold (183 p).

Longley, W. H. 1927. The first autochromes from the ocean bottom: life on a coral reef. *Nat. Geogr. Mag.* vol. 51, p. 56–83.

Manton, S. M.; Stephenson, T. A. 1935. Ecological surveys of coral reefs. *Sci. Repts Gt Barrier Reef Exped. 1928–29,* vol. 3, p. 273–312.

Ransonnet, E. de 1867. *Sketches of the habitants, animal life and vegetation around the lowland and high mountains of Ceylon, as well as of the submarine scenery near the coast, taken in a diving bell.* Vienna: Gerold and Son.

11

Data collection and recording

J. F. Peake[1], A. J. Sinclair[1] and
S. Lomas[1]

INTRODUCTION

During the development of many research projects difficulties frequently arise in the organization of information in a manner which permits its full potential to be realized. Problems may be encountered at all stages from the initial recording of the data to its final presentation. Failure to realize or anticipate these difficulties may diminish the value of the end product, and, in extreme cases, even result in the loss of important facts. Whether the research project is organized on a multi-disciplinary basis, as a long-term study, or as a more modest individual project, the pattern is probably a familiar one. Whenever the investigation concerns a study of the biological or physical properties of a remote land-mass like an atoll another dimension in data organization is apparent. The logistics of reaching such locations are often immense involving considerable expenditure, planning and, as a consequence, infrequent visits. Any information concerning such areas, therefore, has increased importance as archival material. Certainly considerable attention is often given to the preservation of objects associated with such areas, but the storage of data in a systematic manner to permit their use at a future date by a wide range of individuals tends to be forgotten.

A potential solution to these problems exists in the use of computerized data-processing schemes, but only where these are linked to suitable programmes for collecting and organizing the information generated from the initial investigations. Despite the obvious advantages of this type of operation, it should not be undertaken lightly and great care must be taken to ensure that the data are deposited in a format and location which will secure both their long-term survival and availability. Further, a distinction must be recognized between systems for storage and retrieval of information and those for the analysis of such data. This review is concerned with the former and will describe a system which is already in operation: an example of storage for analysis, as applied to

1. Department of Zoology, British Museum (Natural History), Cromwell Road, London SW7 5BD, United Kingdom.

123

tropical reef ecosystems, is reported by Sachet and Dahl (1974). This is not to imply that data collection is divorced from analysis; the relationship must be both complementary and evolutionary. Elton (1966) in quoting Whitehead made a very pertinent comment on this relationship, 'In 1925 Whitehead wrote, "Classification is necessary. But unless you progress from classification to mathematics, your reasoning will not take you very far." But he must have been aware of the relatively enormous amount of qualitative information that has to be mastered in field biology, and the absolute necessity of mastering it, before setting up elaborate technical and quantitative experiments.'

The development of a computerized data bank for information associated with Aldabra, a raised atoll in the western Indian Ocean, provides a suitable model for discussing the problems that can be encountered and the solutions that were proposed.

ALDABRA PROJECT

With the establishment in 1967 of a major research commitment on Aldabra by the Royal Society of London, it was foreseen that an 'information problem' would eventually be encountered. This would be generated not only by the vast array of data that would accrue from the organized research and monitoring programmes, but also from casual observations made by visiting scientists, as well as data obtained from the abstraction of information from publications and manuscripts. The possibilities of applying computerized data-processing schemes to this type of situation were recognized. Nevertheless, the utilization of such methods implied that the data could be collected in an organized and systematic manner, thus permitting such techniques to be used. In designing the scheme it was imperative that the user's needs were considered and that the formats for data collection and retrieval were pragmatic and simplistic. Further, the absence of sophisticated surveys of the atoll implies that the methods for classifying and organizing the data had to be undertaken in an empirical manner, extrapolating wherever possible from previous work on the atoll.

The organization of the data scheme will be considered under four headings: computer program, data structure and organization, data fields and recording formats.

COMPUTER PROGRAM

The capabilities of the scheme to handle a wide variety of data, produce the required form of retrieval and still have the potential to meet any additional demands will depend to a considerable degree on the constraints imposed by the type of computer and programs available. Whichever package is selected it must be sufficiently flexible to accommodate a wide variety of data with differing degrees of sophistication and yet retain the possibility of further expansion and incorporation of additional information. Emphasis is laid on the property of flexibility in the program package, and therefore the data structure, because as any project develops there always remains the possibility that it will be necessary to broaden the data structure to include new categories or further divide existing groups. It is important that the program package can accept such developments. The one adopted for the Aldabra project was devised by Cutbill and Williams (1971) and is employed in a modified form at both the Sedgwick Museum, Cambridge and the British Museum (Natural History). It accepts records with a variable number of characters and without the necessity of codification, but with the data organized in a hierarchical structure. As the data are converted into a structured record, a tagging system (Tables 1 and 2) is employed for recognition of each unit of information, that is each data field; this is simply a form of label which permits recognition of a particular part of of the record. Tagging is employed as opposed to 'fixed field', fixed sequence, and free format methods of organizing each record; the latter all tend to impose several restrictions on the flexibility of the scheme or the form of the data structure. In the Aldabra project, the tags were introduced as the data were transferred to paper tape prior to transference to magnetic tape and input into the computer. The simultaneous use of a control loop passing through a reader attached to the punch-tape typewriter ensures that the data fields are organized in the required sequence with the tags being inserted automatically.

The program package for the computer permits output to be in a readable format with the ability to edit, update the record and print selected areas of the total data file in an organized format. An index or vocabulary is produced covering every level of the data structure.

DATA STRUCTURE AND ORGANIZATION

The data fields are organized in a simple hierarchical manner with each field being assigned to a fixed level (Table 1). This formalized structure imposes a rather strict mode of organization on the data being considered, with the information being grouped into meaningful related fields; this will determine the nature of the computerized output and the success of the vocabulary or index. However, it still permits the inclusion of additional fields with increasing refinement of the system or volume of records. It is obvious that the data structure will also influence the manner in which the original information is collected, yet it must accommodate records with widely differing degrees of sophistication and contents.

The data structure (Table 1) is largely self-explanatory and probably only needs further amplification in two areas, those considering habitat description and events (Fields 6 and 11). In preparing this scheme a number of other works have been consulted and particular concepts or methods employed (Heath and Scott, 1972). The Biological Records Centre at Monks Wood Experimental Station has undertaken various surveys of biological phenomena, the mapping

TABLE 1. Data structure, illustrating the hierarchical organization of data input and the tags used for recognition of each unit of information

1	⟨SN⟩ Specimen number
2	⟨CDA⟩ Collection data
2.1	⟨RCD⟩ Recorded by
2.2	⟨CDT⟩ Date
2.3	⟨CTM⟩ Time of day
2.4	⟨CMD⟩ Collection method
3	⟨ID⟩ Identification
3.1	⟨P⟩ Phylum
3.2	⟨C⟩ Class
3.3	⟨O⟩ Order
3.4	⟨SPF⟩ Superfamily
3.5	⟨F⟩ Family
3.6	⟨T⟩ Species
3.7	⟨TI⟩ Determined by
3.8	⟨TID⟩ Date
4	⟨OA⟩ Observation area
4.1	⟨L⟩ Locality
4.2	⟨GR⟩ Grid reference
4.3	⟨A⟩ Altitude
5	⟨SPD⟩ Specimen details
5.1	⟨AB⟩ Abundance
5.2	⟨NC⟩ Number collected
5.3	⟨PSV⟩ Preservation
5.4	⟨LS⟩ Life stages
5.5	⟨IS⟩ Sex
6	⟨HAB⟩ Habitat data
6.1	⟨MGP⟩ Major habitat group
6.1.1	⟨MGN⟩ Major habitat group name
	Terrestrial, Aquatic-terrestrial, Marine
6.1.2	⟨MGQ⟩ Major habitat group qualifier
	Domestic, Disturbed
6.2	⟨TYP⟩ Habitat type
6.2.1	⟨GTN⟩ Habitat type name
	Woodland, Scrub, Low scrub, Tall herb, Low vegetation,
	Bare ground, Gardens, General
6.2.2	⟨LEV⟩ Level of type
6.2.3	⟨GTQ⟩ Habitat qualifier
6.2.3.1	⟨ARA⟩ Area
6.2.3.2	⟨EUM⟩ Edge/uniform/mixture
6.2.4	⟨CVS⟩ Sub-dominant cover type
6.2.4.1	⟨SFM⟩ Sub-dominant form
	Woodland, Scrub, Low scrub, Tall herb, Low vegetation,
	Bare ground, Garden
6.2.4.2	⟨PAR⟩ Percentage cover
6.3	⟨GEN⟩ General
	Fungi, Dung, Nest, Burrow, Carrion, Dead wood, Equipment,
	Building, Special relationship
6.4	⟨GMP⟩ Geomorphological type
	Granular substrate, Rock: platin
	Rock: champignon, Rock: pave
6.5	⟨STG⟩ Stratum group
6.5.1	⟨STN⟩ Stratum name
	Air above, Canopy, Scrub, Low scrub or herb,
	Ground zone, Surface, Soil, Subterranean
6.5.2	⟨NAT⟩ Nature of stratum

126

TABLE 1—*continued*

	Roots or stem bases, Stems or trunks, Leaves, Flowers, Fruits or seeds, Litter or humus, Rock slabs, Shingle, Sand, Silt, Soil	
6.5.3	⟨POS⟩ Position of specimen	
	In, On or Under	
6.6	⟨ASP⟩ Associated species	
7	⟨NTS⟩ Notes	
8	⟨ARN⟩ Associated record numbers (T, E or SC at present)	
9	⟨BIB⟩ Bibliographic data	
10	⟨GEO⟩ Geographic distribution	
11	⟨EV⟩ Event Record (see Table 2)	
11.1	⟨TEV⟩ Type of event	(e.g. Plants, Research survey)
11.2	⟨SBJ⟩ Subject title	(e.g. Vegetation mapping)
11.3	⟨IDT⟩ Individual title	(e.g. Distribution of *Casuarina* on South Island)

schemes of which have received extensive publicity (Perring and Walters, 1962). The development of a program for recording events on Aldabra was derived from a scheme which had already been tested by the Centre; the purpose and mode of action of this are discussed below. The systems of classifying habitats owe a profound debt to the work of Elton (1966) and his proposals for classifying habitats in the British Isles. Of course reference was made to other methods, for example, those of Braun-Blanquet *et al.* (1932) for vegetation, but it was considered impractical to apply many of these schemes as there was insufficient information concerning the environment found on the atoll. Undoubtedly these problems are not unique to the Aldabra situation; nevertheless, it is important that the classification of habitats employed should reflect certain criteria (Elton, 1966) which are:

1. That discrete and recognizable discontinuities exist in the environment;
2. That the units produced are grouped on the basis of overall similarity, although it is accepted that these are not entirely discreet;
3. It is presumed that the units have some ecological importance.

Probably there would be no dispute regarding the application of these attributes to any classification; nevertheless, attempts to produce a concensus regarding the recognition of meaningful units on Aldabra met with many obstacles, except on a very broad basis. Complex classifications of the vegetation and the geomorphology of the atoll (Fosberg, 1971, 1972) failed to fulfil the criteria outlined, although this does not negate the interest of such studies in other contexts. Problems were encountered in defining recognizable features that could readily be applied; for example, many elements of the flora are difficult to recognize in a vegetative state and the surface topography of the limestone could be considered as forming a continuum from the fretted form of the coastal strip to the flat surface of inland areas. The value of a simplistic approach to these problems,

TABLE 2. Simple method of classifying events showing both 'type of event' and 'subject title' for the Aldabra project

	A Conservation	B Research survey	C Human activities	D Natural events
1. Plants	Eradication of weeds Cutting paths	Vegetation mapping Pemphis study Collecting Photographs	Introductions (gardening) Clearing	Windblow Defoliation Large number of species Debris washed up on shore
2. Animals	Shooting cats Trapping rats	Light trapping Soil surveys Lagoon surveys Inter-tidal investigation Tortoise marking Marine sighting + surveys Bird surveys Photographs Tortoise culling	Shooting for food Fishing Tortoise export Accidental introduction	Large number of species Debris washed up on shore
3. Soil + Rock		Geological survey Dune growth	Litter dumping Extant tracks	Sand blow
4. Water + Air (Freshwater)		Met. Recording		Flooding Droughts Thunderstorms
5. Sea		Floating vegetation and logs	Sewage pollution Ship sightings Oil pollution Litter dumping at sea	Storms
6. Construction	Nest boxes Fencing	Aviary cages Bird holes	Research station Huts, camp sites Renewal of constructions Path maintenance or cutting	Natural damage to buildings
7. Fire			Celebration bonfires	Uncontrolled fires of unknown origin
8. Man	Visits by scientists Clearing litter Movements around reserve	Archaeological finds Enclosures Water holes Old tracks Movements around reserve	Visits by yachts Resumes	Accidents
9. Other	Changes in reserve status		Export agreements Extant tracks	Ship wrecks

as exemplified by Stoddart *et al.* (1971) in their interpretation of the geomorphology of the atoll, cannot be over emphasized.

The proposed solution recognizes only the major discontinuities that are apparent in the environment. It permits the choice of various features which describe the habitat and, therefore, allows the recorder to determine which combination is suited to a particular situation. In the proposed scheme a number of permutations are possible and additional information concerning the vegetation can be added at low levels in the hierarchy. It is recognized that it was impossible to produce units of comparatively equal ecological importance at each hierarchical level; instead, the emphasis was placed on the recognition of distinct units and the grouping of similar forms. As previously stressed many of the alternative schemes would have required considerable prior knowledge, which was not available, and would have had the disadvantage of being either finite in scope, and therefore inflexible, or unstable because of the need to incorporate modifications.

Difficulties were encountered in defining methods for describing the various mosaics that exist between habitat types, and it was impossible to reach an agreement. Although Braun-Blanquet *et al.* (1932) proposed an arbitrary system of scales, reflecting percentage cover of the various elements to cope with such situations, these were difficult to recognize with any confidence in the field. For instance, in many areas on Aldabra there are variations in the form of the mosaics between shrubs and low herb habitats, but the nature of the terrain and the vegetation frequently preclude an estimate of the relative importance of the components being made, even presuming that it is stable over a given area. It is important that descriptions are not made on an *ad hoc* basis by each research worker and, therefore, a compromise was reached: the separate constituents of a mosaic should be recorded and comments could be made on the relative importance of each, but it was important that the recorder indicated the size of the area being considered, for it was this variable which produced major differences in interpretation.

DATA FIELDS

The following annotated notes indicate the definitions applied to the various data fields scored (Table 1). Each record is recognized by a unique combination of letters and numbers; this enables rapid recovery of the data block, cross-referencing between records and very simple methods of indexing. Usually the *date* covers a single day, but with the event records there may be additional entries under this heading to deal with cases where a particular activity is summarized over a period. Entries under *time of day* can also be multiple. *Locality* uses standardized names from a gazetteer, while the *grid reference* provides a check on the locality or a more accurate reference point. Fortunately, a large scale map and air photographs were available for Aldabra; the former had a unique grid overlay which had been prepared prior to the Royal Society's

K

activities. Occasionally multiple entries are recorded under both *locality* and *grid reference*, for example, where a record refers to information collected along a transect.

(a) Habitat

Major habitat group (6.1.1). The two extremes of *terrestrial* and *aquatic* present few problems; although in the case of the latter no detailed classification has been produced which has universal acceptance; nevertheless, a distinction between marine and freshwater is recorded. *Aquatic-terrestrial* includes all transitional areas, particularly the extensive mangrove, but also such areas as the intertidal zone and locations subjected to regular flooding. Two qualifiers (6.1.2) are applied to cover habitats subjected to human disturbance; where this is ongoing, regular and of high intensity the term *domestic* is used, while *disturbed* includes low-level interference and areas where human activity has been abandoned, although the effect is still recognizable.

Habitat types and sub-dominant cover types: (6.2.1 and 6.2.4 respectively) these record the dominant habitat type using the criterion of *area* (6.2.3.1) covered. The divisions are based initially on height of vegetation with the demarcation heights proposed by Elton (1966) being retained as they appear to define valid units on the atoll. Thus the division between *woodland* and *scrub* is 4.5 m, *scrub* and *low scrub* or *tall herb* is 2 m, and *low scrub* or *tall herb* and *low vegetation* is 15 cm. A convention is employed in separating *low vegetation* and *bare ground,* because isolated pockets of vegetation are almost invariably found associated with bare ground; this type is, therefore, included in the definition of this division of *low vegetation,* while *bare ground* is reserved for truely naked surface area. Qualifiers refer to the area of the location being described; while *edge* refers to records considering the interface between two habitats, *uniform* and *mixture* distinguish the areas which consist of mosaics. Where mixtures are considered then the *sub-dominant cover type* is recorded and the relative cover of both can be given whether on a percentage basis or an arbitrary scale (Braun-Blanquet *et al.,* 1932). *Special relationship* includes the parasitic, commensal or symbiotic associations.

General type (6.3). This includes a diverse series of discrete habitats where the organism does not utilize green plant material as a major energy resource; their distribution is often independent of the main habitat types.

Geomorphological type (6.4). The rock formations of platin, champignon and pave follow definitions of Stoddart *et al.* (1971), but in habitats where there is development of soil, or some other feature obscuring the underlying rock surface, the nature of the substratum is often granular, and this can be recorded.

Stratum (6.5). Together with associated qualifiers this field permits the position of the specimen to be recorded. The distinctions between the various groups follow those given above under habitat types.

Associated species (6.6). Records of other taxa implicated in other fields are included here; for example, hosts or parasites.

Associated record numbers (8). These refer to any other records made within the 'study' area at the same time, or whenever the user needs to be referred to any particularly relevant information held in other records; these record cards may be variable in type (see below in Event Records).

Notes (7). Any further details still to be recorded and which cannot be entered appropriately under previous data fields. This may include prevailing weather conditions, the state of the specimen under consideration and more often general behavioural observations.

(b) Event records

Event records (11). The aim of this type of recording is to ensure the availability of information concerning all events which could be of importance to the future understanding of the biology of the atoll. The system is beneficial, or of some assistance, to research workers familiarizing themselves with the atoll and also activities associated with earlier research programmes. This type of information also provides an important base-line for managers undertaking conservation legislation and activities (Perring *et al.*, 1973). In this context an event can be defined as any one of the following:

1. An action by any person liable to lead to a change in the ecosystem;
2. Research surveys and other recording activities (the detailed accounts of which are stored separately);
3. Natural occurrences, usually departures from the normal state, which are likely to have a lasting effect on the ecosystem or which represent an extreme in the variation of natural phenomena;
4. Visits away from the Research Station.

RECORDING FORMATS

A wide range of field studies have demonstrated the advantages of recording observations either against a check-list or on a printed form; not only does it stimulate the recording of information, but it ensures that it is collected in a systematic manner. There is, nevertheless, a danger that information which cannot readily be included in an organized format will be excluded. Yet, conversely, there is the added danger that the scheme will not be utilized merely because all data fields cannot be completed. Although it is obviously desirable to have information in all the major fields, it is still possible to utilize the scheme adequately when only minimal data are available.

At least one scheme has overcome the problem of transferring the data from field records to the computer input; this was achieved by developing forms for recording geological information in a manner that could then be read directly by a machine, an IBM Handwriting reader (Piper, 1971). However, such sophistication requires the objectives of the scheme to be both clearly defined and finite and here again considerable background knowledge is needed.

For the Aldabra project a number of field cards were prepared to cover the general requirements of the research programme. However, other specialized recording formats were prepared, for example, those for noting catches from automatic insect traps and tortoise marking projects. Yet, where systems were already available, as was the case with bird nest and moult record cards, their use was recommended. Moreover, care was taken to ensure that all the information included in these formats could be accommodated in the data structure.

Examples of the formats used on Aldabra are shown in Figures 1–4. The cards were printed in a colour that contrasted with any ink or pencil used by the field recorder; pale blue was found to be suitable. Thus, when the data were finally transcribed to punch tape, it was immediately obvious to the operator which fields contained data.

Similar formats were used for extracting information from museum collections and bibliographic sources, but here the data on habitats are usually minimal and, even when they are recorded, there is no way of checking if similar criteria were employed.

CONCLUSION

The use of data-processing schemes offers enormous possibilities for handling and organizing both a wide range and a large volume of information. Examples of the final output from the computerized data bank, including the basic data and vocabulary are given in Table 3. It is possible to develop the vocabulary still further by including cross-references and subsidiary headings. Special print-outs of selected blocks of data may also be obtained. Nevertheless, the success of the scheme is dependent on an ability to capture information in a suitable format and, in the case of corporate schemes such as Aldabra, the ability to ensure the cooperation of a wide range of individuals. Thus the development of the organization must be reviewed both in terms of methods and public relations.

ACKNOWLEDGEMENTS

The data programme for Aldabra was initiated at the request of the Royal Society's Aldabra Research Committee; the authors' thanks are offered to its

ALDABRA FIELD RECORD   T

Recorded by	Date		Time of day	
Order		Family		
Species			Abundance	
Locality	Grid Ref. E	N+/−	Altitude	m.
Collecting method				
No. of specimens	Preservation			
Life stages			Determined by	

TERRESTRIAL ☐   AQUATIC–TERRESTRIAL ☐   Domestic ☐ Disturbed ☐

HABITAT TYPE   Qualifiers   Area [   ] sq. m.
Woodland   [ ]   Low vegetation   [ ]
Scrub   [ ]   Bare ground   [ ]   Edge ☐ Uniform ☐ Mixture ☐
Low scrub   [ ]   Gardens   [ ]
Tall herb   [ ]   General – see below [ ]   COVER TYPE
                       Special relationship [ ]   Dominant (area)   Sub-Dominant (area)
                                                   Woodland   [ ]   Woodland   [ ]
GENERAL TYPE   Scrub   [ ]   Scrub   [ ]
Fungi   [ ]   Carrion   [ ]   Low scrub   [ ]   Low scrub   [ ]
Dung   [ ]   Dead wood   [ ]   Tall herb   [ ]   Tall herb   [ ]
Nest   [ ]   Equipment   [ ]   Low vegetation [ ]   Low vegetation [ ]
Burrow   [ ]   Building   [ ]   Bare ground   [ ]   Bare ground   [ ]
                                                   Gardens   [ ]   Gardens   [ ]

(a)

GEOMORPHOLOGICAL TYPE   [ ]
Granular substrate
Rock : platin
Rock : champignon
Rock : pave

STRATUM   [ ]
Air above   Roots/stem bases [ ]   Rock slabs [ ]
Canopy   Stems/trunks   [ ]   Shingle   [ ]
Scrub   Leaves   [ ]   Sand   [ ]
Low scrub or herb   Flowers   [ ]   Silt   [ ]
Ground zone   Fruits/seeds   [ ]   Soil   [ ]
Surface   Litter/humus   [ ]
Soil
Subterranean   In ☐ On ☐ Under ☐

Associated species

| Notes | |
| Associated Record No.   T | E |

(b)

Figure 1—(a) front (b) back
Terrestrial field card for recording information concerning a *single* record
or observation.

133

EVENT RECORD		E
Grid Ref. E N +/−	Station	
Date : Start	End	Recorder
Surveys and recording	Other human activities	Natural Occurrences
Title		
Record Numbers	File	
Notes		

(a)

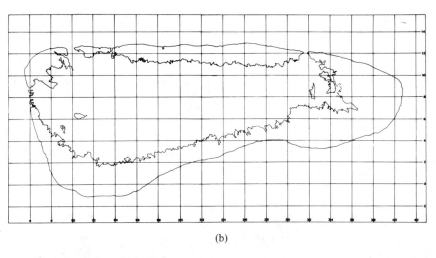

(b)

Figure 2—(a) front (b) back
Event card: the map is used for illustrating routes and areas covered by
record.

ALDABRA SPECIES CARD

Species   Year

Order   Family

Recorder

Terrestrial ☐   Aquatic–Terrestrial ☐   Aquatic ☐

Date	Locality	E Grid Ref. N+/-	Habitat	Abund.	Notes	Assoc. Cards

Figure 3
Species card for recording *multiple* observations on a *single species* where
only limited habitat information is required.

TERRESTRIAL INVERTEBRATES – TRAP CARD   No.

Locality

Trap:	Heath		Water		
	Rothamsted		Window		
	Johnson Taylor		Netting		
	Malaise				

Date   Time

Met. conditions:	Cloud	/8	Temp.	°C	
	Humidity		Wind speed	knots	
	Rainfall	mm			

No. of specimens

Notes

Figure 4
Trap card for recording information concerning various invertebrate
collecting programmes; numbers of animals listed on reverse.

135

members for their constant encouragement and especially to Dr D. R. Stoddart. The authors are grateful to the Natural Environment Research Council for providing financial support and to the Trustees of the British Museum (Natural History) for the use of facilities at that institution. The many individuals who provided specialized knowledge and assistance during the initiation and continuation of this programme, in particular Dr D. B. Williams of the Electronic Data Processing Group at the Museum, Dr F. H. Perring of the Biological Records Centre and Dr J. D. Taylor, are thanked. Finally, the authors are enormously grateful to all those research workers on Aldabra itself, who spent many weary hours completing field cards, for without their cooperation there would have been no data. Constant encouragement and management of the field programme was provided by Mrs Lorise Topliffe, who was initially in

TABLE 3. Part of computer print-out: *upper section*, a single record with tags retained, *middle section*, part of vocabulary illustrating a sort for 'locality', *lower section*, a sort for 'species'

〈recno,SN〉 T 6127
〈cda,RCD〉 L.F.H. Merton
 〈cdt,DAY〉 14 Aug 1974 to 16 Aug 1974
〈id,C〉 Reptilia 〈O〉 Testudines 〈F〉 Testudiniae 〈T〉
 Testudo gigantea
〈oa,L〉 Anse Cedres, SI 〈GR〉 360113
〈hab,mgp,MGN〉 Aquatic-Terrestrial
 〈typ,HTN〉 Bare ground 〈LEV〉
 〈htq,EUM〉 Edge
 〈cvs,SFM〉 Woodland 〈PAR〉
〈NTS〉 Among the many tortoises seen around the camp,
 3 were marked with sunk metal discs: 0452, 0454, 0469,
 〈BIB〉 Disc nos. 0452, 0454, 0469

Ile Malabar, MI (eJst end)	.T 6282. (1).
Ile Picard	.T 6262. (1).
Iles Moustique	.T6304. (1).
inland Gros Ilot Cavalier	.T6260. (1).
La Gigi, WI	.T 4160. La Gigi, WI .T 660. (2).
Middle Camp, MI	.T 332. Middle Camp, MI .T 4912, T 1, T 129, T 1139, T 2104, T 4126, T 4263, T 4502. (14)
Middle Camp, MI (AB 83)	.T 4716. (1).
Middle Camp, MI (AB 84)	.T 4715. (1).
Capra hircus Linnaeus	.T 1. Capra hircus Linnaeus .T 2, T 6, T 12, T 67, T 129, T 183, T 190, T 193, T 195, T 214, T 416, T 418, T 435, T 540, T 645, T 646, T 660, T 1123, T 1138, T 1139, T 1175, T 1181, T 2104, T 4164, T 4165, T 4166, T 4167, T 4172, T 4223, T 4343, T 4344, T 4345, T 4358, T 4369, T 4384, T 4476, T 4477, T 4479, T 4491, T 4492, T 4493, T 4642, T 4705, T 4711, T 4715, T 4716, T 4723,.
Centropus toulou	.T6294. (1).
Corvus albus	.T6295. Corvus albus .T6300, T6303, T6316,
Dicrurus aldabranus	.T6317. Dircrurus aldabranus .T 6265. (2).
Egretta alba	.T6319. (1).

charge of the considerable task of putting the data scheme into operation on the atoll.

References

BRAUN-BLANQUET, J. 1932. *Plant sociology: the study of plant communities.* (Translated, revised and edited by G. D. Fuller and H. S. Conrad). New York, McGraw-Hill (439 p.).

CUTBILL, J. L.; WILLIAMS, D. B. 1971. A program package for experimental data banking. In: J. L. Cutbill (ed.). *Data processing in biology and geology.* Systematics Association, Special Volume no. 3, p. 105–13.

ELTON, C. S. 1966. *The pattern of animal communities.* London, Methuen: New York; John Wiley.

FOSBERG, F. R. 1971. Preliminary survey of Aldabra vegetation. *Phil. Trans. R. Soc. Lond.* (B: *Biol. Sci.*) vol. 260, p. 215–25.

——. 1972. Geomorphic cycle on Aldabra—hypothesis. In: *Proc. Symp. corals and coral reefs,* Mar. Biol. Assoc. India. *12–16 January 1969.*

HEATH, J.; SCOTT, D. 1972. *Instructions for recorders.* Biological Records Centre, Natural Environment Research Council.

PERRING, F. H.; WALTERS, S. M. 1962. *Atlas of the British flora.* London; Nelson.

——.; RADFORD, G. L.; PETERKEN, G. F. 1973. *Reserve recording: instructions for warders.* Biological Records Centre, Natural Environment Research Council.

PIPER, D. J. W. 1971. The use of the D-Mac pencil follower in routine determinations of sedimentary parameters. In: J. L. Cutbill (ed.). *Data processing in biology and geology.* Systematics Association, Special Volume no. 3, p. 97–103.

SACHET, M-H.; DAHL, A. L. (eds.). 1974. Comparative investigations of tropical reef ecosystems: background on an integrated coral reef program. *Atoll Res. Bull.,* vol. 172, p. 1–169.

STODDART, D. R.; TAYLOR, J. D.; FOSBERG, F. R.; FARROW, G. E. 1971. Geomorphology of Aldabra Atoll. *Phil. Trans. R. Soc. Lond.* (B: *Biol. Sci.*), vol. 260, p. 31–65.

12

Zonation of rocky intertidal surfaces

J. D. Taylor[1]

The intertidal rocky shore represents a complex environmental gradient between the sea and land, modified by many factors which include the rise and fall of the tides, wave action, climatic factors, topography of the shore, nature of the substratum and the organisms present. It is one of the steepest of ecological gradients.

Rocky shores have received a great deal of attention, and the advantages of intertidal areas for biological study have been emphasized by Connell (1972), who lists such features as accessibility; usually sessile or slow moving animals, which are often well known taxonomically; the animals are usually easily visible, facilitating studies on abundance and population characteristics. Furthermore, the populations are amenable to experimental field manipulation.

The correlation between various physical factors of the intertidal gradient and the distribution of organisms into distinct zones has been recognized for a long time (see review: Doty, 1957). The vertical zonation phenomena have been described from many parts of the world (reviews: Southward, 1958; Stephenson and Stephenson, 1972). Many earlier studies have described zonation patterns almost as an end in themselves, with little or no attempt at correlation with environmental factors. Also, great attention has been given to the physiological tolerances of organisms to the conditions of the intertidal gradient (general reviews: see Newell, 1970; Kinne, 1970–1972). More recently however, attention is being paid to the biological interactions affecting the distribution of organisms on shores. (review: Connell, 1972; Paine, 1966, 1969, 1971, 1974; Dayton, 1971) and it is being increasingly realized that these interactions are important in the formation and maintenance of zonation patterns.

ZONAL SCHEMES

A great deal of attention has been paid to the formulation of zonation schemes,

1. Department of Zoology, British Museum (Natural History), Cromwell Road, London SW7 5BD, United Kingdom.

for these are useful in providing a descriptive framework within which inter-tidal communities may be described, and they also facilitate the comparison of shores in different parts of the world. Any particular shore may show quite complex zonation features which are often developed in response to local conditions. However, Stephenson and Stephenson (1949) showed that upon widely separated shores throughout the world, there is an underlying similarity of basic zonation patterns, resulting from the presence of similar or ecologically equivalent organisms, occupying similar positions upon the shore.

There has been an extensive and often sterile discussion on zonal termi-nology, but the tripartite system developed by Stephenson and Stephenson (1949) and modified by Lewis (1964) has found a measure of common accept-ance, and has been further modified for use on tropical reef shores (Taylor, 1968, 1971; Morton, 1973; Womersley and Bailey, 1969). The tripartite scheme used by French workers (Plante, 1964; Baissac *et al.*, 1962; Faure, 1974) is essentially similar.

The system is developed from the concept of biotic zones as being bio-logical entities which should be defined by biological means, the organisms themselves being the most sensitive indicators of physical conditions. Physical definitions for shore zones are rejected, because of the complexities of measuring factors of the shore environment other than tides and the many inconsistencies found when attempting to correlate the distribution of organisms with physical criteria. For instance, Lewis (1964) points out that 'the littoral zone can have no constant relation to tidal levels for its extent depends upon the aspect, latitude, topography and composition of its population.' The scheme modified from Lewis (1964) (Fig. 1) has two major zones, the sublittoral and the littoral; these are biological zones, and littoral zone in this sense is not synonymous with intertidal zone which is a physical definition. The frequently used term supralittoral is rejected as a marine zone and should be restricted in use for

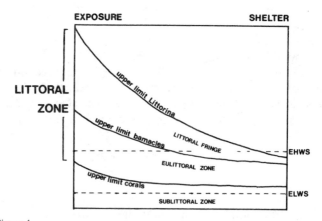

Figure 1
The zonation scheme, showing major zones and the expected variation in relative width from sheltered to exposed conditions.

the lowermost belt of terrestrial vegetation. The littoral zone is divided further into the *littoral fringe* and the *eulittoral zone*. The littoral fringe extends at its upper limits to the maximum range of marine organisms, usually species of the gastropod family Littorinidae, and at its lowest limit to the uppermost occurrence of barnacles. The littoral fringe is characterized particularly by blue–green algae and lichen (blackening organisms), isopods, species of Littorinidae and other gastropods such as *Melampus* and *Truncatella*. In temperate areas, the eulittoral zone extends downwards from the upper limit of barnacles to the first appearance of laminarian algae. In the tropics, *Laminaria* or similar algae are absent, and the top of the sublittoral is marked by the first appearance of corals, marine angiosperms and calcareous red algae. Typical organisms of the eulittoral zone are barnacles, although on some shores in the tropics they may be uncommon (Newman, 1960), limpets, whether they be genera of Patellacea or the pulmonate limpet *Siphonaria,* neritid and thaiid gastropods, mussels and large chitons, particularly *Acanthopleura*. Densities of algae in the eulittoral zone on tropical shores are usually much less than on temperate shores.

The upper limit of the sublittoral zone is defined by the first appearance of corals and the other organisms listed above. Frequently in coral reef areas, the upper parts of the sublittoral zone may be sufficiently distinct from the deeper areas for the recognition of a sublittoral fringe zone. The width of the littoral zone is affected by the shore topography, tidal range, and the degree of wave exposure; thus in exposed situations, littoral species may occur far above the theoretical high tide level, and the biological sublittoral may extend upwards into the intertidal area. (Fig. 1). French workers, for example Baissac *et al.* (1962) and Faure (1974) use the terms supra-littoral, medio-littoral and infralittoral, which seem, in general, to correspond with the littoral fringe, eulittoral, and sublittoral zones respectively.

Although Stephenson and Stephenson (1949) and Stephenson (1958) recognized the equivalence of corals and *Laminaria* as indicators of the top of the sublittoral zone, it was Doty and Morrison (1954) working in the Tuamotus who first formally demonstrated the position of reefs in zonal schemes. Doty (1957) later suggested that the reef flats of coral reefs might be considered as large sublittoral-fringe tidal pools, and that atoll lagoons are essentially large, deep, sublittoral pools. Subsequent studies, basically similar, relating reefs to zonal schemes are: Endean *et al.* (1956), Baissac *et al.* (1962), Kalk (1958), Taylor (1968, 1971), Morton and Challis (1969), Morton (1973), Womersley and Bailey (1969).

A currently accepted general view of reefs in relation to the tripartite zonation scheme is shown in Figure 2. Assemblages of organisms in the higher parts of the sublittoral zone on reefs are usually different from those in the deeper parts of the zone, and it is often convenient for descriptive purposes to separate this as a sublittoral fringe-zone. Reef flats usually support extremely variable assemblages of organisms reflecting the variation in hydrographic, microclimatic and substrata conditions. These assemblages are often arranged

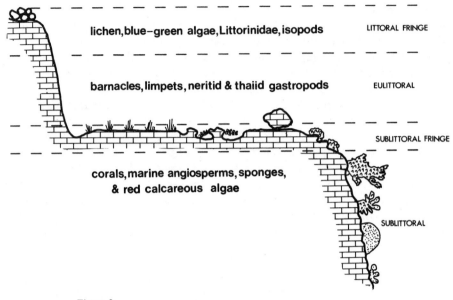

Figure 2
Diagrammatic representation of zones on a typical fringing reef with a
rocky shore. Not to scale.

in belts, parallel to the shore, which occur at more or less the same vertical
level; they are not zones in the zonation scheme sense, but represent the
different responses of organisms to a variety of conditions at one level on the
intertidal gradient.

MODIFYING FACTORS

The extent and character of the littoral zones and the distribution of organisms
within them may be modified by a wide variety of physical factors and the
more important of these are discussed briefly below. Greater detail may be
found in the reviews of intertidal ecology previously cited.

Tides

The essential feature that tides impose upon the shores is the alternation of
periods of emergence and submergence, however irregular in frequency and
duration these may be. Tidal range is one of the main factors influencing the
width of the intertidal zone. Useful straightforward discussions of tidal types
and the possible relation to shore ecology are given in Doty (1957), Lewis
(1964) and King (1961). A map of the character and maximum range of the
tides on the shores of the world is provided by Doty (1957); more detail for

the Indian Ocean is given by Stoddart (1971, Fig. 7). Local data may be obtained from published predictions, permanent or temporary tide gauges and graduated tide poles.

Various workers have attempted to correlate tidal levels with the actual zonation pattern (Doty 1946, 1957) but as Lewis (1964) points out, it is only in very sheltered waters where any close similarity between actual conditions and those calculated from tidal data might be expected. Doty (1946, 1957) discusses what are known as tide factors; on shores with mixed tidal regime the inter-tidal region is not exposed on a time height gradient, but between successive heights there may be a two or three-fold increase in the time of exposure. It would be expected that the vertical range limits of organisms correlate with these critical features of the tides. However, in real conditions these tidal factors are usually modified and obscured by other variables such as wave action. Where tidal data are available, the positions of organisms on shores are levelled to a bench mark or other mark of known height. It is then possible to calculate the emergence time of any position on the shore from data given in the tide tables. Where tidal data are not available, observations may be made with a graduated tide pole or temporary tide gauge. Positions on the shore can then be levelled to the tide pole.

Exposure

To a large extent, both the width of the littoral zone and the variation in inter-tidal zonation pattern are correlated with degree of exposure or wave action. Although methods are now available for the direct measurement of wave action (Jones and Demetropoulos, 1968; Harger, 1970), these are usually time consuming to set up. Assessments of degree of exposure of an area are usually made qualitatively and quantified to some extent by reference to wind speed and constancy over fairly long periods, care being taken to assess possible seasonal variations. Approximate assessments of exposure conditions can be made using measurements of wave height and frequency. Some data con-cerning winds, cyclones, swell, and waves affecting shores are usefully sum-marized in Davies (1972).

It is usual to produce a local exposure scale with sites ranked in order of degree of exposure; however, it is difficult to compare shores in different areas. Ballantine (1961) produced a biological exposure scale for Pembroke, whereby an inspection of the organisms and zonation pattern present would inform the observer of the relative exposure of the shore. A similar scale was attempted by Taylor (1971) at Aldabra Atoll.

Climatic factors

Rainfall, insolation, wind speed and direction are important factors influencing the shore and modifying the intertidal gradient. General data are usually available from meteorological records, however small scale; local effects are

143

often more important and should, if necessary, be measured on site. An array of micro-meteorological devices is now available (Forstner and Rützler, 1970; Monteith, 1972) many of which can be adapted for use on the shore. The effects of violent but irregular climatic events such as hurricanes and severe storms must be considered.

Substrata

Factors of the substrata which need to be considered are aspect, rock type, rock hardness, friability, porosity, microtopography, surface texture and colour. The microtopography and surface texture of the rock substrata will be important factors, influencing the settlement and colonization success of intertidal organisms. Recent work is showing the importance of topographical complexity in influencing the population density and species diversity of rock substrata. Rock type has obvious effects; for instance, shales and sandstones may be too friable and erode too rapidly for permanent successful colonization by organisms; igneous and metamorphic rocks may be too hard for penetration by boring organisms, and hence major components of some food webs may be absent. Organisms which bore by means of acidic secretion can only colonize calcareous substrata. The greatest diversity of organisms on tropical shores is usually found upon calcareous substrata which it is thought allow the greatest exploitation of habitat space. The porosity of the rock will affect the water retention properties of the substrata. Heller (1975) has demonstrated for *Littorina,* an association between shell colour and the colour of the rock substrata.

QUANTITATIVE METHODS

Standard methods of quadrat survey along transects are widely used (Southward 1958, Holme and McIntyre 1971), although the topographical complexity of the shore often causes sampling difficulties. The quadrat size selected depends upon the size and abundance of the organisms to be sampled. Methods of estimating biomass, production and energy flow are given in Holme and McIntyre (1971) and examples from reef shores by Hughes (1971a, b). Semi-quantitative methods of timed counts such as used by Crisp and Southward (1958) may be useful for rapid broad-scale surveys.

A standard procedure in intertidal studies is to record the distribution and abundance of organisms along the complex intertidal gradient represented by the vertical position upon the shore. This is the same procedure as that practised by plant ecologists (review: Whittaker, 1967). This information is used to give indications of the physical tolerances of the organisms, usually considered in relation to the percentage of time the organisms remain exposed. However, the shore gradient represents a much more complex set of environmental variables, and experiment is necessary to separate the various factors involved. More recently, the arrangement of distributions of ecologically similar organisms along the gradient has been interpreted as resulting from partitioning of the habitat-food resource, arising from possible competition interactions between the species.

The position an organism occupies on the gradient may also be controlled by grazing or predation (Paine, 1966, 1974). Manipulation experiments may be used to study the dynamics of such interactions. The intertidal rocky shore is very suitable for this type of experiment, although these have so far been carried out mainly in temperate areas. Two basic types of exclusion experiment have been carried out, either by the total removal of some organisms from the rock area, or by the use of exclusion cages. Cages have been used by a number of workers (Connell, 1961, 1970; Dayton, 1971; Paine, 1974). Holes are bored into the rock using a portable generator and electric drill, a plastic or nylon sleeve is placed in the hole and the cage secured by brass or stainless steel screws. Paine (1974) records such screws, used at Mukkaw Bay, Washington State, as being still in place up to nine years after installation. Harger (1970) used cages to transplant mussels.

Clearance of particular areas is relatively simple in principle, but it is difficult to exclude organisms completely. The methods and difficulties encountered in the removal of the starfish *Pisaster* are discussed by Paine (1969, 1974). Animals living within the rock substrata can be sampled quantitatively by extracting a piece of rock, measuring the volume, and then carefully breaking it into small pieces. Kohn and Lloyd (1973), using this method on $100 \, cm^2 \times 5 \, cm$ deep limestone samples, extracted average yields of $49,000/m^2$ polychaetes. The morphology of the burrow and the volume of the rock occupied by burrowing organisms may be studied by embedding the rock *in vacuo* in wax or polyester resin and then dissolving the rock away by means of hydrochloric acid.

Time lapse photography can be a useful technique in studying long term changes in zonation patterns (Wilson 1974, Paine 1974).

INTERTIDAL STUDIES ON CORAL REEF AREAS

The references below give a brief guide to the literature on intertidal zonation patterns of coral reef areas. Most of the studies are qualitative, as there is a general lack of quantitative data from tropical areas.

Indian Ocean

Rodriguez (Faure, 1974); Réunion (Faure and Montaggioni, 1971); Mauritius (Hodgkin and Michel, 1963; Baissac *et al.*, 1962); Mozambique (Kalk, 1958); Madagascar (Plante, 1964); East Africa (Lawson, 1969, Hartnoll, 1976); Aldabra (Taylor, 1971); Seychelles (Taylor, 1968); Red Sea (Hughes, 1977); Singapore (Purchon and Enoch, 1954).

Pacific Ocean

Solomon Islands (Morton and Challis, 1969; Morton, 1973; Womersley and Bailey, 1969); Queensland (Endean *et al.*, 1956; Stephenson *et al.*, 1958); Raroia (Doty and Morrison, 1954); Tuamotus (Salvat, 1970); Fanning Island (Kay, 1971); Cócos Islands (Bakus, 1975).

Atlantic Ocean

Barbados (Lewis, 1960); Bahamas (Newell *et al.*, 1959; Storr, 1964); Bermuda (Stephenson and Stephenson, 1972); Florida Keys (Stephenson and Stephenson, 1950); Brazil (Laborel, 1969).

References

BAISSAC, J. de B.; LUBET, P. E.; MICHEL, C. M. 1962. Les biocoenoses benthiques littorales de l'Ile Maurice. *Rec. Trav. Stn mar. Endoume*, vol. 29, p. 253–91.

BAKUS, G. J. 1975. Marine zonation and ecology of Cócos Island, off Central America. *Atoll Res. Bull.* vol. 179, p. 1–9.

BALLANTINE, W. J. 1961. A biologically-defined exposure scale for the comparative description of rocky shores. *Field Studies*, vol. 1, 3, 19p.

CONNELL, J. H. 1961. The influence of interspecific competition and other factors on the distribution of the barnacle. *Chthamalus stellatus. Ecology*, vol. 42, p. 710–23.

——. 1970. A predator-prey system in the marine intertidal region I. *Balanus glandula* and several predatory species of *Thais. Ecol. Monogr.*, vol. 40, p. 49–78.

——. 1972. Community interactions on marine rocky intertidal shores. *Ann. Rev. Ecol. Syst.*, vol. 3, p. 169–92.

CRISP, D. J.; SOUTHWARD, A. J. 1958. The distribution of intertidal organisms along the coast of the English Channel. *J. mar. Biol. Assoc. U.K.*, vol. 37, p. 157–208.

DAVIES, J. L. 1972. *Geographical variation in coastal development.* Edinburgh, Oliver & Boyd (204 p.).

DAYTON, P. K. 1971. Competition, disturbance and community organisation; the provision and subsequent utilization of space in a rocky intertidal community. *Ecol. Monogr.*, vol. 41, p. 351–89.

DOTY, M. S. 1946. Critical tide factors that are correlated with the vertical distribution of marine algae and other organisms along the Pacific Coast. *Ecology*, vol. 27, vol. 27, p. 315–28.

——. 1957. Rocky intertidal surfaces. *Geol. Soc. Am. Mem.*, vol. 67, p. 535–85.

——.; MORRISON, J. P. E. 1954. Inter-relationships of organisms on Raroia, aside from man. *Atoll. Res. Bull.*, vol. 35, p. 1–61.

ENDEAN, R.; STEPHENSON, W.; KENNY, R. 1956. The ecology and distribution of intertidal organisms on certain islands off the Queensland coast. *Aust. J. mar. Freshwat. Res.*, vol. 7, p. 317–42.

FAURE, G. 1974. Contribution a l'étude de la zonation littorale sur substrats durs de l'Ile Rodrigue (Archipel des Mascareignes, Océan Indien). *Tethys* vol. 5, p. 437–48.

——; MONTAGGIONI, L. 1971. Etude lithologique et bionomique des calcaires littoraux sub-actuels de la région de St. Leu (Ile de la Réunion, Océan Indien). *Téthys* suppl. 1, p. 281–98.

FORSTNER, H.; RÜTZLER, K. 1970. Measurement of micro-climate in littoral marine habitats. *Oceanogr. mar. Biol. Ann. Rev.*, vol. 8, p. 225–49.

HARGER, J. R. E. 1970. The effect of wave impact on some aspects of the biology of sea mussels. *Veliger*, vol. 12, p. 401–14.

HARTNOLL, R. G. 1976. The ecology of some rocky shows in tropical East Africa. *Est. Coastl. Mar. Sci.*, vol. 4, p. 1–21.

HELLER, J. 1975. Visual selection of shell colour in two littoral prosobranchs. *Zool. J. Linn. Soc.* vol. 56, p. 153–70.

HODGKIN, E. P.; MICHEL, C. M. 1963. Zonation of plants and animals on the rocky shores of Mauritius. *Proc. R. Soc. Arts Sci. Mauritius*, vol. 11, p. 121–42.

HOLME, N. A.; MCINTYRE, A. D. (eds). 1971. *Methods for the study of marine benthos.* Oxford, Blackwell Science Publications. (IBP Handbook no. 16) (334 p.).

HUGHES, R. N. 1971a. Ecological energetics of *Nerita* (Archaeogastropoda, Neritacea) populations on Barbados, West Indies. *Mar. Biol.,* vol. 11, p. 12–22.

——. 1971b. Ecological energetics of the Keyhole limpet *Fissurella barbadensis* Gmelin. *J. exp. mar. Biol. Ecol.,* vol. 6, p. 167–78.

——. 1977. The biota of reef flats and limestone cliffs near Jeddah, Saudi Arabia. *J. Nat. Hist.,* vol. 11, p. 77–96.

JONES, W. E.; DEMETROPOULOS, A. 1968. Exposure to wave action: measurements of an important ecological parameter on rocky shores on Angelsey. *J. exp. mar. Biol. Ecol.,* vol. 2, p. 46–63.

KALK, M. 1958. The intertidal fauna of rocks at Inhaca Island, Mocambique. *Ann. Natal. Mus.* vol. 14, p. 189–242.

KAY, E. A. 1971. The littoral marine molluscs of Fanning Island. *Pac. Sci.,* vol. 25, p. 260–81.

KING, C. A. M. 1961. *Beaches and coasts.* London, Arnold, (403 p.)

KINNE, O. (ed.). 1970–1972. *Marine ecology. A comprehensive, integrated treatise on life in oceans coastal waters.* vol. 1 (Parts 1–3) Environmental factors. London, New York, Wiley-Interscience.

KOHN, A. J.; LLOYD, M. C. 1973. Polychaetes of truncated limestone substrates on eastern Indian Ocean coral reefs: diversity, abundance and taxonomy. *Int. Rev. gesamt Hydrobiol.,* vol. 58, p. 369–99.

LABOREL, J. 1969. Les peuplements de madreporaires des côtes tropicales de Brésil. *Ann. Univ. Abidjan,* Ser. E., vol. 2, p. 1–260.

LAWSON, G. W. 1969. Some observations on the littoral ecology of rocky shores in East Africa (Kenya and Tanzania). *Trans. R. Soc. S. Afr.,* vol. 38, p. 329–40.

LEWIS, J. B. 1960. The fauna of the rocky shores of Barbados, West Indies. *Can. J. Zool.,* vol. 38, p. 391–435.

——. 1964. *The ecology of rocky shores.* London, English Universities Press (323 p.).

MONTEITH, J. L. 1972. *Survey of instruments for micrometerology.* Oxford, Blackwell Scientific Publications. (IBP Handbook no 22) (263 p.).

MORTON, J. E. 1973. The intertidal ecology of the British Solomon Islands. I. The zonation patterns of the weather coasts. *Phil. Trans. R. Soc. Lond.* (B: *Biol. Sci.*), vol. 265, p. 491–542.

——; CHALLIS, D. A. 1969. The biomorphology of Solomon Islands shores, with a discussion of and ecological terminology. *Phil. Trans. R. Soc. Lond.* (B: Biol. Sci.), vol. 255, p. 459–516.

NEWELL, N. D.; IMBRIE, J.; PURDY, E. G.; THURBER, D. L. 1959. Organism communities and bottom facies, Great Bahama Bank. *Bull. Am. Mus. Nat. Hist.,* vol. 117, p. 177–228.

NEWELL, R. C. 1970. *Biology of intertidal animals.* London, Longmans (555 p.).

NEWMAN, W. A. 1960. On the paucity of intertidal barnacles in the tropical West Pacific. *Veliger,* vol. 2, p. 89–94.

PAINE, R. T. 1966. Food web complexity and species diversity. *Am. Nat.* vol. 100, p. 65–75.

——. 1969. The *Pisaster–Tegula* interaction: prey patches, predator food preference and intertidal community structure. *Ecology,* vol. 50, p. 950–61.

——. 1971. A short-term experimental investigation of resource partitioning in a New Zealand rocky intertidal habitat. *Ecology,* vol. 52, p. 1096–106.

——. 1974. Intertidal community structure. Experimental studies on the relationship between a dominant competitor and its principal predator. *Oecologia,* vol. 15, p. 93–120.

PLANTE, R. 1964. Contribution à l'étude des peuplements de hauts niveaux sur substrats solides non récifaux dans la région de Tuléar. *Rec. Trav. Stn. mar. Endoume,* Suppl. Hors série 2, p.206–315.

PURCHON, R. D.; ENOCH, I. 1954. Zonation of the marine fauna and flora on a rocky shore near Singapore. *Bull. Raffles Mus.* vol. 25, p. 47–65.

SALVAT, B. 1970. Études quantitatives sur les mollusques récifaux de l'atoll de Fangataufa (Tuamotu, Polynésie). *Cah. Pacif.,* vol. 14, p. 1–57.

SOUTHWARD, A. J. 1958. The zonation of plants and animals on rocky sea shores. *Biol. Rev. Camb. Philos. Soc.,* vol. 33, p. 137–77.

STEPHENSON, T. A. 1958. Coral reefs regarded as sea-shores. In: *Proc. XV Int. Congr. zool. Lond.,* p. 244–46.

——; STEPHENSON, A. 1949. The universal features of zonation between tide-marks on rocky coasts. *J. Ecol.* vol. 37, p. 289–305.

——; STEPHENSON, A. 1950. Life between the tide-marks in North America. I. The Florida Keys. *J. Ecol.,* vol. 38, p. 345–402.

——; STEPHENSON, A. 1972. *Life between tide marks on rocky shores.* San Francisco, Freeman, (425 p.).

——; ENDEAN, R.; BENNETT, I. 1958. An ecological survey of the marine fauna of Low Isles, Queensland. *Aust. J. mar. Freshwat. Res.,* vol. 9, p. 261–318.

STODDART, D. R. 1971. Environment and history in Indian Ocean reef morphology. *Symp. zool. Soc. Lond.,* vol. 28, p. 3–38.

STORR, J. F. 1964. Ecology and oceanography of the coral-reef tract, Abaco Island, Bahamas. *Geol. Soc. Am. Spec. Pap.,* vol. 79, p. 1–98.

TAYLOR, J. D. 1968. Coral reef and associated invertebrate communities (mainly molluscan) around Mahé, Seychelles, *Phil. Trans. R. Soc. Lond.* (B: Biol. Sci.), vol. 254, p. 129–206.

——. 1971. Intertidal zonation at Aldabra Atoll. *Phil. Trans. R. Soc. Lond.* (B: *Biol. Sci.*), vol. 260, p. 175–215.

WHITTAKER, R. H. 1967. Gradient analysis of vegetation. *Biol. Rev. Camb. Philos. Soc.,* vol. 42, p. 207–64.

WILSON, D. P. 1974. *Sabellaria* colonies at Duckpool, North Cornwall, with a note for May 1973. *J. mar. Biol. Assoc. U.K.,* vol. 54, p. 393–436.

WOMERSLEY, H. B. S.; BAILEY, A. 1969. The marine algae of the Solomon Islands and their place in biotic reefs. *Phil. Trans. R. Soc. Lond.* (B: *Biol. Sci.*), vol. 255, p. 433–42.

13

Visual surveys of large areas of coral reefs

R. A. Kenchington[1]

INTRODUCTION

Surveys of large areas of coral reefs are necessary from time to time for the purposes of description, for baseline studies, for the selection of representative areas for detailed study, or for monitoring the effect of such traumatic influences as tropical storms, oil spills or coral predators. An increase in demand for such surveys may be expected from the requirement by governments of many nations for statements about the effect of these on the environment as a part of development planning.

There is as yet no means of obtaining simple physical indices of the extent and nature of the coral coverage of a large area of reef on a scale comparable to the information available to terrestrial ecologists from aerial photographs. Existing quantitative techniques for quadrat or line transect studies are too demanding in their time requirements to be generally applicable. Visual assessment remains the only means of conducting extensive surveys of large reef areas.

It is apparent from the literature on reef ecology and morphology that many visual surveys have been conducted but that the information obtained has been used sparingly. Whilst there is general reluctance to place reliance on subjective visual assessments, work in progress indicates that it should be possible to develop training procedures and scales of assessment which would enable valid comparisons to be made between observations both in space and time.

General surveys are usually undertaken with specific management objectives and are thus goal oriented, operating within defined constraints of time and cost. The exact form of a survey will be determined by the information required but two general approaches may be recognized: 'Census', whereby an estimate of population of such organisms as Holothurians, Asteroids, Echinoderms, Tridacnid clams or particular coral forms is obtained, or 'General assessment' in which observers report on aspects of reef condition. The two approaches may

1. Great Barrier Reef Marine Park Authority, P.O. Box. 5575, M.S.O. Townsville, Queensland, Australia 4810.

be used in parallel, as in the case of surveys conducted as a result of widespread concern over the predatory activity of large populations of the Crown-of-Thorns starfish, *Acanthaster planci* (Chesher, 1969; Endean and Stablum, 1973; Kenchington and Morton, 1976; Ormond and Campbell, 1971) which were undertaken with the twin tasks of estimating *A. planci* populations and assessing their destructive impact on coral reefs.

CENSUS SURVEYS

The subject of a census survey should fulfil, or leave density dependent indications of its presence which fulfil a number of conditions: large size, limited mobility, ease of recognition, diurnal detectability and a normal level of abundance which can be easily counted by an observer. Extremely high levels of abundance present a problem since an observer may be unable to count all individuals present by the general survey method. This problem of observer saturation may be controlled by observers reporting saturation conditions and subsequently revisiting the location for a detailed subsample search (Kenchington and Morton, 1976).

If the subject of the survey fulfils the conditions outlined above and provision is made for saturation situations the task of the observer is relatively simple; to count recognizable objects with which he is familiar by experience or training. Recording results is simple but interpretation is complicated by local variations in water clarity, reef profile and extent of coral cover.

Endean and Stablum (1973) in discussing their survey technique for *Acanthaster planci*, have estimated that depending on local conditions an observer looking from above onto a section of reef face would be able to see between 10 and 80 per cent of the population of *A. planci* present. Kenchington and Morton (1976) supported their general census technique with routine formalized subsample area searches which were conducted to provide an estimate of the efficiency of the technique in different locations and to provide estimates of abundance of *A. planci* populations in areas from which saturation counts were reported from the primary survey.

Under some circumstances *A. planci* behave cryptically during the day, however they leave feeding scars, which are small areas of coral skeleton, exposed when the living tissue of the coral has been digested. Feeding scars are concealed in time as algae colonize the area, they are however readily recognizable for approximately 14–21 days (Endean and Stablum, 1973) and they have been used as an index of the presence of *A. planci* in surveys by Chesher, 1969; Endean and Stablum, 1973; Kenchington and Morton, 1976 and Ormond and Campbell, 1971. *A. planci* and feeding scar counts made during the general survey were compared with counts of *A. planci* from detailed bed subsample searches (Kenchington and Morton, 1976). The results of the comparisons, presented in Tables 1 and 2, indicate a general comparability of ranking of results by the two techniques but show that the results obtained by the primary

TABLE 1. Comparative analysis by quartiles of ranked *A. planci* results obtained by tow and trident techniques

Trident results: Range (No.)	Tow results *A. planci*			
	0	0–2	3–10	10–'40'
0–3	18	3	0	0
3–18	2	11	6	2
19–51	0	5	10	6
52–523	0	2	6	14

TABLE 2. Comparative analysis by quartiles of feeding scar records obtained by the tow technique and *A. planci* observed by the trident technique.

Trident results: Range (No.)	Tow results feeding scars			
	0–3	3–6	6–32	'40'
0–3	13	4	4	0
3–18	4	9	4	4
19–51	2	8	9	2
52–523	1	1	5	15

survey techniques should be regarded as indices of abundance and not as absolute values. Much of the variation of the tables may be attributed to local variations in the nature of the reef face and the extent of coral cover but discrepancies remain. Some may be explained by the occasional cryptic behaviour of *A. planci* and some by the presence of areas of recently exposed coral skeleton caused by destructive agents other than *A. planci*. The census survey can provide a useful index of the abundance of large recognizable objects in reef areas. The interpretation of the index requires local knowledge which may be obtained by conducting detailed subsample searches.

GENERAL ASSESSMENT SURVEYS

The assessment of coral or other benthic community cover in reef areas presents more intractable problems since the condition being assessed is subject to considerable local variability and cannot readily be indexed for quantification by an observer. In consideration of survey techniques due weight must be placed on the variability of cover and on the psychological basis of the perception of proportional area coverage.

VARIABILITY OF CORAL COVER

Many of the studies described in the literature detail local variability in coral cover arising from zonation and horizontal discontinuity. For the purposes of

151

this discussion the results of Laxton and Stablum (1974) are cited since their photogrammetric technique appears to correspond most closely to visual assessment, being subject to the same limitations in assessment of the third dimension of coral cover.

Laxton and Stablum (1974) studied 25 metre and 100 metre transects by means of 1 square metre photographed quadrat areas. The range of their data, which yield values for 1 square metre quadrats and mean values for complete transects in reef top and reef slope areas, is summarized in Table 3.

TABLE 3. Living hard coral cover measurements (from Laxton and Stablum, 1974)

Location	Maximum 1 m² quadrat	Minimum 1 m² quadrat	Transect mean
Reef slope:			
Hedley Reef	100%	11%	63.5%
Reef top:			
Channel Reef	83%	0%	23.5%

The same techniques were adopted by Endean and Stablum (1973), in assessing coral cover on areas of a number of reefs in the central region of the Great Barrier Reef province. They present mean values for a series of transects which were sited to run from reef crest across the reef top and down the reef slope in a number of weather side and lee side locations. The range of their data is summarized in Table 4.

TABLE 4. Mean coral cover assessments (Endean and Stablum 1973)

Location	No. of records	Minimum	Maximum	Grand mean
Weather face	46	8.7	63.5	38.2
Back reef	11	15.0	69.5	41.7
Reef flat	1	—	—	48.0

In any general survey the gross variations in mean coral cover levels which are the subject of assessment must be considered against the background of local 'microvariability'.

TRAINING

Surveys have generally been conducted by experienced observers. Kenchington and Morton (1976) had as observers Royal Australian Navy divers who were trained by a lecture with colour transparencies followed by demonstration swims and trial tows in the field. During the survey a number of replicate studies were conducted to assess the consistency of assessments. The divers operated as teams, each with a scientist attached. An analysis of the distribution of results for each team was carried out to determine whether there was any consistent difference between teams. Comparisons of initial and replicate results for *A. planci* counts and Live coral assessments are presented in Tables 5 and 6 and team comparisons for the same determinations in Tables 7 and 8. It may be seen that there is considerable agreement between teams and by replicate studies on the proportional distribution of *A. planci*. It is apparent that more difficulty was experienced in coral assessment.

TABLE 5. Comparison of initial and replicate counts of *A. planci* by records per category (from Kenchington and Morton, 1976)

Replicate Survey		Initial Survey				
	Category	0	1	2	3	4
		Number sighted				
		0	1–3	4–6	7–18	18
	0	107	6	1	—	1
	1	6	7	1	—	—
	2	—	—	2	—	1
	3	—	1	1	4	5
	4	—	—	—	1	3

TABLE 6. Comparison of initial and replicate assessments of live coral cover by number of records per category (from Kenchington and Morton 1976)

Replicate Survey		Initial Survey			
	Category	0	1	2	3
		Approximate percentage of coral cover			
		0–1	1–10	10–50	50–100
	0	—	5	—	—
	1	1	27	19	1
	2	6	20	48	7
	3	—	4	4	4

TABLE 7. Analysis by team of percentage distribution of records of *A. planci* abundance (from Kenchington and Morton, 1976)

Category	1	2	3	4
Number sighted	0	1–3	4–18	18
Team:				
1	83	8	3	5
2	84	10	3	4
3	77	9	4	9
Total	81	9	4	6

153

TABLE 8. Analysis by team of percentage distribution of records of live coral cover (from Kenchington and Morton, 1976)

Category	1	2	3	4
Approximate percentage of coral cover	0–1	1–10	10–50	50–100
Team:				
1	0	38	57	5
2	1	62	31	4
3	3	58	35	4
Total	2	53	41	4

SCALES OF ASSESSMENT

Psychophysics, the investigation of observer response to known levels of physical stimulation, has indicated a number of criteria for the development of scales of assessment and the interpretation of their results (Woodworth and Schlosberg, 1938).

The most commonly used scale of assessment of relative area cover is that for recording cloud cover in routine meteorological reports. National weather recording systems use either 8 or 10 point scales, records are determined subjectively and results are routinely used in comparative studies.

Investigations on the design of assessment scales have shown that in any subjective scale there is a tendency for observers to be reluctant to score records in the extreme upper or lower categories of a scale. There is in addition a tendency for observers working with a scale with an uneven number of divisions to score an excessive number of records in the central division. It is thus advised that subjective assessment scales should have an even number of divisions and that these should be selected after study of the minimum difference between levels which can be consistently discriminated (Woodworth and Schlosberg, 1938).

Coral cover assessments have been made using scales of two divisions, (Ormond and Campbell, 1971), three divisions (Endean and Stablum, 1973), four divisions (Kenchington and Morton, 1976) and five divisions (Ormond and Campbell, 1974). All may be criticized for having a limited uneven number of divisions. The four point scale of Kenchington and Morton (1976) was in effect a three point scale operating over a largely redundant zero point.

TESTS OF AREA ASSESSMENT ABILITY

Seventy two unprepared subjects were tested to determine estimates of relative area coverage in a laboratory situation. Twenty two subjects were retested immediately in order to determine whether familiarity with the test procedure changed performance. During the test, observers were shown a sequence of thirty-three transparencies upon which known proportions of the test field were masked with opaque material.

The test showed that observer response is essentially linear and may be described by a regression coefficient. There was a wide range of individual coefficients, minimum 0.685, maximum 1.338 and of Standard Error values, minimum 5.35, maximum 14.99: 70 per cent of the test subjects had Standard Error values less than 10 per cent. There was no difference in the performance of the twenty two observers in their second test.

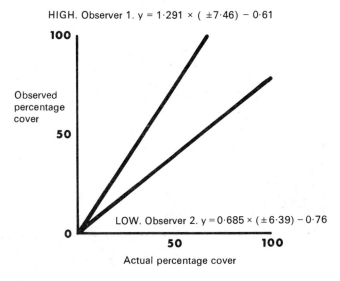

Figure 1
Sample regression slopes for consistent high scoring and low scoring observers in a laboratory area assessment test.

A programme of further tests is in progress to determine whether laboratory performance can be validly related to field performance and to determine whether a suitable training procedure can be developed to improve observer performance.

In initial field trials observers assessed coral cover of 51 small areas, each of which was a circle of approximately two metres radius with the centre defined by a moored buoy. Coral cover of the test areas was measured as the mean of three photogrammetric determinations made with the technique of Laxton and Stablum (1974). Eight observers were tested; two had previous experience of coral assessment, the remainder had reef diving experience but no previous involvement with coral cover assessment.

The results are summarized in Figure 2 in which the mean and range of values for each assessment area are plotted. They indicate that a six-point scale for coral assessment, indicated in Figure 3, is reasonable. If the mean values of

155

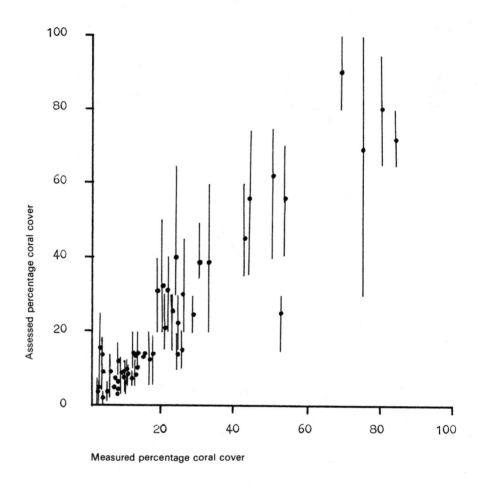

Figure 2
Plot of mean and range of visually assessed coral cover values against
photogrammetrically measured mean values: 4 observations per set visual
assessment, 3 records per set photogrammetric assessment.

the 51 assessments are expressed in the suggested scale intervals, 33 correspond
with the measured values, 16 show a discrepancy of one scale interval and the
remaining two show a discrepancy of two intervals.

Further trials are planned to assess whether or not consistency in the field
can be improved by training in the laboratory, the slope of individual observer
response relationships (see Fig. 1) can be 'corrected' to unity and group means
results can be significantly improved by the exclusion of observers whose initial
laboratory test results were inconsistent.

156

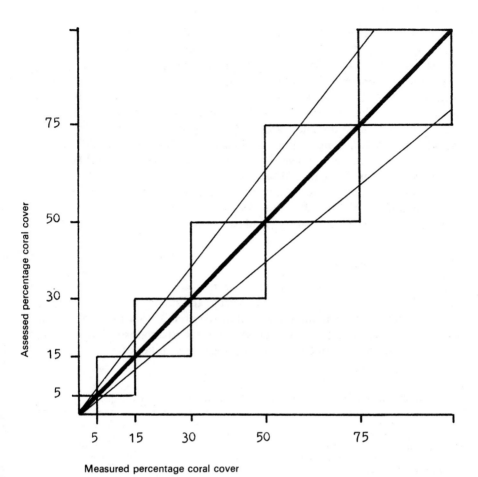

Figure 3
Diagram of possible six-point coral assessment scale superimposed upon a
typical observer regression slope of 1·0 with a standard error of 7·5 at a
a mean value of 30·0 per cent.

FIELD METHODS

Navigation and mapping

Whether the purpose of a general survey is one of mapping distribution or
of selection of study area the ability to relocate an area in which a specific
observation has been made is an essential requirement.

High resolution aerial photographs have been used by Kenchington and
Morton (1976), and Pearson and Garrett (1976). For most situations in the
Great Barrier Reef they enable detailed identification of topographic features,
such as lagoonal coral pinnacles or reef crest pools, which can be recognized

157

by a field observer and thus used to determine his position relative to them. Kenchington and Morton (1976) used enlargements with a scale whereby 1 cm. represented 80 metres, making it possible to identify features as small as 20 metres in diameter. They supported the method with a system of regular position fixes on the workboats using the gyro compass and the radar of the survey mother ship. The precision of the photographic navigation technique is related to the local abundance of distinctive topographic features and is considerably reduced on long straight sections of weather reef face with no tidal pools or coral pinnacles; under these circumstances fixes on workboats are necessary for the maintenance of precision.

Distortion in photographs may require correction for mapping purposes (Kenchington and Morton, 1976) but for most purposes it is of limited concern if the photographs are the primary field navigation aid.

Observation methods

The choice of survey technique is made on the basis of considerations of the extent of the area to be surveyed, the object of the survey and the time and resources available. Depending on the detail required a wide range of possible area coverage is available. Table 9 presents the approximate area which can be covered by an observer in one hour using various techniques.

TABLE 9. Approximate coverage per hour by various reef survey techniques

Method	Area or linear coverage
Quadrat mapping	0.5 m^2
Continuous recording linear transect[a]	30 m
Photographic transect[b]	100 m
Free swimming observer	2000 m
Towed observer[c]	5000 m
Spot check—200 m interval[d]	8000 m
Spot check—500 m interval[d]	12000 m

a. Method developed by Loya (1972).
b. Laxton and Stablum (1974).
c. Kenchington and Morton (1976).
d. Pearson and Garrett (1976).

The values quoted in Table 9 are reasonable approximations based on field experience. They concern only the time spent during observation and make no allowance for preparation and recovery of observers using scuba equipment. Quadrat and transect methods are included in the table for comparison, and although valuable as subsample techniques within a broad survey they are not discussed further.

Free swimming observation, with or without scuba equipment has probably been the most widely used technique in qualitative or semi-quantitative assessment. The advantage of the method is that the observer is free to modify his speed and direction and can thus investigate specific phenomena in detail. The disadvantages are that the observer frequently has little navigational information to enable him to relate sightings to locations and may unwittingly cover the same area more than once.

Chesher (1969) and Pearson and Endean (1969) used free swimming observers to study the distribution of *Acanthaster planci* in the U.S. Pacific Territories and the central region of the Great Barrier Reef respectively. A basis of quantification of results was provided by expressing observations as numbers of records per 20 minute swim.

Towed observation. Chesher (1969) towed observers who held on to the side of the workboat by a strop. Ormond and Campbell 1971) introduced the manta board, a diving plane or sled with which the observer is able to control his position in the water.

The advantage of the manta board is that the observer can control his vertical position in the water and can cover a large area with minimal fatigue. Navigation is the responsibility of the controller of the tow boat.

The chief disadvantage is loss of information with speed; the observer may become saturated with information in a rich area since he is unable to decrease speed or pause to study an interesting situation. This problem can be partially overcome by the adoption of a detailed subsample study technique as a general control and for the investigation of saturation situations (Kenchington and Morton, 1976).

Assuming adequate navigation, the precision of relationship of observations to locations is determined by the frequency with which observers are debriefed. Ormond and Campbell (1971) had their observers maintain a spoken commentary by underwater radio communication. Chesher (1969) and Endean (1974) debriefed observers after periods of 20 or 30 minutes. Kenchington and Morton (1976) adopted a standard 10 minute tow period and debriefed by a system of hand signals at 2 minute intervals with a complete debrief at the conclusion of the 10 minute tow.

Spot check surveys. Pearson and Garrett (1976), operating with limited resources on a project to determine the extent of *Acanthaster planci* populations in the Great Barrier Reef, developed a rapid spot check technique. They were concerned with areas other than the reef flat and circumnavigated a reef in an outboard powered dinghy pausing at predetermined intervals whilst an observer wearing a face mask placed his head under water and studied the area immediately beneath him for approximately 1 minute as the boat moved slowly towards the reef crest. The dinghy moved at speed between check points.

The advantage of the technique is that it enables an observer to cover a very large area. In addition, since the observer does not enter the water it can be used with confidence in areas where sharks are abundant.

The disadvantage is that it is a subsample technique covering a very small proportion of total area. However, comparison of results obtained by this method with those obtained by towed observers using the detailed manta board technique of Kenchington and Morton (1976) indicates that the sub-

TABLE 10. Comparison of the distribution of density classes of abundance of *A. planci* on reefs included in spot check[a] and transect surveys[b]

Reef	Date	Technique Tow Spot check	Percentage distribution of records in each category of abundance			
			0 0	1–3 1	4–18 2–10	>18 >10
Bowden	7/72	Spot check	70	0	30	0
	11/73	Tow	31	29	33	7
	10/74	Tow	27	37	29	7
Prawn	7/72	Spot check	97	3	0	0
	11/73	Tow	40	26	26	8
	10/74	Tow	42	27	24	7
Shrimp	7/72	Spot check	57	24	12	7
	11/73	Tow	56	22	17	5
	10/74	Tow	93	7	0	0
Viper	7/72	Spot check	91	5	5	0
	11/73	Tow	100	0	0	0
	10/74	Tow	100	0	0	0
Faith	11/72	Spot check	100	0	0	0
	11/73	Tow	97	3	0	0
	10/74	Tow	100	0	0	0
Hope	11/72	Spot check	46	17	21	17
	11/73	Tow	81	8	9	2
	10/74	Tow	47	32	21	0
Charity	11/72	Spot check	100	0	0	0
	11/73	Tow	98	2	0	0
	10/74	Tow	88	11	1	0
Line	3/73	Spot check	87	3	3	7
	6/74	Tow	53	19	21	7
	11/74	Tow	86	7	4	3
Big Tideway	7/73	Spot check	73	3	18	6
	6/74	Tow	89	5	3	4
	11/74	Tow	92	3	4	1
Little Tideway	6/74	Tow	36	18	36	9
	11/74	Tow	46	50	4	0
	11/74	Spot check	50	31	19	0

a. Pearson and Garrett (1976).
b. Kenchington and Morton (1976).

sample is satisfactory. Table 10 presents a comparison of distribution of records into categories of abundance by the two techniques for a number of reefs which were surveyed by both techniques, including one reef upon which synoptic surveys were conducted.

SUMMARY

Subjective assessments by observers are a less than ideal basis for recording environmental information. However, in the absence of an effective photographic or electronic means of quantifying reef condition over wide areas it appears that surveys by teams of observers will continue to be necessary.

Selection of the technique most appropriate for a particular survey usually involves a compromise between area and detail of coverage required and the availability of time, personnel and facilities. The combination of a rapid initial survey method with detailed subsamples appears to be the most appropriate compromise for most purposes.

Observer performance is most consistent in census type surveys. There is considerable variation in the ability of observers to assess relative area coverage under laboratory conditions, but it is probable that scales of assessment and procedures for selection and training of observers will be developed which will considerably improve the comparative value of such assessments.

References

CHESHER, R. H. 1969. *Acanthaster planci: Impact on Pacific coral reefs.* Westinghouse Elec. Corp. Report to the U.S. Department Interior, Doc. No. PB187631 (155 p.).

ENDEAN, R. 1974. *Acanthaster planci* on the Great Barrier Reef. In: *Proc. Second Int. Coral Reef Symp.* Brisbane, Great Barrier Reef Committee, vol. 1, p. 563–76.

——; STABLUM, W. J. 1973. A study of some aspects of the Crown-of-Thorns starfish (*Acanthaster planci*) infestations of reefs of Australia's Great Barrier Reef. *Atoll. Res. Bull.,* vol. 167, p. 1–62.

KENCHINGTON, R. A.; MORTON, B. 1976. *Two surveys of the Crown-of-Thorns Starfish over a section of the Great Barrier Reef.* Canberra, Australian Government Publishing Service, (v + 186 p.).

LAXTON, J. H.; STABLUM, W. J. 1974. Sample design for quantitative estimation of sedentary organisms on coral reefs. *Biol. J. Linn. Soc.,* vol. 6, no. 1, p. 1–18.

LOYA, Y. 1972. Community structure and species diversity of hermatypic corals at Eilat, Red Sea. *Mar. Biol.,* vol. 13, p. 100–23.

ORMOND, R. F. G.; CAMPBELL, A. C. 1971. Observations on *Acanthaster planci* and other coral reef echinoderms in the Sudanese Red Sea. *Symp. zool. Soc. Lond.,* vol. 28, p. 433–54.

——.; CAMPBELL, A. C. 1974. Formation and breakdown of *Acanthaster planci* aggregations in the Red Sea. *Proc. Second Int. Coral Reef Symp.* Brisbane, Great Barrier Reef Committee, vol. 1, p. 595–620.

PEARSON, R. G.; ENDEAN, R. 1969. A preliminary study of the coral predator *Acanthaster planci* (L.) (Asteroidea) on the Great Barrier Reef. *Fisheries Notes,* Qd Dept. Harbours Marine (Brisbane), vol. 3, p. 27–55.

——.; GARRETT, R. N. 1976. *Acanthaster planci* on the Great Barrier Reef; General Surveys 1972–1975. *Biol. Conserv.,* vol. 9, p. 157–64.

WOODWORTH, R. S.; SCHLOSBERG, H. 1938. *Experimental Psychology.* (Revised and edited J. W. King and L. A. Riggs, 1971). New York, Holt. Rinehart and Winston.

14

Quantitative benthic ecology of Tuléar reefs

Michel Pichon[1]

INTRODUCTION: A TENTATIVE CLASSIFICATION OF THE MAJOR BIOTA

The various benthic coral reef communities in the vicinity of Tuléar are investigated simultaneously, from both a qualitative and, as far as possible, quantitative point of view. The following communities are included in the present studies:

Hard bottoms → Endobiotic	Epibiotic communities	1
	Limestone boring or destroying organisms	2
	Cryptobiotic communities	3
Soft bottoms	Endobiotic communities	4
	Epibiotic communities	5
Algal or Phanerogamic vegetation	Sessile epiphytic	6
	Mobile faunas { swimming between the 'fronds'	7
	creeping on the 'fronds'	7
Fishes	Permanent stock	8
	Temporary stock (tide migrating species)	9

(Fish communities are not strictly benthic, but most coral reef fishes have very strong trophic relations with coral reef invertebrates; consequently they are involved in the study.)

HISTORICAL BACKGROUND

All the methods which are now in use for benthic studies in Tuléar are derived

1. Station marine d'Endoume et Centre d'océanographie, Marseille, France. Present address: Department of Marine Biology, James Cook University of North Queensland, Townsville, 4811, Australia.

163

from the 'quadrat' method used in terrestrial plant sociology by the Zurich-Montpellier school. The methodology of Braun-Blanquet (1951) was first used in the marine biota by Molinier and Picard (1953) for an ecological study of Mediterranean rock bottoms. This methodology was then improved by Laborel and Vacelet (1958), when they started to investigate the dark cave communities in Marseilles. Later, Picard (1962, 1965) successfully adapted the same method to soft bottom ecology and used it for a study of soft bottom communities in the Mediterranean. All these techniques are a generalization of the original Braun-Blanquet method. After they were developed and tested in Marseilles, they were easily transposed at Tuléar, leading to a systematic use of a 'generalized pluridimensional method' in coral reef benthic ecology.

THE 'GENERALIZED PLURIDIMENSIONAL METHOD': THE MAIN COMMON PRINCIPLES OF THE ORIGINAL METHOD AND OF ITS DERIVATIVES

A detailed analysis of the original and typical 'quadrat' method is given by Scheer, Chapter 15. Reference will be made here to only some of the fundamental principles of the method, principles which remain basically unaltered through all the applications or derivatives of the primary 'quadrat' method.

Surface and volume
Whether hard bottoms or soft bottoms are considered, surface or volume can be used for the sample element or unit:

Surfaces are used in the study of *epibiotic* communities, for instance, on hard bottoms: 1, or on soft bottoms: 5.

Volumes are used for the study of *infaunal* (*endobiotic*) communities such as 2: limestone boring or destroying organisms, 3: cryptobiotic communities, 4: endobiotic communities in soft bottoms.

When regarding the dimensions of the sampling unit, the main reef biota listed above, can be arranged as follows:

Surface (two-dimensional sampling unit)	Hard bottoms, epibiotic communities . . . 1	
	Soft bottoms, epibiotic communities . . . 5	
	algal or phanerogamic vegetation (sessile epiphytic community) 6	
Volume (three-dimensional sampling unit)	Limestone boring or destroying organisms . 2	
	Cryptobiotic communities 3	
	Soft bottoms, endobiotic communities . . 4	
	algal or phanerogamic vegetation (mobile faunas) 7	
	Fishes (permanent stock) 8	
	Fishes (temporary stock) 9	

164

Homogeneous surface (or volume)

The concept of homogeneous surface or volume is developed to ensure that the sample is made in one and only one biological type of bottom: a 'quadrat' sample will be worth processing and reliable only when referring to only one community, sub-community, facies or aspect (sampling in the transition zones must be avoided). Consequently, for epibiotic communities (or their sub-divisions), the quadrat sample locations must be chosen amidst surfaces on which the composition of the faunas and floras appears to be homogeneous to the eye. When working on endobiotic communities (and especially on soft bottoms) the aspect of the substrata (of the sediment) will provide *a priori* a suitable basis: each zone in which the substrata (the sediment) shows a similar appearance is considered as a homogenous volume.

Minimum surface (or volume)

The importance of a 'quadrat' sample must be kept as low as possible, for greater convenience, but at the same time, it must provide the widest range of information on the structure of the community. Therefore a 'quadrat' sample must include most of the living species. The minimum size will depend on the dimensions of the community and on the distribution patterns and the density of the species and individuals within the community. The minimum surface or volume sampled is defined experimentally. The method used to determine the 'minimum volume' when working on soft bottoms is summarized below (for more details see Picard, 1965).

The infaunas are separately extracted from several samples of sediments of regularly increasing volumes ($V = 10 \, \text{dm}^3, 20 \, \text{dm}^3, 30 \, \text{dm}^3, \ldots$) and the number of species n) in each sample is calculated. A graph can be drawn: number of species as a function of the sampled volumes (Fig. 1); generally such a curve has an indeterminate shape. In each of these samples of regularly increasing volume, there is generally one, or a few, species represented by only one individual. (As a rule, these species subsequently prove to be of little ecological significance).

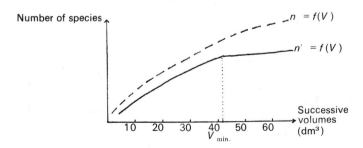

Figure 1
Determination of the minimum volume

Scale to evaluate abundance

| + | 1
<1/20 | 2
1/20–1/4 | 3
1/4–1/2 | 4
1/2–3/4 | 5
>3/4 |

Scale to evaluate Sociability:

| 1
isolated | 2 | 3 | 4 | 5
thick, dense |

Figure 2 *(continued)*

Sociability of colonial species, according to Laborel and Vacelet (1958)

a. Isolated colonies, covering 20 per cent of the area.
   Abundance 2: Sociability 1.
b. Colonies covering the same area, but forming small groups.
   Abundance 2: Sociability 2.
c. Only one large colony, more or less massive or compact, but still covering the same area.
   Abundance 2: Sociability ⊕

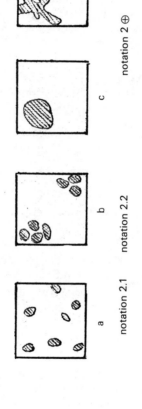

a   b   c   d

notation 2.1   notation 2.2   notation 2 ⊕

Figure 2
Evaluation of abundance and sociability.

167

If we do not take into account these species with one individual when summing up the number of species in each sample, we will obtain a new total $n' \leqslant n$. The graph $n' = f(V)$ will show a singular point, the absciss of which gives the value of the minimum volume V_m. (The second part of the curve, for $V > V_m$ is almost horizontal).

Coefficients and indexes

The generalized pluridimensional method (i.e. the original 'quadrat' method and its derivatives) basically relies on the calculation of *two* coefficients or indexes:

Surface biota. For epibiotic communities (and in fact primarily on hard bottoms) these coefficients are:

$$A = \text{Abundance}$$
$$S = \text{Sociability}$$

The value of these two coefficients is estimated according to the scales given in Figure 2 (including the example of colonial species). Secondary symbols may be used when necessary:

$<$ reduced vitality
E epiphytic
SE upper stratum
SS lower stratum

Volume biota. For endobiotic communities the two coefficients to be used for each species are:

A = Abundance = number of individuals

D = Dominance = $\dfrac{\text{number of individuals} \times 100}{\text{total nb of individuals of all the species present in the sample}}$

$= \dfrac{A \times 100}{I}$

Statistically, it is necessary to consider *ten* samples within each community (in fact within each homogeneous surface or volume), each sample being processed as explained above. The A and S data, or A and D data are then gathered in tables, each table referring to one homogeneous surface or volume. From such tables synthetic coefficients can be calculated for each species:

Mean Abundance $A_m = \Sigma A$

Mean Dominance $D_m = \dfrac{\Sigma A \times 100}{\Sigma I} = \Sigma D$

$$\text{Frequency} = \frac{\text{Number of samples in which the species is present}}{\text{Total number of samples*}}$$

* usually ten.

Other coefficients or indexes may be used for a comparison between two samples or between two communities, eg:

The Similarity index (Sorensen, 1948; Gamulin-Brida, 1962)

$$S_i = \frac{2w \times 100}{n_1 + n_2}$$

w = number of species common to the communities 1 and 2
n_1 = number of species in the community 1
n_2 = number of species in the community 2

The affinity index, as defined by Sanders (1960).

THE GENERALIZED PLURIDIMENSIONAL METHOD IN TULÉAR: PRACTICAL BASES OF FIELD WORK AND DATA PROCESSING

1. Epibiotic communities on hard bottoms

Sciaphilic communities: Sciaphilic communities occur chiefly in the dark caves and tunnels of the outer reef slope. The minimum quadrat size is dependent on the area covered by the community investigated, on the bottom topography, and may vary accordingly. The following quadrat sizes were used: 20×20 cm, 25×25, 30×30, 40×40, 50×50, 60×60, 80×80, and 100×100 cm.

Photophilic communities with scleractinian corals: The sample size is generally $1 \text{ m} \times 1 \text{ m}$, but in some cases a larger size may be necessary (up to 5×5 m).

Other photophilic communities. Blocks of the boulder tract, for instance.

The minimum quadrat size is 40×40 cm. In order to give a more accurate description of the populations of scattered animals, the first two values of the Abundance index (usually marked $+$ and 1) are subdivided according to the number of individuals in the sample as follows:

Σ_1: less than 5 individuals in the minimum quadrat (40×40 cm)
Σ_2: 5 to 10 individuals in the minimum quadrat (40×40 cm)
Σ_3: 10–20 individuals in the minimum quadrat (40×40 cm)
  1: more than 20 individuals in the minimum quadrat (and up to 1/20 of the area of the quadrat (40×40 cm).

2. Limestone boring or destroying organisms

Minimum volume: 1.5 dm^2

3. Cryptobiotic communities

Invertebrates living in the cavities of corals, calcareous Algae, massive formations of animal tubes. Minimum volume: 1 dm^3

4. Soft bottom endobiotic communities

Minimum volume: 50 dm^3. Sampling with a spade (intertidal), with a dredge or, better, with a hydropneumatic 'sucker'.

5. Soft bottom epibiotic communities

As a rule, endobiotic faunas and epibiotic faunas (or floras) do not represent two different communities, but only two aspects, corresponding to two different strata of one and the same community. The epifaunal stock generally consists of tall-sized animals, more or less scattered on the bottom. Practically the epifaunal stock does not deserve a special treatment, and although it could be considered as a surface problem it is more convenient to study it together with the rest of the same biota (endofaunal stock.) See: Soft bottom endobiotic communities above.

6. Sessile epiphytic community of an algal or phanerogamic vegetation

The work already done on hydroids epiphytic on sea grasses (Gravier, 1970) is only semi-quantitative. Hydroid colonies were not numbered with reference to a defined surface, but two indexes of presence were calculated:
  (a): percentage of presence of each species of Hydroid on the various sea grasses.
  (b): percentage of presence of the various species of Hydroid on each species of sea grass.

7. Mobile faunas of algal or phanerogamic vegetation

Faunas swimming between the 'ponds' or thalli or creeping on the 'ponds' or thalli.
    Faunas are sampled by 'mowing' with a small net, 20 or 30 cm in diameter; the mesh size is 0.65 mm (Fig. 3). The volume filtered (corresponding to the sampled volume) is 2 m^3.

8. Fishes: Permanent stock

Fish collecting is done by poisoning a defined area on the reef flat, at low tide. The sampled area is determined on the reef flat by encircling a given zone with a fishing net or with a light sheet iron. When the substratum is uneven, the latter can be fitted with a flexible skirt, taking the shape of the bottom irregu-

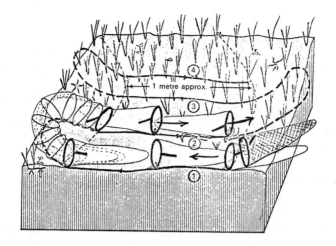

Figure 3
Schematic diagram of the 'moving' technique (after Ledoyer, 1969).

larities. The area sampled ranges from 4 to 100 m². This method is inadequate when coral growth is dense.

9. Fishes: Temporary stock

From a methodological standpoint, the following are included:
    Fishes on the reef slopes (outer slope, inner slope) and of the lagoon
    Fishes swimming on the reef flat at high tide (when the tide range is important)
    Fast swimmers of the permanent stock, i.e. fishes that escape when setting the fishing net or the sheet iron.
    To date the quantitative methodology is unsatisfactory. The two methods used at Tuléar are as follows:

Visual census: Visual census primarily give qualitative results, but an experienced ichthyologist, with the use of scuba may obtain a fairly reliable idea of the relative abundance of the various species. Even for preliminary surveys, visual census are improved by the use of two indexes which give an estimate of the relative abundance of fishes as follows (but this remains partly somewhat subjective):

Abundance (number of sightings of the species during one dive)	Sociability (Mean number of individuals for each sighting of the species)
1 1	1 1
2 2	2 2
3 .... ≤ 4	3 .... ≤ 5

$$4 \ldots \leqslant 8 \qquad\qquad 4 \ldots \leqslant 10$$
$$5 \ldots \leqslant 16 \qquad\qquad 5 \ldots\ldots \text{School} \leqslant 100$$
$$+ \ldots > 16 \qquad\qquad + \ldots\ldots \text{School} > 100$$

(The standard duration of one dive is one hour or 30 minutes according to the depth)

Dynamiting. The use of explosives for fish collecting in open water (but close to the reef) does not refer to a well-defined volume since the sample volume varies for each species, according to its shock wave resistance. Furthermore, species living in holes or crevices of the substratum (or in the sediment, if any) will not be retrieved as a rule.

QUANTITATIVE STUDIES OF REEF FISH FEEDING BEHAVIOUR

Although reef fishes were not subject to quantitative ecology, in Tuléar, their feeding behaviour was investigated from a quantitative standpoint. The following indexes were calculated for each species of fish and for each prey-species:

V = vacuity coefficient: percentage of empty stomach for the total number N of stomachs examined.

f = frequency index: ratio between the number n of stomachs containing a given prey, and the total number of stomachs:

$$f = \frac{n}{N}$$

C_n = ratio between the number of individuals of a given species of prey and the total number N_p of prey individuals:

$$C_n = \frac{\text{No. of indiv. of a prey} \times 100}{N_p}$$

C_p = ratio between the weight of all the individuals of a given species of prey and the total weight P_p of all the categories of preys:

$$C_p = \frac{\text{Weight of all the indiv. of a prey} \times 100}{P_p}$$

Q = feeding coefficient = $C_n \times C_p$

BIOMASS STUDIES

It is to be noticed that biomass studies (Reys and Reys, 1966) were carried on in Tuléar on soft bottoms of terrigeneous origin (littoral zone, but not reef zone) which were previously investigated by Mireille Pichon (1967) who analysed the structure of these communities.

172

The methodology employed for such biomass studies can readily be applied to reef communities without making any change. This method is basically the same as that commonly used by Reys (1964, 1968) in the Mediterranean. (A comprehensive review of the technology of biomass studies on a world-wide basis is given by Reys and Salvat (1971) and by Holme and McIntyre (1971).)

References and selected bibliography

BRAUN-BLANQUET, J. 1964. *Pflanzensoziologie: grundzüge der Vegetationkunde, 3. Auf.* Wien and New York, Springer Verlag (855 p.).

CLAUSADE, M. 1970. Importance et variations du peuplement mobile des cavités au sein des formations épirécifales: modalités d'échantillonnage en vue de son évaluation. *Rec. Trav. Stn mar. Endoume.* Suppl. Hors série 10, p. 107–9.

——. 1971. Peuplement annélidien des levées détritiques et de leurs biotopes de substitution dans la région du Tuléar (Madagascar). *Téthys.*, suppl. I, p. 127–35.

GAMULIN-BRIDA, H. 1962. Biocoenoses du littoral plus profond (circalittoral) dans les canaux de l'Adriatique moyenne. *Acta Adriat.*, vol. 9, no. 1, p. 1–196.

GRAVIER, N. 1970. Etude des Hydraires épiphytes des Phanérogames marines de la région de Tuléar (S. W. de Madagascar) *Rev. Trav. Stn mar. Endoume.* Suppl. Hors série 10, p. 111–62.

GUERIN-ANCEY, D. 1970. Etude des intrusions terrigènes fluviatiles dans les complexes récifaux: délimitation dynamique des peuplements des vases et des sables vaseux du chenal post récifal de Tuléar (S. W. de Madagascar) *Rec. Trav. Stn mar. Endoume.* Suppl. Hors séries 10, p. 1–46.

HOLME, N. A.; McINTYRE, A. D. (eds). 1971. *Methods for the study of marine benthos.* Oxford, Blackwell Scientific Publications. (IBP Handbook no. 16) (334 p.).

LABOREL, J.; VACELET, J. 1958. Etude des peuplements d'une grotte sous marine du golfe de Marseille. *Bull. Inst. Océanogr.* Monaco no. 1120.

LEDOYER, M. 1962. Etude de la faune vagile des herbiers superficiels de Zosteracées et de quelques biotopes d'Algues littorales. *Rec. Trav. Stn mar. Endoume*, vol. 25, no. 39, p. 117–235.

——. 1967. Amphipodes gammariens des herbiers de Phanérogames marines de la région de Tuléar (République malgache) Etude systématique et écologique. *Rec. Trav. Stn mar. Endoume.* Suppl. Hors série 7, p. 7–56.

——. 1969a. Les Caridea de la frondaison des herbiers de Phanérogrames marines de la région de Tuléar. Etude systématique et écologique. *Rec. Trav. Stn mar. Endoume.* Suppl. Hors série 8, p. 63–126.

——. 1969b. La faune vagile des sables fins des hauts niveaux (S.F.H.N.), Signification bionomique de ce biotope vue sous l'angle de la faune vagile. *Téthys*, vol. 1, no. 2, p. 275–80.

MOLINIER, R.; PICARD, J. 1953. Recherches analytiques sur less peuplements littoraux mediterranéens se développant sur substrat solides. *Rec. Trav. Stn mar. Endoume*, vol. 9, no. 4.

PICARD, J. 1962. Méthode d'étude qualitative des biocoenoses des substrats meubles. *Rec. Trav. Stn mar. Endoume*, vol. 39, no. 25, p. 239–43.

——. 1965. Recherches qualitatives sur les biocoenoses marines des substrats meubles dragables de la région marseillaise. *Rec. Trav. Stn mar. Endoume*, vol. 52, no. 36, p. 1–160.

PICHON, MICHEL. 1964. Contribution à l'étude de la répartition des Madréporaires sur le récif de Tuléar (Madagascar). *Rec. Trav. Stn mar. Endoume*, Suppl. Hors série 2, p. 79–203.

PICHON, MIREILLE. 1967. Contribution à l'étude des peuplements de la zone intertidale sur sables fins et sables vaseux non fixés dans la région de Tuléar. *Rec. Trav. Stn mar. Endoume*, Suppl. Hors série 7, p. 57–100.

PLANTE, R. 1964. Contribution à l'étude des peuplements de hauts niveaux sur substrats solides non récifaux dans la région de Tuléar (Madagascar). *Rec. Trav. Stn mar. Endoume*, Suppl. Hors série 2, p. 205–315.

REYS, J. P. 1964. Les prélèvements quantitatifs du benthos de substrat meuble. *La Terre et la Vie*, p. 94–105.

——. 1968. Quelques données quantitatives sur les biocoenoses benthiques du Golfe de Marseille. *Rapp. P.-V. Réun. CIESMM*, vol. 19, no. 2.

——; REYS, S. 1966. Répartition quantitative du benthos de la région de Tuléar. *Rec. Trav. Stn mar. Endoume*, Suppl. Hors série 5, p. 71–86.

——; SALVAT, B. 1971. L'échantillonnage de la macrofaune des sédiments meubles marins. In: *Echantillonnage en milieu aquatique*. Paris, Masson.

SANDERS, H. L. 1960. Benthic studies in Buzzards Bay. III The structure of the soft bottom community. *Limnol. Oceanogr.*, vol. 5, no. 2, p. 138–53.

SØRENSEN, T. 1948. A method of establishing groups of equivalent amplitude in plant sociology based on the similarity of species content and its application to analysis of the vegetation on Danish commons. *K. daroska vid. Selsk. Bot. Skr.*, vol. 5, p. 1–34.

THOMASSIN, B. 1969. Peuplement de deux biotopes de sables coralliens sur le Grand Récif de Tuléar, Sud Ouest de Madagascar. *Rec. Trav. Stn mar. Endoume*, Suppl. Hors série 9, p. 59–133.

VASSEUR, P. 1964. Contribution à l'étude bionomique des peuplements sciaphiles infralittoraux de substrat dur dans les récifs de Tuléar (Madagascar). *Rec. Trav. Stn mar. Endoume*, Suppl. Hors série 2, p. 1–77.

VIVIEN, M. 1973a. Ecology of the fishes of the inner coral reef flat in Tuléar (Madagascar). *J. mar. Biol. Assoc. India*, vol. 15, p. 20–45.

——. 1973b. Contribution à la connaissance de l'éthologie alimentaire de l'ichtyofaune du platier interne des récifs coralliens de Tuléar (Madagascar). *Téthys*, suppl. vol. 5, p. 221–308.

15

Application of phytosociologic methods

G. Scheer[1]

INTRODUCTION

Many authors (listed by Stoddart, 1969) have used quadrats along transects for studying coral reefs. The present report does not consider those works, but deals with a quadrat method derived from phytosociology.

Phytosociology or plant sociology (the expression was established shortly before the turn of this century) developed from the classic plant geography of the last century and from its methods of description of vegetation. The expression plant sociology was criticized from several sides because the second part of the word could give rise to erroneous comparisons with sociology as a doctrine of the human society. Therefore the expression phytocoenology was suggested. In the angloamerican literature the expression plant ecology is sometimes used for plant sociology.

At a congress of botanists at Paris in 1954 plant sociology was defined as follows: 'La phytosociologie est l'étude des communautés végétales du point de vue floristique, écologique, dynamique, chorologique et historique'. After Braun-Blanquet (1964) the main tasks of plant sociology are:

1. Investigation of the composition of plant communities (structural phytosociology).
2. Investigation of the environmental factors conditioning the communities (synecology).
3. Investigation of the development of plant communities (syngenetics and history of communities).
4. Investigation of the distribution of plant communities (synchorology).
5. Elaboration of a distinct division and classification of plant communities (taxonomical plant sociology).

All these problems arise in the course of investigations of coral reefs. Therefore it is quite natural to accept the methods of plant sociology and to profit by its experiences gained over decades.

1. Hessisches Landesmuseum, Zoologische Abteilung, Friedensplatz 1, D6100 Darmstadt, Federal Republic of Germany.

Different authors have referred to the use of phytosociological methods for investigations in marine biology: Petersen (1913, 1915), Prenant (1927), Remane (1940), Molinier and Picard (1953), Laborel and Vacelet (1958), Pérès and Picard (1958), Molinier (1960) and Laborel (1960). Vasseur (1964) applied the method to the coral reefs at Tuléar, Madagascar, and Rosen (1971) also mentioned this method.

During the 2nd Xarifa Expedition 1957/58 (leader Dr Hans Hass) the author applied this method to the investigation of coral reefs in the Maldives (Scheer, 1960, 1967, 1972, 1974). The present paper does not discuss the advantages and disadvantages of the method but deals with its practical application.

INVESTIGATION OF CORAL REEFS

Some fundamentals

No organism lives in isolation in the field, and corals are associated with individuals of the same or another species and with other organisms of fauna and flora. Such a total community was called by Möbius (1877) biocoenosis.

Two other expressions must be made clear here. The composition of a coral community depends on the location. The term location or habitat means the qualities of a certain section of a reef, i.e. the totality of exogenous factors influencing the community. In contrast, locality or station means a geographically circumscribed place. A coral community can be found at many localities, but it flourishes only at a quite distinct, ecologically characterized location.

Coral communities are distinguished by regularly recurring alliances of species, evolving by selection from the competitors for settlement. Only such species can settle as are able to endure the ecological factors of the location and can compete with other species. A coral community reflects to some extent its location, although a special location will not always house the same coral community. A coral community cannot be considered as an organic whole or be compared with an organism. It is rather a combination of several coral individuals conditioned by competition.

The following is a brief description of the working method according to Braun-Blanquet (1964) with reference to Knapp (1971) and Fukarek (1964).

Growth records

Before starting the work it is essential to obtain a general view of the area of investigation by swimming over it and diving with or without scuba. This will indicate differences in coral communities in different parts of the reef (reef flat, reef margin, reef edge, reef front, reef slope). Attention can be directed to typical areas for special study.

The growth records (in phytosociology vegetation records), stand records or shortly stands are the fundamentals of coral-sociological research. A growth record means the analysis of the composition of species together with notes concerning easily noticeable features on limited areas or sample plots.

176

Knowledge of species

To gain a general view of the composition of a reef knowledge of species is indispensable, although it is practically impossible during an expedition to determine the names of all the corals on the spot, since time and specialized book references are insufficient. In practice it is possible to identify the genera of the corals, and to provide them with numbers or other signs. This technique has been mentioned by Gardiner (1903, p. 330) and more recently by Odum and Odum (1957) and by Davies and Stoddart (Stoddart 1966, p. 43).

Choice of sample plot

The right choice of a sample plot is of great importance because all conclusions depend on the result of the record made there. The sample plot has to fulfil three conditions: It must be large enough to ensure that it contains nearly all species ranging regularly in the coral community, be homogeneous and not dominated in different parts by different species and reflect the uniform conditions of the location, for example, uniform water movement, inclination, lighting conditions and so on.

Size of sample plot

The bigger the coralla and the richer the reef is in species the larger the sample plot has to be. It must be large enough to contain the greater part, that is one half to about two thirds of the coral species of the reef area under examination. The necessary size may be found by counting the number of species first on a small plot, for example 0.1 m^2. Then the area is progressively enlarged, for instance to 0.25 m^2, 0.5 m^2, 1 m^2, then to 2, 4, 10, 25, 50, 72 and 100 m^2. The respective newly occurring species are noted. If the number of coral species found in the different samples are recorded graphically the result is the species-number–area curve, which first increases rapidly then always more slowly.

Figure 1a shows the species–area curve for the outer part of the reef flat on the inner reef off the island of Weligandu in the Rasdu Atoll of the Maldives. Figure 1b indicates the curve for the reef flat south of Heron Island, Great Barrier Reef. This curve was obtained in a somewhat different way. Because the major part of the reef flat was covered with sand, dead corals, calcareous algae and soft corals, patches with living corals were chosen and framed with rectangles. The size of the first rectangle was measured and the coral species found there counted. This made the first point of the species–area curve. The size of the second rectangle was added as well as the number of the newly supervening species. From that the second point of the curve resulted. Altogether the species in 15 rectangles of an average size of 4 m^2 were counted.

The species–area curves first increase rapidly then more slowly. The minimum size of the sample plot is obtained where the curve begins to level off, in Figure 1a about 22 m^2, in Figure 1b about 37 m^2. An approximate value of

N

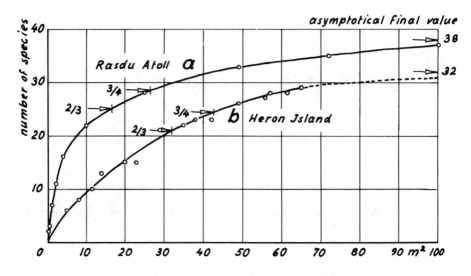

Figure 1
Species-number-area curves for the evaluation of the size of sample plots:
(a) reef flat of the inner reef off the island of Weligandu, Rasdu Atoll,
    Maldives,
(b) reef flat south of Heron Island, Great Barrier Reef.

the size is found by taking $\frac{2}{3}$ to $\frac{3}{4}$ of the asymptotically reached final value of the species number.

Form of the sample plot

Generally a quadrat is chosen, but in itself the form of the sample plot is insignificant. At places in which the chosen quadrats are so large, that one can already observe a zonation of the corals, for example with depth or distance from the shore, it is more convenient to choose a rectangle, whose longer sides are parallel to the shore or to the reef edge. Loya and Slobodkin (1971) and Loya (1972) are even going so far as to use a transect and record the corals lying under this line.

Analysis of species composition

To mark the quadrat or area of otherwise formed sample plot, a nylon rope can be used and the edges marked with short wooden sticks, fastened with string loops to corals.

The first estimate to be made is of the area (as a percentage of the bottom) covered with living corals, sand, dead corals, coral debris etc. For the determination of the extent, the vertical projections of the coralla on the bottom are used. Next the predominant and frequent species are registered on a plastic sheet, then the sample plot is searched for less frequent and rare species.

This list of species however is not sufficient, it has to be completed by information about the quantity.

Quantity of coral species

Quantity has two components: the number of individuals of a species (abundance) and the cover or extent of this species (dominance). Braun-Blanquet (1964) has developed a simple but sufficiently correct method, which combines abundance and dominance. According to this, the following scale with seven steps of the extent of cover can be used:

r   a few isolated specimens, cover negligible,
+   sparsely present, cover low,
1   more frequently present, though covering less than 5 per cent of the sample plot, or only isolated with the same cover,
2   abundant, or covering 5–25 per cent of sample plot,
3   any number of specimens, covering 25–50 per cent of sample plot;
4   any number, covering 50–75 per cent,
5   any number, covering 75–100 per cent.

For the abundance–dominance combination the term 'Artmächtigkeit' was introduced by Schwickerath (1940). The low values r, $+$, 1 and 2 depend on abundance, the higher more on the degree of cover or spread.

Examination of cover shares

It is advantageous to determine, after having finished a growth record, the sum of the percentage extent of all the species and to compare it with the area occupied by all the living corals. Using the above mentioned scale it is sufficient to apply the following values to the calculation of the sum: $+ = 0.25$ per cent, $1 = 2.5$ per cent, $3 = 37.5$ per cent, $4 = 62.5$ per cent, $5 = 87.5$ per cent; r is not considered.

Stratification

Certain coral communities are composed of species of about the same size living side by side in one stratum. In other communities corals of quite different size are growing one upon the other in clearly distinguishable strata. Then the covering degree of the whole sample plot can be more than 100 percent. On stands with stratified coral communities the different strata can be considered separately.

Sociability or gregariousness

Some coral species settle gregariously over large areas (such as *Acropora* sp.), others occur only as single individuals (such as *Fungia* sp.) or single coralla.

179

For this different size of gregariousness, Braun-Blanquet has introduced in phytosociology a scale of five steps: (1) singly growing; (2) growing in groups or horsts; (3) growing in troops (small patches or cushions); (4) growing in small colonies or forming extensive patches or carpets; (5) growing in large herds.

This scale cannot be accepted directly for a coral sociology. How should for example a *Porites* block with a diameter of 3 m, occurring as the only one in the sample plot, be classified? It is suggested that the sociability should be estimated with the following modified scale which takes the size of the coralla into consideration.

1. Small isolated coralla, or isolated solitary corals;
2. Small coralla or solitary corals growing in small groups or forming patches of the size of a hand (about 10×20 cm or circles with 16 cm diameter);
3. Small coralla growing in troops or forming small hedges or patches of 0.2–0.4 m^2 (up to 65×65 cm or 70 cm diameter), or bigger coralla of this size;
4. Coralla of 0.7–2 m diameter, or hedges and patches of 0.4–4 m^2;
5. Coralla larger than 2 m diameter, or hedges and patches bigger than 4 m^2.

The value for the sociability is given after the value for the quantity, separated by a full stop.

A different proposal for abundance-dominance and sociability has been made by Vasseur (1964, p. 20).

Vitality

Different species of corals may show different vitality at different locations. A weak growth or reduced vitality can be indicated by an exponential zero behind the sociability figure (for example $+.1^0$). A luxuriant growth is marked as follows: $\bullet$ (for example $3.3^\bullet$).

Ecological data concerning the growth record

The following data are necessary:
(a) date,
(b) place and locality of sample plot on the reef,
(c) depth of sample plot under sea level,
(d) direction of slope or exposition and slant of sample plot,
(e) shape and size of sample plot in m^2,
(f) percentage of area covered by live corals,
(g) data concerning substratum not covered by live corals,
(h) movement of water, swell, surf,
(i) currents.

The following data are desirable:
(k) clearness of water and sedimentation,

  (l) temperature of water at sample plot,
(m) salinity of water,
 (n) light conditions under water at sample plot.

Graphic representation of the distribution of species in a sample plot

Normally growth records can be drawn up in tables. In addition a graph, in form of a plan view, can be of great help. It shows the coral distribution in the sample plot (see for example Manton and Stephenson, 1935; or Scheer, 1960, 1971).

Evaluation of growth records

In order to be able to make statements about a coral reef several growth records are required from the area of investigation. All the coral species found are listed in a table one beneath the other, along with their occurrence in stands, absolutely and as a percentage. Then the coral species are listed in a second table in order of their frequency, followed by their cover/sociability values. When frequencies are equal, priority is given to the species with the greater cover.

The table shall (a) convey a clear conception of the essential characters of the coral community in question, (b) enable small accidental deviations to be noted in the species composition of the stands as well as showing an average, (c) indicate the peculiarity (characteristic) of the coral community concerned, (d) show which are separated from other communities and (e) which are joined to them.

The arrangement of such a table is illustrated by an example. In the east of Rasdu Atoll in the Maldives (Indian Ocean) the small uninhabited island of Weligandu is situated on the ring-shaped reef of the atoll (Fig. 2). The task was to investigate the coral community of the outer reef. Four stands were chosen on the outer part of the reef flat east of the island, and six stands on the reef flat south-east of the island. By observation while swimming over the reef it was noted that coral settlement was different in the northern and southern part of the reef flat. The evaluation of the growth records resulted in the following table which includes some ecological data.

Presence and constancy

Table 1 indicates that there are species which occur regularly and others which occur only in a small part of the stands or merely in one stand. This different occurrence is called presence. If the areas of the sample plots are equally large, the term constancy is used. Presence and constancy respectively are characteristic qualities of coral communities.

To clarify presentation only five presence classes are adopted: class I has a presence constancy of 1–20 per cent (seldom present), class II 21–40 per cent (not often present), class III 41–60 per cent (often present), class IV 61–80 per cent (mostly present), class V 81–100 per cent (constantly present).

181

TABLE 1. Growth records of the outer reef flat off the island of Weligandu, Rasdu Atoll, Maldives

No. of sample plot	1	2	3	4	5	6	7	8	9	10	Frequency percentage	Constancy class
Date	12.3.1958				18.3	17.3.1958			18.3			
Depth in m	1–2				1	1–3	1–2	1–2	1	1		
Incline	5–10°				0°	25°	10°	10°	0°	0°		
Size in m	5 × 5											
Coral covering in percentage	40	50	40	50	40	80	80	100	70	70		
Dead corals in percentage	40	40	40	40	40	20	20	0	30	30		
Coral fragments in percentage	20	10	20	10	20	0	0	0	0	0		
Water movement	Slight surf							quiet				
Current				slight current to the south								
Coral species	cover . sociability											
Pocillopora eydouxi	2.3	2.3	2.2	2.3	1.3	1.3	2.3	2.3	1.3	1.3	100	V
Acropora irregularis	+.3	+.2	+.3	+.2	2.4	1.4		1.4	3.4	3.4	90	
Acropora palifera	1.2	1.2	1.2	1.3		2.3	3.4	4.5		1.1	80	IV
Acropora humilis	1.2	2.3	2.3	1.3	1.3	2.3			1.3	1.3		
Galaxea fascicularis	+.2	+.2	+.2	+.2	r.1				r.1	+.1		
Porites (Synarea) convexa	r.2	r.2	+.2	+.2		+.3	1.3	+.2			70	
Gardineroseris ponderosa[a]	+.2	+.2	+.2	+.2		+.2	+.2	+.2				
Fungia fungites	+.1	+.2	+.1	+.2		+.2	+.2	+.2				
Acropora hyacinthus	1.2	1.2	1.2	1.2	1.3				1.3		60	III
Goniastrea retiformis	+.2	+.2	+.2	+.2		r.2		r.1				
Porites solida	2.4	2.4	2.3	2.4		3.5					50	

TABLE 1 (continued)

							II (40)	II (30)	I (20)	I (10)
Acropora formosa	1.2	1.2	1.2	1.2	1.3	1.3	2.3	2.3	2.4	2.3
Pocillopora molokensis	+.2	+.2	+.2	+.2	1.3	1.3	1.3	1.3	1.2	1.2
Leptoria phrygia	+.3	+.3	+.3	+.3	r.1	r.1		1.4		
Lobophyllia corymbosa	+.3	+.3	+.1	+.1	1.3					
Acropora abrotanoides	+.2	+.2								
Pavona varians						+.2				
Acropora surculosa	1.4	1.4	1.3	1.3	2.3	2.4	+.3	1.3		
Porites murrayensis	1.3	1.3	1.3	1.3						
Porites lutea	+.3	+.2	+.3	1.3						
Acropora hemprichi	+.2	+.2	+.2	+.3						
Favites abdita	+.1	+.1	+.1	1.2						
Favia pallida	r.1	r.1	+.1	+.1						
Montipora sinensis	r.1	r.1	r.1	+.1						
Platygyra lamellina	r.1	r.1	r.1	r.1						
Echinopora lamellosa	r.1	+.2		r.1						
Porites lichen	+.1	+.1		+.2						
Hydnophora microconos				+.1						
Favia stelligera	r.1	r.1	+.1	+.1						
Favites melicerum	r.1		+.1							
Goniastrea pectinata	r.1		r.1	r.1						
Acropora corymbosa	+.1		+.2	+.2						
Fungia scutaria	r.1									
Astreopora listeri		r.1	r.1							
Pavona explanulata		r.1	r.1							
Psammocora togianensis					+.2					
Porites andrewsi							+.2			
Goniopora planulata					r.1					
Leptastrea transversa		r.1	r.1							
Total 39 coral species										
Number of species in the different stands	29	29	30	28	9	15	9	11	7	7

a. New generic name (see Scheer and Pillai, 1974).

183

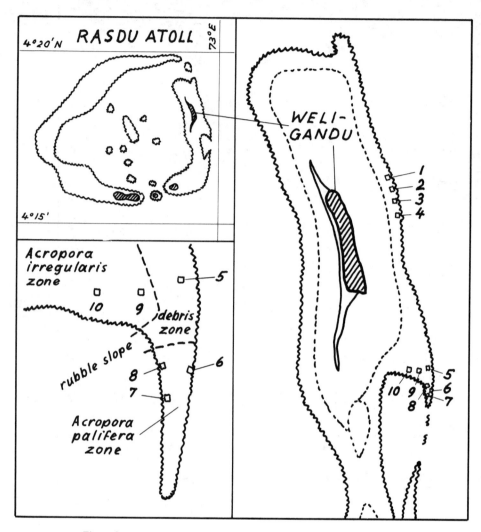

Figure 2
Rasdu Atoll, Maldives, with the reefs around the island of Weligandu and
the position of the stands at the outer reef flat.

When the species numbers of the different constancy classes from Table 1
are drawn graphically Figure 3 results. This diagram shows a very inhomo-
geneous coral growth; class V almost disappears and the lower classes pre-
ponderate.

Number of species

A further and important diagnostic feature of a coral community is the number
of species. Well-developed stands of a coral community, in general, do not

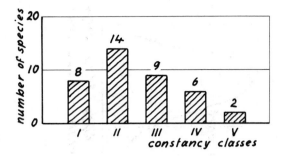

Figure 3
Frequency diagram of the outer reef off Weligandu, all stands together.

differ very much in their species numbers. If, however, great differences occur, this may indicate more than one community.

In Figure 4 the number of stands, resulting from Table 1, is plotted against the species number. This variation curve of the species numbers shows two maxima, lying far apart, and proves that two different coral communities exist at the investigated outer reef. The species *Pocillopora eydouxi,* found in all 10 stands, combines the two communities.

Arranging of a table with growth records of several coral communities

The subjective inspection of the outer reef-flat, made by swimming over it, indicated that coral growth was not uniform. This was confirmed objectively by the curve of Figure 4. It necessitates rewriting Table 1. In this version the coral species of stands 1 to 4 are arranged according to their constancy and coefficients as shown in Table 2. The species of the stands 5 to 10, occurring in more than one stand and not occurring in stands 1 to 4, are within the frame at the top of the right part of Table 2.

When the frequency diagrams for the northern part of the outer reef-flat (stands 1–4) and the southern part (5–10) are drawn separately, Figure 5 results. Table 2 shows at first sight the coral community of stands 1–4 being completely uniform. The same is also presented by Figure 5a with high constancy class V.

Species which occur only here are *Porites murrayensis, Porites lutea, Acropora hemprichi, Favites abdita, Favia pallida, Montipora sinensis,* as well as *Porites lichen, Hydnophora microconos, Favia stelligera* and *Acropora corymbosa* too. Species with a cover of "*r*" are omitted.

The coral community of the southern part, stands 5–10, is not uniform, as Table 2 and Figure 5b indicate.

The right hand part of Table 2 can be rewritten with a change in the order of the stands and arrangement of the species according to their constancy, as shown in Table 3.

In spite of the inhomogeneity it is not possible to separate different coral

185

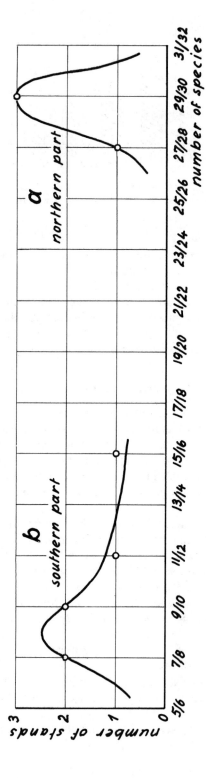

Figure 4
Variation curve of the species numbers of the stands at the outer reef off
Weligandu:
(a) northern part,
(b) southern part.

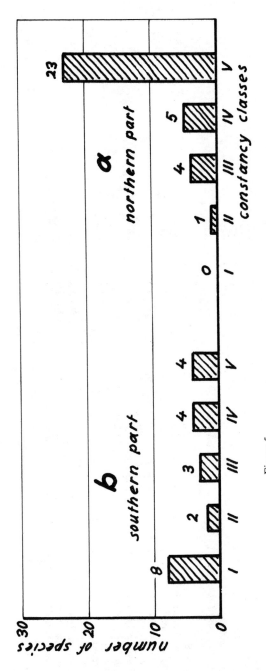

Figure 5
Frequency diagram of the outer reef off Weligandu:
(a) northern part,
(b) southern part.

TABLE 2. Growth records of the outer reef flat, rearranged Table 1

No. of sample plot	1	2	3	4	5	6	7	8	9	10
Coral species					cover . sociability					
Acropora formosa						1.3	2.3	2.3	2.4	2.3
Pocillopora molokensis						1.3	1.3	1.3	1.2	1.2
Acropora surculosa					2.3	2.4	+.3	1.3		
Psammocora togianensis					+.2					
Porites andrewsi							+.2			
Goniopora planulata					r.1					
Porites solida	2.4	2.4	2.3	2.4		3.5				
Pocillopora eydouxi	2.3	2.3	2.2	2.3		1.3	2.3	2.3	1.3	1.3
Acropora humilis	1.2	2.3	2.3	1.3	1.3	2.3			1.3	1.3
Porites murrayensis	1.4	1.4	1.3	1.3	1.3					
Porites lutea	1.3	1.3	1.3	1.3						
Acropora palifera	1.2	1.2	1.2	1.3						
Acropora hyacinthus	1.2	1.2	1.2	1.2	1.3	2.3	3.4	4.5		1.1
Leptoria phrygia	1.2	1.2	1.2	1.2					1.3	
Acropora hemprichi	+.3	+.2	+.3	1.3		r.1				
Favites abdita	+.2	+.2	+.2	1.2						
Acropora irregularis	+.3	+.2	+.3	+.2	2.4	1.4		1.4	3.4	3.4
Acropora abrotanoides	+.3	+.3	+.3	+.3	1.3					
Galaxea fascicularis	+.2	+.2	+.2	+.2	r.1	r.1			r.1	r.1
Goniastrea retiformis	+.2	+.2	+.2	+.2		r.1		r.1	r.1	
Lobophyllia corymbosa	+.2	+.2	+.2	+.2				1.4		

TABLE 2 (continued)

Gardineroseris ponderosa	+.2	+.2	+.1	+.2		+.2		+.2	+.2	+.2
Fungia fungites	+.1	+.2	+.1	+.2		+.2		+.2	+.2	+.2
Pavona varians	+.2	+.2	+.1	+.1		+.2				
Favia pallida	+.1	+.1	+.1	+.1				+.2		
Porites (Synarea) convexa	r.2	r.2	-+.2	+.2		+.3			1.3	+.2
Montipora sinensis	r.1	r.1	+.1	+.1						
Platygyra lamellina	r.1	r.1	r.1	r.1						
Echinopora lamellosa	r.1	r.1	r.1	r.1						
Porites lichen	+.1	+.2	+.1	+.2						
Hydnophora microconos		+.1	+.1	+.1						
Favia stelligera	r.1		+.1	+.1						
Favites melicerum	r.1	r.1	r.1	r.1						
Goniastrea pectinata	r.1		r.1	r.1						
Acropora corymbosa	+.1			+.2						
Fungia scutaria	r.1	r.1								
Astreopora listeri		r.1	r.1							
Pavona explanulata		r.1	r.1							
Lepetastrea transversa			r.1							
Total 39 coral species										
Number of species in the different stands	29	29	30	28	9	15	9	11	7	7

189

TABLE 3. Growth records of the southern part of the outer reef flat, right hand part of Table 2 rearranged

No. of sample plot	10	9	5	6	8	7	Frequency percentage	Constant class
Coral species	cover . sociability							
Pocillopora eydouxi	1.3	1.3	1.3	1.3	2.3	2.3	100	V
Acropora irregularis	3.4	3.4	2.4	1.4	1.4		83.3	
Acropora formosa	2.3	2.4	.	1.3	2.3	2.3		
Pocillopora molokensis	1.2	1.2		1.3	1.3	1.3		
Acropora palifera	1.1		2.3	2.3	4.5	3.4	66.7	IV
Acropora surculosa			1.3	2.4	1.3	+.2		
Acropora humilis	1.3	1.3		2.3				
Galaxea fascicularis	r.1	r.1	r.1	r.1				
Porites (Synarea) convexa				+.3	+.2	1.3	50	III
Gardineroseris ponderosa				+.2	+.2	+.2		
Fungia fungites				+.2	+.2	+.2		
Acropora hyacinthus		1.3	1.3				33.3	II
Goniastrea retiformis				r.1	r.1			
Porites solida				3.5			16.7	I
Lobophyllia corymbosa			1.3		1.4			
Acropora abrotanoides			+.2					
Psammocora togianensis								
Porites andrewsi						+.2		
Pavona varians			r.1	+.2				
Goniopora planulata								
Leptoria phrygia				r.1				
Total 21 coral species								
Number of species in the different stands	7	7	9	15	11	9		

communities, but zones or subcommunities, characterized by dominant species, can be distinguished. In the stands 9 and 10 it is *Acropora irregularis,* in the stands 7 and 8 *Acropora palifera.* Stand 6 is marked by *Porites solida.*

Comparison of the table with the reality

By swimming from north to south over the reef-flat of the outer reef it is noticeable, that the number of species, although still uniform in the stands 1–4, decreases markedly from an average of 29 species to 9 in stand 5. The amount of dead corals and coral debris, caused by the often strong surf, remains about the same, but increases south of stand 5 (debris zone) and culminates in a rubble slope between stands 9/10 and 7/8 (see Fig. 2).

West of the debris zone, marked by a distinct boundary, the bottom is far more extensively covered with corals (stands 9 and 10), in which large patches of the elkhorn-shaped *Acropora irregularis* are conspicuous, giving its name to the zone in Figure 2. South of the debris zone, separated by a sharp boundary, the reef terminates in a spur. The bottom is almost completely covered with corals (stands 7 and 8). This zone was named in Figure 2 after the dominant species, the very bulky and robust *Acropora palifera.*

Stand 6 which lies on the outer side of the spur, on the slope of the outer reef, is inclined and has a somewhat higher species number (15) than stands 7 and 8, as a result of a better supply of oxygen and nutriment. Stand 6 is distinguished from the other stands of the zone by great stocks and heads of the dominant coral *Porites solida* and by round compact tables of *Acropora humilis.*

Interlacing of the stands

In Figure 6 the interlacing of the stands with one another and the supposed, but hypothetical direction of colonization of the different species is drawn graphically. From the north (1–4) *Acropora humilis, A. abrotanoides* and *A. hyacinthus* advanced as far as stand 5. *Acropora hyacinthus* reached in addition stand 9, *Acropora humilis* 9, 10 and 6, but not 7 and 8. *Lobophyllia corymbosa* reached stand 8, and a whole group, i.e. *Porites solida, Porites convexa, Gardineroseris ponderosa, Fungia fungites* and *Goniastrea retiformis,* all characteristic of the reef margin, settled in stand 6. *Porites solida* became dominant there, the other four species advanced to 7 and 8.

The species, characteristic of the northern coral community, are listed in Figure 6 beside the frame of stands 1–4. The characteristic coral species of the southern community, i.e. *Acropora formosa* and *Pocillopora molokensis* (6, 7, 8, 9, 10) as well as *Acropora surculosa* (5, 6, 7, 8), framed in Table 2, are marked by full lines without arrows.

Acropora irregularis, the dominant species of stands 9 and 10, settled in 5, 6, 8 and also in stands 1–4. The dominant species of stands 7 and 8, *Acropora palifera,* spread out to 6 and 10 as well as to 1–4.

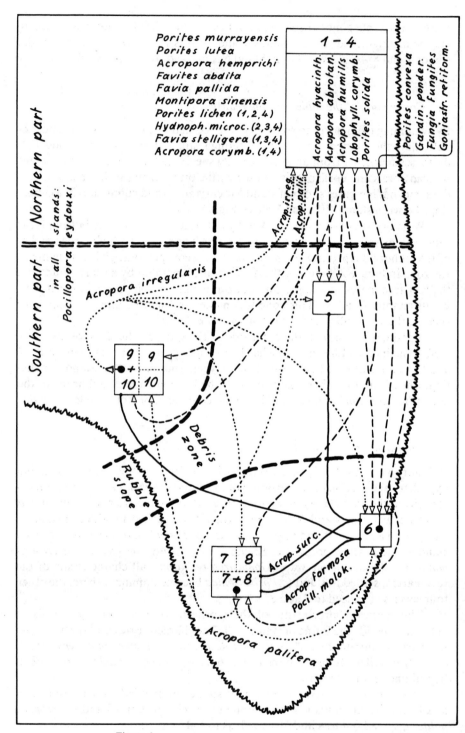

Figure 6
Interlacing of the stands at the outer reef off Weligandu.

THOUGHTS ABOUT THE ESTABLISHMENT OF CORAL COMMUNITIES

In the Introduction, the fifth task of plant sociology was given as: 'Elaboration of a distinct division and classification of plant communities'. This is also valid for a coral sociology. It should be the aim of all growth records to find, as basic units, coral communities corresponding to the associations of phytosociology. The more or less narrow restriction of the occurrence of certain species in certain coral communities can serve as the basic element of a classification. For that purpose these species can be divided into three groups with particular qualities (after Knapp, 1971).

Dominant species

These species cover a greater part of the bottom than the other species growing in the same stand. Thus they determine largely the physiognomy of a coral community.

Different coral communities, with the same dominant species, externally possess a great similarity with each other, but they are not always closely related in their species composition and their ecological claims.

Differential species

The boundary of the settlement of a coral community can be recognized by the appearance of some new species, and often by the disappearance of some other corals. These species, by which coral communities differ, are called differential species.

A certain differential species can occur in various communities. Therefore differential species serve solely for the distinction of side-by-side growing or nearly related coral communities.

Characteristic species

The linkage of a coral species to a community is called fidelity . The phyto-sociology formerly distinguished five degrees of fidelity:

5. Exclusive species with complete or almost complete linkage to a certain community.
4. Selective species with distinct preference to one community, but occasionally occurring in other communities as well.
3. Preferential species present in several communities with equal presence or constancy, but preferring one community by a greater dominance,
2. Indifferent species without pronounced connection to a community,
1. Strange, rare or accidental species.

o

Today only two groups are distinguished: the characteristic species with degrees of fidelity from 5 to 3, and the attendants with degrees 2 and 1.

The great value of the characteristic species lies in the ease with which certain units from the multiplicity of coral communities can be recognized. They are discerned by the comparison of the coral communities of the investigation area. The more extensive the area the more probable it is that the characteristic species are valid for a wider range.

Basic units of the system depending on fidelity

The phytosociology divides its plant communities into classes, orders and alliances, followed by the most important units, the associations, which are subdivided into sub-associations, variants and facies.

A coral sociology can use the same systematical units.

Association. The basic unit of the classification is the association. It was defined originally as follows: 'An association is a plant community with a distinct floristic composition, uniform conditions of the location and uniform physiognomy'.

The basic structure of an association is built by its 'characteristic combination of species', that is a minimum of characteristic and differential species and important companions with a presence of more than 60 per cent. The higher the ratio of species with high presence to the total number of species, the more uniform is the association; and the higher the ratio of the differential species to the total number, the better characterized is the association.

Sub-association. Communities deviating from the type of the association and lacking specific characteristic species can be interpreted as sub-associations. They differ from the typical formation of the association by differential species which do not occur, or are seldom found in the main type, and which indicate slight ecological differences.

Variant. Small deviations from the type, which are worthy of being distinguished for any reason whatever, can be called variants.

Facies. Small areas within a community, which are distinguished by differential species (associations, sub-associations or variants), and in which one species is dominant, are called facies. They are very prominent physiognomically.

Alliance, order, class. On grounds of common characteristic species, several associations are united in an alliance. By analogy further characteristic species group several alliances as an order and several related order as a class.

Outlook

It is difficult to fix characteristic and differential species and to classify coral communities in associations. But at the turn of the century the phytosociology had similar problems and today an immense literature exists.

Biologists, geologists and geographers have already agreed to a considerable extent on a subdivision of the reefs. As far as atolls are concerned there are the outer reef slope, the groove-and-spur system, the outer reef flat, etc. Leeward and windward reefs are distinguished. For the lagoon reef the expressions reef flat, reef edge, reef slope and lagoon floor are applied. In general, coral genera and even coral species serve as names for reef zones. Thus there exists an *Acropora palifera* zone, a *Heliopara* zone, a *Porites lutea* zone, etc. (see for example Manton and Stephenson, 1935; Emery *et al.*, 1954; Wells, 1957; Goreau, 1959; Yonge, 1963; Pichon, 1964; Stoddart, 1969; Mergner and Schuhmacher, 1974). It is always the main aim of any investigation of coral reefs, whether a transect, quadrat or zoning method is applied, to determine the coral species and their cover and to find out the ecological factors which are responsible for the specific distribution of corals.

The application of the methods of phytosociology to the investigation of coral reefs could standardize the results and simplify the procedure. This could be of great advantage considering the usual lack of time on expeditions. Also the tiresome multiplicity of the *Acropora, Porites, Montipora* and other species could be clarified. But this would make necessary a team-work of scientists in order to provide the systematic preliminary conditions for a coral sociology.

References

BRAUN-BLANQUET, J. 1964. *Pflanzensoziologie,* 3rd edit. Wien and New York. Springer-Verlag (865 p.).

EMERY, K. O.; TRACEY, J. I.; LADD, H. S. 1954. *The geology of Bikini and nearby atolls*: Part 1, Geology. U.S. Geol. Surv. (Prof. Paper 260-A), p. 1–265.

FUKAREK, F. 1964. *Pflanzensoziologie.* Berlin, Wissensch. Taschenbücher 14 (160 p.).

GARDINER, J. S. 1903. The Maldive and Laccadive groups, with notes on other coral formations in the Indian Ocean. In: J. S. Gardiner (ed.). *The fauna and geography of the Maldive and Laccadive Archipelagoes.* Cambridge, University Press, vol. 1, p. 12–50, p. 146–83, p. 313–46, p. 376–423.

GOREAU, T. F. 1959. The ecology of Jamaican coral reefs. I. Species composition and zonation. *Ecology,* vol. 40, p. 47–90.

KNAPP, R. 1971. *Einführung in die Pflanzensoziologie.* 3rd edit. Stuttgart, (388 p.).

LABOREL, J. 1960. Contribution à l'étude directe des peuplements benthiques sciaphiles sur substrat rocheux en Méditerranée. *Rec. Trav. Stn mar. Endoume,* fasc. 33, Bull. 20.

LABOREL, J.; VACELET, J. 1958. Etude des peuplements d'une grotte sous-marine du Golfe de Marseille. *Bull. Inst. Océanogr. Monaco,* vol. 55, no. 1120.

LOYA, Y. 1972. Community structure and species diversity of hermatypic corals at Eilat, Red Sea. *Mar. Biol.,* vol. 13, p. 100–23.

——; SLOBODKIN, L. B. 1971. The coral reefs of Eilat (Gulf of Eilat, Red Sea). *Symp. zool. Soc. London,* vol. 28, p. 117–39.

MANTON, S. M.; STEPHENSON, T. A. 1935. Ecological surveys of coral reefs. *Sci. Repts Gt Barrier Reef Exped. 1928–29,* vol. 3, p. 273–312.

MERGNER, H.; SCHUHMACHER, H. 1974. Morphologie, Ökologie und Zonierung von Korallenriffen bei Aqaba (Golf von Aqaba, Rotes Meer). *Helgol. Wiss. Meeresunters.* vol. 26, p. 238–358.

MÖBIUS, K. 1877. *Die Auster und die Austernwirtschaft.* Berlin.

MOLINIER, R. 1960. Etude des biocénoses marines du cap Corse (France). *Vegetatio,* vol. 9.

MOLINIER, R.; PICARD, J. 1953. Recherches analytiques sur les peuplements littoraux méditerranéens se développant sur substrat solide. *Rec. Trav. Stn mar. Endoume*, fasc. 9, Bull. 4.

ODUM, E. P.; ODUM, H. T. 1957. Zonation of corals on Japtan Reet, Eniwetok Atoll. *Atoll Res. Bull.*, no. 52, p. 1–3.

PÉRÈS, J. M.; PICARD, J. 1958. Manuel de bionomie benthique de la mer Méditerranée. *Rec. Trav. Stn mar. Endoume*, fasc. 23, Bull. 14.

PETERSEN, C. G. J. 1913. Valuation of the sea II. The animal communities of the sea bottom and their importance for marine zoo-geography. *Rep. Danish Biol. Stn*, vol. 23.

——. 1915. On the animal communities of the sea bottom of Skagerak, the Christiania Fjord and the Danish waters. *Rep. Danish Biol. Stn*, vol. 23.

PICHON, M. 1964. Contribution à l'étude de la répartition des Madréporaires sur le récif de Tuléar, Madagascar. *Rec. Trav. Stn mar. Endoume*, Suppl. Hors Série 2, p. 79–202.

PRENANT, M. 1927. Notes éthologiques sur la faune marine sessile des environs de Roscoff. *Trav. Stn Biol. Roscoff*, fasc. 6.

REMANE, A. 1940. Einführung in die zoologische Ökologie der Nord- und Ostsee. In: G. Grimpe (ed.). *Die Tierwelt der Nord- und Ostsee*. Leipzig, vol. 1, pt. Ia, p. 1–238.

ROSEN, B. R. 1971. Principal features of reef coral ecology in shallow water environments of Mahé, Seychelles. *Symp. zool. Soc. London*, vol. 28, p. 163–83.

SCHEER, G. 1960. Der Lebensraum der Riffkorallen. *Bericht 1959/60 Naturwiss. Verein Darmstadt*, p. 29–44.

——. 1967. Über die Methodik der Untersuchung von Korallenriffen. *Z. Morph. Ökol. Tiere*, vol. 60, p. 105–14,

——. 1971. Coral reefs and coral general in the Red Sea and Indian Ocean. *Symp. zool. Soc. London*, vol. 28, p. 329–67.

——. 1972. Investigation of coral reefs in the Maldive Islands with notes on lagoon patch reefs and the method of coral sociology. In: *Proc. Symp. Corals and Coral Reefs 1969*. Mar. Biol. Assoc. India, p. 87–120.

——. 1974. Investigation of coral reefs at Rasdu Atoll in the Maldives with the quadrat method according to phytosociology. In: *Proc. Second Int. Coral Reef. Symp.* Brisbane, Great Barrier Reef Committee, vol. 2, p. 655–70.

——; PILLAI, C. S. G. 1974. Report on the Scleractinia from the Nicobar Islands. *Zoologica, Stuttg.*, no. 122, p. 1–75.

SCHWICKERATH, M. 1940. *Die Artmächtigkeit*. Rep. Spec. Nov., vol. 121.

STODDART, D. R. 1966. Reef studies at Addu Atoll, Maldive Islands. *Atoll. Res. Bull.*, no. 116, p. 1–122.

——. 1969. Ecology and morphology of recent coral reefs. *Biol. Rev. Camb. Philos. Soc.*, vol. 44, p. 433–98.

VASSEUR, P. 1964. Contribution à l'étude bionomique des peuplements sciaphiles infralittoraux de substrat dur dans les récifs de Tuléar (Madagascar). *Rec. Trav. Stn mar. Endoume*, Suppl. Hors série 2, p. 1–77.

WELLS, J. W. 1957. Coral reefs. *Mem. Geol. Soc. Am.*, vol. 67, no. 1, p. 609–31.

YONGE, C. M. 1963. The biology of coral reefs. In: F. S. Russell (ed.). *Advances in marine biology*. London and New York, Academic Press, vol. 1, p. 209–60.

16

Plotless and transect methods

Y. Loya[1]

INTRODUCTION

Most of the studies of coral-reef benthic-communities deal with their systematics, physiology, behaviour or some qualitative characteristics of their ecology. Very little work has been done in the past on quantitative description of coral-reef communities. Problems such as species composition, species abundance and distribution as well as zonal patterns of different species have been, usually, qualitatively described. It is not surprising, therefore, that one can rarely find any publication dealing with the spatial distribution of coral-reef benthic-communities, which require, of course, quantitative information for the analysis and presentation of the data.

As our knowledge of coral-reef benthic-communities increases, greater and greater need has been felt by coral-reef students for quantitative analysis and description of coral-reef communities and for methods to measure the characteristics of these communities. Thus, one of the major purposes of the SCOR working group on methods in quantitative ecology of coral reefs was 'to evaluate and test existing methods for the quantitative description of abundance, composition and distribution of benthic invertebrate and plant communities on reefs and to recommend standard field techniques suitable for these problems'.

Most of the invertebrate communities of coral-reefs are stationary or limited in their mobility. In this sense, there is a great similarity between coral-reef invertebrate communities and terrestrial plant communities. It may be, therefore, justified to adopt and test concepts and techniques used by plant ecologists for the study of benthic communities of coral-reefs. (See also Scheer, 1967; Barnes *et al.*, 1971; Stoddart, 1971; Loya, 1972.) The present paper aims to review some of the major plotless and transect methods used by ecologists and discuss their possible application for quantitative studies of coral communities.

1. Department of Zoology, The George S. Wise Centre for Life Sciences, Tel-Aviv University, Tel-Aviv, Israel.

QUANTITATIVE STUDIES OF CORAL COMMUNITIES USING LINE
TRANSECTS

Stoddart (1969, 1972) reviewed field methods and quantitative studies of
hermatypic corals with special attention to the problems of sampling design,
sampling unit and problems of data recording. He divides the linear transect
studies done on coral-reefs into two main categories: (a) some form of continuous recording and (b) sampling along transects. However, all the publications falling in these categories deal in one way or another with quadrat
sampling (see Mayor, 1918, 1924; Edmondson, 1928; Manton, 1935; Odum
and Odum, 1955; Hiatt, 1935, 1957; Newell *et al.,* 1959; Storr, 1964; Stoddart
et al., 1966). Most of these studies are confined to accessible reef-flats, while
fore-reef slopes have been neglected. Some of these studies record the number of
species or genera per quadrat, but, in general, most of them have no usable
data for quantitative comparisons of different reef systems, nor do they emphasize the importance of studying the various zones of the reef. The transect line
in these studies is used only as a reference line for the establishment of quadrats
or as a belt transect with specified length and width, all individuals within it
being measured. The disadvantages of using these methods are discussed in the
next section.

Loya and Slobodkin (1971) and Loya (1972) used for the first time transect
sampling in the sense of category (b) above in the line transect methods (i.e. the
line transect has specified length but no breadth). This method was especially
designed to study the community structure of hermatypic corals in terms of
species composition, zonation and diversity patterns in different zones of the
reef. Line transects were run underwater to a depth of 30 m. Each transect was
10 m long. (See later section for the determination of sample size.) Any coral
species which underlay the line was recorded and its projected length which
intercepted the line was measured to the nearest centimetre (Fig. 1). The
transects were run along depth contours parallel to the shore and parallel to
each other at fixed intervals of one metre on the reef flat and five metres along
the fore-reef (Fig. 2). For the purpose of this work an individual was defined as

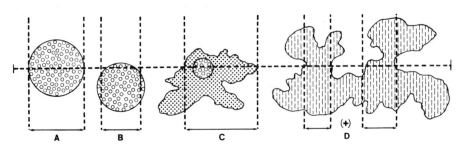

Figure 1
Line transect method for quantitative studies of corals (Loya and
Slobodkin, 1971; Loya, 1972). See text for explanation.

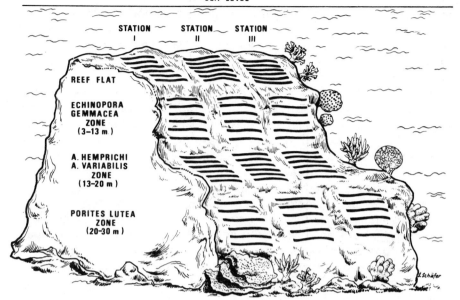

SEA LEVEL

STATION I   STATION II   STATION III

REEF FLAT

ECHINOPORA
GEMMACEA
ZONE
(3-13 m)

A. HEMPRICHI
A. VARIABILIS
ZONE
(13-20 m)

PORITES LUTEA
ZONE
(20-30 m)

Figure 2
The coral reef of Eilat, Red Sea. Quantitative studies of the community
structure and species diversity of hermatypic corals were done using line
transects run along depth contours parallel to the shore and parallel to each
other (Loya, 1972).

any colony growing independently of its neighbours (i.e. whenever an empty
space was recorded between two adjacent colonies). In cases where an individual
colony was clearly separated into two or more portions by the death of the
intervening parts, the separate parts were considered as one individual. In the
case of two or more colonies growing one above the other and underlying the
transect, the projected length of the largest colony was recorded for living
coverage analysis and the length and species of all overlapping colonies, which
underlay the line, were recorded for the coral species diversity analysis.

Porter (1972a, b) studied the species diversity of hermatypic corals at the
San Blas coral reefs, the Atlantic coast of Panama, in a somewhat modified
methodology. A 10 m long chain with links 1.3 cm in length was laid parallel
to the depth contour at 3 m intervals down the reef face. The number of chain
links covering each species of living coral was then recorded. Wallace (1974)
studied distribution patterns of the coral genus *Acropora* at Big Broadhurst
Reef in the Great Barrier Reef, northeast of Townsville, Australia. She adopted
the methods used by Loya (1972). Line transects of 10 m length were run
parallel to the reef front at 1 m intervals, from 12 m before the drop-off, to the
sea floor at 33 m. Ott (1975) has quantitatively analysed the community
pattern and structure of a coral-reef bank in Barbados, West Indies, using a

photographic line transect method. He placed a nylon line marked at one metre intervals normal to the direction of the bank top. Photographs were taken of each one-metre line segment so that a continuous strip along the transect was photographed. Information recorded from the slides was limited to one-metre line segments under the nylon transect line. Comparison between photo and field transects did not vary significantly with respect to species enumerated nor to the linear measure of tissue used. Laxton and Stablum (1974) described a photographic method for estimates of percentage cover of sedentary organisms on coral reefs. Photographs were taken every fourth metre along transect was photographed. Information recorded from the slides was limited weights were expressed as percentages of the total weight. Nevertheless, any photographic method is limited to reef habitats with very low diversity of benthic organisms because of identification difficulties and habitat preference of some species that grow typically beneath coral colonies and do not show up in the photographs. Recently, the author has used the line transect methodology as previously described (Loya, 1972) in two quantitative studies: one which deals with possible effects of water pollution on the community structure of Red Sea corals (Loya, 1975) and the other concerns sedimentation effects on the community structure of hermatypic corals at Punta Ostiones, the west coast of Puerto Rico (Loya, 1976).

RELATIVE ADVANTAGES OF PLOTLESS TECHNIQUES

Usually the members of an entire community cannot be counted or measured because of the enormous number of individuals involved; even if this were done, the information would not be more useful than the information derived from an adequate set of data acquired by proper sampling. However, survey of the literature suggests that sampling is one of the least well understood aspects of quantitative ecology. Ecological sampling in the past has most frequently been plot sampling, such as the methods developed by the Braun-Blanquet school for plant communities (Braun-Blanquet, 1932) and much descriptive and quantitative work carried out by animal and plant ecologists. There is an extensive literature dealing with the problem of quadrat size usually involving the concept of minimal area, or species-log area curves (see next section). Minimal area, however, is a dubious concept and in some instances can appear to be meaningless (Poore, 1964).

A survey of the ecological literature concerned with the structure of animal and plant communities reveals an interesting trend of changing shape and decreasing sample size required for an analysis of a community. Thus, there has been some attempt to get away from quadrat sampling by the development of plotless distance techniques, which essentially reduce quadrat measurements into linear recordings of distances among random points. Further developments of these techniques reduced the sampling unit into a point, which avoids problems of sample size or sample shape. In a new method for a study

200

of plant distributional patterns of plant communities, Yarranton (1966) uses random points sampling. His major argument against quadrat sampling lies in the determination of species which occur together. In quadrat sampling occurring together means within a range of distance from zero to the longest diameter of the quadrat. It is clear from this why associations derived from the quadrat method depend on the nature of the sample.

In general, all of the distance or plotless sampling techniques possess certain obvious advantages when compared to the standard plot techniques, since they are more efficient in terms of results obtained per man-time expended. In studying plant communities, Cottam and Curtis (1956) report savings of 90 per cent or more in time required to obtain equivalent results.

In considering the proper sampling techniques for studies of coral-reef communities, one has always to bear in mind the practical difficulties involved, i.e. the physiological and physical limitations dictated by the aquatic environment (see Jones, 1971). Any underwater study is several times more complicated, tedious, time consuming and expensive than a comparable operation in terrestrial studies.

Loya and Slobodkin (1971) and Loya (1972) discussed the relative advantages of using continuous transect sampling in a study of community structure and species diversity of corals at Eilat, Red Sea. Transect sampling proved to be very efficient in information gained per time spent underwater and also in avoiding problems of bottom topography. Thus, a line may be put along depth contours, while quadrat sampling is much more complicated to interpret and handle underwater. Moreover, the amount of information derived from line transects is for many purposes as useful as that derived from quadrat sampling techniques. Due to efficiency limitations of quadrat sampling a much smaller dimension of the reef can be covered when compared to line transect techniques in terms of results obtained per equal labour time.

Scheer (1967, 1972) adopted methods of plant sociology using quadrat sampling in investigations of coral reefs. Although this method is relatively fast, it is of very little use for quantitative studies of benthic organisms of coral reefs, when problems, such as species diversity, spatial distribution or interspecific association are involved. Recently, Maragos (1974) studied the coral community structure of the leeward ocean reef slope at Fanning Island, Pacific Ocean. He used the continuous quadrat method since he has used it in the past and found it to be 'efficient means of acquiring data when time in the field is limited'. Goldberg (1973) used similar methodology in his studies of the geomorphology, species composition and zonation of coral–octocoral communities off the southeast Florida coast. Both studies, however, are limited to very narrow dimensions of the reefs studied and cannot, therefore, represent the entire area.

SAMPLE SIZE AND NUMBER OF SAMPLES

The considerations involved in determining the size of sample which is adequate

201

to represent a certain animal or plant community are not as straight forward. The necessary sample size may vary for different species within an area as well as varying from area to area, a situation which is commonly met within any investigation involving a sampling technique.

Gleason (1922) pointed out in his vegetation studies that as the area sampled increased the number of unrecorded species added decreased, a concept referred to as the species-area curve which has often been used and disputed in plant ecology (Cain, 1938; Vestal, 1949; Goodall, 1952; Evans et al., 1955; Aberdeen, 1958; Kilburn, 1966). A full treatment of the methods of selecting the optimum sampling unit is given in Cochran (1963) and other textbooks (Greig-Smith, 1964; Kershaw, 1973; Williams, 1964; Southwood,

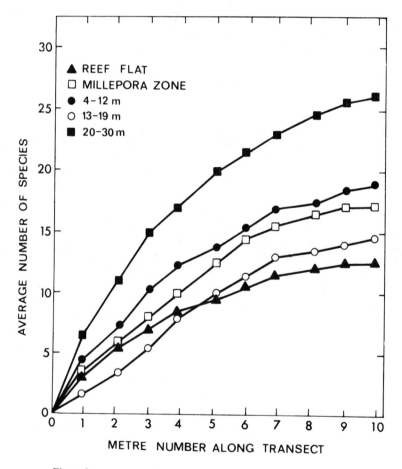

Figure 3
Cumulative number of hermatypic coral species (Eilat, Red Sea) as a function of metre number along a line transect. The curves tend to level off after 9–10 metres of line were recorded (after Loya, 1972).

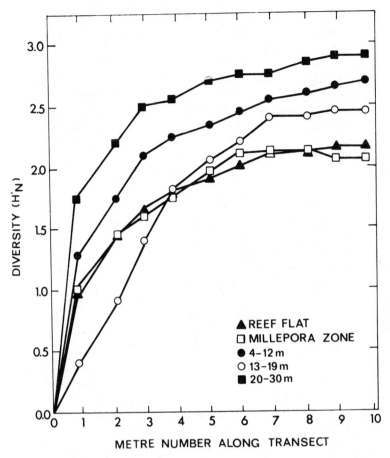

Figure 4
Cumulative number of Shannon and Weaver's (1948) $H'n$ index of diversity
as a function of metre number along a line transect. The curves tend to
level off after 5–6 metres of line were recorded (after Loya, 1972).

1966). The point where the species–area curve starts to level off is usually considered as an adequate sample size. The same considerations may apply to the species versus transect length curve. This approach was taken by Loya (1972) in determining the appropriate transect length in a study of the community structure of hermatypic corals (Figs. 3 and 4). The practical and theoretical limitations of this approach are discussed by Southwood (1966). A 10 m line transect proved to be an adequate sample size for a quantitative study of hermatypic corals in different reefs investigated, such as Eilat, Red Sea (Loya, 1972), San Blas, Atlantic coast of Panama (Porter, 1972a), Big Broadhurst reef, Great Barrier Reef, Australia (Wallace, 1974), Punta Ostiones, Puerto Rico (Loya, 1976). However, the necessary sample size should be determined in a preliminary study of the area investigated. Thus, on the reef flat of Heron

Island, Great Barrier Reef, Australia. The species versus transect length curve started levelling off only after 30 m of a line (Loya, unpublished data).

The number of samples required for an adequate representation and analysis of a particular community is another question. Kuno (1969) suggested a modified method for sequential sampling, which has been previously suggested and used by Waters (1955) and Southwood (1966). In this type of sampling, the total number of samples taken is variable and depends on whether or not the results obtained so far are within the tolerable limits of precision aimed at in the beginning of the study. This problem, however, is not easy to solve, since in biological populations the variance of the count per sampling unit is rarely stable but fluctuates in close relation with the mean density. Kuno's (1969) method, in contrast to the ordinary method (see Southwood, 1966) involves the procedures of successive graphical plotting of the cumulative total counts against corresponding numbers of sampling units examined. The basic difference of this method is in the criterion of judgment at a given point whether to continue or stop sampling. In Kuno's method, the criterion is not concerned with the level of the mean itself, but is the level of precision so far attained for estimating the mean. The criterion is represented graphically by a line (usually a curve) showing the theoretical relationship of cumulative total count to sample size for the specified level of precision. The critical line is called 'stop line'. Kuno suggests his method for wide application to sampling field populations under various situations since it is simply based upon the relationship of variance to mean. More recently, Green (1970) suggested a modification in Kuno's (1969) method by using logarithmic axis in the sequential sampling graph. It has the advantage that the 'stop line' is a straight line rather than a curve for most distributions of organisms encountered in the field (see Fig. 5).

PLOTLESS AND TRANSECT METHODS

There are basically two major approaches in plotless distance-measuring methods. One may either select individuals at random from the whole population and from each of these measure the distance to its nearest neighbouring individual (see nearest neighbour method and random pairs method, 2 and 3 below) or alternatively, one may locate sampling points at random throughout the area and measure the distance from each point to the nearest or nth nearest individuals (see closest individual method, point centred quadrat method and wandering quarter method, 1, 4 and 5 below). The line transect methods basically involve the recording of the length of random-spaced parallel lines which are intercepted by plants or sessile animals.

All these techniques are most easily used with relatively sessile discrete, easily mapped organisms and thus have been used extensively by plant ecologists (Greig-Smith, 1964). It is obvious, therefore, why it would be of great advantage to adopt these methods for quantitative studies of coral reef benthic-

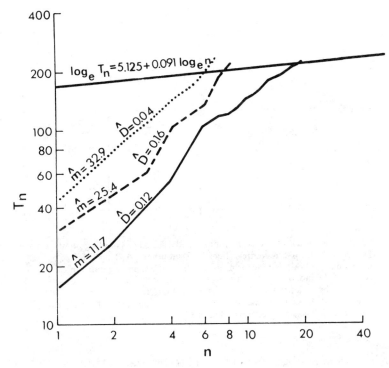

Figure 5
A sequential sampling graph for density of the bivalve *Notospisula parva*
at Crib Island, Queensland. Both T_n (cumulative total for sample n) and n
are logarithmic scales. Three sequential sample runs to the 'stop line' are
shown with estimates of mean density m and standard error to mean ratio
D (after Green, 1970).

communities. It should be mentioned, however, that these methods have been
applied by terrestrial animal ecologists (see Southwood, 1966) in studies on
grasshoppers (Blackith, 1958), frogs (Turner, 1960) and snails (Keuls *et al.,*
1963). Cox (1972) provides an excellent laboratory manual, which deals with
most of the methods mentioned below, including specific exercise on the
formation of testable ecological hypotheses.

Plotless distance methods

1. *Closest individual method.* In this method a point is selected at random, and the
distance between this point and the nearest individual is measured, regardless
of direction (Fig. 6).

This method was introduced by Cottam (1947). The mean-value obtained
by this method was found empirically to be half the square root of the mean
area per individual (Cottam *et al.,* 1953). The mean area per individual represents the average area of ground surface on which one individual occurs. The

205

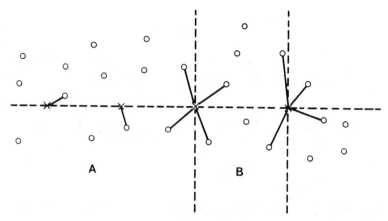

Figure 6
Point to individual methods (methods 1 and 4). X's are sampling points.
Dotted lines are paced compass lines between points. A. The closest
individual method: distance is measured from the sampling point to the
centre of the individual closest to it, regardless of direction B. The quarter
method: the area around the point is divided into four 90° quarters (dashed
lines) and distance is measured from the point to the centre of the closest
individual in each quarter (revised after Cottam and Curtis, 1956).

same relationship has been found to hold theoretically (Morisita, 1954; Clark
and Evans, 1954). The average distance obtained is multiplied by a correction
factor of 2.0 to convert it to square root of the mean area per individual.

Cottam and Curtis (1956) compare different distance measurements and
find that the major advantage of this method is its simplicity. Only one individual and one distance are measured. However, a disadvantage is the extreme
variability of results, which necessitates the sampling of many points before an
adequate sample is obtained, and also the susceptibility of the method to
subjective bias. They conclude that it is the least reliable method.

A different opinion is expressed by Pielou (1959, 1960, 1969) who uses and
discusses this method for a study of pattern of plant populations. She compares the closest individual method to the nearest neighbour method and argues
that, in addition to its greater convenience in the field, the closest individual
method has also theoretical advantage. A non-random population may
exhibit patchiness of several scales—thus, plants may exhibit clumps within
clumps. In such cases an index based on nearest neighbour distances will
indicate only the smallest scale of nonrandomness present, whereas one based
on closest individual distances will be affected by most, if not all, the levels of
non-randomness in the population.

Keuls et al. (1963) have used successfully the closest individual method
for a study of animal populations of limited mobility such as snails. They
provide multiplication factors for estimating the density of a population by
this method with 95 per cent confidence limits and the coefficient of variance of

the estimate of density. The confidence limits become narrower with higher numbers of nearest individuals being measured. Probably the most practical number of nearest individuals to be measured are between three to five considering the labour involved (Southwood, 1966). Keuls *et al.* (1963) suggest that the method could be applied even to mobile animals by recording the nearest individual at *S* moments, perhaps photographically.

2. *Nearest neighbour method.* In this method a point is selected at random and then one searches around in tight concentric rings until an individual is found. The distance between this individual and its nearest neighbour is measured (Fig. 7).

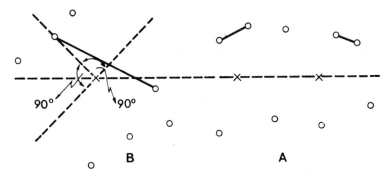

Figure 7
Nearest neighbour methods (methods 2 and 3). In both methods, the individual closest to the sampling point is located. A. Nearest neighbour distance is measured between the two individuals at each point. B. For the random pairs method, an angle of exclusion of 180° is erected with its vertex at the sampling point and its bisector extending through the closest individual. Distance is measured from the closest individual to the individual closest to it that is outside the angle of exclusion (revised after Cottam and Curtis, 1956).

The mean value obtained by this method has been shown theoretically to be half the square root of the mean area per individual (Morisita, 1954; Clark and Evans, 1954). However, Cottam *et al.* (1953) found that the correction factor for this method should be 1.67 instead of the theoretical 2.0. Yet, Greig-Smith (1964) argues that this correction factor was determined empirically from a synthetic random population and it should not be used uncritically. Also, Pielou (1959) points out that it is unlikely that any correction factor can be found which would counterbalance the error introduced by taking a biased sample of distances. Such a factor would inevitably be a function of the degree of aggregation, which is unknown at the start of an investigation.

The nearest neighbour method was first suggested by Dice (1952) to detect non-randomness in plant populations. Since then it has been applied and discussed by many other investigators including Cottam *et al.* (1953) and Cottam and Curtis (1956) who studied plotless distance measurements on a comparative basis. Hopkins (1954) compared the average distance between nearest neighbours with the average distance between random points and closest individuals as a means of measuring aggregation. This measurement had been suggested independently by Moore (1954) who also used it to determine densities. Clark and Evans (1954) used this method as a measure of the departures from randomness in a population of plants. Cottam and Curtis (1956) found that the nearest neighbour method gives less variable results than the closest individual method, but still requires a larger number of sampling points than either of the other distance measurements. Morisita (1954) and Thompson (1956) discuss the use of the second, third, ... *n*th nearest neighbour measurements. Apart from the increase in accuracy of density determination in a random population, pointed out by Morisita (1954), the method described by Thompson (1956) indicates to a greater degree than is possible using only the nearest neighbour, the nature as well as the degree of non-randomness present in a plant population. However, Pielou (1959, 1969) argues that the only way to ensure truly random distance measurements of nearest neighbour individuals is to attach numbered labels to every individual in the area, then consult a random numbers table to decide which are the chosen individuals. She showed how misleading the results can be if 'random' plants are selected by short cut methods, i.e. by selecting a plant nearest to a random point as a 'random' plant. By this method relatively isolated plants have a greater chance of being selected than have those which are members of clumps. For the selection of random points from which to measure distances, Pielou advised taking pairs of coordinates from a random numbers table. The random points may then be reached by measuring with a tape from suitably placed axis laid down beforehand.

3. *Random pairs method.* This method is based on the use of angle of exclusion to denote a series of pairs of individuals for further sampling of species, size and spacing distance. From the sampling point a line is laid to the nearest individual and a 90° exclusion angle erected on either side of it. The distance from the individual to the nearest one lying outside the exclusion angle is measured (Fig. 7). As originally described (Cottam and Curtis, 1949) an exclusion angle of 160° was recommended, but it was later shown (Cottam *et al.*, 1953) that the average distance between pairs was a linear function of the angle of exclusion for 0° to 260°. Cottam and Curtis (1955) found that the correction factor to obtain the square root of the mean area per individual is 0.8. Thus, the mean area per individual, divided into the unit area of density, gives the total density of all species in the sampling area. Comparing this method with other plotless distance measurements, Cottam and Curtis (1956) concluded that with a 180° angle of exclusion this method yielded less variable results than the two methods discussed previously.

Shanks (1954) compared this method with conventional plot sampling in a maple forest. He found this method to be superior to plot sampling in yield of information per man-hour. A disadvantage of this method, in his opinion, is that it does not adequately sample the inferior layers or inferior size classes in the forest stand. A comparison of the data from the complete tree census was done by Rice and Penfound (1955). They concluded that the random pairs technique proved to be useful for procuring data on density, frequency, and basal area, but was insufficiently accurate due probably to the small sample utilized.

4. *Point centred quadrat method.* Each random sampling point along a transect line is considered as a centre of four quarters (quadrants), i.e. the area around the point is divided into four 90° quarters, with orientation fixed in advance by a compass. The distance from the sampling point to the nearest individual in each quadrant is measured. The species and the areal coverage of each individual involved is also recorded (Fig. 6). The mean of the four distances measured from each sampling point has been shown empirically (Cottam et al., 1953) and theoretically (Morisita, 1954) to be equal to the square root of the mean area per individual. The total density of individuals in the area sampled is then obtained by dividing the mean area per individual into the unit area on the basis of which density is to be expressed.

This method, which has been adopted for ecological use by Curtis (1950) was used in the middle of the last century by Federal surveyors making the original survey of government lands (Stearns, 1949). Cottam and Curtis (1956) found that this method is the least variable for distance determinations, provides more data on individual species per sampling point, and is least susceptible to subjective bias. The apparent disadvantage of requiring more time per point is compensated by the necessity for sampling fewer points. They conclude that this method is superior to the other three distance methods discussed previously. Dix (1961) adopted this method for grasslands and found it as accurate as any other grassland sampling method, in addition to being considerably faster. Cox (1972) emphasized that point-to-plant distances should be measured to the centre of the crown, or to the centre of the rooted base, rather than to the edge of the crown. Similarly, Ashby (1972) cautioned that plotless vegetation sampling including the quarter method results in a systematic bias, if measurements 'to the tree' are used in place of 'to the centre of the tree trunk'. It should be mentioned that in making conclusions for density in both the random pairs and the point centred quadrat method, the assumption is made that individuals of all species are randomly dispersed (Cottam and Curtis, 1956). Greig-Smith (1964) cautioned that when the quarter method is applied to grasslands, it should be checked against quadrat density counts. The justification for his reservation is the known tendency for the quarter method to underestimate the density of aggregated populations. Because of this, the mean distance, and hence the mean area of the population, is overestimated. Risser and Zedler (1968) applied the point centred quadrat

209

method to six prairie stands at Wisconsin. Comparisons of quadrat density counts with those obtained by the quarter method showed the two to be significantly correlated. However, the relative difference of the estimates was highly and significantly correlated with the aggregation characteristics of the stands measured by Pielou's index (Pielou, 1959). Their conclusion was that the quarter method on grasslands is subject to question, unless careful checks against quadrat counts are made.

5. *Wandering quarter method.* A modification of the point centred quadrat method is the wandering quarter method of Catana (1963), who suggested studying a sequence of measurements through the population rather than four measurements at randomly selected sampling points. The sequence of measurement is obtained by starting at a randomly selected point and choosing the nearest individual within a 90° angle of inclusion around a previously chosen compass azimuth; then, constructing another 90° angle of inclusion with this individual as a vertex and the compass line as a bisector, the distance to the nearest individual within this angle is measured (Fig. 8). This procedure is continued for 25 distance measurements through the sampling area along each of four transects.

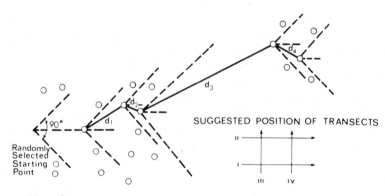

Figure 8
The wandering quater method (after Catana, 1963). See text for explanation.

Line transect methods

Recording under equally spaced points along a transect. A line transect is divided into contiguous units (blocks) of equal size. Each block is divided by a fixed number of equally spaced points. The frequency in each block is determined by summing the presences of each species from all the points within the block. In this way a series of contiguous frequency records may be obtained for each species. Kershaw (1957) was the first to suggest this method. He also described (Kershaw, 1958) a perspex frame designed to enable continuous cover readings to be taken at small intervals along a transect. Thin needles are lowered, or optical measure taken and recorded by sighting through two sets of holes on the ground layer. The general reliability of this approach has been tested by trials on artificial layouts of different types (Kershaw, 1957). He concluded that as long as the basic unit is smaller than the smallest scale of pattern to be detected, the results are reliably consistent. Each set of adjacent readings within a block are grouped together and expressed as a percentage cover reading. The cover readings are blocked up and analysed for the scale of pattern obtained (Kershaw, 1973).

Pielou (1965, 1967) made field investigations of a dry woodland vegetation by laying a transect line across it and recording what plant species occurred at each of the successive points equally spaced along the transect. She discussed the mathematical implications of this method and suggested statistical tests for the study of random mingling of vegetation mosaics. Kilburn (1966) used this method for the study of plant pattern analysis, using 1.7 cm blocks along a line transect with 0.32 cm intervals. This method has also been used for surveys of aquatic vegetation in Long Lake, Minnesota, by Schmid (1965). He recorded the substratum texture and the plant species that overlapped the transect line for each one foot interval. The transects were run along 1 m depth-contours to a depth of 11 m.

Continuous transect recording. This is probably the oldest transect method used mainly by plant ecologists for recording of frequency and coverage of vegetation. Any individual that is intercepted by the line is recorded and the portion of the line being intercepted is measured. Although the line transect itself has practically no breadth, measurements of the coverage of individual species along its length are possible, since they would be proportional to the areas covered by each species concerned. The method is based, therefore, on the expectation that total transect length/total population area = total transect length being intercepted/total area of living population. Cox (1972) suggested to measure also the maximum width of the individual perpendicular to the transect line and the length of the transect segments overlying bare ground. Equations for calculations of the relative density, relative dominance and relative frequency are provided and comprehensively discussed by Cox (1972).

Plant ecologists began to use this method as an alternative to sampling plots because it was easier and quicker and the results obtained were not less accurate (Canfield, 1941; Anderson, 1942; Bauer, 1943). By this method, McIntyre (1953) derived expressions for estimating plant density based on the sum of reciprocals of the longest chord parallel to the intercepted chord length. The latter modification was suggested to eliminate a potential bias in measurements of plants with irregular boundaries. Strong (1966) suggested taking measurements perpendicular to the transect across the greatest extent of each intercepted individual. The sum of the reciprocals of these measurements is multiplied by the desired unit-area and divided by the length of the transect to obtain the density statistic. Strong claims that the results obtained are valid

211

'without regard to whether plants are circular or systematically distorted'. However, Westman (1971) makes the reservation (see Fig. 9) that in cases of aggregation, systematic distortion may produce very large variations in density estimates, because increased interception lengths will be serially correlated. It is unlikely, however, that one would get such a systematic distortion in aggregations of coral-reef benthic populations.

The line transect method has been adopted for benthic studies in various modifications. Neushul (1966) has used it for a study of the distributional and structural features of algal associations in the Puget Sound region at Washington. Loya and Slobodkin (1971), Loya (1972), Porter (1972a, b), Wallace (1974), Ott (1975) and Loya (1975, 1976) have used it in regional studies of the community structure and species diversity of hermatypic corals.

Westman (1971) suggested a new modification of the continuous transect

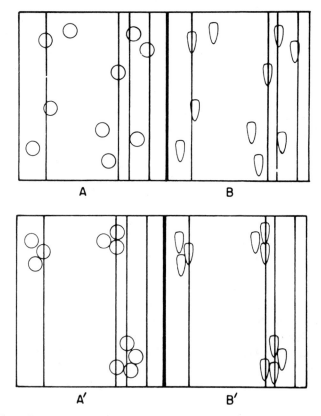

Figure 9
Effect of systematic distortion and aggregation on variance of density estimates by line transect method. Total area of each element is equal. A, B: random distribution; total chord length intercepted remains same in A and B. A', B': aggregated distribution; total chord length intercepted is greater in B' (after Westman, 1971).

recording (the systematic distance method) which was originally designed for density estimates of forest trees. Line transects are established in a random direction, or oriented parallel to any suspected environmental gradients. The distance from the line to all trees within $2 \times$ mean forest point-to-tree ($\bar{n}$) is systematically measured on each side of the line (see Fig. 10). The distance ($\bar{n}$) may be approximated by assuming temporarily a random distribution of trees, and determining ($\bar{n}$) by the point centred quadrat methods from a small number of points.

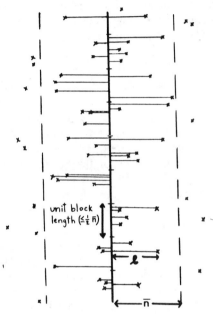

Figure 10
The systematic distance method (after Westman, 1971). See text for explanation.

DISCUSSION AND CONCLUSIONS

Although some of the considerable literature on the general subject of benthic sampling deals with hard-bottom communities (see Thorson, 1957; Holme, 1964; Holme and McIntyre, 1971; Hulings and Gray, 1971) very little of it applies to coral-reefs. The first attempt to introduce quantitative methods for the investigation of coral-reef benthic communities was done in the *Handbook for Atoll Research* (Fosberg and Sachet, 1953) which is outdated today by many significant advancements in this field.

In considering various methods used by plant ecologists for quantitative sampling of terrestrial vegetation, and the possible adoption of these techniques to coral reef work, three basic guide lines should be borne in mind:

(a) the major purpose of the study, (b) the relative efficiency of different field methods in providing the desirable data, (c) the statistical and computational procedures required for each specific method.

Certainly there is no one quantitative method that can answer all possible questions. One of the major purposes of the present handbook is the quantitative description of abundance, composition and distribution of coral reef animal and plant communities. The spatial arrangement of these communities may be deduced from a quantitative knowledge of these aspects. The main distinction lies between regular, random and aggregated distributions with the respective implications that the animals compete, have no effect on each other, or are in clumps. However the sampling method chosen by the investigator may largely affect the apparent distribution. Thus, a careful testing of the pattern and size of sampling unit is needed in order to avoid artifacts.

Although random sampling has the advantage of eliminating any personal bias it is not desirable for use in the reef ecosystem because of the marked zonation and patchiness typical of many reefs. On the other hand, the systematic sampling pattern, although it seems very attractive in analysing abundance and distribution of species along environmental gradients, may cause serious statistical difficulties (Southwood, 1966). It seems, therefore, that the stratified random sampling would be preferable for coral-reef communities studies. Here, the reef area selected for study is divided into a number of sub-divisions (every five metres depth, for example) and several random samples are taken within each sub-division in proportion to its size. Such an approach maximizes the accuracy of the estimate of the population. It is useless, however, to standardize or make a general rule of the number of samples and their size. The use of standard samples (either quadrats or transects) is impractical because it does not give ecologically equivalent results for different community types which exhibit different physical scales of intra-regional variation. Also, as Pielou (1959) pointed out for the plotless distance methods, it is unlikely that a single correction factor can be found which will always allow for the bias in the sample. This does not mean, however, that intra-regional quantitative comparisons are impossible, since these problems can easily be solved by statistical procedures when the same field methods are used. It is pointless, however, to recommend at this stage the 'best method' for general use, because excluding the continuous recording along line transects (Loya and Slobodkin, 1971) none of these methods have ever been tried in the coral reef environment. The field methods reviewed in this paper are suggested for further investigations of their possible applicability for quantitative population studies of coral reef benthic communities.

ACKNOWLEDGEMENTS

I wish to acknowledge permission to reprint figures 5, 8, 9 and 10 in the present paper from the following: Figure 5 (reprinted after R. H. Green, *Res. Popul.*

Ecol. 1970, Japanese Society of Sakyo-Ku, Kyoto, Japan. Figure 8 (reprinted after A. J. Catana) copyright 1963 by the Ecological Society of America. Figures 9 and 10 (reprinted after W. E. Westman in: *Statistical ecology* Vol. 1: Spatial patterns and statistical distributions, edited by G. P. Patil, E. C. Pielou and W. E. Waters 1971). Pennsylvania State University Press.

References

ABERDEEN, J. E. C. 1958. The effect of quadrat size, and plant distribution on frequency estimates in plant ecology. *Aust. J. Bot.*, vol. 6, p. 47–59.

ANDERSON, K. L. 1942. A comparison of line transects and permanent quadrats in evaluating composition and density of pasture vegetation of the tall prairie grass type. *J. Am. Soc. Agron.*, vol. 34, p. 805–22.

ASHBY, W. C. 1972. Distance measurements in vegetation study. *Ecology,* vol. 53, p. 980–81.

BARNES, J.; BELLAMY, D. J.; JONES, D. J.; WHITTON, B. A.; DREW, E. A.; KENYON, L.; LYTHGOE, J. N.; ROSEN, B. R. 1971. Morphology and ecology of the reef front of Aldabra. *Symp. zool. Soc. Lond.,* vol. 28, p. 87–114. In: D. R. Stoddart and C. M. Yonge, (eds.). *Regional variation in Indian Ocean coral reefs.* London and New York, Academic Press (584 p.).

BAUER, H. L. 1943. The statistical analysis of chaparral and other plant communities by means of transect samples. *Ecology,* vol. 24, p. 45–60

BLACKITH, R. E. 1958. Nearest-neighbour distance measurement for the estimation of animal populations. *Ecology,* vol. 39, p. 147–50.

BRAUN-BLANQUET, J. 1932. *Plant sociology: the study of plant communities.* Translated, revised and edited by G. D. Fuller and H. S. Conard. New York, McGraw-Hill, (439 p.)

CAIN, S. A. 1938. The species area curve. *Am. Midl. Nat.,* vol. 19, p. 573–81.

CANFIELD, R. H. 1941. Application of the line interception method in sampling range vegetation. *J. Forestry,* vol. 39, p. 388–94.

CATANA, A. J. 1963. The wandering quarter method of estimating population density. *Ecology,* vol. 44, p. 349–60.

CLARK, P. J.; EVANS, F. C. 1954. Distance to nearest neighbour as a measure of spatial relationships in populations. *Ecology,* vol. 35, p. 445–53.

COCHRAN, W. G. 1963. *Sampling techniques,* 2nd edit. New York, John Wiley. (413 p.).

COTTAM, G. 1947. A point method for making rapid surveys of woodlands. *Bull. ecol. Soc. Am.,* vol. 28, p. 60.

——.; CURTIS, J. T. 1949. A method for making rapid surveys of woodlands by means of pairs of randomly selected trees. *Ecology,* vol. 30, p. 101–4.

——.; CURTIS, J. T.; HALE, B. W. 1953. Some sampling characteristics of a population of randomly dispersed individuals. *Ecology,* vol. 34, p. 741–57.

——.; CURTIS, J. T. 1955. Correction for various exclusion angles in the random pairs method. *Ecology,* vol. 36, p. 767.

——.; CURTIS, J. T. 1956. The use of distance measures in phytosociological sampling. *Ecology,* vol. 37, p. 451–60.

COX, G. W. 1972 *Laboratory manual of general ecology.* Dubuqe, Iowa, W. C. Brown (195 p.).

CURTIS, J. T. 1950. *Original forest structure.* In: *AAAS symposium on structure of plant communities.* Cleveland, 30 December.

DICE, L. R. 1952. Measure of the spacing between individuals within a population. *Contr. Lab. Vertebr. Biol. Univ. Mich.,* vol 55, p. 1–23.

DIX, R. L. 1961. An application of the point-centered quarter method to the sampling of grassland vegetation. *J. Range Mgmt.,* vol. 14, p. 63–9.

EDMONDSON, C. H. 1928. The ecology of an Hawaiian coral reef. *Bishop Mus. Bull.,* vol. 45, p. 1–64.

EVANS, F. C.; CLARK, P. J.; BRAND, R. H. 1955. Estimation of the number of species present in a given area. *Ecology,* vol. 36, p. 342–43.

FOSBERG, F. R.; SACHET, M. H. (eds). 1953. Handbook for atoll research. (2nd prelim. edit.). *Atoll. Res. Bull.,* vol. 17, p. 1–29.

215

GLEASON, H. A. 1922. On the relation between species and area. *Ecology,* vol. 3, p. 158–62.

GOLDBERG, W. M. 1973. The ecology of the coral–octocoral communities off the southeast Florida coast: Geomorphology, species composition and zonation. *Bull. mar. Sci.,* vol. 23, p. 465–88.

GOODALL, D. W. 1952. Quantitative aspects of plant distribution. *Biol. Rev. Camb. Philos. Soc.,* vol. 27, p. 194–245.

GREEN, R. H. 1970. On fixed precision level sequential sampling. *Res. Popul. Ecol.,* vol 12, p. 249–51.

GREIG-SMITH, P. 1964. *Quantitative plant ecology.* 2nd edit. London, Butterworth (242 p.).

HIATT, R. W. 1935. Instructions for marine ecological work on coral atolls. *Atoll. Res. Bull.,* vol. 17, p. 100–8.

HIATT, R. W. 1957. Factors influencing the distribution of corals on the reefs of Arno Atoll, Marshall Islands. In: *Proc. 8th Pacific Sci. Congr.,* vol. 3, p. 929–70.

HOLME, N. A. 1964. Methods of sampling the benthos. *Adv. Mar. Biol.,* vol. 2, p. 171–260.

——.; MCINTYRE, A. D. (eds). 1971. *Methods for the study of marine benthos.* Oxford, Blackwell Science Publications. (IBP Handbook no. 16). (334 p.).

HOPKINS, B. 1954. A new method for determining the type of distribution of plant individuals. *Ann. Bot. N.S.,* vol 18, p. 213–27.

HULINGS, N. C.; GRAY, J. S. 1971. A manual for the study of meiofauna. *Smith. Contr. Zool.,* vol. 78, p. 1–84.

JONES, N. S. 1971. Diving. In: N. A. Holme and A. D. McIntyre, (eds). *Methods for the study of marine benthos.* Oxford, Blackwell Science Publications. (IBP Handbook no. 16) p. 71–79.

KERSHAW, K. A. 1957. The use of cover and frequency in the detection of pattern in plant communities. *Ecology,* vol. 38, p. 291–99.

——. 1958. An investigation of the structure of a grassland community. I. The pattern of *Agrostis tenuis. J. Ecol.,* vol. 46, p. 571–92.

——. 1973. *Quantitative and dynamic plant ecology,* 2nd edit. London, Arnold, (308 p.).

KEULS, M.; OLIVER, H. J.; DE WITT, C. T. 1963. The distance method for estimating densities. *Statistica Neerlandica,* vol. 17, p. 71–91.

KILBURN, P. D. 1966. Analysis of the species-area relation. *Ecology,* vol. 47, p. 831–43.

KUNO, E. 1969. A new method of sequential sampling to obtain the population estimates with a fixed level of precision. *Res. Popul. Ecol.,* vol. 11, p. 127–36.

LAXTON, J. H.; W. J. STABLUM, 1974. Sample design for quantitative esitmation of sedentary organisms of coral reefs. *Biol. J. Linn. Soc.,* vol. 6, p. 1–18.

LOYA, Y. 1972. Community structure and species diversity of hermatypic corals at Eilat, Red Sea. *Mar. Biol.,* vol. 13, p. 100–23.

——. 1975. Possible effects of water pollution on the community structure of Red Sea corals. *Mar. Biol.,* vol. 29, p. 177–85.

——. 1976. Effects of water turbidity and sedimentation on the community structure of Puerto Rican corals. *Bull. mar. Sci.,* vol. 26, p. 450–66.

——; SLOBODKIN, L. B. 1971. The coral reefs of Eilat (Gulf of Eilat, Red Sea). *Symp. zool. Soc. Lond.,* vol. 28, p. 117–39. In: D. R. Stoddart and C. M. Yonge, (eds). *Regional variation in Indian Ocean coral reefs.* London and New York, Academic Press (584 p.).

MANTON, S. M. 1935. Ecological surveys of coral reefs. Sci. Repts, Gt Barrier Reef Exped. 1928–29 vol. 3, p. 273–312.

MARAGOS, J. E. 1974. Coral communities on a seaward reef slope, Fanning Island. *Pac. Sci.,* vol. 28, p. 257–78.

MAYOR, A. G. 1918. Ecology of the Murray Island coral reef. Papers Dept. Mar. Biol. Carnegie Inst., vol. 9, p. 1–48.

——. 1924. Structure and ecology of Samoan reefs. Papers Dept. Mar. Biol. Carnegie Inst., vol. 19, p. 1–25.

MCINTYRE, G. A. 1953. Estimation of plant density using line transects. *J. Ecol.,* vol. 41, p. 319–30.

MOORE, P. G. 1954. Spacing in plant populations. *Ecology,* vol. 35, p. 222–7.

MORISITA, M. 1954. Estimation of population density by spacing method. *Mem. Fac. Sci. Kyushu Univ.,* Ser. E., vol. I, p. 187–97.

NEUSHUL, M. 1966. Studies on subtidal marine vegetation in western Washington. *Ecology,* vol. 48, p. 83–94.

NEWELL, N. D.; IMBRIE, J.; PURDY, E. G.; THURBER, D. L. 1959. Organism communities and bottom facies, Great Bahama Bank. *Bull. Am. Mus. Nat. Hist.,* vol. 117, p. 181–228.

ODUM, H. T.; ODUM, E. P. 1955. Trophic structure and productivity of a windward coral reef community on Eniwetok Atoll. *Ecol. Monog.,* vol. 25, p. 291–320.

216

OTT, B. 1975. Quantitative analysis of community pattern and structure on a coral reef bank in Barbados, West Indies. Ph.D. thesis, McGill University (156 p.).

PIELOU, E. C. 1959. The use of point to plant distances in the study of the patterns of plant populations. *J. Ecol.,* vol. 47, p. 607–13.

——. 1960. A single mechanism to account for regular, random and aggregated populations. *J. Ecol.,* vol. 48, p. 575–84.

——. 1965. The concept of randomness in the patterns of mosaics. *Biometrics,* vol. 21, p. 908–20.

——. 1967. A test for random mingling of the phases of a mosaic. *Biometrics,* vol. 23, p. 657–70.

——. 1969. *An introduction to mathematical ecology.* New York, Wiley–Interscience (286 p.).

POORE, M. E. D. 1964. Investigation in the plant community. *J. Ecol.,* vol. 52 (Suppl.), p. 213–26.

PORTER, J. W. 1972a. Ecology and species diversity of coral reefs on opposite sides of the Isthmus of Panama. In: M. L. Jones, (ed.). *The Panama Biota—A symposium prior to the sea level canal. Bull. Biol. Soc. Wash.,* vol. 2, p. 89–116.

——. 1972b. Patterns of species diversity in Caribbean reef corals. *Ecology,* vol. 53, p. 745–8.

RICE, E. L.; PENFOUND, W. T. 1955. An evaluation of the variable radius and paired tree methods in the black jack-post oak forest. *Ecology,* vol. 36, p. 315–20.

RISSER, P. G.; ZEDLER, P. H. 1968. An evaluation of the grassland quarter method. *Ecology,* vol. 49, p. 1006–9.

SCHEER, G. 1967. Über die Methodik der Untersuchung von Korallenriffen. *Z. Morp. Ökol. Tiere.,* vol 60, 105–14.

——. 1972. Investigations of coral reefs in the Maldive Islands with notes on lagoon patch reefs and the method of coral sociology. In: *Proc. Symp. Corals and Coral Reefs.* Mar. Biol. Assoc. India, p. 87–120.

SCHMID, W. D. 1965. Distribution of aquatic vegetation as measured by line intercept with SCUBA. *Ecology,* vol. 46, p. 816–23.

SHANKS, R. E. 1954. Plotless sampling trials in appalachian forest types. *Ecology,* vol. 35, p. 237–44.

SHANNON, C. E.; WEAVER, W. 1948. *The mathematical theory of communication.* Urbana, University of Illinois Press (117 p.).

SOUTHWOOD, T. R. E. 1966. *Ecological methods with particular reference to the study of insect populations.* London, Methuen, (391 p.).

STEARNS, F. W. 1949. Ninety years change in a northern hardwood forest in Wisconsin. *Ecology,* vol. 30, p. 350–8.

STODDART, D. R. 1969. Ecology and morphology of recent coral reefs. *Biol. Rev. Camb. Philos. Soc.,* vol. 44, p. 433–98.

——. 1971. Problems and prospects in Indian Ocean reef studies. *Symp. zool. Soc. Lond.,* vol. 28, p. 549–593. In: D. R. Stoddart and C. M. Yonge (eds.). *Regional variation in Indian Ocean coral reefs.* London and New York, Academic Press (584 p.).

——. 1972. Field methods in the study of coral reefs. In: *Proc. Symp. Corals and Coral Reefs.* Mar. Biol. Assoc. India, p. 71–80.

——. DAVIES, P. S.; KEITH, A. C. 1966. Geomorphology of Addu Atoll. *Atoll. Res. Bull.,* vol. 116, p. 13–41.

STORR, J. F. 1964. Ecology and oceanography of the coral reef tract, Abaco Island, Bahamas. *Geol. Soc. Am.* Spec. Paper 79, p. 1–98.

STRONG, C. W. 1966. An improved method of obtaining density from line-transect data. *Ecology,* vol. 47, p. 311–3.

THOMPSON, H. R. 1956. Distribution of distance to *n*th neighbour in a population of randomly distributed individuals. *Ecology,* vol. 37, p. 391–4.

THORSON, G. 1957. Sampling the benthos. *Mem. Geol. Soc. Am.,* vol 67 (part 1), p. 61–73.

TURNER, F. B. 1960. Size and dispersion of a Louisiana population of the cricket frog *Acris gryllus. Ecology,* vol. 41, p. 258–68.

VESTAL, A. G. 1949. Minimum areas for different vegetations. *III. Biol. Mang.,* vol. 20, p. 1–129.

WALLACE, C. 1974. Distribution patterns of the coral genus *Acropora* on the reef slope: A preliminary report. Paper presented at the 2nd Crown of Thorns Symposium, Brisbane, September 1974. (18 p., 5 figs, 4 appendices)

WATERS, W. E. 1955. Sequential sampling in forest insect surveys. *Forestry Sci.,* vol. 1, p. 68–79.

WESTMAN, W. E. 1971. Density and basal area sampling techniques. In: G. P. Patil, E. C. Pielou and W. E. Waters, (eds.). *Statistical Ecology,* Vol. I, p. 515–536. London, The Pennsylvania State University Press (582 p.).

WILLIAMS, C. B. 1964. *Patterns in the balance of nature and related problems in quantitative ecology.* London and New York, Academic Press, (324 p.).

YARRANTON, G. A. 1966. A plotless method of sampling vegetation. *J. Ecol.,* vol. 54, p. 229–37.

17

Problems of measuring and mapping coral reef colonies

Michel Pichon[1]

INTRODUCTION

Measuring and mapping coral reef colonies are important parts of field work when studying coral reef communities from a quantitative standpoint. Whatever method (linear transect or quadrat) is used for an ecological study, it will be necessary at some stage to measure (linear transet) or to map (quadrat) coral colonies. These problems involve several difficulties caused by some of the most striking features of coral reefs (especially hermatypic) which are *colonial* invertebrates and have a *calcareous* (that is to say a rigid) skeleton.

Owing to these two characteristics, hermatypic coral reefs may be unusually tall for marine invertebrates, and their morphology may be highly variable: colonies sometimes assume uncommon shapes.

COLONY DEFINITION AND COLONY NUMBERING

From a zoological standpoint, one colony is a formation originating from only one planula. Planulae generally settle on a pre-existing hard substratum (which may be sometimes a dead coral skeleton) and give birth to clearly separated colonies.

Planulae may also settle on the dead part of colonies of the same species. After these new colonies grow for some time, they fuse with the older one. Such a phenomenon, when constantly repeated, lead to a continuous living coral formation, composed of elements belonging to different generations, which remain indistinguishable. These supracolonies may extend over several tens of square metres: even 100 m² or more in some places. This is the case for several species belonging to genera such as: *Acropora* (phenomenon found for tall branched species), *Montipora* which often show superimposed plates or bowl-shaped constructions fitted into each other, *Pavona*, and *Porites*.

1. Station marine d'Endoume et Centre d'océanographie, Marseille, France. Present address: Department of Marine Biology, James Cook University of North Queensland, Townsville, 4811, Australia.

In branched or foliated species (*Acropora, Pavona*) the lower part of the supracolonies may subsequently die, so that the living parts are no longer continuous. Furthermore these lower parts are frequently embedded in a layer of sediment or in limestone deposited by calcareous algae. In such instances, it will be particularly difficult to decide whether it is a supracolony or a dense growth of true colonies, very close to each other.

Manton's assumption (1935) that 1 sq ft of branching coral is equivalent to 1 colony may prove to be valid for one given species but generalization is unwise. An estimate of the importance of a supracolony can be obtained by comparing the area it covers, with the average area of one single, normal-sized colony of the *same species*: then the ratio gives, for each supracolony, the number of equivalent true colonies.

Supracolonies may be so large that they represent by themselves a whole ecological entity (subcommunity, facies or aspect). In most cases, this is not so, although they may far exceed the size of the sampling unit (i.e., the length of the line transect or the area of the quadrat). This does not raise any particular difficulty in data processing, but such an important feature in coral reef physiography deserves a special mention, apart from the limit value taken by the indices (A and S in the quadrat method and coverage and species diversity in the linear transect). When the problem of colony definition is solved, numbering becomes easy: it has long been considered that in colonial invertebrates one colony is equivalent to one individual of solitary species. Supracolonies are numbered also by considering the number of equivalent colonies calculated as explained above.

MORPHOLOGY OF THE CORALLUM: GROWTH FORM AND SHAPE OF THE COLONIES

Growth form of coral colonies is highly variable, according to the species, and also, within one and the same species, according to environmental factors. Most of coral colonies however have a corallum whose shape tends to be close to one of the several typical growth forms which have been recognized, although one can find all the intergrading forms. These typical growth forms can be classified according to the relations between their vertical and horizontal dimensions. (Fig. 1).

The height index is defined by the expression:

$$h = \frac{2H}{D + d}$$

H: maximum height of the colony
D: maximum horizontal dimension of the colony
d: maximum dimension of the colony along a direction perpendicular to that of D.

220

Measuring coral colonies

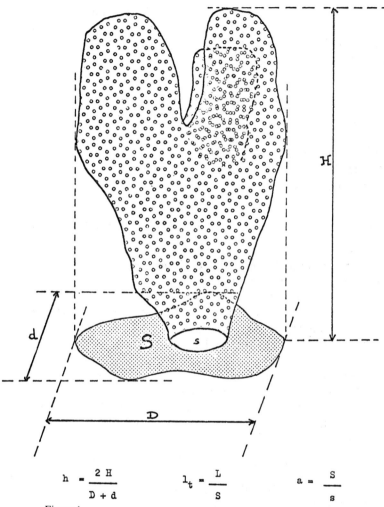

$$h = \frac{2H}{D+d} \qquad l_t = \frac{L}{S} \qquad a = \frac{S}{s}$$

Figure 1
Measuring coral colonies.

(This expression will give for dendroid colonies, which are often fan-shaped, h values comparable to that of other tall-sized colonies.)

If productivity studies are borne in mind, a better classification would take into account the ratio between L, the living surface of the tissues, and S, the horizontal projection of the colonies ($l_t = L/S$). Unfortunately the area of the living surface of the tissues can be estimated only very roughly, making the significance of the ratio of lesser value.

When considering the vertical and horizontal dimensions of the colonies one can group the typical coral growth forms into three categories: (1) developed mostly vertically, (2) equally developed vertically and horizontally, and (3) developed mostly horizontally.

(Within each of these categories the colony shapes can be classified according to the value of the ratio between S, the surface of the horizontal projection of the colony, and s, the surface of attachment on the bottom: attachment index $a = S/s$).

Category (1): colonies developed mostly vertically ($h \geqslant 2$)

This category includes the following growth forms:
    dendroid: $h > 2$, 1_t important ($\geqslant 3$), $a > 4$
    branched (or ramose): $h > 2$, $1_t \geqslant 3$, $a > 4$
    clavate: $h > 2$, $1_t \geqslant 4$, $a \geqslant 2$
    columnar: $h > 2$, $1_t > 4$, $a \# 1$

Category (2): colonies developed equally vertically and horizontally ($0.5 \leqslant h \leqslant 1,5$)

The most important and typical growth forms are:
    clump-shaped: 1_t important, $2 < a < 9$
    fasciculate: 1_t important, $2 < a < 9$
    massive, ranging from a thick encrusting plate to hemispherical and almost spherical colonies:
        thick encrusting plate: $1_t \# 1$, $a \# 1$
        hemispherical: $1_t = 2$, $a = 1$
        spherical: $1_t = 4$; a important (the true spherical colonies are free living and there is no corresponding value for a)
        cupolate: (free living forms such as *Halomitra* for instance) $1_t \neq 2$, no value for a.

Category (3): colonies developed mostly horizontally ($h < 0.5$)

This category includes the following growth forms:
    discoidal (and elongate oval): $1_t \# 1$
    tabulate: $1_t \# 1$, a important ($\geqslant 10$)
    bowl-shaped: $1 < 1_t < 2$, a important ($\geqslant 10$)
    digitate: 1_t important, a important
    console: such growth forms raise the problem of inclined substrates which will be discussed later.

One must emphasize that such a tentative classification is necessarily schematic and incomplete and that a series of intermediate growth forms exist between all the above-mentioned typical ones.

The values given for the h, 1_t and a indexes are only indicative. They will probably need alterations after further discussions and field measurements.

PROBLEM OF STRATA

An example of stratification in coral reefs has been given by Rosen (1971), who considers the existence of three strata, as follows:

Stratum A: sand infauna
Stratum B: rocky platform
　　　　　　isolated coral colonies on soft bottoms
　　　　　　microatolls
　　　　　　cobbles and debris
Stratum C: corals on rocky platform
　　　　　　corals on microatolls
　　　　　　corals on cobbles and debris.

From an ecological standpoint as well as from a methodological one, we must make a distinction between substrata and communities (or living) strata. Then, we may consider sandy bottoms and rocky bottoms are equivalent as substrata and they can be considered as belonging to the same stratum, the primary one. Both of them indeed contain endobiotic communities:

soft bottoms: infauna
hard bottoms: limestone boring or destroying community; cryptobiotic community.

These endobiotic communities represent the inner stratum of living organisms.

(Cobbles are generally considered as intermediate between hard bottom and soft bottoms, but as a rule, they have no true endobiotic community.)

Epibiotic communities include corals, on both hard bottoms and soft bottoms. On the latter, corals are generally free living in adult stages (several genera of the family *Fungiidae* and some species of *Siderastrea, Goniopora, Leptoseris, Heteropsammia, Heterocyathus* . . .)

The living organisms of epibiotic communities can be generally divided into two living strata:

the *lower* stratum, which is composed of organisms generally only slightly elevated above the bottom and sometimes largely spreading over it.
the *upper* stratum, which is composed of tall sized, very photophilic organisms.

Reef corals belong to both of these strata. Some species of the upper living stratum may serve as secondary substrata, such as large coral colonies and microatolls, stems and leaves of sea grasses or algae thalli. The fauna and flora secondarily growing on large coral colonies or on microatolls is often so complex that the whole can be considered independently as a microcosm. Such microcosms in coral reef deserve detailed studies such as that done by McCloskey (1970) in a subtropical environment (see Table 1).

223

TABLE 1. Relationships between substrata stratification and community stratification.

Substratum stratification			Living strata	
Primary	Soft bottom	Sand (mud) infauna		Inner — Endobiotic community
	Cobbles	Limestone boring or destroying organisms		
	Hard bottom	Cryptofauna		
		Corals		
		Various sessile plants or invertebrates	Lower	Epibiotic community
		Mobile fauna		
Secondary	Hard bottom	Corals including microatolls		
	Semi-hard bottom	Algae or Phanerogames	Upper	
		Other tall sized organisms		

When considering coral distribution alone, it would be more accurate to study each stratum independently, but this technique generally proves inconvenient during field work. Measuring and mapping colonies is generally done simultaneously for various strata, each of them, however, can subsequently be referred to by means of an identification symbol for each stratum.

Lastly, it is to be noticed that the lower living stratum is more or less sciaphilic, depending on the upper stratum density. In some cases, when the growth of the upper stratum is very dense, or under large coral colonies (tabulate or console-shaped, for instance), the lower stratum will no longer belong to the same community, or even to the same zone or subzone (with the signification of layer, in the vertical zonation of marine benthic communities). In such circumstances, the lower living stratum must be considered as an enclave of a more sciaphilic community or possibly belonging to a normally deeper layer, in a photophilic community. This situation occurs, for example, when ahermatypic corals (circalittoral layer) grow on the rocky substratum under the shade of large hermatypic corals (infralittoral layer). In such instances the study of the upper stratum and of the lower stratum, which belong to two decidedly different communities must be done absolutely independently.

DIFFERENCES IN THE SCALE OF THE COLONIES

An important difficulty in the study of coral community structure lies in the difference in the scale of the various colonies. This problem which is related to the existence of very large colonies and of supracolonies as mentioned above, may partly explain the inequality between quadrat sizes so far used, ranging from 1 to 900 m². (For some coral reef communities devoid of any hermatypic coral growth, such as the dark cave communities described by Vasseur (1964) in Tuléar, the optimum quadrat size is as low as 0.2×0.2 m.).

Most hermatypic coral colonies in the reef environment are of decimetric size and suitable dimensions for quadrat sampling would be of metric size ($1 \to 5$ m² for instance). However, in all the reef biota (reef flat, lagoon slope, outer slope) large colonies or supracolonies of metric (or even decametric) size may be found. To take them into account, quadrats of metric size would not be adequate and quadrats of decametric size ($25 \to 100$ m² for instance) have to be used simultaneously with metric-sized quadrats. (Decametric sized quadrats cannot be used alone because of the difficulty in estimating the number and percentage coverage of the very numerous colonies of decimetric size). In some instances, even a decametric-sized recording unit will not be sufficient to encircle huge colonies or large supracolonies, which consequently are almost impossible to quantify, in the scope of a quantitative study of coral community structure. The same difficulty arises when using linear transects: the length of transect best fitted to the size of most of the colonies may prove to be insufficient for very large colonies or supracolonies, and a linear transect of standard length, taken at random, can be entirely contained in a very large colony or in

225

a supracolony. It remains to be seen, however, if these features cannot be better considered as microcosms, and investigated independently of the surrounding coral community.

PROBLEM OF INCLINED SUBSTRATA

The problem of inclined substrata does not arise when studying coral community structure with line transects, which are run along depth contours. Yet in some instances, such as in the spur and groove zone, depth contours show a rapid alternation of two different communities and even small transect length will prove to be of little value.

(a) Horizontal substrata

When using the quadrat technique, coral recording is done by measuring the surface of each colony as seen in plan, i.e. by measuring the surface of the vertical projection of the colony on the substrata which, as a rule are considered as practically horizontal. The projection is perpendicular to the reference surface, on the substrata. (Attention has already been drawn to the fact that the ratio between the surface of the vertical projection of a coral colony, and the surface of the living tissues is highly variable). (Fig. 2).

(b) Slightly inclined substrata (up to 45°)

The reference surface S_r of the recording unit is defined and measured on the inclined substrata, for greater convenience. A number of colonies settled on these slightly inclined substrata grow vertically (category (1), as defined above: dendroid, branched, columnar or clavate colonies); their mapping can only be done by measuring the surface of their vertical projection. This can be related to a sample on a fictitious horizontal surface S_h, the area of which depends on the inclination of the substratum, according to the formula:

$S_h = S_r \cos \alpha$ (α = inclination of the substrata) When $\alpha = 45°$, the fictitious horizontal surface of the sampling unit is only 70 per cent of the reference surface on the substrata. This must be taken into account when comparing the results of quadrats referring to substrata of various inclinations. (The best way is to increase the reference surface taken on the inclined surface, by introducing a coefficient $I/\cos \alpha$, so that its vertical projection has the same area as the reference surface on a horizontal bottom.)

When slightly inclined substrata are settled by coral colonies of categories (2) and (3), these colonies are mapped by projecting them perpendicularly on to the inclined substrata containing the reference surface. Therefore, no correction is needed for the substrata inclination.

Generally, colonies of category (1) are growing intermingled with colonies of categories (2) and (3), and the correction coefficient can be estimated according

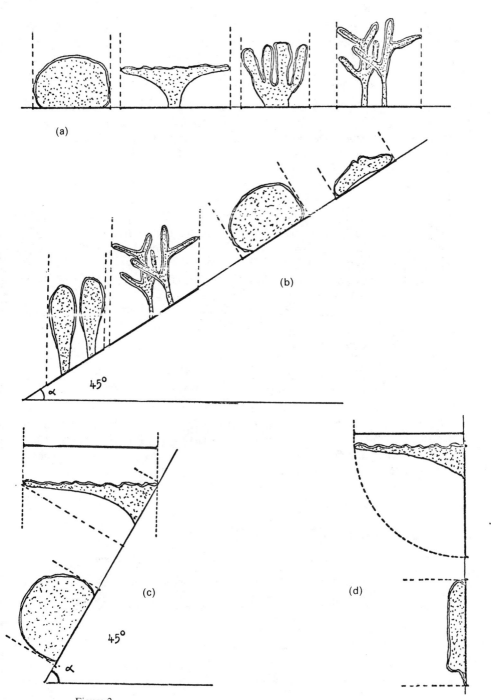

Figure 2
(a) Horizontal substratum; (b) Slightly inclined substratum; (c) Strongly
inclined substratum; (d) Vertical substratum.

to the inclination of the substrata and the ratio between the coverage by category (1) colonies and the coverage by category (2) and category (3) colonies.

Strongly inclined substrata (45° *to vertical*)

Strongly inclined surfaces are generally covered with coral colonies belonging to categories (2) and (3), and only very exceptionally with coral colonies in category (1). Mapping these colonies can be done by projecting them perpendicularly on to the inclined (or vertical) substrata. The only difficulty arises from console-shaped colonies for which the projection perpendicularly to the substrata has no signification. In such exceptional instances, mapping console-shaped colonies can be done by considering their horizontal surface, and not the projected surface on the substrata. In that way, the projected surface is replaced by the surface of the living tissues, which is even better. In such circumstances, the percentage of coverage by coral colonies remains lower than 100 per cent for two reasons:

On subvertical or vertical substrata, coral colonies are not generally very dense, but they are more or less scattered.

Under a console-shaped colony, the part of the substrata lying in the shade of the colony is generally devoid of coral growth. When invertebrates or algae settle there, they belong to the lower strata showing sciaphilic affinities, and, as a rule, belong to another community or an enclave of a normally deeper layer. In neither case should they be taken into account as members of the coral community being sampled by the quadrat method.

The above mentioned considerations are valid when the substratum is almost even. When the bottom topography is very irregular or rough within the recording unit (which should be avoided as far as possible) the general methods are no longer appropriate and a special treatment is necessary.

Selected Bibliography

Abe, N. 1937. Ecological survey of Iwayama Bay, Palao. *Palao Trop. Biol. Stn Stud.,* vol. 1, p. 217–324.

——; Eguchi, M.; Hiro, F. 1937. Preliminary survey of the coral reef of Iwayama Bay, Palao. *Palao Trop. Biol. Stn Stud.,* vol. 1, p. 17–35.

Baker, J. R. 1925. A coral reef in the New Hebrides. *Proc. zool. Soc. London,* p. 1007–19.

Catala, R. 1950. Contribution à l'étude écologique des îlots coralliens du Pacifique Sud. *Bull. biol. France Belgique,* vol. 84, p. 234–310.

Davies, P. S.; Stoddart, D. R.; Sigee, D. C. 1971. Reef forms of Addu atoll, Maldive Islands. *Symp. Zool. Soc. London,* vol. 28, p. 217–59.

Edmondson, C. H. 1928. The ecology of an Hawaiian coral reef. *Bull. Bishop Mus.,* vol. 45, p. 1–64.

Endean, R.; Kenny, R.; Stephenson, W. 1956. The ecology and distribution of intertidal organisms on certain islands off the Queensland coast. *Aust. J.mar.Freshwat. Res.,* vol. 7, p. 317–22. 317–42.

Goreau, T. F. 1959. The ecology of Jamaican coral reefs. Species composition and zonation. *Ecology,* vol. 40, p. 69–90.

HIATT, R. W. 1953a. Methods of collecting marine invertebrates on coral atolls. *Atoll Research Bull.*, 17, p. 78–89.

——. 1953b. Instructions for marine ecological work on coral atolls. *Atoll Research Bull.*, 17, p. 100–8.

——. 1957. Factors influencing the distribution of corals of the reefs of Arno atoll, Marshall Islands. *Proc. 8th Pacific Sci. Congr.*, vol. 3a, p. 929–70.

KISSLING, D. L. 1965. Coral distribution on a shoal in Spanish Harbour, Florida Keys. *Bull. mar. Sci.*, vol. 15, p. 600–11.

KORNICKER, L. S.; BOYD, D. W. 1962. Shallow water geology and environments of Alacran reef complex, Campeche Bank, Mexico. *Bull. Am. Assoc. petrol. Geol.*, vol. 46, p. 640–73.

KÜHLMANN, D. H. H. 1971a. Die Korallenriffe Kubas. II. Zur ökologie der bankriffe und ihrer Korallen. *Int. Rev. gesamt. Hydrobiol.*, vol. 51, no. 2, p. 145–99.

——. 1971b. Zur methodik der Korallenriffuntersuchung. *Wiss. Z. Humboldt Univ. Berlin,Math.-Nat. R.*, vol. 20, p. 697–705.

LOYA, Y. 1972. Community structure and species diversity of hermatypic corals at Eilat, Red Sea. *Mar. Biol.*, vol. 13, p. 100–23.

——; SLOBODKIN, L. B. 1971. The coral reefs of Eilat (Gulf of Eilat, Red Sea) *Symp. zool. Soc. London*, vol. 28, p. 117–39.

McCLOSKEY, L. R. 1970. The dynamics of the community associated with a marine scleractinian coral. *Int. Rev. gesamt. Hydrobiol.*, vol. 55, no. 1, p. 13–81.

MANTON, S. M. 1935. Ecological surveys of coral reefs. *Sci. Repts Gt Barrier Reef Exped. 1928–29*, vol. 3, no. 10, p. 273–312.

MAYOR, A. G. 1918. Ecology of the Murray islands coral reef. *Papers Dept. Mar. Biol. Carnegie Inst.*, vol. 9, p. 1–48.

——. 1924. Structure and ecology of Samoan reefs. *Papers Dept. Mar. Biol. Carnegie Inst.*, vol. 19, p. 1–25.

MOTODA, S. 1939. Submarine illumination, silt content and quantity of food planckton of reef corals in Iwayama Bay, Palao. *Palao Trop. Biol. Stn Stud.*, vol. 1, p. 637–47.

NEWELL, N. D.; RIGBY, J. K.; WHITEMAN, A. J.; BRADLEY, J. S. 1951. Shoal water geology and environments, Eastern Andros Island, Bahamas. *Bull. Am. Mus. Nat. Hist.*, vol. 97, p. 1–29.

——; IMBRIS, J.; PURDY, E. G.; THURBER, D. L. 1959. Organism communities and bottom facies, Great Bahamas Bank. *Bull. Am. Mus. Nat. Hist.*, vol. 117, p. 181–228.

ODUM, H. T.; ODUM, E. P. 1955. Trophic structure and productivity of a windward coral reef community on Eniwetok atoll. *Ecol. Monogr.*, vol. 25, p. 291–320.

PICHON, MICHEL. 1964. Contribution à l'étude de la répartition des Madréporaires sur le récif de Tuléar. *Rec. Trav. Stn mar. Endoume*, Suppl. Hors série 2, p. 79–203.

PLANTE, R. 1964. Contribution à l'étude des peuplements de hauts niveaux sur substrats solides non récifaux dans le région du Tuléar (Madagascar). *Rec. Trav. Stn mar. Endoume*, Suppl. Hors série 2, p. 205–316.

ROSEN, B. R. 1971. Principal features of reef coral ecology in shallow water environment of Mahé, Seychelles. *Symp. zool. Soc. London*, vol. 28, p. 163–83.

SCHEER, G. 1960. Der Lebensraum der Riffkorallen. *Ber. Natur. Ver. Darmstadt*, vol. 59/60, p. 29–44.

——. 1967. Uber de Methodik der Untersuchung von Korallenriffen. *Z. Morphol. Ökol. Tiere*, vol. 60, p. 105–14.

——. 1972. Investigations of coral reefs in the Maldive Islands with notes on lagoon patch reefs and the method of coral sociology. In: *Proc. Symp. Corals and Coral Reefs, 1969 Mar. Biol. Assoc. India*, p. 87–120.

——. 1971. Coral reefs and coral genera in the Red Sea and the Indian Ocean. *Symp. zool. Soc. Lond.*, vol. 28, p. 329–67.

STEPHENSON, T. A.; STEPHENSON, A.; TANDY, G.; SPENDER, M. 1931. The structure and ecology of Low Islands and other reefs. *Sci. Repts Gt Barrier Reef Exped. 1928–29*, vol. 3, p. 17–112.

STEPHENSON, W.; ENDEAN, R.; BENNETT, I. 1958. An ecological survey of the marine fauna of low isles, Queensland. *Aust. J. mar. Freshwat. Res.*, vol. 9, p. 261–318.

STODDART, D. R. 1966. Reef studies at Addu atoll, Maldive Islands: preliminary results of an expedition to Addu atoll in 1964. *Atoll Res. Bull.*, vol. 116, p. 1–122.

——. 1969. Ecology and morphology of recent coral reefs. *Biol. Rev. Camb. Philos. Soc.*, vol. 44, p. 433–98.

——. 1972. Field methods in the study of coral reefs. In: *Proc. Symp. Corals and Coral Reefs, 1969. Mar. Biol. Assoc. India*, p. 71–80.

STORR, J. F. 1964. Ecology and oceanography of the coral reef tract, Abaco island, Bahamas. *Spec. Papers Geol. Soc. Am.,* vol. 79, p. 1–98.

TAYLOR, J. E. 1968. Coral reefs and associated invertebrate communities (mainly molluscan) around Mahé, Seychelles. *Phil. Trans. R. Soc.* (B: *Biol. Sci.*), vol. 254, p. 129–206.

UMBGROVE, J. H. F. 1947. Coral reefs of the East Indies. *Bull. Geol. Soc. Am.,* vol. 58, p. 729–78.

VASSEUR, P. 1964. Contribution à l'étude bionomique des peuplements sciaphiles infralittoraux de substrat dur dans les récifs de Tuléar (Madagascar). *Rec. Trav. Stn mar. Endoume,* Suppl. Hors série 2, p. 1–77.

18

A simulation study of coral reef survey methods

R. A. Kinzie III and R. H. Snider[1]

INTRODUCTION

A number of different quantitative survey techniques have been developed for use on coral reefs. These methods are usually modifications of transect or quadrat techniques used in plant ecological surveys. Much of the theoretical background, strengths and weaknesses of these methods have been discussed by workers on plant communities. Summaries of this work can be found in Greig-Smith (1964), Pielou (1969), Kershaw (1964) and Mueller-Dombois and Ellenberg (1974). More general discussions are to be found in Poole (1974), Southwood (1966), and in the series edited by Patil, Pielou and Walters (1971) especially volume 1.

The questions asked in coral reef surveys are very often similar to those asked by plant ecologists: What is the cover? This can be total coral (or plant) cover or the cover of a single species. What is the abundance? This is usually asked in terms of density—how many individuals of a particular species occur per unit area? What are the dispersion patterns of each species? Is a species dispersed randomly, regularly or contagiously?

While a number of the theoretical aspects of these questions have been discussed (see references above), there is little information on comparative evaluations of different methods in the field. This is, at least partly, due to two factors. The first is that a great deal of time would be needed to collect enough data to permit valid comparisons to be made because of the observed high variability between replicates. The second is that once significant differences have been shown to exist between methods, there remains the question of which one is right. Unless a complete census has been made over the sampled plot, there is no objective basis for making this judgment. These problems have been approached by the use of artificial populations and artificial sampling methods which strive to duplicate, as far as possible, relevant aspects of the field situation. Such simulations have been done manually (Pielou, 1960) and by using computers (Wiebe 1970; Errington, 1973; and Herczynski, 1975).

1. Zoology Department, University of Hawaii, 2538 The Mall, Honolulu, Hawaii 96822, U.S.A.

The project discussed here is an example of the latter approach. Simulated reefs were generated using a particular set of rules which specified the parameters of interest. One of the two aims of this paper is to discuss, in some detail, the program which produces the reefs and to describe the three sampling programs. Subsequently these 'reefs' were sampled using a variety of methods of the same design as those in use on reefs in the field. The second purpose of this paper is to compare the accuracy of these different sampling techniques in estimating known reef parameters. In order to do this, suites of reefs with configurations of particular interest were made and sampled.

METHODS

Description of computer simulation techniques

The four programs used in this study were written so as to be flexible and allow their use in many possible additional studies. A fully documented program package will soon be available from the authors. A brief description of these programs follows.

REEF—Reef generating program

This program places circles representing corals, in a square area with 12-metre sides. The placement of the 'corals' follows certain rules. The 'reef' consists of lists of 'coral' localities and sizes which are printed, and produced in machine-readable output for use as data by the sampling programmes.

The use of round 'corals' is justified on the basis that many massive and branching corals are at least roughly circular in outline. Furthermore, as will be seen below, overlaps result in noncircular corals. Spatial relationships are restricted to two dimensions on the grounds that the survey methods being simulated also ignore the third (vertical) dimension. Multi-layered reefs can be produced and sampled using slight modifications of the existing programs, but so far this additional factor has been avoided due to difficulty of analysis.

The input parameters for generating the reef are: (a) the number of species, (b) the cover for each species, (c) the head size and variability for each species. The procedure consists of randomly placing centres of corals and selecting their sizes from the predetermined Gaussian distribution set by the input parameters. If two corals are placed so that they overlap, the area occupied by both is assigned to the one originally placed. In cases of multiple overlap each occurrence of overlap is evaluated (Fig. 1). Individuals of a species are placed until the accumulated cover for that species reaches the pre-set cover value, then the heads of the next species are assigned.

The printed output from the REEF programme gives the following information: the number of individuals and total cover of each species, the mean and variability of the head area for each species, the number of overlapping pairs of corals and a list of the members of each pair. In addition, a map of the 12×12 metre reef is produced showing the number of coral centres in each of the 144 square metres of the reef.

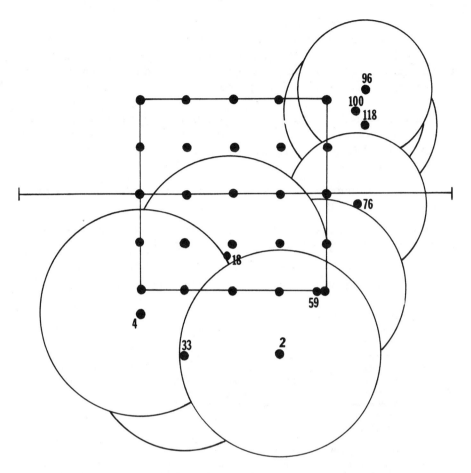

Figure 1
This is a drawing of a portion of an actual reef-run showing the complexity
of overlap situations that are obtained. Each species with a higher
identification number (placed later) loses area to corals with lower numbers
(placed first). The long horizontal line is a part of one of the 10 m transect
lines. Corals nos. 18 and 76 will contribute to the line intercept method
'chord'. The square with 25 points is one of the 3 quadrats placed by LINE.
Coral no. 2 will get 3 points, coral no. 4 will get 4 points, coral no. 18 will
get 6 points, etc. Note corals nos. 33, 59, 100 and 118 have lost their centres.

LINE—Transect and quadrat sampling program
(a) Transects: A set of 10 parallel 10 metre transects is placed randomly on the
reef with the restriction that no part may come closer than the diameter of the
largest coral head to the edge of the reef. This prevents sampling in the areas
of reduced density near the edges of the reef.

In simulating the chain link or line intercept method (Porter 1972, 1974;
Loya, 1972; and Dollar, 1975), the method called chord is used. The length of
the transect line passing through each coral is taken as the datum.

In addition, the point intercept method (Roy and Smith, 1971) is simulated with two intensities. In the higher level 40 points are placed at 0.25 metre intervals along the 10 metre transect line (40 points) while at the lower level 20 points are placed at 0.5 metre intervals (20 points). If a point falls on a coral the point is added to the list of hits for the species.

(b) Quadrats: Three one-square metre quadrats are placed along each transect line with their centres at 2, 5, and 8 metres (the program allows the quadrat size to vary but the results discussed in this paper all deal with 1×1 m quadrats). The quadrat techniques simulated are:

heads—the number of coral heads of each species that fall either wholly or partially in the quadrat.

points—each quadrat has 25 uniformly spaced points, which constitute the third point intercept estimate (points per quadrat).

Table 1 gives the information printed by LINE. Accuracy of the methods (chord, points per quadrat, 40 points and 20 points) (item 10) is defined as the

TABLE 1. Output generated by line

For each 10-metre transect
(1) Location of the left end of the 10-metre transect.
(2) Identification number of each head intersected by the transect line and the length of the chord.
(3) The number of chords for each species (abundance estimate).
(4) The cumulative chord lengths for each species (cover estimate).
(5) The average (and S.D.) chord length for each species (head size estimate).
(6) For each of the three quadrats: How many heads of each species appear in the quadrat (abundance estimates).
(7) For each of the three quadrats: How many centres (after overlap correction) are in the quadrat for each species (abundance estimate including dispersion).
(8) For each of the three quadrats: How many of the 25 points fall on each species (cover estimate).
(9) For each of the species, the average (and S.D.) of the number of points per quadrat (cover estimate).
(10) For each of the species, the average number of heads per quadrat (abundance estimate).
(11) For each species, the number of points per head (head size estimate).
(12) A map showing the identification number of the coral (if any) lying under each of the 25 grid points in each of the 3 quadrats is printed.

For each set of 10 '10-metre transects'
(1) Running mean (and S.D.) (over each of the 10 transects) of the number of points per head (head size estimate).
(2) Mean (and S.D.) of average number of chords (abundance estimate).
(3) Mean (and S.D.) of average cumulative chord (cover estimate).
(4) Mean (and S.D.) of transect chord averages (between-transect-variability measure).
(5) Mean (and S.D.) of number of heads per quadrat (abundance estimate).
(6) Mean (and S.D.) of number of adjusted centres per quadrat (abundance estimate including dispersion).
(7) Mean (and S.D.) number of points per 75 points of three quadrats (cover estimate)
(8) Mean (and S.D.) hit by the 40 points every $\frac{1}{4}$ metre (cover estimate).
(9) Mean (and S.D.) hit by the 20 points every $\frac{1}{2}$ metre (cover estimate).
(10) Accuracy $\pm 5\%$, 10% and 20% for each species of the following cover estimates. Total Chord: Points per quadrat: 40 points and 20 points.

number of times out of ten these cover estimates are within 5, 10 and 20 per cent of the known cover for each species. Three series of sets of ten were run to obtain confidence estimates of these accuracy values. The method simulated by chord is the most laborious and time consuming. Points per quadrat, 40 points and 20 points are increasingly faster.

QUADSIZE—Variable quadrat size simulating program

The problems associated with quadrat size in quantitative survey techniques have long been recognized. (Greig-Smith, 1964; Kershaw, 1964; Pielou, 1969). In addition, quadrats of different sizes have been used to identify dispersion patterns (Greig-Smith, 1964; Morisita, 1959). QUADSIZE calculates dispersion indices based on a series of progressively larger quadrats formed by combining adjacent 1 × 1 metre divisions into 2 × 2, 3 × 3 and 4 × 4 metre sampling units. The dispersion indices given for each quadrat size and species are: Morisita's index of dispersion (Morisita, 1959), and the variance: mean ratio (Stitler and Patil, 1971). The observed frequency distribution of the number of heads per quadrat is listed along with the distributions expected both by the Poisson and the Binomial. In addition the χ^2 values for the deviations from these two expected distributions are calculated and the values are listed for the individual terms contributing most to the χ^2 value.

The dispersion indices are based on the number of heads per quadrat. The centre of a head determines to which quadrat the coral is assigned. In corals which are overlapped, the original centre may no longer accurately represent the centre of its remaining area. Thus methods using the original centres of circles would give misleading estimates of dispersion. To correct for this a new centre was calculated for each coral that was overlapped. The new centre was in effect a centre of gravity of the remaining portion. It was calculated by placing a grid of points over the original position of the head and determining which points remained after points lost through overlap were deleted. The average location of these points was defined as the new centre of the coral. The effect of this shifting of centres of overlapped corals is to increase the distance between corals. It was expected that this would increase uniformity of dispersion.

POINT—Plotless techniques simulating program

Plotless techniques are also commonly used to determine dispersion patterns. The methods simulated here were the Clark and Evans distance to nearest neighbour (Clark and Evans, 1954) and Pielou's alpha$_i$ and alpha$_p$ (Pielou, 1960). The first two methods are based on the distances between individuals and the last on distances between randomly placed points and the nearest individual.

Description of REEFS *used in the sampling study*

Cover and abundance. Three series of reefs (called A, B and C) were designed to study the cover estimates. Table 2 gives the parameters of these reefs. The

235

TABLE 2. Parameters of the reefs of the A, B, and C series

	Species			
	1	2	3	4
	"A" series constant cover (15%)			
A1				
Cover (m²)	22.0709	21.8842	21.6167	21.6194
Avg. head area (after overlaps)	0.6897	0.3908	0.0252	0.0162
Radius (S.D.)	0.5 (0.05)	0.4 (0.04)	0.1 (0.01)	0.09 (0.009)
Number of heads	32	56	859	1332
A2				
Cover (m²)	21.6057	21.6744	21.6345	21.6430
Avg. head area (after overlaps)	0.3087	0.1885	0.1209	0.0668
Radius (S.D.)	0.32 (0.032)	0.28 (0.028)	0.24 (0.024)	0.2 (0.02)
Number of heads	70	115	179	324
A2				
Cover (m²)	21.8257	21.8440	21.6010	21.6015
Avg. head area (after overlaps)	0.3074	0.2121	0.1234	0.0673
Radius (S.D.)	0.32 (0.032)	0.28 (0.028)	0.24 (0.024)	0.2 (0.02)
Number of heads	71	103	175	321
A3				
Cover (m²)	22.5237	22.0525	21.6752	21.6025
Avg. head area (after overlaps)	1.2513	0.5251	0.1582	0.0109
Radius (S.D.)	0.65 (0.074)	0.46 (0.05)	0.26 (0.03)	0.07 (0.007)
Number of heads	18	42	137	1985
A3				
Cover (m²)	22.3052	22.1809	21.6885	21.6308
Avg. head area (after overlaps)	0.9294	0.5410	0.3143	0.1133
Radius (S.D.)	0.58 (0.058)	0.49 (0.049)	0.39 (0.039)	0.24 (0.024)
Number of heads	24	41	69	191

TABLE 2—*continued*

	Species			
	1	2	3	4
	"B" series head size for each species constant			
B1				
Cover (m²)	20.1202	19.7590	19.5542	19.5090
Avg. head area (after overlaps)	1.0590	0.2325	0.0584	0.0131
Radius (S.D.)	0.6 (0.06)	0.3 (0.03)	0.15 (0.015)	0.08 (0.008)
Number of heads	19	85	335	1486
B1 (different randomization)				
Cover (m²)	19.7677	19.5763	19.5027	19.5037
Avg. head area (after overlaps)	1.0404	0.2331	0.0567	0.0131
Radius (S.D.)	0.6 (0.06)	0.3 (0.03)	0.15 (0.015)	0.075 (0.0075)
Number of heads	19	84	334	1495
B2				
Cover (m²)	8.3761	31.2262	31.2137	7.8170
Avg. Head area (after overlaps)	1.0470	0.2548	0.0525	0.0129
Radius (S.D.)	0.6 (0.06)	0.3 (0.03)	0.15 (0.015)	0.075 (0.0075)
Number of heads	8	127	595	604
B3				
Cover (m²)	31.8251	7.8064	7.8030	31.2070
Avg. Head area (after overlaps)	1.0266	0.2440	0.0624	0.0137
Radius (S.D.)	0.6 (0.06)	0.3 (0.03)	0.15 (0.015)	0.075 (0.0075)
Number of heads	31	32	125	273
B4				
Cover (m²)	43.4521	11.8889	11.7020	11.7179
Avg. head area (after overlaps)	1.0863	0.2162	0.0563	0.0141
Radius (S.D.)	0.6 (0.06)	0.3 (0.03)	0.15 (0.015)	0.075 (0.0075)
Number of heads	40	55	208	829
B5				
Cover (m²)	12.2320	11.7200	11.7422	42.9079
Avg. head area (after overlaps)	1.2230	0.2791	0.0631	0.0130
Radius (S.D.)	0.6 (0.06)	0.3 (0.03)	0.15 (0.015)	0.075 (0.0075)
Number of heads	10	42	186	2209

continues overleaf

Table 2—*continued*

			Species			
	1	2	3	4	5	6
		"C" series relative cover of all species constant				
C2						
Cover (m²)	0.3603	1.0805	2.1717	29.0180	10.8203	7.2054
Avg. head area (after overlaps)	0.0021	0.0037	0.0034	0.1677	0.2924	0.0071
Radius (S.D.)	0.025 (0.005)	0.025 (0.02)	0.025 (0.02)	0.2 (0.1)	0.25 (0.2)	0.05 (0.01)
Number of head	175	289	632	173	10	1009
C3						
Cover (m²)	0.1812	0.5418	1.0809	14.4660	5.8515	3.6076
Avg. head area (after overlaps)	0.0021	0.0036	0.0035	0.1523	0.3080	0.0076
Radius (S.D.)	0.025 (0.005)	0.025 (0.02)	0.025 (0.02)	0.2 (0.1)	0.25 (0.2)	0.05 (0.01)
Number of head	88	149	313	95	19	475
C4						
Cover (m²)	0.0905	0.2752	0.5419	7.2856	3.0870	1.8061
Avg. head area (after overlaps)	0.0021	0.0032	0.0032	0.1821	0.2806	0.0078
Radius (S.D.)	0.025 (0.005)	0.025 (0.02)	0.025 (0.02)	0.2 (0.1)	0.25 (0.2)	0.05 (0.01)
Number of heads	43	86	168	40	11	232
C5						
Cover (m²)	0.0447	0.1357	0.2729	3.8159	1.3647	0.9004
Avg. head area (after overlaps)	0.0024	0.0041	0.0040	0.1659	0.6823	0.0084
Radius (S.D.)	0.025 (0.005)	0.025 (0.02)	0.025 (0.02)	0.2 (0.1)	0.25 (0.2)	0.05 (0.01)
Number of heads	19	33	68	23	2	107

five reefs of the A series each had four species with equal cover (15 per cent), which varied in head size and abundance.

In the six reefs of the B series, each of the four species had a mean radius twice that of the next smaller species. These sizes remained constant through the series while the abundance and hence cover were manipulated together.

In the C series, relative head size and relative abundance remained constant while the cover was reduced by a factor of two in each reef of the series. An additional factor of this series is that the six species approximate abundances, size relationships and variabilities of a real reef that was intensively studied in a preliminary part of this project in the field. That is to say it is the most real of the reefs.

Dispersion. A series of reefs was produced that kept factors of cover, abundance and head size constant, but was expected to show differences in dispersion patterns (Table 3). The factors expected to produce differences were: (a) The first corals placed were expected to be more random than those later placed species which might be expected to have more restrictions on their possible locations. (b) When large species are placed first, the small species placed later would be forced to fit into the remaining spaces and might be expected to show clumped patterns (Pielou, 1960). (c) Increased variability in head size might be expected to result in clumped dispersion patterns. (Note that the model is somewhat different from Pielou's 1960 model where the sizes of her root systems are not predetermined but expand, within limits, until they fill the available space). (d) The amount of overlap permitted was reduced in two of the reefs. This was expected to result in more uniform patterns.

One of the difficulties in analysing the ability of different sampling methods to assess dispersion patterns correctly is that, whereas the cover, abundance and coral head size of the simulated reefs are known precisely, there is no analogous true value of uniformity, contagion, or randomness. These terms are relative and depend on the frame of reference.

RESULTS

Cover

A series. The accuracy of methods for estimating cover for the A reefs is shown in Figure 2. Three points of interest emerge from these results:

(a) In no case was the accuracy of a cover estimate greater than 7 out of 10 and usually accuracy was less than five out of ten, i.e. estimates of cover were within a 40 per cent range of the known cover less than half the time.
(b) There is a tendency for the smaller (more abundant) heads to have their cover more correctly estimated than larger heads. That is to say for any method, results for small (abundant) heads are usually more reliable than those from large heads *independent of total cover*.

TABLE 3. Attributes of the six reefs used in determining dispersion patterns

These reefs are placed in increasing order of expected uniformity, but different species in the same reef are expected to show different patterns.

Reef number	Limitations on overlap	Order of species placement	Variability of head size	Expected patterns
183	none	large to small	S.D. = 10% of radius	first species placed random later species clumped
505	none	large to small	S.D. = 5% of radius	same as above slightly more uniform
241	none	small to large	S.D. = 10% of radius	first species placed random later species?
514	none	small to large	S.D. = 5% of radius	Same as above slightly more uniform
162	no overlap more than 20 per cent	large to small	S.D. = 10% of radius	all species tending to uniform dispersion
133	no heads overlap more than 10 per cent	large to small	S.D. = 10% of radius	Strongest uniformity

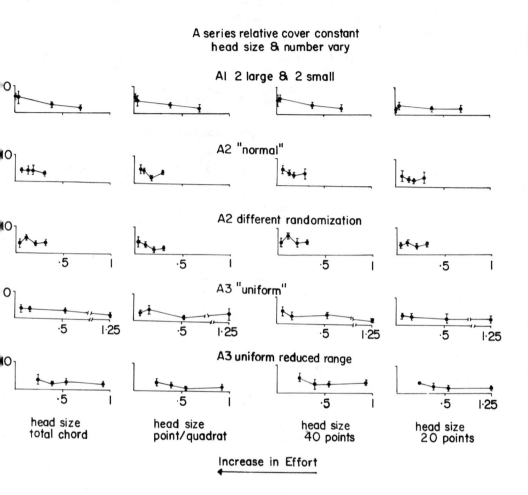

Figure 2
This figure shows the accuracy of the four different cover estimates (Total Chord, Points/Quadrat, 40 Points, and 20 Points) on the reefs of the A series. Each column of graphs refers to a method, and each row to a reef. The accuracy of a method (number correct ±20 per cent) is the number of times, in a set of 10 trials, the estimate was within 20 per cent of the known cover. Each point is the mean accuracy, ±1 standard deviation, obtained from 3 sets of trials. Figures 2, 3 and 4 have the same format, but refer to different reef series. In this figure the species are arranged in the individual graphs by head size, with the smallest (most abundant) species at the left of each graph and the largest of the four species at the right. The values for head size are head area in m^2. Each species has 15 per cent cover. The description of each of the A series reefs refers to the relative differences between the head sizes of the four species in each reef. Two sets of A2 reefs were run differing only in the randomization procedure.

R

(c) Since the accuracy of all the methods is poor, there is little to recommend the more laborious and time consuming methods over the more rapid methods.

B series. The results of cover estimates for the B series are shown in Figure 3.

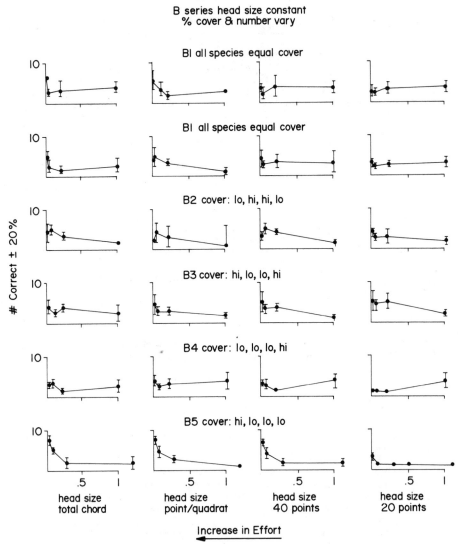

Figure 3
This figure shows the accuracy of the cover estimates of the four different methods on the six reefs of the B series. The format is identical to Figure 2. In the B series each species has a constant head area in all of the reefs (except the largest species in B5). The relative cover of the species is different in each of the reefs. The description of the B reefs indicates the relative cover values. The actual values are in Table 2.

The effect of effort on accuracy is similar to that seen in the A reefs. The 20 point method is apparently not sensitive to the high abundance in B1, B2 and B5 reefs. The B4 series shows that when cover (and hence abundance since head sizes are kept constant) of large corals is increased, the accuracy increases as indicated by the rising right end of the curves. The B5 reef shows that when a species is very abundant it may be correctly estimated (± 20 per cent) most of the time. However it should be noted that this species has an uncommon density of 14 heads per m². These results again indicate that abundance may be a key factor in determining accuracy of cover estimates. One way of visualizing this is seen in Figure 4. This figure shows the same accuracy values as the

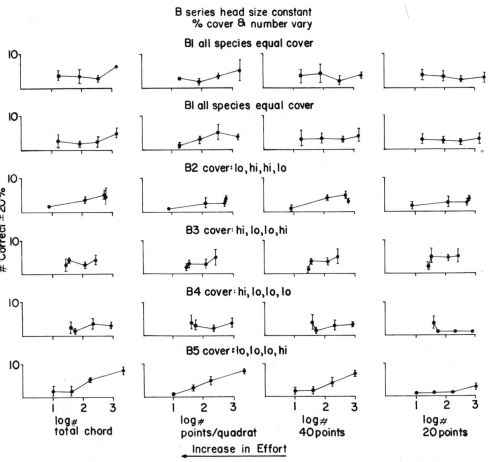

Figure 4
This figure shows the accuracy of the cover estimates of the four different methods of the four species of the six B reefs. The format is similar to Figures 2 and 3. The data are identical to those plotted in Figure 3, but the abscissae of the individual graphs show abundances (log of the total number) of each of the species. Thus the species are arranged in reverse (right to left) order of Figure 3.

previous figure, plotted against abundance (log of total number in the 144 m^2 reef).

When plotted in this manner the relative insensitivity of the 40 and 20 point methods to the abundance of corals becomes clearer. However, due to the great variability, these methods are still not significantly worse than the more laborious total chord and points per quadrat methods. The B3 reef shows that for all methods, corals with low abundance (0.2 heads per m^2) the accuracy of the estimates is low whether the cover is high (hence large heads) or not. The B5 reef shows an interesting and probably significant decrease of accuracy with increasing rarity, and this is progressively worse with the faster sampling methods.

C series. The C series shows the most marked differences between the methods tested (Fig. 5). The total chord method begins to register some correct values at about 10 per cent cover. The other methods apparently require increasing amounts of cover for any correct values to be obtained. It appears as though the methods requiring less effort require increasingly more cover before registering *any* correct values. Small heads in the C series generally have low cover while large heads are usually high cover species. However, in the range of 10 to 15 per cent cover both large and small heads occur (indicated by different symbols in Figure 5). In this range of cover the true cover value of the smaller heads was more accurately estimated. This is consistent with the earlier results which indicate that corals with small size (and in these cases high abundance) will be more correctly estimated than rarer, larger corals with the same cover.

Abundance

Since abundance appears to be such an important factor in the accurate estimation of cover, the ability of the survey methods to estimate abundance correctly was next investigated. The results of one of these tests are shown in Figure 6. The method used in this case was the heads per quadrat technique. The lower graph shows that at densities greater than about one head per m^2, there is a clear linear (slope = 0.023 r^2 = 0.964) relationship between the number of heads per quadrat and the total number of heads on the reef. In most cases these are the smaller heads, but the data from all the C reefs were included in this figure. At densities below one head per m^2 the relationship is less clear. The upper graph is an expanded portion of the low density part of the lower graph (note that there are more points since some were eliminated from the lower graph for clarity). In cases where there is less than one head per m^2 the great variability obscures the fact that the low density data are really an extension of the line (Slope = 0.023 r^2 = 0.560). Note that there is no apparent effect of head size on these low density abundance estimates.

Dispersion

There is a large body of literature dealing with methods of detecting differences

244

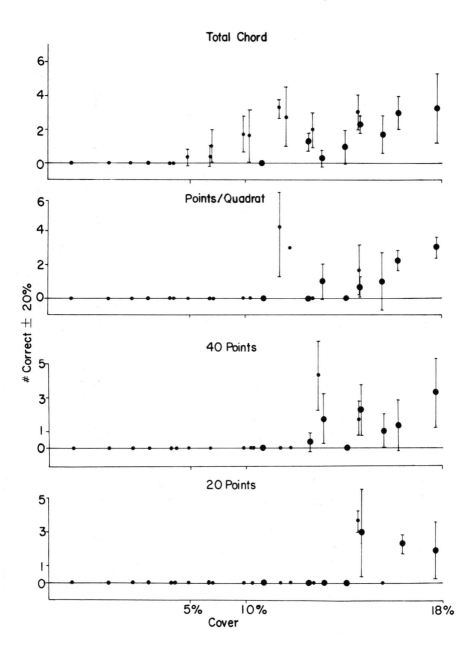

Figure 5
This figure shows the accuracy of the four cover estimates on all of the
species of the C series. Each graph shows the accuracy (number correct
±20 per cent) for one of the four methods. The large dots represent large
species (radius at least 0.2 m): the small dots, the small species (radius less
than 0.1 m). The vertical lines represent one standard deviation on each side
of the mean. Note that the cover given on the abscissae is on a log scale.

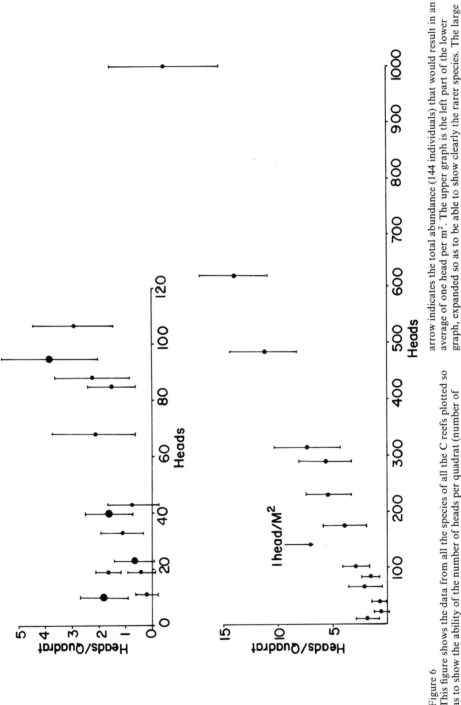

Figure 6
This figure shows the data from all the species of all the C reefs plotted so as to show the ability of the number of heads per quadrat (number of heads/quadrat) method to estimate true abundance (number of heads). The lower (larger) graph includes all the very abundant species, but some of the less common heads (left side of the graph) are eliminated for clarity. The arrow indicates the total abundance (144 individuals) that would result in an average of one head per m². The upper graph is the left part of the lower graph, expanded so as to be able to show clearly the rarer species. The large dots represent the large species (radius at least 0.2 m); the small dots the small species (radius less than 0.1 m). The vertical lines are one standard deviation on each side of the mean.

in dispersion patterns of organisms (see references given earlier). A longer and more detailed report of findings on the results of different sampling methods to detect dispersion patterns is being prepared by the authors of this paper. Only the preliminary results are summarized here.

A priori assumptions are made about the patterns expected, based on the differences among the reefs discussed in the Methods Section. These are reflected in the ordering of the reefs in Figure 7. As expected the first species placed in the upper reefs (nos. 183, 505, 241) appear to be randomly distributed. The last two species placed in large-to-small reefs (nos. 183 and 505) are clumped as predicted. The two reefs with reduced overlap (nos 162 and 133) appear to have more regularly spaced corals. The intermediate reefs give mixed results.

The adjustment of centres to take overlap into account (as discussed in earlier section on Methods) was expected to increase significantly the degree of uniformity, but such an assumption was not supported by results.

It should be noted that while the quadrat method appears to give a larger number of significant results, this is partly a problem of sampling. The QUADRAT program utilizes every coral of the roof while POINT is a true sampling simulation.

CONCLUSIONS

Cover

This is the most commonly measured parameter in reef studies, and the authors feel that the results lead to some definite conclusions regarding its estimation. It appears that all four methods simulated are almost equally bad, and that the best procedure is not to make a few very detailed surveys, but rather to make as many 'quick and dirty' short transects in the study area as possible. There is other justification for this approach. Since the variability of results from both real reefs (unpublished observation) and these simulated reefs is so high, an intensive survey would give detailed information about only a small part of the reef studied while not detecting more general patterns. Numerous fast transects placed throughout the study area not only give more information about the entire site but apparently are not significantly less informative about cover than the more laborious methods.

Abundance

The question of measures of abundance has not been investigated by the authors as thoroughly as those of cover, but the suggestion is that for corals occurring in realistic numbers (less than $1/m^2$) more extensive measures may be required. The authors are currently working on this question.

	FIRST	SECOND	THIRD	LAST
183	—	—	●	●
505	—	—	●	—
241	—	●	—	—
514	O?	O?	—	●?
162	O	—	O	O
133	O?	—	—	—

	FIRST	SECOND	THIRD	LAST
183	—	—	●	●
505	—	—	●	●
241	—	●	—	O?
514	O?	●?	—	—
162	O	O	O	O?
133	O	O?	O?	—

	FIRST	SECOND	THIRD	LAST
183	—	—	●	—
505	—	●	—	—
241	—	—	—	—
519	—	—	—	—
162	O	O	O	O
133	—	●	—	O?

O REGULAR
● CLUMPED

Dispersion

The results of analyses of measures of dispersion are even less clear. The plotless methods simulated all require a good method of randomization. This is often difficult to achieve under water due to limitations on time, visibility and movement. In addition, the models, upon which these methods are based, assume the individuals to be points. While this is no problem for small widely dispersed organisms, it has become apparent that there are systematic differences between the point models and situations where the individuals are large relative to the distances between them, or which may be touching one or more adjacent individuals. The authors are investigating the dispersion properties of such high density situations. While the quadrat methods require more equipment and do not appear as simple at first they may prove to be superior.

ACKNOWLEDGEMENTS

This research was supported by NSF Grant GA 36836. The manuscript was read and improved by Dieter Mueller-Dombois, Paul Jokiel and John Stimson.

References

CLARK, P. J.; EVANS, F. C. 1954. Distance to nearest neighbour as a measure of spatial relationships in populations. *Ecology*, vol. 35, 445–53.
DOLLAR, S. 1975. Zonation of reef corals off the Kona Coast of Hawaii. M.S. Thesis, Univ. of Hawaii.
ERRINGTON, J. C. 1973. The effect of regular and random distribution on the analysis of pattern. *J. Ecol.*, vol. 61, p. 99–105.
GREIG-SMITH, P. 1964. *Quantitative plant ecology*, 2nd edit. London, Butterworth (xii + 256 p.).
HERCZYNSKI, R. 1975. Distribution function for random distribution of spheres. *Nature* (Lond.), vol. 255, p. 540–41.
KERSHAW, K. A. 1964. *Quantitative and dynamic ecology*, 2nd edit. London, Arnold (308 p.).

Figure 7
A summary of the results of the estimates of dispersion. The results of three different kinds of methods Quadrat, Quadrat with adjusted centres and Point are shown. The differences between the reefs are discussed in the text and Table 3. The reefs are arranged with the reef expected to be most uniform (no. 133) at the bottom. The results are shown for each species in its order of placement. The results of two quadrat methods are based on Morisita's index of dispersion, the variance: mean ratio and deviations from frequency distributions expected by either Poisson or Binomial distributions. The Point results are based on the Clark and Evans nearest neighbour method and Pielou's Alpha i and Alpha p. The dashes indicate no significant departure from randomness. The solid circles show clumped patterns and the open circles show regular dispersion. If more than one test indicated departure from randomness no question mark is shown. If only one of the methods indicated a non-random pattern a question mark is added.

LOYA, Y. 1972. Community structure and species diversity of hermatypic corals at Eilat, Red Sea. *Mar. Biol.,* vol. 13, p. 100–23.

MORISITA, M. 1959. Measuring of the dispersion of individuals and analysis of the distributional patterns. *Mem. Fac. Sci. Kyushu Univ.* (Ser. E) vol. 2, p. 215–35.

MUELLER-DOMBOIS, D.; ELLENBERG, H. 1974. *Aims and methods of vegetation ecology.* New York, John Wiley (xv + 547 p.).

PATIL, G. P.; PIELOU, E. C.; WATERS, W. E. (eds). 1971. *Statistical ecology:* vol. 1 *Spatial patterns and statical distributions.* University Park Pennsylvania, Pennsylvania State Univ. Press (xxviii + 582 p.).

PIELOU, E. C. 1960. A single mechanism to account for regular, random and aggregated popula-tions. *J. Ecol.,* vol. 48, p. 575–84.

——. 1969. *An introduction to mathematical ecology,* New York, London, Wiley-Interscience (viii + 286 p.).

POOLE, R. W. 1974. *An introduction to quantitative ecology.* New York, McGraw-Hill (x + 532 p.).

PORTER, J. W. 1972. Ecology and species diversity of coral reefs on opposite sides of the Isthmus of Panama. *Bull. biol. Soc. Wash.,* vol. 2, p. 89–116.

——. 1974. Community structure of coral reefs on opposite sides of the Isthmus of Panama. *Science,* vol. 186, p. 543–45.

ROY, K. J.; SMITH, S. V. 1971. Sedimentation and coral reef development in turbid water: Fanning Lagoon. *Pac. Sci.,* vol. 25, p. 234–48.

SOUTHWOOD, T. R. E. 1966. *Ecological methods.* London, Methuen (xviii + 391 p.).

STITLER, W. M.; PATIL, G. P. 1971. Variance-to-mean ratio and Morisita's index as measures of spatial patterns in ecological populations. In: G. P. Patil, E. C. Pielou and W. E. Waters (eds). *Statistical ecology.* London, Pennsylvania State Univ. Press, p. 423–52.

WIEBE, P. H. 1970. Small-scale distribution in oceanic zooplankton. *Limnol. and Oceanogr.,* vol. 15, p. 205–17.

19

Non-colonial cryptofauna

P. A. Hutchings[1]

INTRODUCTION

Definition of cryptofauna

The term cryptofauna refers to all those organisms which live in cavities, crevices or clefts in coral. These include boring animals (e.g. sponges—Goreau and Hartman, 1963; bivalves—Yonge, 1963; Gohar and Soliman, 1963a-d; and polychaetes—Hartman, 1954; Marsden, 1962) as well as the so called 'opportunistic' species. (For methods of boring by sponges see Rützler and Rieger, 1973). Opportunistic species are not themselves able to bore into coral but may gain access via burrows and crevices created by the activity of borers, or live at the bases of long coral branches where they are completely hidden.

Presence and significance of cryptofauna

The existence of this cryptofauna, although known for many years (Ebbs, 1966; Garth, 1964; Gibbs, 1971; Grassle, 1973; Hartman, 1954; Patton, 1963, 1966; Reish, 1968), has only recently been studied quantitatively (Brander et al., 1971; Clausade, 1970a, 1971a; Hutchings, 1974; Kohn and Lloyd, 1973a, b; McCloskey, 1970; Peyrot-Clausade, 1974a). These studies, from various geographical localities, have shown that the cryptofauna is a rich and varied one, with high densities of animals being recorded (Grassle, 1973; Kohn and Lloyd, 1973a, b). Two recent studies have shown that some reef organisms utilize cryptofaunal polychaetes as food (Kohn, 1959, 1968; Kohn and Nybakken, 1975; Vivien and Peyrot, 1974).

It, therefore, seems important to collect quantitative data on the cryptofauna of coral reefs and, if possible, to achieve some standardization of methods so that data from different reefs may be comparable. The methods which have been used are described and discussed below.

---

1. Australian Museum, Box A285, Sydney South, New South Wales, 2000 Australia.

METHODS

Selection of habitat

All quantitative studies require the use of replicate samples and this means that the habitat must be easily identifiable so that it can be returned to on numerous occasions. Ideally, the habitat should also be recognizable in other localities, both of that particular reef and on other reefs. Therefore, the zone from which the habitats are assessed for quantitative determinations of the cryptofauna must be accurately described for future reference. (For a discussion of the particular zones in each biotope found on the reef, e.g. lagoon, reef flat, reef crest and slope, see Pichon, 1974). Several different techniques have been evolved for studying the physical and biological characteristics of the various coral zones. These are briefly outlined below, but line transect and quadrat methods are treated in more detail elsewhere in this monograph (Loya, Chapter 16; Scheer, Chapter 15).

Quadrat method. A quadrat is laid at repeated intervals, either along a horizontal or a vertical gradient of the zone, and the number of species and colonies present in the quadrat, together with the size of the colonies, is measured. The percentage cover of each species is also either subjectively assessed or rated on a scale of abundance. Sedentary organisms, such as sponges, ascidians, echinoderms or molluscs, occurring in the quadrat can be recorded, together with information on the percentage coverage by coralline algae, sand, etc. The size of the quadrat to be used in a particular area is determined by counting the number of coral species occurring in sample quadrats of increasing size. The results are then plotted and the sample area which includes at least two thirds of the total number of coral species recorded is an ideal quadrat size which should be used for the habitat (for further details see Scheer, 1967, 1971, 1972, 1974).

Photographed quadrats. This involves a slight modification of the quadrat method and is designed to reduce diving time (Laxton and Stablum, 1974). Each quadrat is photographed both at a fixed distance from the frame and at a constant magnification. The photographic prints are cut up and each species or faunal group weighed and expressed as a percentage.

Line transect method. In this method, which has been developed by Loya (1972), a line transect 10 m in length and marked at 1 m intervals is laid across a particular zone and the size of the coral colony lying directly below the line is measured. The species of coral present may be determined on site or from specimens brought back to the laboratory. Other components such as sponges, ascidians, coralline algae, sand etc., lying underneath the line, can easily be measured.

Chain link method. A slight modification of the line transect method has been used by Porter (1972). A 10 m chain with links 1.3 cm in length is laid across

252

the reef and the number of chain links covering each species of coral determined.

All these methods give satisfactory results, but in the case of the quadrat method a subjective estimation of the percentage cover of the corals has to be made. This criticism is eliminated when the quadrats are photographed but this method requires both clear visibility and calm water and there is always the possibility of camera malfunction. The line transect method of Loya's is very rapid and efficient, and since it does not rely on subjective estimations not all transects need to be carried out by a single diver, a very important factor when transects are being made below 16 m depth because of problems of recompression. Finally, providing specimens of the corals are returned to the laboratory, no identifications need to be carried out in the field.

Actual selection of cryptofaunal habitat

The above methods are not satisfactory for collecting quantitative cryptofaunal samples, as they are sampling the reef on too large a scale. For example, Brander et al. (1971) collected all material to a depth of 10 cm from a quadrat of a quarter of a square metre and then divided the substrata into sand, live and dead coral before analysing each component for its cryptofauna. The results, however, were very misleading as effectively several different habitats were being sampled at once. It is therefore not a suitable method for collecting quantitative data on cryptofauna. Instead only one homogeneous microhabitat must be sampled at any one time. Kohn (pers. comm.) prefers the term of 'minihabitat'. Two main approaches for selecting habitats for cryptofauna have been used. In one, a particular type of microhabitat, which is common over the entire reef, is selected and repetitively sampled in a number of zones which have been defined by means of one of the above techniques. This may easily be extended to sampling in a number of geographical localities. This microhabitat could be one particular species of coral (e.g. *Oculina arbuscula* Verrill was used by McCloskey (1970)) or else one particular substratum (like boulders of truncated limestone (Kohn and Lloyd, 1973a)). The other approach is to define within a particular zone of the reef a number of easily recognizable microhabitats such as thin plates of dead coral, dead branching *Acropora* or small pieces of massive coral (Hutchings, 1974), and to sample them repetitively within the zone. This can be extended to sampling several different habitats within each of the characteristic zones of the reef (Clausade, 1970b, 1971a; Peyrot-Clausade, 1974b).

Prior to the collection from the microhabitat it may be useful to define the specific surface under which the cryptofauna is to be sample, or the specific characteristics of that particular part of the zone, by using the quadrat technique. Such factors as the presence of caves or overhangs may be very important local factors in determining the amount of cryptofauna. The major problem in these methods is the choice of the habitat and collecting repetitive samples is purely subjective or dependent on questions being posed of certain taxa or microhabitats by the researcher. For example, Brander et al. (1971) purposely

253

chose coral heads of a similar size. Up to the present time no worker has satisfactorily eliminated this subjectivity in the selection of the samples. A good photographic record of each habitat sampled both *in situ* and in the laboratory prior to the extraction of the cryptofauna, is also very useful in analysing the results.

SAMPLING

Minimum volume of sample

The minimum volume of sample which must be collected so as to include a significant proportion of the species and provide the widest range of information on the structure of the community can be determined by using Picard's (1965) method. This method is clearly explained by Pichon (Chapter 14) for the collection of soft bottom samples but it is equally applicable to collecting coral samples for cryptofauna. An indication of the volume of sample which may have to be collected is 1 dm^3, as calculated by Clausade (1970a) working a Tuléar, Madagascar. The minimum volume may vary between habitats and ideally should be determined by workers for each habitat using Picard's technique.

Collection of sample and extraction of cryptofauna

After selecting the habitat and describing carefully both its position and immediate surroundings, a sample is broken off with a hammer and chisel and immediately placed into a polythene bag and sealed to prevent loss of cryptofauna. It is more satisfactory if the polythene bag can be put over the sample before it is broken off. When several samples are being collected at one time the diver must be equipped with a buoyancy compensator in order to be able to swim the samples back to the boat with safety and ease.

Several methods of cryptofaunal extraction have been used. Kirsteuer (1972) extracts nemerteans from coral by placing the samples in sea water in glass jars which are kept in the shade except for one small area. Decreasing O_2 supply and increasing CO_2 content in the water of the sample forces the nemerteans to leave the habitat and migrate to the lighter area of the jar. This method, however, is not generally effective for the majority of cryptofauna which are either sessile (bivalves) or sedentary (sipunculans and many polychaetes) and die within the coral. Reimer (pers. comm.) breaks up her samples into small pieces and places them in a refrigerator for a few hours to bring out most of the polychaetes, but the coral rubble still has to be broken into smaller pieces to extract sipunculans. A variation on this is to put small pieces of coral overnight into a flat gravel tray containing 51 ml of sea water and 20 ml of 4 per cent formalin and hand sort the next day (Brander *et al.*, 1971).

Providing that sufficient time and adequate laboratory facilities are available it is far easier and more pleasant to sort fresh material. The colour and movement of animals present also tends to make them more obvious. In addition, information on the colouring of cryptic fauna can be obtained; for example, some molluscs and crustaceans are exactly the same colour as some of the coralline algae. Because of the total time necessary for sorting to group level, it is probably advisable to preserve the coral rubble in neutralized formalin before the final extraction of the cryptofauna under a microscope. If field time is limited, the entire narcotized sample can be fixed in formalin (McCloskey, 1970), although if the sample is large it should be broken up into pieces to allow adequate penetration by the fixative. The coral rubble or debris is then virtually pulverized in order to extract the rest of the cryptofauna. The pulverized coral is repeatedly washed through sieves to separate the fauna. The mesh size of the sieves used depends upon the needs of the workers. If only biomass is needed a far larger mesh size can be used than if the number of individuals is required. This was clearly shown by Reish (1959) who passed five grab samples from a shallow water muddy ground through a series of 11 sieves with apertures ranging from 4.7 to 0.15 mm, and counted the number of individuals retained on each. If cumulative percentages of the main species are calculated from Reish's figures (Birkett and McIntyre, 1971), a screen of 0.85 mm would have been suitable for 95 per cent extraction of molluscs but a finer mesh was needed for nematodes and crustaceans. Analysis of polychaete species shows that considerable variation can occur within a taxonomic class. For example, about 95 per cent of *Lumbrineris* were retained by a 1.0 mm mesh but to attain this level of separation for small polychaetes, like *Cossura candida* Hartman, required a mesh of 0.27 mm. When the total faunal assemblage is considered over 95 per cent was retained by 0.27 mm mesh but for biomass over 90 per cent was retained by a 1.4 mm sieve. Other mesh sizes which have been used are 0.25 mm by Grassle (1973) and 0.21 mm by McCloskey (1970).

An approximate indication of the time necessary for extracting the cryptofauna and sorting to group level is as follows. For a sample of 1000 gm, approximately 1 hour is needed for breaking up the coral into small pieces, and an additional 2 hours to extract and sort the cryptofauna to group level. Additional time is needed to sort the groups into genera or species and this may both take a considerable time or involve sending off groups to taxonomic specialists.

Weight of sample collected

The wet and dry weights of the entire sample and of the extracted cryptofauna are useful measurements for expressing biomass. This poses some problems in the complete removal of all the coralline algae and boring sponges from the sample. It may also be useful to split up the cryptofauna into component groups and weigh either each group or the dominant species of the groups. Dry weight determinations of the cryptofauna, or determinations of calorific value, cannot be made until identifications have been completed. The non-calcareous fraction of the habitat, which in some instances may be significant, can be determined by treatment with 10 per cent HCl to dissolve the carbonate fraction (McCloskey, 1970).

PHYSICAL AND BIOLOGICAL PARAMETERS

Several workers (Brander *et al.*, 1971; Grassle, 1973; Hutchings, 1974; Kirsteuer, 1972; Kohn, 1968; Kohn and Lloyd, 1973a) have clearly demonstrated the importance of some physical and biological parameters in influencing the distribution and abundance of cryptofauna. These include surface area (or, as Kirsteuer refers to it, the outer cavity system), porosity, percentage of live coral, and percentage of epifauna and epiflora. Some attempts at measuring, or assessing, these factors should be made and the methods which have been used to date are described below.

Surface area. The surface area can be subjectively assessed (Hutchings, 1974; Kirsteuer, 1972), but actual measurements are needed if the work is to be repeatable. Kohn and Lloyd (1973a), working on samples from truncated reef limestone; measured the surface area by projection. The samples, which had fairly smooth, flat surfaces and were almost rectangular (see Fig. 1; Kohn and Lloyd), were placed on paper, each surface of the sample was outlined and the total surface area estimated. Such a method is only suitable for samples with almost flat surfaces. Dahl (1973) describes a method for measuring the surface area of coral reef algae which could equally well be used for hard substrata. The area to be measured is modelled by a series of scales, such as spheres, cones and squares. For each of these scales the surface variation is measured and referred to as the surface index (SI), which is defined as the ratio of actual surface to that of a plane with similar boundaries, giving a dimensionless number. An SI is calculated for each significant surface variation; these are then multiplied to give a total SI for the area being measured. Some of the methods, developed from geological techniques, for measuring the surface area of structures inside living cells could perhaps be adapted to measuring the surface area of corals. These methods are fully explained by Underwood (1970) and Weibel (1969).

A far simpler method of measuring surface area is to coat all the surfaces of the sample, except the one where it was attached to the reef, with a solution of black latex rubber (Fig. 1). Several layers of latex (Ashtex Products) are built up gradually over the coral surface by allowing each layer to dry partially before applying the next coat. The latex mould is left to dry overnight before it is peeled off the coral. The mould is then laid out and flattened by a sheet of perspex. In some cases it may be necessary to cut the mould in order to get it to lie flat. By illuminating from below, an outline of the mould can be traced on to a sheet of paper lying on top of the perspex. Two traces of each would are made and the area of the traced outline measured by means of a polar planimeter. The average of the two traces is then taken (Hutchings and Weate,

(a)

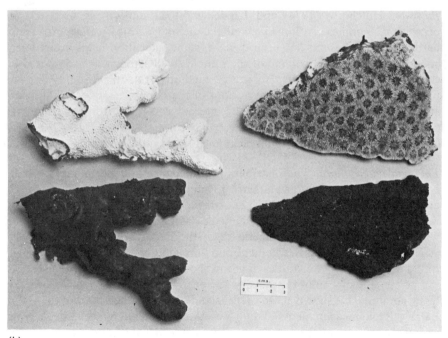

(b)

Figure 1
(a) Coating the coral sample with liquid latex.
(b) Two coral samples and the latex moulds which were made of them. (photo: Gregory Millen.)

in preparation). Because the latex mould must be left on the sample until completely dry, it is not possible to use the sample which is to be subsequently broken up for the extraction of cryptofauna. An additional sample should be collected from each habitat for the sole purpose of estimating the surface area. which means that the actual surface area of the sample analysed for cryptofauna is not determined but a representative value for the surface area of that particular type of habitat is assessed. This type of measurement is totally adequate for between-habitat comparisons of surface area. Table 1 gives the surface areas for the habitats shown in Figure 1.

TABLE 1. The relationship of wet weight, volume to surface area of three coral microhabitats.

	Total wet weight (gm)	Total volume (cc)	Surface area (cm^2)	Percentage weight of invertebrate
Massive coral with high percentage of live coral	545	170	137	1.54
Dead *Acropora*	662	242	186	0.35
Massive dead coral	1776	625	429	0.81

Porosity. Hutchings (1974) and Kirsteuer (1972) subjectively assessed the porosity of samples. Although no direct method of measuring porosity or hardness of the habitat has been devized, some indication is given by determining the weight and volume of the sample as all samples are composed of calcium carbonate. Another subjective method (Hutchings and Weate, in preparation), is to cut transverse sections of the sample using a diamond saw and photograph the cut surfaces. The internal structure of different habitats can then be compared. Finally engineers and geologists have scales of hardness for material which perhaps could be applied to corals.

Epifauna and epiflora. The distribution, abundance and presumably species composition of the epifauna and flora are important in determining the abundance of cryptofauna. Ideally the area occupied by each of the major groups of epifauna and flora should be determined or assessed. Dahl's (1973) technique would be suitable. The characteristics of the major groups should also be assessed, for instance, as to whether or not it is a low encrusting coralline algae, tufted brown algae, etc., and each group should be removed and weighed. As the percentage of epiflora may vary seasonally, as Larkum and Borowitzka (pers. comm.) have shown at One Tree Island on the southern part of the Great Barrier Reef, measurements should be taken for all habitats either during various seasons or at the same time of year in order that direct comparisons may be made. Hutchings (1974) suggested that the surface algae provided protection for the larvae of the cryptofauna whilst they were gaining access into the habitat. If this is the correct interpretation one might expect to find that

258

the time of breeding of the cryptofauna is correlated with maximum algal growth, but as yet there are no supporting data.

The percentage of live coral. Live coral has a very sparse and different crypto-fauna to that found in dead coral (Brander *et al.*, 1971; Grassle, 1973; Hutchings, 1974). Certain species of crustaceans and fish are typically associated with particular species of live coral and the serpulid polychaete, *Spirobranchus giganteus* (Pallas) is almost entirely restricted to live coral. Once the coral dies its cryptofauna changes markedly. The percentage of live coral can be determined by removing it from the sample and expressing its volume, surface area or weight as a percentage of the total. A slight complication occurs when the boundary between the live and dead coral is indistinct, which is common (Brander *et al.*, 1971).

DISCUSSION OF FUTURE WORK

Now that baseline data on the distribution and abundance of cryptofauna are beginning to accumulate, the establishment, succession and maintenance of this community should be investigated. Peyrot-Clausade (Clausade, 1971b, 1974b) has begun to investigate the establishment of the cryptofaunal community. Pieces of coral fragments in nylon net bags are suspended in water above the reef for varying lengths of time, and the rate of colonization and its composition determined. The techniques of Schoener (1974), developed for the study of colonization of marine mini-islands, could also be applied to studying the establishment of cryptofaunal communities.

Work done by McCloskey (1970) and unpublished data from Tuléar, Madagascar (Pichon, pers. comm.) indicates that a distinct succession in the boring organisms exists both temporally and spatially within the habitat. Pichon also states that there is a distinct zoning of borers from the outer reef to the lagoon. These phenomena need further documentation before they can be applied generally to cryptofaunal communities.

Finally, the role of the cryptofaunal community in the total reef ecosystem cannot be fully understood until the following points have been investigated: the food sources and requirements of the cryptofauna themselves, their energy requirements, and detailed information on the feeding habits of other reef organisms. Only then will the role of the cryptofauna, which is probably highly significant, be understood, and the collection of good quantitative data on the cryptofauna is the first step in this direction.

ACKNOWLEDGEMENTS

I sincerely thank the following: Professor M. Pichon and Drs Kohn, Recher, Peyrot-Clausade and Talbot for reading the manuscript and making many useful suggestions.

References

BIRKETT, L.; McINTYRE, A. D. 1971. Treatment and sorting of samples. In: N. A. Holme and A. D. McIntyre (eds). *Methods for the study of marine benthos*. Oxford, Blackwell Sci. (IBP Handbook 16), p. 156–68.

BRANDER, K. M.; McLEOD, A. A.; HUMPHREYS, W. F. 1971. Comparison of species diversity and ecology of reef-living invertebrates on Aldabra Atoll and at Watamu, Kenya. *Symp. zool. Soc. Lond.*, vol. 28, p. 397–431.

CLAUSADE, M. 1970a. Importance et variations du peuplement mobile des cavités au sein des formations épirécifales, et modalités d'échantillonnage en vue de son évaluation. *Rec. Trav. Stn mar. Endoume*, Suppl. Hors série 10, p. 107–09.

——. 1970b. Répartition qualitative et quantitative des Polychètes vivant dans les alvéoles des constructions organogènes épirécifales de la portion septentrionale du Grand Récif de Tuléar. *Rec. Trav Stn mar. Endoume*, Suppl. Hors série 10, p. 259–70.

——. 1971a. Peuplement Annelidien des levées détritiques et de leurs biotopes de substitution dans la région de Tuléar (Madagascar). *Téthys*, Suppl. 1, p. 127–36.

——. 1971b. Colonisation d'un milieu alvéolaire récifal par la faune vagile: Introduction à l'étude expérimentale. *Téthys*, Suppl. 1, p. 137–40.

DAHL, A. L. 1973. Surface area in ecological analysis: Quantification of benthic coral-reef algae. *Mar. Biol.*, vol. 23, p. 239–49.

EBBS, N. K. 1966. The coral-inhabiting Polychaetes of the Northern Florida Reef Tract. Part 1— Aphroditidae, Polynoidae, Amphinomidae, Eunicidae and Lysaretidae. *Bull. mar. Sci.*, vol. 16, no. 3, p. 485–555.

GARTH, J. S. 1964. The Crustacea Decapoda (Brachyura and Anomura) of Eniwetok Atoll, Marshall Islands, with special reference to the obligate commensals of branching corals. *Micronesica*, vol. 1, p. 137–44.

GIBBS, P. E. 1971. The Polychaete fauna of the Solomon Islands. *Bull. Brit. Mus. Nat. Hist. (Zool.)* vol. 21, no. 5, p. 101–211.

GOHAR, H. A. F.; SOLIMAN, G. N. 1963a. On three Mytilid species boring in living corals. *Publ. Mar. Biol. Stn Ghardaa, Red Sea*, vol. 12, p. 66–98.

——. 1963b. On the biology of three Coralliophilids boring in living corals. *Publ. Mar. Biol. Stn Ghardaa, Red Sea*, vol. 12, p. 99–126.

——. 1963c. On the rock-boring lamellibranch *Rocellaria ruppelli* (Deshayes). *Publ. Mar. Biol. Stn Ghardaa, Red Sea*, vol. 12, p. 145–58.

——. 1963d. On two Mytilids boring in dead coral. *Publ. Mar. Biol. Stn Ghardaa, Red Sea*, vol. 12, p. 205–18.

GOREAU, T. F.; HARTMAN, W. D. 1963. Boring sponges as controlling factors in the formation and maintenance of coral reefs. In: R. F. Sognnaes (ed.) *Mechanisms of hard tissue destruction*, Washington, D.C. Am. Assoc. Adv. Sci., Publ. no. 75, p. 25–54.

GRASSLE, J. F. 1973. Variety in coral reef communities. In: O. A. Jones and R. Endean (eds). *Biology and geology of coral reefs.* Academic Press, vol. 2, p. 247–70.

HARTMAN, O. 1954. *Marine Annelida from the northern Marshall Islands, Bikini and nearby atolls, Marshall Islands.* U.S. Geol. Survey (Prof. Paper 260–Q). p. 617–44.

HUTCHINGS, P. A. 1974. A preliminary report on the density and distribution of invertebrates living on coral reefs. In: *Proc. Second Int. Coral Reef. Symp.* Brisbane, Great Barrier Reef Committee, vol. 2, p. 285–96.

KIRSTEUER, E. 1972. Quantitative and qualitative aspects of the nemertean fauna in tropical coral reefs. In: *Proc. Symp. Corals and Coral Reefs 1969.* Mar. Biol. Assoc. India, vol. 1, p. 363–71.

KOHN, A. J. 1959. The Ecology of *Conus* in Hawaii. *Ecol. Monogr.*, vol. 29, p. 47–90.

——. 1968. Microhabitats, abundance and food of *Conus* on atoll reefs in the Maldive and Chagos Islands. *Ecology*, vol. 49, p. 1046–62.

KOHN, A. J.; LLOYD, M. C. 1973a. Polychaetes of truncated reef limestone substrates on Eastern Indian Ocean coral reefs: diversity, abundance and taxonomy. *Int. Rev. gesamt. Hydrobiol.*, vol. 58, p. 369–99.

——. 1973b. Marine Polychaete Annelids of Easter Island. *Int. Rev. gesamt. Hydrobiol.*, vol. 58, p. 691–712.

KOHN, A. J.; NYBAKKEN, J. W. 1975. Ecology of *Conus* on Eastern Indian Ocean fringing reefs: diversity of species and resource utilization. *Mar. Biol.*, vol. 29, p. 211–34.

Laxton, J. H.; Stablum, W. J. 1974. Sample design for quantitative estimation of sedentary organisms of coral reefs. *Biol. J. Linn. Soc.,* vol. 6, p. 1–19.

Loya, Y. 1972. Community structure and species diversity of hermatypic corals at Eilat, Red Sea. *Mar. Biol.,* vol. 13, p. 100–23.

Marsden, J. R. 1962. A coral-eating polychaete. *Nature* (Lond.), vol. 193, p. 598.

McCloskey, L. R. 1970. The dynamics of the community associated with a marine scleractinian coral. *Int. Rev. gesamt. Hydrobiol.,* vol. 55, p. 13–81.

Patton, W. K. 1963. Studies on the decapod crustacea commensal with branching corals of Queensland, Australia, *Proc. XVI Int. Cong. Zool., Wash. D.C.,* vol. 1, p. 104.

——. 1966. Decapod crustacea commensal with Queensland branching corals. *Crustaceana,* vol. 10, p. 271–95.

Peyrot-Clausade, M. 1974a. Colonisation d'un milieu expérimental par les Polychètes de la crypto-faune épirécifale. *Téthys,* vol. 5, p. 409–24.

——. 1974b. Ecological study of coral reef cryptobiotic communities. An analysis of the polychaete cryptofauna. In: *Proc. Second Int. Coral Reef Symp.* Brisbane, Great Barrier Reef Committee, vol. 2, p. 269–83.

Picard, J. 1965. Recherches qualitatives sur les biocoenoses marine des substrats meubles dragables de la région Marseillaise. *Rec. Trav. Stn mar. Endoume,* vol. 52, p. 1–160.

Pichon, M. 1974. Free living scleractinian coral communities in the coral reefs of Madagascar. In: *Proc. Second Int. Coral Reef Symp.* Brisbane, Great Barrier Reef Committee, vol. 2, p. 173–83.

Porter, J. W. 1972. Patterns of species diversity in Caribbean Reef Corals. *Ecology,* vol. 53, p. 745–48.

Reish, D. J. 1959. A discussion of the importance of the screen size in washing quantitative marine bottom samples. *Ecology,* vol. 40, p. 307–09.

——. 1968. The Polychaetous Annelids of the Marshall Islands. *Pac. Sci.,* vol. 22, p. 208–31.

Rützler, K.; Rieger, G. 1973. Sponge burrowing: fine structure of *Cliona lampa* penetrating calcareous substrata. *Mar. Biol.,* vol. 21, p. 144–62.

Scheer, G., 1967. Über die Methodik der Untersuchung von Korallen-riffen. *Z. Morph Ökol. Tiere,* vol. 60, p. 105–14.

——. 1971. Coral reefs and coral genera in the Red Sea and Indian Ocean. *Symp. zool. Soc. London,* vol. 28, p. 329–67.

——. 1972. Investigations of coral reefs in the Maldive Islands with notes on lagoon patches and the method of coral sociology. In: *Proc. Symp. Corals and Coral Reefs 1969.* Mar. Biol. Ass. India, vol. 1, p. 87–120.

——. 1974. Investigations of coral reefs at Rasdu Atoll in the Maldives with the quadrat method according to phytosociology. In: *Proc. Second Int. Coral Reef Symp.,* Brisbane, Great Barrier Reef Committee, vol. 2, p. 655–70.

Schoener, A. 1974. Experimental zoogeography: colonization of marine mini-islands. *Am. Nat.,* vol. 108, p. 715–39.

Underwood, E. E. 1970. *Quantitative stereology.* Massachusetts, Addison–Wesley, (274 p.).

Vivien, M. L.; Peyrot-Clausade, M. 1974. Comparative study of the feeding behaviour of three coral reef fishes (Holocentridae), with special reference to the Polychaeta of the reef crypto-fauna as prey. In: *Proc. Second Int. Coral Reef Symp.* Brisbane, Great Barrier Reef Committee, vol. 2, p. 179–92.

Weibel, E. R. 1969. Stereological principles for morphometry in electron microscopic cytology. *Int. Rev. Cytology,* vol. 26, p. 235–302.

Yonge, C. M. 1963. The biology of coral reefs. In: F. S. Russell (ed.). *Advances in marine biology.* London and New York, Academic Press. vol. 1, p. 209–60.

20

Soft-bottom communities

B. Thomassin[1]

INTRODUCTION

In coral reef complexes such as those of the Tuléar area of Madagascar, carbonate sediments derived from the reefs generally spread over greater areas than those of hard substrata, especially on inner reef flats and in lagoons. In barrier and fringing reef situations, these sediments may be in contact with terrigenous deposits and the boundaries often interdigitate. Because of the vertical and horizontal movement of species (mainly fishes, crabs, and shrimps) induced by diurnal and tidal changes, epifaunal and endofaunal communities play important roles both in the elaboration of food chains in the reef ecosystem and in reef sedimentation (by trapping, fixing and bioturbation).

Complete qualitative faunistic inventories of these soft-bottom communities have only recently been provided (Stephenson et al., 1958; MacNae and Kalk, 1962; Thomassin, 1973, 1978; Thomassin et al., 1978; Gibbs, 1975). However, these are few in number and generally only one or two systematic groups are studied, e.g. crustaceans (Garth, 1964; Thomassin, 1974) and molluscs (Maes, 1967; Taylor, 1968, 1971; Salvat, 1967, 1970, 1972; Salvat and Renaud-Mornant, 1969; Renaud-Mornant et al, 1971). Quantitative studies, either by enumerating individuals of various species by surface area or volume, or by calculation of biomass, are just beginning. Most still deal with a single taxonomic group, generally with large individuals—molluscs (Taylor, 1971; Salvat, 1972; Richard and Salvat, 1972), echinoids, holothuroids, and to a limited extent, polychaetes (Gibbs, 1972).

As Thorson (1957) argued, it is advantageous to describe animal communities on a quantitative basis. This is particularly true when sampling techniques can be standardized and when the sorting of the material is reasonably straightforward. If reef soft-bottom communities are to be compared effectively with

1. Station marine d'Endoume et Centre d'Océanographie, Université d'Aix-Marseille, rue de la Batterie des Lions. 13007 Marseille, France.

terrigenous soft-bottom communities (particularly in tropical environments close to the reefs), the methods employed must be identical. This is essential, in spite of the problems arising from the use of sampling equipment from small boats, from the scattered distribution of soft bottoms between coral patches, and from the difficulties of penetration by samplers in some gravelly and coarse sands mixed with coral branches and rubble.

PROBLEM OF SAMPLING

Various sampling techniques used in the Tuléar coral reef environments are reviewed, and the results are discussed and compared with those generally used elsewhere.

1. Definition of surface and volume units in reef sediments

All methods used for soft bottom epi- and endobiotic communities are derived from the quadrat method used by the Zurich-Montpellier school in terrestrial plant sociology (Braun-Blanquet, 1964). Picard (1962, 1965a) adapted it to marine soft-bottom endofaunal studies, replacing the phytological concept of the 'homogeneous surface' by species counts in a 'homogeneous volume' of sediments.

First of all, samples must be taken from one biological type of substratum, since quadrat samples must refer to only one community, facies or aspect. Thus, locations of the quadrat sample must be chosen on surfaces where the fauna or flora (e.g. sea-grass beds, *Halimeda* flats, or *Caulerpa* meadows) and the nature of the sediments and bottom topography appear to be uniform. However, in studies of endobiotic communities this uniformity must be verified vertically as well as horizontally. Often, for example, layered sediments occur in sandy channels between coral ridges of inner reef flats, and the layers are characterized by different faunistic assemblages (Thomassin, 1969).

2. Samping methods

Numerical data (presence, abundance, frequency) are always based on samples, and it is important that these data are not biased by the sampling method used. In soft-bottom macrofaunal studies a defined volume is generally sampled, and the animals isolated by hand, by sieving, or by other methods. Sampling methods may be grouped as follows into three types according to the areas being studied:

(*a*) *On intertidal flats, completely exposed at low tide.*

Digging is the preferred technique as the exposed sandy substrata of sand bars and beaches are compact enough to be dug with a shovel to depths of 25 cm. At Tuléar, in littoral (sandy and muddy) areas and mangroves, digging was

264

employed by Derijard (1965) and Mireille Pichon (1967) in terrigenous material. For biomass studies, Reys and Reys (1966) and Le Fur (1973) used, in addition, a cylindrical metal frame driven into the substratum, the sediment within being excavated to a depth of 30 cm.

Advantages: simplicity.

Disadvantages: the method is limited to intertidal areas, though Harmelin (1964) used digging during scuba diving to sample mats of the sea-grass *Posidonia* in the Mediterranean area; it could similarly be used on lagoonal submerged *Thalassodendron* or *Thalassia* banks.

(*b*) *Intertidal flats, pools or channels not completely exposed at low tides* (*0.3–1 m deep*).

The *Brett hydraulic suction sieve* (Brett, 1964) has been modified by Massé (1967, 1970) to sample fine thixotropic terrigenous sand communities from shallow bottoms (2–25 m deep). On the Tuléar reefs it was used in furrows on the outer reef flat, on the floors of tidal channels, and on the boulder tract to sample gravelly coarse sand beds 10–15 cm thick in water 0.5 m deep at low spring tides; these places are not accessible at high tides or during neap tides because of surf.

This sampler (Fig. 1) is used under water. It consists of:

A *galvanized pipe* (chimney pipe), 15 cm diameter, curved at one end. The short part, or suction chamber, is 25 cm long. The longer exhaust pipe is 110 cm long. At the right side of the bend a small pipe (15–21 cm), or injector, V-shaped, is brazed at right angles; the inner part of this pipe, in the axis of the exhaust pipe, is 35 cm long; on the outer part (used as a handle) is a three-way tap to control the water pressure flow or shut it off. A handle is soldered on to the middle of the exhaust pipe, and a ring at the end to attach the nylon net-bag.

A *petrol motor pump* (3.5 h.p.) (Fig. 2) for pumping water is placed in a dry part of the reef flat (or the boulder tract or coral head) or in a dinghy (taking care to to damage inflatable compartments with the exhaust silencer). To the pump are attached a ringed rubber suction-pipe 5 m long and 40 mm diameter, with a strainer, and a back flow rubber pipe 10–15 m long and 30 mm diameter.

A *nylon net bag* with 1.3–1.5 mm square mesh. This must be changed when it is full and at least three net bags must be carried for one sample.

When sand is not abundant on the floor, a reducer-pipe is placed at the end of the suction chamber. This sampler is used by the operator in a bent-over position, with his head under water surveying the work with mask and snorkel.

Advantages: visual control of the operation; possibility of sampling in shallow pools (0.3–0.6 m deep) or in sandy channels between coral ridges just accessible at low tides. In sheltered waters, this device can be used at depths up to 30 m with a long water-flow pipe and the pump on a boat (Massé, 1967). If the same net-bag is used on this sampler as on the hydropneumatic air sucker (see below), useful comparisons can be made.

265

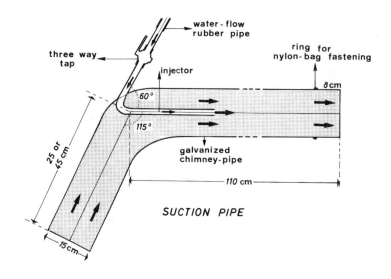

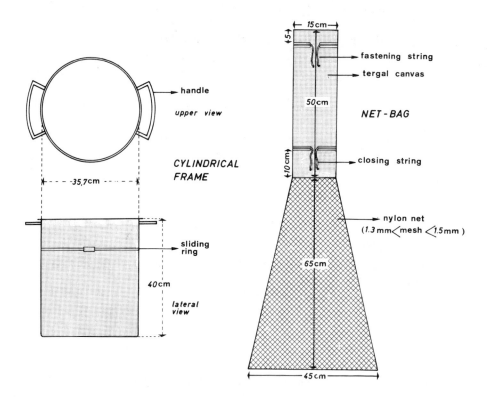

Figure 1
The Brett modified hydraulic sucker (from Massé, 1970, plate 1).

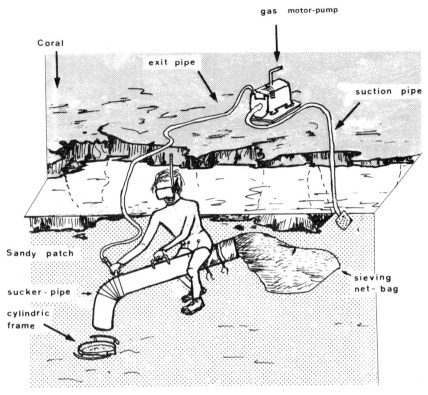

Figure 2
General arrangement of suction pipe used by a scuba diver for sampling
with the Brett modified hydraulic sucker.

Disadvantages: the equipment is bulky and heavy (20–25 kg), especially
when the reef flat is traversed on foot with the pump carried on a back-pack.
The starting of the engine can be difficult if the spark plugs get wet.

A collector bucket has been used to sample various bottoms: on reef flats
at low or neap tides, in sandy channels and channels in sea-grass beds, on inner
lagoon slopes, on outer reef slopes, in variable sediments of groove systems, and
in detrital material of coral hard grounds where most other devices cannot be
used. It consists of a trapezoidal box, with two handles, in sheet iron 2 mm thick,
total volume 12 dm^3 (Fig. 3a).

In depths of 0.5–1 m, between reef-flat coral ridges, in microatoll flats and
in seagrass hollows, the box is used during diving with mask and snorkel and
a 8 kg weight belt. Two persons are required. The diver fills the bucket with
water, dives down, and pushes it into the sand to a depth of 15 cm. When it is
full, the diver brings it to the surface in a vertical position. The contents, sand
and water, are poured into a mason sieve handled by another member of the
team, and the material retained is placed in containers (milk cans).

267

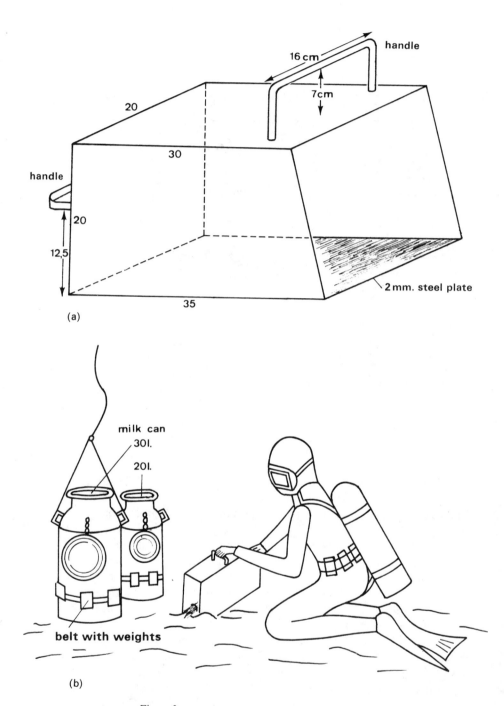

(a)

(b)

Figure 3
(a) The collector bucket
(b) Using the collector bucket in scuba diving.

At greater depths (2–45 m) the collector bucket is used by scuba divers in the same way, but the sediment is poured gently into 20- or 30-litre plastic milk containers (Fig. 3b). These are linked by rope to the boat; when full, they are either hauled up or floated up with bag-balloons inflated under water with a small compressed air-bottle.

Advantages: visual control of the sample; efficient when used by a good diver with some practice; light weight (4 kg).

Disadvantages: depth of sample is not uniform.

(c) *On submerged bottoms*

A modified version of Charcot's dredge (Picard, 1965a), without scuba-diving control, was used by Picard in the Tuléar region on shallow lagoon bottoms (for results see Guérin-Ancey, 1970, Thomassin, 1973, 1978), shallow terrigenous bottoms, and deeper seaward reef bottoms (up to 200 m deep). Pichon (Michel) (1966) used this dredge to collect samples of terrigenous muddy sands in the Nosy Bé area, northwest of Madagascar.

Advantages: useful to map known communities and to sample larger macrofauna in the top few centimetres of the sediment.

Disadvantages: penetration (up to 15 cm) into the substratum is only satisfactory in muds and muddy sands (e.g. *Macoma candida fallax* and *Ensiculus philippianus* communities). In coral sands which are generally more difficult to sample, the dredge skids and samples only the superficial layers. Hence it is impossible to relate the samples to a standard surface area, and to make quantitative comparisons of the results between different samples.

Charcot's dredge with scuba-diving control was used by Massé (1963 survey) for sampling lagoonal and submerged reef-flat sand banks (*Amphioxus* sands; for results see Thomassin, 1973). The dredge is guided and burrowed (up to 20 cm) into the sediment by the diver.

Advantages: in contrast to ordinary dredging it is possible to sample (not without difficulty) between coral growths; visual control.

Disadvantages: restricted thickness of sample (maximum 20 cm); the sampled surface is not precisely delimited; it is difficult to dredge using a boat with less than a 20 hp engine.

The orange-peel grab is described by Holme and McIntyre (1971). It has been used at Tuléar by Reys (unpublished) for biomass studies of lagoonal terrigenous muds and muddy sands; then samples are taken at each station. For criticisms, see Reys 1965, 1968; Reys and Salvat, 1971).

Advantages: can be operated from a small boat.

Disadvantages: poor penetration into compact or gravelly sands and into fine terrigenous or coral sands; high cost.

(d) *In all bottom types* (*reef slopes, lagoons, pools*).

Sampling with a hydropneumatic air-sucker used by scuba diver. This device was

269

built in 1969 (Fig. 4). A compressed air-lift that expands in bubbles running up a pipe is used to draw up the sediment through a pipe ending in a sieve net. Normally the suction pipe (diameter 8 cm) is composed of two plastic (PVC)

Figure 4
Operation of hydropneumatic air sucker by scuba diver.

270

pipes, each 1 m long, joined together. In water only 1 m deep a single pipe is needed. The mouth of the sucker is slightly oblique. A small copper injector pipe, diameter 8 mm, is fixed 5 cm from the mouth, at the level of the handle, and curves back into the suction pipe. A vacuum aspirator rubber pipe connects the injector with a compressed air bottle (3 m^3 air at 180 kg/cm^2), by means of a union nut, but without pressure reducer. At the upper end of the suction pipe a nylon sieve net is laced at two places; the net is cone-shaped with a 1.5 mm square mesh and a nylon canvas sleeve. This is the same type of net as that used on the Brett suction device. A crown metal frame, normally with a volume of 7 dm^3, is used for driving into the substratum to determine the sampled surface and volume. Several subsamples (usually 7) are taken in very close promiximity.

Operation takes place in the following stages:

All materials (in this order: crown frame, scuba diving bottle—4 m^3, suction pipe with a sieve net laced, 2 or 3 additional sieve nets, a rolled balloon bag) are fastened on the end of a nylon rope 40 m long and 8–12 mm diameter by means of snap hooks, and lowered from the boat or buoy.

On the bottom, the scuba diver first unhooks the crown frame and drives it into the sand, then unhooks the pipe and joins it to the compressed air bottle. The sample is taken kneeling down, provided that an additional weight belt is used, or, where wave action is strong, lying down with the pipe wedged on the right shoulder. The right hand holds the pipe; the left hand turns on the tap of the air bottle and controls the flow. It is important to begin with the mouth 10 cm above the sediment because otherwise the outflow may disturb the surface. Immediately after starting, the mouth is lowered onto the surface and the sand is drawn up the pipe. Sieve nets must be changed when they get too heavy, and should be securely closed.

After the sample has been collected, all the equipment should be fastened in the correct order on the rope. The balloon bag is inflated with a small compressed air bottle to bring the equipment to the surface while diving continues.

Advantages: Not expensive; robust and light; not bulky. Easy to operate while scuba diving, even on groove floors of the upper seaward reef slope. It has a good suction and even coral fragments are drawn up, although these could clog the pipe if they are too big. Compressed air is easy to obtain and to carry: 2 m^3 of compressed air is enough to sample 50 dm^3 in medium sand; 4 m^3 is required to sample the same volume in coarse sand.

Disadvantages: none. This quantitative sampler is easier to use on coral reef bottoms than the air sucker of Barnett and Hardy (1967) or Christie and Allen (1972). Except perhaps in fine lagoonal sands, the cylinder of their models generally cannot be sunk correctly by itself into the substratum, which is often coarse or rubbly. The use of a suction pipe 5 m long with a buoy is very cumbersome, particularly in the wave zone. On the other hand, the use of air injection by means of a collar-diffuser could possibly be more effective, though this has not yet been tested.

(e) Other methods of sampling macrofauna on reef soft bottoms.

Poisoning: This method, usually used in fish sampling, was adapted for crustacean sampling by Manning (1960), using a rotenone-base ('pro-noxfix').

On Tuléar reefs, the author used poison for two types of samples:

(i) For study of the vagile and sedentary fauna of the boulder tracts (crag-and-tail boulder tract or boulder rampart) (during 1965 survey, results not yet published).

Samples were taken at low spring tides. Before emergence of the boulder tracts (50 cm water height), a net of 60 cm height (mesh = 1 mm around, mosquito-net), bordered at base by a 40 cm band of pack-cloth, is laid in a square of 4 × 4 m, supported by pegs at the corners and every metre. In a corner, another net demarcates a square of 1 m². When water is 10 cm high, a mixture of rotenone + endrin (or feldrin) + formalin (at 40 per cent) is sprinkled on the floor within the square-net. This mixture kills all the fauna (vagile and cryptic fauna, also the algal flora) and endofauna when the water is percolating down into the substratum of coarse and gravelly sediments:

rotenone kills fishes, crustaceans,
endrin often kills crustaceans,
formalin often kills worms (polychaetes, echiurids, sipunculids).

After 10 minutes, the vagile fauna (up to 5 cm down to 2 cm) are picked out in the 15 m², all the vagile fauna, cryptic fauna and sand infauna are sampled in the 1 m², to 20 cm depth in substratum.

The poison mixture kills all flora and fauna only on the sampled area and tests of restocking show that after 3 days a new vagile fauna colonize the place (boulder tract fauna being over-populated), after 15 days new algae begin to grow.

This method, used with caution, is the best for sampling such a biotope inhabited by many very active species, often crustaceans. Net-fishing is used by fish workers but generally without specific surface areas or volumes. At Tuléar, Harmelin-Vivien recently proposed a useful nylon enclosure and net, and Plessis (1973) proposed a metal enclosure (ictotrèfe) covering 5 m², to be used in very shallow water less than 1 m deep. The latter is bulky, however, and difficult to handle except on flat surfaces.

(ii) For study of sand infauna, generally in scuba-diving.

A tube-frame of 1 m² with 4 iron points of 35 cm long at each corner is covered with a transparent plastic-sheet cut on the top; this opening of 20 cm long is bordered by nylon canvas and can be closed by means of a velcro closing (Maugé and Thomassin built; 1972-survey) (Fig. 5).

This frame is laid on the bottom, the corner-points sunk into the sediment (in bottom stream zone the frame is weighted with a chain and a small anchor of 5 kg). Through the opening, poison (feldrin + rotenone) is injected under the sheet using a plastic bottle. A time of 30 minutes is sufficient to obtain all

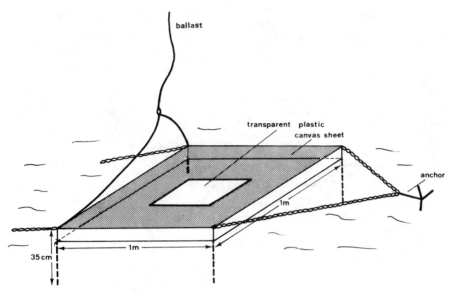

Figure 5
Frame with canvas sheet used for poisoning of endofauna

the sand-burrowed fishes (Ammoditidae, eel-fishes), crustaceans (shrimps, crabs), molluscs and worms of the infauna. Harmelin-Vivien (personal comment) used a transparent plastic enclosure 1.5 m high and 1 m in diameter weighted with a sandbag to poison fishes living in sandy bottoms.

Where infaunal communities of a coral reef region are well-known (from 50 dm^3 sediment samples), these methods are best for mapping. The 30 minute time required for the poison to be effective can be spent taking sediment samples, notes and photographs.

Trapping: Two types of bow-nets were used to study feeding ethnology of the sand-bottom epi- and infauna. To catch fish, big crabs and molluscs, eel-traps are used, then for the small species a type of bow-net (built by the author) is used by group of 5, interspaced by 50 cm, on a rope-scale. Various baits have been tested by Thomassin, (unpublished results).

Trawling: With epibenthic dredges (as Forest's epibenthic dredge or S.M.E. dredge, Fig. 6) or with small perch-trawl, swimming epifauna can be caught.

Net-sweeping: The net-sweeping method was used by Ledoyer (1962, 1967) and by the author to sample bottom or sea-grass leaf epifauna. Fifty arm-strikes to and fro are made with the small net (mesh = 0.5 mm square) just above the surface of the sediments or into the foliage.

T

273

Figure 6
S.M.E. epibenthic (vagile fauna) dredge.

3. Remarks concerning position of samples along a transect

When a coral reef flat is studied using the transect method, from the seaward front to the lagoonal edge, it is strongly recommended to do this transect along the reef 'morphological axis' defined by Weydert (1973a, b). This axis, generally directed along the dominant wind directions (and to the seaward swell propagation direction), shows a good sequence of all the biotopes of the reef flat and for this reason it is the most characteristic transect. In contrast, the study of the outer reef slope must be made using a transect perpendicular to the reef front (as in the 1969 Tuléar IBP survey: Gravier *et al.*, 1970; Weydert, 1974).

Bionomic studies on coral reefs often use transect methods (perpendicular to beach or reef front lines). (For coral studies, see: Stoddart, 1969; Loya, 1972; for soft bottom studies, see: Salvat and Renaud-Mornant, 1969; Thomassin, 1969; Gibbs *et al.*, 1971; Fishelson, 1971; Richard and Salvat, 1972), with samples taken at various intervals:

1 m by Fishelson (1971), in Eilat Gulf;

33 m by MacNae and Kalk (1962), in Inhaca flats;

50 m by Thomassin (1969), on Tuléar reef flat;

contiguous stations of 3 × 2 m for epifauna, some stations (2 or 3 times by 0.5 m², picking out without sieving) for endofauna, by Salvat (1972), on Reao atoll:

station of 2.5 m long × 2 m broad, along the transect axis, spaced by 10 m,

274

for malacological researches, by Richard and Salvat (1972), on the Tiahura reef complex.

Coral endofaunal samples (all the material left after sieving) is temporarily preserved in 10 per cent formalin in sea-water (industrial formalin is itself a 40 per cent solution of formaldehyde: the 10 per cent solution is based on this level of dilution, i.e. add 3 litres of industrial (40 per cent) formalin to 27 litres sea-water). Be careful to put some 10 per cent formalin into the containers before adding the sample and then complete by adding more solution and shaking; this assumes adequate fixing of all the material. Animals with calcareous cuticles or tests, however, should be preserved in 60 per cent alcohol. Small crustaceans such as copepods can be preserved in a mixture of one third alcohol, one third water and one third glycerin (if the alcohol used is 100 per cent, consult Gay-Lussac tables for the quantity of water required). All other animals, including hydroids and actiniarians, are preserved in buffered formalin. Meiofaunal samples are split, one part being preserved in 60 per cent alcohol (for crustacean studies), the other in formalin (for opisthobranchs and nematodes).

Samples taken for biomass studies must be preserved in 10 per cent buffered formalin, because in alcohol the lipids are dissolved.

Sorting is easier in the laboratory than in the field. Hand-picking is facilitated if the animals are stained with Rose Bengal (4–5 mm^3 in 2 litres of water to prepare the stain, and 10 cc poured on the sieve contents). Wait a few hours and then wash the material on a 40 μ sieve. Sort in quantities of 1 or 2 litres on a large white dish (50 × 30 × 7 cm) covered with water. Hand-picking is continued until no animals are seen after five complete remixings of the contents. Coloration techniques which aid sorting are reviewed by Williams (1974). The meiofauna are sorted using a binocular. Thomassin constructed an apparatus giving differential flotation of sediments and animals (Fig. 7), and a larger version was built by Falconetti (1973).

1. Evaluation of the sampled volume

A quadrat sample must include most of the living species of the studied community, but the time spent in collecting must be as short as possible (Pichon, Chapter 14).

The theoretical minimum volume defined by Picard (1962, 1965a) is the smallest volume of sediment that is necessary in order to obtain the greater part of the macrofauna of a given biotope. In practice, this theoretical minimum volume of sediment is obtained when few additional species are found by

275

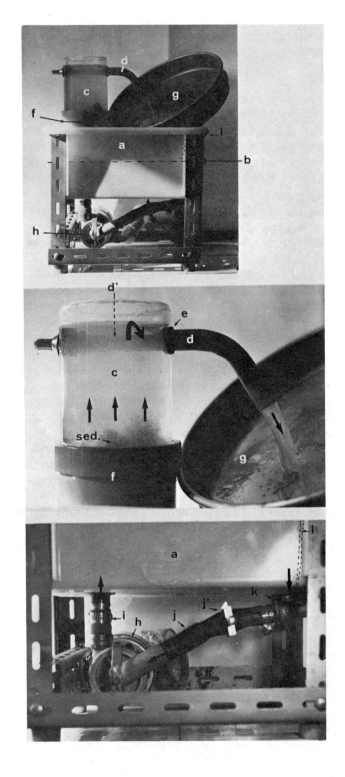

increasing the volume sampled. It is equivalent to the minimum area used in surface studies. The minimum volume is easily determined in temperate regions where taxa are well known, but it is very difficult or even impossible to evaluate in little-known tropical regions. This is particularly true on coral reefs, where it is not possible to identify all the sampled species in the field because of the great species diversity and the small size of many benthic animals such as isopods and amphipods.

Several methods can be used to determine the minimum volume (see data used in Figure 8 in Thomassin, 1973):

The cumulative curve (Gleason 1922; Reys and Salvat, 1971): the number of species taken by volume of sediment sampled (see the species-area curve: Tüxen, 1970).

The curve allows one to determine the volume above which the number

---

Figure 7
Sediment-washing apparatus (constructed by Thomassin and Lienhart in 1968).
(a) 10-litre plastic tank screwed on to a metal frame mounted on rubber blocks.
(b) level of 2 per cent formalin in water. This mixture is a better emulsifier than water alone.
(c) removable transparent plexiglass cylinder (diameter 11 cm) with (2 cm above its base) a plate perforated with several rings of oblique holes, some 1 cm in diameter others 0.4 cm in diameter, covered by a nylon sieve (0.2 mm mesh). This cylinder is fitted into a PVC tube (dilaplast) (f).
(d) plastic pipe, with central U-shaped opening (d^1) to act as a collector. The pipe can turn so that the opening of the collector is downward when the sediment is poured into the cylinder (c).
(e) rubber joint.
(f) PVC plastic tube (dilaplast), (11 cm inside diameter with rubber joint.
(g) 40 μ mesh sieve, tilted so that the animals can be concentrated undamaged in the lower part of the sieve out of the waterfall.
(h) electric water pump.
(i) pipe connecting pump (h) and dilaplast (f).
(j) rubber suction-pipe with screw-valve (j^1) to regulate the flow of water according to the grain size of the sediment being washed.
(k) three-way connector (one way is to a drain plug) screwed into the bottom of the tank (a)
(l) narrow rubber pipe connected to suction pipe (j) to act as an air intake.
← direction of water flow.
sed sediment.
To use:
1. Pour formalin solution into the tank (a).
2. Turn downwards the collector opening (d^1) in pipe (d).
3. Pur 200cc of sediment in the bottom of cylinder (c).
4. Fit the lladed cylinder (c) into the dilaplast (f).
5. Turn pipe (d) so that the collector opening (d^1) opens upwards.
6. Switch on the water pump (h).
7. Adjust the water stream with screw (j^1).
8. Leave the sediment to wash for 10 minutes.
9. Record the animals in sieve (g).

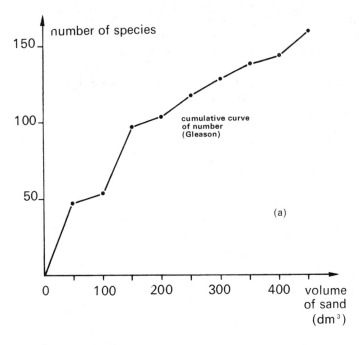

cumulative curve
of number
(Gleason)

(a)

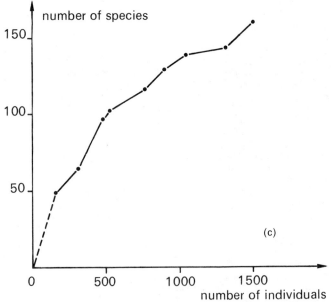

(c)

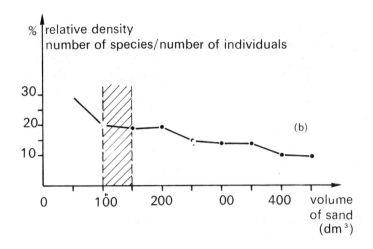

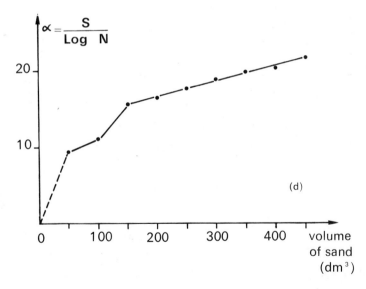

Figure 8
Evaluation of the sample, for example, in the coarse sands of inner channels
(see Thomassin, 1969).
(a) cumulative curve of number of species.
(b) relative densities of of individuals in sample.
(c) rarefraction curve.
(d) species diversity curve (according to Williams).

279

of additional species will not markedly increase. For example, in the poorly-sorted coarse sands of channels and pools on the reef flat at Tuléar, the minimum volume is approximately 150 dm³ (Fig. 8a). From Godron's method (1971); it is also possible to compute a mathematical model of the volume-species curve; the comparison with the observed curve allows one to infer ecological limits.

Relative densities of individuals in the sampled species curve. The number of species/number of individuals (Longhurst, 1959) shows a similar result: in the examples (Fig. 8b, Table 1), the inflexion point is between 100 and 150 dm³.

The rarefaction curve (Sanders, 1960), which expresses the species diversity. In our example it shows an intersection at 150–200 dm³ (Fig. 8c).

The species-diversity curve, defined by $s = \alpha \log_e N$, shows α is a constant (Fisher *et al.*, 1943) (Fig. 8d).

TABLE 1. Cumulative number of species and individuals in increasing volume of sediment sampled in the inner moat (from Thomassin, 1969).

Volume of samples	Number of species	Number of individuals	No. of species/No. of ind.
50 dm³	48	160	0.300
100 dm³	64	309	0.207
160 dm³	97	486	0.199
200 dm³	103	530	0.194
250 dm³	117	767	0.152
300 dm³	129	909	0.141
350 dm³	138	1046	0.131
400 dm³	144	1313	0.110
450 dm³	160	1502	0.106

The statistical test of Cancela de Fonseca (1965), which allows an approximate determination of the minimum volume using the formula $t = \bar{x}\sqrt{n}/s$ where t is Student probability, $\bar{x} =$ individual mean, $n =$ number of samples, $s =$ standard deviation. $\bar{x}$ and s being considered as constant, n is varied until the calculated t value is greater than that given by t-tables for $n - 1$ degrees of freedom at the desired significance level. In the examples given, for a probability of 5 per cent generally acceptable in biology (Lamotte, 1957), the calculated volume is 4 samples each of 50 dm³, or a total of 200 dm³.

2. Evaluation of the number of samples

Examination of species records show that it is impossible, using all the species recorded, to define the structure of the biocoenosis or community studied. For

2. The number of samples in which at least one specimen of the species is present divided by the total number of samples; usually this total number of samples is ten (e.g. Picard, 1965a, Thomassin, 1973). This is equivalent to 'frequency' as misused by Picard (1965a) and Pichon (Chapter 14).

this reason, representative species are used, selected on the basis of constancy as defined by Dajoz (1972)[2]. To define the number of samples, a practical method is to use the progressive means $\bar{x}_i$ of the number of the records in ten samples (Ricou, 1967):

$$\bar{x}_i = \frac{1 + 2 + \ldots i}{i}(1 < i < 10)$$

Table 2 gives progressive means of the few species in the coarse sand community of sandy channels on the Tuléar reef flat: we can see how many samples are required for the mean to be close enough to the total mean ($\bar{x}_{10}$) to be acceptable. The approximation from 9 samples is within 10 per cent. This method is useful because it can be estimated graphically; it is valuable for populations which are typical of the biocoenosis, and which have high constancy, even if the number of individuals is few.

3. Evaluation of sieve mesh size

Usually the sampled sediment is sorted through one or more sieves of chosen mesh (Morrison, 1953), though sieving is not always appropriate. MacNae and Kalk (1962), for example, report that polychaetes are often missed, while these and Enteropneusta may be fragmented.

Table 3 lists the mesh sizes used in benthic community studies in coral reef and other tropical areas; the general problem of mesh size is discussed by Reish (1959). Contrary to the views of Picard (1965a, 1965b) and Pichon (Chapter 14) that a 2 mm mesh size is required in tropical benthic studies, several workers have recommended a 1.4-mm square mesh to avoid missing numerous small animals, especially polychaetes and small crustaceans. Ledoyer (1969) has noted this problem relating to amphipods in sea-greass sediments. The following data illustrate the importance of mesh size in sediments from the Tuléar reef flat:

1.9 × 1.9-mm mesh 50 dm³ sand: 67 animals in 17 species (few polychaetes, no amphipods or isopods).

1.4 × 1.4-mm mesh 50 dm³ sand: 149–237 animals in 40–81 species.

A 1.4 mm square mesh (diagonal equivalent to 1.98-mm diameter circular mesh) is therefore recommended. MacIntyre (1969) defines macrobenthos as those animals retained by a 0.5-mm mesh.

4. Definition of characteristics of biocoenosis

(a) Coefficients and indexes used. Reviews of this subject are given by Reys and Salvat (1971) and by Boudouresque (1971). According to the Braun-Blanquet phytosociologic method, two coefficients are assigned to each species in every sample:

the abundance (A) = number of individuals (presence of the large species near the samples can be noticed by sign (+)),

the dominance (D) (= frequency sensu Dajoz, 1972) = percentage of number of individuals of one species (A)/total number of individuals of all the species present (ΣA).

TABLE 2. Evaluation of the number of minimum volume samples for study of one homogeneous biotope (example from Thomassin, 1969)

Number of 50 dm3 samples	Progressive means of the number of individuals caught (Ricou's method)									
	1	2	3	4	5	6	7	8	9	10
Otopleura auriscati	7.0	7.0	5.3	4.7	4.4	3.6	3.1	3.0	2.7	2.4
Nassarius albescens	9.0	22.5	15.6	12.2	13.2	12.5	11.7	11.9	11.0	11.2
Terebra affinis	5.0	5.5	7.3	7.2	5.8	6.0	5.1	7.0	6.2	5.6
Terebra babylonia	1.0	1.0	1.6	1.5	1.2	1.0	1.4	1.2	1.2	1.6
Lembos caputphotis	14.0	7.5	5.0	3.7	8.6	10.0	8.6	8.4	11.7	—
Grandidierella grossimana	0.0	0.0	1.0	0.7	0.8	1.3	1.4	2.4	2.2	—
Diogenes sp. 1 (aff. senex)	5.0	8.0	9.0	6.7	7.2	6.0	5.1	5.7	5.4	5.9
Ophiuroides sp. 6	3.0	2.0	1.3	1.0	2.8	2.5	2.3	3.0	2.7	2.7
Asymmetron lucayanum	3.0	2.0	1.6	1.5	1.8	1.5	1.3	1.5	1.3	1.2
Glycera tesselata	14.0	8.0	7.0	7.7	7.8	8.3	9.6	10.6	10.8	9.7
Pista cristata	2.0	1.0	1.0	0.7	0.8	0.8	0.9	1.0	1.1	1.2
Diopatra neapolitana	1.0	3.5	2.7	2.0	8.8	13.3	13.0	18.5	19.1	17.2
Aonides oxycephala	16.0	10.0	7.3	5.5	10.0	9.3	9.4	9.9	9.1	8.2
Cirriformia tentaculata	4.0	2.5	3.6	3.2	2.8	2.3	2.0	5.0	4.4	4.1

282

TABLE 3. Mesh-size of sieve used in tropical studies.

Authors	Work locality	Mesh	Biotopes
Morrison (1953)	Pacific atolls (Raroic)	0.8 mm ⎤ 0.3 mm ⎥ 0.15 mm ⎦	coral sands
MacNae and Kalk (1962)	Inhaca Island	picking out of the fauna on successive screens ⎤⎦	sandy and muddy areas
McNulty et al. (1962)	Florida	down to 1.0 m	sandy areas
Derijard (1965)	Tuléar	picking out, and 2 mm	mangrove muds, algal band muds, muddy sands, tidal flats
Reys and Reys (1965)	Tuléar	1.7 mm	medio- and infralittoral beaches
Picard (1965a, 1965b)	Tuléar	2.0 mm	sea-grass beds (on coral reefs and tidal flats)
Pichon (Mireille) (1967)	Tuléar	2.0 mm	beaches and tidal flats
Plante (1967), Plante and Cuny (1971)	Nosy Bé	2.0 mm	infralittoral and circalittoral bottoms
Moore et al. (1968)	Biscayne Bay	1.6 mm	tidal-flats with eel-grass beds
O'Gower and Wacasey (1967)	Florida	3.0 mm	sea-grass beds (Thalassia)
Kikuchi (1966)	Amakusa Bay	1.0 mm	eel-grass beds (Zostera)
Chabanne and Plante (1969)	Nosy Bé (Ambaro bay)	2.0 mm	terrigenous muddy sands
Thomassin (1969, 1973)	Tuléar	1.4 mm	coral sands
Stephenson et al. (1970)	Moreton Bay	picking out then sieving on 6.0 mm	terrigenous lagoonal bottoms
Gibbs et al. (1971)	Cook Islands	1.00 mm	littoral
		0.5, 1.0, 2.0 mm	lagoonal bottoms
Stephenson and Williams (1971)	New Guinea	2.00 mm	infralittoral bottoms
Wade (1972)	Jamaica	0.5 mm	infralittoral bottoms
Le Fur (1973)	Tuléar	2.0, 1.4, 1.0 mm	infralittoral beaches
Salvat (1972)	Reao I.	3 mm	lagoon bottoms (no sieving in very coarse sands on reef flat and lagoonal slopes)

To these two coefficients must be added the *diversity index* (according to Shannon's formula or the simplified Stirling's formula: see below).

As Odum (1971) has noted, the species-dominance is derived from their density, their weight (biomass notion) and their breeding potential; it is the basis of the biological balance.

Results of samples of the same biota (minimum number of samples, with a minimum volume) are gathered in a table. Then several synthetic parameters can be calculated in view of the numerical-quantitative study for every species:

the *mean-abundance* $(A\overline{m}) = \Sigma A/N$ (N = number of samples)

the *mean-dominance* $(D\overline{m})$: 2 methods are being used to calculate it:

. the Picard's method (1962, 1965a) (Reys and Salvat, 1971):

$$D\overline{m} = A\overline{m}/\Sigma \, A\overline{m} \text{ of all species} \times 100$$

. the Guille's (1970) method (Pichon, Chapter 14):

$$D\overline{m} = \Sigma \, A/N \times 100 \, (N = \text{number of samples}).$$

Statistically, Picard's method is the better.

From this two synthetic coefficients $(A\overline{m}, D\overline{m})$ calculated for each species, Picard distinguishes:

The exclusive characteristic species of the biocoenosis—the species which by their abundance and dominance are limited to one biocoenosis (and to the corresponding biotope); they could be found as a few individuals (often sickly or sterile) in other biota where they are considered as *accidental species*.

The preferential characteristic species of the biocoenosis, which are those species present in at least 4/10 samples of a biotope with a mean-dominance $D\overline{m} \geqslant 2 \times D\overline{m}$ in other biotopes (where they are considered as *accompanying species*, among which can be distinguished: muddy species, sandy species, polymodal species, according to the granulometric features of the bottoms colonized).

The presence (P_i) *sensu* Picard = number of samples where the species is present/total number of samples considered. Generally, this coefficient is a percentage, but Picard as well as the author have used a scale from 1 to 10 (for 10 to 100 per cent), that must be named in this case *constancy*. This presence coefficient *is* named frequency (F) by Pichon (Chapter 14). But, presence (P_i) is a synthetic parameter corresponding to frequency (F_i), which is an analytic parameter. Glémarec (1969) gives frequency F_i = number of samples where the species i is taken/total number of considered samples for one community; and, presence $P_i = F_i/\Sigma F_i$ in other samples from other communities. In several quadrat samples, frequency F_i = number of quadrats where species i is present/total number of quadrats $\times 100$, see Boudouresque (1971).

(In Thomassin, 1969, 1973, the author broadens the presence concept to consider all the species present *in* or *near* the sample quadrat.)

From the presence coefficient, several coefficients are derived:

284

The relative abundance index (Harmelin, 1969) (=the dominance-presence coefficient In: Thomassin, 1973; Le Fur, 1973):

$$\text{relative abundance index (R.A.I.)} = D\overline{m} \times P_i \times 100$$

The abundance frequency coefficient (A.F.) (Ledoyer, 1968):

$$\text{A.F.} = A\overline{m}_i/F_i \quad \text{or} \quad \text{A.F.} = \frac{n_x/n_a}{(n_A/n_A) \cdot 100}$$

coefficient principally used to characterize the sessile epifauna species.

The dominance-frequency coefficient (D.F.) (Glémarec, 1964, 1969)

$$\text{D.F.} = D\overline{m}_a \cdot P_{i_1}$$

Species having the highest values $D\overline{m} \times p_i$ are called leaders (from leading dominant species).

The rank correlation and the *biological index* (I_b) (Fager, 1967; Sanders, 1960; Guille, 1970; Thomassin, 1973), where in each sample the species are classified by decreasing abundance order and the ten first species are given an index with values from 10 to 1. For all the considered samples, the total of these values is derived. Biological indices (I_b) indicate the most characteristic species that have a high rank.

(b) *The similarity coefficients.* To compare two or several samples or communities, several indices are used (reviews by Dagnélie, 1960; Goodall, 1967; Cheetham and Hazel, 1969; Blanc *et al.,* 1976) mostly based on binary (presence–absence) similarity.

(i) *Comparison of the number of species in common* (based on the presence–absence concept).

The fourfold point correlation coefficient (Φ):

$$\Phi = \frac{N_t \cdot C_{i1} - N_i \cdot N_j}{[N_i \cdot N_j(N_t - N_i)(N_t - N_j)]^{1/2}}$$

where N_t = total number of species,
$\quad C_{ij}$ = number of samples where species i and j are present together,
$\quad N_i$ = number of samples where species i is present
$\quad N_j$ = number of samples where species j is present.

The similarity coefficient of Sørensen (1948), derived from the Jaccard's coefficient (1912), (*index of biotal dispersity*, for Koch, 1957):

$$\text{Jaccard's coefficient: } S_j = \frac{C_{pq}}{n_p + n_q - C_{pq}} = \frac{C_{pq}}{C_{pq} + U_{pq}}$$

285

where C_{pq} = number of species present in both samples p and q
n_p = number of species present in sample p
n_q = number of species present in sample q
U_{pq} = number of species just present in one sample, p or q.

The 'indice de parenté' of Ledoyer is the same:

$$I_p\% = C_{pq} \cdot 100/n + n_q = C_{pq} \cdot 100/C_{pq} + U_{0q}$$

Sørensen's coefficient: $S_s = \dfrac{2 \cdot C_{pq}}{n_p + n_q - C_{pq}} = \dfrac{2 \cdot C_{pq}}{C_{pq} + U_{pq}}$

Indices of similarity used by O'Gower and Wacasey (1967):

the *Fager's index* (1963) $= c/\sqrt{ab} - \frac{1}{2}\sqrt{b}$, where $b \geqslant a$
the *Webb's index* (1950) $= c/(a + b + c)$

where a = number of occurrences of species A,
b = number of occurrences of species B,
c = number of joint occurrences of species A and B.

O'Gower and Wacasey discussed these coefficients.

(ii) *Comparison of dominance of the species in common*

The similarity coefficient of Kulczynski (1927):

$$S_K = \frac{2 \sum\limits_{i=1}^{n} \inf(D_{ip}, D_{iq})}{\sum\limits_{i=1}^{n} D_{ip} = \sum\limits_{i=1}^{n} D_{iq}}$$

where $\inf(D_{ip}, D_{iq})$ = smallest of the two values D_{ip} and D_{iq}

D_{ip} = dominance of species i in sample p
D_{iq} = dominance of species i in sample q

The affinity degree of Sanders (1960) (used by Wieser, 1960, and Sanders, 1960; Guille and Soyer, 1968; Guille, 1970; Thomassin, 1973):

$$D_{aff} = \sum_{i=1}^{n} \inf(D_{ip}, D_{iq})$$

where $\inf(D_{ip}, D_{iq})$ = the smallest of the two values D_{ip} and D_{iq} of the dominance of species i in the samples p and q.

(Following Boudouresque's opinion, the author is of the opinion that the Gamulin–Brida's coefficient 'Quotient de similitude' (1960):

$$QS = \frac{a'_1 + b'_1}{a_1 - b_1}$$

where a_1 = mean abundance of species of sample A
b_1 = mean abundance of species of sample B
a'_1 = mean abundance of species of sample A encountered also in sample B
b'_1 = mean abundance of species of sample B encountered also in sample A

is a hybrid of qualitative and quantitative concepts and in fact is not correct.

The Bravais–Pearson correlation index (Cassie and Michael, 1968). It is beginning to be used in benthic studies, but as yet has not been employed in coral reef studies.

$$r_{ij} = \frac{\dfrac{1}{n}\sum_{p=1}^{n}(D_{ip} - \bar{D}_i)(D_{jp} - \bar{D}_j)}{s_i \cdot s_j}$$

where s_i = standard deviation of dominance of species i,
s_j = standard deviation of dominance of species j,
D_{ip} and D_{jp} the transformed dominance of species i and j in the sample p,
$\bar{D}_i$ and $\bar{D}_j$ the means of the transformed dominances of the species i and j.

(c) *The diversity measures.* The simplest measure of diversity is the number of species per unit area or volume(S). Standard samples of different sizes are not simply comparable, though the approximately logarithmic relation of species number to sample area or volumes makes some comparisons possible. More species per quadrat measurement are also subject to rather large dispersions because of the variations of the species distribution (microdistribution is generally very irregular in benthic species) and the inclusion of rare species (Whittaker, 1972; MacArthur, 1965).

Several diversity measures can be used; they are discussed in Travers (1971). They are subdivided in two groups:

(i) Those based on the relation of species number of the logarithm of sample size. The more frequently used are:

The Gleason (1922) index:
$d = S/\log A$
S = number of species
A = sample area or volume.
This index must not be used when $N < 20$ (Travers, 1971).

The Fisher et al. *(1943) index:*

$$S = \ln\left(1 + \frac{N}{\alpha}\right) \text{ or}$$

$S = \alpha \cdot \ln N$ assuming N very high in comparison with α.

The measure of species richness of Margalef (1951):

$d = (S - 1)/\log N$
N = number of individuals.

This index must not be used when $N < 35$ (Travers, 1971).
Both the last two (indices) measures are equivalent, it is just a question of units.

(ii) Those derived from the information theory. The most commonly used is that of Shannon (1948):

$H' = -p_i \cdot \log_2 p_i \, (\Sigma p_i = 1)$
p_i = relative frequency (or occurring probability = proportion of individuals belonging to the ith species) of the species of rank i
S = total number of species
H' is expressed generally in bit units.

To compute Shannon index easily without using a computer, Frontier (1969) gives a table of the value of $-p \cdot \log_2 p$; a more precise value was computed by the author.

Species diversity has two components, number of species (S) and 'equitability' (J) (or evenness of the different species) (Lloyd and Gherlardi, 1964);

$$J = H'/\log_e S \text{ (Pielou, 1966)}$$

J is the best index when the number of individuals (N) is low. Criticisms of these indices are made by Swartz *et al.*, 1973.

Redundancy (R_h) which is a good expression of the level of organization is also derived from Shannon index:

$$R_h = 100 \left(\frac{1 - H}{\log_2 S} \right)$$

TENTATIVE EVALUATION OF THE ACTUAL POPULATIONS OVER LARGE AREAS

Estimation of the actual population is only valuable at the time during which the sample was made.

All the estimations of population densities are derived from the calculation of the confidence interval which must be assigned to the arithmetical means calculated.

Now the dispersion of the data around the mean-value is classically measured by the standard error. In the case of non-normal distributions, as in benthic distributions, the standard errors have no statistical significance. The densities generally vary from 0 to n individuals for the benthic species collected in 50 dm^3 of sediments.

Salvat (1970, 1972) used this method to estimate molluscan and holothurian populations on Pacific atolls (densities per hectare). Recently it was used for meiofaunal populations in coarse sands from channels and pools of the inner flat (Thomassin *et al.*, 1976).

MEASUREMENT OF OTHER ABIOTIC AND BIOTIC PARAMETERS.

1. *Granulometrical parameters* (Stoddart, Chapter 5)

Samples of sediment must be taken from the surface as well as from the deepest layers.

Weydert (1971, 1973a, 1973b), working on coral reef sediments, perfected granulometric analysis, pointing out some coefficients that can be used successfully by biologists (see Thomassin 1973). They are in measuring size of the sediment particles):

(a) the maximum dimension (D_{max}) and minimum dimension (D_{min}) of the grains,
(b) the mean size (Folk and Ward, 1957),
(c) the sorting (Folk and Ward, 1957)
(d) the kurtosis K_G (Folk and Ward, 1957),
(e) the determination of the various sedimentary facies, from use of the probability ordinate curves (Visher, 1969), cross points being calculated by the logarithmic spiral method (Weydert, 1973a): exceptional moving, occasional moving, traction, momentary saltation, continuous saltation, momentary suspension, continuous suspension.

To study the deep structure of the reef substrata, particularly in the seagrass beds, the use of a corer of 10 cm internal diameter, 50 cm long, derived from the Deguen and Molinier corer (1959), is appropriate (Thomassin, in press).

In general, the granulometric analyses are made on quantities too small to be representative (50 g by Renaud-Mornant *et al.,* 1971; 100 g by Guilcher *et al.,* 1965). A quantity of 150–200 g is recommended for fine coral sands, 250–300 g for medium and coarse coral sands, and more (up to 1 kg for gravelly coral sands of the deepest layer of the boulder tract).

The Endoume team at Tuléar has extended Picard's (1965a) general terminology for benthic studies to describe biologically significant granulometric properties in the reef environment. Picard's terms have no specific English equivalents and are as follows:

vasicole
    vasicole stricte .... pure mud or mud dominant
    vasicole tolérante.................. all substrata but always with presence of mud
sabulicole
    sabulicole stricte .... clean fine sands
    sabulicole tolérante .... all substrata but always with presence of sands
gravellicole .... gravels or coarse sands
mixticole .... mixing of muds, fine sands and coarse sands
minuticole............................... mixing of muds and fine sands, but without coarse sands.

Glémarec (1969) has extended and redefined this terminology to give greater precision as follows:

sabulicole

sabulicole stricte	sands (medium and coarse) $\geqslant 30\%$
sabulicole fine	sands $(200\,\mu)$ without gravels, but tolerance of pelites (up to 30%).
sabulicole sale	mixed sands $(500\,\mu)$ with tolerance of gravels $(\leqslant 10\%)$ and muds (up to 30–50%).
sabulicole propre	mixed sands $(200$–$1000\,\mu)$ with tolerance of muds $(\leqslant 10\%)$, and gravels $(\leqslant 30\%)$
sabulicole tolérante	mixed sands, always with sands $\geqslant 70\%$.
vasicole	with $\leqslant 30\%$ of muds, less than 10% of gravels
gravellicole	with $\leqslant 30\%$ of gravels, less than 5% of muds
sabulicole-vasicole	muddy sands (muds = 3 to 100%), but always with gravels $\leqslant 10\%$.
sabulicole-gravellicole.................	clean gravels and sands (muds $\leqslant 5\%$)
mixticole	mixed sands $(100$–$1000\,\mu)$, gravels + sands + muds, in equal proportions.

Because of the complexity of deposits in coral reef areas, the more comprehensive scheme of Glémarec is more appropriate (Thomassin 1978).

2. $CaCO_3$ content

In coral reef complexes under important terrigenous alluvial deposits, the $CaCO_3$ content is a good parameter to explain distribution of species related to high $CaCO_3$ content (reef sediment generally) or to silicious sands (littoral tidal flats) or ubiquitous species.

Maxwell's classification (1968) could be validly used in the Tuléar reef complex:

$> 80\%$ acid-soluble materials	high carbonate facies
60–80% acid-soluble materials	impure carbonate facies
40–60% acid-soluble materials	transitional facies
$< 40\%$ acid-soluble materials	terrigenous facies.

On the other hand, Maxwell and Swinchatt's classification (1970) is used with more difficulty. It is:

terrigenous sands.......................	quartz $\geqslant 60\%$, mud $\leqslant 1\%$

terrigenous muddy sands and muds	from pure terrigenous muds to muddy sands with 10% clay, to muddy quartzose–carbonate sands
inter-reef carbonate sands	fine to coarse carbonate sands with local accumulation of gravel and mud.
non-reef carbonate sands and muddy sands	low percentage of coral and foraminifera
carbonate muddy sands	increase of foraminifera
carbonate mud facies	
reef facies	

3. Porosity

Porosity and compaction are two very important parameters to which endo-faunal communities are related. Porosity, however, cannot be measured in the field whilst diving, and transport of sediment destroys the substratum structure. Salvat (1967) proposed an approximate method—measurement of porosity with sand shifted and porosity of the sand compacted, then a mean is calculated— but this method gives two extreme limits and is not very representative of the field structure. Recently, Beard and Weyl (1973) showed that porosity is inde-pendent of grain-size of sand of the same sorting index, but varies with sorting, and permeability decreases as grain size becomes finer and as sorting becomes poorer.

In situ measurements of the porosity of sediments by electrical conduction properties could offer satisfying results. Conductivity must be greater in well-percolated sediments with large spaces between particles and conversely it must be less in clogged or compacted sediments. Conductivity could be easily obtained by potential difference between two electrodes sunk into the sediment, measured on a water-tight potentiometer suitably calibrated. (Apparatus is under construction by the author, but one based on different concepts is used by B. F. Keegan, University College, Galway; personal comment).

4. pH, t°, dissolved O₂ variation measurements

4. pH, $t°$, dissolved O_2 variation measurements

The variations in these parameters were estimated on the Tuléar coral flats using an *in situ* multi-sensor recorder (self-contained, self-acting) built by Jaubert (Technocean group, Univ. Nice) (Fig. 9).

pH and O_2 measurements using small corers are very difficult to do, and penetration into coarse, non-compacted sediments mixing the water layers and giving incorrect values.

5. Organic matter (organic C, total N) measurements.

In coral reef surveys for the fixation of sediment for future analysis, the

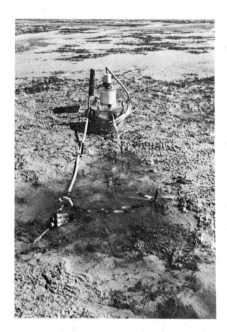

Figure 9
The portable, self-contained, self-acting *in situ* recorder, registering pH, t°, dissolved O_2 meter (Jaubert's prototype, Technocian Group, Nice) in sea-grass beds and in enclosed lagoon bottom on the Great Reef of Talcar (1972 survey, photo Vasseur).

Frontier–Abou's method (1970) (sediment dried at 35°C during 36 hrs.) seems the most practical.

Organic carbon and total nitrogen measures are made according to the common methods (Thomassin and Cauwet, paper in preparation).

Amino acid contents in sediments richest in organic N sometimes gives good results (Daumas and Thomassin, 1977; Müller and Suess, in press).

Permeability, porosity, granulometric size and depth of the well-oxygenated layer are abiotic parameters on which the endofaunal species are dependent. Taking these parameters as a basis, Chassé (1971) proposed a new index, the instability edaphic gradient (I.S.E.), that is:

$$\text{I.S.E.} = \log_{10}(1{,}000 \cdot K \cdot Ox)$$

where K = the permeability in darcy unit

Ox = the summer depth of oxygenated layer in cm = depth of the redox discontinuity.

The instability edaphic gradient, used by this author, represents the best edaphic synthetic criterion in this environment; it allows one to map studied areas (particularly beaches) by means of iso-value curves.

6. Conclusions

All these measures must be correlated with species distribution and abundance, using multivariate analysis, particularly the factor analysis (using the combined R- and Q-type procedures grouping species that occurred together in samples and grouping samples with species occurring together, respectively) (Cassie and Michael, 1968; Popham and Ellis, 1971; Field, 1971; Hughes and Thomas, 1971; Erman and Helm 1971; Monbet, 1972; Blanc and Leveau,1973).

CONCLUSIONS

In conclusion, studies of the coral reef soft bottom communities (very diversified and with difficult approaches) must use several techniques to advance knowledge, most of them fitted to the substrata types or to the research topics.

Descriptions of the coral sand communities must be done using quantitative methods that can be easily compared with results obtained from other soft-bottom communities in order to enlarge the knowledge of tropical soft-bottom biotopes.

ACKNOWLEDGEMENTS

I am particularly grateful to Dr Stoddart (Cambridge University) for his kindness in helping to translate the manuscript.

This contribution is no. 810 of the Station Marine d'Endoume and Centre d'Océanographie (CNRS/LA no. 41), Marseille.

References

AMOUROUX, J.-M.; GUILLE, A. 1973. Premières estimations des biomasses dans l'infralittoral à l'aide d'une suçeuse à pompe immergeable. *Rapp. P.-V. Réun. CIESMM,* vol. 21, no. 29, p. 605–7.

ANON, 1969. Finnish I.B.P.-P.M. Group. Quantitative sampling equipment for littoral benthos. *Int. Rev. gesamt Hydrobiol.,* vol. 54, p. 185–93.

BARNETT, P. R.; HARDY, B. L. 1967. A diver-operated quantitative bottom sampler for sand macrofauna. *Helgoländer Wiss. Meeresunters,* vol. 15, p. 390–8.

BEARD, D. C.; WEYL, P. K., 1973. Influence of texture on porosity and permeability of unconsolidated sand. *Bull. Am. Assoc. petrol. Geol.,* 57, no. 2, p. 349–69.

BLANC, F.; CHARDY, P.; LAUREC, A.; REYS, J.-P. 1976. Choix des métriques qualitatives en analyse d'inertie. Implications en écologie marine benthique. *Mar. Biol.,* vol. 35, p. 49–67.

——; LEVEAU, M. 1973. Plancton et eutrophie: Aire d'épandage rhodanienne et Golfe de Fos (Traitement mathématique des données). Thèse Doct. ès-science, Univ. Aix-Marseille, Archives originales CNRS no AO 7907 (2 vols, xxxix + 681 p.).

BOUDOURESQUE, C. F. 1971. Méthodes d'étude qualitative et quantitative du benthos (en particulier du phytobenthos). *Tethys,* vol. 3, no. 1, p. 79–104.

BRAUN-BLANQUET, J. 1964. *Pflanzensoziologie.* 3rd edit. Wien and New York, Springer Verlag, (865 p.).

BRETT, C. F. 1964. A portable hydraulic diver-operated dredge sieve for sampling subtidal macrofauna. *J. mar. Res.,* vol. 22, no. 2, p. 205–9.

CANSELA DA FONSECA, J.-P. 1965. L'outil statistique en biologie du sol. 1. Distribution de fréquence et tests de signification. *Rev. Ecol. Biol. du Sol.,* vol. 2, no. 3, p. 299–332.

CARPINE, C. 1970. Ecologie de l'étage bathyal dans la Méditerranée occidentale. *Mém. Inst. océanogr., Monaco,* vol. 2 (146 p.).

——. 1972. Standardisation des méthodes, prélèvements benthiques. Rapport "Etude en commun de la Méditerranée—Unité opérationnelle" ECH/655 (15 p. mimeo.).

CASSIE, R. M.; MICHAEL, A. D. 1968. Fauna and sediments of an intertidal mud flat: a multivariate analysis. *J. exp. mar. Biol. Ecol.,* vol. 2, p. 1–23.

CHABANNE, J.; PLANTE, R. 1969. Les populations benthiques (endofaune, crevettes penaeides, poissons) d'une baie de la côte nord-ouest de Madagascar: écologie, biologie et pêche. *Cah. ORSTOM,* (Océanogr.), vol. 7, no. 1, p. 41–71.

CHASSÉ, C. 1971. Distribution qualitative et quantitative des peuplements littoraux des sédiments meubles au long d'un gradient édaphique synthétique quantifié, l'instabilité. E.M.B.S. III, Arcachon, 1968. *Vie et Milieu,* suppl. 22, p. 657–75.

CHEETHAM, A. H.; HAZEL, J. E. 1969. Binary (presence–absence) similarity coefficients. *J. Paleontol.,* vol. 43, no. 5 (1 and 2), p. 1130–6.

CHRISTIE, N. D.; ALLEN, J. C. 1972. A self-contained diver-operated quantitative sampler for investigating the macrofauna of soft substrates. *Trans. R. Soc. S. Afr.,* vol. 40, no. 4, p. 299–307.

DAGNÉLIE, P. 1960. *Théorie et méthodes statistiques,* vol. 1, Gembloux, Duculot (378 p.).

DAJOZ, R. 1972. *Précis d'écologie.* Paris, Dunod (434 p.).

DAUMAS, R.; THOMASSIN, B. A. 1977. Proteic fractions in coral and zoantharian mucus; possible evolution in coral reef environment. *Proc. 3rd Int. Symp. on Coral Reefs,* Miami, May 1977.

DEGUEN, F.; MOLINIER, R. 1959. Un appareil de prélèvement de sédiments destiné à l'étude pédologique des sols phanérogamiques marins. *Bull. Soc. linn. Provence,* vol. 22, p. 54–7.

DELLA CROCE, N.; CHIARABINI, A. 1971. A suction pipe for sampling mid-water and bottom organisms in the sea. *Deep-sea Res.,* vol. 18, p. 851–54.

DERIJARD, R. 1965. Contribution à l'étude du peuplement des sédiments sablo-vaseux et vaseux intertidaux compactés ou fixés par la végétation de la région de Tuléar (Madagascar). *Rec. Trav. Stn mar. Endoume, Suppl.* 3 (94 p.).

ERMAN, D. C.; HELM, W. T. 1971. Comparison of some species importance values and ordination technique used to analyse benthic invertebrate communities. *Oikos,* vol. 22, p. 240–7.

FAGER, E. W. 1957. Determination and analysis of recurrent groups. *Ecology,* vol. 38, p. 586–95.

——. 1963. Communities of organisms. In: M. N. Hill (ed.). *The Sea,* vol. 2. New York, John Wiley, p. 415–37.

FALCONETTI, C. 1973. Fonctionnement d'un appareil de tri-semi-automatique. *Rapp. CIESMM,* vol. 22, no. 4, p. 125–7 (2 fig.).

FIELD, J. H. 1971. A numerical analysis of changes in the soft-bottom fauna along a transect across False Bay, South Africa. *J. exp. mar. Biol. Ecol.,* vol. 7, p. 215–53.

FISHELSON, L. 1971. Ecology and distribution of the benthic fauna in the shallow waters of Red Sea. *Mar. Biol.,* vol. 10, no. 2, p. 113–33.

FISHER, R. A.; CORBET, A. S.; WILLIAMS, C. B. 1943. The relation between the number of individuals in a random sample of an animal population. *J. anim. Ecol.,* vol. 12, p. 42–58.

FOLK, R. L.; WARD, N. C. 1957. Brazos River Bar: a study in the significance of grain size parameters. *J. sedim. Petrol.* vol. 27, p. 3–26.

FOSS, G. 1968. Behaviour of *Myxine glutinosa* L. in natural habitat. Investigation of a mud biotope by suction technique. *Sarsia,* vol. 31, p. 1–14.

FRONTIER, S. 1969. Méthode d'analyse statistique applicables à l'écologie du plancton. *ORSTOM, Nosy Bé, Océanogr., Document scientifique,* no. 7 (33 p. mimeo.).

FRONTIER-ABOU, D. 1970. Dosage de l'azote sur 60 échantillons de sédiment superficiel de la Baie d'Ambaro. *ORSTOM, Nosy Bé, Document scientifique,* no. 15 (16 p. mimeo.).

GAMULIN-BRIDA, H. 1960. Primjena Sorensenove metode pri istrazivanjn bentoskish populacija. *Bioloski Glasnik,* vol. 13, no. 1, p. 21–47.

GARTH, J. S. 1964. The crustacea decapoda (brachyura and anomura) of Eniwetok Atoll, Marshall Islands, with special reference to the obligate commensals of branching corals. *Micronesica,* vol. 1, p. 137–44.

GIBBS, P. E. 1972. Polychaete annelids from the Cook Islands. *J. Zool.,* vol. 168, p. 199–220.

——. 1975. Survey of the macrofauna inhabiting lagoon deposits on Aitutaki (p. 123–31). In: D. R. Stoddart, P. E. Gibbs (eds). Almost-atoll of Aitutaki: Reef studies in the Cook Islands, South Pacific. *Atoll Res. Bull.,* no. 190, p. 1–158.

——.; STODDART, D. R.; VEVERS, H. G. 1971. Coral reefs and associated communities in the Cook Islands. *Bull. R. Soc. N.Z.*, vol. 8, p. 91–105.

GLEASON, H. A. 1922. On the relation between species and area. *Ecology*, vol. 3, p. 158–62.

GLÉMAREC, M. 1964. Bionomie benthique de la partie orientale du Golfe du Morbihan. *Cah. Biol. mar.*, vol. 5, p. 33–96.

——. 1969. Les peuplements benthiques du plateau continental Nord-Gascogne. Thèse Doct. Sciences, Univ. Paris, Archives originales CNRS n° A.O. 3422. 2 vols.

GODRON, M. 1971. Comparaison d'une courbe aire-espèces et de son modèle. *Oecol. Plant.*, Paris, vol. 6, p. 189–96.

GOODALL, D. W. 1967. The distribution of the matching coefficient. *Biometrics*, vol. 23, no. 4, p. 647–56.

GRAVIER, N.; HARMELIN, J. G.; PICHON, M.; THOMASSIN, B.; VASSEUR, P.; WEYDERT, P. 1970. Les récifs coralliens de Tuléar (Madagascar): morphologie de la pente externe. *C.R. Acad. Sci., Paris*, (D) 270, p. 1130–33.

GUÉRIN-ANCEY, O. 1970. Etude des intrusions terrigènes fluviatiles dans les complexes récifaux: délimitation et dynamique des peuplements des vases et des sables vaseux du chenal post-récifal de Tuléar (S. W. de Madagascar). *Rec. Trav. Stn mar. Endoume*, Suppl. 10, p. 3–46.

GUILCHER, A.; BERTHOIS, L.; LE CALVEZ, Y.; BATTISTINI, R.; CROSNIER, A. 1965. Les récifs coralliens et le lagon de l'île Mayotte (Archipel des Comores, Océan Indien). *Mém. ORSTOM*, vol. 11 (210 p.).

GUILLE, A. 1970. Bionomie benthique du plateau continental de la côte catalane française. II. Les communautés de la macrofaune. *Vie et Milieu*, vol. 17, no. 1B, p. 149–280.

——; SOYER, J. 1968. La faune benthique des substrats meubles de Banyuls-sur-Mer. Premières données qualitatives et quantitatives. *Vie et Milieu*, vol. 10, no. 2B, p. 323–59.

HARMELIN, J. G. 1964. Etude des "mattes" d'herbiers de *Posidonia oceanica* Delile. *Rec. Trav. Stn mar. Endoume*, vol. 35, no. 51, p. 43–105.

——. 1969. Bryozaires des grottes obscures sous-marines de la région marseillaise. Faunistique et écologie. *Téthys*, vol. 1, no. 3, p. 793–806.

HIATT, R. W. 1953. Methods of collecting marine invertebrates on coral atolls: In: F. R. Fosberg, M.-H. Sachet, Handbook for atoll research (2nd prelim. edit.). *Atoll. Res. Bull.*, no. 17, p. 78–89.

HOLME, N. A.; McINTYRE, A. D. 1971. *Methods for the study of marine benthos.* Oxford, Blackwell Science Publications. (I.B.P. Handbook 16) (334 p.).

HUGHES, R. N.; THOMAS, M. L. H. 1971. The classification and ordination of shallow-water benthic samples from Prince Edwards Island, Canada. *J. exp. mar. Biol. Ecol.*, vol. 7, p. 1–39.

JACCARD, P. 1912. The distribution of the flora in the alpine zone. *New Phytol.*, vol. 11, p. 37–50.

KEEGAN, B. F.; KÖNNECKER, G. 1973. In situ quantitative sampling of benthic organisms. *Helgoländer wiss. Meersunters.*, vol. 24, p. 256–63.

KIKUCHI, T. 1966. An ecological study on animal communities of the *Zostera marina* belt in Tomioka Bay, Amakusa, Kyushu. *Publ. Amakusa mar. biol. Lab.*, vol. 1, no. 1, p. 1–106.

KOCH, L. F. 1957. Index of biotal dispersity. *Ecology*, vol. 38, p. 145–8.

KULCZINSKI, S. 1927. Die Pflanzenassoziationen des Pieninen. *Bull. Inst. Acad. Pol. Sci. Lett. Classe Sci. Math.*, (B) Suppl. 2, p. 57–203.

LAMOTTE, M. 1957. *Initiation aux méthodes statistiques en biologie.* Paris, Masson, 144 p.

LEDOYER, M. 1962. Etude de la faune vagile des herbiers superficiels de Zosteracées et de quelques biotopes d'Algues littorales. *Rec. Trav. Stn. mar. Endoume*, vol. 25 no. 39, p. 117–235.

——. 1968. Ecologie de la faune vagile des biotopes méditerranéns accessibles en scaphandre autonome. IV: Synthèse de l'étude écologique. *Rec. Trav. Stn mar. Endoume*, Bull. 44, fasc. 60, p. 125–295.

——. 1969. Amphipodes Gammariens du sédiment des herbiers de Phanérogames marines et des dunes hydrauliques du Grand Récif du Tuléar (Madagascar) *Rec. Trav. Stn mar. Endoume*, Suppl. 8, p. 15–62.

LE FUR, C. 1973. Etude quantitative et dynamique d'un peuplement intertidal d'une plage tropicale (Sud-Ouest de Madagascar). Thèse Doct. spéc., Univ. Aix-Marseille (54 p. mimeo.).

LLOYD, M., GHELARDI, R. J. 1964. A table for calculating the "equitability" component of species diversity. *J. anim. Ecol.*, vol. 33, p. 217–25.

LONGHURST, A. R. 1959. The sampling problem in benthic ecology. *Proc. N.Z. Ecol. Soc.*, vol. 6, p. 8–12.

LOYA, Y. 1972. Community structure and species diversity of hermatypic corals at Eilat, Red Sea. *Mar. Biol.*, vol. 13, no. 2, p. 100–23.

MacNae, W.; Kalk, M. 1962. The fauna and flora of sand flats at Inhaca Island, Moçambique. *J. anim. Ecol.*, vol. 31, p. 93–128.

Maes, V. O. 1967. The littoral marine Mollusks of Cocos-Keeling Islands (Indian Ocean). *Proc. Acad. nat. Sci. Phil.*, vol. 119, no. 4, p. 93–217.

Manning, R. B. 1960. A useful method for collecting crustacea. *Crustaceana*, vol. 1, no. 4, p. 272.

Margalef, R. 1951. Diversidad de especies en las comunidades naturales. *Publnes Inst. Biol. apl.*, Barcelona, vol. 9, p. 5–27.

Massé, H. 1967. Emploi d'une suçeuse hydraulique transformée pour les prélèvements quantitatifs dans les substrats meubles infralittoraux. *Helgoländer wiss. Meeresunters.*, vol. 15, p. 500–5.

——. 1970. La suçeuse hydraulique, bilan de quatre années d'emploi, sa manipulation, ses avantages et inconvénients, peuplements benthiques. *Téthys*, vol. 2, no. 2, p. 547–56.

Maxwell, W. G. H. 1968. *Atlas of the Great Barrier Reef.* Amsterdam, Elsevier (258 p.).

——; Swinchatt, J. P. 1970. Great Barrier Reef: regional variation in a terrigenous-carbonate province. *Geol. Soc. Am. Bull.*, vol. 81, p. 691–724.

McArthur, R. H. 1965. Patterns of species diversity. *Biol. Rev.*, vol. 40, p. 510–33.

McIntyre, A. D. 1969. Ecology of marine meiobenthos. *Biol. Rev.*, vol. 44, p. 245–90.

McNulty, J. K.; Work, R. C.; Moore, H. B. 1962. Level sea bottom communities in Biscayne Bay and neighbouring areas. *Bull. mar. Sci. Gulf Caribb.*, vol. 12, p. 204–33.

Monbet, Y. 1972. Etude bionomique du plateau continental au large d'Arcachon (Application de l'analyse factorielle). Thèse Doct. spéc., Univ. Aix-Marseille (98 p. mimeo.).

Moore, H. B.; Davies, L. T.; Fraser, T. H.; Gore, R. H.; Lopez, N. R. 1968. Some biomass figures from a tidal flat in Biscayne Bay, Florida. *Bull. mar. Sci.*, vol. 18, no. 2, p. 261–79.

Morrison, J. P. E. 1953. Collecting mollusks on and around atolls. In: F. R. Fosberg and M.-H. Sachet (eds). Handbook for atoll research, (2nd prelim. edit.). *Atoll Res. Bull.*, no. 17, p. 74–7.

Müller, P. J.; Suess, E. in press. Interaction of organic compounds with calcium carbonate. III. Amino acid composition of sorbed layers.

Odum, E. P. 1971. *Fundamentals of ecology.* 3rd edit., 1959. Philadelphia, Saunders (574 p.).

O'Gower, A. K.; Wacasey, J. W. 1967. Animal communities associated with *Thalassia, Diplanthera,* and sands beds in Biscayne Bay. I. Analysis of communities in relation to water movements. *Bull. mar. Sci.*, vol. 17, no. 1, p. 175–210.

Picard, J. 1962. Méthode d'étude qualitative des biocoenoses des substrats meubles. *Rec. Trav. Stn mar. Endoume*, vol. 25, no. 39, p. 239–44.

——. 1965a. Recherches qualitatives sur les biocénoses marines des substrats meubles dragables de la région marseillaise. *Rec. Trav. Stn mar. Endoume.*, vol. 36, no. 52, p. 1–160.

——. 1965b. Propositions pour une subdivision des benthontes en fonction de la taille. In: Méthodes quantitatives d'étude du benthos et échelle dimensionnelle des benthontes. Comm. intern. Explor. sci. mer Méditerranée, Colloque du Comité du Benthos 1963.

Pichon, Michel, 1966. Note sur la faune des substrats sablo-vaseux infralittoraux de la Baie d'Ambaro (côte nord-ouest de Madagascar). *Cah. ORSTOM, (océanogr.)*, vol. 4, no. 1, p. 79–94.

Pichon, Mireille, 1967. Contribution à l'étude des peuplements de la zone intertidale sur sables fins et sables vaseux non fixés dans la région du Tuléar. *Rec. Trav. Stn mar. Endoume*, Suppl. 7, p. 57–100.

Pielou, E. C. 1966. Šhannon's formula as a measurement of species diversity: its use and misuse. *Am. Nat.*, vol. 100, p. 463–5.

Plante, R. 1967. Etude quantitative du benthos dans la région de Nosy-Bé; note préliminaire. *Cah. ORSTOM, (océanogr.)*, vol. 5, no. 2, p. 95–108.

——; Plante-Cuny, M. R. 1971. Premiers résultats de l'étude des populations du macrobenthos et des diatomées benthiques dans une baie un milieu tropical (Madagascar). *Ann. Univ. Madagascar*, vol. 8, p. 245–53.

Plessis, Y. 1973. Comptage ichtyologique par "ictotrefe". Nouvelle méthode d'approche pour l'obtention d'un bilan biologique. In: *Eaux et Pêches outre-mer: Inventaire, écologie, utilisation, Journées d'études 23–24 mars 1973*, Paris, Muséum natl. Hist. nat.

Popham, J. D.; Ellis, D. V. 1971. A comparison of traditional cluster and Zürich-Montpellier analyses of infaunal peleopod associations from two adjacent sediment beds. *Mar. Biol.*, vol. 8, no. 3, p. 260–6.

Reish, D. J. 1959. A discussion of the importance of the screen size in washing quantitative marine bottom samples. *Ecology*, vol. 40, no. 2, p. 307–9.

RENAUD-MORNAND, J. C.; SALVAT, B.; BOSSY, C. 1971. Macrobenthos and meiobenthos from the closed lagoon of a Polynesian Atoll, Maturei Vavao (Tuamotu). *Biotropica*, vol. 3, no. 1, p. 36–55.

REYS, J. P. 1965. Remarques sur les prélèvements quantitatifs du benthos de substrats meubles. In: *Méthodes quantiatives d'étude du benthos et échelle dimensionnelle des benthontes*. Comm. Intern. Explor. sci. mer Méditerranée, Monaco.

——. 1968. Quelques données quantitatives sur les biocoenoses benthiques du Golfe de Marseille. *Rapp. P.-V. Réun. CIESMM*, vol. 19, no. 2.

——; REYS, S. 1966. Répartition quantitative du benthos dans la région de Tuléar. *Rec. Trav. Stn mar. Endoume*, Suppl. 5, p. 71–86.

——; SALVAT, B. 1971. L'échantillonnage de la macrofaune des sédiments meubles marins. In: M. Lamotte et coll. (eds). *Echantillonnage en milieu aquatique*. Paris, Masson, p. 185–242.

RICHARD, G.; SALVAT, B. 1972. Ecologie quantitative des Mollusques du lagon de Tiahura, île de Moorea, Polynésie française. *C.R. Acad. Sci., Paris* (D), vol. 275, p. 1547–50.

RICOU, G. 1967. Etude biocoenotique d'un milieu "natural" la prairie permanente pâturée. Thèse Doct. Sciences, Univ. Paris, Inst. Nat. Recherch. Agro. Paris (154 p.).

SALVAT, B. 1967. Importance de la faune malacologique dans les atolls polynésiens. *Cah. Pac.*, vol. 11, p. 7–49.

——. 1970. Etudes quantitatives (comptages et biomasses) sur les mollusques récifaux de l'atoll de Fangataufa (Tuamotu, Polynésie). *Cah. Pac.*, vol. 14, p. 1–57.

——. 1972. La faune benthique du lagon de l'atoll de Reao (Tuamotu, Polynésie). *Cah. Pac.*, vol. 16, p. 29–109.

——; RENAUD-MORNANT, J. 1969. Etude écologique du macrobenthos et du méiobenthos d'un fond sableux du lagon de Mururoa (Tuamotu, Polynésie). *Cah. Pac.*, vol. 13, p. 159–79.

SANDERS, H. L. 1960. Benthic studies in Buzzards Bay. III. The Structure of the soft-bottom community. *Limnol. Oceanogr.*, vol. 5, no. 2, p. 138–53.

SHANNON, C. E. 1948. The mathematical theory of communication. *Bell Syst. tech. J.*, vol. 27, p. 379–423, 623–56.

SMITH, S. V.; KAM, D. T. O. 1973. Atlas of Kaneohe Bay: A reef ecosystem under stress. V. Sampling and Methods 19–20. Univ. Hawaii.

SØRENSEN, T. 1948. A method of establishing groups of equal amplitude in plant sociology based on similarity of species content. *K. danske vidensk. Selsk.*, vol. 5, p. 1–34.

STEPHENSON, W.; ENDEAN, R.; BENNETT, I. 1958. An ecological survey of the marine fauna of Low Isles, Queensland. *Aust. J. mar. Freshwat. Res.*, vol. 9, no: 2, p. 261–318.

——; WILLIAMS, W. T. 1971. A study of the benthos of soft bottoms Sek Harbour, New Guinea, using numerical analysis. *Aust. J. mar. Freshwat. Res.*, vol. 22,p. 11–34.

—— ——; LANCE, G. N. 1971. The macrobenthos of Moreton Bay. *Ecol. Monogr.*, vol. 40, p. 459–94.

STODDART, D. R. 1969. Ecology and morphology of recent coral reefs. *Biol. Rev. Camb. Philos. Soc.*, vol. 44, p. 433–98.

SWARTZ, R. C.; DE BEN, W. A.; McERLEAN, A. J. 1973. Comparison of species diversity and faunal homogeneity indices as critera of change in biological communities: 317–334. In: S. S. Verner (ed.), *Proceeding of Seminar on methodology for monitoring the marine environment*, Seattle, Oct. 1973, EPA-600/4-74-004.

TAYLOR, J. D. 1968. Coral reefs and associated invertebrate communities (mainly Molluscan) around Mahé, Seychelles. *Phil. Trans. R. Soc. Lond.* (B: *Biol. Sci.*), vol. 254, p. 129–206.

——. 1971. Reef associated molluscan assemblages in the Western Indian Ocean. *Symp. zool. Soc. Lond.*, vol. 28, p. 501–34.

THOMASSIN, B. A. 1969. Les peuplements de deux biotopes de sables coralliens sur le Grand Récif de Tuléar, S.W. de Madagascar. *Rec. Trav. Stn mar. Endoume*, Suppl. 9, p. 59–133.

——. 1973. Peuplements des sables fins sur les pentes internes des récifs coralliens de Tuléar (S.-W. de Madagascar). Essai d'interprétation dynamique des peuplements de sables mobiles infra-littoraux dans un complexe récifal soumis ou non aux influences terrigènes. *Téthys*, Suppl. 5, p. 157–220.

——. 1974b. Soft bottoms carcinological fauna *sensu lato* on Tuléar coral reef complexes (S.W. Madagascar): distribution, importance roles played in trophic food-chains and in bottom deposits. In: *Proc. Second Int. Coral Reef Symp.*, Brisbane, Great Barrier Reef Committee, vol. 1, p. 297–320.

——. 1978. Peuplements des sédiments coralliens dans la région de Tuléar (S.W. de Madagascar).

Leur insertion dans le contexte côtier indopacifique. Thèse Doct. Sciences, Univ. Aix-Marseille, Archives originales CNRS, n°, A.O. 11.581.

——; JOUIN, C.; RENAUD-MORNANT, J.; RICHARD, G.; SALVAT, B. 1975. Macrofauna and meiofauna in the coral sediments on the Tiahura reef complex, Moorea Island (French Polynesia). 13th Pacific Sci. Congr., Vancouver, 17–30 August (4 p. mimeo., 4 tables, 4 figs.).

——; VIVIER, M. H.; VITIELLO, P. 1976. Distribution de la méiofaune et de la macrofaune des sables coralliens de la retenue d'eau épirécifale du Grand Récif de Tuléar (Madagascar). *J. exp. mar. Biol. Ecol.*, vol. 22, p. 31–53.

THORSON, G. 1957. Bottom communities (sublittoral or shallow shelf). In: J. W. Hedpeth, ed., Treatise on marine ecology and paleoecology. *Geol. Soc. Am. Mem.*, vol. 67, no. 1, p. 461–534.

TRAVERS, M. 1971. Diversité du microplancton du Golfe de Marseille en 1964. *Mar. Biol.*, vol. 8, no. 4, p. 308–43.

TÜXEN, R. 1970. Bibliographie zum Problem des Minimalareals und der Artareal-kurve. *Excerpta Botanica*, (B), vol. 10, no. 4, p. 291–314.

VISHER, G. S. 1969. Grain size distribution and depositional processes. *J. sedim. Petrol.*, vol. 39, p. 1074–106.

WADE, B. A. 1972. A description of a highly diverse soft-bottom community of Kingston Harbour, Jamaica. *Mar. Biol.*, vol. 13, no. 1, p. 57–69.

WEBB, W. L. 1950. Biogeographic regions of Texas and Oklahoma. *Ecology*, vol. 31, p. 426–33.

WEYDERT, P. 1971. Etude sédimentologique et hydrodynamique d'une coupe de la partie médiane du Grand Récif de Tuléar (S.W. de Madagascar). *Téthys*, Suppl. 1, p. 237–79.

——. 1973a. Morphologie et sédimentologie de la partie méridionale du Grand Récif de Tuléar (S.W. de Madagascar): les ensembles sédimentaires de la pente interne. *Téthys*, Suppl. 5, p. 133–56.

——. 1973b. Morphologie et sedimentologie des formations récifales de la région de Tuléar, S.W. de Madagascar. Thèse Doct. Sciences, Univ. Aix-Marseille, Archives originales C.N.R.S. n° A.O. 7201.

——. 1974. Morphologie et sédimentologie de la pente externe de la partie nord du Grand Récif de Tuléar (S.W. de Madagascar). Nature et répartition des éléments organogènes libres. *Mar. Geol.*, vol. 17, p. 299–337.

WHITTAKER, R. H. 1972. Evolution and measurement of species diversity. *Taxon*, vol. 21 (2/3), p. 213–51.

WIESER, W. 1960. Benthic studies in Buzzards Bay. II. The meiofauna. *Limnol. Oceanogr.*, vol. 5, no. 2, p. 121–37.

WILLIAMS III, G. E. 1974. New technique to facilitate hand-picking macrobenthos. *Trans. Am. Microscop. Soc.*, vol. 93, no. 2, p. 220–6.

21

Sponges in coral reefs

K. Rützler[1]

INTRODUCTION

Sponges are sessile aquatic metazoans, bounded by pinacoderm and containing choanocyte chambers. Choanocytes generate a waterflow from small ostia, through an incurrent and excurrent aquiferous system to larger oscula. Most sponges are massive (crust-, cushion-, fan-, tree- or cup-shape) without distinct symmetry. The mesohyle (between pinacoderm and choanoderm) contains a variety of cell types, collagen and related products and, usually, an inorganic skeleton of silicon dioxide or calcium carbonate. Sexually produced larvae are mostly free-swimming and fundamental to the distribution of the adults. All sponges are active filter feeders, and some use symbioses with bacteria and algae to supplement their energy requirements. Many species are tolerant to epi- and endobiotic organisms (for recent summaries on sponge biology see: Fry, 1970 and Brien et al., 1973; for terminology see: Borojević et al., 1968).

Sponges are an important component of all coral reef communities. Their biomass and range of ecological tolerance frequently exceeds that of the reef-building coral species (Fig. 1a, 1b). They cause considerable impact on their environment by effectively filtering large quantities of water (Reiswig, 1917a, b), by destroying the reef framework (Goreau and Hartman, 1963; Rützler, 1975), by competition for space (Goreau and Hartman, 1966; Rützler, 1970, 1975; Sarà, 1970; Glynn, 1973) and by serving as food source and shelter for numerous fishes and invertebrates (Randall and Hartman, 1968; Tyler and Böhlke, 1972; Rützler, 1976). Nevertheless, due to taxonomical problems and to difficulties in quantitative assessment, quantitative studies of reef sponges are rare.

Although many ecological sponge studies have been made in non-reef environments most of the techniques for collecting, processing for systematic study, biomass determination and quantitative evaluation can be applied to coral reefs.

1. Department of Invertebrate Zoology, National Museum of Natural History, Smithsonian Institution, Washington, D.C. 20560, U.S.A.

Figure 1
Sponges in a Caribbean coral reef: a, Massive, tubular and whip-shaped
specimens at the edge of the fore-reef slope, Carrie Bow Cay, Belize, 20 m
deep. A: *Agelas* sp., H: *Haliclona rubens* (Pallas), M: *Mycale* sp., V.c.:
Verongia cauliformis (Carter), V.g.: *Verongia gigantea* (Hyatt), X:
Xestospongia sp.; b. Diver with large *Xestospongia* sp., 1.4 m width of field;
c, Incrusting-burrowing *Anthosgimella varians* (Duchassaing and
Michelotti), 25 cm width of field.

COLLECTING, PRESERVATION AND PROCESSING FOR SYSTEMATIC STUDY

The following is a summary of procedures which can easily be followed by non-specialized field workers. The resulting data and preparations will not only be the basis for ecological analysis but also an invaluable help for conducting and accelerating identification or systematic study (see also: Laubenfels, 1953; Hartman, 1964; Rubió, 1973).

Habitat data. Most reef surveys will be accomplished by wading, skin or scuba diving, or from submersible vessels. These techniques permit detailed data to be collected by direct observation. The following data should be recorded as completely as possible: date; exact locality (use reliable map and bearings); depth (from mean sea level); substratum (nature and inclination); light (estimate exposure to maximum available light in a given depth); visibility (estimate of suspended materials); exposure (to currents, wave action, and to falling dry-intertidal); sediments (possibility of being buried); community (classify according to predominant organisms); photograph (of habitat and specimen *in situ*).

Specimen data. The entire specimen should be removed from the substratum, including basal membrane (using a sharp knife). Particularly thin incrusting and burrowing forms should be taken with the substratum (using a rock hammer, hammer and chisel). Leave in fresh seawater until ready for fixation. Record the following data: shape (e.g. incrusting, massive; amorphous, ramose, cylindrical, tubiform, vasiform); size (surface area covered, diameter, height); colour (use colour chart, if possible[2]); consistency (e.g. hard brittle, soft elastic, compressible; note mucus production if present); surface (texture; structures like conuli, dilated subsurface channels, embedded sediments); apertures (distribution and size of expanded oscula and pori); photographs (colour, total views and close-ups of surface details—submerged in pan of clean seawater, or in air after removal of excess water).

Fixation. Specimens are fixed (separately) in 10 per cent formalin-seawater (concentrated [37–40 per cent] formaldehyde solution: seawater = 1:9). To neutralize and buffer add 20 g Methenamine ($C_6H_{12}N_4$) to each litre of final solution. To insure good fixation for histological purposes representative slices (about 2 cm³, including some surface area) should be cut from large specimens and fixed separately. Large specimens can be air-dried after a small portion has been fixed. For the study of sponges with well-developed spongin skeleton, it is useful to cut a similar slice (about 1 cm thick) before fixation and let it macerate in fresh water (repeated rinsing) and dry. This will facilitate later observation of the skeleton architecture. Formalin–seawater is the best all-purpose fixative for marine sponges but it can be replaced by others for specific purposes. Not before 2 days and not after 3 weeks the specimens should be transferred into 75 per cent ethyl alcohol (at least 1 change). Prolonged preservation of sponges in formalin frequently causes maceration of the tissue. Notes should be made

2. A useful and inexpensive colour chart is published by the Royal Horticultural Society, London.

of any colour changes of the fixing and preservation fluids due to exudations from the sponges. With each specimen a water- and alcohol-proof label must be enclosed, showing, specimen number (matched with data sheet); possibly a descriptive field name; locality and depth; collector and date collected; remarks, if applicable (colour change, etc.).

Thick sections. These serve for microscopic study of the skeleton architecture (Figs. 2a, 2b), i.e. the three-dimensional structure of the spongin fibre network, the position of spicules in relation to each other, to the fibre network or to other morphological features (e.g. ectosome, choanosome differentiation). The

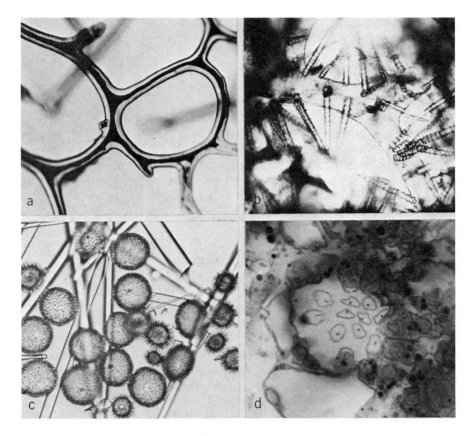

Figure 2
Microscope preparations for systematic study: a, Spongin fibres cleaned from cellular tissue (maceration) of *Verongia fistularis* (Pallas), 1.2 mm width of field; b, Thick section (200 μm) of *Agelas conifera* (Schmidt) showing arrangement of spicules, partially embedded in spongin fibres 500 μm width of field; c, Isolated spicules of *Geodia neptuni* (Sollas), 300 μm width of field; d, Polished thin section of *Cliona lampa* Laubenfels showing choanocyte chamber, safranin-crystal violet stain, 60 μm width of field.

following steps should be taken: transfer a representative piece of the sponge into 96 per cent ethyl alcohol for hardening. Cut with razor blade several slices perpendicular to the surface, as thin as possible (0.2–0.5 mm is usually possible and sufficient). Even thicker sections are permissible (and sometimes necessary) when macerated spongin skeletons are cut. Make sure both ectosomal and choanosomal portions are present on the section. Then make several tangential sections from the surface down to the choanosome. In some species the ecto-some detaches easily and can be peeled off with fine pointed forceps. Stain in basic fuchsin or safranin dissolved in 96 per cent ethyl alcohol (10 seconds to several minutes). Solution can be up to saturation, depending on how readily the sections accept the stain. Stain and subsequent dehydrating and clearing fluids can be kept in small petri dishes. Transfer of sections can be done by spatula or forceps. Dehydrate in two changes, one of 96 per cent and the other of 100 per cent ethyl alcohol (30 seconds minimum in each). Observe under stereo microscope the extent to which stain is washed out. If section is under-stained go back to fuchsin and extend staining time; if overstained extend washing time in 96 per cent alcohol. Dehydrate and clear in saturated solution of phenol in xylene. Transfer to pure xylene and change once. Mount on slide with Canada balsam or similar medium. Thick irregular sections do not hold the cover glass parallel to the slide and balsam tends to run out. This can be avoided by cutting strips of cardboard or short lengths of nylon fishing line (thickness adjusted to section) to support the cover glass. Use small lead weights to press down the cover slips during drying (in oven at 37°C). A label should show specimen number and locality. Near the sections (outside cover glass) the cutting direction can be marked: ⊥ perpendicular, ∅ tangential.

Spicule mounts. Whereas the thick sections serve mainly for higher classification of sponges, study of the type, shape and size of isolated spicules (Fig. 2c) is important for species determination (except in those groups where proper spicules are lacking). For temporary mounts, fragments of the sponge (from the ectosomal as well as the choanosomal region) are placed on a microscope slide and a few drops of sodium hypochlorite are added. After disintegration of the soft parts a cover slip is added. For permanent mounts take the following steps: dissolve soft parts of the sponge fragments in a test tube using cold sodium hypochlorite or boiling concentrated nitric acid (except for calcareous sponges). Wash spicules with tap water by filling the test tube and shaking. Await settling of spicules on the bottom (at least 1 hour) or accelerate this process by centrifuging. Decant carefully. Wash spicules twice in 96 per cent alcohol (as above, settling time at least 30 minutes). Decant carefully. Shake and pour sediment on microscope slide. Allow to dry, then add a few drops of xylene, mounting medium, cover slip and label.

Histological sections. These are routinely used for the study of choanocytes and choanocyte chambers, the location of very small microscleres, spongin traces, reproductive cells and, of course, all other histological observations. The

303

techniques are similar to those which can be found in any general manual or textbook of histological and staining methods. Some special practices are worth pointing out. Calcareous sponges which are usually packed with relatively large spicules can be easily decalcified in 5 per cent nitric acid with subsequent neutralization in 5 per cent sodium sulphate solution (24 hours) and rinsing in tap water (24 hours). The same should be done with all sponges which have large amounts of calcareous particles incorporated in tissue or spongin fibres. The substratum of burrowing (boring) sponges must be removed in the same way: to keep the sponge from falling apart, preliminary embedding in 12 per cent gelatine and decalcification in a cool place are advantageous. Gelatine embedding is useful for all sponges to be cut with a cryostat microtome. An excellent embedding medium for sectioning at room temperature is polyester wax (N. W. Riser, personal communication). Mallory's triple stain is well-suited for routine purposes and for detection of small traces of spongin.

Wet-ground and polished thick and thin sections of epoxy embedded material can be effectively used when demineralization is not desirable and serial sections are not needed (Fig. 2d). The methods are the same as applied to palaeontological preparations, except that tissue is dehydrated in a graded alcohol series and propylene oxide before embedding in epoxy resin. Toluidin blue or, for a double stain, safranin followed by crystal violet (1 per cent aqueous solution, 5–10 mins. at 60°C) give excellent staining results (see also: Rützler, 1974).

DETERMINATION OF BIOMASS

Several methods have been used to express the quantitative importance of sponges within a community. Each has its merits in the context of a particular study and no absolute value judgments are possible. Detailed description of the method used is important to make the results repeatable. Sarà (1966) pointed out two most desirable attributes of a quantitative method, ease of application under difficult field conditions and suitability for statistical elaboration.

Number of individuals. Poriferologists generally agree that a sponge mass bounded by pinacocytes is an individual rather than a colony (Hartman and Reiswig, 1973). Nevertheless, counts of specimens alone are not very useful from a quantitative point of view. The size range, even of sexually mature individuals within a given species can amount to two orders of magnitude (Figs. 1b, 1c).

Surface area. This measure has been used in various ways. Laborel and Vacelet (1958) adopted and modified the Braun–Blanquet phytosociology method where surface area covered by organisms is estimated in percent of the sample square to evaluate abundance. The values obtained were combined with an

304

index of sociability which also distinguishes whether one and the same area coverage is caused by many small or one large individual. Vasseur (1964) employed this method for different taxa, including sponges and introduced designations for reduced vitality and epizoism.

Russ and Rützler (1959), Sarà (1961), Sarà and Siribelli (1960, 1962) and Rützler (1965a, b) used specimen numbers and area of projected surface coverage (in cm²) to study quantitative distribution of predominantly encrusting Mediterranean sponges. A similar method was employed by Storr (1964) for reef biota in the Bahamas; however, there is but little information on sponges. Wiedenmayer (1977) studied the quantitative distribution of massive and erect sponges near Bimini (Bahamas). He too measured projected surface area but oriented the projection plane to obtain maximum area, depending on the growth form of each species. Surface values have been obtained by Rützler (1965a, b) by counting 1 cm² meshes of a overlaying grid drawn on a plexiglas plate or, more accurately, by planimetry of paper traces from projected photographs (Rützler, 1975).

Sarà (1966) introduced a frame counting method by which frequency of occurrence of sponges in a 5 cm grid are recorded. This technique also results in sponge coverage values.

Volume. When one is dealing with large, irregular massive, tree-shaped, tubular and cup-shaped sponges, the projected surface area becomes an inadequate measure for biomass. For this reason Rützler (1972) determined the displacement volume of sponges sampled in a reef off Nossi-Bé (Madagascar). Drip-dried specimens were submerged in a container filled with seawater to the level of an overflow tube. the amount of displaced water could be determined using a graduated cylinder. This method, however, requires collecting of all specimens to be measured. The displacement technique can also be used to estimate the internal space system, available to an endobiotic fauna, in relation to the sponge tissue volume (Rützler, 1976). Whole sponges were enclosed tightly in thin plastic foil and submerged to measure total volume. From this the value of the displacement volume without wrapping can be subtracted to give the interstitial space volume.

A convenient volumetric field method was used by Reiswig (1973, 1974) in a Jamaica reef. Specimen size was determined by measuring the three axes of each specimen *in situ*. The net volume, excluding atrial cavity, where present, was estimated by applying the values of a predetermined regression curve.

In a comparable manner Dayton *et al.* (1974) converted linear measurements, taken from photographs of Antarctic sponges into wet weight values. The length (or diameter) to wet weight regression had been pre-determined for each species.

Weight and calorific content. Although a common practice in ecological studies, weight measurements have not been much used for sponges. The procedures are tedious and require equipment which is not usually available in the field. As with displacement volume determinations, specimens have to be removed from the habitat. The method, however, if properly used, gives the most accurate measure of biomass.

Russ and Rützler (1959) supplemented area coverage with wet-weight data but did not compensate for the varying amount of skeleton material (spicules) in different species. Rützler (1975) determined wet- and dry-weight for 8 species of burrowing sponges and related these data to the size of their papillar fields, a measure that can be readily determined *in situ*. In this example the weight data were important to compensate for specific differences in penetration depth and burrowing patterns. The spicule to soft tissue ratio was fairly constant among all species and could be neglected. Dry-weights proved to be slightly more repeatable than wet-weights.

If accurate biomass comparison of species with very different skeleton contents is required, ash-free weights, or another measure that excludes hard tissue, e.g. organic carbon content, must be determined. Calculation of energy budgets may require measurement of calorific content of tissues.

Randall and Hartman (1968) presented data on the relation of ash content to organic matter in 18 species of sponges which are frequently eaten by West Indian fishes. The content ranges from 0.5 per cent in *Chondrosia* to as much as 70 per cent in *Anthosigmella*.

For comparative study of metabolism in 3 species of Jamaican reef sponges Reiswig (1973, 1974) determined weight and calorific content of tissues. Dry weights were obtained by drying to constant weight at 105°C, ash weights by combustion at 500°–510°C for 2 hours. Corrections were applied for water loss from siliceous spicules (Paine, 1964). The results (Reiswig, 1973) showed relatively low ash values of 31 per cent for *Mycale* (Poecilosclerida) and 34 per cent for *Verongia* (Dictyoceratida) as opposed to 62 per cent for *Tethya* (Hadromerida). Calorific values per ml sponge, obtained by microbomb calorimetry were high in *Verongia* (407 cal/ml), only about half of that amount in *Mycale* (200 cal/ml) and *Tethya* (214 cal/ml). In *Mycale* over 40 per cent of the calories are contained in skeletal spongin.

Similar parameters (dry weight, ash-free dry weight, calorific content of tissue) were measured by Dayton *et al.* (1974) to quantify the standing crop of an Antarctic sponge community.

Oxidizable carbon is considered a 'realistic measure of the energy stored in a crop' (Strickland and Parsons, 1968). In developing a preliminary model of a coral reef ecosystem, the participants in a recent workshop meeting on Glover's Reef (Belize, Central America: 1971) have agreed to use carbon as the universal measure for biomass and material flow (Macintyre *et al.*, 1974). The meeting also stimulated preliminary determinations of wet-weight- dry-weight: carbon ratios in Caribbean reef sponges (Rützler, unpublished). Specimens of ten species of sponges belonging to six orders were collected in Bermuda. Two samples of each species were cleaned from sediments and symbionts under a stereo microscope. Wet-weight was obtained after draining off interstitial water and quick superficial blotting. Dry-weight was determined after drying to constant weight at 95°C over calcium sulphate. Carbon content was measured using a Coleman Model 33 carbon-hydrogen analyser standardized with tartaric acid. Samples of *Dysidea* had been previously decalcified to exclude inorganic carbon from sediment carbonates included in its fibres. The results are summarized in Table 1.

TABLE 1. Wet-weight: Dry-weight: Carbon ratios in Bermuda Sponges[a]

Order and species	Dry-weight as percentage of wet-weight	Organic carbon as percentage of dry-weight
Dictyoceratida		
Ircinia cf. *fasciculata* (Pallas)	13.3	27.8
"Ianthella" ardis Laubenfels	19.3	33.5
Dysidea fragilis (Montagu)	22.0	23.6
Haplosclerida		
Haliclona viridis (Duch. & Mich.)	24.1	24.2
Gelliodes ramosa (Carter)	17.1	33.3
Callyspongia vaginalis (Lamarck)	13.8	34.0
Poecilosclerida		
Tedania ignis (Duch. & Mich.)	19.1	28.0
Halichondrida		
Ulosa sp. (*"Dysidea crawshayi"*)	32.4	21.9
Hadromerida		
Chondrilla nucula Schmidt	16.9	13.7
Spirophorida		
Cinachyra cf. *cavernosa* (Lamarck)	26.9	26.1

[a]. Species allocation following Laubenfels (1950).

QUANTITATIVE SAMPLING METHODS

The ultimate aim of any ecological study is to find cause-effect relationship between environmental parameters (including biotic influences) and distribution patterns of species and individuals (biomass). Each species has developed its own strategies to cope with environmental conditions. The tolerance of a species to factor gradients determines its distributional range (frequency). Approach of optimum conditions is reflected by an increase of individuals or biomass (abundance). The number of coexisting species (diversity) is a measure for environmental complexity (number of available niches).

Problems and methods for the quantitative study of sponge populations are the same as those applying to any other group of sessile organisms. As there is no single best technique, the methods used are generally a compromise between available time and means and required results for a given situation.

Diversity and abundance estimates. Simple distributional principles, as caused by a factor gradient, can be recognized by examining the faunal composition of zones which are defined by different light intensities. For example, Sarà (1961) and Pouliquen (1972) delimited areas of decreasing illumination (e.g.

shaded, obscure and dark) in Mediterranean caves. They listed the sponge species in each zone and determined their relative abundance (e.g. present, rare, abundant, very abundant). Although these data are not suitable for statistical elaborations, they do represent a measure of diversity and permit comparisons with other habitats.

In a similar manner, without having a uniform sample size for statistical treatment, Rützler (1965b) determined the influence of substrata stability on the diversity and growth of a sponge fauna inhabiting the lower surfaces of loose rocks.

The majority of quantitative sponge studies, however, are based on quadrat sampling.

Quadrat size and sampling area. Quadrat size and sampling area are usually not identical. Choice of suitable quadrat size depends on the method of data collecting, the complexity of the environment and the size range and density of the organisms to be studied. If the entire sample is to be removed and brought to the laboratory, if the factor gradients are steep (complex substrata configuration, heterogeneous microclimate), and if the organisms are comparatively small and densely spaced, squares of $\frac{1}{16}$ m^2 (25 × 25 cm) can be used (Russ and Rützler, 1959). For visual census and coarse area coverage estimates involving very large sponges in a homogeneous environment, quadrats of up to 100 m^2 (10 × 10 m) have been considered necessary (Wiedenmayer, 1977). The best suitable sample size has to be found empirically for each application. If the quadrat is too small, distortion in statistical treatment can occur (Ryland, 1973). If it is too large, environmental changes cannot be resolved.

For statistical reasons all sampling units should be of equal size. For applications where this is not possible, a method of conversion based on computer simulation has been introduced (Ryland, 1972). The sum of all samples within a stratum (community) represents the sampling area. Its minimum size can be determined by the species-area curve (Cain, 1938; Riedl, 1953). Another, more recently introduced, method is based on binomial sampling theory (Dennison and Hay, 1967). The minimum proportional presence of a species within the study area must be found empirically. From a graph one can then determine the sampling area required for a desired probability value for collecting efficiency.

Quadrat sampling and evaluation. The phytosociological quadrat method has been applied by Laborel and Vacelet (1958) and Vasseur (1964) for the study of sessile populations (including sponges) in a Mediterranean cave and in Indian Ocean reef habitats. Two coefficients, quantifying abundance and sociability, were estimated *in situ* for a number of species. The data are not statistically usable but serve for recognition and comparison of characteristic plant and animal assemblages and their dependence upon such factors as light, hydrodynamics and silting.

The influence of intertidal exposure, light, water movement and sedimentation on sponge distribution was determined by Russ and Rützler (1959) and Rützler (1965a, 1972) for Mediterranean caves and for an Indian Ocean fringing reef. Transects were selected which represented profiles through factor gradients (e.g. in a cave, from light to dark, from ceiling to bottom). Along these transects, quadrat samples ($\frac{1}{16}$ m^2 or $\frac{1}{4}$ m^2) were marked in fixed distances. Most samples were removed entirely (including burrowed portions of the substratum) and taken to the laboratory for species and biomass determinations. Some quantitative estimates were made *in situ* and from photographs. Where transects were meaningless, random samples had to be chosen within areas of apparently uniform environmental conditions. Sample data were then arranged in groups corresponding to different intensities of a particular parameter. Care was taken to eliminate counteracting factors (e.g. samples representing a light gradient were chosen from vertical substrata with average hydrodynamic exposure, to avoid influences from sediments and excess water-movement). Indices of homogeneity (Riedl, 1953) were calculated to determine faunal similarities between samples assigned to one microclimatic regime, and to compare the community structure of different environments.

Although this method is objective and suitable for statistical treatment, it is tedious and not suitable for large scale application.

With these difficulties in mind Sarà (1966, 1970) introduced a quick quadrat counting method for the quantitative study of Mediterranean shallow-water sponges. A 25 cm × 25 cm frame was subdivided with nylon filament to form a grid of 25 meshes (5 cm × 5 cm). The frame was placed on the substratum and the number of meshes occupied by each species was counted. The frequency of counts is correlated with the surface extension of the individuals. The effect of this method is similar to chain link counts which have been used for coral diversity studies (Porter, 1972). Rützler (1975) adopted the frame counting method for large scale distributional studies of burrowing sponges in Bermuda reefs. It was modified to express estimated coverage values (in cm^2) inside the meshes and calibrated for the surface area-biomass ratio of each species.

SUMMARY AND CONCLUSIONS

Synopsis. Compared with other important reef organisms, sponges have been greatly neglected in quantitative studies. The principal reasons for this are taxonomic problems and difficulties in quantification, due to great variability in shape and size.

Identification of sponge taxa is much facilitated if guidelines for proper preservation, data collecting and micro-anatomical preparation are followed.

Specimen counts have limited quantitative application. Biomass estimates in the field can be based on projected surface area or on measurement of the three main axes of a specimen. It is necessary, however, to correct the data for variations in skeleton contents, or tissue porosity, by submitting subsamples of

309

each species to laboratory analysis. In this manner, quick and reliable estimates of weight, volume or energy content can be obtained, without need to remove the entire sample.

Quadrat sampling along transects and, at random, with defined zones has been used for quantitative sponge studies in rocky sublittoral and coral reef areas. Quadrat size and sample area vary with size classes and distributional characteristics of the fauna. Phytosociological techniques are best suited to uncover characteristic organism assemblages and interactions. Other, more objective methods, involving counts of species presences, or biomass measurements, can be evaluated statistically and have been applied to reveal relationships between factor complexes and faunal distribution patterns.

Methods adopted for I.M.S.W.E. Reef Project. The current Investigations of Marine Shallow Water Ecosystems (I.M.S.W.E., Smithsonian Institution) Coral Reef Project is conducting quantitative studies on reef biota off Carrie Bow Cay, Belize.

The zoning of the reef complex has been mapped, using a permanent main transect. This transect starts in the *Thalassia* zone of the lagoon and extends, perpendicular to the direction of the barrier reef to the 45 m depth mark on the fore-reef slope. Habitats, characterized by dominant organisms (e.g. *Millepora* zone, *Turbinaria* zone) or geological features (e.g. rubble and pavement zone) have been and are still being mapped and their position fixed in relation to the main transect.

Principal organism assemblages in each habitat are quantified using auxiliary transect counts (crossing habitat boundaries) and random quadrat counts (within habitats). (Figs. 3c, 3d). Chain transects (mainly in coral dominated habitats) are compared with quadrat transects (quadrat positioned every 2 m on the transect). Quadrats vary in size from 0.5 m × 0.5 m to 2 m × 2 m, depending on the size classes of organisms. Area coverage of each species (dimension of main axes, for large sponges) is determined *in situ* (Figs. 3a, 3b), subsamples are taken to the laboratory for biomass assessment (wet weight, displacement volume). Substratum complexity is taken into consideration and sample size is corrected for functional surface area (Dahl, 1973).

Each habitat is subdivided into strata, which are defined on the basis of microclimatic conditions and substrata properties. For example, colonized (unburied) lower surfaces of rocks, seagrass rhizomes or leaves, interstitial spaces or burrows in dead coral, sand or rubble are each considered a stratum and sampled separately, after its proportional extension within the habitat had been noted. Volume samples replace surface area counts, where appropriate (e.g. rubble, sand). Interstitial organisms are extracted after anaesthetizing with magnesium chloride or by oxygen depletion (Kirsteuer, 1967).

Environmental parameters applying to each stratum are measured or estimated at the time of sampling. Whenever possible, these factors are monitored or checked over long periods of time to learn about intensity means and extremes.

Figure 3
Quantitative methods applied during coral reef study at Carrie Bow Cay,
Belize: a, Diver holding 25 × 25 cm frame to record height and width of
large tubular *Verongia* sp.; b, Frame on top of tube cluster of *Agelas* sp.;
c, Frame overlaying *Agaricia-Porites* patch (spur and groove system) for
point counting at the intersections of the filament grid; d, Situation like in c,
but frame placed on the pavement with some *Agaricia,* gorgonians and
green algae.

A suitable method of multivariate analysis will be applied (R. G. Domey, pers. comm.), as soon as sufficient amount of data has been processed.

ACKNOWLEDGEMENT

This work was supported by the Smithsonian Research Foundation, by the Smithsonian Environmental Programme and by a grant from the Exxon Corporation. It is Contribution No. 21, Investigations of Marine Shallow Water Ecosystems Project, Smithsonian Institution.

References

BOROJEVIĆ, R.; FRY, W. G.; JONES, W. C.; LÉVI, C.; RASMONT, R.; SARÀ, M.; VACELET, J. 1968. Mise au point actuelle de la terminologie des ésponges [A Reassessment of the Terminology for Sponges]. *Bull. Mus. Natl. Hist. Nat.* vol. 39, p. 1224–35.

BRIEN, P.; LÉVI, C.; SARÀ, M.; TUZET, O.; VACELET, J. 1973. Spongiaires. In: P.-B. Grassé (ed.). *Traité de Zoologie:* vol. 3 (1), Masson, Paris, (716 p).

CAIN, S. A. 1938. The species area curve. *Am. Midl. Nat.,* vol. 19, p. 573–81.

DAHL, A. L. 1973. Surface area in ecological analysis: Quantification of benthic coral-reef algae. *Mar. Biol.,* vol. 23, p. 239–49.

DAYTON, P. K.; ROBILLIARD, G. A.; PAINE, R. T.; DAYTON, L. B., 1974. Biological accommodation in the benthic community at McMurdo Sound, Antarctica. *Ecol. Monogr.,* vol. 44, p. 105–28.

DENNISON, J. M.; HAY, W. W. 1967. Estimating the needed sampling area for subaquatic ecologic studies. *J. Paleontol.,* vol. 41, p. 706–8.

FRY, W. G. (ed.). 1970. *The biology of the Porifera,* Symp. zool. Soc. London, vol. 25, London and New York, Academic Press. (512 p.).

GLYNN, P. W. 1973. Aspects of the ecology of coral reefs in the western Atlantic region. In: O. A. Jones and R. Endean (eds). *Biology and geology of coral reefs,* vol. 1: Biology. London and New York, Academic Press, p. 271–324.

GOREAU, T. F.; HARTMAN, W. D. 1963. Boring sponges as controlling factors in the formation and maintenance of coral reefs. In: R. F. Sognnaes (ed.). *Mechanisms of hard tissue destruction.* Am. Assoc. Adv. Sci., Publ. 75, p. 25–54.

—— ——. 1966. Sponge: Effect on the form of reef corals. *Science,* vol. 151, p. 343–44.

HARTMAN, W. D. 1964. Phylum Porifera. In: R. I. Smith (ed.). *Keys to marine invertebrates of the Woods Hole region,* Systematics-Ecology Program, Marine Biological Laboratory, Woods Hole, Massachusetts, p. 1–7.

——; REISWIG, H. M. 1973. The individuality of sponges. In: R. S. Boardman, A. H. Cheetham and W. A. Oliver, Jr. (eds). *Animal colonies, development and function through time,* Stroudsburg, Pennsylvania, Dowden, Hutchinson and Ross, p. 567–84.

KIRSTEUER, E. 1967. Marine benthonic nemerteans: How to collect and preserve them. *Am. Museum Novitates,* 2290, p. 1–10.

LABOREL, J.; VACELET, J. 1958. Étude des peuplements d'une grotte sous-marine du golfe de Marseille. *Bull. Inst. Ocean.,* vol. 1120, p. 1–20.

LAUBENFELS, M. W. DE. 1950. The Porifera of the Bermuda Archipelago. *Trans. zool. Soc. Lond.* vol. 27, p. 1–154.

——. 1953. A guide to the sponges of Eastern North America. The Marine Laboratory, University of Miami, Special Publication. University of Miami Press (32 p.).

MACINTYRE, I. G.; SMITH, S. V.; ZIEMAN, Jr. J. C., 1974. Carbon flux through a coral-reef ecosystem: A conceptual model. *J. Geol.,* vol. 82, p. 161–71.

PAINE, R. T. 1964. Ash and caloric determinations of sponge and opisthobranch tissues. *Ecology,* vol. 45, p. 384–87.

PORTER, J. W. 1972. Ecology and species diversity of coral reefs on opposite sides of the isthmus of Panamá. In: M. L. Jones (ed.). The Panamic biota: Some observations prior to a sea-level canal. *Bull. biol. Soc. Wash.,* vol. 2, p. 89–116.

POULIQUEN, L. 1972. Les spongiaires des grottes sous-marines de la région de Marseille: Écologie et systématique. *Téthys*, vol. 3, p. 717–58.

RANDALL, J. E.; HARTMAN, W. D. 1968. Sponge-feeding fishes of the West Indies. *Mar. Biol.*, vol. 3, p. 216–25.

REISWIG, H. M. 1971a. In situ pumping activity of tropical Demospongiae, *Mar. Biol.*, vol. 38–50.

——. 1971b. Particle feeding in natural population of three marine demosponges. *Biol. Bull. Mar. Biol. Lab. Woods Hole, Mass.*, vol. 141, p. 568–91.

——. 1973. Population dynamics of three Jamaican Demospongiae. *Bull. mar. Sci.*, vol. 23, p. 191–226.

——. 1974. Water transport, respiration and energetics of three tropical marine sponges. *J. exp. mar. Biol. Ecol.*, vol. 14, p. 231–49.

RIEDL, R. 1953. Quantitativ ökologische Methoden mariner Turbellarienforschung. *Österr. Zool. Zeitschr.*, vol. 4, p. 108–45.

RUBIÓ, M. 1973. Recolección y primera descripción de esponjas: fijación, conservación y preparación. *Inm. y Ciencia*, vol. 3, p. 37–48.

RUSS, K.; RÜTZLER, K. 1959. Zur Kenntnis der Schwammfauna unterseeischer Höhlen. *Pubbl. Staz. Zool. Napoli*, vol. 30 (Suppl.), p. 756–87.

RÜTZLER, K. 1965a. Systematik und Ökologie der Poriferen aus Litoral-Schattengebieten der Nordadria. *Z. Morph. Ökol. Tiere*, vol. 55, p. 1–82.

——. 1965b. Substratstabilität im marinen Benthos als ökologischer Faktor, dargestellt am Beispiel adriatischer Porifera. *Int. Rev. gesamt. Hydrobiol.*, vol. 50, p. 281–92.

——. 1970. Spatial competition among Porifera: Solution by epizoism. *Oecologia* (Berl.), vol. 5, p. 85–95.

——. 1972. Principles of sponge distribution in Indo-Pacific coral reefs. In: *Proc. Symp. Corals and Coral Reefs, 1969*. Mar. Biol. Assoc. India, p. 315–32.

——. 1974. The burrowing sponges of Bermuda. *Smithsonian Contr. Zool.*, vol. 165, p. 1–32.

——. 1975. The role of burrowing sponges in bioerosion. *Oecologia* (Berl.), vol. 19, p. 203–16.

——. 1976. Ecology of Tunisian commercial sponges. *Téthys*, vol. 7, p. 249–64.

RYLAND, J. S. 1972. The analysis of pattern in communities of bryozoa. I. Discrete sampling methods. *J. exp. mar. Biol. Ecol.* vol. 8, p. 277–97.

——. 1973. The analysis of spatial distribution patterns. In: G. P. Larwood (ed.). *Living and fossil Bryozoa: Recent advances in research*. London and New York, Academic Press, p. 165–72.

SARÀ, M. 1961. La fauna di Poriferi delle grotte delle isole Tremiti. Studio ecologico e sistematico. *Arch. Zool. Ital.*, vol. 46, p. 1–59.

——. 1966. Studio quantitativo della distribuzione dei Poriferi in ambienti superficiali della Riviera Ligure di Levante. *Arch. Oceanogr. Limnol.*, vol. 14, p. 365–86.

——. 1970. Competition and co-operation in sponge populations. In: W. G. Fry (ed.). *The biology of the Porifera*, Symp. zool. Soc. London, vol. 25, p. 273–84. London and New York, Academic Press.

——; SIRIBELLI, L. 1960. La fauna di Poriferi delle "secche" del Golfo di Napoli. I. La secca della Gaiola. *Annu. Ist. Mus. Zool. Univ. Napoli*, vol. 12, p. 1–93.

——; SIRIBELLI, L. 1962. La fauna di Poriferi delle "secche" del Golfo di Napoli. II. La secca di Benda Palumno. *Annu. Ist. Mus. Zool. Univ. Napoli*, vol. 14, p. 1–62.

STORR, J. F. 1964. Ecology and oceanography of the coral-reef tract, Abaco Island, Bahamas. *Geol. Soc. Am. Spec. Paper*, 79, p. 1–98.

STRICKLAND, J. D. H.; PARSONS, T. R. 1968. A practical handbook of seawater analysis. *Bull. Fish. Res. Bd Can.*, Ottawa, Queen's Printer, no. 167 (311 p.).

TYLER, J. C.; BÖHLKE, J. E. 1972. Records of sponge-dwelling fishes, primarily of the Caribbean. *Bull. mar. Sci.*, vol. 22, p. 601–42.

VASSEUR, P. 1964. Contribution à l'étude bionomique des peuplements sciaphiles infralittoraux de substrat dur dans les récifs de Tuléar (Madagascar). *Rec. Trav. Stn mar. Endoume*, Supp. Hors série 2, p. 1–77.

WIEDENMAYER, F. 1977. A monograph of the shallow-water sponges of the Western Bahamas. Basel, Birkhäuser. (in press).

22

Coral-associated Nemertina

E. Kirsteuer[1]

INTRODUCTION

The phylum Nemertina comprises approximately 800 described species, ranging in size from 1 mm up to 30 m. The majority of the taxa are marine and nemerteans have been found in all oceans, at all depths, and in almost all habitats. The benthic species are usually slender and have a remarkable capacity for extension and contraction of the body. Mucus secretion by epidermal gland cells is common and enables the animals not only to stick to the substratum but also facilitates their locomotion which is accomplished by ciliary gliding or muscular peristaltic. They are positively thigmotactic and many species are in addition also positively geotactic and negatively phototactic. Hence, benthic nemerteans lead a rather cryptic mode of life, hiding underneath stones, in crevices of rocks and corals, and amongst plant tangles and epizoic growth on hard substrata, and other species are part of the infauna of sediments.

In order to permit proper identification, nemerteans should be studied alive prior to the indispensable histological examination of the internal organization because body colour as well as taxonomically important details of the proboscis armature are difficult to discern in preserved and sectioned specimens. Nemerteans often react violently to strong mechanical or chemical irritation, which may result in complete ejection and loss of the proboscis and in autotomy of the body, and therefore, special procedures are necessary for collecting and fixing these animals.

The degree of knowledge of nemertean faunae varies with geographical regions, the European and North American coasts being the best investigated areas whereas the tropical litoral has hitherto attracted comparatively little attention. Within the tropical realm the nemertean fauna of coral reefs are particularly poorly investigated and, as has been pointed out (Kirsteuer, 1972), they have remained virtually unknown for almost two centuries. Out of about 450 papers on systematics and ecology of nemerteans published up to 1960 only

1. The American Museum of Natural History, Central Park West at 79th St., New York, N.Y. 10024, U.S.A.

20 refer *inter alia* to species found in reef areas, and, for example, of the 73 species of benthic nemerteans described from the Indian Ocean only 11 have been found in reefs or on corals. These records usually refer to species represented by rather large forms which were incidentally encountered when coral heads were broken up into pieces. It is thus apparent that much remains to be learned about the faunistic and zoogeography of nemerteans and also about their ecological requirements and quantitative distribution.

Although investigation of the invertebrate fauna of coral reefs has been intensified during the last few decades, nemerteans are still widely ignored. Clearly, this is partially due to the difficult nature of nemertean systematics and the laborious preparations required for identification of the animals, which may dissuade investigators from studying this group. However, it is also obvious that nemerteans are often either not detected in samples, or specimens which are recovered are unsuitable for identification due to inadequate extraction techniques.

No one method is equally effective for collecting all the invertebrate taxa in a given habitat, and samples and specimens must be dealt with in different ways depending on the morphological, physiological and behavioural peculiarities of the animals to be studied. Attention has to be paid to the resistance of the animals to mechanical damage and to noxious chemical substances, keeping in mind that the condition of the specimens collected should satisfy the needs of the systematist. In addition, the method chosen should have a high extraction efficiency, yet it must not be too tedious so that replicate samples of optimal size can be worked on within a reasonable period of time in the course of quantitative-ecological field surveys. Some methods for collecting coral-associated nemerteans, meeting the aforementioned requirements and allowing for quantitative extraction of living specimens, are described below.

SAMPLING DESIGN

Substrata selection

Since the amount of time normally available for field work does not permit examination of all species of corals and other microhabitats present in a reef it is necessary to decide which types of substrata should be sampled for studying the associated fauna. For a sampling programme conducted in a reef off Madagascar (Kirsteuer, 1968) a number of coral species which exhibited distinctly different growth forms and which were also common in the study area were chosen so that material for several samples of each species could be collected. Furthermore, discriminations were made in regard to the ratio of dead to living coral material, the amount of epigrowth which had developed on the dead portion of the corals, and the extent to which the substratum was permeated with burrows of other organisms. The results of this survey indicated that several of these edaphic conditions had a strong influence on the species composition and population density of the nemertean fauna. The same

316

approach in sample substrata selection was subsequently used to study the distribution of nemerteans in coral reefs in the Red Sea and Caribbean Sea (Kirsteuer, 1972). Similar criteria have also been applied by Hutchings (1974) for selecting coral habitats during an investigation of the invertebrate fauna in the Great Barrier Reef.

Sample size

Nemerteans can be frequently found on corals but they are not as abundant as, for example, the polychaetes, and to obtain a significant portion of the nemertean population present in a selected habitat it is advisable to keep the sample size relatively large. It was found that samples of about 15–20 litres (displacement volume of substratum) are easy to handle (with the water deterioration method; see below) and that three to five replicate samples usually suffice to register all the species of nemerteans inhabiting a particular type of substratum, i.e. additional samples do not produce species previously unrecorded.

Quantification of sample

In situ quantification of samples from a coral reef is extremely difficult and several of the inherent problems have been discussed by Brander *et al.* (1971). Sampling by area, i.e. removing the substratum to a certain depth within a marked quadrate at regular intervals along a transect was frequently found to give mixed samples (sand, gravel, stone, and corals) varying considerably in volume, and the samples had to be roughly subdivided to extract the fauna from the various substrata fractions. The second method used by Brander *et al.* (1971) was to select subjectively rocks or pieces of coral of approximately the same size, thus reducing the variability in the volume and surface area of each sample and making the estimation of the population density of the fauna more accurate.

For a project designed to study the fauna inhabiting quite different types of corals neither of the two methods can be consistently employed. The area method could be used for taking a sample from dense stands such as are formed by *Porites porites* (Fig. 1) though a decision has to be made in regard to the depth to which the substratum is to be removed (digging down 10 cm as was done by Brander *et al.* would, in the case of *P. porites,* result in a sample of only living coral material). If for the purpose of comparing the fauna a sample of *Agaricia agaricites* is required then specification of both area and digging depth become rather meaningless due to the overlapping, shingle-shaped configuration of the substratum (Fig. 2). On the other hand, the similar size method has certain advantages if one is working with a single species of coral or with compactly growing corals such as *Meandrina meandrites* or *Diploria strigosa,* but difficulties arise when collecting colonies of equal size from, for example, the massive *D. strigosa* and the branching *Oculina diffusa,* which (although covering the same horizontal area of the reef) differ considerably in substrata (displacement) volume and coral surface area. Furthermore, it seems well-nigh

317

Figure 1
Stand of *Porites porites* in 1 m depth, Bahia de Villa Concha, north
coast of Colombia, S.A.

impossible to pick up pieces of similar size from branching and plate-forming
colonies.

To avoid some of the restrictions imposed by the two methods discussed
above, samples for the study of coral-associated nemerteans were collected on
the basis of a rough estimation of volume, i.e. substratum was removed to
the amount considered optimal and still manageable with the extraction
technique employed. After a stand or colony of coral was selected, digging
(chiselling or breaking off by hand) commenced at one point and continued
vertically as long as the material was easily recognized (by skeleton structure)
as belonging to the selected species, and horizontally until enough substratum
was collected. Knowing the volume of the glass jar used for extraction of the
fauna (see below) it is possible to estimate the amount of substratum needed by
filling a sack (or any other container) of similar capacity with coral. Since the

Figure 2
Habitat with mainly *Agaricia agaricites* in about 52 m depth, near Discovery Bay, north coast of Jamaica, W.I.

coral is usually broken into pieces during removal, the amount of material of a particular species that can be fitted into the collecting container (and subsequently into the extraction jar) is similar in repeated samples (settling and packing effect of smaller and more equally sized pieces) and differences in the volume of samples from different coral species are also within reasonable limits. This volume method does not provide information regarding the area or three-dimensional space occupied by the sample substratum in the reef, however, it allows comparatively large samples of similar volume to be collected from different kinds of corals, irrespective of their growth patterns, and because the substratum is removed by 'strip mining' it can be assumed that a representative portion of a given stand or colony of coral is sampled. The actual volume of substratum collected and used for extraction is then determined by displacement of water in the extraction jar (see below).

Transport of samples

For collection and subsequent transport of the substratum from the sample station to the site where extraction is performed, sacks of an appropriate size can be used but sturdy plastic containers such as trash cans or dust bins, with a lid, are preferable (if available) because polyethylene sacks are liable to tear because of the weight and rough texture of the sample material. Burlap sacks do not hold the water when the sample is transported over land and animals accidentally dislodged from the substratum may be lost. When working with trash cans, an empty one attached upside down to the full sample container can be employed as a lifting device (by filling it partially with air from the scuba tank). This is particularly useful for bringing back large samples from deeper zones of the reef (Fig. 3).

Figure 3
Divers returning with heavy substratum sample, employing an air-filled bucket as lifting device.

EXTRACTION OF FAUNA

Water deterioration method

Investigations concerned with the reactions of motile aquatic invertebrates to changing conditions in the ambient medium have revealed that many organisms which are under normal circumstances positively geotactic and negatively phototactic become negatively geotactic and positively phototactic when the oxygen supply is reduced and carbon dioxide accumulates in the surrounding water (e.g. Naumann, 1921; Ubrig, 1952). This reversal is obviously an important survival mechanism and it enables the animals to migrate to areas with optimal oxygen content to satisfy their respiratory needs. Based on this modification in the behaviour of animals confronted with a deterioration of their environment, Riedl (1953) developed the method of 'Klimaverschlechterung' which he used effectively for quantitative extraction of marine turbellarians from various types of substrata, and the same principle, i.e. fouling of the water in which the sample is kept, was later found to be efficient for extracting coral-inhabiting nemerteans (Kirsteuer, 1965, 1968, 1972).

Preparation of the sample

At the field station or laboratory the coral material is transferred from the sample container to a glass jar (Fig. 4). Rectangular jars, with height greater than width and with a capacity of 30–40 litres are best suited (in supply catalogues listed as battery jars), however, they are not always available at smaller institutions and to have them shipped to remote areas is usually expensive and risky. To eliminate this problem, sheets of glass cut to the right size (one bottom and four wall pieces) can be taken along and fitted together in the field with clear silicone rubber adhesive sealer to form a rectangular tank. Such tanks have been used on several occasions for collecting nemerteans in the Caribbean and are a good substitute for jars. Conventional aquaria are useless because animals aggregating in the corners are obscured by the metal frame.

Prior to being placed in the jar, all the substratum is briefly examined and conspicuous animals (e.g. echinoderms, crustaceans, and molluscs) are sorted, out, and coral pieces larger than a fist are broken up. Sometimes nemerteans are encountered during this procedure but if a specimen is still entangled in the coral it is better to leave it there because attempts to pull a nemertean out from a crevice will inevitably result in a rupture of the worm's body. After the coral pieces are loosely arranged in the jar the water from the collecting container (and if necessary also fresh seawater) is added in measured portions and the jar filled to a level of about 5 cm above the substratum. The volume of the substratum in the jar is now easily determined by subtracting the amount of water poured into the jar from the total volume of the sample finally contained in the jar.

The sample should be kept undisturbed in the shade, ideally with one corner or side of the jar exposed to stronger light, but extraction is also satis-

Figure 4
Preparation of substratum for transfer to glass jars used for extraction of
nemerteans by water deterioration.

factorily performed under uniform, dim light conditions. Direct sunlight has
to be avoided to prevent the sample water from rapid and excessive heating.

Collecting the animals

Depending on the composition of the substratum (e.g., ratio of living to dead
coral, amount of algal and epizoic growth on dead coral, number of associated
errant animals) and the ambient air temperature, the time span between setting
up the sample and deterioration of the sample to the degree that animals are
forced to come out from the substratum will vary, but usually after four to
eight hours the first nemerteans appear on the walls of the glass jar on which
they continue to move upward. The sample is then checked in intervals of

about 30 min., and nemerteans as well as the other organisms which have aggregated at the water surface along the wall of the jar are picked up with a pipette. Nemerteans are readily distinguished from other worms in the sample (e.g. turbellarians and polychaetes) by their inability to glide backward, but the removal and inspection of all the animals on the water surface ensures that not even very small specimens of nemerteans are overlooked. The nemerteans are then transferred to fresh seawater and subsequently studied alive prior to being fixed for histological examination (Kirsteuer, 1967).

The sample is considered exhausted when no more nemerteans appear on the glass walls and water surface. This coincides with the dying off of the sedentary fauna and of errant animals which could not climb to the surface, discoloration of the sample water, and the beginning of emanation of hydrogen sulphide. Complete deterioration of a coral sample may take from 12 to 24 hours, however, the sample does not need continuous attention and the intervals between checking for nemerteans can be used to work on other animals which have been collected, or to repeat the sampling, hence the method is actually not very time consuming.

Experiments conducted in collaboration with Dr. Klaus Rützler, Smithsonian Institution, during recent field work at Carrie Bow Cay, Belize, disclosed that the migration of nemerteans from the substratum is a constant reaction to the deteriorating environmental conditions. Oxygen concentration measurements made in samples at regular time intervals showed a slight difference between bottom and upper water layer, with the highest concentration values recorded in the near-surface water. Animals in a container with one corner or side exposed to comparatively stronger light migrate toward the lighter area where they subsequently ascend to the surface, whereas animals in a more or less uniformly illuminated container move from the substratum to all sides of the jar and then upward. The latter behaviour also happens when a sample is kept in the dark (e.g. when sample extraction continues during the night) as sporadic checking with a flashlight has shown. However, if only the lower part of a sample jar is exposed to light and the remainder screened off (covered with aluminium foil) then the nemerteans assemble on the jar wall near the bottom and remain there until they die. The fact that the animals can be induced to aggregate in the most unfavourable (lowest oxygen concentration) bottom climate seems to indicate that migration is an obligatory response to general oxygen depletion and that light is the dominant stimulus in guiding the animals, even when leading them into a death trap. Under normal day or night conditions, however, it is the combined effect of positive phototaxis and negative geotaxis which obviously directs the animals to the better oxygenated surface water in the container.

The water deterioration method as described above can also be used for the extraction of nemerteans from other types of hard substrata and from marine plants (Kirsteuer, 1963a, b), but for the separation of nemerteans from sediment samples it has to be modified and additional procedures are necessary (Kirsteuer, 1967, 1971).

Extraction efficiency

In view of the experimental observations one would expect that in a slowly deteriorating, undisturbed sample uniformly exposed to light all the nemerteans would sooner or later arrive at the water surface. Occasional re-examination of such samples has shown that the extraction efficiency was in fact high. The test was made by taking the substratum from completely exhausted samples and shaking it piece by piece vigorously in a bucket with sea water. Sorting the fauna washed out in this way never produced any nemerteans, however, some dead nemerteans were infrequently found when sorting the residue at the bottom of the extraction jar. So far the largest number of individuals per sample recovered in tests was five. This happened at one time in a sample of *Porites porites* from which 44 nemerteans had been extracted by deterioration, and on a second occasion in a sample of *Agaricia agaricites* which had already yielded 35 nemerteans. The extraction efficiency in these two instances is thus 89.8 per cent and 87.5 per cent, respectively, and compared with other tested samples these are the lowest values recorded. All the specimens found in the residue belonged to species which were also registered on the water surface during deterioration of the sample and apparently the method does not have a selective effect as far as nemertean taxa are concerned.

It should be mentioned that the water deterioration method is probably less efficient when employed on board a vessel because the sample cannot rest undisturbed owing to the movements of the craft and vibrations caused by the engines. Nemerteans already on their way to the surface water have been seen to turn back and disappear again in the substratum.

Comparison with other methods

The methods commonly used for quantitative extraction of the errant, coral-reef-associated invertebrate fauna consist mainly of breaking up the substratum into small pieces and sorting out the animals either immediately (e.g. Hutchings, 1974) or after the substratum debris has been fixed in formalin-seawater (e.g. McCloskey, 1970; Brander *et al.,* 1971). The samples treated by chipping and sorting are necessarily always small (about 1 litre or 0.5–2 kg of substratum) but even then careful separation of the fauna can be 'the most time consuming process' (McCloskey, 1970).

Extraction from fixed substratum samples is of little value as far as nemerteans are concerned because they should be studied alive prior to fixation and, furthermore, when sorting the fauna it will occasionally be impossible to distinguish between larger turbellarians and smaller nemerteans. On the other hand, sorting out live nemerteans from the sample debris also poses a problem because smaller, drab-coloured species covered with mucus and sticking tightly to the substratum are difficult to discern whereas specimens found and removed by mechanical means are easily damaged. The inefficiency of this method for collecting nemerteans is best exemplified by the data reported by Hutchings (1974) who examined 100 samples from a wide spectrum of reef habitats whereby 'the samples were broken up into very small pieces and in some cases the coral was virtually pulverized, and all the invertebrates removed'. Sorting of the extracted fauna under a binocular microscope subsequently revealed that only polychaetes, sipunculids, crustaceans, molluscs, echinoderms and echiuroids had been obtained. Although it is true that coral-associated nemerteans occur with much lower population densities than some other invertebrate groups, and could thus be missed when working with small samples, it is, nevertheless, unlikely that in 100 samples nemerteans were not represented at all.

The technical difficulties involved in sorting out live nemerteans from the substratum are also demonstrated by recently obtained data relating to two comparatively large samples of *Agaricia agaricites* which had been taken at the same time from the same habitat in the reef of Carrie Bow Island, Belize. One sample of 15.5 litre substratum was subjected to water deterioration and produced 18 nemerteans belonging to seven species, whereas the second sample of similar (visually approximated) amount of coral material which was broken up and sorted for a general fauna inventory, yielded only two specimens representing two of the species also registered in the deteriorated sample (J. Ferraris, pers. comm.).

A disadvantage of the water deterioration method is that it is only applicable to the extraction of a particular segment of the coral-inhabiting invertebrate fauna, all sessile organisms and sedentary forms as well as all those errant animals which are unable to ascend on a glass wall being *a priori* excluded.

INTERPRETATION OF SAMPLE RESULTS

It was hinted earlier in this paper that certain qualities and conditions of the substratum have an appreciable influence on the distribution of coral-associated nemerteans. Measuring the physical and biological properties of the sampled coral material is, however, usually difficult and sometimes impossible (for available methods see Hutchings, Chapter 18), particularly when large samples are involved. For investigations on nemerteans the characteristics of the substratum have always been subjectively assessed, but based on comparisons of many samples of different kinds of corals collected in different geographical regions and in different zones of the reefs it is, nevertheless, feasible to evaluate the importance of edaphic features in governing the quantitative distribution of nemerteans.

The density of nemertean populations is in general much higher on densely branching corals than on compactly growing species but it is concommitantly also influenced by the ratio of dead to living material of a colony because nemerteans avoid live coral surface (Kirsteuer, 1968). Epigrowth has a significant influence on the faunal density on coral species with basically poor surface configuration, e.g. *Acropora pharaonis* was always found to contain more nemerteans when the dead portions of colonies were already covered with algae (Kirsteuer, 1968, 1972), and comparatively higher densities have also been recorded for *Agaricia agaricites* whenever it had a rich epizoic growth developed on the shaded underside of the flat colonies (unpublished data). However, under certain cirumstances epigrowth can have a negative effect on the population density of nemerteans as was once observed (Kirsteuer, 1973) in a Colombian coral reef where a large stand of *Porites porites* was extensively infiltrated by the tube-building polychaete *Chaetopterus variopedatus*. The worm tubes were confined to the lower, dead portion of the coral and had no discernible influence on the growth of the stand but they caused a significant reduction in the number of nemerteans in this otherwise densely populated species of coral.

Comparison of samples taken from normal growing stands of *Porites porites* in exposed and in protected reef areas has shown that sedimentation can also be involved in governing the distribution of nemerteans, the number of animals always being considerably smaller in the samples with a visibly high content of fine sediment, i.e. in samples from a sheltered station (unpublished data).

As far as the internal cavity system of corals is concerned, it is not yet possible to ascertain whether it is frequently occupied by nemerteans (Kirsteuer, 1972). Occasionally animals have been found when breaking up corals, but during preparation of samples only a minor portion of the existing burrows become accessible for inspection, and extraction with the water deterioration method does not provide information as to which animals were living inside the coral.

ACKNOWLEDGEMENT

Hitherto unpublished information presented herein has been obtained during field work supported by U.S. National Science Foundation Grant GB-7952, and by the U.S. National Museum, Smithsonian Institution (IMSWE—Coral Reef Project; Contribution No. 28).

References

BRANDER, K. M.; McLEOD, A. A.; HUMPHREYS, W. F. 1971. Comparison of species diversity and ecology of reef-living invertebrates on Aldabra Atoll and at Watamu, Kenya. *Symp. zool. Soc., London.* vol. 28, p. 397–431.

HUTCHINGS, P. A. 1974. A preliminary report on the density and distribution of invertebrates living on coral reefs. In: *Proc. Second. Int. Coral Reef. Symp.*, Brisbane, Great Barrier Reef Committee, vol. 2, p. 285–96.

KIRSTEUER, E. 1963a. Beitrag zur Kenntnis der Systematik und Anatomie der adriatischen Nemertinen (Genera *Tetrastemma, Oerstedia, Oerstediella*). *Zool. Jahrb. (Anat.)*, vol. 80, 0. 555–616.

——. 1963b. Zur Ökologie systematischer Einheiten bei Nemertinen. *Zool. Anz.*, vol. 170, p. 343–54.

——. 1965. Über das Vorkommen von Nemertinen in einem tropischen Korallenriff. 4. *Hoplonemertini monostilifera*. *Zool. Jahrb. (Syst.)*, vol. 92, p. 289–326.

——. 1967. Marine benthonic nemerteans: How to collect and preserve them. *Am. Mus. Novitates*, 2290, p. 1–10.

——. 1968. Bermerkungen zu den Aufsammlungen mariner Evertebraten im Nordwesten von Madagaskar, unter besonderer Berücksichtigung der Nemertini. *Zool. Anz.,* vol. 180, p. 165–77.

——. 1971. Nemertini. In: A manual for the study of meiofauna. N. C. Hulings and J. S. Gray (eds). *Smithsonian Contr. Zool.,* vol. 78, p. 1–83.

——. 1972. Quantitative and qualitative aspects of the nemertean fauna in tropical coral reefs. In: *Proc. Symp. Corals and Coral Reefs.* Mar. Biol. Assoc., India, p. 367–71.

——. 1973. Über das Vorkommen von *Chaetopterus variopedatus* (Annelida, Polychaeta) in einem karibischen Korallenriff. *Zool. Anz.,* vol. 190, p. 115–23.

McCLOSKEY, L. R. 1970. The dynamics of the community associated with a marine scleractinian coral. *Int. Rev. gesamt. Hydrobiol.,* vol. 55, p. 13–81.

NAUMANN, E. 1921. Untersuchungen über das Verteilungsproblem des limnischen Biosestons. I. Die allgemeinen reizphysiologischen Verteilungsbedingungen des heliophilen Biosestons. *Kungl. Svenska Vetenskapsakad. Handl.,* vol. 61, no. 6, p. 1–28.

RIEDL, R. 1953. Quantitativ ökologische Methoden mariner Turbellarienforschung. *Österr. zool. Z.,* vol. 4, p. 108–45.

UBRIG, H. 1952. Der Einfluss von Sauerstoff und Kohlendioxyd auf die taktischen Bewegungen einiger Wassertier. *Z. vergl. Physiol.,* vol. 34, p. 479–507.

23

Collection and sampling of reef fishes

B. C. Russell,[1] F. H. Talbot,[1]
G. R. V. Anderson[2]
and B. Goldman[3]

INTRODUCTION

A great deal of attention has been paid to methods of collection and sampling in ecology but the development of such techniques for study on coral reefs has tended to lag. This is in part historical, due largely to the logistic and technical difficulties that faced early coral reef workers. But even though improvements in transport and the development of suitable diving techniques have solved many of the early problems, there have been comparatively few detailed quantitative studies of coral reefs and the animals which live on them. This is especially true of coral reef fishes. The ecology of most coral reef fish species is poorly known and for many species, particularly those of the rich Indo-Pacific region, considerable basic taxonomic work remains to be done.

A major difficulty in quantitative study of coral reef fish communities is that of sampling. Many fishes are highly mobile and this presents a number of problems not encountered in surveying sedentary or sessile organisms. Because of their mobility, fishes are able to respond rapidly to changes in their physical environment and their distribution and abundance is more directly linked with habitat and food requirements. The spatial distribution of many species varies according to the nature of the bottom (Brock, 1954; Bardach, 1959; Randall 1963c; Talbot, 1965; Risk, 1972) and different coral reef habitats may support markedly different assemblages of fishes (Harry, 1953; Hiatt and Strasburg, 1960; Abel, 1960; Eibl-Eibesfeldt, 1965; Jones, 1968; Talbot and Goldman, 1972; Hobson, 1974; Goldman and Talbot, 1976). Intra- and inter-specific interactions play an important part in spacing (Reese, 1964; Low, 1971; Sale, 1972; Smith and Tyler, 1972; Barlow, 1974a, 1974b; Fishelson et al., 1974). Many fishes maintain discrete home ranges (Bardach, 1958; Randall, 1962, 1963a; Springer and MacErlean, 1962; Sale, 1971) or are highly territorial

1. Environmental Studies Program, Macquarie University, North Ryde, New South Wales, 2113 Australia.
2. Australian National Parks and Wildlife Service, P.O. Box 636, Canberra City, A.C.T. 2601 Australia.
3. Lizard Island Research Station, P.M.B. 37, Cairns, Queensland 4870, Australia.

(Salmon *et al.*, 1968; Rasa, 1969; Low, 1971; Myrberg, 1972; Vine, 1974; Barlow, 1974b). Others may be more or less regularly spaced, while still others live in groups or schools and tend to be highly aggregated and patchy in their distribution (Buckman and Ogden, 1973; Ogden and Buckman, 1973; Popper and Fishelson, 1973; Barlow, 1974b; Fishelson *et al.*, 1974; Choat and Robertson, 1975). There are marked diurnal-nocturnal changes in distribution (Hobson, 1965, 1968, 1972, 1974; Stark and Davis, 1966; Schroeder and Stark, 1964; Stark and Schroeder, 1965; Collette and Talbot, 1972; Vivien, 1973) and the range of movement and distribution of some species may vary greatly according to the state of the tide (Woodland and Slack-Smith, 1963; Potts, 1970; Choat and Robertson, 1975). Scarids for example, form tight cohesive schools at certain stages of the tide; at other times they may be widely dispersed over the reef flat, and at night they may be inactive but aggregated into small scattered schools (Choat and Robertson, 1975)

Factors such as these tend to complicate sampling and make it difficult to obtain reliable quantitative data. Standard methods of estimating numbers, such as mark-recapture (Regier and Robson, 1971) which rely on repetitive non-selective sampling procedures, are not applicable to many species and a more direct approach is usually necessary. It is the purpose of this paper to examine the different collecting methods and to evaluate the various sampling techniques which have been used to study coral reef fishes.

GENERAL COLLECTING TECHNIQUES

Ways of collecting fishes are many and varied, ranging from the use of simple traditional methods by a single person to techniques involving large vessels and highly sophisticated technology. As Randall (1963b) points out:

'The diversity of . . . methods not only reflects the varied habits and habitats of the fishes but also the different reasons for taking the fish: for food, for bait, for aquaria, for scientific purposes'.

Lagler (1971), in a general review of methods of fish capture, emphasized that all techniques are selective to varying degrees; the techniques employed in a study will be a compromise between the biases of the method, the available time and manpower, and the information sought. Thus on coral reefs, a general picture of the distribution and abundance of fishes has usually been obtained using a variety of observational techniques in conjunction with spearing, handlining and other methods. In this way, with a good team of workers, an overall appreciation of the distribution of fishes may be built up quickly. A detailed understanding of the comparative abundance and biomass of the fish fauna in an area, however, requires more quantitative techniques. Table 1 summarizes some of the commonly used methods of collecting coral reef fishes.

In general, conventional fishing methods using set nets, seines or trawls are not practicable other than in midwater or over the open sandy parts of reefs such as lagoon floors. Over areas of coral, foul ground seriously limits

Table 1. Commonly used methods of collecting fishes on coral reefs.

Method	Use and effectiveness	Remarks
Seine net / Trawl net / Gill net, set nets	Highly selective methods, feasible only on open bottoms or in midwater	
Fish traps	Highly selective, suitable coral reefs mainly for collection of live fishes for tagging, etc.	
Handlines / Set lines	Highly selective, inefficient methods of collection	
Night-lighting with dip nets	Highly selective, limited to fishes attracted to surface at night, attracts mostly pelagic fishes	
Handspear, Hawaiian sling, Spear gun	Highly selective, inefficient method for general collection, requires skill	
Rotenone: open poison station	Moderately non-selective method, about 75 per cent effective under good conditions, but water movement, currents and temperature affect action of poison	Use with caution, difficult to control. May cause dermal irritation and is injurious to some forms of marine life.
enclosed poison station	Excellent non-selective method, 100 per cent effective on small patch reefs when frame-net used. Technique limited to small areas	
Anaesthetics	Moderately non-selective, but poorly effective in small quantities due to rapid dilution in water. Cost generally prohibits widespread use. Suited to collection of live fishes	Use with caution, some drugs carcinogenic and injurious to marine life
Explosives	Excellent non-selective method, nearly 98 per cent effective	Use with caution, causes local damage to coral.

their use. Other more commonly used methods of catching fish also have their drawbacks. Spearfishing and handlining are both time consuming and extremely selective. Talbot (unpublished data) for example, found that during 360 line hours on Tutia Reef, East Africa, only 24 species were caught by handline. These represented only 12.5 per cent of the 192 species known from the area, and excluding those species of which fewer than 5 individuals were caught, only 9 species were taken often enough to justify the method as a means of collecting samples for biological investigation. Trap fishing similarly tends to be highly selective. Some fishes show a greater propensity than others to enter fish traps, and trap design and predation on the trapped fish also affect catches (High and Beardsley, 1970; Munro *et al.,* 1971).

Poisons and drugs are probably the most widely used methods of collecting fishes for scientific purposes on coral reefs. They have a distinct advantage in that they yield cryptic and burrowing species often missed by other techniques. Powdered *Derris* (7.5 per cent active Rotenone) or one of the commercial Rotenone preparations are the most commonly used fish poisons. Rotenone is an alkaloid derivative present in *Derris* root and is a relatively quick acting respiratory inhibitor. It causes asphyxiation and distress which results in cryptic fishes leaving their burrows and holes, and they may then be easily collected. A number of anaesthetic drugs have also been used for collecting fishes. These have been reviewed by McFarland (1960), Randall (1963b), Bell (1967), and McFarland and Klontz (1969). Quinaldine (2-methylquinoline) is probably the most widely used collecting drug, although there are several others which may be useful underwater and which are less expensive (Randall, 1963b). Anaesthetic drugs have a similar effect to poisons and cause fishes to leave their holes. They have the added advantage, however, that specimens can be collected alive and later returned to the habitat if required. The generally very high cost of many of the drugs makes their use in quantitative collecting work largely impracticable. Collecting chemicals should always be handled and used with care. *Derris* dust and commercial rotenone preparations can cause severe dermal irritation if handled repeatedly without protective clothing. Dust should not be handled in a confined space without dust masks and should be washed off the skin as soon as possible. Some collecting drugs are carcinogenic to man and may be highly toxic to other forms of marine life (Gibson, 1967; Jaap and Wheaton, 1975).

Explosives have been used as an illegal method of fishing and collecting for the aquarium trade in some parts of the world, often with devastating effect on local reef fish faunas (Lubbock and Polunin, 1975). Because the effect of an underwater explosion is more or less instantaneous and confined to a limited area, small explosive charges are a useful method of obtaining good quantitative collections of fishes. The rapid pressure changes at the front of the shock wave generated by an underwater explosion damages compressible organs, particularly the swim-bladder, and almost all fishes regardless of size are affected. Those closest to the blast are killed instantly through massive shock and by rupturing of the air-bladder. Fishes further away are temporarily stunned and may be easily collected. The effects of underwater explosions on fishes are discussed in detail by Aplin (1947), Fitch and Young (1948), Hubbs and Rechnitzer (1952) and Fry and Cox (1953).

QUANTITATIVE SAMPLING METHODS

Scuba diving has greatly facilitated the collection and sampling of fishes on coral reefs. Clear coral reef waters lend themselves well to direct underwater observation, and visual counts and quantitative collection by diving are widely employed sampling methods.

Visual census techniques

This method of sampling was first used by Brock (1954) to count Hawaiian reef fishes, and has subsequently been adopted by a number of workers for estimating numbers and biomass of coral reef fishes (Odum and Odum, 1955; Bardach, 1959; Clark et al., 1968; Risk, 1972; Key, 1973; Hobson, 1974; Nolan et al., 1975; Jones and Chase, 1975; Gundermann and Popper, 1975; Grovhoug and Henderson, 1976). A strip transect is generally swum by one or more divers who record the numbers and sizes of all fishes encountered. Data may be written on underwater writing boards or recorded using a tape recorder sealed in an underwater housing (Fager et al., 1966; Powell, 1967).

If length/weight information is available for a series of specimens of a similar size range to those counted visually, biomass can be estimated using the relationship

$$w = al^b$$

where w = wet weight, and a and b are species specific constants with b usually between 2 and 4 and commonly 3. The estimated length, l, may be either total length (TL) or standard length (SL), whichever measurement was used in deriving a and b (Tesch, 1971). Dry weight may be estimated similarly, either directly from the estimated length, or from the estimated weight, using

$$dry\ weight = k\ (wet\ weight)^c$$

where k and c are species specific constants. For most purposes k may be taken as 1 and c as 0.8. With heavily armoured fishes, very delicate juveniles, and some demersal fishes, these figures may vary. For approximate calculation, dry weight can be assumed to be about 20 per cent of wet weight (Vinogradov, 1953).

Advantages of direct visual censuses are that they provide a quick, non-destructive method suited to studies where successive samples are required in the same place. As an example of the effort involved, Jones and Chase (1975) found that a 100 m transect encompassing a strip 1 m on either side of the transect line and 2 m above it, took about 20 minutes to obtain a complete count. The use of an underwater tape recorder greatly improves the efficiency of counts and also avoids some observer error from fishes which are missed during time spent looking down at the slate when writing. Against direct recording with a tape recorder, however, must be balanced the extra time needed to transcribe the data. Laying a transect line can also be time consuming, but with practice, by swimming at a known speed, it is possible to dispense with the line and obtain accurate counts. We have used this 'free transect' method for obtaining counts of chaetodontid fishes, covering a random transect strip 200 m long by 5 m wide in 15 minutes.

Visual counts have several biases. The affect the diver has on the fishes being observed is a problem in accurately counting numbers of some species. Conventional scuba is noisy and has visible bubbles, and the presence of the diver causes some fishes to move away or to hide while others may be attracted (Chapman *et al.*, 1974), thus affecting counts. Disturbance to fishes may be greatly reduced by the use of closed-circuit re-breathing equipment, and this type of scuba was instrumental in the success of the Tektite II missions studying fishes *in situ* (Earle, 1972; Collette and Talbot, 1972; Smith and Tyler, 1972). Mixed gas re-breathers, however, demand specialized training and are not recommended for general use. Observer error is perhaps the greatest source of bias of visual counts. Larger alert fishes may easily evade sighting and small cryptic fishes and nocturnal species are frequently overlooked: it may be virtually impossible to count some species visually (Russell, 1977). Smaller fishes tend to have more restricted territories or home ranges than larger fishes and move less from the transect area during counts. Thus, there is a built-in bias towards more accurate estimation of numbers of smaller fishes. Estimating numbers of transient and schooling fishes is also difficult, and requires practice. Repeated sampling, sampling over large areas, and duplicate counts by one or more divers may reduce some of these observational errors.

Remote censusing techniques

Underwater movie films or 'cinetransects' have been used for counting fishes in Californian kelp-beds (Ebeling *et al.*, 1971) and on coral reefs (Alevizon and Brooks, 1975). The technique offers advantages in providing a permanent visual record of both the habitat and the fishes. Alevizon and Brooks (1975) obtained fish counts from 60 2.5 minute super-8 mm colour movie film taken by a scuba diver swimming just above the reef substratum. The camera was panned so as to include most or all of the fishes sighted within about 4–5 m to either side of the diver. Each cinetransect covered a distance of approximately 50 m. Films were reviewed using slow motion and stop action projection. Identification errors were a problem, but were partly overcome by counting only those fishes closer than 5 m from the camera. Beyond this range there is a rapid loss of colour and film definition which makes identification difficult. Fishes that were close enough to be counted but which were obscured in the films due to poor lighting, camera angle, extreme motion, or other factors that precluded accurate identification also were omitted from subsequent analysis.

However, Alevizon and Brooks estimate that such errors accounted for less than 5 per cent of the total number of fishes photographed.

Photographic counts are likely to prove most useful in counting some of the larger more mobile fishes which are usually difficult to sample by other means. Underwater visibility and film quality impose serious limitations and cinetransects are possible only in clear, shallow water during the middle of the day. Many of the limitations of visual transects apply also to cinetransects. Because only larger fishes are readily identifiable on film, a sizeable portion of the reef fish fauna is not amenable to this method of sampling. Individuals smaller than about 50 mm and species that are cryptic, secretive or nocturnal will be under-represented or entirely absent from film counts.

Remote-controlled underwater television (UTV) holds promise as a method of counting fishes and has been used recently in several *in situ* underwater studies of fishes. Myrburg (1973) and Smith and Tyler (1973) have both used UTV to obtain census data on the fishes living on a small section of reef in Bimini. The television caused no disturbance to the fishes and permitted relatively accurate counts of species normally too wary to be approached by divers. Underwater television, however, has many of the same drawbacks of underwater photographic techniques in that it is limited mainly to shallow water work at close range. It has one advantage over all methods; by coupling an image intensifier device, night observation is possible.

Rotenone

Rotenone has been widely used to obtain population estimates of coral reef fishes (Randall, 1963c; Clark *et al.,* 1968; Smith and Tyler, 1972; Smith, 1973; Nagelkerken, 1974) and Smith (1973) has discussed its use in quantitative sampling of small patch reefs in some detail. Information on the amount of Rotenone needed to effectively poison a given area is scant, and experience with the poison under local conditions would seem to be the best guide. Lagler (1971), however, suggests that using powdered Derris root (5 per cent Rotenone), a minimum lethal concentration in the water is 0.5 ppm, but applications range as high as 2.0 ppm. Emulsified rotenone concentrates with added synergists, such as the commercially available Pro-noxfish and Chem-fish collector, are more effective than *Derris* dust. Smith (1973) for example, found that 650 ml of emulsified Rotenone applied from a plastic syringe bottle was sufficient to sample effectively a patch reef 20 feet (6 m) in diameter, or a 100 foot (30 m) section of shoreline. An effective substitute for straight emulsified Rotenone which we have used successfully is a mixture of 500 g of *Derris* dust with 2–3 ml of liquid detergent and 250 ml of Chem-fish collector added, the mix being kneaded to a thick paste inside a plastic bag with a small amount of seawater. Taken underwater and spread by divers direct from the bag, this mixture is effective over an area of about 60 m².

The main advantage of Rotenone is that it yields small cryptic species that are often missed in visual field counts. Rotenone tends, however, to be un-

335

predictable. Temperature affects the time of action (Gilderhus 1972) and some groups of fishes, especially juveniles and small pelagic species, such as engraulids, are affected much more rapidly than others, such as eels. Control of the poison is difficult. In areas of only moderate water movement dispersion may be too rapid for effective sampling, while in calm, warm water careless use can easily result in an overkill. Samples may also be somewhat biased because some larger fishes are capable of swimming away from the poison unaffected, while predatory species frequently are attracted to the area by the smaller fishes which have succumbed to the poison. Furthermore, it is difficult to delineate the actual area being sampled unless it is somehow enclosed with a net or walls. On a large scale, enclosed poison stations are not completely successful (e.g. Quast 1968) and only some kinds of bottom can be sampled in this way. Even under ideal conditions a complete kill is rarely obtained from Rotenone and for quantitative sampling repeated poisoning may be necessary (Smith and Tyler, 1972; Smith, 1973).

The use of a collapsible frame-net (Fig. 1) overcomes many of the problems associated with poison stations and one of us (Anderson) has found it particularly useful in sampling small patch reefs and artificial reefs on the Great Barrier Reef. The net, made of 0.5 mm Terylene mesh supported on a galvanized steel frame, completely encloses the area being sampled. The net is designed with a loose skirt about 15 cm wide around the base which can be weighted or buried in the substratum, thereby ensuring that all fishes inside the net are retained. Poison or anaesthetic is introduced from a plastic bag through a hose pushed under the net, and is left for 20–45 minutes before the net is removed. The fine mesh of the net cuts down water flow within the sample area and allows successful operation with small amounts of poison even under difficult conditions of water movement. Moreover, by operating several frame nets, a single diver can successively sample several areas in a short time. Dead fishes are picked up in a hand net, and an air-lift suction tube with a net bag collector is used to collect smaller fishes. In conjunction with pre-poisoning visual counts, this method gives an extremely accurate sample of fishes in small areas.

Explosive sampling

Explosives have been used to sample quantitatively coral reef fish communities by Talbot (1965) and Talbot and Goldman (1974). Four half-pound (225 g) sticks of gelignite are used. This charge is sufficient to kill fishes over a radius of about 5 m in shallow water (less than 2 m depth) and over a radius of about 7 m in deeper water. The charges are laid by hand in the area being sampled and 20–30 minutes allowed to elapse for the fishes to return to normal. The charges are detonated electrically[4] from a boat moored a safe distance away

4. We have used both seismic detonators and ordinary instantaneous detonators, with 100 m Polypropylene insulated lead wires, down to depths of 30 m, with no failures in more than 100 explosive stations. The detonators can be fired using an ordinary 6 volt dry cell battery.

Figure 1
(a) Collapsible hoopnet being placed in position over a small artificial reef
    in preparation for collecting the fishes using Rotenone.
(b) Hoopnet in position and Rotenone being poured in under the net.
(photo: B. A. Anderson.)

(usually about 20 m) and a team of 4–6 divers then collects all dead and stunned fish using handnets.

Providing standardized explosive charges are used, the area of reef from which fish may be collected is reasonably constant, but water depth and bottom topography both affect dissipation of the shock waves and careful attention is needed in placing the charge so as not to create 'shadow' areas. With experienced operators, small explosive charges are safe to use and cause only slight damage to the reef. With a 2 pound (1 kg) charge, local pulping of the coral may occur over about a 1 m radius, with coral heads broken off a further 2 m away. Recovery of the damaged area, however, is usually rapid, and within 12 months it is difficult to distinguish an area which has been sampled using explosives. Explosive samples yield large collections of fishes and immediate preservation is usually necessary to prevent their rapid decay in tropical climates. We have found that the fishes are best placed immediately into a large plastic garbage bin containing dilute (5 per cent) sea water formalin, and all large fishes (more than 10 cm) injected with concentrated formalin at the collection site.

The main bias associated with explosive sampling is failure to collect fishes which are unaffected by the blast. These include species such as eels and some blennies, in which the swimbladder is absent or only poorly developed. Other potential sources of error are loss of fishes which have floated to the surface or have been carried away by currents, but this can be minimized by careful collection and searching both on the bottom and at the surface. With continual repetitive sampling in the same general area, sharks and other predatory fishes may be a nuisance and actively compete with the collectors in picking up fishes. However, this is rarely a serious problem and it can be minimized by taking no more than 2 or 3 samples on consecutive days in any one area.

DISCUSSION

Few workers have given proper consideration to the effectiveness of the different methods used in quantitatively sampling coral reef fishes. Direct observation, although time consuming, is non-destructive and is particularly useful in long-term population studies. But even on small areas of reef, repeated counts may be necessary to obtain reliable census data (Smith and Tyler, 1972, 1973; Jones and Chase, 1975). Larger, fast-moving fishes and schooling species pose special difficulties in sampling, and visual counts may be the only practicable method for estimating their numbers. Reliable counts from transects may be difficult to obtain but with some knowledge of the behaviour of a species, problems of counting may be overcome. For example, by observing the movements of fishes over fixed routes to and from feeding grounds, Ogden and Buckman (1973) were able to obtain accurate population estimates of *Scarus croicensis* on Caribbean reefs.

Community studies over large areas of reef pose greater difficulties: visual censuses are often limited by the sheer diversity and numbers of fishes. Jones and Chase (1975) for example, found that visual counts on Guam reefs under-estimated the number of species present, and that random counts in the same area added as many as 30 per cent more species. Clark *et al.* (1968) likewise found that visual counts seriously under-estimated numbers of species and that Rotenone collections were needed to provide a comprehensive picture of the fish community. Quast (1968) used a combination of these two methods to obtain quantitative estimates of the populations and standing crop of fishes living in southern Californian kelp-beds.

Some of the advantages of using Rotenone have already been pointed out. However, the method has been found particularly useful in studying fish communities of small isolated patch reefs (Smith and Tyler, 1972; Smith, 1973). Because they are spatially isolated from other areas of reef, patchreefs are more easily sampled using Rotenone. Smith (1973) in discussing the effectiveness of small Rotenone stations, estimated that about 75 per cent of the species present are taken in a single sampling and that two or three applications of Rotenone a few hours apart, will effectively kill 85–95 per cent of all the fishes present.

Smith (1973) suggests that an estimate of the total population can be obtained by applying the method of Leslie and Davis (1930) to the repeated sample data. By this method, the number of individuals taken in successive samples when plotted against the previous cumulative total number of individuals collected (Fig. 2) yields a decreasing curve that approaches the abscissa, and the point of intercept gives an estimate of the total population. A problem inherent in sampling by repeated collection, which could give rise to possible errors, however, is that of re-population. Re-colonization of denuded reef areas can be extremely rapid (Bussing, 1972; Russell *et al.,* 1974; Gundermann and Popper, 1975) and this may lead to overestimation of the population.

A more reliable way of sampling fishes from small isolated reefs is by the frame-net technique outlined previously. This method usually ensures that all fishes are taken in a single sample, it minimizes losses from escapees and predation, and is less time consuming than other methods. For sampling over larger areas of reef, explosives probably yield the most consistently reliable results. While not entirely free from bias, this method by itself is relatively quick and efficient and while perhaps equally as labour intensive, explosive sampling is more precisely quantifiable than either visual counting or Rotenone collection on a wide scale.

A general problem with sampling any large complex community is the high within-habitat sampling variance that is usually encountered and the need for replicate samples. Underwater, such repetitive sampling may pose special problems, particularly where deep diving work is involved. In this case it may be necessary to make a compromise between the time able to be spent under-water to avoid decompression, and the minimum number of samples which are needed. An estimate of the minimum sample size is most easily obtained by plotting, from a series of samples, the cumulative number of species collected against the cumulative number of samples. Using standardized explosive

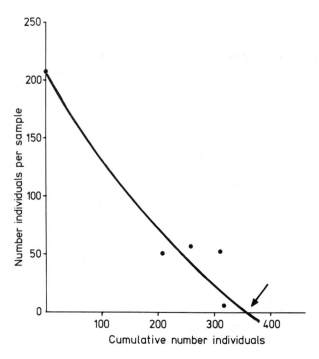

Figure 2
Leslie and Davis's (1930) graphical method of population estimate from
repeated sample data. Data are from Smith (1973), the numbers of fishes
collected in 5 consecutive poisonings of a Bahamas patchreef. The point of
intercept of the curve with the abscissa (arrow) gives an estimate of the
population.

charges, a minimum of 8–10 samples was required to obtain reliable estimates
of the number of species in fish communities on the Great Barrier Reef (Fig. 3).
Using species diversity (H_q''—Pielou, 1966) rather than species number as a
measure of community structure, an asymptote is reached more quickly and
it can be seen that fewer samples are required. This largely reflects the insensitivity of most species diversity measures towards 'rare' species. On coral reefs,
however, such 'rare' species are perhaps the most significant feature of fish
communities and may account for up to 60 per cent of the total number of
species. For this reason we feel species diversity is a poor measure of community structure, and in terms of actual collection, sorting and counting
samples, the extra effort needed to obtain a good estimate of total number of
species is well justified.

To conclude, it is difficult to lay down precise guidelines for use of the
various methods. None is free from selective bias and all have some disadvantages. To this extent, the adoption of any one method must be based upon the
particular problems and aims of the investigation, and the limitations and

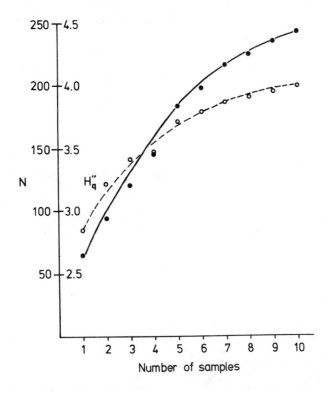

Figure 3
Cumulative number of species N (——) and cumulative diversity H_q''(----)
plotted against number of samples in the order in which they were taken.
Data from Goldman and Talbot (in preparation). The fishes are from
explosive stations in a leeward reef slope habitat at One Tree Reef, Great
Barrier Reef.

biases of the method should always be borne in mind when interpreting results.
For small isolated patch reefs it would seem that visual counts and enclosed
poison stations both provide reliable population estimates, but for larger areas
of reef, explosives, or a combination of visual censusing and poison or explosives,
are probably best. There is a pressing need for further comparative evaluation
of all the sampling methods. Equally important is the necessity to adopt
standard sampling criteria: a major drawback to useful comparison of coral
reef fish community studies is the multiplicity of different sampling methods
which have been used. The authors make a plea for a rational conservation-
minded approach to any sampling programme. All the methods of collection,
apart from those designed specifically to return live fishes to their habitat,
involve the permanent removal of at least a part of the fish community, and
complete recovery may not occur for some time. In many parts of the world
some of the methods which we have discussed are specifically prohibited, and

341

special permission for their scientific use should not be abused. Poisons and explosives are dangerous collecting agents if used carelessly. Steps should be taken to ensure that there is no needless killing, and that there is sufficient labour available to collect all the fishes, especially where collections are made near established recreation areas or close to urban centres.

References

ABEL, E. F. 1960. Zur Kenntnis des Verhaltens und der Ökologie von Fischen an Korallenriffen bei Ghardaqa (Rotes Meer). Z. Morph. Ökol. Tiere, vol. 49, 0. 430–503.

ALEVIZON, W. S.; BROOKS, M. G. 1975. The comparative structure of two western Atlantic reef-fish assemblages. Bull. mar. Sci., vol. 25, p. 482–90.

APLIN, J. A. 1947. The effect of explosives on marine life. Calif. Fish Game, vol. 33, p. 23–30.

BARDACH, J. E. 1958. On the movements of certain Bermuda reef fishes. Ecology, vol. 39, p. 139–46.

——. 1959. The summer standing crop of fish on a shallow Bermuda reef. Limnol. Oceanogr., vol. 4, p. 77–85.

BARLOW, G. W. 1974a. Contrasts in social behaviour between Central American cichlid fishes and coral reef surgeon fishes. Am. Zool., vol. 14, p. 9–34.

——. 1974b. Extraspecific imposition of social grouping among surgeon fishes. J. zool. Soc. Lond., vol. 174, p. 333–40.

BELL, G. R. 1967. A guide to the properties, characteristics, and uses of some general anaesthetics to fish. Bull. Fish. Res. Bd Can., vol. 148, p. 1–4.

BROCK, V. E. 1954. A preliminary report on a method of estimating reef fish populations. J. Wildlife Management, vol. 18, p. 297–308.

BUCKMAN, N. S.; OGDEN, J. C. 1973. Territorial behaviour of the striped parrotfish Scarus croicensis Block (Scaridae). Ecology, vol. 54, p. 589–96.

BUSSING, W. A. 1972. Recolonization of a population of supratidal fishes at Eniwetok Atoll, Marshall Islands. Atoll Res. Bull., no. 154, p. 1–7.

CHAPMAN, C. J.; JOHNSTONE, A. D. F.; DUNN, J. R.; CREASY, D. J. 1974. Reactions of fish to sound generated by diver's open-circuit underwater breathing apparatus. Mar. Biol., vol. 27, p. 357–66.

CHOAT, J. H.; ROBERTSON, D. R. 1975. Protogynous hermaphroditism in fishes of the family Scaridae. In: R. Reinboth (ed.). Intersexuality of the animal kingdom. Berlin, Springer-Verlag, p. 263–83.

CLARK, E.; BEN-TUVIA, A.; STEINITZ, H. 1968. Observations on a coastal fish community, Dahlak Archipelago, Red Sea. Bull. Sea Fish. Res. Stn Haifa, no. 49, p. 15–31.

COLLETTE, B. B.; TALBOT, F. H. 1972. Activity patterns of coral reef fishes with emphasis on nocturnal-diurnal changeover. In: B. B. Collette and S. A. Earle (eds). Results of the Tektite program: ecology of coral reef fishes. Bull. Nat. Hist. Mus. Los Angeles, no. 14, p. 125–70.

EARLE, S. A. 1972. Introduction. In B. B. Collette and S. A. Earle (eds). Results of the Tektite program: ecology of coral reef fishes. Bull. Nat. Hist. Mus. Los Angeles, no. 14, p.1–9.

EBELING, A. W.; LARSON, R.; ALEVIZON, W. S.; DE WITT, F., Jr. 1971. Fishes of the Santa Barbara kelp forest. Abstr. Coastal Shallow Water Res. Conf., no. 2, p. 61.

EIBL-EIBESFELDT, I. 1965. Land of a thousand atolls. Cleveland, New York, World Publishing, (195 p.).

FAGER, E. W.; FLECHSIG, A. O.; FORD, R. F.; CLUTTER, R. I.; GHELARDI, R. J. 1966. Equipment for use in ecological studies using SCUBA. Limnol. Oceanogr., vol. 11, p. 503–9.

FISHELSON, L.; POPPER, D.; AVIDOR, A. 1974. Biosociology and ecology of pomacentrid fishes around the Sinai Peninsula (northern Red Sea). J. Fish Biol., vol. 6, p. 119–33.

FITCH, J. E.; YOUNG, P. H. 1948. Use and effect of explosives in Californian coastal waters. Calif. Fish Game, vol. 34, p. 53–70.

FRY, D. H.; COX, W. 1953. Observations on the effect of black powder explosions on fish life. Calif. Fish Game, vol. 39, p. 233–36.

GIBSON, R. N. 1967. The use of the anaesthetic Quinaldine in fish ecology. J. anim. Ecol., vol. 36, p. 295–301.

GILDERHUS, P. A. 1972. Exposure times necessary for antimycin and rotenone to eliminate certain freshwater fish. *J. Fish. Res. Bd Can.*, vol. 29, p. 199–202.

GOLDMAN, B.; TALBOT, F. H. 1976. Aspects of the ecology of coral reef fishes. In O. A. Jones and R. Endean (eds). *Biology and geology of coral reefs:* vol. 3. *Biology* 2. New York, Academic Press, p. 125–54.

GROVHOUG, J. G.; HENDERSON, R. S. 1976. Distribution of inshore fishes at Canton Atoll. In: S. V. Smith and R. S. Henderson (eds). *An environmental survey of Canton Atoll Lagoon 1973.* San Diego, Naval Undersea Center, p. 99–157.

GUNDERMANN, N.; POPPER, D. 1975. Some aspects of recolonization of coral rocks in Eilat (Gulf of Aqaba) by fish populations after poisoning. *Mar. Biol.*, vol. 33, p. 109–17.

HARRY, R. R. 1953. Ichthyological field data of Raroia Atoll, Tuamotu Archipelago. *Atoll Res. Bull.*, no. 18, p. 1–90.

HIATT, R. W.; STRASBURG, D. W. 1960. Ecological relationships of the fish fauna on coral reefs of the Marshall Islands. *Ecol. Monogr.*, vol. 30, p. 65–127.

HIGH, W. L.; BEARDSLEY, A. J. 1970. Fish behaviour studies from an undersea habitat. *Comm. Fishing Rev.*, vol. 32, no. 10, p. 31–7.

HOBSON, E. S. 1965. Diurnal-nocturnal activity of some inshore fishes in the Gulf of California. *Copeia 1965*, no. 3, p. 291–302.

——. 1968. Predatory behaviour of some shore fishes in the Gulf of California. *Res. Rept U.S. Fish Wildl. Serv.*, no. 73 (92 p.).

——. 1972. Activity of Hawaiian reef fishes during the evening and morning transitions between daylight and darkness. *Fish Bull.*, no. 70, p. 715–40.

——. 1974. Feeding relationships of teleostean fishes on coral reefs in Kona, Hawaii. *Fish. Bull.*, no. 72, p. 915–1031.

HUBBS, C. E.; RECHNITZER, R. 1952. Report on experiments designed to determine effects of underwater explosions on fish life. *Calif. Fish Game*, vol. 38, p. 336–66.

JAAP, W. C.; WHEATON, J. 1975. Observations on Florida reef corals treated with fish collecting chemicals. *Fla mar. Res. Publ.*, no. 10, p. 1–18.

JONES, R. S. 1968. Ecological relationships in Hawaiian and Johnston Island Acanthuridae (Surgeon fishes). *Micronesica*, vol. 4, p. 309–61.

——.; CHASE, J. A. 1975. Community structure and distribution of fishes in an enclosed high island lagoon in Guam. *Micronesica*, vol. 11, p. 127–48.

KEY, G. S. 1973. Reef fishes in the Bay. In: S. V. Smith, K. E. Chave and D. T. O. Kam (eds). *Atlas of Kaneohe Bay: A reef ecosystem under stress.* Honolulu, Univ. Hawaii Sea Grant Program., p. 51–66.

LAGLER, K. F. 1971. Capture, sampling and examination of fishes. In: W. E. Ricker (ed.). *Methods for assessment of fish production in fresh waters.* Oxford, Blackwell Science Publications. (IBP Handbook no. 3, 2nd edit.), p. 7–44.

LESLIE, P. H.; DAVIS, D. H. S. 1930. An attempt to determine the absolute number of rats in a given area. *J. anim. Ecol.*, vol. 8, p. 94–113.

LOW, R. M. 1971. Interspecific territoriality in a pomacentrid reef fish *Pomacentrus flavicauda* Whitley. *Ecology*, vol. 52, p. 648–54.

LUBBOCK, H. R.; POLUNIN, N. V. C. 1975. Conservation and the tropical marine aquarium trade. *Envir. Conserv.*, vol. 2, p. 229–32.

McFARLAND, W. 1960. The use of anaesthetics for the handling and transport of fishes. *Calif. Fish Game*, vol. 46, p. 407–431.

——.; KLONTZ, G. 1969. Anaesthetics in fishes. In: E. V. Miller (ed.). Comparative anaesthesia in laboratory animals. *Federation Proc.*, vol. 28, p. 1535–40.

MUNRO, J. L.; REESON, P. H.; GAUT, V. C. 1971. Dynamic factors affecting the performance of the Antillean fish trap. *Proc. Gulf Caribb. Fish Inst.*, vol. 23, p. 184–94.

MYRBURG, A. A. Jr. 1972. Social dominance and territoriality in the bicolour damselfish, *Eupomacentrus partitus* (Poey) (Pisces: Pomacentridae). *Behaviour*, vol. 41, p. 207–31.

——. 1973. Underwater television—a tool for the marine biologist. *Bull. mar. Sci.*, vol. 23, p. 824–36.

NAGELKERKEN, W. P. 1974. On the occurrence of fishes in relation to corals in Curacao. *Stud. Fauna Curacao*, no. 147, p. 118–41.

NOLAN, R. S.; McCONNOUGHEY, R. R.; STEARNS, C. R. 1975. Fishes inhabiting two small nuclear test craters at Enewetak Atoll, Marshall Islands. *Micronesica*, vol. 11, p. 205–17.

ODUM, H. T.; ODUM, E. P. 1955. Trophic structure and productivity of a windward coral reef community on Eniwetok Atoll. *Ecol. Monogr.*, vol. 25, p. 291–320.

343

OGDEN, J. S.; BUCKMAN, N. S. 1973. Movements, foraging groups, and diurnal migrations of the striped parrotfish *Scarus croicensis* Bloch (Scaridae). *Ecology*, vol. 54, p. 589–96.

PIELOU, E. C. 1966. Shannon's formula as a measure of specific diversity. Its use and misuse. *Am. Nat.*, vol. 100, p. 463–5.

POPPER, D.; FISHELSON, L. 1973. Ecology and behaviour of *Anthias squammipinnis* (Peters 1855) (Anthiidae, Teleostei) in the coral habitat of Eilat (Red Sea). *J. exp. Zool.*, vol. 184, p. 409–24.

POTTS, G. W. 1970. The schooling ethology of *Lutjanus monostigma* (Pisces) in the shallow water environment of Aldabra. *J. Zool., Lond.*, vol. 161, p. 223–35.

POWELL, J. 1967. Underwater tape recorder. *Skin Diver*, vol. 16, no. 2, p. 28–9.

QUAST, J. C. 1968. Estimates of the populations and the standing crop of fishes. In: W. J. North and C. L. Hubbs (eds). Utilisation of kelp-bed resources in southern California. *Calif. Fish Game, Fish Bull.*, no. 391, p. 57–79.

RANDALL, J. E. 1962. Tagging reef fishes in the Virgin Islands. *Proc. Gulf Caribb. Fish Inst.*, vol. 14, p. 201–41.

——. 1963a. Additional recoveries of tagged reef fishes from the Virgin Islands. *Proc. Gulf Caribb. Fish Inst.*, vol. 15, p. 155–7.

——. 1963b. Methods of collecting small fishes. *Underwat. Nat.*, vol. 1, no. 2, p. 6–11. and 32–6.

——. 1963c. An analysis of the fish populations of artificial and natural reefs in the Virgin Islands. *Caribb. J. Sci.*, vol. 3, p. 31–47.

RASA, O. A. E. 1969. Territoriality and the establishment of dominance by means of visual cues in *Pomacentrus jenkinsi* (Pisces: Pomacentridae). *Z. Tierpsychol.*, vol. 26, p. 825–45.

REESE, E. S. 1964. Ethology and marine zoology. *Oceanogr. Mar. biol. Ann. Rev.*, vol. 2, p. 455–88.

REGIER, H. A.; ROBSON, D. S. 1971. Estimating population number and mortality rates. In: W. E. Ricker (ed.). *Methods for assessment of fish production in fresh waters*. Oxford, Blackwell Science Publications. (IBP Handbook no. 3, 2nd edit.), p. 131–65.

RISK, M. J. 1972. Fish diversity on a coral reef in the Virgin Islands. *Atoll Res. Bull.*, no. 153, pp. 1–6.

RUSSELL, B. C. 1977. Population and standing crop estimates for rocky reef fishes of north-eastern New Zealand. *N.Z. J. mar. Freshwat. Res.* vol. 11, p. 23–36.

——; TALBOT, F. H.; DOMM, S. 1974. Patterns of colonisation of artificial reefs by coral reef fishes. In: *Proc. Second Int. Coral Reef Symp.* Brisbane, Great Barrier Reef Committee, vol. 1, p. 207–15.

SALE, P. F. 1971. Extremely limited home range in a coral reef fish *Dascyllus aruanus* (Pisces: Pomacentridae). *Copeia 1971*, no. 2, p. 324–7.

——. 1972. Effect of cover on agonistic behaviour of a reef fish: a possible spacing mechanism. *Ecology*, vol. 53, p. 753–8.

SALMON, M.; WINN, H. E.; SARGENT, N. 1968. Sound production and associated behaviour in trigger fishes. *Pac. Sci.*, vol. 22, p. 11–20.

SCHROEDER, R. E.; STARK, W. A. 1964. Diving at night on a coral reef. *Natn. Geogr.*, vol. 125, no. 1, p. 128–54.

SMITH, C. L. 1973. Small rotenone stations: a tool for studying coral reef fish communities. *Am. Mus. Novit.*, no. 2512, p. 1–21.

——; TYLER, J. C. 1972. Space resource sharing in a coral reef fish community. In: B. B. Collette and S. A. Earle (eds). Results of the Tektite program: ecology of coral reef fishes. *Bull. Nat. Hist. Mus. Los Angeles*, no. 14, p. 125–70.

——; ——. 1973. Population ecology of a Bahamian suprabenthic shore fish assemblage. *Am. Mus. Novit.*, no. 2528, p. 1–38.

SPRINGER, V. G.; McERLEAN, A. J. 1962. A study of the behaviour of some tagged South Florida coral reef fishes. *Am. Midl. Nat.*, vol. 67, p. 386–97.

STARK, W. A.; DAVIS, W. P. 1966. Night habits of fishes on Alligator Reef, Florida. *Ichthyologica*, vol. 38, p. 313–356.

——; SCHROEDER, R. E. 1965. A coral reef at night. *Sea Frontiers*, vol. 11, no. 2, p. 66–79.

TALBOT, F. H. 1965. A description of the coral structure of Tutia Reef (Tanganyika Territory, East Africa) and its fish fauna. *Proc. zool. Soc. Lond.*, vol. 145, p. 431–70.

——; GOLDMAN, B. 1974. A preliminary report on the diversity and feeding relationships of the reef fishes at One Tree Island, Great Barrier Reef. In: *Proc. Symp. Corals and Coral Reefs, 1969, Mar. Biol. Assoc. India*, p. 425–44.

TESCH, W. F. 1971. Age and growth. In: W. E. Ricker (ed.). *Methods for assessment of fish production in fresh waters*. Oxford, Blackwell Science Publications. (IBP Handbook no. 3, 2nd edit.), p. 98–130.

VINE, P. J. 1974. Effects of algal grazing and aggressive behaviour of the fishes *Pomacentrus lividus* and *Acanthurus sohal* on coral-reef ecology. *Mar. Biol.,* vol. 24, p. 131–6.

VINOGRADOV, A. P. 1953. The elementary chemical composition of marine organisms. *Sears Found Mar. Res. Mem.,* no. 2, Yale Univ. (647 p.).

VIVIEN, M. 1973. Ecology of the fishes of the inner coral reef flat in Tulear (Madagascar). *J. mar. Biol. Assoc. India,* vol. 15, p. 20–45.

WOODLAND, D. F.; SLACK-SMITH, R. J. 1963. Fishes of Heron Island, Capricorn Group, Great Barrier Reef. *Univ. Qld Pap. Dept. Zool.,* vol. 2, no. 2, p. 15–69.

Part III

Energy and nutrient flux

Introduction

R. E. Johannes[1]

This section of the Monograph is devoted largely to methods for studying the flux of nutrients and energy through coral-reef communities, sub-communities and individual reef organisms. Most of these methods have undergone significant development and modification during the past four years since Project Symbios at Enewetak Atoll when many were first tested extensively in the field. Most of the authors are Symbios participants which, for better and for worse, results in a much greater harmony of objectives than one might otherwise find in such a collection of papers.

Let me touch briefly on what appear to me to be the major ultimate objectives of such studies.

Ecologists supported by public funds are charged with two increasingly important duties: (1) the preservation of ecosystems, and, in the case of food-producing ecosystems, (2) discovering how to extract optimum sustainable yields from them. On the basis of these criteria, coral reef ecologists have a long way to go, but by extending some of the techniques described in the following papers we have an opportunity to make some important contributions to these objectives.

Just as medical doctors measure various components of an individual's excreta to monitor his health, so might ecologists some day monitor the health of whole ecosystems using homologous flow methods pioneered by coral reef ecologists. The approach has more to commend it than mere elegance.

Most of today's practical criteria of ecosystem 'health' are structural; that is, the effects of pollutants or other environmental stresses must usually bring about structural alterations in ecosystems before their effects can be detected. But surely ecosystems, like individuals, also manifest their pathologies in metabolic changes, some of which predate any structural change.

The ability to detect such changes and an understanding of their significance would enable us to diagnose ecosystem stresses and remedy them before any

1. Hawaii Institute of Marine Biology, P.O. Box 1346, Kaneohe, Hawaii, 96744, U.S.A.

irreversible structural damage to the ecosystem commenced. Coral reef ecologists have made a good start in the direction of developing such an early warning system. Because of Project Symbios at Enewetak, and Kinsey's pioneering work on reef metabolism on the Great Barrier Reef, we have a good preliminary understanding of the metabolism of healthy shallow reef communities. The time is thus ripe to examine the metabolism of stressed reef communities.

At the outset of Project Symbios some of us were also optimistic that a better understanding of energy and nutrient flux in reef communities would provide us with some insight into the problems of harvesting edible reef organisms efficiently. But, whereas we knew a lot more about how reef communities function after the expedition, we had learned nothing of consequence about how to harvest them. We do know enough, however, to piece together a hypothesis concerning what might limit fish production.

Gross primary productivity is unusually high in reef communities. Fish biomass is also often high on unexploited reefs. But reef fish populations do not seem to be able to withstand sustained commercial fishing pressures of similar magnitude to those in shallow temperate marine communities. It has been argued by way of explanation that, because the P/R ratios in these communities are often close to one, there is little excess production to be skimmed off by man. This argument seems wanting. A fisherman is a predator. When a new predator enters a community there is no theoretical reason why, under normal circumstances, it cannot consume sizeable quantities of prey without reducing the P/R ratio and unbalancing the system. It can accomplish this simply by consuming at the expenses of other predators (e.g. carnivorous reef fish) with the total amount of prey consumed in the community remaining more or less unaltered.

A fisherman is not a normal predator, however, in that he removes the nutrients in his prey from the marine ecosystem. A comparatively high proportion of the available nutrients in reef communities is tied up in fish biomass, and a relatively low proportion resides in an exchangeable reserve in the sediments and in algae. Thus the harvesting of fish results in the removal of proportionally more nutrients from a reef community than from typical shallow temperate marine communities. The fact that a comparatively small percentage of reef fish biomass constitutes 'trash' fish—almost all species of adequate size are used—amplifies the trend, as does the use of a wide variety of invertebrate types not generally eaten in the temperate zone. In addition the low levels of dissolved and particulate nutrients characteristic of tropical waters implies a reduced capacity of reef communities to import and replace exported nutrients relative to shallow temperate marine communities. Thus nutrient reserves, rather than initial net community productivity, may set the upper limit on sustainable yields of reef fish.

If this hypothesis were to prove true, it might influence our methods of coral reef management. It would elevate prospects, for example, for the success of controlled fertilization (pioneered experimentally, by the way, by Kinsey, using methods described in this volume). This possibility troubles me because it raises the spectre of sparkling reef waters turning to green soup. However experiments in lakes have demonstrated that fish yields can be raised through controlled fertilization without inducing environmental degradation. Perhaps the same might prove true in coral lagoons.

Studies of both stress metabolism and nutrient limitation in coral communities require their experimental manipulation. For this reason studies of reef metabolism in the near future will probably depend less on large expanses of reef such as those studied by the Symbios team, and more upon small, more easily manageable communities such as the tank experiments of Jokiel and the isolated reef communities used by Kinsey—both described in detail in the following pages.

24

Measurement of water volume transport for flow studies

J. E. Maragos[1]

INTRODUCTION

Submerged shallow reef platforms extending across barrier and atoll reef rims provide ideal sites for the study of reef community metabolism and ecology, especially where continuous uni-directional currents prevail. Changes in the rate at which certain substances are expelled into or removed from seawater give clues on nutrient utilization, productivity, respiration, and other functional relationships within benthic reef flat communities. Two kinds of information are required to measure the flux of substances across reef platforms: (a) the changes in the concentration of substances in the flowing seawater, and (b) the amount of the flowing seawater or volume transport. Volume transport data are needed to convert concentration differences into absolute quantities of substances and the rates at which these quantities change as they cross reef flat communities. This report outlines the fundamental problems and procedures regarding volume transport measurements on shallow submerged reefs. Sample data from a study site at Enewetak Atoll, Marshall Islands, are also analysed.

METHODS

Location and frequency of measurement on transects

For reef sites showing consistent dimension, depth, and current flow characteristics, it usually suffices to take volume transport measurements at only one point along the transect. Under such circumstances, the product of the current velocity and water depth will be essentially constant at any given time, thereby insuring that volume transport will also be constant at any point along the transect. For example, currents may be swift at shallow portions of the reef transect such as near the algal ridge. Slower currents downstream, however,

1. Hawaii Institute of Marine Biology, University of Hawaii, P.O. Box 1346, Kaneohe, Hawaii, 96744, U.S.A. Present address: Environmental Resources Section, U.S. Army Corps of Engineers, Pacific Ocean Division, Bldg 230, Fort Shafter, Honolulu, Hawaii APO 96558, U.S.A.

will be 'compensated' by greater water depths so that the volume of water flowing past both locations will be the same at any given instance.

Data for water transport calculations should be collected consistently at the same locations and at the same times that water samples are collected for chemical analyses.

Once a tentative reef transect site is selected, the investigator should conduct preliminary investigations on currents and water depth in order to estimate the maximum range in these variables. The investigator should also consult published tide records for the area to determine if expected tides are in time phase with those observed on the reef. Such information is important for decisions regarding instrumentation design and location and the frequency of data acquisition.

Data acquisition for volume transport calculations

In estimating volume transport, one is attempting to determine the rate at which a three dimensional volume of water flows past a reference point on the reef (Fig. 1). This requires that a time interval (t) be established and that data

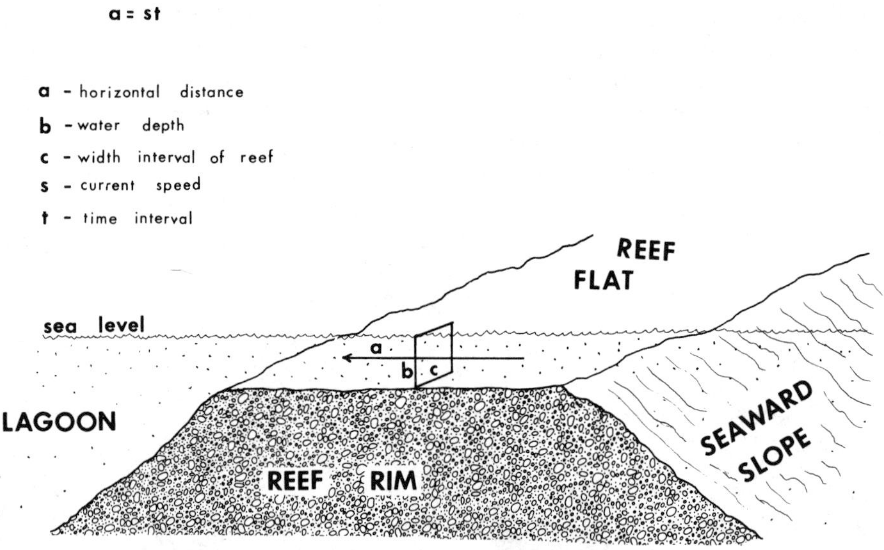

$$a = st$$

a – horizontal distance

b – water depth

c – width interval of reef

s – current speed

t – time interval

Figure 1
Diagrammatic sketch of a cross section through an atoll reef rim showing the information needed for the computation of volume transport of flowing waters. Depicted is an 'ideal' reef site showing uncomplicated form and dimension. The distance value (a) is computed from the product of the current speed (s) and time interval (t). Both (t) and (c) (reef width interval) are assigned arbitrary values by the investigator while (s) and (b) (water depth) are variables which are measured *in situ*. Current direction is lagoonward from the ocean side.

on each of the three linear dimensions of the water mass (a, b, c) be acquired. The product of the three dimensions then give an estimate of water volume where

$$V = abc \qquad (1.1)$$

where a = length of flowing water
$\quad b$ = depth of flowing water
$\quad c$ = width of flowing water

The distance (a) is conveniently estimated from the product of the current velocity (s) and the time interval (t) or:

$$a = st \qquad (1.2)$$

The linear dimension (b) is determined by measuring the depth of the water. The width value (c) is arbitrarily chosen by the investigator; most often in the past (c) has been assigned a value of 1 m. The time interval (t) is also arbitrarily assigned a constant value such as 1 hr.

Thus of the four kinds of information required (s, t, b, c) only the current velocity (s) and water depth (b) are actually measured on the reef. If the values used for (c) and (t) are the same throughout the study, then the calculation of volume transport rate (V_t) is essentially reduced to determining the product of the current velocity and water depth or:

$$\boxed{V_t = sb} \qquad (1.3)$$

Both current velocity and water depth fluctuate considerably with time on reef flats, and therefore, data must be collected *in situ*.

Measuring water depth

The most direct method of estimating water depth (b) involves the use of a calibrated rod such as a metre stick where the investigator manually takes readings of depth at times when water samples and current data are also collected. A more sophisticated approach involves the use of a continuous recording tide staff which is established permanently on the transect. The latter approach has the advantage of acquiring continuous data without requiring substantial field time on the part of the investigator. The principal disadvantage is the difficulty of setting up such equipment on submerged reefs without the need for towers, frames, or other supporting structures.

The placement of tide staffs on shorelines or piers far removed from the reef site is undesirable because of the probable deviations of height and time phase for tidal oscillations at different locations. For example, reef formations may impede the exchange of water between the lagoon and ocean; tidal oscillations in the lagoon may lag behind those of the ocean side and will show smaller amplitude variation. Data on water depth should be acquired at the same time and frequency as for current data and water sample collection.

The rise and fall of the tide causes the major water depth fluctuations. A build up of waves may elevate sea level 20–30 cm above normal (Munk and Sargent, 1948; Tait, 1972, 1974).

Measuring current velocity

There are two ways of measuring current velocities. One involves the placement of neutrally buoyant devices in the water at an upstream location, after which the investigator records the time and distance covered by the device during its movement downstream. Acceptable drifting devices include dyes, current crosses, current-drogues, drift-cards, and even the body of a diver who drifts downstream and records his progress at the same time. It is important that the drifting device be neutrally buoyant and not project so far above the surface of the water that winds deflect the device and cause errors in current velocity and direction. Since vertical gradients in current velocity frequently exist, the device should also be positioned low enough in the water in order to obtain data on mean current velocities. The 'drift device' approach produces accurate information on current velocity and direction although data acquired in this way may vary from time to time. (S. Smith, pers. comm.). The approach unfortunately requires considerable field time relative to the amount of data collected. However, the drift device approach should be employed for preliminary observations on the current characteristics at prospective reef sites in order to determine the degree of deviation of the direction of the current from the transect line. The drift approach is inexpensive and manual depth readings and water samples can be conveniently obtained at the same time and location.

The second approach in measuring currents involves the use of current meters which are anchored at specific reef locations. Water flows past the stationary meters causing rotors or other sensors to move or deflect. The more sophisticated meters (ducted, magnetic field-type, Savonius, Eckman, etc.) give estimates of instantaneous current velocity which are recorded on paper, tape or drums. Less sophisticated meters employ counters which sum the number of revolutions of rotor-like devices; the investigator must keep a record of the time the meter is on station. These meters are calibrated prior to their establishment on the reef so that the number of revolutions can be converted to distance (value 'a' of Fig. 1).

The principal advantage of stationary recording current meters is their ability to record continuous and comprehensive current data with only minimal amounts of field time required by the investigator. The principal disadvantage is the lack of precise information on possible current eddies or reversals which cannot be detected if only one or two meters are in operation on a lengthy transect. Although some current meters record both direction and velocity of currents, potential deflection of currents at one point along the transect may not correspond to those at other points. If current direction is found to deviate significantly from that of the transect line, then the investigator must alter the location of the collection of water samples; determination of these sites are rendered more difficult if stationary recording current-meters are employed.

Thus the investigator should have reasonable assurance of uni-directional current flow on study reefs where stationary meters are utilized.

RESULTS

Sample data and calculation of volume transport

Figure 2a shows some uni-directional current data collected on a windward reef flat transect near Japtan Island, Enewetak Atoll, during a study in June 1971. A Hydroproducts Ducted Current Meter was anchored to a rigid frame 20 cm above the substratum approximately 100 m behind the breaker zone near the seaward reef edge. Continuous records of current velocity were provided over an 18-hour period on 9 June. Water depth readings (Fig. 2b) were taken manually during the same time interval at the site of the current meter.

A low tide of 0.3 m occurred at approximately 1200 hrs while high tides of 1.5 m occurred at 0530 and 1900 hrs. Due to a rise in sea level of approximately 30 cm due to wave action (Pilson and Smith, unpub.) currents flowed from the ocean side across the reef and into the lagoon during the entire 18-hour period. Note that the times of maximum and minimum current velocity coincided with those of water depth (Fig. 2a and 2b).

Current velocities tended to fluctuate much less during low tides. The coming and going of wave sets (surf beat) appeared to cause the regular oscillations in current velocities during low tide. Evidently only larger waves travel across the reef, thereby noticeably affecting current velocity. At high tide most waves, large or small, travel across the outer reef flat causing more variable currents (Fig. 2a). At no time did currents fall below 10 cm/sec (low tide) and maximum velocities often exceeded 120 cm/sec (at high tide). Munk and Sargent (1948) reported currents of up to 110 cm/sec driven by a rise in sea level due to wave action on reef flats at Bikini Atoll, Marshall Islands.

The data of Figures 2a and 2b provided the basis of estimates of volume transport rates shown in Figure 2c. Using equation (1.3), the mean current data (solid curve of Figure 2a) was multiplied by the water depth data to yield volume transport rates. The values (t) and (c) were assigned the numbers 1 sec and 1 m, respectively.

At high tide, volume transport is calculated to be $(1.5) (0.6) = 0.9 \text{ m}^3/\text{sec}/\text{m}$ using average current data. The corresponding transport at low tide is computed as $(0.2)(0.3) = 0.06 \text{ m}^3/\text{sec}/\text{m}$. Hence, data provided in Figure 2c show that volume transport rate varies fifteen-fold during the course of a single tide cycle. substituting the maximum current velocity in the equation, the maximum volume transport at high tide increases to $(1.5) (1.5) = 2.25 \text{ m}^3/\text{sec}/\text{m}$, and substituting the minimum current velocity into the low tide equation yields a minimum volume transport rate of $(0.2) (0.1) = 0.02 \text{ m}^3/\text{sec}/\text{m}$. This corresponds to a hundred-fold variation in transport rates during a tidal cycle. It is conceivable that such variations may be prolonged and commonplace during

357

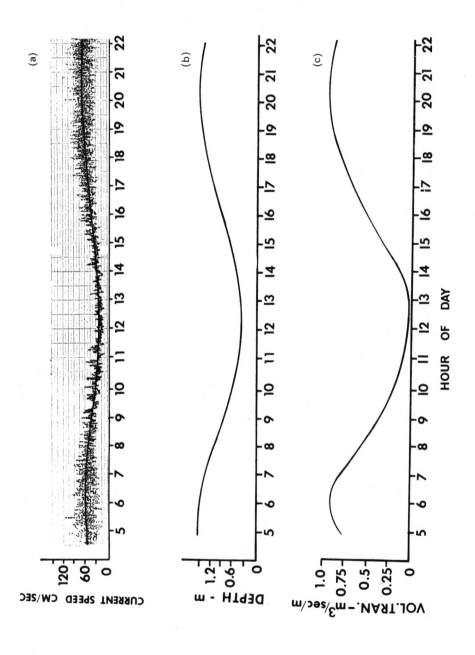

spring tides on some reef flats when both currents and water depth would be expected to achieve their extreme maximum and minimum levels.

DISCUSSION

Although current velocities and water depth fluctuations might be greater on reef flats in the Marshall Islands than in many other locations, the results emphasize the need for accurate and frequent field data for calculation of volume transport rates. In many Pacific reef areas, normal spring tidal range is 1.5 m or more (Munk and Sargent, 1948; Newell and Bloom, 1970). Review of past studies on water currents indicate that current velocities commonly vary between 0 and 50 cm/sec or more on reefs (Munk and Sargent, 1948; von Arx, 1948; Odum and Odum, 1955; Inman et al., 1963; Kopenski and Wennekens, 1966; Bathen, 1968; Gallagher et al., 1971; Tait, 1972, 1974; etc.). For reefs showing more moderate fluctuations in currents and tides, volume transport variations may still vary tenfold or more during a normal tidal cycle.

It appears to be a misdirected effort for those carrying out flow-type community metabolism studies to devote most of their time to refinement of chemical analyses if the collection of volume transport data is not of equal

Figure 2(a)
A record of current velocity collected at Japtan Reef, Enewetak Atoll on 9 June 1971 between the hours 0400–2200. High tides occurred at approximately 0530 hrs and 1900 hrs. Low tide occurred at 1200 hrs. Data were collected from a continuous recording Hydroproducts ducted current meter anchored 20 cm above the substratum near the seaward edge of the reef platform. Currents were uni-directional (lagoonward) for the duration of the record. The solid line shows the mean current velocities for the 18-hr. period.

Figure 2(b)
A rough plot of the water depth over the same time interval.

Figure 2(c)
The bottom transport rate expressed as cubic metre/sec/metre plotted over the same time interval. The values were computed from the product of the current velocity (2a) and water depth (2b) using equation (1.3).

precision. Accurate chemical determinations may show whether the concentration of a substance increases or decreases along a transect, but one cannot determine the absolute quantities of substances or their rates of change per unit reef area without reference to good volume transport data. Since volume transport rates themselves fluctuate as well, then current and depth data should be collected as frequently as the water samples

ACKNOWLEDGEMENTS

The author thanks Robert Clutter, Robert Johannes and Philip Helfrich who assisted during data collection and Stephen Smith who critically reviewed the manuscript. This study was supported by Federal grants to the Alpha Helix Program of the National Science Foundation, to the Atomic Energy Commission, and to the U.S. Sea Grant programme. The Janss Foundation also provided funds for the study.

References

BATHEN, K. H. 1968. A descriptive study of the physical oceanography of Kaneohe Bay, Oahu, Hawaii. *Hawaii Inst. mar. Biol. Tech. Rep.,* 14, p. 1–353.

GALLAGHER, B. S.; SHIMADA, K. M.; GONZALES, Jr., F. I.; STROUP, E. D. 1971. Tides and currents in Fanning Atoll Lagoon. *Pac. Sci.,* vol. 25, p. 191–205.

INMAN, D. L.; GAYMAN, W. R.; COX, D. C. 1963. Littoral sedimentary processes on Kauai, a subtropical high island. *Pac. Sci.,* vol. 17, p. 106.

JOHANNES, R. E.; ALBERTS, J.; D'ELIA, C.; KINZIE, R. A.; POMEROY, L. R.; SOTTILE, W.; WIEBE, W.; MARSH, J. A. JR.; HELFRICH, P.; MARAGOS, J.; MEYER, J.; SMITH, S.; CRABTREE, D.; ROTH, A.; McCLOSKEY, L. R.; BETZER, S.; MARSHALL, N.; PILSON, M. E. Q.; TELEK, G.; CLUTTER, R. I.; DuPAUL, W. D.; WEBB, K. L.; WELLS, J. M. JR.; 1972. The metabolism of some coral reef communities. *BioScience,* vol. 22, no. 9, p. 541–44.

KOPENSKI, R. P.; WENNEKENS, M. P. 1966. *Circulation patterns Johnston Island, Winter–Summer, 1965.* Washington, D.C., U.S. Naval Oceanographic Office (223 p + 41 colour pls.).

MUNK, W. H.; SARGENT, M. C. 1948. Adjustment of Bikini Atoll to ocean waves. *Trans. Am. geophys. Union,* vol. 29, no. 6, p. 855–60.

NEWELL, N. D.; BLOOM, A. L. 1970. The reef flat and two-meter eustatic terrace of some Pacific atolls. *Geol. Soc. Am. Bull.,* vol. 81, p. 1881–94.

ODUM, H. T.; ODUM, E. P. 1955. Trophic structure and productivity of a windward coral reef community. *Ecol. Monogr.,* vol. 25, p. 291–320.

SARGENT, M. C.; AUSTIN, T. S. 1954. *Biologic economy of coral reefs.* U.S. Geol. Surv. (Prof. Paper 260-E), p. 283–300.

TAIT, R. J. 1972. Wave set-up on coral reefs. *J. geophys. Res.,* vol. 77, p. 2207–11.

——. 1974. Water and sediment movement due to wave set-up on coral reefs. Submitted ms. 17 p.

VON ARX, W. S.; 1948. The circulation systems of Bikini and Rongelap lagoons. *Trans. Am. geophys. Union,* vol. 29, no. 6, 861–70.

25

Productivity measurements of coral reefs in flowing water

J. A. Marsh, Jr.[1] and S. V. Smith[2]

INTRODUCTION

The study of coral reef productivity has been focused largely on reef flat communities subjected to a unidirectional flow of water. There have been a sufficient number of such studies to ensure that a general methodology can be presented for those conditions. The principles which lead to this methodology of flowing water respirometry are also applicable in situations of more complex water movement, as shown by lagoonwide metabolic surveys (Smith and Pesret, 1974; Smith and Jokiel, 1975). The method described by Kinsey (Chapter 35) for studying the respirometry of reef communities periodically subjected to 'no flow' conditions demonstrates yet another variation which can be applied.

The basic model of productivity measurements in flowing water entails the measurement of oxygen, carbon dioxide, or other constituents of interest immediately before the water begins its transit across a particular community and immediately downstream of the community. If the change in that water property is divided by the water transit time, then the net rate at which the community alters the water is thereby determined. The approach has its most obvious application in a river or stream, in which the characteristics of water flow are well-defined (Odum, 1956). Many reef flats are subjected to a similar unidirectional flow of water driven by waves breaking on the reef margin. If the sampling transect has biological zones which are perpendicular to the direction of water flow, then lateral mixing of water as it crosses the reef flat will not introduce a significant error into the estimate of changes in water composition along that transect.

GENERAL CONSIDERATIONS AND DEFINITIONS

Productivity should be expressed on an area basis, where area is taken to be

1. The Marine Laboratory, University of Guam, P.O. Box EK, Agana, Guam, 96910, U.S.A.
2. Hawaii Institute of Marine Biology, University of Hawaii, P.O. Box 1346, Kaneohe, Hawaii 96744, U.S.A.

361

the flat map area rather than the absolute three-dimensional surface area actually occupying a given map area. This gives results which are comparable with most observations previously reported in the literature for various aquatic and terrestrial communities having both two-dimensional and three-dimensional structures. Moreover, for a total reef community, the light available to the primary producers cannot exceed the amount of light striking the horizontal water surface overlying that community. Littler (1973), working with individual populations of coralline algae, reported a closer correlation between primary productivity and projected (flat) area than between productivity and absolute area. The area of photosynthetic surface on a reef, of course, may be markedly higher than the horizontal area of the overlying water surface. This point was considered by Dahl (1973), who used surface index as the ratio of actual surface to that of a plane with similar boundaries. Such an index is analogous to the well-established leaf area index used in studies of agricultural crops.

Zonation on reefs has often been described with respect to the structural components of these systems, but metabolic partitioning of an entire transect subjected to continuous water flow has usually not been accomplished. In taking upstream–downstream samples, one often finds that the changes in water composition between the beginning and end of the transect are just barely detectable, so there has been no attempt to determine metabolic activity of various zones by sampling intermediate stations. Kinsey (Chapter 35) has succeeded in such subdivisions under conditions of no water flow. Such attempts should be made. No zone should be ignored on the basis of visual inspection, since areas devoid of conspicuous fleshy algae or coral heads can be the most productive portions of reef flats (Smith and Marsh, 1973). Other zones which have been necessarily ignored in upstream–downstream studies are the reef-face zones in front of the breaking surf and the surf zone itself. Because of their inaccessibility, these zones cannot be sampled adequately by the method presented here. In addition, the great turbulence of the surf zone may lead to rapid equilibration of dissolved gases with the atmosphere, a factor which overwhelms any possible change in these gases brought about by metabolic activity.

Considerable confusion concerning the use of various terms to express community metabolism exists in the literature. Until a unified terminology is finally adopted, each presentation should include careful definition of the terms used therein. Our conventions follow those of Kinsey (Chapter 35) in so far as practical. These terms are given below and are illustrated on the diurnal metabolism curve shown in Figure 1:

r = hourly respiration rate (the measured night-time metabolic rate).

y = hourly rate of net production. (Kinsey calls this 'net photosynthesis'; it is the measured day-time metabolic rate).

p = $y + r$; hourly rate of gross production. (Kinsey calls this photosynthesis).

R = 24 hr (24-hour respiration) calculated on the assumption that r is constant over the diurnal cycle.

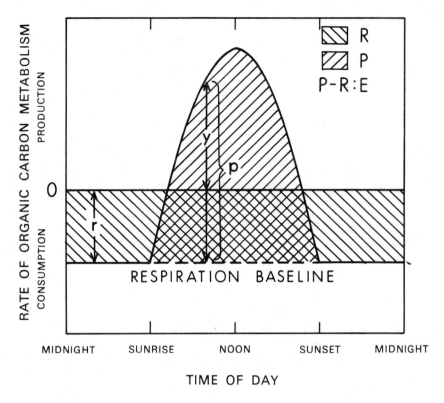

Figure 1
Idealized diurnal curve of community metabolism. Symbols are defined in
the text.

P = daily gross production; the integration of the metabolism curve with
respect to p.

$E = P - R$; excess production (if $E > 0$) or consumption ($E < 0$).

According to the conventions used for the symbols here, individual
measurements or calculations of instantaneous rates are denoted by lower-case
letters. Rates integrated over timespans equalling or exceeding full light or dark
cycles are represented by capital letters. Each of the above processes must be
expressed in terms of mass transfer per unit time. In this presentation, mass
will be given in terms of grams or moles of oxygen, carbon dioxide, or carbon.
The time component given here will be hours or days. Finally, the processes
will be standardized to map area (expressed in square metres).

Only two of the rates given above can be measured directly—y and r. The

363

simplified (and almost certainly incorrect) assumption is frequently made that daylight respiration equals night-time respiration. Of necessity, we make that assumption here. R then equals the hourly night-time respiration rate multiplied by 24. If day-time respiration does not equal night-time respiration, then both P and R are in error accordingly. Research into the diurnal variation of community respiration rate is needed. E is not subject to error from this uncertainty about day-time respiration, as can be seen algebraically.

The common term 'net daily productivity' has been frequently used, but not consistently so. It has been taken to mean E, as defined above; y integrated over the daylight hours; and average y multiplied by 12. In view of this confusion, the term should be explicitly defined if it is to be used at all.

Ratios of reef productivity to respiration can provide insight into the energy dynamics of the community. Again, such ratios have been variously defined. Among the choice of ratios to be found in the literature are the maximum y or p during the day to r; net daily productivity (by any of the above definitions) to 'respiration'; and P to 'respiration'. 'Respiration', in turn, may be night-time respiration, day-time respiration, or R. The single most useful production to respiration ratio seems likely to be the ratio of daily P to R. A ratio of greater than 1.0 indicates that the community is autotrophic; it is either storing or exporting organic carbon. A ratio of less than 1.0 indicates that the community is heterotrophic and is either importing organic carbon or is utilizing carbon from stored materials within the community. A ratio of 1.0 indicates that community productivity and respiration are in balance. Calculation of $P:R$ ratios should not be considered a sufficient basis for statements of the potential amount of biomass that may be harvested from a given community, since such statements also require a detailed knowledge of internal energy pathways. Various subareas, or zones, of the community may have varying $P:R$ ratios, with some zones exceeding 1.0 and others falling below this. In such cases, the autotrophic and heterotrophic portions of the community are functionally linked; and the community as a whole may have a $P:R$ ratio near unity (Smith and Marsh, 1973).

The upstream–downstream method measures total community productivity. There have been no successful attempts to study the individual P's and R's of the various populations in a reef community in order to compare the sum of these components with total community metabolism. Such a study would be possible (at least with respect to the major components). Differences between summing the individual components and measuring total community metabolism would represent either biases in one of the two levels of analysis or a failure to account for all important organisms in the community, or both.

METHODOLOGY: ADVANTAGES, DISADVANTAGES, ASSUMPTIONS

Two materials have been monitored as primary indicators of reef productivity in flowing waters. Oxygen is the parameter with considerable historical precedent (e.g. Sargent and Austin, 1949, 1954; Odum and Odum, 1955); CO_2 has been measured less frequently. Recent summaries of earlier papers on flow respirometry are provided by Kinsey and Domm (1974), Marsh (1974), and Smith (1974).

The advantages of O_2 analyses are the relative ease of O_2 determinations under field conditions, thus allowing large numbers of replicates; comparability with the bulk of the present literature on coral-reef metabolism; and the possibility of continuous monitoring (Kinsey and Domm, 1974). The major disadvantage is the rapidity of oxygen exchange across the air–sea interface when any partial pressure difference exists between these two media.

Carbon dioxide measurements have as their major advantage a more direct relation than O_2 to organic carbon fixation and a lower susceptibility to gas exchange across the air–sea interface. The major disadvantages are that both the measurement and the calculation of CO_2 changes are more complex than those for O_2; the high level of CO_2 in seawater demands extreme precision in CO_2 measurements if differences between samples are to be detected; and a CO_2 correction for calcium carbonate precipitation must be made for an actively calcifying system such as a coral reef.

Several assumptions are made in most metabolic studies of reef communities. Reference was made above to the assumption that rates of night-time respiration and day-time respiration are equal. It is likely that respiration differs between light and dark, but effective methods for evaluating the differences in natural communities have not been developed. It is generally assumed that vertical mixing of the water mass moving across the reef flat is thorough, so that samples taken from the surface are representative of the entire water mass passing over the benthic community. This assumption can be tested by releasing patches of fluorescein dye at various depths. Lateral movement and flow reversals are assumed to be minimal, so that flow is very nearly unidirectional between paired samples.

Since volume transport across reef flats may be too great at high tides to observe significant changes in the O_2 or CO_2 content between upstream and downstream samples, it will be necessary in most cases to construct diurnal curves from samples taken at low-tide periods of several successive (or closely spaced) days and nights so that a complete coverage of all hours can be obtained. The assumption is therefore made that metabolic activity does not vary significantly from day to day if light conditions are similar. It is further assumed that metabolic activity of the reef community is independent of the tidal state or flow velocity of water and that low tide observations are typical for all tidal states. This assumption has not been tested for reef communities, but Nixon *et al.* (1971) reported a hyperbolic increase of community respiration in mussel beds in response to increasing current speeds up to about $0.1 \, \text{m sec}^{-1}$. Increased metabolism of individual plants with an increase in water movement has been reported by a number of workers (e.g. Westlake, 1967; Whitford and Schumacher, 1961), and a general overview of water movement as an ecological factor has been made by Riedl and Schwenke (1971).

Most workers have based yearly calculations of productivity on the assumption of little seasonality and have extrapolated the results of a particular month to the entire year. Kohn and Helfrich (1957) and Gordon and Kelly (1962) have made observations at two different times of the year in Hawaii; their results indicated that there was moderate but significant seasonal variation. Kinsey (Chapter 35) and Kinsey and Domm (1974) report considerable seasonality in the reefs at One Tree Island, Great Barrier Reef. These reefs are all relatively high-latitude reefs, so the seasonality seen on them may exceed that to be expected of reefs at lower latitudes. Short-term variations in algal standing crop have been reported for one Hawaiian reef (Doty, 1971); it is unclear how such biomass variations might affect community metabolism.

SAMPLING AND ANALYSIS PROCEDURES

The basic procedure for flow respirometry is to collect water samples or make measurements at the upstream and the downstream ends of the transects being studied. Samples should also be taken at intermediate locations along the transect at the beginning and end of each biological zone, for possible determination of metabolism within these zones. It is likely that neither O_2 nor CO_2 changes will be sufficient for reliable determination of metabolism in any zone narrower than about 200 m under any but the slowest current conditions. Temperature should be measured to $\pm 0.5°C$ in the field as the samples are taken. All samples should be collected from immediately upstream of the person taking those samples in order to minimize contamination.

It is important to trace the diurnal variations in O_2 and/or CO_2 changes across the transect. This demands adequate sampling over a complete diurnal cycle. If, as is frequently the case, upstream–downstream changes can only be detected during periods of low tides, then samples must be taken on a sufficient number of successive low tides to establish the characteristics of an average day over that period. At most locations, the time of low tides shifts about 1 hour per day. Therefore sampling at most low tides over a 24-day period in an area with predominantly diurnal tides, or a 12-day period in an area with predominantly semidiurnal tides, should establish the characteristics of such an average day.

As detailed records as possible of weather and sea conditions should be kept. These records should include wind velocity data and cloud cover. The former can be used for calculating gas exchange across the air–sea interface (discussed below), while the latter may serve to explain much of the observed variability in productivity over the average day. Additional measurements of solar insolation made with a pyrheliograph, or similar instrument, would be even more desirable.

Oxygen

If Winkler analyses (see below) are to be utilized for O_2 measurements, the

366

samples may be obtained by scooping water into a plastic bucket and siphoning the water from the bucket through a piece of plastic tubing into standard BOD bottles (glass-stoppered and designed to be filled with no trapped gas). The siphoned water should be allowed to overflow and flush these bottles for at least 30 seconds. Care must be taken to exclude bubbles from both the siphon tube and the sample bottle. The Winkler reagents should be added to the bottles within 15 minutes of sample collection. This may be accomplished either by returning the bottles to the shore or by taking the reagents into the field. Bottles should be shielded from direct sunlight and protected from drastic temperature changes. The entire sampling procedure can usually be handled more efficiently by two people than by one person. Fixed samples may be held for later titration, but this should not be delayed longer than 24 hours.

Oxygen analysis may be by the classical Winkler methods (Amer. Pub. Health Assoc., 1971; Strickland and Parsons, 1968; Carpenter, 1965), or there may be immediate *in situ* readings with an oxygen electrode (discussed more extensively by Kinsey, in Chapter 35). A portable electrode and meter can be used for sampling at discrete times in a manner analogous to taking discrete samples for Winkler analyses. This requires a rugged instrument which can be used under rigorous field conditions. Alternatively, meters and probes can be mounted for continuous *in situ* recording. Conversions from partial pressure readings on the oxygen meter to absolute values of oxygen concentration require a saturation table. Since the O_2 saturation tables available are derived from modified Winkler titrations (Green and Carritt 1967; Weiss, 1970), the accuracy of this technique would appear to be the factor limiting accuracy of all O_2 determinations. It should be realized, however, that the ability to estimate metabolism from O_2 changes as water crosses the reef is ultimately limited by the precision rather than the accuracy of the O_2 measurement.

Carbon dioxide

Characterizing the CO_2 system in seawater requires the measurement of two CO_2-related parameters (most commonly pH and total alkalinity in field situations). Analytical details of CO_2 analysis are reported by Smith and Kinsey (Chapter 36). The techniques of sample collection can be identical to those described for O_2 sampling.

Alternatively, the water may be collected simply by immersing a glass or polyethylene bottle to the desired sampling depth, filling it once for a rinse, emptying and then refilling it, and finally capping it underwater to eliminate air pockets in the bottle. If the salinity of the water is suspected to change by as much as 0.1 parts per thousand (from rainfall, evaporation, or groundwater seepage) as the water crosses the transect, then sufficient water should be collected for salinity determinations. That amount of salinity change is unlikely under most circumstances of water flow across a reef flat.

Samples should be returned to the laboratory and analysed as rapidly as possible. There is no satisfactory method of preserving either the total CO_2

content or the CO_2 speciation in the water to the required degree of precision, so analyses should be performed within an hour after collection.

CALCULATIONS

Both the oxygen and the carbon dioxide content of water crossing a reef flat change in response to a variety of processes, in particular organic carbon metabolic activity, other chemical reactions, gas exchange, and the physical processes of advection and eddy diffusion. The calculation of reef-community metabolism then involves two quite separate considerations: the ability to quantify the total changes which occur as water crosses the reef, and the ability to apportion these changes among the various causal processes.

Total rate of change

The first of these considerations, that of quantifying the total O_2 or CO_2 change, is largely a matter of precision and accuracy. The analytical precision of determining the difference between paired upstream and downstream samples ultimately limits the quantification of these differences, while the accuracy of volume transport measurements limits the degree to which concentration changes can be appropriately scaled into metabolic rates.

Smith and Marsh (1973) reported a within-sample precision (standard deviation) of 1.56 µmoles litre^{-1} for duplicate O_2 Winkler titrations on each of two bottles from a given sample. This value is equivalent to a standard error (s.e.) on four replicates of 0.78 µmoles litre^{-1}, close to the limits quoted by Vollenweider (1969) and Strickland and Parsons (1968) for Winkler titrations. The standard error of the difference between two samples is given by (s.e.$_1^2$ + s.e.$_2^2$)$^{\frac{1}{2}}$ or 1.10 µmoles litre^{-1}. The 95 per cent confidence interval for distinguishing between two samples is approximately two standard error units (Strickland and Parsons, 1968), or 2.2 µmoles litre^{-1}. Similar precision can be achieved with an O_2 metre.

Smith and Kinsey (Chapter 36) estimate that with duplicate analyses the precision standard error on CO_2 measurements is approximately 5 µmoles litre^{-1}. For four replicates (analogous to the O_2 precision figures quoted above) the standard error would be 3.5 µmoles litre^{-1}, for a standard error of the difference of 5 µmoles litre^{-1}. If one assumes that the CO_2 uptake and release rate by a reef community equals the O_2 release and uptake rate (that is, the metabolic quotient of the community = 1.0), then the O_2 measurements are about twice as sensitive to metabolic alterations of the water composition as are CO_2 measurements.

Volume transport calculations impose different, but equally important, limitations on the determination of O_2 and CO_2 changes. Errors in the measurement of volume transport will introduce multiplicative (or scaling) errors in the calculation of rates of change from concentration differences. The product of volume transport per unit width of reef perpendicular to the direction of water flow ($m^3 hr^{-1} m^{-1}$, or $m^2 hr^{-1}$) and change in O_2 or CO_2 concentration between upstream and downstream stations (in μmoles litre^{-1}, or mmoles m^{-3}) is a rate in moles m^{-1} hr^{-1}. Division by the distance (m) between upstream and downstream stations yields the rate per unit area: moles m^{-2} hr^{-1}. Maragos (Chapter 24) discusses the methodology of measuring flow rates and converting these rates to volume transport calculations.

Partitioning the total changes

Advection and eddy diffusion. Having recognized that these processes are conceptually of some importance, we can dismiss them rapidly by the following considerations. Changes in material concentrations due to advection are effectively and implicitly handled by the analysis of paired upstream and downstream samples. In theory, the upstream sample should be collected, and then one should wait until that water has had just enough time to reach each downstream sampling site. In practice, the rate of variation in the upstream water is often insufficient to justify that care; an exception was reported by Marsh (1974). The need for eddy diffusion corrections is obviated if the transect site is zoned similarly to the reef for some distance to either side of the transect. Then water properties diffusing to or from the transect should be essentially identical to those of the transect itself. Thus the practices of choosing and sampling a site for flow respirometry are the reasons these processes need not be considered further.

Gas exchange. Gas exchange across the air–sea interface can be of considerable importance to the net flux of O_2 or CO_2 as water crosses a reef flat. First, consider the lesser of two processes of gas exchange—the formation and subsequent escape of bubbles.

Bubbles may be introduced into the water by two major processes. Breaking waves will carry bubbles under the water surface, where increased hydrostatic pressure may cause partial or total solution of these bubbles. Such bubble solution will always tend to supersaturate the water with respect to all atmospheric gases (see, for example, the discussion by Kanwisher, 1963). As oxygen is liberated during the day by photosynthesis, the water becomes supersaturated and some of the excess gas may go into the production of bubbles. Bubbles introduced into the water by either process will rapidly achieve a gas composition approximately that of air saturated with water vapour (that is, about 80 per cent N_2, 20 per cent O_2, and 0.03 per cent CO_2), and the rise of these bubbles to the sea surface will strip these gases from the water. In general, the escape of gas from seawater by this process is probably more spectacular than significant (see also Kinsey, Chapter 35), but more information is needed on this point. In a situation where this process should be significant, it will be so only with respect to O_2 and N_2 (Kanwisher, 1963). If there is the likelihood that bubble escape may be significant in a particular situation, then a correction factor may be obtained by collecting bubbles over a known area for a known time and measuring the O_2 composition of these bubbles. J. Maragos (pers. comm.) has found that an inverted funnel with a test tube fitted tightly over the stem is a convenient collection device. Such a device has also been used in other environments by Odum (1956). The assembly is flooded with water, the accumulation rate of a gas in the test tube is noted, and the composition of that gas is measured with an oxygen metre and electrode. The area of the funnel opening is the appropriate surface area to be used in converting gas accumulation rates in the test tube to rates per unit area.

Gas exchange by diffusion across the air–sea interface is a far more serious and complex potential problem to flow respirometry than is bubble escape. Again, O_2 is more susceptible to this exchange than is CO_2 (Kanwisher, 1963). Therefore, most of the discussion presented below will specifically address the subject of O_2 diffusion.

The basic procedure for calculating diffusion rates in flowing waters was given by Odum (1956) and further elaborated with a specific example by Odum and Hoskin (1958). The diffusion rate, D (moles $m^{-2} hr^{-1}$ diffusion from the water) is given by the equation:

$$D = KS \qquad (1)$$

where K (expressed as moles $m^{-2} hr^{-1}$ per 'per cent saturation deficit') is a constant which can be determined empirically for the particular field conditions, and S is the per cent saturation deficit, or the per cent deviation of oxygen concentration in the water from its saturation level at the particular temperature and salinity in question. The tables of Green and Carritt (1967) or Weiss (1970) may be used for calculating per cent saturation, or this value may be determined directly from an oxygen meter.

The measured per cent saturation minus 100 yields the per cent saturation deficit; this 'deficit' will thus be positive if the water is supersaturated.

K may be influenced by temperature, salinity, velocity of the wind blowing across the surface of the water, and the degree of surface roughness. The latter factor not only controls the actual surface area on the irregular air–water interface per unit of map area but also affects the diffusion constant directly through physical influence on movements of molecules, as pointed out by Kanwisher (1963).

The constant K may be calculated according to the following formula derived from equation (1):

$$K = \frac{q_m - q_e}{S_m - S_e} \qquad (2)$$

where q_m is the total rate of change (moles $O_2 \, m^{-2} hr^{-1}$) in the water just before dawn, q_e is the rate of change in the water just after sunset, S_m is the morning per cent saturation deficit, and S_e is the evening per cent saturation deficit. Note that the rates of change used here are area-based; these are converted from the whole-transect rates of change as discussed previously. Equation (2) gives an 'average' K value for the entire night-time interval between evening and morning sampling times. Respiration throughout the night is assumed to be constant, and morning-to-evening differences in q are assumed to be due solely to diffusion. The algebraic value of K should be positive if there are no sampling artifacts due to changing wind velocity or other complicating factors, but Gordon and Kelly (1962), using a slight modification of equation (2), got negative values in some of their calculations. They then took the absolute value of K for use in further calculations. The justification for such a procedure is not clear and is not recommended here.

Kinsey (Chapter 35) and Kinsey and Domm (1974) offer a modification of the above procedure. In brief, q is obtained on successive days at 'standard times' and under comparable wind conditions. The assumption is then made that, from one day to another at the same time of day, community metabolism is constant. Differences in q and S then become attributable to day-to-day variations in water volume per unit area of reef. The approach can be applied at any time of day, but night-time measurements should be free from the vagaries of large changes in metabolic rate in response to subtle variations in available light (or other limiting constraints). Moreover, measurements near low tide should maximize S, thus making q more readily discernible than would otherwise be the case.

Once an average K value is derived, it can then be applied in equation (1) to calculate D for each sampling time. The D values so calculated are positive when gas diffuses out of the water (day-time) and negative when it diffuses in (night-time).

A comparison can be made between wind tunnel data reported by Kanwisher (1963) and the biologically derived estimates reported by Kinsey (Chapter 35). Figure 2 shows Kanwisher's values (as calculated for a temperature of 25°C from the exit coefficients which he reports) and the best exponential regression line through those points. Kinsey's average estimates under two different field situations are also shown. Kanwisher's wind speeds were measured 10 cm above the water surface, while Kinsey's wind speeds are estimates. Nevertheless, the comparison is useful. Kinsey's values are higher than those of Kanwisher at low wind speeds but increase less rapidly with increasing wind. Kanwisher noted that waves seem to accelerate exchange at low wind speeds and decrease it at high speeds. It is possible that this effect explains the difference between his data and those of Kinsey. Nevertheless, over the range of normal tradewinds (about 5 to 9 metres sec^{-1}) the two sets of data agree remarkably well.

It is reasonable to suggest, therefore, that detailed field studies of O_2 gas exchange under the conditions encountered on reef flats are in order. In the absence of data from such detailed studies, the curve presented in Figure 2 probably provides adequate means for making diffusion corrections in most studies. Corrections obtained from such a curve are probably at least as accurate as corrections which might be obtained from a relatively small amount of data collected according to the Odum (1956), Gordon and Kelley (1960), or

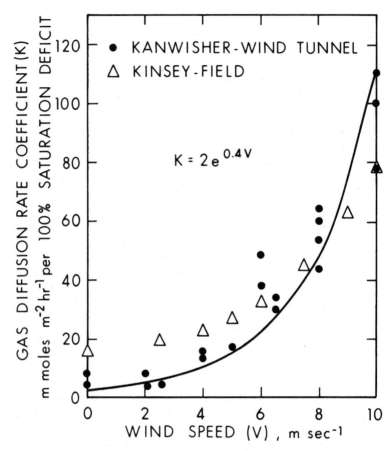

Figure 2
O_2 diffusion as a function of wind velocity.

Kinsey (Chapter 35) techniques. In any case, procedures for making diffusion corrections should be considered as provisional until more detailed studies have been made.

Data on CO_2 gas exchange under field conditions are very limited. Those data which are available (in particular Sigiura et al., 1963, and Park and Hood, 1963) do not yield a clear relationship between the exchange rate and wind velocity, although such a relationship probably does exist. With presently available data, only a likely typical exchange rate can be presented. Let us define an equation similar, but not identical, to equation (1):

$$D = K(P_w - P_a) \tag{3}$$

Again, D is the diffusion rate from the water in moles $m^{-2} hr^{-1}$. The exchange rate constant K has the units moles $m^{-2} hr^{-1}$ per μatm CO_2 partial pressure difference between water and air. P_w is the CO_2 partial pressure in the water (expressed as parts per million, or micro-atmospheres), and P_a is the CO_2 partial pressure of air (about 330 μatm). Until adequate experimental techniques are derived for measuring K under the conditions prevailing on a reef flat, the nominal value of 2×10^{-5} can be used for K. Under most flow respirometry conditions, the CO_2 diffusion rate is probably negligible (see Smith, 1973).

Chemical reactions other than organic carbon metabolism

Chemical reactions other than photosynthesis–respiration alter the CO_2 and O_2 content of waters crossing reef flats. With the present techniques of flow respirometry, these processes will be included with the metabolic processes. Abiotic processes affecting O_2 are probably too slow to be of consequence here. However, the precipitation or solution of $CaCO_3$ lowers or raises the CO_2 content of the water. Smith (1973) estimated that $CaCO_3$ precipitation accounted for up to 40 per cent of the total CO_2 change in water crossing the reef flat. As discussed by Smith and Kinsey (Chapter 36) it is relatively easy to estimate the contribution of $CaCO_3$ reactions to the total CO_2 changes. CO_2 changes from such reactions equal half the change in total alkalinity. It is imperative that two CO_2-related parameters (in practice, usually pH and total alkalinity) be measured in order that the appropriate corrections and calculations can be made.

Measured changes in total O_2 or CO_2 must be corrected for diffusion and chemical changes other than photosynthesis-respiration if accurate productivity estimates are to be obtained. The calculation of the changes and the apportioning thereof can be summarized by the following equations, where X is the mass (in moles) of the material measured, $[X]$ is the molar concentration of the material, $\Delta[X]$ is the change in molar concentration, $\Delta X/\Delta t$ is the rate of change (moles hr^{-1}), D is the area-based rate of diffusion out of the water (moles $m^{-2} hr^{-1}$), T is the volume transport ($m^3 hr^{-1}$) per unit width of reef front (assumed to be 1 m) perpendicular to the direction of water flow, and area (m^2) is calculated as the transect length (m) multiplied by a unit width of reef face (again assumed to be 1 m),

$$\Delta[X] \text{ (whole transect)} = [X] \text{ downstream} - [X] \text{ upstream} \qquad (4)$$

$$\frac{\Delta X}{\Delta t} \text{ (whole transect)} = T \, \Delta[X] \text{ (whole transect)} \qquad (5)$$

$$\frac{\Delta X/\Delta t \text{ (whole transect)}}{\text{Area}} = \text{Net } \frac{\Delta X}{\Delta t} \text{ (per unit area)} \qquad (6)$$

All succeeding calculations are area-based.

$$\text{Net } \frac{\Delta X}{\Delta t} \quad \frac{\Delta X}{\Delta t} \text{ (metabolism)} - D - \frac{\Delta X}{\Delta t} \text{ (other)} \qquad (7)$$

$$\frac{\Delta X}{\Delta t} \text{(metabolism)} = \frac{\Delta X}{\Delta t} \text{(net)} + D + \frac{\Delta X}{\Delta t} \text{(other)} \tag{8}$$

As was discussed above, $\Delta X/\Delta t$ (other) is significant primarily in the case of CO_2 removal by calcification, while D has its primary significance in the case of O_2 measurements. Thus, the choice of the gas to be examined allows some simplification of equation (8).

The diurnal metabolism curve

Values for O_2 or CO_2 changes as a result of metabolic activity can be generated by the procedures which were outlined in the previous section, and these values corrected for diffusion and calcification may be plotted as a function of time of day. The diurnal pattern may be handled in one of several ways. If there is a clear diurnal trend, then a smooth curve may be fitted through the points either by eye or by one of several regression techniques. If the day and night data show too much scatter for the fitting of such a smooth diurnal curve, then the calculation of mean day-time and mean night-time values of O_2 or CO_2 metabolic flux may be the only valid treatment of the data. If community metabolism remains directly responsive to light throughout the day (i.e. saturation light intensities do not occur), then the resultant metabolic curve may be visualized as a day-time half-sine wave and a constant night-time segment (Fig. 1); the latter will yield a square wave of metabolic flux versus time of day. In either case, the resultant curves show the rate of metabolism (moles $m^{-2} hr^{-1}$) between the upstream and the downstream stations as a function of time of day. This rate of change will ordinarily indicate net day-time organic carbon production (on Fig. 1, y is positive; hence O_2 in the water increases and CO_2 decreases) and net organic carbon consumption at night. There are two complications. The times of compensation light intensity (i.e. $y = 0$) may not coincide with sunrise and sunset. Secondly, apparent metabolic lags immediately after sunrise and sunset have been reported.

To calculate the various metabolic parameters, one must initially draw a "respiration baseline' on the diurnal curve (Fig. 1). This line is drawn through the night-time respiration rates after they have achieved a constant value free of any apparent lags. The difference between the 0 metabolism line and the baseline equals r. R is r multiplied by 24, that is the integrated area between the baseline and the 0 line. The parameter y is any instantaneous rate above the 0 line, while p is the instantaneous rate above the baseline. P is the integrated area between the baseline and metabolism curve. E equals P minus R.

The measurement of areas represented on Figure 1 may be accomplished by direct integration if a curve has been fitted to the data by some regression technique. Alternatively, counting squares enclosed by a plot on graph paper, planimetry, or weighing cutouts of the curve and comparing those cutouts with the weights of 'standard areas' may be used.

Comparison of O_2 and CO_2 data

Past studies of O_2 production on coral reefs have usually reported the data in terms of grams O_2 per unit volume of water or per unit (map) area of reef surface. For simplicity of comparison, it seems most reasonable to report both O_2 and CO_2 in terms of molar concentrations. According to the simplified and generalized photosynthetic equation, one mole of CO_2 utilized equals one mole of O_2 released:

$$CO_2 + H_2O = CH_2O + O_2 \tag{9}$$

Hence, the comparison between O_2 and CO_2 is facilitated by reporting the values in the molar quantities. Most reef metabolism studies in which the conversion from O_2 metabolic flux to carbon metabolism has been reported have assumed, implicitly or otherwise, that the $O_2:CO_2$ ratio (the metabolic quotient) is 1.0. Qasim and Sankaranarayanan (1970) have used Ryther's (1956) suggested value of 1.2 for aquatic communities. The data of Smith and Marsh (1973) and Kinsey (Chapter 35) suggest that the most appropriate metabolic quotient for coral reef communities may lie between this suggested value and 1.0. Smith and Marsh (1973) point out that the assumption of any value for this quotient other than 1.0 is probably not justified in the absence of an explicit gas exchange correction to the O_2 data.

SUMMARY

The methodology for measuring the productivity of coral reefs in simple flowing water regimes is straightforward, and this methodology can be modified for use in other, more complex régimes.

Imprecise uses of terms and statements of assumptions have produced some confusion in the literature. Such imprecisions should be avoided in the future.

Both O_2 and CO_2 have advantages and disadvantages as metabolic indicators. The authors recommend that the two be examined together.

The total rates of O_2 and CO_2 changes need to be apportioned between both biotic and abiotic processes in order that a diurnal metabolic curve be constructed.

ACKNOWLEDGEMENTS

This work was partly supported by EPA Grant No R800906, awarded to the University of Hawaii and the paper is contribution No. 58 from the Marine Laboratory of the University of Guam; contribution No. 530 from the Hawaii Institute of Marine Biology.

References

AMERICAN PUBLIC HEALTH ASSOCIATION. 1971. *Standard methods for the examination of water, sewage, and industrial wastes*, 13th edit. Washington, APHA.

CARPENTER, J. H. 1965. The Chesapeake Bay Institute technique for the Winkler dissolved oxygen method. *Limnol. Oceanogr.*, vol. 10, p. 141–3.

DAHL, A. L. 1973. Surface area in ecological analysis: quantification of benthic coral-reef algae. *Mar. Biol.*, vol. 23, p. 239–49.

DOTY, M. S. 1971. Antecedent event influence on benthic algal standing crops in Hawaii. *J. exp. mar. Biol. Ecol.*, vol. 6, p. 161–6.

GORDON, M. S.; KELLY, H. M. 1962. Primary productivity of an Hawaiian coral reef: a critique of flow respirometry in turbulent waters. *Ecology*, vol. 43, p. 473–80.

GREEN, E. J.; CARRITT, D. E. 1967. New tables for oxygen saturation of seawater. *J. mar. Res.*, vol. 25, p. 140–7.

KANWISHER, J. 1963. On the exchange of gases between the atmosphere and the sea. *Deep-sea Res.*, vol. 10, p. 195–207.

KINSEY, D. W.; DOMM, ALISON. 1974. Effects of fertilization on a coral reef environment—primary production studies. In: *Proc. Second. Int. Coral Reef Symp.* Brisbane, Great Barrier Reef Committee, vol. 1, p. 49–66.

KOHN, A. J.; HELFRICH, P. 1957. Primary organic productivity of a Hawaiian coral reef. *Limnol. Oceanogr.*, vol. 2, p. 241–51.

LITTLER, M. M. 1973. The productivity of Hawaiian fringing-reef crustose Corallinaceae and an experimental evaluation of production methodology. *Limnol. Oceanogr.*, vol. 18, p. 946–52.

MARSH, J. A. Jr. 1974. Preliminary observations on the productivity of a Guam reef flat community. *Proc. Second Int. Coral Reef Symp.* Brisbane, Great Barrier Reef Committee, vol. 1, p. 139–45.

NIXON, R. S.; OVIATT, C. A.; ROGERS, C.; TAYLOR, K. 1971. Mass and metabolism of a mussel bed. *Oecologia*, vol. 81, p. 21–30.

ODUM, H. T. 1956. Primary production in flowing waters. *Limnol. Oceanogr.*, vol. 1, p. 102–17.

——; HOSKIN, C. M. 1958. Comparative studies on the metabolism of marine waters. *Publ. Inst. Mar. Sci.*, Univ. Texas, vol. 5, p. 16–46.

——; ODUM, E. P. 1955. Trophic structure and productivity of a windward coral reef community on Eniwetok Atol. *Ecol. Monogr.*, vol. 25, p. 291–320.

PARK, P. K.; HOOD, D. W. 1963. Radiometric field measurements of CO_2 exchange from the atmosphere to the sea. *Limnol. Oceanogr.*, vol. 8, p. 287–9.

QASIM, S. A.; SANKARANARAYANAN, V. N. 1970. Production of particulate matter by the reef on Kavaratti Atoll (Laccadives). *Limnol. Oceanogr.*, vol. 15, p. 574–8.

RIEDL, R.; SCHWENKE, H. 1971. In: Kinne, O. (ed.). *Marine ecology*, New York, Wiley–Interscience, vol. 1, part 2, Chap. 5.

RYTHER, J. H. 1956. The measurement of primary production. *Limnol. Oceanogr.*, vol. 1, p. 72–84.

SARGENT, M. C.; AUSTIN, T. S. 1949. Organic productivity of an atoll. *Trans. Am. geophys. Union*, vol. 30, p. 245–9.

——; ——. 1954 *Biologic economy of coral reefs*. U.S. Geol. Survey (Prof. Paper. 260-E), p. 293–300.

SMITH, S. V. 1973. Carbon dioxide dynamics: a record of organic carbon production, respiration, and calcification in the Eniwetok reef flat community. *Limnol. Oceanogr.*, vol. 18, p. 106–20.

——. 1974. Coral reef carbon dioxide metabolism. In: *Proc. Second Int. Coral Reef Symp.* Brisbane, Great Barrier Reef Committee, vol. 1, p. 79–85.

——; JOKIEL, P. L. 1975. Water composition and biochemical gradients in Canton Atoll Lagoon. 2. Budgets of phosphorus, nitrogen, carbon dioxide and particulate material. *Mar. Science Comm.* vol. 1, p. 165–207.

——. MARSH, Jr., J. A. 1973. Organic carbon production on the windward reef flat of Eniwetok Atoll. *Limnol. Oceanogr.*, vol. 18, p. 953–61.

——; PESRET, F. 1974. Processes of carbon dioxide flux in the Fanning Island Lagoon. *Pac. Sci.*, vol. 28, p. 225–45.

STRICKLAND, J. D. H.; PARSONS, T. R. 1968. A practical handbook of seawater analysis. *Bull. Fish. Res. Bd Can.*, Ottawa, Queen's Printer, no. 167, (311 p.).

SUGIURA, Y.; IBERT, E. R.; HOOD, D. W. 1963. Mass transfer of CO_2 across sea surfaces. *J. mar. Res.*, vol. 21, p. 11–24.

VOLLENWEIDER, R. A. (ed.). 1969. *A manual on methods for measuring primary production in aquatic environments*. Oxford and Edinburgh, Blackwell Scientific Publications. (IBP Handbook 12). (224 p.).

WEISS, R. F. 1970. The solubility of nitrogen, oxygen, and argon in water and seawater. *Deep-sea Res.*, vol. 17, p. 721–35.

WESTLAKE, D. F. 1967. Some effects of low-velocity currents on the metabolism of aquatic macrophytes. *J. exp. Bot.*, vol. 18, p. 187–205.

WHITFORD, L. A.; SCHUMACHER, G. J. 1961. Effect of current on mineral uptake and respiration by a freshwater alga. *Limnol. Oceanogr.*, vol. 6, p. 423–5.

26

Measurement and interpretation of photosynthesis and respiration in reef corals

L. R. McCloskey[1], D. S. Wethey[2]
and J. W. Porter[3]

The metabolism of coelenterates harbouring symbiotic dinoflagellates has intrigued investigators since the Hertwig brothers (1879) first suggested that the 'yellow cells' in actinians were algae. Subsequently, Brandt (1883) postulated that the zooxanthellae act as analogues of chloroplasts by supplying dissolved photosynthates to their host tissues. Research since then has diverged into studies concentrating on the biochemical aspects of this symbiotic relationship (reviewed in Muscatine, 1973) and studies focusing on the oxygen balance of these organisms (Table 1). The stated, or implied, objective of most of the oxygen studies was to compare rates of photosynthesis and respiration in an attempt to reveal the degree to which carbon fixed by the zooxanthellae meets the needs of the symbiotic complex. This paper has three interconnecting objectives: 1, to point out the metabolic complexities and theoretical assumptions implicit in studies of this kind; 2, to review the methodology best suited for acquiring interpretable data in oxygen studies of these symbionts; and 3, to suggest lines of investigation useful in uniting the biochemical and physiological researches as they pertain to the construction of total carbon and total energy budgets for these organisms.

INTERPRETATION OF PHOTOSYNTHETIC AND RESPIRATORY DATA

Production (P) and respiration (R) are often expressed as a simple ratio (P/R). Since the ratio is a dimensionless quantity, it is not necessary to make estimates of an organism's biomass or its surface area when using this expression of production. Since both biomass and surface area have proved exceptionally difficult to measure in corals, this ratio has been frequently utilized in coral physiology studies (Beyers, 1966; Kanwisher and Wainwright, 1967; Roffman, 1968; Franzisket, 1969; McCloskey and Chesher, 1971; Pillai and Nair, 1972;

1. Department of Biological Sciences, Walla Walla College, College Place, Washington 99324, U.S.A.
2. Division of Biological Sciences, University of Michigan, Ann Arbor, Michigan 48109, U.S.A.
3. School of Natural Resources, University of Michigan, Ann Arbor, Michigan 48109, U.S.A.

TABLE 1. Respiration, production, and P/R ratios given in the literature for reef corals. Numbers italicized have been calculated from data in the original paper.

Reference/Locality Species	Size	(R) O_2 uptake per hour	(P_n) O_2 generation per hour	gross P/R	length of expt. (hrs.)	units of O_2/hr
Verwey (1930)/Indonesia						
Acropora hebes	61.0 g	1.483	1.55	2.05 max	6 (P)	cc/1
Verwey (1931)/Indonesia						
Acropora hebes	71.3 g	0.0129 (0.087)	ng	} 3.4–5.1[a]	7½ (R)	,,
,, ,,	73.1 g	ng	0.316 (0.358)		8 (P)	,,
,, ,,	60.9 g	ng	1.623	} 2.09	5½ (P)	,,
,, ,,	60.5 g	1.483	ng		7⅓ (R)	,,
Yonge and Nicholls (1931)/ GBR						
Psammocora gonagra	9 cc	0.063	−0.032	0·51[b]	9	,,
,, ,,	9 cc	0.069	−0.017	0.24[b]	,,	,,
,, ,,	7.5 cc	0.067	−0.014	0.22[b]	,,	,,
,, ,,	6 cc	0.047	0.002	1.05[b]	,,	,,
Yonge et al. (1932)/GBR						
Hydnophora microconus	53 cc	0.178	0.431	3.43	,,	,,
Psammocora gonagra	190 cc	0.303	−0.103	0·66	,,	,,
Lobophyllia corymbosa	150 cc	0.288	0.051	1.18	,,	,,
Pavona danae	45 cc	0.213	0.066	1.31	,,	,,
Cyphastrea chalcidicum	200 cc	0.231	0.061	1.26	,,	,,
Porites sp.	145 cc	0.237	0.171	1.72	,,	,,
,,	130 cc	0.301	0.365	2.21	,,	,,
Favia sp.	157 cc	0.331	0.329	1.99	,,	,,
,,	120 cc	0.273	0.421	2.54	,,	,,
Galaxea fascicularis	45 cc	0.121	0.099	1.82	,,	,,
,, ,,	43 cc	0.192	0.186	1.96	,,	,,
Fungia danae	31 cc	0.210	0.281	2.34	,,	,,
,, ,,	32 cc	0.252	0.512	3.03	,,	,,
Pocillopora bulbosa	28 cc	0.314	0.650	3.07	,,	,,
,, ,,	45 cc	0.350	0.874	3.50	,,	,,
Flabellum rubrum	6 cc	0.054	0.048	1.88	,,	,,
Millepora sp.	23 cc	0.127	0.092	1.73	,,	,,
,,	30 cc	0.187	0.075	1.40	,,	,,
Heliopora sp.	35 cc	0.132	0.091	1.69	,,	,,
,,	90 cc	0.256	0.140	1.55	,,	,,
Fungia danae	75 cc	0.587	−0.063	0.89 (11½ hrs) 0.43 (24 hrs)	27	,,
,, ,,	39 cc	0.481	−0.048	0.90 (11½ hrs) 0.43 (24 hrs)	,,	,,
Galaxea fascicularis	74 cc	0.348	0.175	1.50 (11½ hrs) 0.72 (24 hrs)	,,	,,
,, ,,	70 cc	0.311	0.211	1.68 (11½ hrs) 0.80 (24 hrs)	,,	,,
Psammocora gonagra	56 cc	0.769	−0.288	0.81 (11½ hrs) 0.39 (24 hrs)	,,	,,
,, ,,	48 cc	0.714	0.117	1.16 (11½ hrs) 0.56 (24 hrs)	,,	,,
Favia sp.	119 cc	0.547	−0.101	0.82 (11½ hrs) 0.39 (24 hrs)	,,	,,
Porites sp.	142 cc	0.211	−0.032	0.85 (11½ hrs) 0.41 (24 hrs)	,,	,,

TABLE 1—*continued*

Reference/Locality Species	Size	(R) O_2 uptake per hr	(P_n) O_2 generation per hour	P/R gross	length of expt. (hrs.)	units of O_2/hr
Kawaguti (1937)/Palau						
Pavona praetorta (dark)	7.2 g	0·0271	ng	6.7 max	1.7	mg/g
	6.0 g	ng	0.1656		1.0	
Merulina ampliata	11.2 g	0.0086	ng	9.1	1.7	,,
	13.5 g	ng	0.0714		1.0	
Millepora	6.0 g	0.0200	ng	3.7	1.5	,,
	5.8 g	ng	0.0526		1.0	
Lobophyllia (flat)	29.0 g	0.0171	ng	3.2	1.7	,,
	32.0 g	ng	0.0386		1.0	
Acrehelia horrescens	9.0 g	0.0343	ng	5.9	0.5	,,
	5.5 g	ng	0.1699		1.5	
Seriatopora hystrix	10.5 g	0.0257	ng	5.3	0.6	,,
	7.0 g	ng	0.1128		1.5	
Fungia actiniformis	13.2 g	0.0428	ng	7.7	2.0	,,
	4.0 g	ng	0.2999		1.0	
Montipora ramosa	9.0 g	0.0288	ng	4.2	3.5	,,
	12.0 g	ng	0.1628		3.0	
Psammocora contigua (brown)	12.0 g	0.0300	ng	4.5	1.0	,,
	9.0 g	ng	0.1042		1.5	
Goniastrea aspera	25.5 g	0.0300	ng	1.7	1.0	,,
	61 5 g	ng	0.0200		1.0	
Acropora palawensis	13.0 g	0.0243	ng	2.9	2.0	,,
	13.0 g	ng	0.0443		1.5	
Porites sp.	35.0 g	0.0139	ng	2.1	1.5	,,
	10.5 g	ng	0.0157		1.0	
Halomitra robusta	325.0 g	0.0129	ng	3.7	3.0	,,
	12.0 g	ng	0.0343		1.0	
Goniopora sp.	28.0 g	0.0043	ng	2.7	1.6	,,
	52.0 g	ng	0.0071		2.0	
Pocillopora damicornis	34.0 g	0.0157	ng	5.9	1.5	,,
	6.2 g	gn	0.1171		1·0	
Psammocora contigua (green)	10.0 g	0.0386	ng	1.8	1.0	,,
	16.0 g	ng	0.0300		1.5	
Pachseris speciosa	10.5 g	0.0300	ng	1.7	1.6	,,
	11.0 g	ng	0.0228		2.0	
Mycedium sp.	12.0 g	0.0257	ng	1.6 max	3.0	,,
	12.0 g	ng	0.0157		1.0	
Acropora (purple)	7.3 g	0.0457	ng	2.9	3.0	,,
	15.0 g	ng	0.0900		3.7	
Caulastrea furcata	12.0 g	0.0171	ng	4.0	1.7	,,
	22.0 g	ng	0.0400		1.0	
Motoda (1940)/Palau						
Goniastrea aspera	8.6 cm^2	0.0288	0.0457	3.0		mg/cm^{2c}
	$\bar{x}25$	$\bar{x}12$	$\bar{x}13$			
Odum and Odum (1955)/ Eniwetok						
Millepora	ng	ng	ng	>1.0	24	
Porites sp.	ng	ng	ng	>1.0	24	
Heliopora sp.	ng	ng	ng	>1.0	24	
Odum et al. (1959) Puerto Rico						

381

TABLE 1—*continued*

Reference/Locality Species	Size	(R) O_2 uptake per hr	(P_n) O_2 generation per hour	P/R gross	length of expt. (hrs.)	units of O_2/hr
Porites	ng	ng	ng	>1.0	24	
Goreau (1960)/Jamaica						
Meandrina brasiliensis	ng	*0.0017*	*0.0003*	*0.17*	ng	mg/mgN
Beyers (1966)/Puerto Rico						
Porites furcata	10.8 cm^2	11.1	10.7	0.96[d]	24	gCO / m^2/day
Millepora alcicornis	32.7 cm^2	4.4	3.3	0.75[d]	,,	,,
Roos (1967)/Curacao						
Porites astreoides	ng	0.624	−0.174	*0.72*[e]	ng	mg/l
,, ,,	,,	0.624	−0.354	*0.43*[e]	,,	,,
,, ,,	,,	0.624	−0.420	*0.33*	,,	,,
Kanwisher and Wainwright (1967)/Florida						
Siderastrea siderea	ng	ng	ng	2.10 max	>1	ng
Porites divaricata	,,	,,	,,	3.40 ,,	,,	,,
Favia fragum	,,	,,	,,	2.30 ,,	,,	,,
Manicina areolata	,,	,,	,,	2.40 ,,	,,	,,
Montastrea annularis	,,	,,	,,	2.90 ,,	,,	,,
Oculina diffusa	,,	,,	,,	5.00 ,,	,,	,,
Mussa angulosa	,,	,,	,,	1.90 ,,	,,	,,
Isophyllia multiflora	,,	,,	,,	5.00 ,,	,,	,,
Colypophyllia sp.	,,	,,	,,	3.20 ,,	,,	,,
Roffman (1968)/Eniwetok						
Fungia fungites	,,	ng 1.8	ng 4.7	5.10 max 3.90 $\bar{x}^4$	$\frac{1}{2}$–2 ,,	mg O_2
Acropora reticulata	,,	ng 8.4	ng 5.9	2.70 max 1.90 $\bar{x}$ 11	,,	,,
Acropora diversa	,,	ng 2.7	ng 1.4	1.70 max 1.50 $\bar{x}$ 10	,,	,,
Porites (?) lutea	,,	ng 0.67	ng 0.87	2.90 max 2.40 $\bar{x}$ 6	,,	,,
Porites monticulosa	,,	ng 2.2	ng 2.6	2.90 max 2.30 $\bar{x}$ 11	,,	,,
Pavona clavus	,,	ng 1.25	ng 0.90	2.10 max 1.75 $\bar{x}$ 4	,,	,,
Pocillopora verrucosa/elegans	,,	ng 2.3	ng 2.4	2.80 max 2.25 $\bar{x}$ 33	,,	,,
Gramoni (1968)/Galapagos						
Pocillopora sp.	,,	0.304	0.453	1.49	ng	mg/g
,,	,,	0.146	0.374	2.56	,,	,,
Psammocora sp.	,,	0.126	0.407	3.23	,,	,,
Pavona sp.	,,	0.116	0.193	1.66	,,	,,
Porites sp.	,,	0.072	0.075	1.04	,,	,,
Franzisket (1959)/Hawaii						
Porites compressa	30–50 g	ng	ng	2.92–4.35	ng	ml O_2
Pocillopora meandrina	,,	,,	,,	3.12–3.38	,,	,,
Montipora verrucosa	,,	,,	,,	3.45–3.91	,,	,,
Fungia scutaria	,,	,,	,,	3.25–4.05	,,	,,

382

TABLE 1—*continued*

Reference/Locality Species	Size	(R) O_2 uptake per hr	(P_n) O_2 generation per hour	P/R gross	length of expt. (hrs.)	units of O_2/hr
Pillai and Nair (1972)/India						
Acropora corymbosa	90 g	0.0257	0.0301	2.17 max	1	mg/g
	72 g	0.0275	0.0411	2.49 ,,	,,	,,
Acropora erythraea	72 g	0.0233	0.0453	2.94 ,,	,,	,,
	70 g	0.0211	0.0334	2.58 ,,	,,	,,
Cyphastrea microphthalma	110 g	0.0082	0.0121	2.47 ,,	,,	,,
	102 g	0.0066	0.0085	2.29 ,,	,,	,,
Favia pallida	142 g	0.0077	0.0126	2.64 ,,	,,	,,
	115 g	0.0066	0.0127	2.92 ,,	,,	,,
Favites abdita	88 g	0.0059	0.0034	1.57 ,,	,,	,,
	84 g	0.0031	0.0132	4.94 ,,	,,	,,
Goniastrea pectinata	98 g	0.0027	0.0035	2.30 ,,	,,	,,
	102 g	0.0066	0.0055	2.20 ,,	,,	,,
Goniopora stokesi	125 g	0.0154	0.0379	3.46 ,,	,,	,,
	90 g	0.0158	0.0270	2.71 ,,	,,	,,
Montipora divaricata	107 g	0.0170	0.0321	2.89 ,,	,,	,,
	70 g	0.0186	0.0509	3.74 ,,	,,	,,
Pocillopora damicornis	64 g	0.0314	0.0628	3.00 ,,	,,	,,
	90 g	0.0261	0.0529	3.03 ,,	,,	,,
Porites solida	100 g	0.0058	0.0107	2.84 ,,	,,	,,
	107 g	0.0037	0.0136	4.68 ,,	,,	,,
Wells et al. (1973)/Virgin Islands						
Acropora cervicornis	ng	ng	ng	2.76 max 0.87[f]	ng	ml O_2
		,,	,,			
Montastrea cavernosa	,,	,,	,,	2.90 max 0.89[f]	,,	,,
		,,	,,			
Manicina areolàta var. danaei	,,	,,	,,	2.84 max 0.79[f]	,,	,,
		,,	,,		,,	,,
Mussa angulosa	,,	,,	,,	1.15 max	,,	,,
Manicina aerolata var. areolata	,,	,,	,,	2.91 max	,,	,,
Colpophyllia natans	,,	,,	,,	1.87 max	,,	,,
Siderastrea siderea	,,	,,	,,	2.15 max		
Drew (1973)/Red Sea						
Millepora tenera	,,	0.0048	0.0086	1.89	,,	mg/g
Goniastrea sp.	,,	0.0015	0.0021	1.70	,,	,,
Acropora sp.	,,	0.0048	0.0102	2.05	,,	,,

a. dependent upon calculation of respiration due to unfiltered water
b. subjected to following pretreatment for 137 days: 0.51—starved in light; 0.24—fed in dark; 0.22—starved in dark; 1.05—fed in light
c. assuming 2 polyps occupy 1.0 cm^2
d. note that this is based on CO_2 rather than O_2; each value on average of 3
e. dependent upon angle of incidence of light
f. integrated values with P being considered + values of O_2 only

Drew, 1973; Wethey and Porter, 1976b). The use of this ratio came from studies of phytoplankton in which photosynthesis releases carbohydrates within the cell where they are metabolized. In a symbiotic association, this is not necessarily the case: the zooxanthellae photosynthesize short-chain carbon compounds such as glycerol and alanine (among other things), use some of these photosynthates for their own basal and growth metabolism, and translocate some to the animal partner (Muscatine 1967; Von Holt and Von Holt, 1968; Muscatine and Cernichiari, 1969; Muscatine et al., 1972; Lewis and Smith, 1971; Trench, 1971a, 1974). The P/R ratio of a coral head does not reveal how much, if any, of the photosynthetically fixed carbon is actually shared with the host tissue. It has been estimated that 35 to 50 per cent of the algal photosynthate is actually translocated (Muscatine and Cernichiari, 1969; see also Trench, 1971a, 1974). Presumably the other 50 to 65 per cent of the photosynthate is used by the zooxanthellae in growth, reproduction, and repair.

Originally, the P/R ratio was used to estimate the compensation light intensity for the symbiotic association where the P/R ratio equalled unity. It was assumed that a value of 1.0 for the ratio meant that as much carbon was fixed in photosynthesis as was utilized in respiration by the coral and zooxanthellae. A P/R ratio > 1.0 was interpreted to mean that photosynthetically fixed carbon exceeded basal metabolic demands and was available for growth and reproduction. Conversely, a P/R ratio < 1.0 was interpreted to mean that the coral utilized more carbon than was fixed. If a coral with a $P/R < 1.0$ is not retrogressing, then additional carbon must be supplied by zooplankton feeding (Porter 1974), uptake of dissolved organics (Stephens, 1962), bacterial feeding (Sorokin, 1972, 1973, 1974; Di Salvo, 1971), deposit feeding (Goreau et al., 1971), or by several of these methods. If only 30 to 50 per cent of the photosynthate is actually incorporated into host coral tissue, it is likely that a true compensation depth will be shallower since P/R ratios in excess of 1.0 will be required to meet fully the metabolic requirements of the coral–algal association. The high (2.0 to 5.0) P/R values reported in some of the studies (Table 1) make more plausible, but do not prove, the possibility that the zooxanthellae supply at least the basal metabolic requirements of the coral under the conditions in those experiments. A coral with a P/R ratio less than 1.0 may still, however, be receiving translocation products.

Adding to the difficulty inherent in using the P/R ratio is the fact that neither P nor R has been uniformly defined. In most of the studies in which values of production or respiration for symbiotic coelenterates are reported, P and R are not defined at all, making interpretation, or meaningful comparisons, of the data impossible. P has been expressed as the total amount of oxygen produced over a 24-hour cycle, as an oxygen production rate per unit time, as the net production without correction for coral or algal respiration, and as a gross production after some respiration value is added to the daytime evolution of oxygen. Respiration has been expressed as a night-time oxygen or carbon consumption value without a day-time consumption value being included, as a value double the 12 hour nightly consumption value, or as a rate of consumption during night-time or simulated dark conditions during the day. A variety of combinations and permutations of these 'values' have been used to compute a P/R ratio. Of the studies presenting P/R ratios, we have placed only those for scleractinian corals in Table 1.

TERMINOLOGY

If the P/R ratio can be adequately defined, it will be valuable for several reasons: 1, it does not require laborious determination of biomass or area units; 2, it is a sound measure of the relative trophic dependence of a coral head on its internally autotrophically fixed carbon, and, by subtraction, on heterotrophically derived carbon; and 3, it should permit a clearer understanding of the disproportionately high animal to plant biomass apparently sustained on coral reefs. On the other hand, P and R of host coral and algae should be known individually too. P will, and R may, change over time and environmental gradients such as depth or sediment load in the water. Thus, coral animal and algal metabolic rates must be known separately before an accurate evaluation of the effect of environmental variables can be made. The respiratory and caloric requirements of the coral animal can be met from other sources, and consequently its respiratory demands must be known in isolation from those of its zooxanthellae. This accurately compartmentalized data will also relate to the question of the carbon and caloric dependence of the coral animal upon its zooxanthellae.

The following procedure and formulae are largely adapted from Muscatine et al. (in preparation) and Muscatine and Porter (1977). A reasonable approach to the oxygen and carbon balance of corals and other algal–animal associations is facilitated by redefining P/R as the per centage of the total daily carbon required by the animal (coelenterate tissue alone) which is supplied by its symbiotic algae (zooxanthellae). Net photosynthesis (P_z net) represents the pool of fixed carbon which potentially can be shared with the host animal; but, as mentioned, only a part of the net production is actually translocated to the host. Therefore, to obtain the percent of required carbon which is supplied to the host, P_z net must be corrected for translocation. The formula for P/R then becomes

$$P/R = \frac{\% \text{ contribution}}{\text{by zooxanthellae}} = \frac{(P_z \text{ net}) (\% \text{ translocation})}{R_a 24} \tag{1}$$

where $R_a 24 =$ the total carbon catabolism by the host animal over a 24 hour period. We assume that R_z night is satisfied by non-translocated photosynthetic products retained within the algae. Hence the estimate of the per centage contribution of the algae to animal carbon requirements does not include the night-time respiration value for the algae.

Practically, there are technical difficulties with obtaining this ideal P/R.

Foremost, neither P_z net nor R_a24 are directly measurable. R_a and R_z (respiration of animal and algal fractions respectively) must be calculated by applying a 'biomass ratio' (ideally the relative proportion of metabolically active animal and algal biomass) to total coral respiration (R_c). $P_z$net, then, would be calculated as

$$P_z \text{ net daylight } = \int P_z \text{ gross } - R_z \text{ daylight} \qquad (2)^4$$

where P_z gross = total apparent or measured productivity of the coral head in the light (or P_c net) + respiration of the coral colony (R_a daylight + R_z daylight), and R_z daylight is assumed to be = night respiration rate (animal + algae × time of photosynthetic activity × biomass ratio of zooxanthellae

$$\left[\text{i.e. } \frac{R_z}{(R_a + R_z)} \right],$$

or

$$R_z \text{ daylight} = R_c \text{ dark } \times \text{ time } \times \frac{R_z}{R_a + R_z}. \qquad (3)$$

R_a24, in turn, is calculated as

$$R_a24 = 24\{(\bar{x}R_c/\text{hr}) \text{ (animal biomass ratio)}\} \qquad (4)$$

where the animal biomass ratio is $R_a/(R_a + R_z)$.

Direct measurements of P_z net have not been possible since to do so would require the zooxanthellae to be removed from the coral colony. Some other value might be measured on the free-living stage of the zooxanthellae while separate from the animal, but the zooxanthellae behave differently in the coral than when removed from it (Trench, 1971b; Muscatine *et al.*, 1972). Thus the extrapolation of production or respiration data from isolated zooxanthellae to those in the living animal is not useful.[5]

R_c must be estimated during the day from measurements made during the night. Direct respiration measurements of its subcomponents, R_a and R_z, can not be made (either day or night) since the animal tissue contains the respiring algal cells; removal of the algal cells would cause unnatural stresses.

Estimation of R_a and R_z by multiplying the measured respiration rate of

4. The derivation of formula (2) is:

$$P_z \text{ net daylight} = P_z \text{ gross} - R_z24$$
$$= P_z \text{ gross} - R_z \text{ daylight} - R_z \text{ night}-$$

But, since R_z night is satisfied by translocation, then,

$$P_z \text{ net daylight} = P_z \text{ gross} - R_z \text{ daylight}.$$

5. A potentially fruitful line of investigation for directly determining P_z gross could come from the complete inhibition of R_c (including both R_a and R_z) for very short time intervals (with zooxanthellae respiration stopped, long inhibitory time intervals would also affect production). Another area in which considerable research might be directed is toward differential inhibition of R_a and R_z. This would allow a more direct and accurate determination of P_z net. As this paper goes to print, the authors have not been able to do this, although respiratory inhibitors tested to date show some promise (R. Tetley, pers. comm.).

the coral head (R_c) by the per cent biomass of the plant versus animal tissue, assumes that equal biomasses of plant and animal tissue respire equal quantities of oxygen. The percentage of protein in the animal and algal fractions of a coral head can be obtained by separation of the zooxanthellae and coral tissue through density gradient centrifugation (Muscatine *et al.*, in preparation). The best estimates of biomass ratios are from measurements by Muscatine *et al.* (in preparation) on homogenates of *Pocillopora damicornis* and *Fungia scutaria* in which approximately 5 per cent of the total protein in the coral head is algal protein, and from estimates by Patton *et al.* (in preparation) on *P. damicornis* in which 10 to 15 per cent of the total protein is algal. In contrast, Muscatine and Cernichiari (1969) initially reported 39 to 59 per cent algal protein in *P. damicornis*. It may not, however, be safe to assume parity of respiration rates between plant and animal tissue based on these experiments.[6] In any case, it appears likely that considerably less than half of the observed respiration is due to the algal component. Any estimates of total caloric requirements of the coral animal, based on respiration rates of an intact coral head, must be decreased by the relative proportion of animal biomass (Porter, 1974).

R_c rate, obtained by simply measuring the oxygen metabolized by the coral at night, is assumed to be indicative of daytime respiration as well. This is obviously a tenuous and untested assumption, R_c during daylight possibly could be measured using photosynthetic inhibitors like DCMU for short durations, but cannot at present be directly measured.[7]

Given the technical difficulties of determining translocation factors and biomass ratios, and the fact that much potentially useful data on coral respiration would be lost if the P/R ratio of formula (1) were rigidly held, we present an alternate method for determining P/R in corals.

In practice, one actually measures 'apparent' production, or P_c net. P_c net plus respiration of the animal alone (R_a) during the period of photosynthesis is the net production of the zooxanthellae:

$$P_z \text{ net} = \int P_c \text{ net} + R_a(t) \qquad (5)$$

where R_a = respiration rate of the coral corrected for per cent biomass; i.e. $(R_c)[R_a/(R_a + R_z)]$; (t) is the time period of measurable photosynthetic activity. On the other hand, gross production $[P_z \text{ gross}]$ is more readily obtained with-

6. R_a might be measured after the zooxanthellae have been removed from the coral by application of an artificial stress (such as retaining the coral in prolonged darkness), or by the measurement of the respiration rate of an ahermatypic coral (species lacking zooxanthellae); but these methods seem too stressful or indirect to prove useful at this stage of research. Since correlations have been reported between cytochrome-c oxidase activity and respiration measurements, perhaps a technique for assaying the activity of this enzyme in the animal fraction could be developed. This would provide a more valid estimate of the per cent animal respiration in a whole coral head.
7. Vandermuelen *et al.* (1972) reported that R_c daylight might be measured with the application of DCMU, a photosynthesis inhibitor. The problem with this is that DCMU also inhibits calcification via a shutdown of the photosynthetic process. Calcification requires respiration (Chalker and Taylor 1975) and is a normal part of R_c daylight. Consequently, R_c daylight values measured under DCMU inhibition will give artificially low readings.

out application of a biomass factor:

$$P_z \text{ gross} = \int P_c \text{ net} + R_c(t) \qquad (6)$$

Since $R_c = R_a + R_z$, as R_a increases relative to R_z, P_z net approaches P_z gross. And, by the same reasoning, R_a 24 approaches R_c 24. Therefore, if 80 to 95 per cent of the coral is animal biomass (op. cit.),

$$\frac{P_z \text{ gross}}{R_c 24} \rightarrow \frac{P_z \text{ net}}{R_a 24}. \qquad (7)$$

This still does not incorporate the per cent of translocation. We do not yet know the translocation rate for many species of coelenterates. Where data are available, they fall between 35 and 50 per cent. For *Pocillopora damicornis*, the translocation factor is 40 per cent (Muscatine *et al.*, in preparation). We tentatively suggest that one may approximate true P/R, then, as

$$P/R \approx \frac{[P_z \text{ gross}](0.4)}{R_c 24} \qquad (8)$$

where 0.4 is an approximation of the amount of carbon translocated.

P/R data presented simply as

$$P/R = \frac{P_z \text{ gross}}{R_c 24} \qquad (9)$$

will make it possible for later correction of the data when precise metabolic biomass and translocation values become available. All of the P/R data in Table 1 are calculated as in formula (9).

In all these equations, P's and R's can be expressed as rates or as total quantities normalized to biomass. Because P and R differentially shift in magnitude constantly throughout the day we prefer measurement of the net productivity and calculation of the P/R ratio using daily integrated values only. This will prevent further confusion in the literature and be more closely in keeping with their ecological meanings. Finally, respiration or production values are used by the authors to mean either carbon or oxygen metabolism as discussed in the next section.

METHODS OF MEASUREMENT

Environmental conditions

Coral respiration studies have consistently ignored three biological characteristics of corals:

(a) Although photosynthesis does not appear to be deleteriously affected by handling or artificial confinement in incubation chambers, the respiration of a coral head (presumably of the animal tissue primarily) does. This can measurably affect the P/R ratio. An incubation time of more than two hours, in a small chamber without flushing, stresses the organism so much that any interpretation of data collected on corals so treated is highly suspect. As far as possible, the authors have limited incubation times so that the oxygen concentration does not fall below 75 per cent of the original ambient value. This incubation time should also be less than one hour with complete flushing of the chamber between measurement cycles to prevent the buildup of noxious waste products from the experimental coral. Frequent flushing avoids the buildup of mucus which may affect respiration rate measurements in long term incubations (Yonge, 1937; Franzisket, 1970). The best methods to achieve this are the *in situ* semicontinuous automatic flushing system of McCloskey *et al.* (1976, in preparation; see also Wethey and Porter, 1976a), or the *in vivo* flow method of Franzisket (1964) with a flow of one litre per hour in a one litre chamber. Some authors (Roffman, 1968) use a recirculating flow system which does no more than stir the medium, and permits accumulation of metabolic byproducts which may be inhibitory.

Another difficult problem is the treatment of coral specimens underwater. One is faced with the dilemma of handling the specimen as little as possible as it is picked from the reef and placed in the experimental chamber, and the need to be usre that there are no algae or invertebrates attached or in the coral head.[8] Based upon considerable experience in collecting and handling corals, 60 minutes underwater in a good locality may produce only one or two specimens acceptable for respiration experiments.

(b) As it is nearly impossible to duplicate *in situ* light flux, spectral quality, and intensity under laboratory conditions, experiments must be conducted at the depth of experimental interest and with corals acquired at that depth. Probably in response to these depth-related light parameters, coral pigment quality and quantity varies closely with depth: corals collected from as shallow as five metres have an increased chlorophyll concentration compared with corals from one metre (Margalef, 1959; Maragos, 1972; Roth and McCloskey, unpublished manuscript; Kawaguti and Nakayama, 1973; but see also Drew, 1972). The same differences appear to hold true for accessory pigments (Margalef, 1959). Related to these depth dependent pigment changes is the acclimation of the photosynthetic system of the zooxanthellae to ambient light regime (Wethey and Porter, 1976a, b).

(c) Short term measurements of P made under maximum light conditions cannot be extrapolated to a 12-hour daylight period. This is because maximum production [P_c max gross] does not consider the substantial period of non-saturation conditions early and late in the day, nor cloud cover which can decrease the light level below saturation values, or below compensation levels, even in shallow water. Continuous measurements, done *in situ,* and integrated

---

8. Corals usually harbour an astonishing assortment of associates, and it is suspected that many reported measurements of coral metabolism have included these organisms.

over 24 hours produce the only P/R ratio that realistically reflect natural environmental conditions.

Estimation of P/R in varying weather conditions

When P/R is measured *in situ,* the results will be influenced by the particular pattern of cloudy spells and sunshine which characterize that particular day. Light flux, therefore, should be measured, and ideally recorded simultaneously on the same chart recorder tape as the oxygen measurements. The light sensor should be positioned at the same site as the coral undergoing *in situ* measurement. The photosynthesis–radiant flux relationship for the coral may thereby be established (Wethey and Porter, 1976a) by fitting the data to the Michaelis–Menten[9] function (Bliss and James, 1966; Hanson *et al.,* 1967). *In situ* radiant flux on cloudless, overcast, and extremely dark days might be simulated from shore-based radiant flux measurements, and by knowing the vertical extinction coefficient of the water at the study site. The daily light flux may be split into 15 minute increments, the expected productivity estimated from the Michaelis–Menten regression equation, and the productivity values are summed over the entire day along with the night-time respiration values (Wethey and Porter, 1976). P/R can be then estimated as described in earlier sections, for sunny or overcast days.

Compounds measured and preferred units

P and R are usually measured by determining O_2 or CO_2 changes. P/R ratios based upon O_2 changes have been reported (Roffman, 1968); others (Kanwisher and Wainwright, 1967) prefer to change O_2 into CO_2 equivalents, assuming a photosynthetic quotient (PQ) of 1.0 (Smith and Marsh, 1973), and then convert CO_2 to carbon equivalents (CE). All of these are acceptable when presented as ratios (P/R), but if one intends to use the P and R data for assimilation or translocation studies, then carbon equivalents are preferable.[10] When

9. Michaelis–Menten equation.
$$P = \frac{P_{max} \times I}{K_m + I}.$$

10. Considerable confusion exists regarding the conversion of O_2 to CO_2 to C equivalents. The general formula for conversion of ml O_2 to mg C is:

$$\text{mg C} = (1.428 \text{ mg } O_2/\text{ml } O_2) \times \text{ml } O_2 \times \left(\frac{C}{CO_2} = \frac{12}{44}\right) \times \left(\frac{CO_2}{O_2} = \frac{44}{32}\right) \begin{bmatrix} \div PQ = \dfrac{+\Delta O_2}{-\Delta CO_2} \\ \text{or} \\ \times RQ = \dfrac{+\Delta CO_2}{-\Delta O_2} \end{bmatrix}$$

$$= 1{\cdot}428 \times \text{ml } O_2 \times \frac{12}{32} [\div PQ \text{ or } \times RQ]$$

$$= 0.5355 \times \text{ml } O_2 [\div PQ \text{ or } \times RQ]$$

PQ should be used in calculating production values, and RQ for respiration measurements (see Strickland and Parsons, 1972, p. 262, 265). If, as Drew (1973) has pointed out, glycerol is the major photosynthetic product, the PQ is $7/6 = 1.167$. In Drew's experiment, however, glycerol as the major *labelled* photosynthetic product may simply reflect a small pool of glycerol with a high turnover rate. A PQ of 1.167, therefore, may only be used very tentatively. Because of this uncertainty, and the fact that the RQ of corals has not been experimentally determined, we propose the use of a PQ and an RQ of 1.0 until more data become available. See also Raven (1976).

oxygen changes are reported, they should be expressed as mg O_2 rather than ml O_2. In an *in situ* study at 50 metres depth, there is questionable utility in expressing oxygen as the volume it would occupy at the surface. The mass of oxygen is invariate with depth and pressure, and is a better unit.

Biomass measured and preferred units

If ecological comparisons with other organisms are made, or ecological efficiencies are determined, then *P* and *R* data (preferably in carbon units) must be normalized by means of a biomass estimate. In the case of corals this is very difficult. A volume, or wet weight, of an entire colony, rather than being representative of currently living tissue, is an estimate of the biomass history of the colony over its whole life since it includes an extremely high percentage of old skeleton. Since metabolic rates are concerned only with living tissue, the inclusion of the weight of calcium carbonate skeleton only confuses the issue. There are several means of separating tissue components from the skeleton for separate consideration. Chlorophyll can be extracted in acetone (Maragos, 1972; Jeffrey and Humphrey, 1975), and the colony can then be extracted in KOH for Lowry or biuret protein analysis. The colony can be decalcified and wet and dry weights of residues determined, or Kjeldahl nitrogen content measured. This requires large amounts of acid and destroys the skeleton, which might otherwise be used in growth or surface area studies. The tissue can be stripped off with a Water Pik (Johannes and Weibe, 1970). This disrupts the tissue and adds fluid, so wet weights are meaningless, but it is quite satisfactory for preparation of samples for chlorophyll (after filtration), Lowry, or Kjeldahl assay.

Surface area measurements are particularly useful. Since surface area is related to photosynthesis, and to a certain extent feeding capability (Porter, 1976), it is a biologically meaningful quantity which is related to the interaction of the organism with its environment. The estimation of surface area by the aluminium foil method of Marsh (1970) is the most straightforward. Aluminium foil is carefully fitted to the surface of the colony, and is trimmed to avoid overlap. The weight of the foil is a measure of its planar area. Each colony should be wrapped several times, and the mean and variance estimated. Ten estimates usually give confidence limits of plus or minus 5 per cent (Student's *t*, $p < 0.05$). In the case of a species with a high degree of surface relief, such as those in *Acropora* or *Pocillopora*, the surface estimate will be too low, and metabolic rates may be overestimated as a result. Despite this shortcoming, the method allows analysis of data in the field because only a roll of foil and a balance are required. The vaseline method (Odum and Odum, 1955) for measuring surface area relies on its approximation to coral tissue thickness when a cleaned skeleton is dipped in the molten liquid. Dead spots on a colony cannot be discounted with this method which nevertheless may be the most satisfactory for branching morphologies. Differential adhesion to surfaces of greater or less fine surface sculpturing might also bias the method considerably.

A newer, hopefully more promising, colorimetric technique is under development (McCloskey, unpublished). The geometrical method (Dahl, 1973) requires the extrapolation from ideal geometrical forms: cylinders, cones, hemispheres, with corrections applied for surface corrugation for sinusoidal character. This method is most useful in the nondestructive transect sampling of a reef community. In physiological measurements, where the tissue and skeleton will probably be analysed in different ways, this method is of limited use. The planar projection of a coral shadow on a grid for measuring areas (Kanwisher and Wainwright, 1967; Beyers, 1966) assumes that underwater light is unidirectional and that a projection of a surface is the best estimate of the area which is exposed to light. On a reef, however, light is multidirectional (Roos, 1967; Brakel, 1976) and there is a great deal of scattering from suspended particles in the water and reflection from white sand. Unless experimental chambers are covered in black velvet on all sides except that of the light source, the laboratory measurements which assume planar projection area will be biased toward a gross underestimation of the photosynthetically active surface area. This method has been used to allow comparison with the flow respirometry studies (Sargent and Austin, 1949, 1954; Odum and Odum, 1955; Kohn and Helfrich, 1957; Odum *et al.*, 1959; Gordon and Kelly, 1962; Milliman and Mahnken, 1969; Smith and Marsh, 1973) which employed planimeter measurement of hydrographic charts for surface area estimation. It is not recommended for individual corals. Metabolic rates are artificially high when calculated by these means. The authors suggest that in future work, a biomass measurement be made on total living surface area (cm^2), weight of chlorophyll (per gm Chl), chlorophyll per unit surface area, or Lowry or Kjeldahl nitrogen (per gm N). In this way, the great confusion existing in the literature today, with each experimenter using his own method, will not be continued. By determining the coefficient of variation for these three against respiration data, the best parameter for use can be readily determined.

DISCUSSION AND LITERATURE SYNTHESIS

A survey of selected literature on coral photosynthesis, respiration, and P/R is summarized in Table 1. The per hour rate values in the table are expressed, whenever possible, in milligrams oxygen per dry gram tissue, per milligram total nitrogen, or per square centimetre, to allow comparison among the papers using the same units; as yet, no conversion factors between different units have been established. Authors who standardize against colony weight have done so as total weight including skeleton (Kawaguti, 1937; Pillai and Nair, 1972); or as wet weight of organic residue after decalcification (Mayor, 1924); while others express it as 'weight' without giving any indication of what this means (Cary, 1918).

Flow respirometry measurements on whole reefs show a range of possibilities from reef heterotrophy (Gordon and Kelly, 1962; Pillai and Nair, 1972), to balance (Smith and Marsh, 1973), to slight autotrophy (Odum *et al.*, 1959; Odum and Odum, 1955; Kohn and Helfrich, 1957), and to untrustworthy high autotrophy (Pillai and Nair, 1972; Milliman and Mahnken, 1969).

In continuous measurements, done *in situ* under the conditions described previously, integrated P/R ratios give values between 0.7 and 1.8 for most reef corals depending on the depth (McCloskey *et al.*, 1976; Wethey and Porter, 1976b). The wide range of experimental conditions and units of measure applied to previous research in coral physiology makes comparisons of values in the literature questionable at best. The order of magnitude of photosynthesis and respiration has probably been established from these studies, but careful, sensitive measurements need to be made over the full range of environmental conditions and depths experienced by natural populations of the animals before any far-reaching ecological or physiological conclusions can be drawn. A possible cautious conclusion that can be drawn from the literature is that corals are trophically flexible (see also Trench, 1974; Porter, 1974, 1976), that they are autotrophic when light conditions permit, and heterotrophic (in terms of total O_2 or carbon flux) when they do not.

ACKNOWLEDGEMENTS

The research was supported by a U.S. National Science Foundation grant GA-27941 (to LRM); an Organization for Tropical Studies Fellowship from the Rackham School of Graduate Studies, University of Michigan, and an NSF Graduate Fellowship (to DSW); and NSF Grant OCE-7726781, a NOAA–MUST Research Grant 74–1090, and a Rackham Faculty Research Fellowship and Grant (to JWP). Additional support came from à U.S. ERDA grant through the University of Hawaii–Mid Pacific Marine Laboratory, and from U.S. National Science Foundation grants through the Scripps Institution of Oceanography R/V Alpha Helix Program.

R. K. Trench and Leonard Muscatine provided helpful comments on the manuscript.

References

BEYERS, R. J. 1966. Metabolic similarities between symbiotic coelenterates and aquatic ecosystems. *Arch. Hydrobiol.,* vol. 62, p. 273–84.

BLISS, C. I.; JAMES, A. T. 1966. Fitting the rectangular hyperbola. *Biometrics,* vol. 22, p. 573–602.

BRACKEL, W. 1976. The ecology of coral shapes: microhabitat variations in the growth form and skeletal structure of *Porites* on a Jamaican reef. Ph.D. Dissertation, Yale University.

BRANDT, K. 1883. Über die morphologische und physiologisch Bedeutung des Chlorophylls bei Thieren. II. *Mitt. Zool. St. Neapel,* vol. 4, p. 191–302.

CARY, L. R. 1918. A study of respiration in Alcyonaria. *Pap. Dept. Mar. Biol. Carnegie Inst. Wash.,* vol. 12, p. 185–91.

CHALKER, B. E.; TAYLOR, D. L. 1975. Light enhanced calcification, and the role of oxidative phosphorylation in calcification of the coral *Acropora cervicornis. Proc. R. Soc. Lond.* (B: *Biol. Sci.*), vol. 190, p. 323–31.

DAHL, A. L. 1973. Surface area in ecological analysis: quantification of benthic coral-reef algae. *Mar. Biol.*, vol. 23, p. 239–49.

DiSALVO, L. H. 1971. Ingestion and assimilation of bacteria by two scleractian coral species. In H. M. Lenhoff *et al.* (eds.). *Experimental coelenterate biology.* Honolulu, University of Hawaii Press, p. 129–136.

DREW, E. A. 1972. The biology and physiology of alga-invertebrate symbiosis. II. The density of symbiotic algal cells in a number of hermatypic hard corals and alcyonarians from various depths. *J. Exp. mar. Biol. Ecol.*, vol. 9, p. 71–5.

——. 1973. The biology and physiology of alga-invertebrate symbiosis. III. *In situ* measurements of photosynthesis and calcification in some hermatypic corals. *J. Exp. mar. Biol. Ecol.*, vol. 13, p. 165–79.

FRANZISKET, L. 1964. Die Stoffwechselintensität der Riffkorallen und ihre ökologische, phylogenetische und soziologische Bedeutung. *Z. vergl. Physiol.*, vol. 49, p. 91–113.

——. 1969. The ratio of photosynthesis to respiration of reef building corals during a 24 hour period. *Forma et Functio*, vol. 1, p. 153–58.

——. 1970. The effect of mucus on respirometry of reef corals. *Int. Rev. gesamt. Hydrobiol.*, vol. 55, p. 409–12.

GORDON, M. S.; KELLY, H. M. 1962. Primary productivity of an Hawaiian coral reef: a critique of flow respirometry in turbulent waters. *Ecology*, vol. 43, p. 473–80.

GOREAU, T. F. 1960. On the physiological ecology of the coral *Meandrina brasiliensis* (Milne-Edwards and Haime) in Jamaica. *Assoc. Island Mar. Labs. Third Meeting*, p. 17–8. (Abstr.).

——; GOREAU, N. I.; YONGE, C. M. 1971 Reef corals: autotrophs or heterotrophs? *Biol. Bull. Mar. Biol. Lab. Woods. Hole Mass.*, vol. 141, p. 247–260.

GRAMONI, R. 1968. Respiration and photosynthesis in Galápagos corals. *Stanford Oceanogr. Exp. Rept.*, vol. 17, p. 263–70.

HANSON, K. R.; LING, R.; HAVIR, E. 1967. A computer program for fitting Michaelis–Menten data. *Biochem. Biophys. Res. Commun.*, vol. 29, p. 194–97.

HERTWIG, O.; HERTWIG, R. 1879. Die Actinien anatomische und histologische mit besonderer Berücksichtigund des Nervenmuskelsystems untersucht. *Jena Z. Naturw.*, vol. 13, p. 457–640.

JEFFREY, S. W.; HUMPHREY, G. F. 1975. New spectrophotometric equations for determining chlorophylls a, b, c_1, and c_2 in higher plants, algae, and natural phytoplankton. *Biochem. Physiol. Pflanz.*, vol. 167, p. 191–94.

JOHANNES, R. E.; WIEBE, W. J. 1970. A method for determination of coral tissue biomass and composition. *Limnol. Oceanogr.*, vol. 15, p. 822–24.

KANWISHER, J. W.; WAINWRIGHT, S. A. 1967. Oxygen balance in some reef corals. *Biol. Bull. Mar. Biol. Lab. Woods Hole, Mass.*, vol. 133, p. 378–90.

KAWAGUTI, S. 1937. On the physiology of reef corals. 1. On the oxygen exchanges of reef corals. *Palao Trop. biol. Stn Stud.*, vol. 1, p. 187–98.

——; NAKAYAMA, T. 1973. Population densities of zooxanthellae in some reef corals. *Biol. J. Okayama U.*, vol. 16, p. 67–71.

KOHN, A. J.; HELFRICH, P. 1957. Primary organic productivity of a Hawaiian coral reef. *Limnol. Oceanogr.*, vol. 2, p. 241–51.

LEWIS, D. H.; SMITH, D. C. 1971. The autotrophic nutrition of symbiotic marine coelenterates with special reference to hermatypic corals. I. Movement of photosynthetic products between the symbionts. *Proc. R. Soc. Lond.* (B: *Biol. Sci.*), vol. 178, p. 111–29.

MARAGOS, J. E. 1972. A study of the ecology of Hawaiian reef corals. Ph.D. Dissertation, University of Hawaii, 290 p.

MARGALEF, R. 1959. Pigmentos asimiladores extraídos de las colonias de celentéreos de los arrecifes de coral y su significado ecológico. *Invest. Pesq.*, vol. 15, p. 81–101.

MARSH, J. A. 1970. Primary productivity of reef-building calcareous red algae. *Ecology*, vol. 51, p. 255–63.

MAYOR, A. G. 1924. Structure and ecology of Samoan reefs. *Pap. Dept. Mar. Biol. Carnegie Inst. Wash.*, vol. 19, p. 1–25.

McCLOSKEY, L. R.; CHESHER, R. H. 1971. Effects of man-made pollution on the dynamics of coral reefs. In: *Tektite 2: Scientists in the sea.* Washington, D.C., U.S. Dept. of the Interior, p. vi229–vi237.

——; KANWISHER, J. W.; LAWSON, K. D. 1976. *In situ* measurement of coral productivity and a description of an *in situ* respirometer. In: *Third Int. Symp. Coelenterate Biol.* (Abstract).

MILLIMAN, J. D.; MAHNKEN, C. V. W. 1969. Reef productivity measurements. *Atoll. Res. Bull.*, vol. 129, p. 23–41.

Motoda, S. 1940. The environment and the life of the massive reef coral *Goniastrea aspera* Verrill, inhabiting the reef flat in Palao. *Palao Trop. biol. Stn Stud.*, vol. 2, p. 61–104.

Muscatine, L. 1967. Glycerol excretion by symbiotic algae from corals and *Tridacna* and its control by the host. *Science,* vol. 156, p. 516–19.

——. 1973. Nutrition of corals. In: O. A. Jones and R. Endean (eds.). *Biology and geology of coral reefs*, New York, Academic Press, vol. II, p. 77–115.

——; Cernichiari, E. 1969. Assimilation of photosynthetic products of zooxanthellae by a reef coral. *Biol. Bull.,* vol. 137, p. 506–23.

——; Pool, R. R.; Cernichiari, E. 1972. Some factors influencing selective release of soluble organic material by zooxanthellae from reef corals. *Mar. Biol.*, vol. 13, p. 298–308.

——; Porter, J. W. 1977. Reef corals: Mutualistic symbiosis adapted to nutrient-poor environments, *Bio Science,* vol. 27, p. 454–60.

Odum, H. T.; Odum, E. P. 1955. Trophic structure and productivity of a windward coral reef community on Eniwetok Atoll. *Ecol. Monogr.,* vol. 25, p. 291–320.

——; Burkholder, P. R.; Rivero, J. 1959. Measurement of productivity of turtle grass flats, reefs and the Bahia Fosforescente of southern Puerto Rico. *Publ. Inst. Mar. Sci. Univ. Texas,* vol. 6, p. 159–70.

Pillai, C. S. G.; Nair, P. V. R. 1972. Productivity studies on some hermatypic corals by means of both oxygen measurements and ^{14}C method. In: *Proc. Symp. Corals and Coral Reefs, 1969.* Mar. Biol. Ass. India, p. 43–58.

Porter, J. W. 1974. Zooplankton feeding by the Caribbean reef-building coral *Monastrea cavernosa.* In: *Proc. Second. Int. Coral Reef Symp.* Brisbane, Great Barrier Reef Committee, vol. 1, p. 111–25.

——. 1976. Autotrophy, heterotrophy, and resource partitioning in Caribbean reef corals. *Am. Nat.,* vol. 110, p. 731–42.

Raven, J. A. 1976. The quantitative role of 'dark' respiratory processes in heterotrophic and photolithotrophic plant growth. *Ann. Bot.* vol. 40. p. 587–602.

Roffman, B. 1968. Patterns of oxygen exchange in some Pacific corals. *Comp. Biochem. Physiol.,* vol. 27, p. 405–18.

Roos, P. J. 1967. Growth and occurrence of the reef coral *Porites astreoides* Lamarck in relation to submarine radiance distribution. Utrecht, Netherlands, Drukkerij Elinkwijk (72 p.).

Sargent, M. C.; Austin, T. S. 1949. Organic productivity of an atoll. *Trans. Am. geophys. Union,* vol. 30, p. 243–49.

——; Austin, T. S. 1954 *Biologic economy of coral reefs.* U.S. Geol. (Prof. Paper. 260-E), p. 293–300.

Smith, S. V.; Marsh, J. A. 1973. Organic carbon production on the windward reef flat of Eniwetok Atoll. *Limnol. Oceanogr.,* vol. 18, p. 953–61.

Sorokin, Yu. I. 1972. Bacteria as a food of coral reef fauna. *Oceanologia,* vol. 12, p. 195–204 (Russian).

——. 1973. Microbial aspects of the productivity of coral reefs. In: O. A. Jones and R. Endean (eds.). *Biology and geology of coral reefs.* New York, Academic Press, vol. II, p. 17–46.

——. 1974. Bacteria as a component of the coral reef community. In: *Proc. Second Int. Coral Reef Symp.,* Brisbane, Great Barrier Reef Committee, vol. 1, p. 3–10.

Stephens, G. C. 1962. Uptake of organic material by aquatic invertebrates. I. Uptake of glucose by the solitary coral *Fungia scutaria. Biol. Bull. Mar. Biol. Lab. Woods Hole, Mass.,* vol. 123, p. 648–59.

Strickland, J. D. H.; Parsons, T. R. 1972. A Practical Handbook of Seawater Analysis. *Bull. Fish. Res. Bd Can.,* Ottawa, Queens Printer, no. 167 (310 p.).

Trench, R. K. 1971a. The physiology and biochemistry of zooxanthellae symbiotic with marine coelenterates. I. The assimilation of photosynthetic products of zooxanthellae by two marine coelenterates. *Proc. R. Soc. Lond.* (B: *Biol. Soc.*), vol. 177, p. 225–35.

——. 1971b. The physiology and biochemistry of zooxanthellae symbiotic with marine coelenterates. III. The effect of homogenates of host tissues on the excretion of photosynthetic products *in vitro* by zooxanthellae from two marine coelenterates. *Proc. R. Soc. Lond.* (B: *Biol. Sci.*), vol. 177, p. 251–64.

——. 1974. Nutritional potentials in *Zoanthus sociatus* (Coelenterata, Anthozoa). *Helgol. wiss. Meeresunters.,* vol. 26, p. 174–216.

Vandermeulen, J. H.; Davis, N. D.; Muscatine, L. 1972. The effect of inhibitors of photosynthesis on zooxanthellae in corals and other marine invertebrates. *Mar. Biol.,* vol. 16, p. 185–91.

VERWEY, J. 1930. Depth of coral reefs and penetration of light. With notes on oxygen consumption of corals. In: *Proc. Pacific Sci. Congr.*, Fourth, Batavia, IIa, p. 227–99.

——. 1931. Coral reef studies. II. The depth of coral reefs in relation to their oxygen consumption and the penetration of light in the water. *Treubia,* vol. 13, p. 169–98.

VON HOLT, C.; VON HOLT, M. 1968. Transfer of photosynthetic products from zooxanthellae to coelenterate hosts. *Comp. Biochem. Physiol.,* vol. 24, p. 63–81.

WELLS, J. M.; WELLS, A. H.; VANDERWALKER, J. G. 1973. *In situ* studies of metabolism in benthic reef communities. *Helgol. wiss. Meeresunters.,* vol. 24, p. 78–81.

WETHEY, D. S.; PORTER, J. W. 1976a. Sun and shade differences in productivity of reef corals. *Nature* (Lond.) vol. 262, p. 281–82.

——; ——. 1976b. Habitat-related patterns of productivity of the foliaceous reef coral, *Pavona praetorta.* in: G. O. Mackie (ed.). *Coelenterate Ecology and Behavior.* New York Plenum Publishing, p. 59–69.

YONGE, C. M. 1937. Studies on the biology of Tortugas corals. III. The effect of mucus on oxygen consumption. *Pap. Tortugas Lab. Carnegie Inst., Wash.* vol. 31, p. 207–14.

——; NICHOLLS, A. G. 1931. Studies on the physiology of corals. V. The effect of starvation in light on the relationship between corals and zooxanthellae. *Sci. Repts. Gt Barrier Reef Exped. 1928–29,* vol. 1, p. 177–211.

——; YONGE, M. J.; NICHOLLS, A. G. 1932. Studies on the physiology of corals. VI. The relationship between respiration in corals and the production of oxygen by their zooxanthellae. *Sci. Repts. Gt Barrier Reef Exped. 1928–29,* vol. 1, p. 213–51.

NB. Author's change of address (April 1978): J. W. Porter, Department of Zoology, University of Georgia, Athens, Georgia 30602, U.S.A.

396

27

Alkalinity depletion to estimate the calcification of coral reefs in flowing waters

S. V. Smith[1]

INTRODUCTION

Two separate approaches have been used to estimate the $CaCO_3$ production rate of coral reefs.[2] The approach with considerable historical precedent consists of estimating the standing crop and turnover rates of the calcifying organisms in the community. Chave *et al.* (1972) have reviewed much of the literature on this subject. Because of the large amount of information required by this approach, no such study has been truly comprehensive.

An alternative procedure can, in many instances, more nearly gauge the total calcification rate of coral reef communities. The procedure consists of estimating the rate at which $CaCO_3$ production in the community depletes the overlying water column with respect to some $CaCO_3$-related dissolved constituent. Calcium itself is the dissolved constituent most directly related to calcification, while magnesium, strontium, and other cations are common coprecipitates with calcium. The amount by which any of these materials is depleted is generally below conventional "wet chemical" detection limits, and detection of isotopic changes is an intriguing but ordinarily impractical alternative for estimating calcification rates in natural environments.

The depletion of total alkalinity is an alternative chemical measure of calcification, and this measurement is analytically feasible in many coral reef systems. This paper deals with alkalinity-derived estimates of reef calcification in flowing waters. A second paper in this volume (by Kinsey, Chapter 35) discusses the use of the method in still waters; and a third paper (by Smith and Kinsey, Chapter 36) presents the analytical methodology of the approach, particularly as it applies to the incubation of calcifying organisms in controlled laboratory aquaria. Smith and Kinsey (1976) review relevant papers using this approach.

---

1. Hawaii Institute of Marine Biology, University of Hawaii, P.O. 1346, Kaneohe, Hawaii 96744, U.S.A.
2. The term $CaCO_3$ is used here to include both calcite and aragonite, including Mg, Sr, and the other common coprecipitates with Ca. In terms of mass of material precipitated, the error in this usage is negligible—less than 2 per cent for a calcite with 30 per cent Mg substitution for Ca.

Alkalinity depletion studies have been undertaken at relatively few localities, and it is useful to consider those studies briefly. The calcification study most nearly resembling the 'flow respirometry' model which has been used for oxygen metabolism studies of coral reefs was conducted by Smith (1973), who analysed the calcification rate of two communities on the windward interisland reef flats of Enewetak Atoll. Water crosses the reef flats there in a few minutes; the alkalinity of that water is depleted by less than 0.01 meq/litre during its crossing; and the calcification rate is about $10 \, g \, CaCO_3 \, m^{-2} \, day^{-1}$.

Broecker and Takahashi (1966) estimated the calcification rate on the Bahama Banks. That study might be considered a long-term flow respirometry study, as the water takes approximately 200 days to cross the Banks. Those authors did not consider the $CaCO_3$ precipitation there to be biogenic, but subsequent investigations (Stockman et al., 1967; Neumann and Land, 1975) suggest otherwise. Whether or not the precipitation is biogenic does not alter the central fact that the $CaCO_3$ precipitation lowers alkalinity. Alkalinity[3] changed by up to about 0.9 meq/litre, and the calcification rate was about $1.5 \, gm^{-2} \, day^{-1}$.

Smith and Pesret (1974) and Smith and Jokiel (1976) have estimated the $CaCO_3$ production rate of the lagoons at Fanning and Canton Atolls respectively. In both situations, lagoon water exchanged with ocean water in response to tidal flushing. The mean residence time for water in these two lagoons was about 30 and 50 days respectively; and the respective $CaCO_3$ production rates were about 3 and $1.5 \, gm^{-2} \, day^{-1}$.

Kinsey (1972 and Chapter 35) has studied coral reef communities which are periodically subjected to a cessation of water flow for several hours and subsequently flushed. Alkalinity changed by about 0.1 meq/litre, and the calcification rate was about $11 \, gm^{-2} \, day^{-1}$.

The calcification rate of two atoll lagoons flushed only by tidal exchange has also been determined. The residence time of water in the lagoon of Fanning Island is about 30 days; alkalinity depletion is about 0.5 meq/litre; and the calcification rate is about $3 \, g \, m^{-2} \, day^{-1}$ (Smith and Pesret, 1974). At Canton Island, the lagoon water residence time is about 60 days; alkalinity depletion is about 0.2 meq/litre; and the calcification rate is about $2 \, g \, m^{-2} \, day^{-1}$ (Smith and Jokiel, in preparation).

THE MODEL

In its simplest form, the alkalinity depletion model is as follows. For each mole (100 g) of $CaCO_3$ precipitated from a given volume of water, total alkalinity is lowered by two equivalents (see Smith and Kinsey, Chapter 36, for discussion and references); and each volume of water remains in contact with a given map

---

3. Broecker and Takahashi (1966) used carbonate, rather than total, alkalinity in their calculations. Because pH was relatively constant, total alkalinity depletions approximately equalled carbonate alkalinity depletions in that study.

area of the reef community some measurable length of time. Therefore, the $CaCO_3$ production rate equals the decrease in alkalinity (ΔT.A., in eq m^{-3}) times 50 g $CaCO_3$ eq^{-3} times the water volume per unit area (which equals the mean water depth, in m) divided by the period of time the water remains in the system (τ, in days or other useful units). Application of this alkalinity depletion method is limited by the resolution of ΔT.A. and τ, and by interferences with ΔT.A. The alkalinity depletion method has so far been applied in relatively few reef systems, and each system has been quite different. Therefore, the presentation of a 'methodology' for measuring calcification from alkalinity depletion is more nearly a consideration of these interferences and limitations.

RESIDENCE TIME

Maragos (Chapter 24) discusses the measurement of volume transport of water crossing a reef flat and the use of this measurement in flow respirometry studies. In the present paper, it is more useful to consider residence time (τ) and to relate the volume transport measurement to τ.

Let us define τ as the timespan which a particular volume of water remains in the system of interest. In the case of water flow across a reef flat, τ, in seconds, is the volume of water on that reef flat (m^3) divided by the volume transport of water across the reef flat (m^3 sec^{-1}). In practice, both the volume of water on the reef flat and the volume transport are expressed per unit width of reef perpendicular to flow. This evaluation of residence time in a particular system is applicable when there is a simple unidirectional flow of water across a reef flat. Smith (1973) has applied the method for estimating the calcification rate of two transects on the windward interisland reef flats of Eniwetok Atoll, and the approach has seen wide application in oxygen flow respirometry studies (Marsh and Smith, Chapter 25).

More complex systems which lack such a simple pattern of unidirectional water flow through them have been the subject of an alternative approach to estimating τ. Two studies have utilized budgets of salt and water flux as a primary estimate of τ (Smith and Pesret, 1974; Smith and Jokiel, 1976), while a third study (Broecker and Takahashi, 1966) has used the approach as a secondary check on τ. Whereas the volume transport approach is most easily applied in reef flat situations where τ is likely to be an hour or less, the salt-water budget approach is applicable to systems with τ being several days. In fact, the three studies to which this approach has been applied have had τ values equalling or exceeding one month.

Smith and Pesret (1974) present the model in some detail, and their model needs only the addition of an explicit term for evaporation.[4]

$$\tau = (z)(e - p)^{-1}(S_\tau - S_0)(S_0)^{-1} \qquad (1)$$

4. Rainfall exceeded evaporation at Fanning Island by such an amount that evaporation could be neglected from explicit consideration in that system.

τ is the now-familiar residence time term, in days; z is the mean water depth in the system, in metres; e and p are the daily evaporation and precipitation rates, in metres per day[5]; S_0 is the salinity of ocean water entering the system; and S_τ is the salinity of the water after it has resided in the system. The equation is based on the assumption that S_τ is being maintained at a constant, steady-state value and that rainfall and constant-composition ocean water are the only two water sources for the system. Unless the sampling has been undertaken during a period of greatly changing weather conditions (e.g. transition from the wet season to the dry season), the first assumption is not likely to be seriously violated. Variability of the evaporation and rainfall parameters over timespans which are short relative to the residence time of water in the system (e.g. occasional cloudbursts) should not be a significant problem, because these short-term variations will be averaged out in the data. If the second assumption is seriously violated (e.g. there is a large influx of groundwater), then the alkalinity depletion approach to calcification studies may be invalidated anyway.

Equation (1) is most safely applied to evaluate the mean residence time of water in a system. That is, the mean salinity of water in the system is inserted for S_τ, and the equation is solved for the mean age of that water. The equation can also be applied, albeit somewhat more tenuously, by inserting the value 1 for $(S_\tau - S_0)$ and solving the equation for the residence time per unit salinity change.

If this method is to be used and data on rainfall and evaporation at the field site are not available, these parameters can be evaluated. Both evaporation and rainfall estimates should be obtained during the course of the alkalinity studies and preferably for a period of time previous to those studies approximating to the mean residence time of water in the system.

Other approaches to estimating τ can be devised for particular situations. For example, Broecker and Takahashi (1966) used the relationship between bomb-produced ^{14}C in the atmosphere and the ^{14}C of water crossing the Bahama Banks to estimate the residence time of that water. Smith and Pesret (1974) used data on tidal flux and salinity as a method of calculating τ. Von Arx (1954) built hydrodynamic models which yielded estimates of τ in the lagoons of Bikini and Rongelap Atolls. Kinsey (1972 and Chapter 35) has described systems which periodically undergo effective isolation from the neighbouring ocean water for directly observable spans of time. Even open reef flat areas may be subjected to periods of sufficiently slow water flow that samples at a single location over discrete intervals of time provide an adequate record of change (Emery, 1962).

Let us briefly consider the effect of an error in residence time on calcification rate studies. τ is always a positive quantity, and this quantity is multiplied by the alkalinity change as the water incubates in the system of interest. Hence, τ is a scaling factor, and an error in estimating τ will impose a proportional error in the estimate of calcification.

5. The method represented by equation (1) can be applied to the calculation of τ only if evaporation does not equal rainfall; in such a case, the equation cannot be solved.

ALKALINITY CHANGES (ΔT.A.)

The precise measurement of alkalinity and the separation of calcification-induced alkalinity changes, from changes induced by various interferences, are central to this method of estimating calcification. The direct analytical considerations of alkalinity measurement are given elsewhere in this volume (by Smith and Kinsey, Chapter 36); this section is devoted to the strategies of sampling and analysis. ΔT.A. must be well-known in order that the approach be applied. Erroneous values for T.A. before and after the water has incubated in the system of interest can easily yield apparent 'negative calcification' (that is, solution) rates in obvious net calcifying systems.

The total alkalinity of water flowing through a coral-reef system can change in response to several processes in addition to the precipitation and solution of $CaCO_3$. Chief among these are lowering of the alkalinity by rainfall, alteration (either lowering or raising) by groundwater, and raising of alkalinity by evaporation. Dilution by rainfall and concentration by evaporation affect the alkalinity in an easily predictable fashion. They add or remove alkalinity-free water, so they change salinity and total alkalinity in proportion to one another. The term 'specific alkalinity' is defined as the ratio of total alkalinity to chlorinity. There is a proportional relationship between chlorinity and salinity, so specific alkalinity equals 1.805 times the ratio of total alkalinity to salinity.[6] Hence, if seawater undergoes alkalinity changes only from evaporation, rainfall, and $CaCO_3$ reactions, the processes are easily separated:

$$TA_c = (TA_0)(S_0)^{-1}(S_\tau) - TA_\tau \qquad (2)$$

TA_c is the alkalinity change from calcification; TA_0 is the total alkalinity of the ocean water; TA_τ is the alkalinity of the water after it has incubated in the system; S_0 is oceanic salinity; and S_τ is the salinity of the water after it has incubated in the system.

If there is an input of fresh water from sources other than rain, the alkalinity alteration pattern may become complex. The groundwater from coral islands tends to have a high and variable alkalinity, so the influence of such water on the alkalinity of the diluted ocean water is not subject to unambiguous prediction. Fortunately, the data presented by Smith and Pesret (1974) suggest that even in extreme situations the groundwater influence may be minor and at least crudely predictable in a large system such as an atoll lagoon. Peculiar alkalinity anomalies such as those described by Davies and Kinsey (1973) for small (5–20 cm deep) beachrock pools are perhaps explained in terms of excessive groundwater interference.

Another class of alkalinity interferences might rarely be encountered in

---

6. Salinity actually equals 0.03 + 1.805 (chlorinity). The value 0.03 is negligible with respect to calculating specific alkalinity. The specific alkalinity of most open ocean surface water is between 0.120 and 0.125.

portions of a coral reef. Certain seawater constituents which are usually minor or absent in low-nutrient, aerated waters of a coral reef (e.g. sulphide, nitrate or ammonia) can contribute to total alkalinity and can vary in a manner which interferes with the calcification calculations. If the variability of these interfering materials exceeds about 0.01 meq/litre in any particular situation, then the alkalinity depletion method described here may no longer be applicable without allowance for these terms.

All of these interferences may be minimized by working with systems in which alkalinity changes can be detected over short intervals of time. Under such circumstances, the precipitation of $CaCO_3$ is likely to be the only process significantly altering the total alkalinity of the water.[7] A different problem then emerges with these short-residence time systems—that of resolving the alkalinity change as the water incubates in the particular system. The strategy of water sampling and analysis is strongly influenced by whichever of these considerations limits detection of calcification—interferences to recognizing the calcification effect or analytical resolution.

As has been discussed, the relationship between salinity and alkalinity is helpful in recognizing interferences. Most systems with a long residence time— hence large potential interference—are also geographically large systems which cannot be adequately sampled in a single day. Adequate definition of the relationship between salinity and alkalinity demands adequate day-to-day precision. That is, a day-to-day drift in standardization cannot be tolerated, because all samples must be compared with one another and with the open ocean water. On the other hand, the total alkalinity changes which occur in such systems are likely to be large, so sample-to-sample precision is not critical in determining the salinity-to-alkalinity pattern. Therefore, the analytical interference introduced by holding the samples for several hours before analysis or by not performing replicate analyses is tolerable; but day-to-day care must be taken in standardizing the pH meter, the reagents, the glassware, and the analytical procedures.

By contrast, detection of small alkalinity changes as water crosses a reef in a matter of minutes is accomplished only by taking extreme care in comparing the 'before' sample with its companion 'after' sample. Samples should be returned to the laboratory within minutes of collection, filtered immediately, and analysed at least in duplicate. It is the pair of samples which is being compared, so the conditions at the time of analysis must be carefully controlled. Day-to-day differences in the various analytical considerations are not critical to the detection of the slight alkalinity differences to be expected. Finally, such data should be subject to careful statistical analyses to determine the significance of differences observed.

---

7. $CaCO_3$ solution raises the alkalinity, so the alkalinity depletion method actually yields an estimate of the net value ($CaCO_3$ precipitation—$CaCO_3$ solution). This net is clearly positive in most coral reef systems, as evidenced by the net accumulation of calcareous materials growing in those systems.

PLANNING AND IMPLEMENTING AN ALKALINITY DEPLETION STUDY

In most instances, it should be possible to plan the strategy of a particular alkalinity depletion study, including the feasibility of that study. Most reef environments calcify at rates in excess of $1\,\mathrm{g\,CaCO_3\,m^{-2}\,day^{-1}}$, and 3 to $15\,\mathrm{g\,CaCO_3\,m^{-2}\,day^{-1}}$ is probably a reasonable range for most environments with significant coral cover (Smith and Kinsey, 1976). Given the value $3\,\mathrm{g\,m^{-2}\,day^{-1}}$ as a lower limit to calcification rates in most reef environments, assumptions about the dimensions of a particular environment, and the likely residence time of water there, one can calculate the analytical resolution needed to detect that calcification. This necessary resolution can be compared with the practical resolution of the method (Smith and Kinsey, Chapter 36). In the case of a reef flat, these calculations may suggest the minimum width over which the water must flow, the maximum tolerable depth of that water, or the maximum flow rate at which calcification could be detected. Smith (1973) detected barely measurable alkalinity changes as water about 1 metre deep crossed reef flat environments about 300 metres wide at speeds between 4 and 60 cm/sec. Such a study is limited by analytical resolution, and the study must be designed to optimize that resolution.

The potential effects of the various interferences can also be anticipated. Given assumptions on the geometry of the particular system of interest, and the residence time of water in it, one can calculate the approximate rate of rainfall and evaporation necessary to alter the salinity by as much as 0.1 parts per thousand. If as much alteration as that is likely to occur, then sampling of the environment should be designed to cope with that salinity variation, and to correct for it according to equation (2). Groundwater influence is likely to be significant only if the reef in question is associated with a landmass which has a large fresh water lens. Unless the groundwater is likely to dilute the ocean water by as much as 0.1 parts per thousand, such an influence can usually be excluded from consideration. In the event that the potential groundwater influence is so great, alkalinity measurements of the water should be made. Samples grading from groundwater towards seawater (such as one might encounter in sampling vertically through a groundwater lens into the underlying seawater) will be helpful in recognizing the groundwater influence on a plot of alkalinity versus salinity (see Smith and Pesret, 1974).

Water sampling for salinity and/or alkalinity measurements in a coral reef environment should include at least some sampling to look for the possibility of vertical gradients or stratification in the water mass. If there is little or no such vertical variation, then subsequent sampling can be confined to surface waters. In water several metres deep, subsurface samples are easily taken from a boat by means of a small battery-powered bilge pump attached to the end of a hose and lowered to the desired sampling depth. Insulated electric wire can be run from the pump, along the hose, to a battery kept in the boat. Before the

403

water sample is taken, the pump should be allowed sufficient time to flush the hose.

Water sampling at specific sites should also be undertaken to consider possible diurnal or tidal variations in the water properties. Such variations are more likely to be significant in systems with residence times shorter than one day than in longer residence-time systems which exhibit changes integrated over several days.

Finally, it should be recognized that calcification is but one of the metabolic processes altering the CO_2 content of water in a coral reef system. Therefore, studies of coral reef calcification should be regarded as incomplete unless they include a consideration of these other processes, discussed by Marsh and Smith (Chapter 25), Kinsey (Chapter 35), and Smith (1974).

ACKNOWLEDGEMENTS

This paper is HIMB contribution No. 528. The research was partially supported by Grant No. R800906 awarded by the U.S. Environmental Protection Agency to the University of Hawaii.

References

BROECKER, W. S.; TAKAHASHI, T. 1966. Calcium carbonate precipitation on the Bahama Banks. *J. geophys. Res.*, vol. 71, p. 1575–602.

CHAVE, K. E.; SMITH, S. V.; ROY, K. J. 1972. Carbonate production by coral reefs. *Mar. Geol.*, vol. 12, p. 123–40.

DAVIES, P. J.; KINSEY, D. W. 1973. Organic and inorganic factors in recent beach rock formation, Heron Island, Great Barrier Reef. *J. sedim. Petrol.*, vol. 43, p. 59–81.

EMERY, K. O. 1962. *Marine Geology of Guam.* U.S. Geol. Survey (Prof. Paper 403B) (76 p.).

KINSEY, D. W. 1972. Preliminary observations on community metabolism and primary productivity of the pseudo-atoll reef at One Tree Island, Great Barrier Reef. In: *Proc. Symp. Corals and Coral Reefs, 1969.* Mar. Biol. Assoc. India, p. 13–32.

NEUMANN, A. C.; LAND, L. S. 1975. Lime mud deposition and calcareous algae in the Bight of Abaco, Bahamas: a budget. *J. sedim. Petrol.*, vol. 45, p. 763–86.

SMITH, S. V. 1973. Carbon dioxide dynamics: a record of organic carbon production, respiration, and calcification in the Eniwetok reef flat community. *Limnol. Oceanogr.* vol. 18, p. 106–20.

——, 1974. Coral reef carbon dioxide metabolism. In. *Proc. Second Int. Coral Reef Symp.*, Brisbane, Great Barrier Reef Committee, vol. 1. p. 77–85.

——; JOKIEL, P. L. 1976. Water composition and biogeochemical gradients in the Canton Atoll Lagoon. In S. V. Smith and R. S. Henderson (eds). *An environmental survey of Canton Atoll Lagoon, 1973.* U.S. Naval Undersea Center Tech. Publ. 395, p. 15–53. (Also to be issued as a number of *Atoll Res. Bull.*).

——; KINSEY, D. W. 1976. Calcium carbonate production, coral reef growth, and sea level change *Science,* vol. 194, p. 937–9.

——; PESRET, F. 1974. Processes of carbon dioxide flux in the Fanning Atoll lagoon. *Pac. Sci.,* vol. 48, p. 225–45.

STOCKMAN, K. W.; GINSBURG, R. N.; SHINN, E. A. 1967. The production of lime mud by algae in south Florida. *J. sedim. Petrol.,* vol. 37, p. 633–48.

VON ARX, W. S. 1954. *Circulation systems of Bikini and Rongelap lagoons.* U.S. Geol. Survey (Prof. Paper 260-B), p. 265–73.

28

Total organic carbon

D. C. Gordon, Jr.[1]

INTRODUCTION

The measurement of total organic carbon in seawater can provide valuable information about coral reef production and energy requirements; for example, the import, production, and export of organic matter at a particular part of a reef or for an entire reef system. Very few measurements of this type have been made because organic carbon analysis is an exacting and involved process and methodology has yet to be standardized.

DEFINITION OF TERMS

Studies of organic carbon in natural waters generally include fractionation into two parts by filtration. Organic carbon retained on a filter (about 1 μm pore size) is generally referred to as particulate or suspended while that which passes through is called dissolved or soluble. These definitions, although practical, are misleading. Organic carbon in sea water cannot be cleanly divided into two such separate fractions. It actually consists of a wide and continuous spectrum of components ranging in size from methane molecules to whales. Filtration merely removes those particles larger than the effective pore size of the filter. This demarcation is not sharp and is dependent upon filter type and porosity, volume of water filtered, and particle composition and concentration (Sheldon, 1972). In addition to organic compounds in true aqueous solution, the filter-passing fraction also contains colloidal-sized organic material (1 nm–1 μm). Sharp (1973a) has demonstrated using dialysis membranes that approximately 25 per cent of the organic carbon in open seawater falls into this category.

In most instances, a very minor portion of the total organic carbon in sea water is contained in particles large enough to be retained on a filter of about

1. Marine Ecology Laboratories, Bedford Institute of Oceanography, Dartmouth, Nova Scotia, Canada B2Y 4A2.

1 μm porosity. Sharp (1973a) lists percentages ranging from 0.7 to 24 in different environments. Gordon (1971) observed that in the lagoon of Fanning Island, a Pacific atoll, only 5 per cent of the total organic carbon was retained on a filter. Since the precision of analytical methods for measuring filter-passing organic carbon is between 5–10 per cent at best, observed concentrations are rarely significantly different from total organic carbon concentrations.

For the reasons outlined above, it is recommended that instead of measuring the organic carbon concentration of filtered sea-water and calling it dissolved (or soluble), *unfiltered* sea-water should be analysed and the results expressed as *total* organic carbon. If particulate organic carbon data are required, a separate volume of water can be filtered and the filter analysed appropriately (Marshall, Chapter 29).

CHOICE OF AN ANALYTICAL METHOD

Before attempting to measure total organic carbon in sea water, investigators should realize that there is no universally accepted method available. In recent years, at least six different methods have been developed (see Table 8 in Gordon and Sutcliffe, 1973). The most widely used is the wet oxidation procedure developed by Menzel and Vacarro (1964) which has been modified slightly by Strickland and Parsons (1968). However, the results of high temperature combustion methods (Skopintsev et al., 1966; Sharp, 1973b; Gordon and Sutcliffe, 1973) suggest that the wet oxidation procedure may miss some of the organic carbon present, especially in deep ocean water. Possible reasons for the discrepancies between the results of different methods are offered by Sharp (1973b), Gordon and Sutcliffe (1973), and MacKinnon (1977).

Although these different analytical methods for measuring total organic carbon have never been compared using sea water collected from coral reef environments, it is logical to conclude on the basis of comparisons made in open ocean water that each method could yield different concentrations. It will probably take a number of years for chemical oceanographers to decide which method is the most accurate and should be recommended for general use. Until this matter is settled, it is recommended that investigators wishing to measure total organic carbon in reef environments use the wet oxidation procedure as outlined by Strickland and Parsons (1968) with the alterations listed in the next section. This method is recommended at this time because it is the least expensive and easiest to perform. It must be remembered, however, that the total organic carbon concentrations obtained may be underestimated and that absolute concentrations and perhaps even relative concentrations may prove impossible to interpret accurately. If the necessary equipment is readily available, it is recommended that this method be compared using reef water, with one of the dry combustion methods, such as that of Gordon and Sutcliffe (1973) which uses standard instruments and also provide total nitrogen data simultaneously.

RECOMMENDED ALTERATIONS TO STRICKLAND AND PARSONS PROCEDURE

1. Water samples should be collected in clean glass containers (plastic containers can exude organic compounds). A 100 ml sample is sufficient. If sampling is done from a boat, uncontaminated surface (0–3 mm) and shallow water (0.5–10 m) can be easily collected using the equipment described by Gordon and Keizer (1974). If sampling is performed by someone wading or swimming, shallow water can be collected with hand-held glass bottles.
2. The handling of sea water must be kept to a minimum. Every time water is transferred from one container to another, organic carbon can be lost by adsorption or gained by contamination.
3. Sea water should *not* be filtered. However, it should be screened through a 160 μm sieve to remove any zooplankton or large particles present.
4. The analytical grade 85 per cent (syrupy) phosphoric acid can be used directly; diluting it with distilled water (which is never carbon free) merely increases the magnitude of blanks (Gordon and Sutcliffe, 1973). One μl of acid should be added for each ml of sea water; this quantity should be enough to bring the pH well below 4.5, the pH at which all inorganic carbon (mostly bicarbonate and some carbonate at normal sea water pH) is converted to CO_2. The pH of a few samples should be measured to insure that sufficient acid is being added. High levels of suspended carbonate particles in some reef environments make this step particularly important. Any inorganic carbon not removed from sea water samples at this stage will be detected as organic carbon.
5. The analytical grade potassium persulphate produced by some chemical suppliers is relatively organic-free and therefore does not require re-crystallization. Therefore, this step can be omitted if checks indicate that a particular shipment of the chemical is 'clean'.
6. The potassium persulphate should not be added until after the acidifica-tion and nitrogen purging steps. After its addition, samples should be purged only 20 seconds before sealing. If added with the acid, potassium per-sulphate can apparently dissolve and begin oxidizing organic carbon during the 5 minutes purging period (Sharp, 1973b).
7. If the effluent gas from the infrared analyser can escape to a hood or in some other way is drawn outside of the laboratory building, the potassium iodide trap (for removing chlorine) can be omitted. Chlorine does not give appreciable infrared absorption and will not harm the inner components of the infrared analyser.

ACKNOWLEDGEMENTS

The author thanks Drs R. Pocklington, J. Sharp, W. Sutcliffe, and P. Wangersky for reading this manuscript and offering numerous suggestions for improving it.

407

References

GORDON, D. C., JR. 1971. Organic carbon budget of Fanning Island Lagoon. *Pac. Sci.*, vol. 25, p. 222–7.

——; KEIZER, P. D. 1974. Estimation of petroleum hydrocarbons in seawater by fluorescence spectroscopy: improved sampling and analytical methods. *Fisheries and Marine Service Tech. Report*, no. 481.

——; SUTCLIFFE, JR., W. H. 1973. A new dry combustion method for the simultaneous determination of total organic carbon and nitrogen in seawater. *Mar. Chem.*, vol. 1, p. 231–44.

MacKINNON, M. D. 1977. Analysis of total organic carbon in seawater. Ph.D. Thesis, Dalhousie University (200 p.).

MENZEL, D. W.; VACCARO, R. F. 1964. The measurement of dissolved organic and particulate carbon in seawater. *Limnol. Oceanogr.*, vol. 9, p. 138–42.

SHARP, J. H. 1973a. Size classes of organic carbon in seawater. *Limnol. Oceanogr.*, vol. 18, p. 441–7.

——. 1973b. Total organic carbon in seawater—comparison of measurements using persulfate oxidation and high temperature combustion. *Mar. Chem.*, vol. 1, p. 211–29.

SHELDON, R. W. 1972. Size separation of marine seston by membrane and glass fiber filters. *Limnol. Oceanogr.*, vol. 17, p. 494–8.

SKOPINTSEV, B. A.; TIMOFEYEVA, S. N.; VERSHININA, O. H. 1966. Organic carbon in the near-equatorial and southern Atlantic and in the Mediterranean. *Okeanologiya/Oceanology*, vol. 6, p. 201–10.

STRICKLAND, J. D. H.; PARSONS, T. R. 1968. A practical handbook of seawater analysis. *Bull. Fish. Res. Bd Can.*, Ottawa, Queen's Printer, no. 167, p. 153–8.

29

Particulate organic carbon

N. Marshall[1]

Particulate organic matter is usually collected onto filters, thus the first step is to select the filter best suited for the desired retention. Since the assays are to be for carbon, the polycarbonate membranes (General Electric Nuclepore) and cellulose ester membranes (Millipore) cannot be used, leaving metal membranes (Selas Flotronics) and glass-fibre filters for consideration. The metal or silver membranes have the advantage of a stated pore size and Sheldon (1972) points out that, prior to overloading when finer particles are screened out, the retention is directly governed by this pore size. He also shows that glass-fibre filters perform comparably, for example, the retentions of a 0.45 Selas Flotronics membrane and a Whatman GFC are similar.

Prior to use, glass-fibre and silver filters are freed of carbon by combusting at 450°C for at least two hours. Since replicate samples using both types give considerably higher carbon values for the total retention on glass, there is little doubt that during filtration the glass-fibres adsorb more dissolved carbon than the metal. D. C. Gordon, Jr. and W. H. Sutcliffe, Jr. (1974) offer data which strongly suggest there is no uptake of dissolved matter of consequence by the silver filters but, until this is firmly established under varied circumstances, it seems necessary, even for silver, to screen through at least two filters using the carbon values from the underlying layer as a blank. This layer is largely free of particulate matter while indicative of any adsorption that might occur, though it does not clearly correct for any unidentified filter effect such as Gordon and Sutcliffe have found in testing silver filters.[2] To achieve more complete freedom from possible error due to dissolved organics, Banoub and Williams (1972) went to the trouble of using three layers of glass filters, subtracting 2 × the value of the bottom filter from the sum of the top two; however, this does not seem necessary for general work.

Summing up, the glass-fibre filter is recommended for screening for two reasons: (1) filtration is relatively rapid even for volumes as large as ten litres;

---

1. Graduate School of Oceanography, University of Rhode Island, Kingston, Rhode Island 02881, U.S.A.
2. Discrepancies in the non-carbon blank levels have been observed for different packaged lots of silver filters. Thus it is important not to mix lots in setting up an overlying-underlying filter pair.

(2) a satisfactory correction for dissolved organic carbon is easily made by using two filters.

Once the water has been screened through the filters, the retained organic carbon can be determined with a CHN analyser either: (1) by the method of Telek and Marshall (1974) combusting at about 720°C, which is appreciably below the temperature of carbonate dissociation; or (2) by the method of Hirota and Szyper (1975) in which organic carbon is driven off by baking one sample of each replicate pair at 500°C, then combusting all samples on the analyser at the usual 1100°C with the difference between baked and untreated samples interpreted as organic matter. Both methods obviate the need for an acid wash, which is questionable around reefs where carbonate nuclei may be coated with resistant organic films. Filters prepared in the field can be held under dessication, preferably in a vacuum, for several months before being analysed. Some of the features and limitations of these methods have been elaborated by the authors cited. Although Sharp (1974) recommends an acid wash procedure, not considered adequate around reefs for reasons stated herein, his paper offers a wealth of suggestions as to CHN techniques. In my opinion his comments as to artificial sources of organic matter adhering to filters reinforces the need to use an underlying filter for a blank reading.

In reef waters, which characteristically have low levels of particulate matter (commonly < 0.1 mg C/L), filtering as much as ten litres on to 47-mm membranes is recommended though this is next to impossible with silver filters. The large volume suggested increases the different between true values and the imprecisions of the measurement procedures. It also lessens the relative size of any errors which might arise from the filter blank or from inadequate corrections for adsorbed dissolved matter which, according to some data in Manzel (1966), may quickly reach saturation. Sheldon (1972) gives reassuring comments that the degree of vacuum is not important when using filters only for retention. Thus the task of vacuum control, often awkward especially in field operations, can be by-passed.

With these techniques, one can readily discern differences that may occur between particulate organic levels as sampled offshore, over the reef, and in lagoon environments. Since the CHN procedure also gives nitrogen values, C/N ratios in the suspended particulates can be obtained in this way. Assuming one has also assayed for the total organic carbon and nitrogen of the water being sampled, the appropriate values of particulate matter i.e. total particles as retained by the specified filter, can be subtracted to obtain data on the dissolved components. In fact, because of the unknown effects of filtration on dissolved levels, this calculation is preferred over assays on filtrates.

References

BANOUB, M. W.; WILLIAMS, P. J. LeB. 1972. Measurements of microbial activity and organic material in the western Mediterranean Sea. *Deep-sea Res.,* vol. 19, p. 433–43.

GORDON, D. D. JR.; SUTCLIFFE, W. H. JR. 1974. Filtration of seawater using silver filter for particulate nitrogen and carbon analysis. *Limnol. Oceanogr.,* vol. 19, p. 989–93.

HIROTA, J.; SZYPER, J. P. 1975. Separation of total particulate carbon into inorganic and organic components. *Limnol. Oceanogr.,* vol. 20, p. 896–900.

MENZEL, D. W. 1966. Bubbling of sea water and the production of organic particles: a re-evaluation. *Deep-sea Res.,* vol. 13, p. 963–6.

SHARP, J. H. 1974. Improved analyses for particulate organic carbon and nitrogen from seawater. *Limnol. Oceanogr.,* vol. 19, p. 984–9.

SHELDON, R. W. 1972. Size separation of marine seston by membrane and glass-fiber filters. *Limnol. Oceanogr.,* vol. 17, p. 984–9.

TELEK, G.; MARSHALL, N. 1974. Using a CHN analyser to reduce carbonate interference in particulate organic carbon analyses. *Mar. Biol.,* vol. 24, p. 219–21.

411

30

Nitrogen determination

K. L. Webb[1]

Nitrogenous nutrients, in waters surrounding coral reef communities, are usually extremely low in concentration as are other elements such as phosphorus. Colorimetric analysis will normally require a spectrophotometer with a 10 cm light path and the processing of about 50 ml of sea water per sample analysis. Such sample volumes are normally available in flow studies or from other studies of environmental concentrations. If fluxes between organisms and the environment are also being measured (D'Elia, Chapter 37), it is advantageous to scale down the volume of the colorimetric determinations. Samplings of incubation media would thus have less effect on the total volume of the system and possibly simplify kinetic calculations (D'Elia, Chapter 37).

The determinations which follow can all be scaled down to 5 ml of sample simply by reducing proportionately the volumes of all reagents added. Additional advantages of the scaled down sample volumes include a savings in cost of chemicals, and reduction in both size and physical bulk of glassware required. Reduction of bulk may be advantageous in the transport of materials to remote areas. Disadvantages of sample size reduction include probable modification of spectrophotometer cuvette holder to hold a 10 cm, 5 ml volume cuvette (5 ml, 10 cm cells available from Pyrocell Manufacturing Co., P.O. Box 176, Westwood, NJ 07675, U.S.A. Catalog S18-260 no. 5010; a cell adapter no. 5010A is also available).

The 5 ml cell holder can be made from aluminium turned to the same diameter as the normal 30 ml, 10 cm cell (i.e. 22 mm for the Beckman Du-2) and cut to about 10 cm in length (Fig. 1). A hole is bored on centre with a 10 mm (the diameter of the 10 cm, 5 ml cell) bit to within about 1 mm of the end. The remaining length is bored with a 9 mm bit and the cylinder is cut in half lengthwise, forming two cell adapters with a lip at one end. The light beam will probably have to be restricted to pass through the smaller diameter cell; if the spectrophotometer is not equipped with a variable aperture, a small aperture can be constructed from stiff black paper. The method of scaling down sample size to 5 ml is based on suggestions of J. J. McCarthy (Harvard University, pers. comms.). Disadvantages of the scaled down determinations also include the additional expense of micropipettes for dispensing reagent volumes in the range of 100–400 µl and the need for extra precaution in mixing between reagent additions. Use of a Vortex type mixer is virtually a necessity

1. Virginia Institute of Marine Science, Gloucester Point, Virginia, 23062, U.S.A.

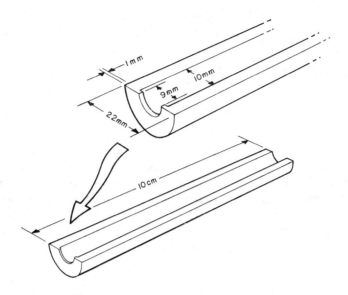

Figure 1
Illustration of adapter to hold 5 ml, 10 cm cell.

for the DAM (di-acetyl-monoxime)-urea determination. Thorough cleanliness is always necessary, it is worth noting that any contamination in the reduced volume analysis will introduce ten times greater an error than it would otherwise.

NH_4^+ is adequately determined with the Solórzano method (Solórzano, 1969). In reef environments, the turbidity is generally low enough to allow determinations to be made without either filtering or using turbidity blanks. If filtering cannot be avoided, great care must be taken to avoid introducing ammonia positive material into the samples from the filters (Marvin *et al.,* 1972). Glass fibre filters generally produce lower blanks than acetate filters but extensive prewashing (as for phosphorous determinations) may be necessary. Swinnet® filter holders (Millipore Corp.) fitted to a syringe for sampling make a convenient device for filtering. Samples for NH_4^+ should be analysed as soon as possible; otherwise freezing is the best preservation technique. Samples should be kept in closed containers until analysed and processed in a low ammonia atmosphere. It is desirable to keep all ammonia containing chemicals out of the immediate laboratory, and to choose a well-ventilated smoke-free work area.

After the addition of reagents to the sample, no further contamination by ammonia will affect colour development and thus the sample reaction vessels need not be covered. Aluminium foil has been reported to promote spurious colour development if in contact with samples (McCarthy and Kamykowski, 1972). Laboratory conditions such as temperature are likely to vary considerably in field laboratories; consequently, it is a wise precaution to determine colour development versus time to see if a 1 hour colour development is optimum for the specific conditions. If samples are analysed daily, the sample plus reagents may remain in the glassware. Just before reuse, the flasks or test tubes can be emptied, rinsed several times with NH_4^+ free water and reused (D'Elia, pers. comm.).

Water for reagent blank determinations is critical if absolute levels of NH_4^+, or any other constituent, are to be determined. Fortunately for flow studies, the concentration difference between two samples can be calculated without reagent blanks. A good grade of freshly distilled water, or such water freshly run through a strongly acidic cation exchange column, may produce a good NH_4^+ reagent blank. Phytoplankton in the light are also effective removers of ammonia from sea water and may in some cases be utilized to produce 'ammonia free' water for a reagent blank.

A good quality of sodium hypochlorite solution (e.g. the commercial bleach, Chlorox®) is essential for good NH_4^+ results. The solution slowly loses its potency with time and should be fresh. Shortly before departing for remote locations, it is a good procedure to try small bottles of bleach from different sources and take along several from the acceptable supply. Strickland and Parsons (1968) alternatively suggest checking the strength periodically.

Beer's Law is obeyed over the NH_4^+ concentration range encountered and only one concentration of standard need be used to calculate the factor for relating absorbance to concentration. For precise work, however, it is a good check on procedures to calculate the factor from a computed linear regression of absorbance at several concentrations.

NO_3^- and NO_2^- are effectively determined by the method of Wood et al. (1967). Undiluted samples should be utilized. Despite the recommendations of Strickland and Parsons (1968), the author prefers to use EDTA rather than ammonium chloride as the activator when ammonia determinations are being carried out in the same laboratory. Suitable precautions will be necessary to avoid contamination of NH_4^+ analysis if it is decided to use NH_4Cl. Nitrite will often be below the limit of precision of this method in reef environments; in this case, it will be necessary to concentrate the azo dye produced in a litre or more of water by the anion-exchange method of Wada and Hattori (1971). The delivery arrangement suggested by Wood et al. (1967) to introduce copperized cadmium to the reduction column without exposure to air is unnecessary; the cadmium filings may be processed in a volumetric flask and subsequently introduced into the column, without air, simply by inverting the flask into the water-filled reservoir of the column. Samples may be preserved effectively for short periods with Hg^{++} by adding several drops of a saturated $HgCl_2$ solution to 100 ml of sample.

Total dissolved organic nitrogen (DON) is currently most effectively determined by oxidizing the DON with ultra violet light (Armstrong, et al., 1966; Armstrong and Tibbitts, 1968). NH_4^+, NO_3^- and NO_2^- must be measured on the untreated and the irradiated samples, the difference being attributed to N arising from the UV treatment. There seems to be variation, among laboratories and equipment used, in the effectiveness of this technique in oxidizing various DON components. Consequently, each investigator must determine oxidation time versus completeness of oxidation for natural DON and known compounds. Theoretically, oxidation should be complete to NO_3^- although in practice various amounts of deaminated ammonia remain unoxidized. This procedure can be effectively scaled down in volume enabling as many as two 6-hour runs of 24 samples each to be carried out in a day.

In designing the equipment, the volumes of sample required must be taken into account. This will be determined by the number of repeated analyses to be made on each oxidation sample, the volume required for analysis, and whether or not dissolved organic phosphorus (DOP) is to be determined on the same sample. DOP is effectively oxidized in shorter times than DON and ultra violet oxidation is clearly the method of choice for DOP if the equipment is available. Contrary to indications in the literature that urea is resistant to this oxidation procedure, it is the experience of the author that urea can be completely oxidized by this method. Consequently, urea is perhaps a good material to use to determine operational conditions of specific apparatus.

If ultra violet oxidation is out of the question, one must resort to the Kjeldahl method. The author has used the Kjeldahl as described by Strickland and Parsons (1968) coupled to the Solórzano (1969) ammonia determination. The method adopted by the author was to neutralize the Kjeldahl digest with NaOH, titrate the sample with dilute NaOH and pH meter to a final pH of 8–8.5 and volume of 50 ml, followed by immediate addition of the Solórzano reagents. The precipitate which developed upon pH adjustment was removed by centrifugating after the colour development and before reading the optical density.

Specific components of the DON pool are numerous and a significant fraction may be refractory. Specific components may be important in coral reef community metabolism and consideration should be given to measurements more specific than total DON. Urea is considered by some investigators to be as important as NH_4^+ in marine nitrogen cycles although urea is largely uninvestigated on coral reefs. Methods described by McCarthy (1970) and Newell et al. (1967) are both effective and the choice is largely left to the individual investigator. McCarthy's urease-urea method will be increasingly less precise as the ratio of NH_4^+ to urea increases, because it depends upon the determination of NH_4^+ before and after hydrolysis of urea. Obtaining suitable active enzyme preparations with low ammonia blank values may be a problem (see suggestions in McCarthy and Kamykowski, 1972). On the other hand, the author has found that in some circumstances the DAM method of Newell et al. (1967) measures some constituent in seawater which is not biologically active urea. Despite this, the DAM method is preferred; concentrations have ranged from about 0.4 to 2.0 µg-at DAM urea N/1 for Kaneohe Bay, Hawaii and Enewetak coral reef environments. This range of values is, surprisingly, about the same as those for Chesapeake Bay. Reagent C for the DAM method

416

containing $MnCl_2$ seems to be light sensitive; the method has worked only when this reagent is stored in the dark.

Glassware contamination of human origin is an extremely serious problem in urea determinations as well as being moderately serious for NH_4^+ determinations. Urea amounts within the range of 0.05–0.15 µg at urea N/cm^2 have been measured on the hand. Precautions against contamination must be carried to the extreme. The author has found it successful to rinse reaction glassware with tap water after the determination, soak overnight in mild detergent, rinse thoroughly and oven dry inverted. Freshly washed glassware is used and rubber gloves worn during the washing procedure. An automatic dishwasher would probably also produce good results.

Reagent blanks, if needed, can be determined on freshly distilled water and should be below 0.10 O.D. units for a 10 cm cell. The best blanks have been consistently obtained with UV oxidized seawater (<0.02 O.D. units).

Free amino acids (FAA) can be quantitatively determined by the method of Webb and Wood (1967). This method has been further modified for precise work. For those FAA to be measured, low concentrations (relative to natural concentration) of ^{14}C labelled internal standards are added to the sample prior to desalting. During the subsequent chromatography, absolute recovery rates of the ^{14}C labelled FAA are determined. An anthracene-packed flow cell (Nuclear-Chicago Model 6900) in a liquid scintillation counter is contained in the analytical train just before addition of the ninhydrin reagents to the column effluent. The assumption is made that recoveries of added ^{14}C-FAA are the same as the same naturally occurring FAA. Frozen samples are best returned to a sophisticated laboratory for FAA analysis. This analysis is too costly and time consuming for extensive data collection but there may be occasions when the identification of FAA components of the DON pool will warrant the effort.

A relatively new determination, of intermediate level of specificity between DON and FAA, shows promise for the analysis of primary amines in the picomole range (Undenfriend et al., 1972). This analysis requires either a fluorometer or, ideally, a spectrophotofluorometer. The total FAA in as little as 1 ml of seawater can be determined by buffering to pH 9 and adding a solution of Fluram® (Hoffman-La Roche Inc) in acetone while vigorously mixing the sample on a vortex type mixer. This step is necessary because the reagent is unstable in water. Excitation at 390 nm produces fluorescence at 480 nm. Background fluorescence of the seawater may cause a high blank value, use of spectrophotofluorometer may optimize the sample to background readings. Data should be calculated in glycine units in the absence of other guidelines since glycine is the most abundant FAA in seawater (Webb and Wood, 1967). Use of these kinds of data may point to specific situations where it is worth the effort to analyse for individual FAA.

Particulate organic nitrogen can best be determined by a dedicated gas chromatograph or a commercially fabricated unit for this purpose. This function is often combined with the analysis for carbon in a commercial unit such as the Perkin–Elmer Model 240. CHN analyser; working instructions with the equipment are adequate. As much as 4 litres of water must be filtered onto a Flotronics silver membrane (pore size 0.45 μm); precombusted glass fibre filters may also be used. Samples can be stored under vacuum dessication. For related information on POC analysis see Marshall (Chapter 29) or Telek and Marshall (1974).

If a nitrogen analyser is not available, one must make use of the Kjeldahl determination (Strickland and Parsons, 1968). The author suggests coupling the Kjeldahl to the Solórzano (1969), or whichever NH_4^+ determination is being used, rather than using two or more NH_4^+ determinations.

If the author were to carry out another nitrogen budget for a coral reef using the flow study approach, he would investigate the possibility of automating as much of the sampling and chemistry as possible. Modular constructed automated chemistry devices have progressed to a high level of sophistication (Technicon Instruments Corp., Tarrytown, N.Y. 10591 U.S.A.). A slight disadvantage of this apparatus for low concentration nutrient determinations compared to manual methods is the use of a 5 cm light path compared to the 10 cm path of the spectrophotometer for manual determinations. This disadvantage is most apparent where low absolute concentrations have to be determined. The problems associated with evaluating the true reagent blank value render the accuracy of low values questionable in any case.

Commercially available automated methodologies for NH_4^+, NO_3^- and Kjeldahl N are satisfactory. Atlas et al. (1971) provide a good review of the methodology. Automated methodologies have been published for creatine (Whitledge and Dugdale, 1972), urea (DeManche et al., 1973) and DON (Afghan et al., 1971) which should prove satisfactory. Automating the Fluram® method for primary amines should be fairly straightforward using Technicon modules and the automated chemistry adapter for spectrofluorometers (Turner Associates, 2524 Pulgas Ave., Palo Alto, CA 94303 U.S.A.). In practice, some investigators have found it more efficient to UV oxidize the DON samples manually, utilizing automated chemistry to obtain the before and after inorganic N values. It may be equally efficient to run urea determinations manually as well. Generally, however, automated chemistry will allow more data points to be obtained per unit time. This is, of course, of great advantage in obtaining statistically significant results.

If automated chemistry is available, establishment of several sampling stations along the flow study transect becomes feasible. In analogous fashion to other rate determinations, it is desirable to have data points from several stations along a transect rather than just a starting and terminal value. For a study, with the order of magnitude as Symbios (Johannes et al., 1972), after preliminary investigation for station placement, sampling from instrument towers is recommended. For flow studies of nutrient flux, the minimum automated equipment must include current and depth measuring devices to provide volume transport information in conjunction with an automated water-sampling device. Up to 28, sequential 70–490 ml samples at predetermined time intervals (0.5–6 h) can be taken by a sampler such as the ISCO Model 1391

(Instrument Specialities Company, Lincoln, Nebraska, U.S.A.). This should be ultimately well-suited for the study of nutrients such as NO_3^- which can be preserved for short periods of time by preaddition of a preservative such as $HgCl_2$ to the sample bottles. The ingenuous investigator is left to carry the suggestion further, e.g. utilizing existing technology to sample larger volumes of water for PON, etc.

References

AFGHAN, B. K.; GOULDEN, P. D.; RYAN, J. F. 1971. Use of ultraviolet irradiation in the determination of nutrients in water with special reference to nitrogen. *Tech. Bull.* No. 40. Inland Waters Branch, Department of Energy, Mines, and Resources. Ottawa, Canada.

ARMSTRONG, F. A. J.; TIBBITTS, S. 1968. Photochemical combustion of organic matter in sea water for nitrogen, phosphorus and carbon determination. *J. mar. Biol. Ass. U.K.,* vol. 48, p. 143–52.

——; WILLIAMS, P. M.; STRICKLAND, J. D. H. 1966. Photo-oxidation of organic matter in seawater by ultra-violet radiation, analytical and other applications. *Nature* (Lond.), vol. 211, p. 481–3.

ATLAS, E. L.; GORDON, L. I.; HAGER, S. W.; PARK, P. K. 1971. A practical manual for use of the Technicon® Autoanalyzer® in seawater nutrient analyses; revised. Technical Report 215 Dept. Oceanography. Oregon State Univ. Corvallis. OR. 97331.

DeMANCHE, J. M.; CURL, H.; COUGHENOWER, D. D. 1973. An automated analysis for urea in seawater. *Limnol. Oceanogr.,* vol. 18, p. 686–9.

JOHANNES, R. E.; ALBERTS, J.; D'ELIA, C.; KINZIE, R. A.; POMEROY, L. R.; SOTTILE, W.; WIEBE, W.; MARSH, J. A. JR.; HELFRICH, P.; MARAGOS, J.; MEYER, J.; SMITH, S.; CRABTREE, D.; ROTH, A.; McCLOSKEY, L. R.; BETZER, S.; MARSHALL, N.; PILSON, M. E. Q.; TELEK, G.; CLUTTER, R. I.; DU PAUL, W. D.; WEBB, K. L.; WELLS, J. M., JR.; 1972. The metabolism of some coral reef communities: a team study of nutrient and energy flux at Eniwetok. *BioScience,* vol. 22, p. 541–3.

MARVIN, K. T.; PROCTOR, JR., R. R.; NEAL, R. A. 1972. Some effects of filtration on the determination of nutrients in fresh and salt water. *Limnol. Oceanogr.,* vol. 17, p. 777–84.

McCARTHY, J. J. 1970. A Urease method for urea in seawater. *Limnol. Oceanogr.,* vol. 15, p. 309–13.

——; KAMYKOWSKI, D. 1972. Urea and other nitrogenous nutrients in La Jolla Bay during February, March and April 1970. *Fish. Bull.,* vol. 70, p. 1261–74.

NEWELL, B. S.; MORGAN, B.; CUNDY, J. 1967. The determination of urea in seawater. *J. mar. Res.,* vol. 25, p. 201–2.

SOLÓRZANO, L. 1969. Determination of ammonia in natural waters by the phenohypochlorite method. *Limnol. Oceanogr.,* vol. p. 799–801.

STRICKLAND, J. D. H.; PARSONS, T. R. 1968. A practical handbook of seawater analysis. *Bull. Fish. Res. Bd Can.,* Ottawa, Queen's Printer, no. 167, p. 143–7.

TELEK, G.; MARSHALL, N. 1974. Using a CHN analyser to reduce carbonate interference in particulate organic carbon analysis. *Mar. Biol.,* vol. 24, p. 219–21.

UNDENFRIEND, S.; STEIN, S.; BÖHLEN, P.; DAIRMAN, W.; LEIMGRUBER, W.; WEIGELE, M. 1972. Fluorescamine: A reagent for assay of amino acids, peptides, proteins, and primary amines in the picomole range. *Science,* vol. 178, p. 871–2.

WADA, E.; HATTORI, A. 1971. Spectrophotometric determination of traces of nitrite by concentration of azo dye on an anion-exchange resin. Application to sea waters. *Anal. Chim. Acta,* vol. 56, p. 233–40.

WEBB, K. L.; WOOD, L. 1967. Improved techniques for analysis of free amino acids in seawater. In: *Automation in analytical chemistry* (Technicon Symposia 1966). White Plains, New York, Mediad, vol. 1, p. 440–4.

WHITLEDGE, T. E.; DUGDALE, R. C. 1972. Creatine in seawater. *Limnol. Oceanogr.,* vol. 17, p. 309–14

WOOD, E. D.; ARMSTRONG, A. J.; RICHARDS, F. A. 1967. Determination of nitrate in sea water by cadmium–copper reduction to nitrite. *J. mar. Biol. Assoc. U.K.,* vol. 47, p. 23–31.

31

Determination of phosphorus

M. E. Q. Pilson[1]

The majority of coral reefs are found in regions where the concentrations of nutrient elements are low. Methods used to measure these nutrients must be both accurate and precise; the requirement for precision is especially important for flow studies, where it is necessary to measure small differences between samples.

The two most readily distinguishable forms of phosphorus in seawater are (a) 'reactive', which reacts with molybdate in the usual procedures, and (b) 'total', which is measured after digestion of the sample in some way. The difference between the two determinations yields an estimate of 'organic' phosphorus. In surface waters, the 'organic' forms may constitute more than 50 per cent of the total, and it is essential to measure this in order to understand phosphorus cycles.

During field work at Enewetak and other tropical regions with low nutrient concentrations the following methods have proved accurate, precise and reliable: (a) for reactive phosphorus, the method of Murphy and Riley (1962) as conveniently presented by Strickland and Parsons (1968); and (b) for total phosphorus, the method of Menzel and Corwin (1965), for digestion, followed by measurement of the phosphorus by the method of Murphy and Riley. It has proven possible at concentration levels between 30 and 500 nM (nannomolar) to determine reactive phosphorus to a precision of ± 8 nM (2 standard errors of the mean, based on duplicate determinations) and total phosphorus to ± 13 nM. These data are based on an extensive series of field observations (Pilson and Betzer, 1973); under laboratory conditions, with standards, the precision is better.

Given below are a number of notes, which, if followed, should tend to improve the quality of the resulting data.

1. Samples should be processed within 1–2 hours of collection, if possible. No methods of preservation have so far proven unequivocally satisfactory. Collection of samples in large (1–4 litre) containers will minimize the surface to volume ratio and thus the loss of phosphorus to the walls by adsorption.

1. Graduate School of Oceanography, University of Rhode Island, Kingston, Rhode Island, 02881, U.S.A.

If storage is necessary, the investigator should determine the rate and reproducibility of loss under his own conditions.

2. All volumes should be carefully measured. It is convenient to pipette 40-ml samples into 125 ml Erlenmeyer flasks (or 70-ml test tubes with ground glass stoppers). With this volume, only 4 ml of mixed reagent is required. The mixed reagent should be discharged vigorously into the sample and mixed immediately. This procedure seems to improve precision. The rapid discharge may be accomplished using a rubber bulb and a pipette but it is more convenient and faster to use a 'Repipette' automatic syringe-type pipette to deliver the reagent.

3. A standard should be included with each set of samples, and all standards and blanks should also be run in duplicate. Dilute working standards (about 500 nM) lose measurable phosphate to the walls of containers in a few hours and should be made fresh for each run.

4. All sea water contains measurable arsenate, generally about 10–50 nM (Johnson and Pilson 1972a and b) and this also produces a blue colour with the reagent, although the wavelength maximum is slightly different. This arsenate may be removed by reduction according to the method of Johnson (1971). For the highest precision in, for example, flow studies, where one is interested primarily in differences in phosphorus concentration, it may be preferable to leave the arsenate in the solution. If this is done then the solutions should be allowed to rest for at least $\frac{1}{2}$ hour before the absorbance is measured, because the rate of colour formation by the arsenate is slower than by the phosphate.

5. All glassware should be used for one purpose only, and should be rinsed with deionized water after each use. *Washing* of glassware, once it is in use, should be avoided, if possible.

6. In ordinary clear surface waters such as are usually found around coral reefs there is not enough particulate phosphorus for this form to be detected by using differences between filtered and unfiltered samples. If needed it should be directly determined by filtration of much larger samples.

7. It is a bad practice, with ordinary clear surface waters, to filter water samples before analysis. Millipore filters contain phosphorus and release measurable quantities to the filtrate. They can be cleaned before use by soaking in hot water or in hot dilute HCl, and by passing these fluids through them. One cannot be sure, however, that such clean filters will not adsorb organic phosphorus from solution. If samples are turbid, they must, of course, be filtered. Otherwise a more reliable approach is to use unfiltered samples and measure any particulate phosphorus as in (6) above.

8. The solvent extraction procedure of Stephens (1963) for low levels of phosphorus is suggested as possibly suitable where the concentrations of reactive phosphorus are below acceptable limits (perhaps 30 nM) for the standard procedure. The sensitivity is potentially greater by a factor of about 10, but the procedure is more time consuming and the greater number of reagents and glassware offers more opportunities for contamiantion. Solvent extraction procedures have not been adequately tested for use with sea water, either in the

laboratory or under field conditions so there is no basis for predicting the degree of success. The possible extraction of arseno-molybdate compounds must be allowed for, and no generally acceptable procedure for this has yet been developed.

References

JOHNSON, D. L. 1971. Simultaneous determination of arsenate and phosphate in natural waters. *Environ. Sci. Technol.* vol. 5, p. 411–4.

——; PILSON, M. E. Q. 1972a. Spectroscophotometric determination of arsenite, arsenate and phosphate in natural waters. *Anal. Chim. Acta.* vol. 58, p. 289–99.

——; ——. 1972b. Arsenate in the western North Atlantic and adjacent regions. *J. mar. Res.* vol. 30, p. 140–9.

MENZEL, D.; CORWIN, N. 1965. The measurement of total phosphorus in seawater based on the liberation of organically bound fractions by persulfate oxidation. *Limnol. Oceangr.*, vol 10, p. 280–2.

MURPHY, J.; RILEY, J. P. 1962. A modified single solution method for the determination of phosphate in natural waters. *Anal. Chim. Acta*, vol. 27, p. 31–6.

PILSON, M. E. Q.; BETZER, S. B. 1973. Phosphorus flux across a coral reef. *Ecology*, vol. 54, p. 581–8.

STEPHENS, K. 1963. Determination of low phosphate concentrations in lake and marine waters. *Limnol. Oceangr.*, vol. 8, p. 361–2.

STRICKLAND, J. D. H.; PARSONS, T. R. 1968. A practical handbook of seawater analysis. *Bull. Fish. Res. Bd Can.*, Ottawa, Queen's Printer. no. 167. (311 p).

32

Phytoplankton consumption

O. Holm-Hansen[1]

INTRODUCTION

Many investigators have estimated the net flux of detrital material, zooplankton, or nutrients to or from coral reef communities by measurement of these constituents at points where the water enters and leaves the reef. This section describes methodology for the estimation of phytoplankton biomass in water samples so that algal consumption by the reef may be similarly calculated.

It is assumed in this discussion that the currents across the reef are uni-directional and that the distance across the reef is long enough for significant changes in biomass to result from grazing activities of animals. Significant changes in the phytoplankton biomass from one end of the reef to the other may conceivably be the result of the following additional processes.

1. Growth of the algae during flow across the reef. Estimates of the rate of increase in biomass must be obtained from separate productivity experiments.
2. Respiratory losses. Corrections for respiration may be either estimated from the measured growth rates or biomass, or measured by direct oxygen-consumption techniques.
3. Losses by settling. This would include all live or dead cells which settle onto the bottom and are not grazed.
4. Losses due to grazing by animal populations.

The biomass of phytoplankton sampled at different points on the reef may be estimated by a variety of methods as outlined below.

ESTIMATION OF PHYTOPLANKTON BIOMASS

The easiest method of estimating phytoplankton biomass is to measure chlorophyll concentrations and to assume a certain factor between chlorophyll

1. Sverdrup Hall, University of California, La Jolla, California 92093, U.S.A.

a and total cellular organic carbon. Although the ratio of carbon/chl. *a* may vary from about 10 to over 300, many investigators have used a ratio of either 75 or 100, which is the range most commonly encountered in marine samples. The reliability of this ratio may be estimated by comparing the biomass values so obtained with the estimates obtained from measurements outlined below, as well as from measurement of the total particular organic carbon. Methods of chlorophyll estimation based on light absorption measurements (Marshall, 1965) or chromatographic separations (Jeffrey, 1968) will not be discussed below because they require too large volumes of samples and are too time-consuming. The chlorophyll *a* concentrations generally found in reef waters are in the range of 0.05 to 1.0 µg chl. *a*/litre. In recent years, the use of fluorescence measurements (Yentsch and Menzel, 1963) for chlorophyll estimation have almost entirely replaced the earlier procedures based on spectrophotometry.

Fluorescence of extracted samples. Water samples are filtered through glass fibre filters (which permit more rapid filtration than through membrane filters) and extracted in 90 per cent acetone. After separation in a centrifuge, the fluorescence of the supernatant liquid is read in a fluorometer. This reading is then converted to absolute chlorophyll units based on calibration of the fluorometer with spectrophotometric readings. The sensitivity of this method is so high that a few hundred millilitres of water sample should suffice for all coral reef studies. Phaeophytin can also be measured on the same samples by acidification of the extract and again measuring the fluorescence. The methodology employed in these determinations has been described by Holm-Hansen *et al.* (1965) and Kiefer (1973a).

In vivo fluorescence techniques. The sensitivity of the fluorometers commonly used in these studies permits chlorophyll to be estimated without any concentration of the cells. Water samples may be placed directly in the fluorometer and the reading converted to chlorophyll concentration. Continuous profiling or transects across the reef is also possible by pumping the water through a chamber in the instrument. It should be noted that *in vivo* fluorescence measurements are not as accurate as measuring extracted chlorophyll, as the fluorescence per unit chlorophyll in the cells varies with light conditions, species composition, nutritional state of the cells, etc. In spite of these limitations, the method of continuous monitoring of *in vivo* fluorescence is of great value in oceanography and should be most valuable in coral reef studies. Kiefer (1973b) has recently described the methodology and limitations of this method.

Microscopic methods. Probably the most reliable method for the determination of total phytoplankton biomass is still by conventional microscopic enumeration of total cell counts combined with measurements of cell volumes. These data are usually obtained by fixing the cells in Lugol's iodine solution or formalin solution and counting all phytoplankton cells on the inverted microscope as described by Utermohl (1958). The equations for converting cell

426

numbers to total cellular organic carbon has been described by Kovala and Larrance (1966) and Mullin *et al.* (1966). This methodology is laborious and time-consuming (one sample will often require one day for microscopic examination) and hence is not generally amenable to a study involving numerous samples. It can be of great value, however, if used on selected samples which are then used to compare the reliability of the other methods described in this section.

Electronic particle counters can be used to monitor the cell numbers and cell volumes in natural samples (Sheldon *et al.*, 1973). One difficulty in applying this method to the reef community, however, is that it measures the effective volume of all particulate material, without any distinction between live/dead or organic/inorganic materials. In view of the abundant suspended inorganic particles characteristic of reef environments, this method probably will not be very useful for coral reef studies.

Measurement of ATP. The methodology for determination of adenosine triphosphate and its extrapolation to biomass units (e.g. organic carbon) has been described by Holm-Hansen (1973). This method gives the total microbial biomass and does not yield information regarding the type of cells in the water sample. For most euphotic zone samples, however, the bulk of the biomass is represented by the phytoplankton, and hence this method could be used to estimate changes in phytoplankton concentrations with time. It is recommended, however, that such ATP data be supported by occasional measurements of chlorophyll concentrations and total cell volumes as described above.

References

HOLM-HANSEN, O. 1973. Determination of total microbial biomass by measurement of adenosine triphosphate. In: L. H. Stevenson and R. R. Colwell (eds). *Estuarine microbial ecology.* Columbia, South Carolina. Univ. of South Carolina Press, p. 73–89.

——; LORENZEN, C. J.; HOLMES, R. W.; STRICKLAND, J. D. H. 1965. Fluorometric determination of chlorophyll. *J. Cons. CIEM,* vol. 30, p. 3–15.

JEFFREY, S. W. 1968. Photosynthetic pigments of the phytoplankton of some coral reef waters. *Limnol. Oceanogr.,* vol. 13, no. 2, p. 350–5.

KIEFER, D. 1973a. The *in vivo* measurement of chlorophyll by fluorometry. In: L. H. Stevenson and R. R. Colwell (eds). *Estuarine microbial ecology.* Columbia, South Carolina, Univ. of South Carolina Press, p. 421–430.

——. 1973b. Fluorescence properties of natural phytoplankton populations. *Mar. Biol.,* vol. 22, p. 263–9.

KOVALA, P. E.; LARRANCE, J. D. 1966. Computation of phytoplankton cell numbers, cell volume, cell surface and plasma volume per liter, from microscopical counts. Spec. Rep. 38, Dept. Oceanog., Univ. Wash., Seattle.

MARSHALL, N. 1965. Detritus over the reef and its potential contribution to adjacent waters of Eniwetok Atoll. *Ecology,* vol. 46, p. 343–4.

MULLIN, M. M.; SLOAN, P. R.; EPPLEY, R. W. 1966. Relationship between carbon content, cell volume, and area in phytoplankton. *Limnol. Oceanogr.,* vol. 11, no. 2, p. 307–11.

SHELDON, R. W.; SUTCLIFFE, Jr., W. H.; PRAKASH, A. 1973. The production of particles in the surface waters of the ocean with particular reference to the Sargasso Sea. *Limnol. Oceanogr.,* vol. 18, no. 5, p. 719–33.

UTERMÖHL, H. 1958. Zur Vervollkomnung der quantativen Phytoplankton-Methodik. *Int. Verein. Theor. Angew. Limnol.*, vol. 9, p. 1–38.

YENTSCH, C. S.; MENZEL, D. W. 1963. A method for the determination of phytoplankton chlorophyll and phaeophytin by fluorescence. *Deep-sea Res.*, vol. 10, 221–31.

33

Flux of zooplankton and benthic algal detritus

R. E. Johannes[1]

When working in shallow reef communities situated in unidirectional currents one can measure the net flux of zooplankton and detritus to or from the community by monitoring changes in numbers or biomass in water as it crosses the reef (Odum and Odum, 1955; Tranter and George, 1972; Johannes et al., 1972; Glynn, 1973; Johannes and Gerber, 1974).

Reef communities import and consume holoplankton and meroplankton as well as exporting considerable numbers and variety of meroplankton (Glynn, 1973; Johannes and Gerber, 1974). To quantify this flux it is necessary to sample the zooplankton at upstream and downstream stations across the reef. A shallow site should be chosen in order to maximize the impact of the reef community on the water's contents and thereby facilitate the measurement of this impact. At such sites it is usually not possible to tow plankton nets.

It is practical however to use fixed nets by anchoring them at the site if the current is unidirectional and continuous. Plankton net frames can be easily constructed to avoid the problem of the advance pressure wave created by the bridle and line on a conventional towed plankton net.

Such sampling is subject to most of the same sources of error as conventional towed net sampling. The author will not reiterate them here since they have been discussed at length elsewhere (e.g. Tranter, 1968). It suffices to say that different sizes and species will be caught with different efficiencies and that these efficiencies will vary with current velocity. (The use of plankton pumps has never been attempted in connection with zooplankton flux studies on reefs, but would be subject to similar variations in size and species catching efficiency).

Drifting zooplankton are often comparatively sparse in reef waters and anchored nets are usually fairly small because the water in which they are used is very shallow. They may therefore have to be used for several hours to get samples of adequate size. This may create problems. Firstly, since plant detritus is often abundant in reef waters (e.g. Johannes and Gerber, 1974), clogging may become a problem. Secondly, the zooplankton are held in the net for so long that predation may alter the species composition significantly.

1. Hawaii Institute of Marine Biology, P.O. Box 1346, University of Hawaii, Kaneohe, Hawaii, 96744, U.S.A.

Johannes and Gerber (1974) used a stationary net, designed by Robert Clutter, for reef transect sampling. The net mouth was rectangular, providing a cross sectional area larger than that of any round-mouth net that could be immersed in only a few centimetres of water. The netting had a large area relative to the area of the net mouth in order to reduce friction and clogging problems. The collector consisted of three plankton nets of progressively smaller mesh size (1 mm, 330 microns and 60 microns, respectively) inter-locked in tandem on the single frame. This resulted not only in the automatic fractionation of plankton into three size classes, but also further reduced clogging. Each net had a length-wise plastic zipper, facilitating removal of samples without removing the nets from the frame.

When zooplankton is sparse and algal detritus is abundant, quantitative removal of zooplankton from net samples for volume, weight, or chemical determinations has proven very difficult (e.g. Johannes *et al.,* 1972). The author has heard that plant material may be dissolved, rendering zooplankton separation much easier, by adding the enzyme, cellulase, to samples, but has no personal experience with this technique.

It is often assumed that large, sparsely-distributed particles make up such a small proportion of the total particulate load in sea water that small volume water samplers, which do not sample these larger particles, provide an adequate measure of total particulate matter. This is not always the case on coral reefs where unusually large quantities of benthic algal fragments may be in suspen-sion. On an Enewetak windward interisland reef, for example, large clumps of algae made up an important part of the total particulate flux, but were nonethe-less still too sparsely distributed to be sampled adequately with four-litre water samplers (Johannes and Gerber, 1974). Here it was necessary to sample using both plankton nets for the large particles and water samplers for the small particles in order to get an adequate picture of total suspended particulate concentrations and flux rates.

Since benthic algal fragments sometimes float, it may be desirable to position the plankton net in such a way that a portion of it remains above water in order to sample this floating material.

Net filtering efficiency must be measured, preferably using current meters positioned inside and outside the net. The technique is the same as that used with conventional towed nets and is described in detail by Tranter and Smith (1968).

References

GLYNN, P. W. 1973. Ecology of a Caribbean coral reef, the *Porites* reef flat biotope. Part II. Plankton community with evidence for depletion. *Mar. Biol.,* vol. 22, p. 1–21.

JOHANNES, R. E.; COLES, S. L.; KUENZEL, N. T. 1970. The role of zooplankton in the nutrition of some scleractinian corals. *Limnol. Oceanogr.,* vol. 15, p. 579–86.

——; ALBERTS, J.; D'ELIA, C.; KINZIE, R. A.; POMEROY, L. R.; SOTTILE, W.; WIEBE, W.; MARSH, J. A., Jr.; HELFRICH, P.; MARAGOS, J.; MEYER, J.; SMITH, S.; CRABTREE, D.; ROTH, A.; McCLOSKEY, L. R.; BETZER, S.; MARSHALL, N.; PILSON, M. E. Q.; TELEK, G.; CLUTTER, R. I.;

DuPaul, W. D.; Webb, K. L.; Wells, J. M., Jr.; 1972. The metabolism of some coral reef communities. A team study of nutrient and energy flux at Eniwetok. *BioScience,* vol. 22, p. 541–3.

——; Gerber, R. 1974. Import and export of zooplankton and detritus by an Eniwetok coral reef community. *Proc. Second Int. Coral Reef Symp.* Brisbane, Barrier Reef Committee, vol. 1, p. 97–104.

Odum, H. T.; Odum, E. P. 1955. Trophic structure and productivity of a windward coral reef community on Eniwetok Atoll. *Ecol. Monogr.,* vol. 25, p. 291–320.

Tranter, D. J.; Fraser, J. H. (eds). 1968. *Zooplankton sampling.* Paris, Unesco. (Unesco monographs on oceanographic methods, no. 2). (174 p).

——; George, J. 1972. Zooplankton abundance at Kavaratti and Kalpeni Atolls in the Laccadives. In: *Proc. Symp. Corals and Coral Reefs, 1969.* Mar. Biol. Assoc. India, p. 239–56.

——; Smith, P. E. 1968. Filtration performance. In: D. J. Tranter and J. H. Fraser (eds.), 1968, *Zooplankton sampling,* Paris, Unesco. (Unesco monographs on oceanographic methology no. 2) p. 27–36.

34

Flux of bacteria

W. J. Wiebe[1]

INTRODUCTION

Microorganisms possess an extraordinary range of metabolic functions. As it is impossible in this contribution to review all of the methods necessary to deal with this group of organisms, three objectives will be concentrated on: 1. to provide useful references for further inquiry; 2. to discuss the methods used to measure some specific metabolic processes as they apply to coral reefs; and 3, to offer some guidelines concerning the design of microbial experiments on coral reefs. References to oxygen uptake or CO_2 evolution will be excluded from this discussion, as they are included in several other chapters of the Monograph. A community approach is taken in this Chapter. As will be seen, it is not often possible to separate specifically bacteria *per se* from other microorganisms. Indeed this probably should not be done, for in doing so the interactions between organisms are lost. Where methods are adequately described in the open literature, references will be given. Each investigator is cautioned to examine critically the applicability of the methods before accepting them.

MEASUREMENT OF MICROBIAL BIOMASS

Microorganism biomass may be measured in a variety of ways depending upon the investigator's requirements. Each technique has its advantages and drawbacks.

ATP

The use of the adenosine triphosphate (ATP) assay has received wide application in recent years (Holm-Hansen and Booth, 1966; Holm-Hansen, 1973). It is used to estimate the total living biomass in a sample. Techniques are available for water analysis (Holm-Hansen, 1973) and more recently for sediments

1. Department of Microbiology, University of Georgia, Athens, Georgia, 30602, U.S.A.

(Christian *et al.*, 1975). It is a highly sensitive but imprecise measure. Its usefulness lies in the speed of analysis and thus the ability to repeat samples. It is imprecise because one must convert ATP concentrations to some carbon or biomass value. The C:ATP ratio has been shown to be variable even within a single pure culture of bacteria over several phases (Bancroft *et al.*, 1976). Nevertheless, it offers a reasonable and, at present, by far the best estimate of living biomass. It is used to estimate not only bacteria but all living organisms. Holm-Hansen (1976) has suggested that in the euphotic water column, algae provide most of the ATP and thus for reef water this technique probably will not yield a useful bacterial estimate. Within the sandy sediments of the reef it may be better. Sorokin (1974) estimated by direct counting techniques (see below) that there are 0.3 to 9×10^9 bacteria present per gram dry weight of sediment. Campbell and Wiebe (unpublished data) measured ATP for several sandy reef sediments (Enewetak Atoll; Kaneohe Bay, Hawaii) and calculated the total biomass from 0.5 to 5×10^9 bacterial equivalents[2] per gram dry weight of sediment. This agreement does not imply that there are only bacteria present in the sediments but suggests that they make up the majority of the biomass.

Specific assays

Limulus lysate. Limulus lysate clumps when it is mixed with lipopolysaccharide components of gram-negative bacterial (Jorgenson *et al.*, 1973; Sullivan and Watson, 1974). This method is now being tested for use as a specific quantitative measure of these bacteria. Since most of the bacteria in marine environments appear to be gram-negative, this assay should provide a measure of most of the bacteria.

Muramic acid. Moriarty (1975, 1976) suggests the use of muramic acid for the estimation of bacterial biomass. This is not yet evaluated in reef systems but it could provide a specific assay system.

Direct counting

Sorokin and Kadota (1972) have reviewed the techniques for directly counting bacteria in water and sediment. More recently Dale (1974) has presented a detailed analysis of a technique for counting bacteria in marine clay sediments that should be adaptable for reef sediment work. The advantage of direct counting is that only bacteria (in theory) are included in the analysis. Disadvantages include the problem of discriminating between dead and living cells, the recognition of bacteria and the time necessary for each analysis (Wiebe and Pomeroy, 1972). A variety of fluorescent stains have been used to overcome

2. Since one does not know what organisms are present the ATP derived biomass is calculated as bacterial equivalents, i.e. what the biomass would be if all of the ATP were from bacteria of a mean 1 μ^3 size (see Christian *et al.*, 1975, for details).

these problems and Daley and Hobbie (1975) discuss the latest developments in these techniques. Odum and Odum (1955) placed microscope slides in the reef for up to six weeks and attempted to count the bacteria that were present. Slide techniques may work for specific organisms, particularly on hard surface algal flats (see below) but probably are not adequate for water or sandy zones. Scanning electron microscopy is probably inadequate at present for *in situ* identification of bacteria.

Plate and enrichment counts

Commonly agar plate or extinction dilution counts are employed by microbiologists to measure the number of 'total viable bacteria'. As discussed by Wiebe (1971) these are *not* adequate techniques for measuring bacterial biomass. Generally, the numbers of microorganisms estimated by these techniques are much lower than are present. However, they are of use for estimating, in a relative way, specific types of microorganisms, for example in the final stage of the examination of some bacterial process such as nitrification (see below). The investigator who wishes to pursue the use of such techniques can read further in the *Manual of Microbiological methods* (1957) and in papers pertaining to the isolation of some specific type of organism. Aaronson (1971) is a good reference for the different types of media. For taxonomic identification the latest Bergey's Manual (Breed *et al.,* 1974) and Skerman's *Guide to the Genera of Bacteria* (1968) will be essential. As a general rule the identification of microorganisms without functional measurement being made has limited value in ecosystems work.

Fluorescent antibodies

Schmidt (1974) suggested using fluorescent antibodies against specific organisms to quantitate their presence in natural environments. This technique has great potential and has been used in a study of the organisms responsible for nitrification on a coral reef (Webb and Wiebe, 1975). At present the technique is limited to a few organisms but may become widely used for many more species in the future.

MEASUREMENT OF NUTRIENT FLUXES AND ENERGETICS

Few investigators of coral reef ecosystems have specifically measured the energetics and nutrient fluxes of bacteria. However, investigations of oxygen uptake and release, CO_2 exchange, nitrogen and phosphorus turnover include within their results the activities of the bacteria. These matters are covered elsewhere in the Monograph and discussion here is restricted to those techniques that deal with bacteria and in one instance blue-gree algae.

Energetics

Sorokin (1968, 1971, 1973, and 1974) examined bacterial turnover, their contribution to total respiration and their use as food for animals in both water and sediments. Using ^{14}C techniques described in Sorokin and Kadota (1972), he presented a discussion of the rationale and methodologies used. He estimated extremely rapid turnover rates for bacteria of two to five days in sandy sediments. Di Salvo and Gunderson (1971) examined microbial processes within coral rubble and dead coral heads and also found rapid metabolic turnover. In both investigations, emphasis was placed on the importance of bacteria in reef energetics. Such studies need expansion and further amplification for they suggest a major role for bacteria in secondary reef production.

Nutrient flux

Di Salvo (1970, 1974) described methods for estimating bacterial regeneration of phosphorus and amino-nitrogen in coral seef sediments. Webb et al. (1975) measured the nitrogen flux across the Enewetak reef and Wiebe et al. (1975) and Webb and Wiebe (1975) accounted for the microbial contribution to these processes in terms of nitrogen fixation and nitrification (nitrate production). Using the fluorescent antibody technique of Schmidt (1974), Wiebe and Schmidt (unpublished data) identified *Nitrobacter agilis* as the organism responsible for nitrate production. To accomplish this, glass slides were placed on the algal flat for up to one month, fixed in 10 per cent formalin and then treated and examined as described by Schmidt (1974).

COMMENTS

It is advisable when measuring a community process in a container to restrict the incubation time to a short period. If possible the effects of incubation should be examined. Microbial growth rates can be very rapid and populations can change during only a few hours incubation. One should also control light, temperature and water circulation when experiments are performed in a laboratory. Wiebe and Johannes (unpublished data) found that stirring affected the rate of nitrogen fixation by the blue green alga *Hormothamnion* but not *Calothrix*. In experimental systems one important variable not often regulated is oxygen concentration. These systems have high metabolic activity and, if a chamber is overloaded, the O_2 concentration can be rapidly and drastically reduced.

In working with portions of hard substratum, such as algal flat or coral rubble, each sample represents a separate ecosystem. Wiebe et al. (1975) found that nitrogen fixation varied greatly from sample to sample. Thus replicates in the usual sense could not be made. Control rates of nitrogen fixation under standard *in situ* conditions had to be estimated *before* experimental manipulation could be performed. A similar situation existed during the studies in nitrification and its inhibition (Webb and Wiebe, 1975). The rate of nitrate production had to be established *before* the sample could be treated with a metabolic inhibitor.

In both the nitrogen fixation and nitrification studies mentioned above hard surface substrata were incubated. The organisms could not be separated from the substratum; we normalized data by measuring the surface area (see Webb *et al.*, 1975, for details). Dahl (1973) has described a more general technique for measuring a variety of surface areas in reef systems.

Two specific physical conditions in reef complexes are worth mentioning. First, unidirectional current systems as at Enewetak Atoll permit the direct measurement of input and output of some property from a portion of a reef. This is described by Holm-Hansen (1976) for algae and Johannes (Chapter 33) for zooplankton. Secondly, the author has found tide pools, isolated at low tide from water flow, useful for studies on reef flats. Such locations permit direct *in situ* experimental manipulations of the environment. In still water situations, enclosures described by Kinsey (Chapter 35) offer similar advantages.

References

AARONSON, S. 1971. *Experimental microbial ecology.* New York, Academic Press.

BANCROFT, K.; PAUL, E. A.; WIEBE, W. J. 1976. The extraction and measurement of adenosine triphosphate from marine sediments. *Limnol. Oceanogr.,* vol. 21, p. 473–80.

BREED, R. S.; MURRAY, E. G. D.; SMITH, N. R. 1974. *Bergey's manual of determination bacteriology,* 8th edit. London, Bailliere, Tindall and Cox.

CHRISTIAN, R. R.; BANCROFT, K.; WIEBE, W. J. 1974. Distribution of microbial adenosine triphosphate in salt marsh sediments at Sapelo Island, Ga. *Soil Sci.,* vol. 119, p. 89–97.

DAHL, A. L. 1973. Surface area in ecological analysis: quantification of benthic coral reef algae. *Mar. Biol.,* vol. 23, p. 239–249.

DALE, N. E. 1974. Bacteria in intertidal sediments; Factors related to their distribution. *Limnol. Oceanogr.,* vol. 19, p. 509–518.

DALEY, R. J.; HOBBIE, J. E. 1975. Direct counts of aquatic bacteria by a modified epi-fluorescence technique. *Limnol. Oceanogr.* vol. 20, 815–82.

DI SALVO, L. H. 1974. Soluble phosphorus and amino-nitrogen released to sea water during recoveries of coral reef regenerative sediments. In: *Proc. Second Int. Coral Reef Symp.,* Brisbane, Great Barrier Reef Committee, vol. 1, p. 11–20.

——. 1970. Regeneration functions and microbial ecology of coral reefs. Ph.D. Dissertation, University of N. Carolina, Chapel Hill, N.C.

——; GUNDERSON, K. 1971. Regenerative functions and microbial ecology of coral reefs. I. Assays for microbial populations. *Can. J. Microbiol.,* vol. 17, p. 1081–9.

HOLM-HANSEN, O. 1973. Determination of total microbial biomass by measurement of adenosine triphosphate. In: L. H. Stevenson and R. R. Colwell (eds). *Estuarine microbial ecology.* Columbia, S.C., University of S. Carolina Press, p. 73–89.

——; BOOTH, C. R. 1966. The measurement of adenosine triphosphate in the ocean and its ecological significance. *Limnol. Oceanogr.,* vol. 11, 510–9.

JORGENSEN, J. H.; CARVAJAL, H. F.; CHIPPS, B. E.; SMITH, R. F. 1973. Rapid detection of gram-negative bacteria by use of the *Limulus* endotoxin assay. *Appl. Microbial.,* vol. 26, p. 38–42.

Manual of Microbiological Methods. 1957. Society of Am. Bacteriologists, New York, McGraw-Hill.

MORIARTY, D. J. W. 1975. A method for estimating the biomass of bacteria in aquatic sediments and its application to trophic studies. *Oecologia,* vol. 20, p. 219–29.

——. 1976. Quantitative studies on bacteria and algae in the food of the mullet *Mugil cephalus* L. and the prawn *Metapenaeus bennettae* (Racek and Dall). *J. exp. mar. Biol. Ecol.,* vol. 22, p. 131–143.

ODUM, H. T.; ODUM, E. P. 1955. Trophic structure and productivity of a windward coral reef community on Eniwetok Atoll. *Ecol. Monogr.*, vol. 25, p. 192–320.

SCHMIDT, E. L. 1974. Quantitative autoecological study of microorganisms in soil by immuno fluorescence. *Soil Sci.*, vol. 118, p. 141–9.

SKERMAN, V. D. B. 1968. *A Guide to the identification of the genera of bacteria.* Baltimore, Williams and Wilkins.

SOROKIN, Y. I. 1968. The use of C^{14} in the study of aquatic animals. *Comm. Int. Assoc. Theor. Appl. Limnol.* Stuttgart. N16. (41 p.).

——. 1971. On the role of bacteria in the productivity of tropical oceanic waters. *Int. Rev. gesamt. Hydrobiol.*, vol. 56, p. 1–48.

——. 1973. On the feeding of some scleractinian corals with bacteria and dissolved organic matter. *Limnol. Oceanogr.*, vol. 18, p. 380–5.

——. 1974. Bacteria as a component of the coral reef community. In: *Proc. Second Int. Coral Reef Symp.* Brisbane, Greater Reef Committee, vol. 1, p. 3–10.

——; KADOTA, H. (eds.). 1972. *Techniques of the assessment of microbial production and decomposition in fresh water.* Oxford and Edinburgh, Blackwell Scientific Publications. (IBP Handbook no. 13). (104 p.)

SULLIVAN, J. D. Jr.; WATSON, S. W. 1974. Factors affecting the sensitivity of *Limulus* lysate. *Appl. Microbiol.*, vol. 28, p. 1023–26.

WEBB, K. L.; WIEBE, W. J. 1975. Nitrification in a coral reef. *Can. J. Microbiol.*, vol. 21, p. 1427—31.

——; DU PAUL, W.; WIEBE, W. J.; SOTTILE II, W. S.; JOHANNES, R. E. 1975. Enewetak (Eniwetok) Atoll: aspects of the nitrogen cycle on a coral reef. *Limnol. Oceanogr.*, vol. 20, p. 198–210.

WIEBE, W. J. 1971. Perspectives in microbial ecology. In: E. P. Odum (ed.). *Fundamentals of Ecology.* 3rd edit., Philadelphia, Saunders. p. 484–97.

WIEBE, W. J.; POMEROY, L. R. 1972. Microorganisms and their association with aggregates and detritus in the sea: A microscopic study. *Mem. Ist. Ital. Idrobiol.*, vol. 29 Suppl., p. 325–52.

——; JOHANNES, R. E.; WEBB, K. L. 1975. Nitrogen fixation in a coral reef community. *Science*, vol. 188, p. 257–9.

35

Productivity and calcification estimates using slack-water periods and field enclosures

D. W. Kinsey[1]

INTRODUCTION

While it is true that many Central Pacific and some Atlantic reefs are subjected to something approaching unidirectional current flow, there are many other situations in which this is not normal. It is obvious that where tide or wind-induced water flow is variable, flow studies of the kind described earlier cannot be used for other than very short periods of time. In some situations it is likely that there will be periods of slack-water sufficiently protracted to facilitate standing-water observations being made. This is more likely to be at the bottom of the tide than at other time. Metabolic functions, monitored as chemical changes in the water under such conditions, can be related to a very precisely defined community because of the limited mixing which occurs with water from adjacent zones. Also, monitoring is very simple as only one station is required. As a further advantage, the total changes in analytical variables are likely to be relatively great due to the protracted exposure time, and this allows precise data to be more easily obtained. The first mention of a study taking advantage of a very limited standing water situation on a coral reef seems to be that of Emery (1962).

In choosing suitable sites it is obvious that many reefs will not allow the use of a standing-water approach during intermittent periods of standing water except perhaps with the specialized communities of intertidal pools on the reef flat or beach rock zones (Davies and Kinsey, 1973). However, it is equally important to stress that these methods are certainly not restricted to coral reef environments. Any situation subjected to periods of standing water is suitable whether it be physically confined (pools etc.) or open. The ultimate deciding factor is that the 'ratio' of community metabolic activity to water volume has to be sufficient to cause detectable chemical changes in the water.

If one is fortunate enough to be dealing with a reef in an area of relatively large tides, it is likely that there will be large expanses of reef flat and, in some

1. Hawaii Institute of Marine Biology, University of Hawaii, P.O. Box 1346, Kaneohe, Hawaii 96744, U.S.A.

439

cases, lagoon environments and patch reefs which are not only subjected to standing-water conditions at the bottom of the tide, but are actually cut-off from exchange with the surrounding open water by the exposed reef crest for significant periods of time. These conditions apply to a number of reefs on the Australian Great Barrier Reef and are very marked in the Capricorn and Bunker groups. These reefs are relatively small, but wide, and in many cases have a well-developed central lagoon.

One Tree Island reef is in the Capricorn Group and has been the site for a considerable amount of community study work in recent years. It is a perfect case of a reef with the attributes referred to above. A detailed description has been given (Kinsey, 1972) of this reef and its tidal behaviour. For about half of each tidal cycle this lagoonal platform reef is essentially a large saucer full of water to the rim, and completely isolated from the surrounding sea. Because all 'low-tides' are exactly at this constant level much of the coral formation within the enclosed reef reaches the surface at low-water. This effectively prevents wind-induced currents. There is a well developed lagoon with extensive coral growths, and a reef flat which does not expose, but at low tide holds between 0.5 m and 2 m of water over the sand between the coral. The rich coral areas of this flat have been referred to in various publications as 'back-reef' to distinguish them from the more typical reef flat development found in fringing reefs and close to the cays in the same area, but it is acknowledged that this is not really back-reef in the sense that most workers have used the term.

One Tree Island gives standing water conditions over its entire area inside the reef crest for periods of close to five hours, though some slight draining occurs during the first two hours. During this time the following zones can be monitored with complete freedom from interference from the others, using only one fixed station.

Crest pools
Various coral zones of the flat ('back-reef')
Sand flats
Various lagoon types
Depressed centres of patch reefs ('micro-atolls')

The patch reefs are themselves miniatures of the whole reef in that they also have a rim which is level with the water surface at low tide and causes, in many cases, very effective isolation of substantial pools. Hence the expression 'micro-atoll' is used in a general sense and does not mean the centres of *Porites* formations as is sometimes seen in the literature.

Because periods of standing water imply negligible water movement, other than by diffusion, etc., it is possible to extend the general approach to obtain complete isolation of discrete sub-communities by surrounding them with open topped 'fences'. This valuable bonus procedure allows very specific information to be obtained and requires virtually no interference with the naturally occurring conditions during the standing water periods. No such simple extension of procedure is practical in flow systems, though attempts have been made by other workers to channel flow along specific transects.

440

SPECIFIC CONSIDERATIONS

Comparing the still water approach with the flow studies already described in an earlier Chapter, the advantages and disadvantages can be summarized as follows:

Advantages	*Disadvantages*
Simple single station monitoring	Useful monitoring periods discontinuous due to tides (frequently a problem in flow systems also).
Much smaller and more discrete communities can be studied—hence community structure is more easily described.	
Great variation in analytical parameters simplifies instrumental requirements.	Greater variations in water chemistry may lead to levels causing biological limitations thus complicating diurnal extrapolations.
Continuous recording monitors can easily be used without problems of correlation with a second down-stream station.	Greater displacement in O_2 and CO_2 levels from equilibrium aggravates problems from diffusion exchange with atmosphere.
Fences give a logical extension of the approach.	Localized gradients due to inadequate mixing may develop.
Overall it enables a more detailed picture to be built up with generally better precision.	Diurnal integrated data are based on low tide periods only. (i.e. high tide activities assumed to be same as low tide).
	Accurate assessment of the flux of suspended materials is not possible.

MONITORING CONCEPTS

In developing an approach to monitoring variables in the water mass overlying a community it is first necessary to be clear on the ultimate objective of the investigation. Is it primarily aimed at determining community response as a function of concentration of some variable? Is the objective to determine nutrient flux, or net growth rates (organic or inorganic)? If the latter, is it only instantaneous rates that are sought or is it only after diurnal or annual integrations that the objective will be met? Can the objective be satisfied by monitoring only one variable or the flux of only one element? If carbon flux is the principal consideration, will the story be much more valuable if the specific oxygen and carbon dioxide fluxes are both known to enable consideration to be given to respiratory quotient and photosynthetic quotient of the community? Is it necessary to relate the nutrient variations observed to incident light energy? Will the community under study be considered alone, or in relation to the surrounding ecosystem? Will consideration be given to input and output of organic material (soluble or particulate, living or non-living) or is it only the flux of basic nutrients such as O_2, CO_2, N, P, etc which is of interest?

It is not proposed to recommend here which of these should be emphasized most, but in general it is probable that most such investigations will ultimately be concerned with the integration of data into diurnal or annual patterns. Obviously diurnal curves, using the approaches originally defined in detail by Odum (1956) and Odum and Hoskin (1958), and subsequently applied in one form or another by many workers, can be easily applied to standing water situations (Park et al, 1958, Welch, 1968, Hornberger and Kelly, 1974). However, it is equally obvious that standing water for three hours or so in very 12 hours does not allow diurnal curves to be constructed over any one 24 hour period. Consequently, relatively large accumulations of basic data from slack-water periods are required to facilitate the construction of composite diurnal curves. This is based on the somewhat suspect assumption that composite low tide information gives the same overall result which would have been obtained if a continuous diurnal curve had been constructed. The specific application of the diurnal curve approach to the handling of field data from low tide periods will be expanded below. Also the use of such curves as standard curves to simplify the subsequent investigation of perturbations will be mentioned.

It cannot be stressed too strongly that data obtained from one time of the year or in one general weather situation or degree of insolation must never be extrapolated to give annual data. Results quoted later indicate how great such errors can be.

Standing-water conditions at low-tide with substantial protection from water movement effected by coral growth to the surface is ideal for boat-mounted monitors and laboratory facilities. In general this has been the approach used at One Tree Island (see Fig. 1). Monitoring of some variables in situ is extremely simple (e.g. O_2, temperature, pH, Cl). Alternatively, holding time for withdrawn samples where unstable variables such as CO_2 pH, etc., are to be measured, can be kept to an absolute minimum. Other procedures such as specific ion measurements, alkalinity determinations, and filtration of particulate matter can be easily carried out under these conditions saving a great deal of shore based laboratory time.

Continuous, fixed, on-site monitors also have a place in the standing water approach, particularly where long time periods (weeks or months) need to be used at the one site. However, unless automatic cut-outs of some sort are used a large proportion of the total recorded data will be relatively useless—i.e. all except the standing water data during two 3–5 hour periods each day. Nevertheless, this approach has proven very satisfactory in long term fertilization studies of micro-atoll environments (Kinsey and Domm, 1974, see also Figs. 2 and 3).

442

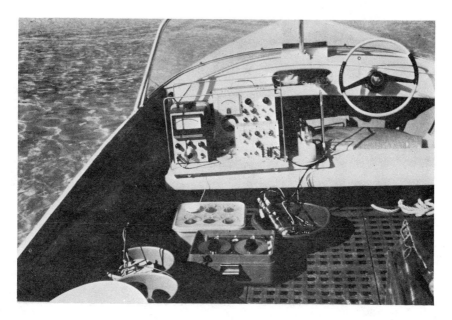

Figure 1
Boat-mounted monitoring equipment used for short time sequences in calm
water. Digital or potentiometric readout systems are necessary where wave
action is pronounced.

Figure 2
General view of tower-mounted continuous-recording monitors. This is a
low tide view across a micro-atoll

Figure 3
Close up of the tower-mounted instrument bundle winched down to the
servicing position and with the tarpaulin removed.

PRODUCTION AND RESPIRATION

General

Assessments of production and respiration in a community reveal a great deal
about metabolic activity, overall carbon flux, photosynthetic self sufficiency (or
lack of it), etc. Given also the input and losses of organic carbon, the absolute
flux and hence the flux (if any) in the standing crop can be determined. In
general it seems that most reefs actually lose somewhat more organic matter
than they consume (Marshall, 1965; Johannes, 1967) and consume slightly
more CO_2 (excluding calcification altogether) than they produce (Odum and
Odum, 1955; Kohn and Helfrich, 1957; Johannes *et al.*, 1972; Smith and
Marsh, 1973). Overall it seems reasonable to suggest that most coral reefs
exhibit a carbon flux close to equilibrium if calcification is discounted. As
mentioned earlier it is unfortunate that the standing-water approach does not
allow this total assessment to be made owing to the impracticability of measuring particulate fluxes. But very accurate estimations of production and respiration are possible.

Measurement of carbon dioxide flux has three marked advantages over
the measurement of oxygen flux. First, it is a direct indication of carbon flux.
Secondly, it gives an estimate of calcification as a bonus (discussed by Smith
and Kinsey, Chapter 36, and later in this paper). Thirdly, the properties of the
CO_2 system in seawater are such that problems of exchange with the atmosphere

444

are minimal, even though standing water experiences considerable displacement from equilibrium due to protracted biological influence. Direct measurement of CO_2 has not yet achieved sufficient precision for coral reef work, and consequently the precise but more cumbersome alkalinity/chlorinity/pH procedures must be used. These do not give a direct estimation which can be continuously recorded on site.

Oxygen flux can also be used to derive rates for production or respiration provided that (a) sufficient CO_2 data are available to establish RQ or PQ values relevant to the community under consideration, (b) corrections for atmospheric exchange can be reliably made and (c) loss of photosynthetically produced oxygen as bubbles is negligible (see later). Oxygen is a direct estimation which can be made with high precision using electrochemical oxygen electrodes and, as such, lends itself to continuous recording. It has been used as the principal monitored parameter in most work at One Tree Island. Oxygen data tell us nothing about calcification.

Parameters to be monitored to enable the above approaches to be applied to communities or sub-communities under conditions of standing water are as follows:

Oxygen based	*Carbon dioxide based*
Oxygen	pH
Temperature	Temperature
Wind velocity	Cl
(Values for the diffusion	Alkalinity
constant must also be	
available or derived)	

All parameters need to be checked for vertical stratification or patchy horizontal distribution and if either is significant, monitoring at more than one point over the site is necessary.

Additionally, records need to be kept of depth, insolation, time and whatever parameters of community structure and size may make the final derived production or respiration figures more meaningful—e.g. percentage of bottom cover, actual surface area of the community (either projected or absolute), community mass per m^2, biomass per m^2, community volume (overall or absolute) per m^2, etc., Data expressed in the simplest form of flux per m^2 of bottom area are the most commonly seen. The other reference bases suggested above are most relevant when discrete communities and sub-communities are being considered.

Data need to be obtained for all times of the 24 hour cycle, all times of the year and all weather conditions for a total picture to be built-up.

Methods

pH and alkalinity are covered in detail elsewhere (Smith and Kinsey, Chapter

36). Chlorinity (Cl) is essential for accurate estimation of CO_2 content. In standing water, evaporation may influence chlorinity substantially. Its influence on oxygen content can generally be ignored except in restricted environments such as tide pools where the change may be sufficient to influence oxygen solubility and of course where it also serves as a potential indicator of volume change due to evaporation. Any conductivity type salinometer capable of giving the second decimal place will be satisfactory but in line with the general preference indicated for on site estimation, the instrument chosen should be suitable for field work.

Temperature is best measured *in situ* with thermistor probes and should be accurate to 0.1°C if O_2 is the monitored variable. It can readily be recorded even on simple galvanometric recorders with the use of a simple bridge circuit.

Wind velocity should be recorded at least to the nearest 5 knots. This value is used in applying diffusion coefficients. Subjective estimation is generally satisfactory after some practice

Oxygen can be determined in the traditional manner using modified Winkler procedures on samples but modern electrochemical techniques properly applied are far more satisfactory. The first use of this approach for on-site reef studies appears to have been by Kinsey in 1961 (Kinsey and Kinsey, 1967) using polarographic probes. The probes still in use at One Tree Island are not substantially different except that they are made commercially and are fully temperature compensated. For total reliability over very long periods of time and particularly where on-site continuous monitors with infrequent calibration checks are to be used, the best results will be obtained using probes with the following characteristics:

polarographic rather than galvanic,
gold cathode rather than platinum (prevents sulphide poisoning),
very large electrolyte reservoir (minimizes chemical changes),
polyethylene membranes, but never polytetrafluoroethylene (PTFE causes serious drift)
temperature compensated to ± 0.5 per cent *with the chosen membrane.*

Additionally oxygen electrodes require movement past the membrane. This can be imparted by raising and lowering the cable by hand in spot measurements or by using battery powered impellers mounted against the electrode (Fig. 4).

Associated circuitry to be used with oxygen probes may be specially designed, or one of the many units now on the market, however, it is essential that it allows an accuracy and repeatability better than ± 1 per cent and that it be virtually devoid of any temperature sensitivity which interferes with its use in the field. The same points apply to recorders used in continuous monitors. Battery-operated solid state equipment is virtually mandatory in these applications.

It should be stressed that even the most precise and fully temperature compensated oxygen meter indicates a value proportional only to oxygen tension (saturation level) and not to actual concentration regardless of what the

446

Figure 4
Underwater view of oxygen (left) and temperature sensors *in situ*. The
rotating impeller can be seen as a blur behind the sensors. Plastic-coated
spirals give physical protection to the assembly without interfering with
water movement.

meter calibration might suggest. Instrument readings are least ambiguous if
recorded as percentage of saturation (S)—i.e. with respect to sea water at the
same temperature saturated with air at a total pressure of 760 mmHg. This can
be converted to concentration (C) only by relating it to the solubility of oxygen at
the Cl and temperature of the measurement. The conversion is a simple matter
of applying values for oxygen solubility from such tabulated data at those of
Carpenter (1966).

Calibration of oxygen electrodes can be done very simply and accurately.
First, any residual signal in the absence of oxygen should be cancelled. This is
best done by placing the electrode in nitrogen gas (or water through which N_2
is bubbled). This is preferred to the use of reducing agents such as metabisulphite

447

which may cause chemical problems, however, it is important to ensure that the gas is supplied oxygen free. By far the most straightforward way to obtain a calibrating oxygen standard is to shake violently (or aerate) a small quantity of sea water (Cl not critical) for about 30 seconds, and repeat with a change of head space air. Then swirl gently until completely clear. This gives a solution which is better than ± 1 per cent of true saturation. A correction for barometric pressure should be applied if necessary, to 760 mmHg. The temperature used should be reasonably close to the range to be encountered experimentally to minimize any error in the electrode's temperature compensator. Ideally, the temperature compensator should have been 'trimmed' to give constant reading from the electrode at any temperature in air saturated sea water rather than in fresh water or dry air (vapour pressure difference).

The instrument calibrated by the procedure outlined should give a precision of ± 1 per cent over a reasonable range of temperature. Calibration checks should be made daily, if practicable, though the system in use at One Tree Island (specially designed) has maintained calibration for up to several weeks. However, long term stability has frequently been upset by algal growth on the membrane with electrodes used in continuous monitoring systems.

As mentioned earlier it is necessary to correct oxygen data for gains from or losses to the atmosphere, if maximum precision in derived biological parameters is to be obtained. To do this, values for the diffusion coefficient K must be determined. The application of this coefficient will be outlined in the next section. In the earliest coral reef studies by Sargent and Austin (1949, 1954) and Odum and Odum (1955) no corrections were applied. In the subsequent work of Kohn and Helfrich (1957) corrections were used based on the Odum (1956) principle of obtaining coefficients from post-dusk and pre-dawn respiration values. This principle requires that there be complete confidence in the constancy of night-time respiration rates. Gordon and Kelly (1962) used a more complex approach, still based on the Odum (1956) and Odum and Hoskin (1958) principle but introducing frequent determinations of values for K during the night and the application of average values from the night to the day-time data.

The approach used at One Tree Island which is described below, has taken advantage of the very substantial differences in oxygen concentrations in the water between the low tide standing water situation and those found during or immediately after the 'flushing' of the lagoon by the high tides. The calculation of standard values for K from large accumulations of data is favoured over redetermination for each experimental series, however, in short term work this is clearly impractical.

Unlike earlier methods, this approach allows the calculation of K equally well from day-time or night-time data. It also is not dependent on the assumption of constant respiration rates throughout the night. However, like all approaches to this problem it is dependent on certain suspect assumptions, viz. production and respiration are assumed to be unaffected by oxygen tension within the range 70–150 per cent of air saturation and values for K are calculated from data within this range. Also light penetration through a water surface disrupted to varying degrees by wind action is assumed to be constant (not relevant to night calculations). The following conventions will be used:

K = areal diffusion coefficient for O_2

S = per cent O_2 saturation with respect to air at 760 mmHg total pressure

C = O_2 concentration in any suitable units

t = time

Z = water depth

D = the mean value of the saturation excess (positive value) or deficit (negative value) at the *water surface* during the period used for experimental determination of dC/dt. i.e. $D = (S' + S'')/2 - 100$ over 100

The reasoning applied to the determination of K is as follows (values quoted refer to 1 m deep back-reef at One Tree Island):

(a) High-tide O_2 range (90–110 per cent satn.) is much smaller than the low-tide slack water range $(14 - >200$ per cent saturation).

(b) Low-tide oxygen concentration for any *particular time*, is therefore dependent on the number of hours since the preceding high tide.

(c) Given constant temperature, insolation and wind velocity, the low-tide oxygen saturation level will be different at any *particular time* during a series of 4–5 consecutive days or nights, due to the decreasing time elapsed since the preceding high tide.

(d) Therefore values obtained for the rate of change of oxygen concentration (dC/dt) at *that time* on each of the days *will* differ but because of differences in diffusion alone. (i.e. real metabolic rates are assumed to be constant).

(e) Thus a value of K relevant to the wind velocity chosen can be calculated by the Odum and Hoskin (1958) procedure, on the premise that net production rate (y) or respiration rate (r) must have remained constant.

(f) Summarizing.—Strictly within the experimental framework outlined under (a)–(e):

$$(dC/dt)'Z + D'K = (dC/dt)''Z + D''K = (dC/dt)'''Z + D'''K, \text{ etc.}$$

for any particular time over a period of several days at the one site.

K is a constant for any particular wind velocity. Thus by solving any pair of the above where a constant wind velocity applies, a value for K is obtained relevant to the site under consideration at its low tide depth, and to the particular wind velocity. The actual value of K once obtained is itself virtually independent of time, season and insolation. It has also been found to be relatively independent of temperature though this is not in line with theoretical considerations. The units for K will be $gO_2 \, m^{-2} \, hr^{-1}$ *at 100 per cent air saturation deficit,* or similar, dependent on the units of oxygen concentration and time chosen.

Constant wind conditions will usually occur sufficiently often to enable such values to be calculated from data accumulated during one field trip of a few weeks.

If comparisons are also made between values of dC/dt subject to the conditions above but with substantially varying wind of say 5, 10 and 20 knots, the relationship between K and wind velocity can readily be determined. Fortunately sudden changes of wind also occur sufficiently often at One Tree Island to make this practical.

Table 1 gives values for K determined as above. The values have been

TABLE 1. Low tide[a] values for the areal oxygen diffusion coefficient (K) (g O_2 m^{-2} hr^{-1} at 100 per cent air saturation deficit)

Back-reef and micro-atoll situations:				1 m deep				
Wind velocity (knots)	0	5	8	10	12	15	18	20
K	0.5	0.6	0.65	0.7	0.8	1.1	1.5	2.0
Shallow lagoon situations between patch reefs:				2–3 m deep				
K	0.5	0.65	0.8	1.0	1.3	1.8	2.5	3.0

a. At low tide in both the areas used in obtaining the values for K, considerable protection of the water surface against wind action is effected by flat-topped 'pie-crust' coral.

N.B. It is not recommended that these values by applied in other situations without first determining tehir suitability.

found to be the same for low or supersaturated levels of O_2. The areas for which values are given are all subject to substantial protection of the water surface at low-tide by the frequency of windrows or reticulum of coral flush with the surface which prevent severe wind wave formation. The values are expressed on the 100 per cent *air* saturation deficit basis and not per atmosphere of pure oxygen.

It must be stressed that values of K must be determined for each type of environment being considered. The physical nature of the bottom, the extent of coral development and other such factors exert a considerable influence on water mixing and wave action and, as such, modify the value of K obtained.

When measuring the production and respiration of coral reef communities it must be borne in mind that information derived from changes in water chemistry will not distinguish between the contributions of the benthic community and those of the planktonic community. Fortunately the activity of planktonic communities over coral reefs has been found to be very low relative to the total (Sargent and Austin, 1949, 1954; Odum and Odum, 1955; Gordon, 1971; Kinsey and Domm, 1974; Gordon et al., 1971; Johannes et al., 1972; Ramachandran and Pillai, 1972). Sophisticated methods of concentrating the plankton before estimating its activity have been used (Pomeroy and Johannes, 1968) elsewhere, however the approach used at One Tree Island has proved to be simple and effective. This involves withdrawing a sample of around 25 litres, bringing it to 100 per cent air saturation (noting temperature), using an aeration system, then enclosing a series of 1 litre sub-samples in polyester bags with the total exclusion of bubbles. The bags are immersed in ambient lagoon water at the site being used for overall monitoring and examined by the procedures in use after 0.5, 1, 2 and 3 hours. Thus each bag is only opened once and the oxygen saturation level and temperature determined by quickly inserting the electrodes into the bag and stirring. No detectable pick up will occur during the time taken for this operation. Water held in bags must not be monitored longer than 3 hours and hence composite results are required for the derivation of a diurnal pattern. During 3 hours, linear rates (allowing for the natural diurnal pattern) will be observed, but if the sample is held longer, rapidly increasing respiration will be found due to settling and development of bacteria on the walls of the bag. Polyester bags are very clear and exhibit a very low diffusion characteristic. Polyethylene is poor from both points of view, particularly the latter. PVC can be used but leaching of toxic plasticizers is a hazard. The total omission of this examination of planktonic activity can usually be assumed not to detract greatly from the value of coral reef community metabolism studies.

The mounting and protection of field instrumentation is an important aspect of methodology. For boat mounting, digital readout systems and potentiometric recorders have the advantage of freedom from inertial problems resulting from movement of the boat. Normal meter movements and galvanometric recorders can behave rather erratically except under the calmest conditions. Generally speaking it is simpler to use low voltage equipment powered by lead acid accumulators, or even built-in dry or mercury cells (if they prove adequate), than to use high voltage A.C. equipment in conjunction with an inverter. It has been found entirely practical to use conventionally assembled electronic equipment on boats (as indicated in Fig. 1), rather than the bulkier and more expensive completely waterproofed equipment. Boats should be fitted with windscreens if possible, and clear plastic covers, either rigid or framed, used to cover the instrument bundle at all times. The assembly should be mounted above the floor level and tied down. During transit the plastic cover should be further protected with an absorbent cover such as a large towel. This is extremely efficient in preventing spray penetration. Careful procedures should also be followed to ensure minimal transfer of salt water to instrument controls. Fresh water may be used for washing hands but this is not really as important as an adequate supply of dry towels. Where possible boats should have flat floors covered with some form of open mesh to allow any loose water on the floor to be clear of the working area. (See Fig. 1.)

For on-site fixed monitors in reef flat and lagoonal situations it has been found simple. safe and practical to mount continuous battery (lead acid) powered monitors on galvanized steel poles with wire guys, and to winch the instrument platform up to a level above the wave crests at high tide. (See Figs 2 and 3). Servicing is normally carried out at low tide when the reef gives a virtually exposed flat working surface. Again it has been found quite practical to use unsealed electronic equipment covered with rigid plastic covers. Additionally, the entire assembly including the accumulators is covered with heavy canvas type material and tied securely.

Processing Data

The handling of raw data to give estimates of changes in CO_2 concentration is covered elsewhere (Smith and Kinsey, Chapter 36). While the handling of oxygen data is also covered elsewhere in this Monograph, relative to other situations, it is desirable that the complete approach used at One Tree Island for still water data should be outlined. This has also been covered in the recent paper given at the Second International Coral Reef Symposium (Kinsey and Domm, 1974).

All oxygen saturation data should first be converted to concentration (C) data by applying the temperature dependent solubility factors referred to earlier. (See Table 2). If stratification has made it necessary to determine oxygen at several depths a vertical mean should next be derived from the various concentrations taking care to weight properly individual figures for the extent of the layer they represent (Kinsey, 1972; and Table 2).

The mean oxygen concentrations obtained for a series of times during the standing water period are next used to obtain values for dC/dt making the assumption that the rate is constant (i.e. $\Delta C/\Delta t = dC/dt$). This assumption is of course not strictly valid because of the changing effect of diffusion interference (dependent on saturation level) and in the day time because of the progressively changing rate of photosynthetic production throughout the daylight period. However, in practice the assumption that dC/dt is constant over periods of one hour, or even three hours near the middle of the day, gives rise to very small errors, and this method of data processing is preferred because of its simplicity.

At this stage the volumetric dC/dt is converted to a rate of change in the quantity of oxygen overlying unit bottom area by multiplying by the mean water depth. (See Table 2.) The resulting dM/dt can then be converted to an hourly rate of net production (y) in daylight or respiration (r) in the dark by applying the diffusion correction according to the principles outlined by Odum and Hoskin (1958). A value for K (determined as discussed earlier) is required and this is assumed to apply across a gradient expressed as the saturation deficit (or excess) at the surface using the mean value for the period (D—see earlier). This value must *not* make any allowance for stratification but use only surface values. This is essential as exchange with the atmosphere is a function only of saturation level at the surface even though the metabolic activity being measured may be influencing the whole overlying water mass.

Thus

y or $r = dC/dt\ Z + DK$ $\begin{bmatrix} \text{N.B. } dC/dt \text{ and } D \text{ may be positive or nega-} \\ \text{tive, } y \text{ is usually positive, } r \text{ must be negative} \end{bmatrix}$

Table 2 gives an example of the processing of data from the saturation values recorded in the field to the derivation of a value for net production rate (y).

Whether CO_2 or oxygen data are used, the overall objective should be to obtain sufficient values for y, each based on a 1–3 hour low-tide period, to cover the whole day-time period. This should be done over the minimum number of days possible (preferably not exceeding 1 week) taking advantage of

TABLE 2. Processing short term low-tide standing water results—typical data from a rich coral area of the reef flat ('back-reef') at One Tree Island

20 September 1968
Insolation 100 per cent
Cl = 19·5 parts per thousand

Tides 0305 186 cm[a]
0907 104 cm
1555 247 cm

1 Time	2 Hour	3 Wind (knots)	4 Total depth (cm)	5 Depth of reading Z (cm)	6 Temp (°C)	7 %O_2 satn S	8 O_2 conc. C (g m^{-3})	9 O_2 conc. C (Vertical mean)	10 dC/dt (g m^{-3} hr^{-1})	11 dM/dt (g m^{-2} hr^{-1})	12 K	13 Mean surface Satn (per cent)	14 satn excess D	15 y (g m^{-2} hr^{-1})	16 Time
0900	0	10	81	2	19.6	94	7.00	6.68							
,,	,,	,,		10	19.6	91	6.78								
,,	,,	,,		70	19.4	87	6.51								
1000	1	10	81	2	20.5	108	7.92	7.85	1.17	+0.95	0.70	101	+0.01	+0.95	0930
,,	,,	,,		10	20.5	108	7.92								
,,	,,	,,		70	20.5	106	7.77								
1200	3	15	80	2	21.4	140	10.11	10.11	1.13	+0.91	0.84	124	+0.24	+1.11	1100
,,	,,	,,		10	21.4	140	10.11								
,,	,,	,,		70	21.4	140	10.11								

a. The lagoon level is at 155 cm above datum. Water level changes little from 0700 to 1200 with only 1 cm drop from 0900–1200. This is the period of standing water conditions.
Special Points. (Relevant to column numbers indicated).

Columns 1–7 are field data. 8–16 are derived data.

4. Slight change in depth over 3 hr causes negligible volume transport to interfere with standing water concept.
5. When no stratification is detected only one monitoring depth need be used.
7. Depressed levels initially reflect standing water conditions near dawn when respiration dominant. Increasing wind responsible for better mixing later in the series.
8. Derived from values under 7 using oxygen solubilities after Carpenter (1966).
9. Vertical means calculated after Kinsey (1972), i.e. assume 80–10 cm band is at the mean value of the oxygen concentrations (8) for 70 and 10 cm and assume the 0–10 cm band is at the mean value of the oxygen concentrations for 2 and 10 cm.
10. Difference between two consecutive vertical means over the time interval between them.
11. $dM/dt = dC/dt \times Z$ (mean relevant values from column 4). This value is the rate of change in the quantity of oxygen overlying unit plane bottom area.
12. Value from Table 1 using mean wind velocity, i.e. 12.5 knots for 1000–1200.
13. Mean value at 2 cm from column 7 for the time period concerned.
14. ((value in column 13)—100)/100.
15. $y = dM/dt + DK$.
16. Time at which the value of Y in column 15 is considered to apply.

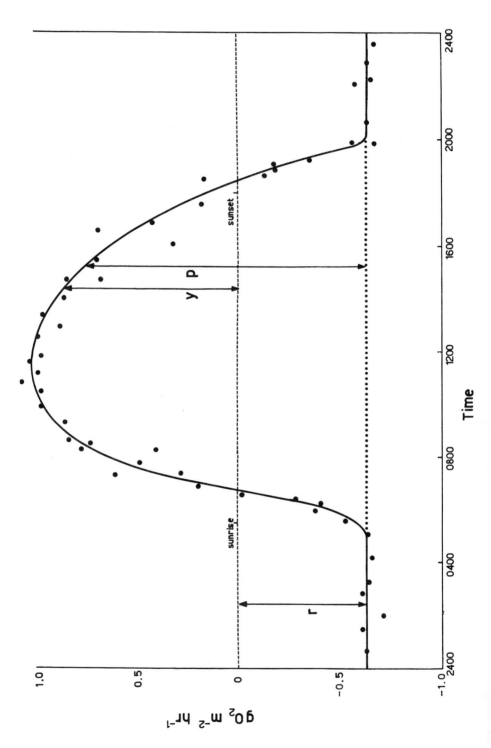

the daily change in the time of the tide. Similarly it is advisable to determine values for r at several times from dusk till dawn in case r is not found to be constant. (In fact r has usually been found to be very nearly constant in all the situations examined at One Tree Island.) The accumulated values for y are then plotted against time of the day to give a composite diurnal curve of the type indicated in Figure 5. Considering this curve and making the conventional though suspect (viz. possibility of photorespiration) assumption that day-time respiration is equal to that at night, the following conventions will be used:

r = hourly respiration rate
y = hourly rate of net photosynthesis
y_{max} = peak hourly rate of net photosynthesis
p = $y + r$ = hourly rate of photosynthesis
p_{max} = peak hourly rate of photosynthesis
R = 24 r (provided r is found to be constant at night)
P = integration of the curve with respect to p which approximates Σp.

Values for all these variables can be expressed on whatever basis relative to the community has been decided in the original experimental plan—i.e. per m^2, or per kg coral mass, or per g tissue nitrogen, etc.

When sufficient data have been accumulated to facilitate the construction of really reliable diurnal curves it is most expeditious, in subsequent work in the same or similar situations, to use these curves as standard curves such that it only becomes necessary to determine as few as one value for y and r to enable a satisfactory prediction of y_{max} and hence p_{max}, P and R. For instance, not only has it been found possible realistically to predict y_{max} (and hence p_{max}) in 'back-reef' situations from individual values obtained for y at times from 0900 to 1500 hrs but the value for P derived by such an approach is remarkably accurate due to a very consistent relationship between p_{max} and P in any one situation at a particular time of the year, e.g. 1 m deep 'back-reef' and micro-atolls at One Tree Island (must not be applied elsewhere):

$P =$ 9 p_{max} at 10th May
$P =$ 8 p_{max} at 30th June
$P =$ 10 p_{max} at 30th September
$P =$ 11 p_{max} at 15th December

(Hours of sunshine vary considerably from roughly 10 hr 40 min. in late June to 13 hr 40 min. in late December).

Figure 5
Diurnal oxygen curve for 1 m deep back-reef ($P/R = 1.1$ based on O_2) in early October. Correction for diffusion has been applied. The curve is a composite of 50 2–5 hour low-tide standing water periods with complete insolation. From each period a single mean value of y or r has been plotted. The asymmetrical form of the peak with y_{max} at midday is usual for diurnal curves based on One Tree Island data. Curves based on such large accumulations of data (over several years) have proved very useful as standard curves.

This simplified approach has proved very satisfactory in studying perturbations to a system already well elucidated in its normal pattern—e.g. fertilization of micro-atolls (Kinsey and Domm, 1974).

Expression of results

While some interesting conclusions can be drawn from considering values for y_{max} and p_{max} and r most significant discussion will usually result from consideration of P, R and P/R. P/R is an indication of the photosynthetic self sufficiency of the environment. If the level of gross diurnal photosynthesis (P) exceeds the level of gross diurnal respiration (R)—i.e. $P/R > 1$—it can be assumed that either the system is exporting organic matter or the standing crop is increasing. If $P/R < 1$ the system must import organic matter to complete its nutritional requirement or else it must be losing standing crop. The resolution of the various alternatives must depend on estimates of standing crop or import/export of organic matter or both.

Carbon dioxide data can be expressed as g CO_2, g mole CO_2, g carbon, g atoms carbon or g organic matter (as $(CHO)n$). Generally grams carbon is the preferred basis.

Oxygen data can be expressed as cc O_2, g O_2, g atoms O_2, g mole O_2 or converted to any of the carbon bases used for expression of CO_2 data. The latter are somewhat arbitrary unless at least some values are obtained by both oxygen and carbon dioxide approaches facilitating the determination of an appropriate conversion factor. The ratio of carbon dioxide produced by respiration to oxygen consumed by respiration is conventionally known as the respiratory quotient ($RQ = \Delta CO_2/\Delta O_2$). This can be obtained by comparing values for r derived from CO_2 and oxygen data respectively (on a molar or carbon equivalent basis). The ratio of oxygen produced by photosynthesis to carbon dioxide consumed by photosynthesis can be termed photosynthetic quotient ($PQ = \Delta O_2/\Delta CO_2$). It can be obtained by comparing values for p on the above basis. A similar ratio based on net photosynthesis (y) can also be useful though its significance is imprecise. While predominantly autotropic systems might be expected to give values of PQ and RQ equal to unity, many values actually obtained at One Tree Island have varied significantly from this value. Unfortunately it is also quite possible that PQ^{-1} will not be equal to RQ which further complicates interpretations (Strickland and Parsons, 1968; Strickland, 1960).

Diurnal data should not be used to derive annual data or data for other times of the year (see next section). Data from days of complete insolation will generally have values higher than those from heavily overcast days.

Interpreting results

It is worth considering some typical, fully processed, information arising from reef investigations. While standing water results from One Tree Island are used as the examples, much the same types of information could be derived from any detailed examination of a reef. The principal advantage of the standing water situation is that it allows more discrete zones to be studied. The results presented have been chosen to stress the importance of caution in making interpretations from incomplete data and particularly of not making generalizations or extrapolations except with great care. Again it should be stressed that the low-tide standing water approach used at One Tree Island is itself making at least one risky assumption—viz. that real diurnal production and respiration involving high tide periods as well as low tide periods is equal to that determined from composite low-tide diurnal curves.

Table 3 gives values for gross production and respiration on a diurnal basis for several lagoon environments. These are based on oxygen data and

TABLE 3. Typical production and respiration patterns[a] for shallow areas at One Tree Island—early October (mid-Spring)

	P ($g O_2 m^{-2} day^{-1}$)	R ($g O_2 m^{-2} day^{-1}$)	P/R
Coral rich reef-flat area—'back-reef' (0.8 m deep, 40 per cent coral cover)	20 (0.8)[a]	18 (1.4)	1.1 (0.05)
Sand flats (0.9 m deep, negligble coral cover)	2.3 (0.6)	3.6 (1.1)	0.6 (0.1)
Central lagoon with extensive coral reticulum (2.5 m deep, 10 per cent coral cover)	9 (0.6)	7.5 (0.8)	1.2 (0.05)
Water overlying reef-flats and shallow lagoon (0.8–2.5 m deep—'bag' Experiments)	0–0.15	0.3–.8	0–0.3

a. Based on low-tide composite diurnal curves of oxygen flux, and giving the standard deviation (in brackets) for the data obtained from a number of composite curves over several years. n varies from 8 for sand flats to 30 for 'back-reef'.

hence have been expressed on that basis. Expressed as carbon the results would be $\frac{12}{32}$ of the value indicated if RQ and PQ were equal to 1. Results obtained for benthic communities are remarkably constant (frequently better than ± 10 per cent) at any particular time of the year and with complete insolation. Results from planktonic communities ('bag' experiments) are not unexpectedly quite variable.

The principal points of interest in Table 3 are:

(a) Photosynthetic activity of plankton is extremely low.

(b) Respiration activity of plankton is much higher but only marginally contributing to overall respiration.

(c) Sand flats exhibiting visible algal films have significant activity but surprisingly low production relative to their respiration.

(d) Both coral zones are 'autotrophic' but this is more marked in the case of the central lagoon.

(e) Values for P, R and P/R obtained in the coral area of the reef flat are in marked general agreement with most other published data for similar areas (Kohn and Helfrich, 1957; Odum and Odum, 1955; Sargent and Austin, 1949, 1954; Ramachandran and Pillai, 1972; Smith and Marsh, 1973), though recent values for P/R (Smith and Marsh, 1973) given for a coral dominated area of a transect at Enewetak (previously spelled 'Eniwetok') were less than 1.

Table 4 gives values for RQ and PQ^{-1} determined in the same coral zone of the reef flat referred to in Table 3. By using the reciprocal of PQ both figures are on a comparative basis (i.e. $\Delta CO_2/\Delta O_2$). Table 4 includes values obtained for typical large coral communities within the same area and isolated during the standing water period by the fencing technique described later. The points of interest are:

(a) The area exhibits a marked difference between RQ and PQ^{-1} and is reasonably in keeping with the popular $RQ = 1$ and $PQ^{-1} = 0.8$ (Strickland and Parsons, 1968).

(b) Considering this difference relative to the values for P, R and P/R for the same site in Table 4 it is apparent that P/R based on carbon should be closer to 1.0.

TABLE 4. Mean values [a] of the respiratory quotient (RQ) and the reciprocal photosynthetic quotient (PQ^{-1}) for the coral rich reef-flat ('back-reef') at One Tree Island—September to November (spring)

	RQ	PQ^{-1}
General area (0.8 m deep 40 per cent coral cover)	1.05 (0.14)[a]	0.90 (0.05)
In-situ outcrop Porites andrewsi (3 m diam., fenced)	0.91 (0.14)	0.87 (0.11)
In-situ outcrop Leptoria phrygia (2 m diam., fenced)	0.88 (0.09)	0.86 (0.03)

a. Based on comparative low-tide composite diurnal curves of oxygen flux and carbon dioxide flux, and giving the standard deviation (in brackets) for a number of estimations during the one year ($n = 8$).

(c) The large and representative outcrops, while giving essentially the same value for PQ^{-1}, give a substantially lower value than the general area for RQ. No certain explanation is indicated but it seems reasonable to postulate that either the sand and rubble between coral outcrops has a very high RQ (approx. 3, indicating pronounced anaerobic activity) or else the outcrops chosen are not suitably representative of the area as a whole.

These values can suggest that oxygen lost as bubbles from benthic communities (at least in the present situation) is quantitatively unimportant. PQ values equivalent to a PQ^{-1} of 0.8 have been used by a number of workers (Ryther, 1956; Strickland, 1960; Welch, 1968; Strickland and Parsons, 1968), and an even higher value of 1 is implied by Smith and Marsh (1973). Bearing in mind that the lower this value becomes the greater is ΔO_2 with respect to ΔCO_2, it seems reasonable to suggest that the present experimental values of 0.86–0.90 are not compatible with any substantial quantity of O_2 having been lost as bubbles. This is even more convincing if considered relative to the very high levels of supersaturation (Table 2) encountered in this standing water situation.

Table 5 makes very clear the extreme hazards of extrapolating from one time of the year to another where there is any significant seasonal pattern. It also stresses that activity can be substantially out of phase with temperature (December and May results). A considerable seasonal variation in the auto-trophic self-sufficiency (P/R) is a feature of this discrete lagoonal community. Either there is considerable flux in standing crop throughout the year, or the community is importing and exporting considerable quantities of organic material. It is interesting to note that this shallow community with its relatively low P/R ratio (0.95 in late September) is within the general lagoon environment (2.5 m deep) indicated in Table 3 which exhibits the usefully high P/R of 1.2 in early October.

TABLE 5. Seasonal variation in production and respiration patterns[a] for a typical enclosed lagoon patch reef ('micro-atoll')[b] at One Tree Island

	Length of day sunrise to sunset (hr)	Diurnal temp. range (°C)	P ($g\,O_2\,m^{-2}day^{-1}$)	R ($g\,O_2\,m^{-2}day^{-1}$)	P/R
Late June	10.7	19–22	4.6	6.5	0.71
Late September	12.0	20–23	8.0	8.4	0.95
Mid-December	13.6	25–28	11.1	10.3	1.08
Mid-May	11.2	23–24	11.0	12.0	1.92

a. Based on low-tide composite diurnal curves of oxygen flux.
b. 1 m deep, 25 m wide with vertical coral walls and 5 per cent bottom cover.

CALCIFICATION

General

All coral reef communities contain large numbers of calcifying organisms varying enormously in the physical and chemical form in which they deposit carbonates. Within the context of overall nutrient flux we are concerned primarily with such matters as—what is total diurnal or annual calcification?—is there any reversal (dissolution) of this process?—is there constant calcification or a pronounced diurnal cycle?—how does calcification vary throughout the various reef zones? If a complete understanding of the inorganic growth of the reef is to be built up it is also necessary to estimate redistribution and total loss of particulate carbonates varying from fine sediments to large boulders.

Many 'calcifying' algae incorporate significant quantities of magnesium as well as calcium in their carbonate deposits. It is therefore more suitable in an overall study to monitor carbonate flux than the flux of calcium itself.

The historical background to reef calcification studies has been discussed in detail (Smith, Chapter 27; Smith, 1973; Chave *et al.*, 1972) and need not be further elaborated here. Similarly the general concept and justification for using alkalinity anomalies as indicators of calcification is well covered elsewhere (Smith, Chapter 27; Smith and Kinsey, Chapter 36; Smith and Pesret, 1974; Smith, 1973; Broecker and Takahashi, 1966; Traganza and Szabo, 1967), though the authors of the two earliest of those papers made the fundamental error of using changes in carbonate alkalinity rather than changes in total alkalinity as their reported parameter. Recent attempts have been made by Alison Domm (working in conjunction with Kinsey at One Tree Island) to correlate actual weight increases of corals over roughly six months with the apparent calcification rate estimated using the alkalinity method. Her results are discussed elsewhere in this volume (Smith and Kinsey, Chapter 36).

The standing-water approach to calcification based on the studies of One Tree Island has proved very satisfactory. Because of the frequent flushing of the low-tide standing water by the intervening high tides, and because the ratio of water to benthic biomass is considerable in most lagoonal situations, the water chemistry is not subject to excessively large changes such as those found in restricted environments such as beach-rock pools (Davies and Kinsey, 1973). In this latter situation the use of alkalinity anomalies as indicators of calcification becomes very risky. While work commenced on calcification studies at One Tree Island in 1968, the picture so far built up for the complete reef is not nearly as detailed or as reliable as that for production and respiration.

All general observations made in preceding sections of this paper relevant to working in discontinuous periods of standing water during low-tides apply and will not be repeated here. Just as productivity studies based on low-tide standing water periods are not accurately able to include estimations of particulate matter (living or non-living) entering or leaving the zone being considered, so does the same limitation apply to standing water periods used for calcification studies where estimates of the movement of sediments cannot be made.

The approach at One Tree Island again has been one of determining a series of rates for calcification during standing water periods throughout the day and night and over as short a period as possible. These may then be used to construct a complete diurnal curve, but the general precision of the calcification studies is such that a mean day-time rate and a mean night-time rate are about as much value as a diurnal curve for estimating diurnal flux.

Again it is important that checks be made for vertical stratification when working in standing water and if necessary sampling should be from several depths.

Methods

Analytical methods are detailed elsewhere (Smith and Kinsey, Chapter 36). Only values for total alkalinity and chlorinity need be determined and even the latter can be omitted if it is certain that no change occurs due to evaporation during the period of the observations. Therefore, calcification can be determined entirely on samples taken back to the laboratory though delays exceeding

48 hours are best avoided particularly if the samples are held unfiltered. When dealing with lagoonal situations it is imperative that all samples be filtered before the actual alkalinity estimation is made, as suspended carbonates will contribute erratically to the determination by dissolving in the added acid. In standing water at One Tree Island, changes in alkalinity found over the monitoring period were well within the precision of the method (± 0.005 equ.m^{-3}) seldom being less than 0.02 equ.m^{-3} hr^{-1}, unlike those found in flowing water situations (Smith, 1973). Even so, alkalinity data can hardly be expected to give the precise estimates of community calcification activity which can be made for production and respiration using O_2 and derived CO_2 data.

The other data to be recorded are the usual physical parameters of the environment such as depth, bottom cover, etc., which have been outlined in detail earlier.

Processing data

Analytical results will be in the form of total alkalinity (TA) in equivalents per m^3. If any change in chlorinity has occurred, indicating evaporation, the value for TA should be corrected accordingly. Next vertical means should be determined, if required, according to the procedure outlined for O_2 data (Table 2). The mean values for TA can be used to obtain a value for dTA/dt which is assumed to equal $\Delta TA/\Delta t$ over the standing water monitoring periods of 1–3 hours.

The value of dTA/dt as calculated above will have the units equivalents m^{-3} hr^{-1}. If the basis for consideration of the results is to be relative to bottom area the value should be multiplied by the depth to give equivalents m^{-2} hr^{-1}.

A change in TA of one equivalent in a given volume of water or overlying a given bottom area, etc., is equivalent to the net precipitation (or dissolution) of 50 g $CaCO_3$. (Smith and Kinsey, Chapter 36). Thus dTA/dt, whether per m^2 or m^3, can be expressed as a net calcification rate by multiplying by 50. It should be stressed that this method does not allow any estimate of gross calcification in the presence of dissolution but can only indicate net calcification. It is doubtful that any field procedure will ever allow that distinction to be made.

When sufficient values for the calcification rate (or rate of dissolution) have been obtained over individual 1–3 hour periods they may be used to construct a diurnal curve. It is simpler, however, and within the precision of the method, to determine a mean rate for the hours of daylight and one for the night-time period. The latter has tended to be erratic and unpredictable at One Tree Island. The day-time values do form a curve somewhat similar to the photosynthesis curve but with a much flatter plateau (Smith and Kinsey, Chapter 36). Diurnal calcification is estimated by multiplying the two rates by the number of hours over which they apply and summing the two results.

Expression of results

As indicated above there is really one one piece of information conveyed by this experimental approach and that is rates of net calcification. These may be mean night time, mean day time, peak day time, diurnal, etc. Only g $CaCO_3$ is used and this can be related to all the physical bases (m², kg skeleton, g tissue nitrogen, etc.) indicated in other sections.

Interpreting results

Calcification data obtained during low-tide standing water periods at One Tree Island have frequently included negative rates at night from some sites. They have also indicated a very pronounced day–night rate difference with the day-time rate always being much higher. The concept of a high day-time rate is in keeping with most of the numerous studies made of hermatypic corals in isolation but is not in agreement with the data of Smith (1973) from Enewetak where the shallow reef flat transects exhibited continuous and fairly constant calcification over the 24 hour cycle.

The data of Alison Domm from isolated coral heads suggest that most *corals* exhibit pronounced day–night cycles of calcification and that the night-time rate varies from zero to 20 per cent of the day-time rate. In one case (*Goniastrea benhami*) a negative night-time rate (-11%) was found but the results with this particular species were unreliable. Thus it seems that overall negative rates obtained at night in the reef flat area are not likely to be a function of the living coral (dissolution of 'living' coral skeleton) but either passive dissolution of dead coral skeleton or carbonate sand, etc., due to the low pH (7.9 is common on the reef flat), or an activity of some other group within the community—perhaps calcareous algae and bacteria may be implicated.

Table 6 gives some rates obtained in the rich coral reef-flat area ('back-reef') for which other data have already been quoted. Values obtained from this area at any particular time of the year have varied ±20 per cent for day-time rates but have been highly erratic at night though always much lower than the day-time rates. There does not appear to be a pronounced seasonal pattern which is interesting when compared with the pattern for production and respiration as indicated in Table 5. At this time there is no known explanation

TABLE 6. Calcification rates[a] for the rich coral reef-flat ('back-reef') at One Tree Island—(0.8 m deep, 40 per cent coral cover)

	Diurnal temp. range (°C)	Mean day-time calcification (g $CaCO_3$ m^{-2}hr^{-1})	Mean night-time calcification (g $CaCO_3$ m^{-2}hr^{-1})	Diurnal estimate (g $CaCO_3$ m^{-2}day^{-1})
Late September 1968	18–27	0.8	0.2	11.5
Mid-July 1973	18–23	1.5		
Late September 1973	20–25	1.0	−0.1	10.8
Late November 1973	25–31	1.1	−0.4	10.0

a. Each value based on low-tide standing water data obtained during four days of a two week period. All day-time values fall in the range ±20 per cent from the mean. Night-time values were low and erratic.

for the conspicuous difference between the 1968 and the 1973 data. The overall diurnal estimate of say $10–11 \text{ g m}^{-2} \text{ day}^{-1}$ is in close agreement with the value of $10 \text{ g m}^{-2} \text{ day}^{-1}$ estimated by Smith for a somewhat similar situation at Enewetak even though his transect exhibited essentially no diurnal variation in rate.

Table 7 indicates the similarity of day-time calcification rates estimated

TABLE 7. Calcification rates[a] for typical isolated (fenced) outcrops compared with those of the general surrounding rich coral reef-flat ('back-reef') area (all expressed per m^2 of actual coral bottom cover)

	Mean day-time calcification ($g \, CaCO_3 \, m^{-2} hr^{-1}$)	Mean night-time calcification ($g \, CaCO_3 \, m^{-2} hr^{-1}$)	Dirunal estimate ($g \, CaCO_3 \, m^{-2} day^{-1}$)
General area—September 1973 (derived from Table 6)	2.5	−0.3	26.4
In situ outcrop *Pocillopora damicornis*[b] September 1970 (50–60 per cent viable, 2.5–3 m diam.)	2.2	0.0 (consistent)	26.4
In situ outcrop *Porites andrewsi*[c] December 1969 (20 per cent viable, 3 m diam.)	1.6	±0.15 (variable)	19.2

a. Each based on low-tide standing water data obtained during four days of a two week period. Daytime values fall within ±20 per cent of the mean.
b. *Pocillopora damicornis* typically does not form a flat top at low-tide level and occasional dead material is spread through the formation.
c. *Porites andrewsi* forms a completely flat topped outcrop with totally viable sides consisting of branches penetrating 8–16 cm. The remainder of the outcrop is 'dead'.

for the general area and for two specific outcrops within the area, isolated during low-tide standing water by the fencing technique described in the next section. All are expressed on the basis of actual area of bottom covered by coral. It is particularly interesting to note that the night-time rates for the isolated outcrops do not exhibit the pronounced negative value (dissolution) found for the area as a whole. The differences indicated for distribution of viable coral within the outcrops probably explain, at least in part, both the frequent low negative night-time rates found with *P. andrewsi* (solution of dead material) and the higher day-time rates together with lack of dissolution at night with *P. damicornis* (relatively low content of dead material). *P. andrewsi* has been examined extensively over much of the year and has been found always to exhibit the erratic night-time behaviour.

FENCING TECHNIQUES

Concept

As mentioned in the introduction, the standing water approach can be extended logically into the isolation of specific *in situ* formations using fences. The rationale of this procedure is that the reef communities are subject to nothing more than gradual water mixing by diffusion and wind action during low-tide standing water periods. No volume transport of water occurs. Therefore if this mixing is further controlled by placing an impervious transparent fence around a sub-community such that it comes just above the water surface and such that the water volume to biomass ratio is approximately the natural one, the organisms enclosed should be essentially unaffected. Obviously normal high tide flushing should occur in some manner approaching that occurring in the rest of the community.

Any monitoring carried out on the water mass within such an enclosure must obviously detect changes brought about by the enclosed community and be unaffected by the activities of the general area. The technique also allows the effects of abnormal influences to be tested on a small scale—e.g. floating oil films (Kinsey, 1973), deliberate decreases in the water volume available, or addition of nutrients or toxins.

A further extension of the enclosure concept has been to use natural large (25–100 m diameter) fully-enclosed lagoon micro-atolls at One Tree Island to study perturbations caused by a fertilization programme (Kinsey and Domm, 1974). Here again the isolation is only during the standing water period, and requires no artificial fence at all.

Methods

The fencing method described by Kinsey (1972) has been in use since 1968 at One Tree Island. It is not considered by any means the ideal system but the development of a more sophisticated approach has not yet been investigated seriously. The material used is 1-metre wide fine wire mesh similar to fly wire coated with a continuous film of *acetate* plastic. The high gas diffusion property of this plastic does not pose quantitative experimental problems (Kinsey, 1973). The material is stiff across its width but sufficiently flexible to facilitate it being readily unrolled, standing in water, around a rigid structure of steel stakes joined with heavy gauge wire. A fence of this kind is illustrated in Figure 6. It has been placed to give a natural water-to-coral ratio. Such fences can be made very stable up to about 7 m in diameter.

Some restrictions obviously exist as to where this type of fence can be placed. The reef-flat area at One Tree Island has a fair amount of sand over the hard platform between the various reef outcrops. This allows the base of the fence to be bedded slightly into sand preventing any significant exchange under the fence. If normal gas diffusion is to occur at the surface it is also necessary that the fence be only slightly higher than the depth of the water. If tidal flow is not too severe after the standing water period is over, the turbulent flushing which occurs as the water passes over the submerging fence has been found to be quite adequate to make the removal of the fence unnecessary. In many situations however the tidal flow will make it physically impossible to leave the fence in place between standing water periods.

Figure 6
Typical reinforced plastic fence around a natural back-reef outcrop of
Porites andrewsi 3 m in diameter. The low-tide standing-water depth (as
shown) is 85 cm. The fence has been placed to give a ratio of coral to sand
bottom which is the mean for the general surroundings. The clear area in
the foreground is atypical.

At Heron Island (Kinsey, 1973) a fence was left in place for 5 weeks during
early spring and during that time no modification was noted to any aspect of
the community. Even the population of small fish remained unchanged. At the
end of this time a population of settling organisms on the fence was starting to
build up. This could be a more serious problem during those times of the year
when colonization is more active (autumn).

The only other method involved in the fencing approach is the measurement of the actual contained water volume. This has been done simply and
reproducibly by mixing into the water 1 ml of 20 per cent w/v filtered fluorescein
solution for approximately every m^3 of water. This should be done after the
completion of monitoring and immediately before high tide flushing. No ill-
effects have been observed after a very large number of repetitions.

When mixing is visually complete at least four samples are withdrawn into
glass bottles (some problems of absorption have been encountered with polyethylene) and their fluorescence determined against a suitable standard using
a fluorimeter. If kept in the dark, together with standards made up at the same
time, results have been found to be reliable even if estimation is delayed 6–8
weeks. S. V. Smith (pers. comm.) has suggested that absorption of fluorescein

by the community during the period before sampling may be a problem but this has not been checked at this time.

The absolute volume of the outcrop being studied can also be determined by subtracting the volume of water obtained, using the above technique, from the calculated total contained volume of the fence derived from accurate physical measurements and compass bearings of the angles of the sides, etc.

Applications

The value of being able to isolate specific representative sub-communities from the whole has already been demonstrated by the data in Table 4 and Table 8. This approach can also be extended to elucidate not just the individual contributions of various types of outcrop to the total metabolism of the community, but also the lesser and frequently very important contributions of the populations within the sand, rubble or hard substrata between outcrops.

By considering results from isolated outcrops against one of the more specific bases than just bottom area of the outcrop, it is possible to determine such things as specific growth rates of actual *in situ* corals without the risks involved in extrapolating from isolated material in aquaria.

For example: The outcrop of *Porites andrewsi* referred to in Table 8 had an approximate diameter of 3.0 m and was 0.75 m high. It was flat topped (dead) with totally viable near-vertical sides. This is the normal configuration for this species.

Diurnal calcification (see Table 8)	$19.2 \text{ g CaCO}_3 \text{ m}^{-2}\text{day}^{-1}$	(1)

This was based on:

Total calcification of the outcrop (monitored in an enclosed water volume of 9.05^3)	$145 \text{ gCaCO}_3 \text{ day}^{-1}$	(2)
Actual bottom area of outcrop	7.55 m^2	(3)

Other physical parameters determined were:

Projected area of living coral cover (i.e. plane area of sides)	7.07 m^2	(4)
Mean horizontal penetration of living branches	11.2 cm	(5)
Total mass of living branches (dry)	183 kg	(6)

Thus alternatives to the bottom cover basis used for expressing the result above are:

Diurnal calcification on a projected living coral cover basis (2)/(4)	$20.5 \text{ g CaCO}_3 \text{ m}^{-2}\text{day}^{-1}$	(7)
or Diurnal calcification on dry 'living' skeleton weight basis (2)/(6)	$0.79 \text{ g CaCO}_3 \text{ kg}^{-1}\text{day}^{-1}$	(8)
or Diurnal rate of lateral growth of the outcrop (radial)—((8).(5))/1000	$0.0088 \text{ cm day}^{-1}$	(9)

466

The mass of living coral was determined by carefully removing all living branches from a vertical strip 32.5 cm wide, air drying and weighing. The mean penetration of living branches is approximate in view of the top to bottom variation of 8 to 16 cm but was nevertheless carefully determined. The lateral growth concept is an interesting one. Because of the shape of the outcrop no vertical growth is possible, and it is easy to predict a lateral expansion on a purely radial basis. The value obtained (9) of 0.0088 cm day^{-1} suggests an annual expansion of 3.2 cm. However, this estimate was made in mid-summer and *Porites andrewsi* has been found by Alison Domm (unpublished data) to exhibit a marked seasonal cycle. Therefore the real annual growth is likely to be considerably less.

It is also interesting that the mean hourly daytime calcification rate for this outcrop, calculated on a living coral skeleton basis, of 66 mg kg^{-1} hr^{-1} (determined in December) is in remarkable agreement with an equivalent mean rate of approximately 50 mg kg^{-1} hr^{-1} determined for isolated heads by Alison Domm (in November).

Finally, it should be stressed that all the above deductions based on calcification of the living coral component of a natural reef outcrop do not make any allowance for the possibility of significant calcification occurring in some of the 'dead' areas due to the activity of calcareous algae, or inorganic in-filling.

The examples given above of the highly specific data which can be obtained for *in situ* communities using the standing water field fencing technique, demonstrate the considerable value which that technique has in situations which allow its application.

ACKNOWLEDGEMENTS

The experimental work used as a source of data for this paper forms part of The Australian Museum's coral reef programme. It has been supported with equipment or funds by the Australian Research Grants Committee (project D 67/16745), The Australian Museum, CSIRO Science and Industry Endowment Fund, and Rural Credits Development Fund. Mauri Brothers and Thomson loaned certain items of equipment.

The author thanks S. V. Smith and R. E. Johannes for their critical comments on this manuscript.

References

BROECKER, W. S.; TAKAHASHI, T. 1966. Calcium carbonate precipitation on the Bahama Banks. *J. geophys. Res.*, vol. 71, p. 1575–602.

CARPENTER, J. H. 1966. New measurements of oxygen solubility in pure and natural water. *Limnol. Oceanogr.*, vol. 11, p. 264–77.

CHAVE, K. E.; SMITH, S. V.; ROY, K. J. 1972. Carbonate production by coral reefs. *Mar. Geol.*, vol. 12, p. 123–40.

DAVIES, P. J.; KINSEY, D. W. 1973. Organic and inorganic factors in recent beach rock formation, Heron Island, Great Barrier Reef. *J. sedim. Petrol.*, vol. 43, p. 59–81.

EMERY, K. O. 1962. *Marine geology of Guam*. U.S. Geol. Surv. (Prof. Paper 403-B).

GORDON, D. C., JNR. 1971. Organic carbon budget of Fanning Island lagoon. *Pac. Sci.*, vol. 25, p. 222–7.

——; FOURNIER, R. O.; KRASNICK, G. J. 1971. Note on the planktonic primary production in Fanning Island lagoon. *Pac. Sci.*, vol. 25, p. 228–33.

GORDON, M. C.; KELLY, H. M. 1962. Primary productivity of a Hawaiian coral reef: a critique of flow respirometry in turbulent waters. *Ecology*, vol. 43, p. 473–80.

HORNBERGER, G. M.; KELLY, M. G. 1974. A new method for estimating productivity in standing waters using free oxygen measurements. *Water Res. Bull.*, vol. 10, p. 265–71.

JOHANNES, R. E. 1967. Ecology of organic aggregates in the vicinity of a coral reef. *Limnol. Oceanogr.*, vol 12, p. 189–95.

——; ALBERTS, J.; D'ELIA, C.; KINZIE, R. A.; POMEROY, L. R.; SOTTILE, W.; WIEBE, W.; MARSH, J. A. JR.; HELFRICH, P.; MARAGOS, J.; MEYER, J.; SMITH, S.; CRABTREE, D.; ROTH, A.; McCLOSKEY, L. R.; BETZER, S.; MARSHALL, N.; PILSON, M. E. Q.; TELEK, G.; CLUTTER, R. I.; DUPAUL, W. D.; WEBB, K. L.; WELLS, J. M. JR. 1972. The metabolism of some coral reef communities: a team study of nutrient and energy flux at Eniwetok. *BioScience*, vol. 22, p. 541–3.

KINSEY, D. W. 1972. Preliminary observations on community metabolism and primary productivity of the pseudo-atoll reef at One Tree Island, Great Barrier Reef. In: *Proc. Symp. Corals and Coral Reefs, 1969*, Mar. Biol. Assoc. India, p. 13–22.

——. 1973. Small scale experiments to determine the effect of crude oil films on gas exchange over the coral back-reef at Heron Island. *Environ. Pollut.*, vol. 4, p. 167–82.

——; DOMM, ALISON. 1974. Effects of fertilisation on a coral reef environment–primary production studies. In: *Proc. Second Int. Coral Reef Symp.* Brisbane, Great Barrier Reef Committee, vol 1, p. 49–66.

——; KINSEY, Barbara E. 1967. Diurnal changes in oxygen content of the water over the coral reef platform at Heron Island. *Aust. J. mar. Freshwat. Res.*, vol. 18, p. 23–4.

KOHN, A. J.; HELFRICH, P. 1957. Primary organic productivity of a Hawaiian coral reef. *Limnol. Oceanogr.*, vol. 2, p. 241–51.

MARSHALL, N. 1965. Detritus over the reef and its potential contribution to adjacent waters of Eniwetok lagoon. *Ecology*, vol. 46, p. 343–4.

ODUM, H. T. 1956. Primary production in flowing waters. *Limnol. Oceanogr.*, vol. 1, p. 102–117.

——; HOSKIN, C. M. 1958. Comparative studies on the metabolism of marine waters. *Publ. Inst. Mar. Sci. Texas*, vol. 5, p. 16–46.

——; ODUM, E. P. 1955. Tropic structure and productivity of a windward coral reef community on Eniwetok Atoll. *Ecol. Mon.*, vol. 25, p. 291–320.

PARK, P. K.; HOOD, D. W.; ODUM, H. T. 1958. Diurnal pH variation in Texas bays, and its application to primary production estimation. *Publ. Inst. Mar. Sci. Texas*, vol. 5, p. 47–64.

POMEROY, L. R.; JOHANNES, R. E. 1968. Occurrence and respiration of ultraplankton in the upper 500 metres of the ocean. *Deep-sea Res.*, vol. 15, p. 381–91.

RAMACHANDRAN, P. V.; PILLAI, C. S. G. 1972. Primary productivity of some coral reefs in the Indian Seas. In: *Proc. Symp. Corals and Coral Reefs, 1969*. Mar. Biol. Assoc. India, p. 33–42.

RYTHER, J. H. 1956. The measurement of primary production. *Limnol. Oceanogr.*, vol. 1, p. 72–84.

SARGENT, M. C.; AUSTIN, T. S. 1949. Organic productivity of an atoll. *Trans. Am. geophys. Union*, vol 30, p. 245–9.

——; ——. 1954. *Biologic economy of coral reefs*. U.S. Geol. Survey. (Prof. Paper 260-E)., p. 293–300.

SMITH, S. V. 1973. Carbon dioxide dynamics: A record of organic carbon production, respiration, and calcification in the Eniwetok reef flat community. *Limnol. Oceanogr.*, vol. 18, p. 106–20.

——; MARSH, Jr., J. A. 1973. Organic carbon production on the windward reef flat of Eniwetok Atoll. *Limnol. Oceanogr.*, vol. 18, p. 953–61.

——; PESRET, F. 1974. Processes of carbon dioxide flux in the Fanning Atoll lagoon. *Hawii Inst. Geophys. Tech. Rep.* (*Second Fanning Atoll Exped.*), p. 21–49.

STRICKLAND, J. D. H. 1960. Measuring the production of marine phytoplankton. *Bull. Fish. Res. Board Can.*, no. 122. (172 p.).

——; PARSONS, T. R. 1968. A practical handbook of sea water analysis. *Bull. Fish. Res. Bd Can.*, Ottawa, Queen's Printer. no. 167. (311 p.).

TRAGANZA, E. D.; SZABO, B. J. 1967. Calculation of calcium anomalies on the Great Bahama Bank from alkalinity and chlorinity data. *Limnol. Oceanogr.*, vol. 12, p. 281–6.

WELCH, H. E. 1968. Use of modified diurnal curves for the measurement of metabolism in standing water. *Limnol. Oceanogr.*, vol. 13, p. 679–87.

468

36

Calcification and organic carbon metabolism as indicated by carbon dioxide

S. V. Smith and D. W. Kinsey[1]

INTRODUCTION

Corals, other calcifying organisms, and even complete reef communities can be considered broadly as metabolizing carbon in two ways: organic carbon production–consumption, and calcification. The present paper presents and examines a method for elucidating CO_2 flux in both of these. The method is based on measurements of the CO_2 system in the surrounding sea water with no modification or sampling of the organisms being studied. All procedures discussed are equally applicable to controlled aquarium situations and to unconfined field situations.

The present method does not indicate organic carbon (soluble or particulate) taken from, or liberated back into the water, or the movement of fine suspended $CaCO_2$ in the water, and consequently does not give total carbon flux through the organisms. However all these additional parameters can be readily estimated using accepted techniques.

Nor is it the purpose of this paper to discuss at length the total scope for application of CO_2 data to metabolic studies, as this subject is covered elsewhere in this Monograph (Marsh and Smith, Chapter 25; Smith, Chapter 27; Kinsey, Chapter 35). This paper presents the basic analytical methodology and its rationale.

What advantages, if any, does the direct measurement of CO_2 related properties in sea water offer over other approaches available for studying the metabolic rates of calcifying organisms? There are in fact at least three marked advantages of this approach: (1) the method allows simultaneous but discrete measurement of CO_2 flux due to organic carbon metabolism within the organism and CO_2 flux due to calcification (or dissolution); (2) the method does not require any direct examination, sampling, or destruction of the actual organism or community so that these can be used repeatedly and over protracted periods (even annual cycles, etc.); and (3) no additions of reagents are made to

1. Hawaii Institute of Marine Biology, University of Hawaii, P.O. Box 1346, Kaneohe, Hawaii 96744, U.S.A.

the incubation water mass; and hence there are few limitations to large scale or field experiments.

All other methods aimed at elucidating CO_2 flux and calcification activity are limited by at least one of the points mentioned above. A few simultaneous measurements of organic carbon production and calcification have been made for both corals and algae using radioisotope techniques (Goreau, 1961; Littler, 1973), but these authors have recognized that their data have not provided internally consistent results. The answer to this inconsistency may well lie, at least in part, in the skeletal uptake of respiratory carbon (Pearse, 1970), or in accounting for all the Ca pools in this system of interest (Böhm and Goreau, 1973). Also, simultaneous measurements of ^{45}Ca and ^{14}C involve the measurement of uptake into the actual skeleton and soft tissues rather than depletion in the water; hence each measurement requires that the organism be sacrificed after a single treatment.

The CO_2 approach is less sensitive than isotope studies of carbon metabolism but is more amenable to estimating absolute levels of uptake or release. Frequently, the results of isotopic analyses are reported in relative rates, in large part because of the difficulty in converting radioactivity to absolute uptake. Moreover, the 'blank' (isotopic exchange or surface adsorption value) is always a potential problem in converting isotope uptake to metabolic rates.

Finally, the CO_2 measurements of organic carbon metabolism are little more trouble than oxygen-based metabolism measurements, but CO_2 measurements provide twice the information return. Oxygen does have the advantages of being more amenable to continuous monitoring than CO_2 and being subject to somewhat more precise measurement.

Figure 1 is an illustration to show sea-water CO_2 changes resulting from incubating a single 400 cm^3 coral head for two days in a 5-litre aquarium. The coral (*Pocillopora danae*) was maintained under natural light conditions in a 5-litre open-topped aquarium which sat in a large water bath. While measurements were not being made, a hose constantly flushed sea water through the aquarium and caused water to overflow into the water bath. During each 50-minute experimental run, the hose was removed from the aquarium (stopping its overflow). The water in the aquarium was constantly mixed by a magnetic stirrer, and the aquarium was flushed for at least 10 minutes between each run. Carbon dioxide analyses were performed on sea-water samples withdrawn from the aquarium at the beginning and end of each run. $\Delta\Sigma CO_2^o$ is the CO_2 change from organic carbon metabolism, while $\Delta\Sigma CO_2^c$ is that change due to calcification. The actual calculation of these values will be explained elsewhere in the text.

The figure illustrates several points about the metabolism of that coral. Graphic integration of the ($\Delta\Sigma CO_2^o$) curve shows that organic carbon production significantly exceeded consumption over a daily cycle. The saturation light intensity for organic carbon production in this coral prevailed during about five midday hours (1000 to 1500), and the light levels were above compensation intensity for about 9 hours (0800 to 1700). Day-time calcification exceeded the

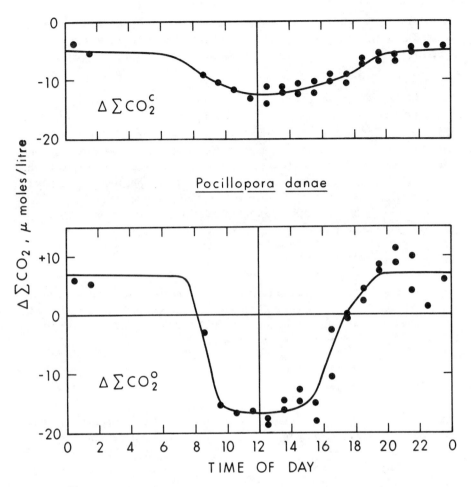

Figure 1
CO_2 changes attributable to calcification (C) and organic carbon production-respiration (O) during successive 50-minute incubations of *Pocillopora danae* in an aquarium.

night-time rate by more than twofold; there appears to have been a saturation period (or light intensity) for calcification approximately coinciding with the period during which organic carbon production was constant. In short, all of these characteristics are in general agreement with our knowledge of coral metabolism.

METHODS

General

Basically, the CO_2 technique involves careful measurement of any two CO_2-

471

related parameters in sea water before and after that water has been used as an incubation medium for the organisms of interest. These parameters can then be used to apportion the CO_2 changes in the water between the metabolic processes of interest (organic carbon production–consumption and calcification–solution).

The physical chemistry of the marine CO_2 system and the basis for estimating metabolism from that system have been considered in some detail elsewhere (Skirrow, 1975; Park, 1969; Smith, 1973; Smith and Key, 1975). Major consideration will be given here to methodology and to possible problems and interferences, as those subjects are not covered extensively in the papers cited above. The analytical methodology described here is applicable in a variety of laboratory and field situations with only minor modifications. The general procedure given here is similar to that of Strickland and Parsons (1968). The present, amplified version is more precise, is more directly amenable to use for coral reef studies, and is tailored to the metabolism calculations of primary interest here.

The two most convenient CO_2-related parameters to measure in this approach are pH and total alkalinity. Table 1 summarizes the equations for calculating total CO_2 from these two parameters and presents a sample calculation. While these calculations can be made by hand, they are very tedious and are most conveniently done by computer or calculator.

Equipment and supplies

Table 2 lists the equipment and supplies necessary for the CO_2 measurements as presented here. The only mandatory major equipment item is a high precision pH meter. Several meters which can be read to ± 0.001 pH units and which are repeatable to ± 0.005 pH units are commercially available. Necessary accessories for the mter include electrodes (glass and reference), pH buffers, measurement vessels, and a thermometer. Combination electrodes can prove both satisfactory and convenient. They can be fitted through a rubber stopper which fits the measurement vessel (most conveniently a test tube), even allowing room for the thermometer to be inserted through a second hole in the stopper. Some combination electrodes introduce both stable and transient errors apparently related to the junction potential. It is important when choosing combination electrodes to check their behaviour and readings against those of conventional high quality separate electrodes. Provided no deficiency is evident, the combined probe may be used.

When the electrodes are not to be used for periods of hours or longer, they should be stored as follows. Either combination electrodes or glass electrodes are stored in weak (≈ 0.01 N) HCl or in pH 4 buffer—but never in unacidified water, sea water, or sea-water buffers. Reference electrodes can be stored dry. The cap of a reference electrode or of a combination electrode should be plugged when the electrode is not in use.

472

TABLE 1. Calculation of the total CO_2 content of seawater from pH, total alkalinity, salinity and temperature[a]

A. General equations	B. Sample problem
	(pH = 8.3; total alkalinity = 2.3 meq/litre; salinity = 35 parts per thousand; temperature = 28°C

$\Sigma B = 0.01 \cdot S$

$\Sigma B = 0.01 \cdot 35 = 0.35$

$$B.A. = \Sigma B \left[\frac{a_H K_{1b} + 2K_{1b}K_{2b}}{a_H^2 + a_H K_{1b} + K_{1b}K_{2b}} \right]$$

$$B.A. = 0.35 \left[\frac{10^{-8.3} \cdot 10^{-8.7} + 2 \cdot 10^{-8.7} \cdot 10^{-9.8}}{(10^{-8.3})^2 + 10^{-8.3} \cdot 10^{-8.7} + 10^{-8.7} \cdot 10^{-9.8}} \right] = 0.109$$

$C.A. = T.A. - B.A.$

$C.A. = 2.3 - 0.109 = 2.191$

$$\Sigma CO_2 = C.A. \left[\frac{K_{1c}a_H + K_{1c}K_{2c} + a_H^2}{K_{1c}a_H + 2K_{1c}K_{2c}} \right]$$

$$\Sigma CO_2 = 2.19 \left[\frac{10^{-6.0} \cdot 10^{-8.3} + 10^{-6.0} \cdot 10^{-9.0} + (10^{-8.3})^2}{10^{-6.0} \cdot 10^{-8.3} + 2 \cdot 10^{-6.0} \cdot 10^{-9.0}} \right] = 1.882$$

a. ΣB = total boron (mmoles/litre); S + salinity (parts per thousand); B.A. = borate alkalinity (meq/litre); C.A. = carbonate alkalinity (meq/litre); T.A. = total alkalinity (meq/litre); CO_2 = total CO_2 (mmoles/litre); a_H = hydrogen ion activity (10^{-pH}); K_{1b}, K_{2b}, K_{1c}, K_{2c} = first and second dissociation constants for boric and carbonic acids.

Values for these dissociation constants are tabulated as functions of temperature and salinity in Riley and Skirrow (1965). Approximate values at 28°C and 35 parts per thousand salinity are: $K_{1b} = 10^{-8.7}$; $K_{2b} = 10^{-9.8}$, $K_{1c} = 10^{-6.0}$; $K_{2c} = 10^{-9.0}$.

TABLE 2. Instrumentation and supplies for CO_2 measurements

Item	Comments
pH meter	Should be high precision, preferably digital output instrument. (Repeatability ± 0.005 pH)
Salinometer	May not be needed; see text discussion
pH electrodes (glass and calomel)	Combination electrodes are convenient and may be satisfactory with certain reservations (see text discussion)
Measurement containers	30-ml test tubes work well with combination electrodes. Larger containers needed for separate electrodes.
Thermometer(s)	To measure both laboratory temperature and sample collection temperature
Stoppers to fit measurement containers, including one with hole(s) to accommodate electrode(s)	
Polyethylene or glass sample containers	Should be gas-tight and have a minimum volume of 100 ml (larger if salinity is also to be measured)
Polyethylene reagent bottles	For storing acid (both stock concentrate and diluted solution). Also for sea water secondary buffers, etc.
Volumetric flask (1 litre)	For diluting stock solution of acid.
Volumetric pipets (100, 30, 20, 10, 5, 3 ml)	The large one is for diluting acid; the others are for alkalinity measurements. See text for discussion of sizes.
Magnetic stirrer, with stirring bars to fit measurement containers.	Desirable, but not essential.
50 cc syringe, in-line filter holder, 0.8 μ membrane filters, short piece of rubber (or tygon) tubing to reach into sample containers.	For filtering sea water.
Aquarium pump, tygon tubing, 2½-litre plastic bottles, tops for each with 2 holes, 3 airstones or other bubbling tips, tubing clamp to regulate bubbling rate.	For air bubbling aparatus; desirable but not always essential (see text)
Water bath	Desirable, but not essential; can simply be a large container filled with water at room temperature.
Standardized HCl	0.010N HCl can be made from stock solution of 0.1N acid, which is commercially available; other concentrations may be used, as discussed in text.
Saturated KCl solution	For the reference electrode.
NaOH pellets	For air bubbler
pH buffers	pH 4.01 and 7.00 buffers are commercially available, and seawater buffer (about 7.7) can be prepared as discussed in the text.
Distilled or deionized water	
Cleaning material such as detergent, technical HCl, H_2SO_4, $K_2Cr_2O_7$, etc.	Readily available in any lab but easy to forget for the field!

Reagents

Buffers. Three buffers are useful for establishing and maintaining the calibration of the pH meter. Two of these, dilute KH phthalate (pH 4.01 at 25°C) and dilute mixed phosphate (pH 7.00 at 25°C) are commercially available or they may be prepared according to standard laboratory recipes (Bates, 1964). The third buffer is a sea water–Tris buffer prepared as described below.

One litre of sea water which has been filtered through a 0.8 μ (or finer) pore-size membrane filter is boiled gently until approximately 50 ml of water have evaporated. To the remaining water are added 21·0 ml of 1.0N HCl, 0.05 moles (6.057 g) of Tris powder (2-Amino-2 (hydroxymethyl)-1,3-propanediol), and sufficient distilled or deionized and boiled water to bring the solution back to 1 litre. Approximately 1 ml of formalin or 0.5 g thymol are added to prevent biological activity in the buffer. The buffer is then stored in a polyethylene bottle, which in turn is kept in a can or some other gas-tight vessel with some CO_2 absorbing agent such as Ascarite.

This buffer serves only as a secondary standard; as such, a stock solution can be used as long as it lasts. The buffer has a pH of approximately 8.37 at 25°C and has a temperature coefficient of about −0.02 pH units per °C. The temperature coefficient of each new batch of buffer should be established between 20°C and 30°C when the buffer is prepared.

Standardized HCl. The only additional analytical reagent required is HCl of precisely known normality. Any normality may be used; the authors recommend 0.01N. The acid may be prepared and standardized according to procedures described in any analytical chemistry textbook. Pre-standardized HCl of a variety of normalities may be purchased and diluted to the desired normality with distilled or deionized and boiled water.

Working procedures for pH meter use

At the beginning of each day of sea water pH-alkalinity measurements, the meter is calibrated and the slope characteristics of the electrodes are established with the two dilute buffers according to manufacturer's specifications for the meter. The electrodes are soaked for an hour in sea water, and then the pH of the sea-water pH buffer is measured. Further calibration is performed against the sea-water buffer, in order to avoid subjecting the electrodes to large shifts from solutions of one ionic strength to another. Such shifts may require up to one hour re-equilibration time to achieve stable readings. At least once every hour (more frequently if instrument drift exceeds 0.01 pH units over that time), the meter should be recalibrated against the sea water–Tris buffer (allowing, of course, for the temperature coefficient established when the buffer was first prepared). The slope characteristics of the electrodes can be assumed to remain constant during a day's run.

During the pH measurement of a series of samples with compositions similar to one another (either a series of sea-water pH samples or a series of samples acidified for alkalinity measurements), the electrodes should not be wiped, nor should they be rinsed with anything other than part of the sample. Wiping the electrodes, or rinsing them with distilled water, will increase electrode response time and decrease precision. Gentle agitation of the solution with a magnetic stirrer and stirring bar will speed response time, although it may sometimes result in erratic readings.

When pH measurements shift between low pH alkalinity measurements and high pH straight sea-water measurements, the electrodes should be rinsed briefly in a dummy sample and then soaked for at least ten minutes in another one. Consequently, it is efficient to batch high or low pH samples as far as is practical.

Sea-water pH

Two separated pH-related measurements are made on the sea-water samples. The first of these is simply the pH of a sea-water sample which has not been filtered, bubbled, or otherwise subjected any more than necessary to gas exchange with the atmosphere. The sample should have been initially collected and held in a bottle with a gas-tight cap and with little or no air trapped in the bottle The sample should have been brought to measurement temperature either in the sample container or in smaller containers with better characteristics for thermal equilibration. For maximum precision, pH analyses should be delayed by no more than an hour, because there is no satisfactory way to stop biochemical alteration of the pH without affecting the pH by the preservation. The pH value and the temperature should be recorded.

Total alkalinity

The second pH-related determination is the measurement of total alkalinity. A slight modification of the Culberson et al. (1970) technique is both rapid and precise. That technique is, in turn, a modification of the method described by Anderson and Robinson (1946), with the bubbling step described below being the only significant addition. For slightly more accurate analyses or analyses of sea water with low oxygen, high and variable nutrient levels, or low salinity (below about 15 parts per thousand) the Gran titration as described by Edmond (1970) is probably preferable. That titration is too time-consuming to be of practical value for analysing large numbers of samples over a short period, nor does it apparently improve the precision over the Culberson technique. CO_2 measurements for metabolic calculations rely on differences between samples, so precision rather than accuracy is ordinarily the limiting consideration to the methods described here.

The technique involves the measurement of the pH of a sea-water/acid mixture; a known volume of HCl (V_a) of known normality (N, usually 0.010) is added to sea water (V_s). The pH of that sample is converted to hydrogen ion

476

activity $(a^H = 10^{-pH})$, and the total alkalinity (T.A.) is calculated according to the following equation:

$$\text{T.A.} = \frac{1000}{V_s} V_a N - \frac{1000}{V_s} (V_s + V_a) a_H / f \qquad (1)$$

According to Culberson et al. (1970) the empirical constant f of equation (1) has a value of 0.74 over the salinity range of 31 to 40 parts per thousand. Kinsey has estimated 0.76 to 0.77 to be a more appropriate choice. It can be seen from equation (1) that choice of f within this range has only a very limited effect on the calculated alkalinity. Therefore, the choice of a value to use for f is not generally critical for the purposes discussed here. Below a salinity of about 15 parts per thousand, f changes rapidly (Strickland and Parsons, 1968). If accuracy of CO_2 measurements, and thus the 'best' choice of f, are critical to a particular investigation, then the most appropriate f value for the water in question should be determined experimentally by measuring the pH of sea-water samples to which have been added constant volume but varying-normality amounts of HCl (discussed, for example, by Culberson et al., 1970).

The measurements of pH on samples acidified for alkalinity measurements should use water which has been filtered before acid addition in order to remove $CaCO_3$ and other particulate materials which can contribute erratically to the alkalinity. A simple and satisfactory filtration apparatus is a 50 cc syringe, plastic in-line filter holder, and a membrane filter (0.8 μ or smaller pore size). A single filter can be used several times, even for relatively turbid water.

The pH of the acid plus sea-water mixture for alkalinity determinations should be in the pH range of 3.2 to 3.9, so the ratio of acid to sea water must be chosen accordingly. The total alkalinity of reef waters commonly lies between about 2.0 and 2.6 meq/litre. Over that alkalinity range, the single most convenient ratio of 0.010N HCl volume to sea-water sample volume for alkalinity measurements is 0.3. Therefore, one needs pipettes of 3 and 10 ml (or some multiple thereof). It is convenient to use an acid : sea water ratio of 0.25 (5 and 20 ml pipettes, for example) for low-alkalinity water, or a ratio of 0.33 (10 and 30 ml pipettes) for high-alkalinity water in order that the pH fall in the prescribed range. Of course, one may also choose other acid : sea-water ratios or other acid normalities and then solve equation (1) accordingly. The optimum pH range remains fixed regardless of these other variations.

The single greatest imprecision in alkalinity measurements is likely to arise in pipetting the acid or the sample. Considerable care should be exercised during this step. After the sample and acid are pipetted into the measurement container, that container should be stoppered, shaken vigorously with at least a 20 per cent gas space in the container, and then bubbled with CO_2-free, water-saturated air (as discussed by Culberson et al., 1970). Both the shaking and the bubbling drive off free CO_2. Measurements of pH in samples so-treated differ only slightly but fairly consistently, from unbubbled samples. The following has been found to be a satisfactory bubbling procedure: a small aquarium pump is used to bubble air through a stoppered, plastic bottle containing ~10N NaOH (to remove the CO_2) and through a second, stoppered bottle with ~ 0.01 N HCl (to saturate the air with water). This CO_2-free, water-saturated air is then bubbled through the sea water + acid sample to remove the air bubbles introduced by shaking. A small-bore syringe needle on the end of the air line provides a stream of fine bubbles that increase the stripping rate.

If expected total alkalinity changes are large (and therefore easily measurable) or too small to be of interest (that is, the system is not a calcifying one), then the bubbling apparatus can be eliminated with little loss of precision. The discussion of Culberson et al. (1970) suggests that there will be some loss of accuracy; but again, precision is more limiting to CO_2 studies of metabolism than is accuracy. If bubbling is not used, several changes of head space gas should be made during a period of very thorough shaking. The use of boiled water in the preparation of the dilute HCl is a further advantage.

A convenient analysis routine is to pipette one sample while a second one is bubbling and a third one is being measured. Neither the electrodes, the measurement vessel, nor the pipets should be rinsed between samples; the previous sample is by far the most effective rinse for all of the components. All glassware used for pH and alkalinity measurements should be reserved exclusively for that purpose.

Additional considerations

With care, it is possible to measure the pH of a sea-water sample to better than ± 0.005 pH units and to measure total alkalinity to better than ± 0.005 meq/litre (standard error on duplicate measurements). If a particular situation necessitates extreme precision, the measurement of each of these parameters can be improved beyond those quoted errors by the simple expedient of additional replicates or direct-sequencing of related samples to minimize effects of instrument drift.

Because all of the constants listed in Table 1 are functions of salinity, the salinity of the samples must also be known. If the salinity is known to remain constant during a CO_2 incubation, then it is sufficient to know it to within about ± 3 parts per thousand. If it is changing, then the salinity of each sample should be known to ± 0.5 parts per thousand. The temperature of the samples, when their pH is measured, should be known to $\pm 0.1 °C$. Original in situ temperature of the incubation water need be known accurately only if the partitioning of the CO_2 species is of interest. In particular, the CO_2 partial pressure is quite sensitive to temperature. A $1 °C$ error in the field temperature introduces approximately a 5 per cent error in CO_2 partial pressure calculated from pH and alkalinity. There is also approximately a 0.01 pH unit shift per $°C$ temperature change of sea-water (Gieskes, 1969; Ben Yaakov, 1970), and this temperature coefficient should be taken into account if incubation or field pH values are to be calculated from laboratory measurements.

It is useful to consider the error introduced by each of the measured parameters in calculating the total CO_2 content of sea water. Approximate measurement errors resulting in a 0.01 mmole/litre (or 0.5 per cent) error in calculating CO_2 are: pH, 0.02 pH units; total alkalinity, 0.01 meq/litre; salinity, 1 part per thousand; and laboratory temperature, 1°C. The accuracy of CO_2 determinations is, of course, also limited by the accuracy of the constants summarized in Table 1. However, the precision with which two samples can be compared is not particularly sensitive to the accuracy of those constants.

APPLICATION OF CO_2 DATA TO ESTIMATION OF METABOLIC ACTIVITIES

In an open aquarium and in all field situations there are three major processes which are likely to alter the CO_2 content of the water: gas exchange across the air–water interface, calcium carbonate precipitation–solution, and organic carbon production–consumption. Park (1969), Smith (1973) and Smith and Key (1975) present the rationale of calculating these processes from pH and total alkalinity. The present discussion describes but does not defend the procedure.

Gas exchange corrections

Kanwisher (1963) provides data on the relative exchange rates of oxygen versus carbon dioxide; the exchange of carbon dioxide from diffusion and gas stripping by bubbles proceeds tens to hundreds of times more slowly than does oxygen exchange. Sugiura *et al.* (1963) present the results of field and laboratory experiments demonstrating the CO_2 exchange rate coefficient to be something less than 25 μmoles m^{-2} hr^{-1} for each micro-atmosphere of sea-water CO_2 partial pressure deviation from the atmospheric value (~ 320 μatm). Under extreme conditions in sea-water aquaria, the CO_2 partial pressure may rise as high as 700 μatm, or about 400 μatm above atmospheric. Under such conditions, the rate of CO_2 escape would be less than about 0.01 moles CO_2 escape m^{-2} hr^{-1}, or less than 0.12 gC m^{-2} hr^{-1}. Coral metabolism is likely to exceed this value sufficiently (Fig. 1), so that under most circumstances a gas exchange term in the CO_2 budget can be neglected. Alternatively, a clear plastic or glass cover over an aquarium will effectively eliminate any CO_2 exchange between the air and water, even at high CO_2 partial pressure.

Calcification

Calculating the amount of CO_2 involved in calcification of dissolution is straightforward. For each mole of $CaCO_3$ (or $MgCO_3$, etc.) precipitated, the total alkalinity is lowered by two equivalents; the converse is true for $CaCO_3$ dissolution. Other processes likely to occur in the aquaria, or in most aerated natural systems, should have little or no effect on the total alkalinity, provided that one works within reasonable natural limits of pH, etc., although they will affect the carbonate alkalinity.

Two studies have been conducted to examine the expected stoichiometric relationship between total alkalinity changes in sea water and biogenic $CaCO_3$ precipitation. In cooperation with A. Roth, Smith incubated tips of *Acropora formosa* in test tubes containing ^{45}Ca-labelled sea water. At the end of a 30-minute incubation, the tips were cleaned and preserved for subsequent measurement of radioactivity, and the total alkalinity of the incubation water was measured. Figure 2 illustrates the results. There is a strong correlation between

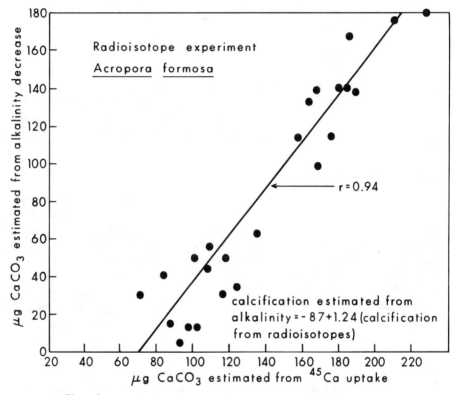

Figure 2
The relationship between coral calcification estimated from ^{45}Ca uptake and that estimated from alkalinity depletion.

the two methods of estimating calcification, but the alkalinity-derived estimates are about 25 per cent above the radioisotope estimates (that is, the slope of the line is about 1.25. The abcissa intercept of the regression line can be interpreted as the uptake of ^{45}Ca, either through inorganic exchange or through physical adsorption of the isotope at the broken bases of the coral tips, but aside from calcification uptake.

A. Domm, working in conjunction with Kinsey has compared the measured monthly skeletal weight increase of six coral species with weight increase calculated from alkalinity depressions during short term incubations. In most cases, the alkalinity approach gave estimates equivalent to 50–75 per cent of the mean dry skeletal weight increases (calculated from wet weight increases). In retrospect, we believe the principal explanation for this moderate but consistent underestimate by the alkalinity approach is that the corals were given only an hour or two acclimatization time in the incubation chambers prior to alkalinity depletion measurements and spent only one day per month in those chambers. The rest of the time the corals lived free in a lagoon environment. It seems reasonable to suggest that none of these organisms achieved completely natural behaviour (or normal metabolic patterns) during these brief periods in incubation chambers. This is further supported by the fact that the poorest agreement was obtained with *Goniopora tenuidens,* a coral normally exhibiting extreme and highly variable polyp extrusion.

These preliminary results suggest that alkalinity values may give higher estimates of calcification than do ^{45}Ca studies but perhaps lower values than direct weight-increase measurements. It remains to be established whether these differences among the various methods are real biases or merely artifacts of limited data. In any event, alkalinity measurements ordinarily appear to give calcification rate estimates within about ± 30 per cent of estimates from other methods.

Organic carbon flux

Organic carbon production–consumption, the major remaining process altering the CO_2 content of aquarium waters during an incubation experiment, can be calculated as the difference between the total CO_2 change observed and the CO_2 change attributable to calicfication ($\frac{1}{2}$ the total alkalinity change). If this model is correct, then there should be a strong negative correlation between non-calcification CO_2 changes in the water. The general shape of the diurnal curve in Figure 1 substantiates the model, as do the data illustrated in Figure 3. A diatom bloom was allowed to develop on the sides and walls of 500-litre flow-through aquaria. Both CO_2 and O_2 were measured in the tank inlets and outlets at approximately hourly intervals for 24 hours. There is an excellent correlation between changes in the two gases, and the -1.05 slope of the regression line indicates that the metabolic quotient for these diatoms is near 1. The correlation between O_2 and CO_2 data is also covered extensively elsewhere in this Monograph by Marsh and Smith (Chapter 25), and by Kinsey (Chapter 35).

Again it should be stressed that this procedure gives a measure of total carbon dioxide fixed by photosynthetic and calcification processes, and released by respiratory processes. The CO_2 procedure above will not detect directly the uptake or release of soluble or particulate organic matter.

DISCUSSION

The CO_2 method for metabolism studies presented here can be contrasted with a simpler method which has been employed for both sea water and fresh water.

2H

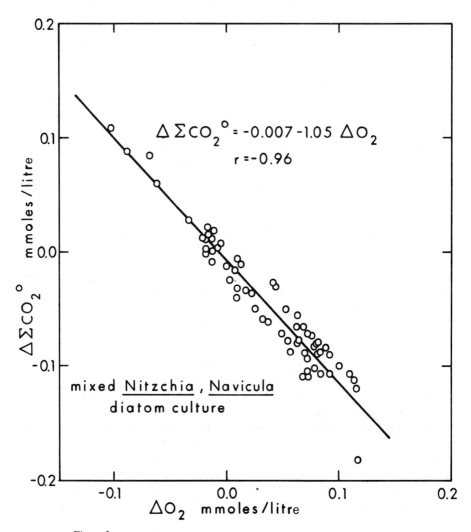

Figure 3
CO_2 versus O_2 changes from organic carbon production-consumption by mixed diatom culture.

Beyers (1966) describes the use of this simplified method for studies of coral metabolism. The approach consists of establishing an empirical relationship between the pH of the water to be used during the incubation and the CO_2 content of that water. Changes in pH are then directly related to changes in CO_2. There are two reasons why that approach is unsatisfactory for calcifying systems. In the first place, as the alkalinity is lowered, the relationship between pH and CO_2 shifts to accommodate the lowered buffer capacity of the water. Unless there is a large change in alkalinity, this error is not likely to be large.

A second and more serious problem is that the approach fails to discriminate between two quite different processes. As an example of the problem, an $O_2:CO_2$ metabolic quotient calculated from CO_2 data so-obtained could include a significant component of calcification-induced CO_2 change. When compared with data on metabolic quotients gather by other methods, or with the composition of organic carbon compounds in the organism, such a ratio would have very little physiological significance. Therefore, such a single-parameter approach to CO_2 metabolism studies should be avoided in actively calcifying systems.

In conclusion, it can be seen that monitoring sea-water CO_2 changes during metabolism studies of corals and other marine biota can yield considerable information. The dearth of information on this subject can probably be attributed both to the complexity of calculations in the marine CO_2 system and to the need for very precise measurements. The analytical and computational tools to overcome both of these problems are readily available.

ACKNOWLEDGEMENT

This research was partially supported by Grant No. R800906 awarded by the U.S. Environmental Protection Agency to the University of Hawaii. This paper is HIMB contribution No. 529.

References

ANDERSON, D. H.; ROBINSON, R. J. 1946. Rapid electrometric determination of the alkalinity of sea water using a glass electrode. *Industrial Engineering Chemistry* (Analytical edition), vol. 18, p. 767–9.

BATES, R. G. 1964. *Determination of pH: theory and practice.* New York, Wiley (435 p).

BEN-YAAKOV, S. 1970. A method for calculating the *in situ* pH of sea water. *Limnol. Oceanogr.,* vol. 15, p. 326–8.

BEYERS, R. J. 1966. Metabolic similarities between symbiotic coelenterates and aquatic ecosystems. *Arch. Hydrobiol.,* vol. 62, p. 273–84.

BÖHM, E. L.; GOREAU, T. F. 1973. Rates of turnover and net accretion of calcium and the role of calcium binding polysaccharides during calcification in the calcareous alga *Halimeda opuntia* (L.).*Int. Rev. gesamt. Hydrobiol.,* vol. 58, p. 723–40.

CULBERSON, C.; PYTKOWICZ, R. M.; HAWLEY, J. E. 1970. Seawater alkalinity determination by the pH method. *J. mar. Res.,* vol. 28, p. 15–21.

EDMUND, J. M. 1970. High precision determination of titration alkalinity and total carbon dioxide content of sea water by potentiometric titration. *Deep-sea Res.,* vol. 17, p. 737–50.

GIESKES, J. M. 1969. Effect of temperature on the pH of seawater. *Limnol. Oceanogr.,* vol. 14, p. 679–85.

GOREAU, T. F. 1961. On the relation of calcification to primary productivity in reef building organisms. In: H. M. Lenhoff and W. F. Loomis (eds). *Biology of Hydra and other coelenterates.* University of Miami Press, p. 269–85.

KANWISHER, J. 1963. On the exchange of gases between the atmosphere and the sea. *Deep-sea Res.* vol. 10, p. 195–207.

KINSEY, D. W. 1972. Preliminary observations on community metabolism and primary productivity of the pseudo-atoll reef at One Tree Island, Great Barrier Reef. In: *Proc. Symp. Corals and Coral Reefs, 1969.* Mar. Biol. Assoc. India, p. 13–32.

LITTLER, M. M. 1973. The productivity of Hawaiian fringing-reef crustose Corallinaceae and an experimental evaluation of production methodology. *Limnol. Oceanogr.,* vol. 18, p. 946–52.

PARK, P. K. 1969. Oceanic CO_2 systems: an evaluation of 10 methods of investigation. *Limnol. Oceanogr.,* vol. 14, p. 179–86.

PEARSE, V. B. 1970. Incorporation of metabolic CO_2 into coral skeleton. *Nature* (Lond.), vol. 228, p. 383.

RILEY, J. P.; SKIRROW, G. (eds). 1975. *Chemical Oceanography.* 2nd edit. London and New York, Academic Press.

SKIRROW, G. 1975. The dissolved gases—carbon dioxide. In: J. P. Riley and G. Skirrow (eds). *Chemical oceanography.* London and New York, Academic Press, vol. 2, p. 1–192.

SMITH, S. V. 1973. Carbon dioxide dynamics: a record of organic carbon production, respiration, and calcification in the Eniwetok reef flat community. *Limnol. Oceanogr.,* vol. 18, p. 106–20.

——; KEY, G. S. 1975. Carbon dioxide and metabolism in marine environments. *Limnol. Oceanogr.,* vol. 20, p. 493–5.

STRICKLAND, J. D. H.; PARSONS, T. R. 1968. A practical handbook of seawater analysis. *Bull. Fish. Res. Bd. Can.,* Ottawa, Queen's Printer, no. 167. (311 p.).

SUGIURA, Y.; IBERT, E. R.; HOOD, D. W. 1963. Mass transfer of CO_2 across sea surfaces. *J. mar. Res.,* vol. 21, p. 11–24.

37

Dissolved nitrogen, phosphorus and organic carbon

C. F. D'Elia[1]

THE UPTAKE AND RELEASE OF DISSOLVED C, N, AND P BY CORALS

Although total community metabolism has been measured in terms of gross changes in water passing over coral reef communities (Odum and Odum, 1955; Johannes *et al.*, 1972; Pilson and Betzer, 1973, Webb *et al.*, 1975), relatively few autecological data are available to indicate what organisms play what roles in producing the overall changes observed. Clearly, more experiments are needed to produce such data. Here some factors which should be considered when designing, performing, and interpreting these experiments are discussed. Although much of the discussion[2] will be directed to corals, the principles covered here are equally applicable to many other reef organisms.

Forms of C, N, and P dissolved in sea water

Table 1 indicates the principal forms of C, N, and P dissolved in sea water that may be affected by the fluxes of dissolved substances into and out of corals. For general reviews dealing with these forms, their measurement, their role as nutrients, and how they are transferred and recycled in marine systems, consult Harvey, 1957; Duursma, 1965; Fogg, 1966; Johannes, 1968; Pomeroy, 1960, 1971; Wagner, 1969; Riley, 1970; Corner and Davies, 1971; Riley and Chester, 1971; Healey, 1973; Parsons and Takahashi, 1973; Strickland and Parsons, 1968.

Processes by which fluxes occur

Through proper experimental control, or manipulation of factors which affect the fluxes of solutes through cell membranes, it may be possible to measure

---

1. Woods Hole Oceanographic Institution, Woods Hole, MA 02543, (Formerly: Department of Biological Sciences, University of Southern California, Los Angeles, California, 90007, U.S.A.).
2. This discussion will be limited solely to the measurement of fluxes of dissolved C, N, and P between organisms and their sea-water medium.

TABLE 1. Principal forms of C, N, or P that have been measured in sea water. References listed are: I. recent ones either reviewing techniques for measuring these forms, or where such information can be found, and II. those which have dealt with measuring C, N, and P dissolved fluxes in corals. For a general discussion of coral nutrition, see also Muscatine, 1973.

C, N, or P form	I. Reference for measurement	II. Reference for past coral work
Inorganic		
Nitrate	Webb, Chapter 30	Franzisket, 1973, 1974
Nitrite	Webb, Chapter 30	Franzisket, 1973, 1974
Ammonia	Webb, Chapter 30	Kawaguti, 1953
Phosphate	Pilson, Chapter 31	Yonge and Nicholls, 1931
	Olsen, 1966	Yamazato, 1970
		Pomeroy and Kuenzler, 1969
		Sorokin, 1973
		D'Elia, 1977,
		Pilson, 1974
		Pomeroy et al., 1974
Polyphosphates	Solórzano and Strickland, 1968	
Organic		
Carbohydrates	Wagner, 1969	Stephens, 1962
Hydrocarbons, lipids, fatty acids	Wagner, 1969	Benson and Muscatine, 1974
Amino acids, peptides, polyproteins	Wagner, 1969	Johannes and Webb, 1970
	Webb, Chapter 30	Stephens, 1962
		Lewis and Smith, 1971
Humic acids	Wagner, 1969	
Nucleic acids, nucleosides, nucleotides, RNA, DNA	Wagner, 1969	
Urea	Webb, Chapter 30	
Vitamins (especially biotin, thiamin, cobalamin)	Wagner, 1969	
Chlorophylls, phaeophytins	Loftus and Carpenter, 1971	
Dissolved organic nitrogen (DON) in general	Webb, Chapter 30	
Dissolved organic carbon (DOC) in general	Marshall, Chapter 29	Sorokin, 1973
Dissolved organic phosphorus (DOP), in general	Pilson, Chapter 31	D'Elia, 1977,
		Sorokin, 1973

naturally occurring C, N, and P flux rates to and from an aquatic organism and to characterize the processes which mediate these fluxes. A general understanding of solute penetration of membranes and of the factors which affect the rates of penetration is necessary for a researcher dealing with these fluxes. For this reason the factors which affect movement of substances across membranes are reviewed.

Endo- and exocytosis. For endocytosis (e.g. Simson and Spicer, 1973; Fawcett, 1965) to have any great consequence in solute interiorization, high solute concentration would be necessary at the sites of endocytosis (pinocytosis) on the surface of the cell membrane. Such high concentrations may occur in the guts of organisms where extracellular digestion of particulate food is occurring, but are unlikely to be encountered in sea water surrounding organisms—particularly in nutrient-poor waters where most corals are found. Hence, endocytosis of small quantities of sea water by coral epidermis (as suggested by Goreau *et al.,* 1971) is not likely to be an *important* uptake mechanism for dissolved substances in sea water. On the other hand, the concentrations of solutes inside cells of organisms are generally quite high relative to environmental concentrations (e.g. Johannes *et al.,* 1969); for this reason, exocytosis of internal substances could potentially represent a significant efflux of C, N, and P. The author is not aware of any studies showing that this occurs in corals, yet any one interested in determining the cellular mechanism of efflux should consider the possibility that it does.

Diffusion and carrier transport. Solutes permeate biological membranes either by diffusion or by what has been described as 'carrier transport' (e.g. Stein, 1967). (Physical, not biological forces control the diffusion of materials across membranes.) This rate is proportional to the concentration inside and outside of the membrane and is affected by the permeability of the membrane to the solute in question (ibid.). The greatest diffusion will occur across the most permeable surfaces of an organism, and factors which control the external and cellular concentration of the solute will affect the rate and direction of flux. In carrier transport, flux rates are characterized by concentration dependence that is suggestive of enzyme kinetics or 'carrier' mediation (ibid.): at higher solute concentrations there is evidence of 'saturation' (i.e. a maximum transport rate is attained). Carrier transport may or may not involve the expenditure of energy by the cell: if it does, it is termed 'active transport', if it does not, it is termed 'facilitated transport' (ibid.). Since energy is required for a substance to move against a concentration gradient, in the case where the cellular concentration of a solute is higher than the external concentration, net inward movement can only occur by active transport.

Since different kinetic and energetic characteristics are exhibited by different flux processes (diffusion, facilitated transport, and active transport), it follows logically that from kinetic analysis of solute flux at different concentrations and by determining the energy requirements for the movement of the solute into or out of organisms, it should be possible to determine whether there is diffusion, facilitated transport, or active transport. Yet, even though making kinetic measurements of solute flux may seem to be an easy way to determine this, it is rarely so in practice, for, in addition to technical difficulties encountered in measuring low nutrient concentrations, the interpretation of the data is often complicated. Net fluxes of solutes between corals and sea water may be the sum of uni- or bi-directional fluxes from various combinations of separate carrier transport systems and diffusion, or may be affected by a number of other physical and biological factors which are discussed below.

Physical factors affecting flux rates

Temperature. Like other metabolic processes, carrier transport is temperature sensitive, with Q_{10} values greater than 2.0 (Giese, 1968). Hence, slight changes in temperature may have profound effects on transport rates. Diffusion, like carrier transport, is temperature sensitive, but has characteristically lower Q_{10} values (typically, between 1.2 and 1.5, ibid.). In addition to affecting permeation rates, a change of temperature, although within the physiological tolerance range of an organism, may occur too suddenly for an organism to acclimatize, resulting in temperature 'shock'. The effects of this on coral metabolism is as yet undetermined (Jokiel and Coles, 1974).

Water movement. Rates of solute movement across membranes are substantially enhanced with increasing current speeds at the membrane surface (e.g. Whitford and Schumacher, 1961, 1964; Gavis, 1976). Kinetic constants for transport are also affected (Winne, 1973). Since corals live in a variety of habitats with varying current velocities, this parameter should be considered.

Light. In photosynthetic organisms, light under some circumstances acts to enhance the uptake of a substance (as for example nitrate uptake by algae; Eppley and Coatsworth, 1968), either by supplying through photosynthesis the necessary energy for transport or acceptors for the transported molecules. In corals that contain zooxanthellae (endozoic algae), light might be expected to affect the flux of C, N, and P compounds, as in free-living algae. Franzisket (1974) reported finding no effects of light on nitrate uptake, whereas D'Elia (1977) found significant effects of light on P fluxes. Certainly, more research into the effects of light on coral nutrient flux is needed.

Dissolved substances and ionic species in sea water

pH. Most metabolic reactions are quite pH sensitive (Giese, 1968); so too are carrier transport systems (Stein, 1967). Due to the high buffering capacity of sea water, pH generally remains fairly constant and is not a problem during most experiments.

Oxygen. Low or high oxygen tension may affect the respiration rate and metabolism of an organism (Hoar, 1966), and hence its C, N, and P fluxes. Coral respiration becomes non-linear at about 50 per cent O_2 saturation (L. R. McCloskey, pers. comm.). The effects of different oxygen tensions on coral C, N, and P fluxes have not been assessed.

External nutrient concentration. The effects of a substance's concentration on its own flux has been discussed briefly above. The concentration of other nutrients may affect that substance's flux also. Lack of a nutrient required as a precursor may conceivably limit the uptake of another. In some cases, transport systems may be unable to function due to lack of a cofactor (Healey, 1973)[3].

3. For example, molybdenum is required for nitrate reductase activity in some algae (Cardenas *et al.*,1971).

In other situations, transport systems may be repressed or inhibited[4]. To my knowledge, whether or not such effects occur in corals has not been determined.

Metabolic factors affecting flux rates

Nutritional state of the organisms. Changes in the concentration of nutrients in internal pools may affect concentration gradients and in turn, nutrient fluxes (Johannes, *et al.,* 1969). Franzisket (1974) has shown that a coral 'saturated with nitrate . . . does not immediately take up nitrate from water with low nitrate concentration.' Changes in energy reserve levels or in amounts of transport enzymes, induced in times of nutrient deficiency or repressed in times of nutrient availability, may also affect transport rates (Healey, 1973)[5]. In times of high nutrient availability, storage pathways may be induced in some algae, allowing nutrient uptake to continue (e.g. 'luxury consumption,' Fitzgerald and Nelson, 1966).

Metabolic rate. Metabolic rates of organisms correlate with body size (Zeuthen, 1953). Johannes (1964) found that the turnover rate of a nutrient (P) increased with decreasing body size and increasing metabolic rate. Short-term changes in metabolic activity are brought about by endogenous rhythms in photosynthetic organisms (e.g. Stross, Chisholm, and Downing, 1973); concomitant changes in nutrient flux rate may also be expected (however, Muscatine and D'Elia (unpubl.) found that uptake of ammonia by a hermatypic coral remained constant over a 24-hour period with a natural light-dark cycle). Finally, increased metabolic activity, and in turn increased C, N, and P fluxes, may be caused by stress due to temperature shock, handling, or crowding (Satomi and Pomeroy, 1965).

EXPERIMENTAL PROTOCOL

Selection and treatment of experimental organisms

Obtaining accurate and ecologically representative nutrient flux data necessitates the appropriate choice of species and specimens for experimental purposes. Certain species are unusually hardy and appear to endure handling and laboratory conditions that others cannot. However, such species (for example, the solitary corals of the genera *Manicina* and *Fungia*) may not be important reef-builders, and may be of doubtful ecological significance in terms of their

4. For instance, nitrate reductase may be repressed by high ammonia concentration (Eppley *et al.,* 1969), and competitive inhibition of phosphate has been reported (Jeanjean and Blasco, 1970).
5. It has been shown for some algae that nitrate reductase activity is affected by nitrogen availability—as NH_4^+ (Eppley *et al.,* 1969) and alkaline phosphatase by phosphorus deficiency (Fitzgerald and Nelson, 1966).

relative contribution to the nutrient fluxes of the entire community. For other species (e.g. *Acroporas*), the converse seems to be true: their relative ecological importance can be inferred from their abundance and rapid growth rates, but these species may be difficult to work with.

For his research, the author used species which: (a) are abundant and available—insuring a large range of specimens from which to choose, (b) are conveniently collected—with plentiful small heads that are easily dislodged from the substratum with a minimum of injury to coral tissue, (c) contain minimal amounts of unremovable epi- or infauna, (d) appear not to be greatly stressed when handled—producing little mucus and readily re-expanding polyps after handling[6], and (e) suit the specific requirements of the experiment being conducted (such as easy separation of zooxanthellae from coral tissue homogenate, or amenability to a particular biomass determination).

Frequently, specimens of appropriate size can be easily found in the field. In many instances, the 'stalk' at the base of a branching coral is dead corallum and the living coral can be broken off in that region without injury. Whether or not breaking the coral in areas where there is living tissue seriously affects C, N, and P fluxes is not known, but corals quite obviously survive injury due to predation and breakage due to wave action. Often, during times of increased wave action, pieces of branching corals are broken off in regions of living tissue. Many of the pieces survive and heal within a week or two so that the broken surface is completely covered with new tissue; the author has used such pieces of *Porites compressa* in his own research[7].

Depending on circumstances (such as hardiness of the experimental species, quality of the sea water in laboratory sea-water systems, or other factors) it may be important to use freshly collected specimens. For instance, corals often do not remain healthy after prolonged retention in laboratory sea-water tables. Perhaps more important in respect to the present discussion, even though corals may appear healthy and even grow for months after being placed in laboratory sea-water tables, they are probably subject to altered nutrient fluxes; for example, they are not receiving the normal input of food when bathed in filtered sea-water.

Chamber incubations

Ideally, one would like to be able to measure fluxes of dissolved C, N, and P of an organism *in situ* in its natural habitat. In practice, this is often not feasible, especially when one needs to do an immediate laboratory analysis on water

6. These are not infallible criteria, but the best we have until such time as exhaustive and rigorous physiological comparisons are made between many species from which we can determine the ability of corals to withstand stress from handling.
7. Similarly, the researcher can break pieces off corals and allow them to heal in this manner for later use.

samples to obtain flux data. Moreover, one may desire to alter natural conditions in the course of the experiment; such alterations may be impossible to effect *in situ*. Consequently, it is standard practice to remove the organism from its natural habitat and to place it in some sort of chamber in which environmental conditions can be easily manipulated.

Control of the chamber environment. Adequate controls for light, temperature, and circulation must be included in the design of the experimental apparatus. Obviously, the best approximation of the natural environment will produce the most realistic results.

Light. Since it is very difficult to duplicate the spectral characteristics of natural sunlight with artificial light sources, natural sunlight should be used, when possible in day-time experiments. But there are difficulties encountered when using natural sunlight. Intensity and spectral characteristics cannot be easily regulated; not only do they vary with time of day and latitude, but also with cloud cover; hence an artificial light source may be required when sustained intensity and controlled spectral distribution is necessary. Hopefully, the source chosen will have strong irradiance at wavelengths in the photosynthetic action spectrum of the experimental organisms. In any case, recording and reporting incident light in terms of irradiance and spectral composition is desirable (e.g. Tyler, 1973)[8].

Temperature. A surrounding water bath can be used to control temperature in the incubation chamber. This bath can be attached to a constant temperature water source, such as a recirculating incubator, in the laboratory. The chamber should be designed with a port for a thermometer to allow monitoring of the temperature in the chamber throughout the experiment.

Circulation. Circulation during a chamber incubation can be controlled by placing a magnetic stirrer inside the chamber or by flow-through flushing of the chamber. Measuring flow rates obtained over a coral surface is a difficult problem, especially when using branching corals with surfaces oriented in different directions to the flow. The problem of flow measurement is further complicated in a chamber where a magnetic stirrer creates a vortex (with different flow rates on the perimeter than in the centre) or in a flow-through system where a jet of water may produce uneven current velocities in the chamber. About the best one can do under such circumstances is to describe the experimental conditions as accurately as possible, and perhaps make rough estimates of the current velocity from observations on rates and direction of movement of a marker dye added to the chamber medium.

Conducting the chamber incubation
  Water treatment. If there is appreciable particulate material in the incuba-

---

8. Measurements should be made, of course, from inside the chamber to allow for absorbance characteristics of the chamber material.

tion water, it may be desirable to filter it before the beginning of the experiment. The author has used Cuno Aquapure® filters for filtering large quantities of sea water. This treatment has been shown to remove most particulate material, including many bacteria (Struhsaker et al., 1973). It may not be advisable to filter water as part of the analytical procedure, because an error may be introduced by sorption or desorption of dissolved materials by the filter (Marvin et al., 1972; Marshall, Chapter 29; Pilson, Chapter 31; Webb, Chapter 30).

Preincubation. Since collection and handling seems to stress corals enough to cause them to contract their polyps and secrete more mucus than normal, the author retains experimental corals in the incubation chamber (concurrently flushing the chamber with fresh sea water) until polyps re-expanded and mucus production ceases (usually within one-half hour), thus presumably allowing them to become acclimatized to the chamber.

Incubation. If an incubation is continued too long, chamber effects will cause spurious results. Frequently, oxygen tensions in the chamber reach a level where the metabolic rate is affected as it would not be in nature. In addition, metabolites could conceivably accumulate in the chamber medium and cause metabolic anomalies. It is probably safe to assume that by monitoring oxygen tension and terminating experiments before oxygen stresses occur, metabolite build-up will not be large enough to be significant (although this is difficult to assess). Another problem in doing chamber incubations is that accurate determination of C, N, and P fluxes may be prevented by nutrient depletion in the chamber (e.g. if one were measuring NH_4^+ flux, and all NH_4^+ was removed from the water, no further uptake could be recorded and uptake would be underestimated). Whether or not this is occurring will be evident if kinetic studies are carried out (see below). Finally, micro-organisms may proliferate and the effects of their C, N, and P fluxes may represent a significant portion of the observed results. This last problem can usually be avoided by limiting the incubations to a few hours at most between vigorous flushings of the chamber.

One of two variations of incubation procedures might be followed. A flow-through system can be used in which the chamber is continuously flushed while inflowing and outflowing water is sampled and analysed. The nutrient flux required to create the observed difference between the samples can be calculated, provided that the water volume in the chamber and its turnover time are known. Unless flow rates are accurately measured and controlled, a significant error can be introduced in calculation of turnover time. A simpler procedure is to stop the flow completely for a short time at intervals, sampling before and at the end of each 'static' interval—the flux rates can be calculated using the water volume in the chamber, the time interval, and the difference in concentration between samples. The chamber is flushed rapidly between such static intervals to insure that the chamber medium is fresh. In this incubation procedure, time between samples is more easily measured accurately than water turnover in 'continuous' flow incubations. Thus, the 'static' approach is often preferable. However, if numerous replicate samples are desired, the 'continuous' flow approach may be desirable. Equivalent changes would occur in either system[9].

Regardless of the incubation procedure used, oxygen stress, metabolite build-up, etc., may occur before chemically measured changes occur in the component of interest. If such proves to be the case, then an alternate analytical procedure (perhaps involving the use of stable or radioactive isotopes) must be sought.

Other experiments

After having determined the natural flux rates of a C, N, or P fraction, one may be interested in characterizing the mechanisms by which that flux occurs and in determining what factors affect the flux rates. Experimental approaches for doing this are discussed below.

Kinetic studies. It was pointed out above that by obtaining kinetic measurements of solute flux at different concentrations one can often determine whether it is governed by diffusion or carrier transport. In a typical experiment, kinetics might be measured during a chamber incubation of an organism by enriching the medium with the substance in question, and monitoring its depletion from the medium[10]. The amount of flux per unit biomass per unit time is determined by multiplying the change in concentration between samples by the chamber volume (which may change significantly due to sample removal) and dividing by time and biomass. A rate of flux versus concentration curve is obtained: if passive diffusion alone is occurring, the resultant curve should approximate one obtained by applying the equation of Fick[11]. The result will be a straight line, indicating that flux rate is dependent on concentration. If unidirectional carrer mediated transport is occurring; the curve may be approximated by the Michaelis–Menten hyperbola[12]; at concentrations which saturate the carrier system, increasing concentration will not increase the rate of flux. In more complicated situations, as for instance when bidirectional fluxes occur, or when more than one transport system is present, the mathematical interpretation is considerably more complicated (cf. Neame and Richards, 1972; Williams, 1973); in such cases, isotopes or inhibitors may be helpful in distinguishing between influxes and effluxes.

9. It is a misconception that by following the first approach one avoids the build-up of external metabolites or the risk of oxygen stress. Although continuous flushing of the chamber turns over (changes) the chamber medium over a period of time, proportionate changes occur in the components of the chamber medium as in a 'static' incubation interval.
10. Or alternatively, monitoring uptake of an isotope with strong β emission (such as P-32) by counting Cherenkov radiation (e.g. Matthews, 1968) at intervals during the experiment (an approach tried by Pomeroy *et al.,* 1974).
11. $J = P \cdot A \cdot S$, where J is the flux rate, P is the permeability coefficient of the membrane, A is the area over which the flux occurs, and S is the concentration difference driving the flux (see Stein, 1967, for a good discussion of the use of this equation).
12. $v = V_{max} \cdot S/(K + S)$, where v is the rate of transport, V_{max} is the maximum obtainable transport rate, K is the Michaelis–Menten constant, and S is the substratum concentration (e.g. Stein, 1967; Neame and Richards, 1972).

The use of isotopes. Neither chemical or isotopic measurement of fluxes will alone provide information about influx and efflux or net flux when bi-directional fluxes occur; both measurements must be made. Unfortunately, many researchers have assumed that fluxes are unidirectional, and that monitoring isotope flux alone was sufficient to determine net transport rates[13]. Briefly, three often neglected aspects must be considered when measuring nutrient fluxes isotopically: (a) Specific activity (the ratio of labelled to un-labelled substance)—saying that an organism took up 1000 dpm of something is meaningless, unless one knows the specific activity, (b) specific activity *changes*—specific activity in experimental compartments[14] must be monitored continuously for changes do occur: the change in specific activity and the rate of isotope influx must be known in order to calculate net flux and gross efflux, and (c) distribution of labelled material within compartments—if it is not homogeneously distributed within compartments, interpretation of the results is not possible.

The use of metabolic inhibitors. Inhibitors may be useful for determining whether there is active transport, and what the immediate source of energy is. Glycolytic and electron transport system inhibitors that may be used to inhibit fluxes include 2,4-dinitrophenol, amytol, rotenone, antimycin A, carbon monoxide, cyanide, fluoride, arsenate and others (e.g. Mahler and Cordes, 1966, pp. 601–602; Avron, 1971). Photosynthetic inhibitors in common use include DCMU, CMU, glucose phloridzin, and the antibiotic Dio-9 (Avron, 1971). Caution is advised in the interpretation of negative evidence: the inhibitor must be able to reach its site of activity to be effective, hence appropriate controls must be carried out to show that inhibitor penetration occurs.

Enzymatic characterization of uptake systems. Certain enzymes are associated with uptake pathways (e.g. nitrate reductase with that for nitrate.—Eppley and Coatsworth, 1968). While demonstration of the presence of the enzyme is conclusive evidence for the presence of a particular uptake pathway in an organism, negative evidence, even with appropriate controls for the effectiveness of the assay may only mean that the enzyme was repressed at the time of assay.

Autoradiography. Sites of uptake of ^{3}H, ^{14}C, ^{35}S, and ^{33}P labelled compounds can be determined by autoradiography, but resolution is very poor if isotopes with greater energies are used (Rogers, 1973). One must be careful to avoid washing soluble labelled compounds from specimens during histological preparations (Roth and Stumpf, 1969; Rogers, 1973). That generally means that standard histological procedures of fixation and dehydration must be

---

13. For an excellent discussion of proper design and interpretation of experiments incorporating isotopes to measure transfer of materials in marine food chains, see Conover and Francis, 1973. Another useful reference is Steele, 1971.
14. i.e. pools into and from which fluxes occur.

abandoned for sectioning frozen tissue with a cryostat, a procedure found difficult when working with corals. Again, as with any experiment involving tracers, caution is urged in the interpretation of the results—the presence of radioactive markers at a particular site in a section is not proof of net uptake of the labelled compound, or proof of the site of active transport. Proper controls must be carried out.

References

AVRON, M. 1971. Biochemistry of photophosphorylation. In: M. Gibbs, (ed.). *Structure and function of chloroplasts.* New York, Springer-Verlag. p. 149–67.

BENSON, A. A.; MUSCATINE, L. 1974. Wax in coral mucus: energy transfer from corals to reef fishers. *Limnol. Oceanogr.,* vol 19, p. 810–14.

CARDENAS, J.; RIVAS, J.; PANEQUE, A.; LOSADA, M. 1971. Molybdenum and the nitrate reducing system from *Chlorella. Arch. Mikrobiol.,* vol. 79, p. 367–76.

CONOVER, R. J.; FRANCIS, V. 1973. The use of radioisotopes to measure the transfer of materials in aquatic food chains. *Mar. Biol.,* vol. 18, p. 272–83.

CORNER, E. D. S.; DAVIES, A. G. 1971. Plankton as a factor in the nitrogen and phosphorus cycles in the sea. *Adv. Mar. Biol.,* vol. 9, p. 102–204.

D'ELIA, C. F. 1977. The uptake and release of dissolved phosphorus by reef corals. *Limnol. Oceanogr.,* vol. 22, p. 301–15.

DUURSMA, E. K. 1965. The dissolved organic constituents of sea water. In: J. P. Riley and G. Skirrow (eds.). *Chemical Oceanography,* New York, Academic Press. p. 433–75.

EPPLEY, R. W.; COATSWORTH, J. L. 1968. Uptake of nitrate and nitrite by *Ditylum brightwellii*—kinetics and mechanisms. *J. Phycol.,* vol. 4, p. 151–56.

——; COATSWORTH, J. L.; SOLÓRZANO, L. 1969. Studies of nitrate reductase in marine phytoplankton. *Limnol. Oceanogr.,* vol. 14, p. 194–205.

FAWCETT, D. W. 1965. Surface specialization of absorbing cells. *J. Histochem. Cytochem.,* vol. 13, p. 75–91.

FITZGERALD, G. P.; NELSON, T. C. 1966. Extractive and enzymatic analyses for limiting and surplus phosphorus in algae. *J. Phycol.,* vol. 2, p. 32–37.

FOGG, G. E. 1966. The extracellular products of algae. *Oceanogr. mar. Biol. Ann. Rev.,* vol. 4, p. 195–212.

FRANZISKET, L. 1973. Uptake and accumulation of nitrate and nitrite by reef corals. *Naturwissenschaften,* vol. 60, p. 552.

——. 1974. Nitrate uptake by reef corals. *Int. Rev. gesamt Hydrobiol.,* vol. 59, p. 1–7.

GAVIS, J. 1976. Munk and Riley revisited; nutrient diffusion transport and rates of phytoplankton growth. *J. mar. Res.* vol. 34, p. 161–79.

GIESE, A. 1968. *Cell physiology,* 3rd edit. Philadelphia, Pa. Saunders.

GOREAU, T. F.; GOREAU, N. I.; YONGE, C. M. 1971. Reef corals: autotrophs or heterotrophs? *Biol. Bull. Mar. Biol. Lab. Woods Hole, Mass.,* vol. 141, p. 247–60.

HARVEY, H. W. 1957. *The chemistry and fertility of sea water,* 2nd edit. Cambridge University Press.

HEALEY, F. P. 1973. Inorganic nutrient uptake and deficiency in algae. *Crit. Rev. Microbiol.,* vol. 3, p. 69–113.

HOAR, W. S. 1966. *General and comparative physiology.* Englewood Cliffs, N.J., Prentice-Hall.

JEANJEAN, R.; BLASCO, F. 1970. Influence des ions arséniate sur l'absorption des ions phosphate par less Chlorelles. *C.R. Acad. Sci., Paris,* vol. 270, p. 1897–1900.

JOHANNES, R. E. 1964. Phosphorus excretion and body size in marine animals: microzooplankton and nutrient regeneration. *Science,* vol. 146, p. 923–4.

——. 1968. Nutrient regeneration in lakes and oceans. In: M. Droop and E. J. F. Wood (eds). *Advances in microbiology in the sea.* New York, Academic Press. p. 203–13.

——; ALBERTS, J.; D'ELIA, C.; KINZIE, R. A.; POMEROY, L. R.; SOTTILE, W.; WIEBE, W.; MARSH, J. A. Jr.; HELFRICH, P.; MARAGOS, J.; MEYER, J.; SMITH, S.; CRABTREE, D.; ROTH, A.;

DuPaul, W. D.; Webb, K. L.; Wells, J. M. Jr. 1972. The metabolism of some coral reef communities: a team study of nutrient and energy flux at Eniwetok. *BioScience*, vol. 22, p. 541–3.
——; Coward, S. J.; Webb, K. L. 1969. Are dissolved amino acids an energy source for marine invertebrates? *Comp. Biochem. Physiol.*, vol. 29, p. 283–8.
——; Webb, K. L. 1970. Release of dissolved organic compounds by marine and freshwater invertebrates. In: D. W. Hood, (ed.). *Organic matter in natural waters*. College, Alaska, Alaska Press, p. 257–73.
Jokiel, P. L.; Coles, S. L. 1974. Effects of heated effluent on hermatypic corals at Kahe Point, Oahu. *Pac. Sci.*, vol. 28, p. 1–18.
Kawaguti, S. 1953. Ammonium metabolism of the reef corals. *Biol. Journ. Okayama Univ.*, vol. 1, p. 171–6.
Lewis, D. H.; Smith, D. C. 1971. The autotrophic nutrition of symbiotic marine coelenterates with special reference to hermatypic corals. I. Movement of photosynthetic products between the symbionts. *Proc. R. Soc. Lond.* (B: *Biol. Sci.*), vol. 178, p. 111–29.
Loftus, M. E.; Carpenter, J. H. 1971. A fluorometric method for determining chlorophylls a, b, and c. *J. mar. Res.*, vol. 29, p. 319–38.
Mahler, H. R.; Cordes, E. H. 1966. *Biological chemistry*. New York, Harper and Row.
Marvin, K. T.; Proctor, R. R., Jr.; Neal, R. A. 1972. Some effects of filtration on the determination of nutrients in fresh and salt water. *Limnol. Oceanogr.*, vol. 17, p. 777–84.
Matthews, H. R. 1968. Application of Cerenkov counting to column chromatography of phosphorus-32-labelled substances. *J. Chromatogr.*, vol. 36, p. 302–8.
Muscatine, L. 1973. Nutrition of corals. In: O. A. Jones and R. Endean (eds). *Biology and geology of coral reefs*. New York, Academic Press, vol. II, p. 77–115.
Neame, K. D.; Richards, T. G. 1972. *Elementary kinetics of membrane carrier transport*. Oxford, Blackwell Scientific Publications.
Odum, H. T.; Odum, E. P. 1955. Trophic structure and productivity of a windward coral reef community on Eniwetok Atoll. *Ecol. Monogr.*, vol. 25, p. 291–320.
Olsen, S. 1966. Recent trends in the determination of orthophosphate in water. In: *Proceedings of an IBP symposium held in Amsterdam and Nieuwersluis*.
Parsons, T. R.; Takahashi, M. 1973. *Biological oceanographic processes*. Oxford, Pergamon Press.
Pilson, M. E. Q. 1974. Arsenate uptake and reduction by *Pocillopora verrucosa*. *Limnol. Oceanogr.*, vol. 19, p. 339–41.
——; Betzer, S. B. 1973. Phosphorus flux across a coral reef. *Ecology*, vol. 54, p. 581–8.
Pomeroy, L. R. 1960. Residence time of dissolved phosphate in natural waters. *Science*, vol. 131, p. 1731–32.
——. 1971. The strategy of mineral cycling. *Ann. Rev. ecol. Systematics*, vol. 1, p. 171–90.
——; Kuenzler, E. J. 1969. Phosphorus turnover by coral reef animals. *Proc. 2nd Conference on Radioecology*. AEC CONF-670503, p. 474–82.
——; Pilson, M. E. Q.; Wiebe, W. J. 1974. Tracer studies of the exchange of phosphorus between reef water and organisms on the windward reef of Eniwetok Atoll. In: *Proc. Second Int. Coral Reef Symp.* Brisbane, Great Barrier Reef Committee, vol. 7, p. 87–96.
Riley, G. A. 1970. Particulate and organic matter in sea water. *Adv. Mar. Biol.*, vol. 8, p. 1–118.
Riley, J. P.; Chester, R. 1971. *Introduction to marine chemistry*. London, Academic Press.
Rogers, A. N. 1973. *Techniques of autoradiography*. New York, Elsevier.
Roth, L. J.; Stumpf, W. E. (eds). 1969. *The autoradiography of diffusible substances*. New York, Academic Press.
Satomi, M.; Pomeroy, L. R. 1965. Respiration and phosphorus excretion in some marine populations. *Ecology*, vol. 46, p. 877–81.
Simson, J. V.; Spicer, S. S. 1973. Activities of specific cell constituents in phagocytosis (endocytosis). *Int. Rev. Exp. Pathol.*, vol. 12, p. 79–118.
Solórzano, L.; Strickland, J. D. H. 1968. Polyphosphate in sea water. *Limnol. Oceanogr.*, vol. 13, p. 515–8.
Sorokin, Yu. I. 1973. Feeding of some scleractinian corals with bacteria and dissolved organic matter. *Limnol. Oceanogr.*, 18, p. 380–5.
Steele, R. 1971. *Tracer probes in steady-state systems*. Springfield, Illinois, Thomas.
Stein, W. D. 1967. *The movement of molecules across cell membranes*. New York, Academic Press.
Stephens, G. C. 1962. Uptake of organic material by aquatic invertebrates. I. Uptake of glucose by the solitary coral, *Fungia scutaria*. *Biol. Bull. Mar. Biol. Lab. Woods Hole, Mass.*, vol. 132, p. 648–59.

496

STRICKLAND, J. D. H.; PARSONS, T. R. 1968. A practical handbook of sea water analysis. *Fish Res. Bd Can. Bull.*, Ottawa, Queen's Printer, no. 167. (311 p.).

STROSS, R. G.; CHISHOLM, S. W.; DOWNING, T. A. 1973. Causes of daily rhythms in photosynthetic rates of phytoplankton. *Biol. Bull. Mar. Biol. Lab. Woods Hole, Mass.,* vol. 145, p. 200–9.

STRUHSAKER, J. W.; HASHIMOTO, D. Y.; GIRARD, S. M.; PRIOR, F. T.; COONEY, T. D. 1973. Effect of antibiotics on survival of carangid fish larvae (*Caranx mate*), reared in the laboratory. *Aquaculture,* vol. 2, p. 53–88.

TYLER, J. E. 1973. Lux vs. quanta. *Limnol. Oceanogr.,* vol. 18, p. 811.

WAGNER, F. S. 1969. Composition of the dissolved organic compounds in sea water: a review. *Contr. Mar. Sci.,* vol. 14, p. 115–53.

WEBB, K. L.; DUPAUL, W. D.; WIEBE, W.; SOTTILE, W.; JOHANNES, R. E. 1975. Enewetak (Eniwetok) Atoll: aspects of the nitrogen cycle on a coral reef. *Limnol. Oceanogr.,* vol. 20, p. 198–210.

WHITFORD, L. A.; SCHUMACHER, G. J. 1961. Effect of current on mineral uptake and respiration by a fresh-water alga. *Limnol. Oceanogr.,* vol. 6, p. 423–25.

——; SCHUMACHER, G. J. 1964. Effect of a current on respiration and mineral uptake in *Spirogyra* and *Oedogonium. Ecology,* vol. 45, p. 168–70.

WILLIAMS, P. J. LEB. 1973. The validity of the application of simple kinetic analysis to heterogeneous microbial populations. *Limnol. Oceanogr.,* vol. 18, p. 159–64.

WINNE, D. 1973. Unstirred layer, source of biased Michaelis constant in membrane transport. *Biochim. Biophys. Acta,* vol. 298, p. 27–31.

YAMAZATO, K. 1970. Calcification in a solitary coral, *Fungia scutaria* L. in relation to environmental factors. *Bulletin of Science and Engineering Division, University of the Ryukyus, Mathematics and Natural Sciences,* vol. 13, p. 57–122.

38

Resident reef plankton

K. G. Porter[1], J. W. Porter[1]
and S. L. Ohlhorst[2]

OBJECTIVES

The near-shore plankton were among the first life forms from the sea to be described. The sails of *Physalia* and phosphorescent tides were noted by the early Phoenicians. This early recognition, however, did not result in rapid advances in understanding of their biology due to the technological requirements for microscopical examination of most forms and the necessity for relatively sophisticated sampling and preservation techniques. As these became widely available near the end of the 19th century, plankton received increasingly intense study, as witnessed by the extensive plankton expeditions during the late 1890's (the German 'Plankton Expedition' and 'Deep-Sea Expedition' among others), and the inception at this time of journals and monographs devoted strictly to this subject (*Nordische Plankton, The Journal of Marine Zoology and Microscopy,* and the *Fauna und Flora des Golfes von Neapel*). This research was restricted in two general ways, both spatial, which prevented an understanding of true coral reef plankton: the most intensive studies were conducted in north temperate waters, rather than in tropical oceans, and the collections were exclusively open water: sailing vessels rarely approached reefs closely enough to do the kind of sampling described below (except when running aground on them, a fate which befell even Captain James Cook during his Great Barrier Reef survey).

This chapter will outline the general sampling techniques which have been successfully employed in collecting, preserving, and enumerating coral reef plankton. This information will be complemented by a literature review and the presentation of original data from the authors' researches where they pertain to collecting procedures. Finally, the authors will present their current thinking on the patterns they have observed in plankton seasonality, as well as abundance, and spatial distribution (in two and three dimensions) over the reef.

1. Department of Zoology, University of Georgia, Athens, Georgia, 30602, U.S.A.
2. Osborn Laboratory, Yale University, New Haven, Connecticut, 06520, U.S.A.

499

PLANKTON NETS

1. Towed plankton nets

Sampling methods should reflect the questions being asked. Only in the last decade, however, has this been so with respect to plankton research on coral reefs. Most earlier studies involved towing or hauling a plankton net of a given mesh size through the open water column for a given period of time, and then counting the catch (see Krämer, 1897). These techniques answer 'what and when' questions for open water tropical plankton. The techniques used in these open water studies have been extensively reviewed by Wickstead (1965), and in handbooks by Josse (1970), Tranter and Fraser (1968), and the Biological Methods Panel (1969).

Nylon nets with mesh size of 390 µ (equal to 0.015 inches on the diagonal) have been recommended for acceptance as 'standard' by the Biological Methods Panel (1969). A net with this mesh can withstand long tows without clogging, while retaining all the larger zooplankton. In using a 75 µ mesh net, the authors found that clogging occurred both day and night after dragging the net less than 20 metres. While this fine mesh size retains a significant proportion of the algae, its rapid clogging makes it only of limited use in quantitative zooplankton sampling. Further, the cone of resistance that builds up in front of a clogging net is likely to be pushed away or avoided by many mobile zooplankton (Fleminger and Clutter, 1965). Several recommendations follow: the authors found that extremely short tows of only a few metres are possible for nets with mesh sizes less than 120 µ. A net diameter of 0.5 m is recommended with a filter area ratio (porosity multiplied by mesh area and divided by mouth area) of 5 to 1 with a reserve filtering catchment bucket on the end. Flow meters are needed: one mounted off centre in the mouth of the net; the other mounted on the outside of the net. The inside meter, after calibration, records the total volume of water filtered; the outside meter indicates unimpended flow, the ratio of these two values gives an estimation of filtering efficiency.

These meters allow one to answer 'how much' questions in terms of number or oganisms per cubic metre. Repeated tows are necessary in order to determine statistical confidence in plankton abundance studies. Average values are not always desirable, however, if questions relating to patchiness of the plankton are under investigation. Here, a large number of small samples will tell more about local variations in plankton composition and abundance than a few long tows. Both will give the same average abundance, but one will be infinitely more useful in determining micro-geographical distributions. Sample size is an extremely difficult parameter to set. The size of an adequate sample will vary greatly from day to night, from day to day, or from one point on the reef to another. One must have the question to be answered clearly in mind before initiating a zooplankton sampling programme. This is why most of the early work is valuable primarily for its taxonomy rather than its ecology.

Numerous studies employing plankton nets have been carried out in open water in tropical areas. (Nets catching on the bottom is a difficulty during shallow

500

water tows from a boat.) In the Pacific, studies of this nature were conducted in Palao (Matsuya, 1937; Motoda, 1939, 1940a, b, and c), in the Marshall Islands (Fleming, 1954; Johnson, 1949), on the Great Barrier Reef (Farran, 1949; Marshall, 1933; Russell, 1934; Russell and Colman, 1931, 1934, 1935; Russell and Orr, 1931; Tattersall, 1936), and in Hawaii (Miller, 1973). In the Caribbean, studies have been conducted in Bermuda (Moore, 1949; Menzel and Ryther, 1961; Deevey, 1964, 1968; Reeve, 1964; Grice and Hart, 1962; Herman and Beers, 1969; Kuenzel, 1972), in Florida (Woodmansee, 1958), and in Puerto Rico (Glynn, 1973a and b; Coker and Gonzalez, 1960; Gonzalez and Bowman, 1965).

2. *Stationary plankton nets*

In this Monograph, Johannes (Chapter 33) has presented techniques related to the use of nets anchored on the bottom. As with all studies, interpretation must relate to the biological question being asked. For instance, stationary nets do not sample larger, actively swimming zooplankton which could leave the net by crawling or swimming out, but sample accurately 'drift' plankton. Also, a drift net's contents do not accurately reflect the 'stomach contents' of a predator whose mouth is ringed by tentacles capable of reaching for and holding actively swimming zooplankters. These plankters would escape the net but not the active benthic filter feeder.

3. *Diver controlled nets*

Emery (1968) appears to have been the first to recognize clearly the difficulty of coral reef zooplankton sampling and do something quantitative about it. Using a diver-held net, Emery pushed the net close to the surface of the reef guiding the path of the moving net near the irregular surface of the reef. Although his tow volumes were not measured, he inferred the existence of a considerable endemic component in his near-reef samples based on their different taxonomic composition compared with open water samples.

The second author initiated a year-long plankton sampling programme, in 1971, in Panama using a diver-pushed net of 120 μ mesh (Porter, 1973). The net was 0.5 m in diameter, 2 m long, with flow meters, and was pushed at three different depths on two different reefs. Pushes were accompanied by an open water vertical haul from 20 metres to the surface, 500 metres away from the reef. Each push was performed twice along a measured 33 metre course at each depth interval, in one direction the first time and in the opposite direction the second time. These paired pushes at each of the three depths were effected once every week in the morning and at night at the same times of day for 52 consecutive weeks. The data are overwhelming. Plankton samples must stand alone in the extremely time-consuming, arduous difficulty of their enumeration.

Certain trends are visible from an analysis of simple, plankton settling volume (Porter, 1973), see Figure 1. In this study, data were collected over a 24-

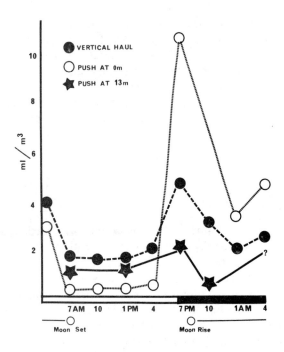

Figure 1
The settling volume of plankton and other particulate matter per m³ of reef-water sampled on a Caribbean reef, San Blas Islands, Panama, on 28–29 May, 1972. Sunrise was at 5.59 a.m., sunset at 6.30 p.m., and moonrise at 7.13 p.m. Open circles and stars represent plankton volumes from net tows made by a diver within a metre of the reef's surface at 0 m and 13 m depth, respectively. The vertical haul was from 13 m to 0 m straight up in an area 500 m offshore from the reef over water 100 m deep. See text for further description of the net and towing procedure (from Porter, 1973).

hour period, and the changes in plankton plus drift material abundance can be seen. The bulk of the plankton, in terms of volume and numbers, comes from the reef itself and not from the open ocean. It is of unique taxonomic composition and behaviour: true reef plankton is of greater taxonomic diversity since it contains juvenile stages of a large number of benthic phyla not found in the holoplankton. True reef plankton is also involved in regular diurnal vertical migrations from the substratum (Porter and Porter, 1977). It is large bodied and can be fed upon when it rises, making it the major caloric source for the benthic animals, not the open water plankton drifting over the reef (Porter, 1974).

Additional studies using diver-pushed nets have also been conducted for short periods of time from underwater habitats such as Tektite in the Virgin Islands (Hickel, 1971; Hentig, 1971) and from Hydro-Lab in the Bahama Islands (Schroeder *et al.*, 1973; Porter, in prep.).

502

PLANKTON PUMPS

Pumps are used to sample open waters (in Edmondson and Winberg, 1971; Barnes, 1949; Tranter and Fraser, 1968) and have been employed in coral atolls (Mathisen, 1964). The three major problems exist in pump sampling: (1) destruction of the plankton in the water sample, (2) differential avoidance of the pump intake by plankton, and (3) restricted and inexact placement of the intake hose in the water column. Large, high speed pumps are only suited for use on large research vessels. This obviates their use in shallow, truly reef-waters. In all systems, water is taken in through a large diameter (> 5 cm) intake hose. Intake water then flows into a large barrel-like chamber with a net or series of nets (Mathisen, 1964) between the points of inflow and outflow from the barrel. The barrel, which is kept full of water, prevents direct ejection of the intake water on to the netting which would damage the plankton severely. If possible, the barrel nets should lie between the intake and the pump to avoid passing the plankton through the pump mechanism. Mortality of 20 to 40 per cent is common in pump sampling. Larger forms such as euphausids and mysids can easily avoid the intake.

SUCTION DEVICES

The plankton which lives in or near the reef surface can be sampled by diver-operated suction devices. The demersal plankton is patchily distributed on the reef. The swarming behaviour of copepods and mysids (Steven, 1961; Emery, 1968) and the habitation of caves, crevices and overhangs produces patches of high density. Swarming species and species which inhabit openings in the reef face can be collected using air-lift systems with self-contained (Emery, 1968) or surface supplied (in Holme and McIntyre, 1971) sources of suction. The suction systems draw animals and water from the surface of the reef and concentrate them in bags of plankton netting. The contents are bottled and preserved when brought to the surface.

MICRO-SAMPLING: THE SAMPLING OF FINE PARTICULATE MATTER

Investigations of the food available to filter-feeding reef invertebrates require the sampling of fine particulate matter in the water. The following technique has been used to provide direct assessment of the rate of filtration of particles by various sponges (Reiswig, 1971). Reiswig (pers. comm.) suggests that it can be used for tunicates as well.

Exhalant water samples are obtained by carefully inserting a capped, clear 25 ml polyethylene syringe into the exhalant stream below the margin of the osculum, taking care not to contact the specimen. The cap is removed

503

while in the stream, the syringe slowly filled and the cap replaced while still in the stream. Ambient samples are taken near the inhalant surface of the sponge immediately following the collection of the exhalant sample.

Within one hour of collection, 15 ml portions of each of the samples are filtered through 25 mm 0.22 μ Millipore type GS membrane filters at a suction of 0.3 atm or less (Holmes and Anderson, 1963). The filters are fixed in formalin fumes for 30 minutes, air dried, and stained in a membrane-filtered solution of 1 per cent erythrosin-phenol for one hour at 60°C (Jannasch and Jones, 1959; Kriss, 1963). They are then rinsed in distilled water, air dried, and mounted in Canada balsam under cover slips on microscope slides and visually examined. See Reiswig (1971) for further details as to the method of volume and carbon determinations.

SAMPLING OF FRAGILE MACROPLANKTONIC FORMS

Many animals (e.g. jellyfish, marine gastropods, salps) are too fragile to be caught and preserved by conventional plankton collecting methods using nets. A group, from the University of California at Davis, under the direction of W. M. Hamner (1975), developed a system to search for and study these animals. This involves open-water diving with each diver linked by rope to a coordinating diver, clear plastic bottles of half pint to quart size (approximately a quarterlitre to one litre) for safe collection, and the use of oblique strobe light and harmless carmine or fluorescent green dye to aid visibility photography. Although more tedious than net towing this method of sampling makes it possible to collect and observe the many animals missed or destroyed by other plankton collecting techniques. Emery (1968) has suggested that a sheet of polarizing plastic aids in making plankton more visible but the authors were unsuccessful with this technique. Electronic image intensifiers which are worn like goggles and enhance whatever light is present could be used for night collection.

LIGHT TRAPS

At night, reef plankton which are attracted to diving lights can be sucked into plastic bags attached to 'slurp guns' available commercially for the capture of small reef fish (personal observation). They may also be collected using the suction collector of Emery (1968). The sample is preserved, filtered and transferred to a suitable storage bottle at the surface.

A light trap consisting of an underwater flashlight inside a 40 × 40 × 40-cm frame with raisable walls of 210 μ plankton netting can be used to encase plankters attracted to the light (Sale, et al., 1976). When raised to the surface, the contents drain through a net cod in the floor of the frame. Of course, all light traps will be selective in capturing only animals that are positively phototropic at the light intensities employed and for the time of day or night employed.

MIGRATION TRAPS

Demersal plankton which exhibit diurnal vertical migration can be captured in traps similar in principle to those used for the sampling of emerging stream insects (Mundie and Morgan, in Edmondson and Winberg, 1971) and vertically migrating freshwater benthic crustacea (Whiteside and Williams, 1975). These traps can be used to document that demersal plankton actually originate from the reef surface. They permit continuous sampling of the plankton as it rises from the reef. The traps consist of a round or square funnel with a mouth area of at least one square metre (Porter and Porter, 1977; Porter et al., 1977). They are made of semi-rigid plastic sheeting or of polyethylene film stretched on a frame, and are anchored with the mouth just above the reef surface. The narrow end leads, through 3 cm I.D. tubing, well into a large 2–10 litre plastic catching bottle. The bottle contains some air to keep the system vertical in the water column and it can be removed and replaced without moving the funnel from its station. This allows a time series of continuous collections to be made. $MgCO_3$ or 5 per cent formalin can be injected into the base of the catch bottle to prevent predatory animals from decimating prey in the catch flask. These substances may, however, inhibit animals from entering the bottle. Patchiness can be assessed by using a series of adjacent traps. Traps can also be placed at varying heights in the water column to determine differences in the degree of vertical rise of various species. A reversed configuration, with the funnel turned upward, will catch animals returning to the reef at dawn. Other trap designs have also been used with success (Aldridge and King, 1977).

MODIFICATIONS OF LACUSTRINE SAMPLING DEVICES

Techniques which permit accurate quantitative sampling of zooplankton populations and the determination of small scale (less than or equal to one metre) vertical and horizontal distributional patterns have been developed to a high degree by limnologists. This is in part due to the ease with which small, calm lakes can be navigated, the accuracy with which each depth in the water column under a smooth surface can be located and repeatedly sampled and the high density of organisms compared to those in the open ocean. Conditions in lagoons and back reef areas approximate those in small lakes and ponds (Johnson, 1949; Boden, 1952), allowing limnological techniques to be applied to them. In particular, traps and bottles which enclose portions of the water column may be used. These are described in detail in Edmondson and Winberg (1971). The ten-litre steel or brass Juday traps (Edmondson and Winberg, 1971) and 12 and 30-litre plexiglass Schindler–Patalas traps (Schindler, 1969) can be worked by hand from small boats in these reefal environments. The square traps are lowered to the desired depth with their tops and bottoms open, triggered or closed automatically, and hauled to the surface where their contents drain into a net cod with a siphon at the bottom. This allows quantitative samples to be collected from any depth in the water column. Water bottles, used to sample phytoplankton and occasionally zooplankton, are easily avoided by large zooplankton and usually contain too small a volume to be useful in reef areas. The large 30 litre plexiglass trap is recommended for reef use but it also may be of insufficient volume.

METHODS OF PRESERVATION

It is best to observe and identify live animals. This allows them to be examined intact and their natural colour and posture to be studied. The enumeration of samples, however, is done on preserved collections to avoid decomposition during the long, tedious process of counting. The ideal preservative is inexpensive, easily obtained, fixes animals with a minimum of bleaching, shrinkage or deformation, is equally effective on all groups, and has a long shelf life.

The best fixative–preservative for general use is formalin. It must be of the best quality available and stored, whenever possible, in glass or polyethylene containers. It should be neutralized so that there is no free acid in solution, and added to the sample as soon as possible. Formalin is a saturated solution of formaldehyde in water, the so-called 40 per cent solution. Commercial formalin supplied in large steel drums contains dissolved iron impurities. If the plankton are preserved with this formalin the iron eventually begins to come out of solution as a brown, flocculant precipitate. This enmeshes the plankton effectively, obscures the small organisms and obliterates the finer structures such as crustacean appendages. This problem does not arise when higher quality formalin from non-metal containers is used. Formalin can be purchased at most pharmacies even in the tropics. If only the commercial quality is available, the iron can be prevented from coming out of solution by adding Rochelle salt (sodium potassium tartrate) which acts as a chelating agent (Wickstead, 1965).

Neutralized (or buffered) formalin is required for tropical plankton samples because of the large proportion of animals with calcareous shells or tests. These body parts are essential for proper identification and un-neutralized formalin contains free acid which promotes the dissolution of these parts. The best method for neutralizing the formalin is to place an excess of calcium carbonate in the bottom of the storage container. Commercial calcium carbonate, marble chips, or coral sand may be used.

The sample should be preserved as soon after collecting as possible. Some percentage of the plankton is dead when the net leaves the water and decomposition occurs rapidly especially in the tropics. Wickstead (1965) cautions that even during the course of the plankton haul animals will have begun to decompose. As undesirable as it is to have formalin aboard a small collecting craft, it must be available to preserve the samples immediately. It can be carried in the sample bottles or can be added from a squeeze bottle. One part of the 40 per cent neutralized formalin solution is added to every eight parts of plankton sample to produce a final concentration of 5 per cent. From 4 to 6 per cent is suitable but higher concentrations cause severe shrinkage and deformation of some specimens. The labelling should be done as soon as possible, as Wickstead reminds us, 'Plankton samples are easily mixed up, and the tropics are notorious for inducing forgetfulness.' Use good waterproof ink or pencil. Metal caps on the jars will invariably corrode so plastic caps should be used if at all possible.

The jars should be stored in the dark to aid in preserving the coloured pigments useful in identification. As mentioned above, marble or coral can be added to maintain neutrality.

The above method is used for preserving plankton for general inspection. Forty per cent ethanol and sea water is, however, the best long-term preservative for animals with calcium carbonate parts. Many analyses cannot be performed on plankton preserved in formalin. Preservation in this manner brings about chemical changes, such a loss of fats. For determination of dry weight, calorific value and biochemical composition it is recommended that animals be dried in an oven at not more than 60°C and stored in a dessicator. Even this treatment can cause loss of volatile compounds and for very accurate work freeze drying is recommended (in Edmondson and Winberg, 1971). For histological work Bouin's fluid is often recommended. Biochemical analysis of preserved specimens should either be done on formalin-fixed samples within 24 hours or on samples which have been deep frozen ($-25°C$) or freeze dried. Ten per cent trichloracetic acid and 70 per cent ethanol are far less satisfactory (Fudge, 1968).

METHODS OF ANALYSIS

The methods of analysis will vary depending on the information desired. There are three major ways of quantifying a plankton sample: by volume, weight (wet weight, dry weight or ash free dry weight) or numbers. Any large non-planktonic animals such as fish or large medusae should be removed and treated separately as they will distort many of the measurements. Contamination of zooplankton with mucus and phytoplankton is often a problem and these may be separated by use of differential settling rates, centrifugation and/or sucrose gradients.

Volume

Volume is measured either in terms of settling volume or displacement volume. Settling volume is measured by putting the plankton into a narrow graduated cylinder and, after settling, the volume occupied by the plankton can be read from the cylinder. The most marked change in volume with time occurs during the first day (Ahlstrom and Thrailkill, 1962) and readings should be taken until there is no further change. This usually takes one to two days. The amount of decrease with time will depend on the faunal composition; the least decrease is for crustaceans and the greatest is for salps and many larval forms. Usually the reason for measuring the volume of an animal is to provide an indirect approximation of its weight although the volume enclosed by the external surface of some animals will include space that is not really occupied by animal tissue (e.g. cladocera and ostracods).

Displacement volume gives more consistent results and there are several techniques for measuring it. The plankton can be placed in a graduated cylinder which is then made up to a certain volume. The sample is then poured through a filter and the volume of the filtrate measured and subtracted from the first gives the displacement volume of the plankton. Alternatively a cylinder is filled to an exact level and the filtered plankton added, the new reading minus the initial gives the displacement volume. The method of water extraction is important and the different water-holding capacities of the plankton (salps versus copepods for example) makes precision tiresome. Wickstead (1965) and Yentsch and Hebard (1956) give more elaborate methods which yield more precise and comparable results.

If the sample is to be counted, an estimate of volume can be determined by measuring various dimensions of the animals and calculating the volume. Johannes *et al.* (1970), Kuenzel (1972), and Heusden (1972) all give procedures for doing this on marine samples. The IBP Handbook no. 17 (Edmondson and Winberg, 1971) includes an extensive list of references using this technique with fresh water zooplankton.

Weight

Wet weight is a straightforward procedure and involves filtering the sample dry and then weighing it. The source of error is the difficulty in removing all the water and if samples are of differing faunal composition it is not possible to compare them accurately with each other. If the composition is such that the animals do not lose water at different rates, this is a very quick method for comparing biomass.

Dry weight determinations should not be made on formalin-preserved samples because there is loss of organic substances (especially fats) from the organisms and because carbon determinations cannot be made on samples preserved with organic compounds such as formalin or alcohol. In a comparison of preservation methods Fudge (1968) found no difference between the dry weight of formalin-treated or fresh samples although biochemical determinations did differ. If formalin-preserved samples cannot be used, the samples should be frozen or freeze dried as soon as possible. Because of rapid decomposition and the rarity of adequate refrigeration in the tropics it is desirable to determine with each investigation whether formalin samples yield adequate information comparable with the frozen samples. If the analyses are comparable then it is desirable to use formalin, both for the above mentioned reasons and because the sample will not have to be split in the field, if both biomass or chemical determinations as well as counting are to be performed.

Although the sample should be rinsed with distilled water to remove the salt, Curl (1962) cautions that such washing can result in an appreciable loss of water soluble carbon-containing compounds. The samples are then placed in weighing bottles and dried to constant weight, at 60°C (Edmondson and Winberg, 1971; Lovegrove, 1962). Higher temperatures will volatilize the fats and break down organics. An alternative method (Biological Methods Panel, 1969) involves homogenization of the frozen sample with aliquots taken for dry weight and carbon and nitrogen analysis. Dry weights are difficult to measure under many of the conditions prevalent in the tropics, the most serious being the high humidity and one must remember to stopper the weighing bottles after removal from the oven to cool before weighing.

The ash weight, or determination of organic matter, is determined by the loss of weight compared to the dry weight after ignition in a muffle furnace at temperatures close to 500°C. If the temperature is higher, disintegration of $CaCO_3$ or loss of alkali chlorides can occur. The IBP Handbook no. 17 should be consulted for further discussion of this and bomb colorimetric determinations as well as for further references.

Curl (1962), Golterman and Climo (1969), Vollenweider (1969), Edmondson and Winberg (1971), and Strickland and Parsons (1968) should be consulted for methods of biochemical analysis of carbon, nitrogen, phosphorus, chitin, etc.

Techniques have been worked out for determining wet weights and calorific values from the dimensions of various zooplankton. The size measurements can be taken at the same time as the sample is counted. Edmondson and Winberg, 1971, Clarke and Bishop (1948), Comita and Schindler (1963), Cummins and Wuycheck (1971) and Porter (1974) should all be consulted for specifics on this technique. Bé (in Tranter and Fraser, 1968) suggests a scheme for biomass measurement based on the use of different meshed nets and size fractionation of plankton filtered through a separatory column.

Number

The counting of marine plankton is especially tedious but provides by far the best way to assess both the community organization of the plankton and its relations to reef trophic dynamics. Temperate water and lacustrine samples contain fewer species than those from the tropics and can be accurately sub-sampled to a much finer degree than tropical samples. The general methods given by Edmondson (Edmondson and Winberg, 1971) are still applicable or one can refer to Wickstead (1965).

The whole sample is poured into a graduated cylinder and made up to a definite volume with preservative. The volume of subsample depends on the commonness of the organisms one is most interested in. If one needs to determine the numbers of both abundant and scarce animals with the same reliability it will be necessary to count at least two different dilutions of the sample.

The sample is poured from the cylinder into a container and stirred in such a manner as to avoid vortices that concentrate the organisms. The subsample is taken using a pipette that will draw up a definite volume of liquid. The Hensen Stemple pipette is designed for this purpose and Edmondson gives details about the best alternative equipment to use. When counting different dilutions all subsampling should be done at one time. From the most concentrated sample small portions are taken for counting scarce organisms. Other portions are taken, made up to a definite volume and subsampled in the same manner as the more concentrated sample. This subsample is used for the more abundant animals.

An alternative method involves the use of one of the various instruments which have been developed for splitting a sample into fractions. These are generally plastic vessels with internal partitions arranged in such a way that after the sample is poured in, rotation of the vessel isolates equal fractions of the sample (McEwen et al., 1954; Wiborg, 1951). Care must be taken to rinse the chamber carefully in order to recover the animals that stick on the walls.

Subsample size, representative subsampling and statistical methods are discussed by M. Cassie in Edmondson and Winberg (1971) and Tranter and Fraser (1968). Statistical methods are included in those volumes. A way to determine the size of a representative subsample using a three way nested analysis of variance is given by Porter (1972).

An open petri dish is convenient for scanning the plankton and pulling out specimens to mount but it is not practical for counting. This is because of the difficulty in keeping one's place, even if there are grids, and the ease of disturbing the liquid and moving the plankton. The most convenient method of counting is with a Bogorov counting tray, a plexiglass chamber with plexiglass partitions which aid in keeping one's place and restricting movement of the plankton. Wickstead (1965) gives clear instructions for the construction of such a tray. A binocular microscope with $250 \times$ magnification is usually sufficient although $500 \times$ or $1000 \times$ oil immersion is often needed for species identification. The animals are viewed with reflected light and although use of a stain will make the plankton more visible it will obscure much of the characteristic coloration helpful in identification. Speed in counting must be balanced with accuracy and ease of identification. Clumps of organisms can be dispersed by addition of a few drops of detergent to the sample. Wickstead (1965), Edmondson and Winberg (1971) and Heusden (1972) describe other counting chamber designs.

Semi-permanent slides can be made by mounting specimens in water-soluble polyvinyl lactophenol sealed with nail polish. Polyvinyl lactophenol is highly toxic, should be used in a well-aired room and not ingested or allowed to come in contact with the skin. An alternative is to use 50 per cent Karo syrup or a concentrated sucrose solution with five to ten per cent formalin added.

Keys for aid to identification of tropical plankton are scarce but the following references are helpful: Wickstead (1965), Owre and Foyo (1967), Tregouboff and Rose (1957), Deevey (1968), Gonzalez and Bowman (1965), Owre (1972) and Sears (1950).

CONCLUSION

Based on the tows and plankton trap samples analysed to date (Porter, 1974; Porter and Porter, 1977; Porter *et al.*, 1977) and the continuing counts, a number of facts and impressions are emerging. (1) Coral reefs harbour a highly abundant and diverse variety of resident zooplankton. (2) This diversity and abundance is in striking contrast to that of the open water plankton as little as 500 metres from the reef area. (3) Most of the plankton on the coral reef comes from the reef itself, and not from the nutrient-poor water surrounding the reef. The predominance of an endemic plankton found on a reef is true both in terms of the total number of zooplankton (75 per cent benthic in origin, 25 per cent open-ocean in origin) and also in terms of the total biomass of zooplankton (85 per cent of the biomass being of local origin). The reef plankton is either meroplanktonic (part of the adult or juvenile stage spent on the bottom) or demersal (most of the adult stage existing on the bottom). The reef thus serves both as nursery and as a home for a large number of partly planktonic organisms. (4) This plankton undergoes marked vertical migration at night when it becomes available to 'planktivorous' fish (Vivien, 1973) and to filter-feeding benthic predators: the stomach contents of these benthic animals reflect the predominance of zooplankton of reefal origin, with open ocean plankton contributing very little to their diets (Porter, 1974). (5) The abundance of plankton rising from a reef surface is related to the structural heterogeneity of the surface: branching coral generate more demersal plankton than plating corals, rubble or sand (Porter and Porter, 1977; Porter *et al.*, 1977; Aldredge and King, 1977). (6) Demersal plankton diversity does not appear to correlate with substratum heterogeneity or structural diversity (Porter *et al.,* 1977). As shown in Figure 1 for the San Blas, Panama (after Porter, 1973), migrating plankton can go directly to the surface. In this study, the reef zooplankton do nôt remain near the reef surface or in mid-water where they might be eaten by benthic filter-feeders or planktivorous fish. In this case, there is less plankton next to the reef's surface during the night than during the day! Thus, while there is more plankton *over* the reef at night, there is actually less *on* it (Fig. 1).

More studies are needed to determine the species composition, life cycles, feeding habits, diurnal movements, lunar cycles and seasonal cycles of this unique group of plankton. Obviously, many more reefs will have to be sampled before zoogeographical trends can be seen. Most 'reef' plankton studies to date have not been directly addressed to this group. This chapter has been written to suggest how studies might be performed on reef plankton, and why this knowledge is of prime importance in understanding the coral reef ecosystem.

ACKNOWLEDGEMENTS

The authors thank Stan Rachootin, John T. Lehman and Richard Werder for field and laboratory help. Helpful comments were received from them and from Dr Willard D. Hartman and David S. Wethey. Research support came from a Predoctoral Fellowship from the Smithsonian Tropical Research Institute, Panama and an NSF Doctoral Dissertation Research Grant in the Field Sciences GA 30979 to J. W. Porter; and from NSF grants DES 74-2419 to the Pennsylvania State University and OFS 74-12888 and OFS 74-01830 to the Scripps Institution of Oceanography for the operation of R/V Alpha Helix. This paper is contribution No. 149 from the Discovery Day Marine Laboratory.

References

ALDREDGE, A. L.; KING, J. M. 1977. Distribution, abundance, and substrate preferences of demersal reef zooplankton at Lizard Island Lagoon, Great Barrier Reef. *Mar. Biol.,* vol. 41, p. 317–33.

AHLSTROM, E. H.; THRAILKILL, J. R. 1962. Plankton volume loss with time of preservation (Abstract). *Rapp. P.-V. Réun. CIEM,* vol. 153, p. 78.

BARNES, H. 1949. On the volume measurement of water filtered by a plankton pump with some observations on the distribution of planktonic animals. *J. mar. Biol. Assoc. U.K.* vol. 28, p. 651–62.

BIOLOGICAL METHODS PANEL COMMITTEE ON OCEANOGRAPHY. 1969. *Recommended procedures for measuring the productivity of plankton standing stock and related oceanic properties.* Washington, D.C., National Academy of Sciences (59 p.).

BODEN, B. P. 1952. Natural conservation of insular plankton. *Nature* (Lond.), vol. 169, p. 697–9.

CLARKE, G. L.; BISHOP, D. W. 1948. The nutritional value of marine zooplankton with a consideration of its use as an emergency food. *Ecology,* vol. 29, p. 54–71.

COKER, R. E.; GONZALEZ, J. G. 1960. Limnetic copepod populations of Bahia Fosforescente and adjacent waters, Puerto Rico. *J. Elisha Mitchell Scient. Soc.* vol. 76, p. 8–28.

COMITA, W. G.; SCHINDLER, D. W. 1963. Calorific values of microcrustacea. *Science,* vol. 140, p. 1394–5.

CUMMINS, K. W.; WUYCHECK, J. C. 1971. Caloric equivalents for investigations in ecological energetics. *Mitt. Int. ver. theor. angew Limnol.* vol. 18, p. 1–158.

CURL, H. 1962. Analyses of carbon in marine plankton. *J. Mar. Res.* vol. 20, p. 181–8.

DEEVEY, G. B. 1964. Annual variations in length of copepods in the Sargasso Sea off Bermuda. *J. mar. Biol. Assoc. U.K.* vol. 44, p. 589–600.

——. 1968. Pelagic ostracods of the Sargasso Sea off Bermuda. *Bull. Peabody Mus. Nat. Hist., Yale Univ.,* vol. 26, p. 1–125.

EDMONDSON, W. T.; WINBERG, G. G. (eds.). 1971. *A manual on methods for the assessment of secondary productivity in fresh waters.* Oxford, Blackwell Science Publications. (IBP Handbook no. 17) (358 p.).

EMERY, A. R. 1968. Preliminary observations on coral reef plankton. *Limnol. Oceanogr.* vol. 13, p. 293–303.

FARRAN, G. P. 1949. The seasonal and vertical distribution of the copepoda. *Sci. Repts Gt Barrier Reef Exped. 1928–29,* vol. 2, p. 291–312.

FLEMING, M. W. 1954. *Plankton of northern Marshall Islands.* U.S. Geol. Surv. (Prof. Paper 260 F), p. 301–14.

FLEMINGER, A.; CLUTTER, R. S. 1965. Avoidance of towed nets by zooplankton. *Limnol. Oceanogr.* vol. 10, p. 96–104.

FUDGE, H. 1968. Biochemical analysis of preserved zooplankton. *Nature* (Lond.), vol 219, p. 380–1.

GLYNN, P. W. 1973a. Ecology of a Caribbean coral reef. The Porites reef-flat biotope: Part I. Meterology and Hydrography. *Mar. Biol.* vol. 20, p. 297–318.

——. 1973b. Ecology of a Caribbean coral reef. The *Porites* reef-flat biotope: Part II. Plankton community with evidence for depletion. *Mar. Biol.* vol. 22, p. 1–21.

GOLTERMAN, H. L.; CLIMO, H. (eds.) 1969. *Methods for chemical analysis of fresh waters.* Oxford, Blackwell Science Publications (IBP Handbook no. 8) (172 p.).

GONZALEZ, J. G.; BOWMAN, T. E. 1965. Planktonic copepods from Bahia Fosforescente, Puerto Rico, and adjacent waters. *Proc. U.S. Nat. Mus.* vol. 117, p. 241–307.

GRICE, G. D.; HART, A. D. 1962. The abundance, seasonal occurrence and distribution of the epizooplankton between New York and Bermuda. *Ecol. Monogr.* vol. 32, p. 287–309.

HAMNER, W. M. 1975. Underwater observations of blue-water plankton: logistics, techniques, and safety procedures for divers at sea. *Limnol. Oceanogr.* vol. 20, p. 1045–51.

HENTIG, R. T. VON. 1971. Planktonic distribution. In: J. W. Miller, J. G. Van Derwalker and R. A. Waller (eds). *Tektite 2: Scientists in the sea.* Washington, D.C., U.S. Dept. of Interior, p. VI-279–VI-284.

HERMAN, S. S.; BEERS, J. R. 1969. The ecology of inshore plankton populations in Bermuda. Part 2. Seasonal abundance and composition of the zooplankton. *Bull. mar. Sci.* vol. 19, p. 483–503.

HEUSDEN, G. P. H. VAN. 1972. Estimation of the biomass of plankton. *Hydrobiologia,* vol. 39, p. 165–208.

HICKEL, W. 1971. Seston composition and distribution in the bottom water of Great Lameshur Bay. In: J. W. Miller, J. G. Vanderwalker and R. A. Waller (eds). *Taktite 2: Scientists in the sea.* Washington, D.C., U.S. Dept. of Interior, p. VI-275–VI-278.

HOLME, N. A.; McINTYRE, A. D. (eds). 1971. *Methods for the study of marine benthos.* Oxford, Blackwell Science Publications. (IBP Handbook. no. 16) (334 p.).

HOLMES, R. W.; ANDERSON, G. C. 1963. Size fractionation of C^{14} labeled natural phytoplankton communities. In: C. Oppenheimer (ed.). *Symposium on marine microbiology.* Springfield, Illinois, Thomas. p. 241–50.

JANNASCH, H. W.; JONES, G. E. 1959. Bacterial populations in sea water as determined by different methods of enumeration. *Limnol. Oceanogr.* vol. 4, p. 128–39.

JOHANNES, R. E.; COLES, S. L.; KUENZEL, W. T. 1970. The role of zooplankton in the nutrition of some scleractinian corals. *Limnol. Oceanogr.* vol. 15, p. 579–86.

JOHNSON, M. W. 1949. Zooplankton as an index of water exchange between Bikini Lagoon and the open sea. *Trans. Am. geophys. Union,* vol. 30, p. 328–44.

JOSSE, J. W. 1970. Annotated bibliography of zooplankton sampling devices. *U.S. Fish. Wild. Serv. Spec. Sci. Rep. Fish.* vol. 609, p. 1–90.

KRÄMER, A. 1897. *Über den Bau der Korallenriffe und die Planktonvertheilung an den Samoanischen Küsten nebst vergleichenden Bemerkungen.* Lipsius und Tisher, Kiel (163 p.).

KRISS, A. E. 1963. Methods used in deep sea microbiological research. (Transl.) In: J. M. Shewan and E. Kahata (eds). *Marine microbiology (Deep Sea),* Chap. 1. Edinburgh, Oliver and Boyd, p. 1–16.

KUENZEL, N. T. 1972. A numerical approach to the study of variations in population size and composition of coral reef zooplankton. M.S. thesis, University of Georgia, Athens, Georgia (vii + 80 p.).

LOVEGROVE, T. 1962. The effect of various factors on dry weight values. *Rapp. P.-V. Réun. CIEM,* vol. 153, p. 86–91.

McEWEN, G. F.; JOHNSON, M. W.; FOLSOM, T. R. 1954. A statistical analysis of the performance of the Folsom plankton splitter, based upon test observations. *Arch. Met. Geophys. Klimatol.* A, vol. 7, p. 502–27.

MARSHALL, S. M. 1933. The production of microplankton in the Great Barrier Reef region. *Sci. Repts Gt Barrier Reef Exped. 1928–29,* vol. 2, p. 111–58.

MATHISON, O. A. 1964. Determination of plankton biomass in Rongelap Atoll, Marshall Islands, by the use of a multinet plankton pump. *Verh. Int. Verein. Limnol.* vol. 15, p. 735–44.

MATSUYA, Z. 1937. Some hydrographical studies of the water of Iwayama Bay in the South Sea Islands. *Palao Trop. Biol. Stn Stud.* vol. 1, p. 95–135.

MENZEL, D. W.; RYTHER, J. H. 1961. Zooplankton in the Sargasso Sea off Bermuda and its relation to organic production. *J. Con. CIEM,* vol. 26, p. 250–8.

MILLER, J. M. 1973. A quantitative push-net system for transect studies of larval fish and macro-zooplankton. *Limnol. Oceanogr.* vol. 18, p. 175–8.

MOORE, H. B. 1949. Zooplankton of the upper waters of the Bermuda area of the North Atlantic. *Bull. Bingham Oceanogr. Coll.* vol. 12, p. 1–97.

MOTODA, S. 1939. Submarine illumination, silt content and quality of food plankton of reef corals in Iwayama Bay, Palao. *Palao Trop. Biol. Stn Stud.,* vol. 1, p. 637–49.

——. 1940a. A study of growth rate in the massive reef coral, *Goniastrea aspera* Verril. *Palao Trop. Biol. Stn Stud.* vol. 2, p. 1–6.

——. 1940b. Comparison of the conditions of water in bay, lagoon, and open ocean in Palao. *Palao Trop. Biol. Stn Stud.* vol. 2, p. 41–8.

——. 1940c. Environmental and life of the massive coral *Goniastrea aspera* Verrill, inhabiting the reef flat in Palao. *Palao Trop. Biol. Stn Stud.,* vol. 2, p. 61–104.

OWRE, H. B. 1972. Marine biological investigations in the Bahamas: the genus *Spadella* and other chaetognaths. *Sarsia,* vol. 49, p. 49–58.

——; FOYO, M. 1967. Copepods of the Florida Current. *Fauna Caribaea,* vol. 1, p. 1–137.

PORTER, J. W. 1973. Biological, physical, and historical forces structuring coral reef communities on opposite sides of the isthmus of Panama. Ph.D. Dissertation; Yale University, New Haven, Connecticut. (xiii + 149 p.).

——. 1974. Zooplankton feeding by the Caribbean reef-building coral *Montastrea cavernosa.* In: *Proc. Second Int. Coral Reef Symp.* Brisbane, Great Barrier Reef Committee, vol. 1, p. 111–25.

——.; PORTER, K. G. 1977. Quantitative sampling of demersal plankton migrating from different coral reef substrates. *Limnol. Oceanogr.* vol. 22, p. 553–6.

——; ——; CATALAN, Z. B. 1977. Quantitative sampling of Indo-Pacific demersal reef plankton. In: *Proc. Third Int. Coral Reef Symp.* Univ. Miami, Miami, vol. 1, p. 105–12.

PORTER, K. G. 1972. A method for the *in situ* study of zooplankton grazing effects on algal species composition and standing crop. *Limnol. Oceanogr.* vol. 17, p. 913–7.

REEVE, M. R. 1964. Studies on the seasonal variation of the zooplankton in a marine subtropical in shore environment. *Bull. mar. Sci. Gulf Carib.* vol. 14, p. 103–22.

REISWIG, H. M. 1971. Particle feeding in natural populations of three marine demosponges. *Biol. Bull. Mar. Biol. Lab. Woods Hole, Mass.* vol. 141, p. 568–91.

RUSSELL, F. S. 1934. The zooplankton. III. A comparison of the abundance of zooplankton in the Barrier Reef Lagoon with that of some regions in northern European waters. *Sci. Repts Gt Barrier Reef Exped. 1928–29,* vol. 2, p. 176–201.

——; COLMAN, J. S. 1931. The zooplankton. I. Gear, methods and station lists. *Sci. Repts Gt Barrier Reef Exped. 1928–29,* vol. 2, p. 5–36.

——; ——. 1934. The zooplankton. II. The composition of the zooplankton of the Barrier Reef Lagoon. *Sci. Repts Gt Barrier Reef Exped. 1928–29,* vol. 2, p. 159–76, 210.

——; ——. 1935. The zooplankton. IV. The occurrence and seasonal distribution of the Tunicata, Mollusca, and Coelenterata (Siphonophora). *Sci. Repts Gt Barrier Reef Exped. 1928–29,* vol. 2, p. 203–76.

——; ORR, A. P. 1931. The work of the boat party. *Sci. Repts Gt Barrier Reef Exped. 1928–29,* vol. 2, p. 1–4.

SALE, P. F.; McWILLIAM, P. S.; ANDERSON, D. T. 1976. Composition of near-reef zooplankton at Heron Reef, Great Barrier Reef. *Mar. Biol.* vol. 34, p. 59–66.

SCHINDLER, D. W. 1969. Two useful devices for vertical plankton investigation. *Trans. Am. Fish. Soc.,* vol. 62, p. 292–303.

SCHROEDER, W. W.; FERRARI, F. D.; SNIDER, J. E. 1973. Preliminary findings of a zooplankton study on the southern coast of Grand Bahama Island. *Hydro-Lab Journal,* vol. 2, p. 85–93.

SEARS, M. 1950. Zooplankton: Notes on Siphonophores 1. Siphonophores from the Marshall Islands. *J. mar. Res.* vol. 9, p. 1–16.

STEVEN, D. M. 1961. Shoaling behaviour in a mysid. *Nature* (Lond.), vol. 192, p. 280–1.

STRICKLAND, J. D. H.; PARSONS, T. R. 1968. A practical handbook of seawater analysis. *Bull. Fish. Res. Bd Can.,* Ottawa, Queen's Printer, no. 167. (311 p.).

TATTERSALL, W. M. 1936. The zooplankton. V. The occurrence and seasonal distribution of the Mysidacea and Euphausiacea. *Sci. Repts Gt Barrier Reef Exped. 1928–29,* vol. 2, p. 277–90.

TRANTER, D. J.; FRASER, J. H. (eds). 1968. *Zooplankton sampling.* Paris, Unesco. (Unesco monographs on oceanographic methodology, 2). (174 p.).

TREGOUBOFF, G.; ROSE, M. 1967. *Manuel de planctonologie Méditerranéenne.* Tome I. Texe. Tome II. Planches. Centre National de la Recherche Scientifique; Paris (587 p.).

VIVIEN, M. L. 1973. Contribution a la connaissance de l'ethologie alimentaire de l'ichtyofaunae du platier interne des récifs coralliens de Tuléar (Madagascar). *Téthys,* suppl. 5, p. 221–308.

VOLLENWEIDER, R. A. (ed.). 1969. *A manual on methods for measuring primary production in aquatic environments.* Oxford, Blackwell Science Publications. (IBP Handbook no. 12) (224 p.).

WHITESIDE, M. C.; WILLIAMS, J. B. 1975. A new sampling technique for aquatic ecologists. *Verh. Int. Verein. Limnol.* vol. 19, p. 1534–9.

WIBORG, K. F. 1951. The whirling vessel. *Rep. Norw. Fish Mar. Invest.* vol. 9, p. 1–16.

WICKSTEAD, J. H. 1965. *An introduction to the study of tropical plankton.* London, Hutchinson Univ. Library (160 p.).

WOODMANSEE, R. A. 1958. The seasonal distribution of the zooplankton ofi Chicken Key in Biscayne Bay, Florida. *Ecology,* vol. 39, p. 247–62.

YENTSCH, C. S.; HEBARD, J. F. 1956. A gauge for determining plankton volume by the mercury immersion method. *J. Cons. CIEM,* vol. 22, p. 184–90.

39

Coral feeding on zooplankton

J. W. Porter[1]

Coelenterates were among the first aquatic animals to be experimentally studied for feeding behaviour and nutritional requirements (Trembley, 1744). This interest has continued, and within the last decade many advances have been made toward understanding the biochemical control of feeding behaviour (Lenhoff, 1968), both in the laboratory and as it applies in field situations (Mariscal and Lenhoff, 1968; Lehman and Porter, 1973). The classic laboratory observations of the researchers on the Great Barrier Reef Expedition (Yonge, 1930a, b) on Indo-Pacific corals, and earlier work on Caribbean species (Vaughan, 1919; Boschma, 1925; and others) has established the effectiveness with which some corals can capture living zooplankton. This ability is coupled with a variety of other feeding mechanisms (reviewed in Goreau et al., 1971) but the relative importance of each of these mechanisms to reef corals in situ has not been worked out. The following chapter describes methods for studying zooplankton feeding in natural populations of corals based on stomach-sampling techniques. These field studies are placed in the context of determination of the caloric and nutrient requirements of the species examined.

EQUIPMENT

1. *Field research*
(a) Extraction: Hypodermic syringe, at least 10 ml capacity
     Large syringe needle, inner diameter about 2 mm
(b) Preservation: Buffered formalin
     Several hundred 5 ml vacuumized test tubes, e.g. Vacutainers
     Small syringe needle for pre-injecting the formalin
     Marker pen for test tube labelling

1. Department of Zoology, University of Georgia, Athens, Georgia, 30602, U.S.A.

(c)   Location: Local tide and lunar cycle tables; data on currents if available
      Conventional scuba apparatus
      Underwater flashlights
      Medium size net bags

2. *Laboratory equipment*
(a)   Filtration: Millipore filter pump
      Millipore filter flask and funnel for 25 mm filters
      25 mm white gridded Millipore filters with the maximum pore size avail-
         able for ease in filtration
      Glass slides 2 in $\times$ 3 in
      25 mm diameter glass cover slips
      Storage boxes for 2 in $\times$ 3 in slides
      Cover sealer: fingernail polish
      Embedding Resin: Polyvinyl lactophenol
      Stains: Alcian Blue (for mucus)
            Eocin-Y Red (for animal tissue)
(b)   Counting: Microscope $\times 10$ to $\times 100$ with oil immersion
      Occular micrometer
      Taxonomic keys for appropriate plankton groups

TEST ORGANISMS

Any sessile polyped animals are suitable for the techniques described below, the size of the needle is determined by the size of polyp under study. The most easily sampled and quantified corals are those whose polyps are arranged in a stellate manner, each distinct polyp then being a discrete sample. Those species with mouths opening out into long grooves lined with tentacles (e.g. the brain corals) are also suitable. In this study, it was important to establish the ability of corals to feed under natural conditions on the reef, and therefore the Caribbean reef-building coral *Montastrea cavernosa* was chosen. Observations in tank experiments (Vaughan, 1919; Lehman and Porter, 1973) and under water at night with plankton artificially attracted by the beam of a flashlight showed that living zooplankton could be captured by the needle. Other corals as well as those with long tentacles should be used since negative results in this study are just as important as positive ones.

With modifications, stomach contents from almost all sessile animal phyla can also be sampled in this way. Special methods have been worked out for those invertebrates which pump water as part of their feeding behaviour. In a series of fascinating experiments on coral reef sponges, Reiswig (1971, 1972) sampled water before it went into the inhalant canal of several sponge species and as it came out the exhalant oscula. The difference in particulate content between the two samples is the amount eaten. Reiswig (pers. comm.) suggests that this technique might be employed successfully on tunicates also.

PROCEDURES FOR CORAL GUT SAMPLING

Gut contents

Blunt the needle to be used in gut content extraction by filing down the point so that the tip of the needle is flat. This will allow the entire tip of the needle to enter the mouth, not just the tip of a sharply pointed edge, and will form a better seal during the extraction process.

For collecting the gut contents, use vacuumized test tubes. The advantage is that when the syringe needle bearing the gut contents penetrates the vacuum seal, the contents are sucked out of the syringe into the tube. When brought back up to the surface, the top does not explode off due to the internal pressure increase caused by the injected liquid. The author recommends 5 ml Vacutainers for several reasons. These tubes come pre-packed with the vacuum established in them and can safely be taken to 15 m depth without implosion. Their soft rubber top can be penetrated with a needle many times without releasing the vacuum. This means they can be pre-injected with small amounts of preservative before gut collection and can be used several times before it is necessary to discard them. The vacuum is re-established by inserting a thin needle through the top and removing as many cubic centimetres of air as the syringe has capacity; with the syringe plunger still out, the needle is pulled out of the rubber stopper, and the tube is left with a vacuum in it. The necessity for pre-injecting formalin into the tube is that it not only preserves the sample, but also stops further digestion of the contents. The amount of formalin to be injected will depend on the volume of the polyp contents to be extracted. The final solution in the tube should be 5–10 per cent formalin. Alternatively, fixation in five per cent glutaraldehyde nicely preserves protozoans and photosynthetic organisms, and allows for fluorescence microscopy later on.

Digestion in all the corals studied to date (Boschma, 1925; Yonge, 1930; Porter, 1974) is rapid. The *M. cavernosa* digestion rate was established in the laboratory by periodic gut sampling of corals which were starved and then fed brine shrimp and assorted plankters. After feeding, the guts were sampled every half-hour to observe the disintegration rate of the plankters. Soft bodied plankters disappear after one-half hour, most crustacea after three. Different stages of the digestive process involving soft-parts, limbs, exoskeletons, and heavily chitinized eyes, jaws or cuticles can be established for each plankton group. This should be done because of its importance in interpreting the results. The rapidity of digestion also indicates that the timing of the gut sampling is very important depending on which 2 to 3-hour period of day or night is chosen for sampling. Lunar and seasonal cycles are also important and must be considered in the sampling programme. Ideally, a complete sampling programme will include at least one set of all-night samples and samples taken under several lunar regimes.

The extraction procedure is straightforward. The coral head to be sampled is rapidly located and immediately tapped to close the polyps. This prevents gut enrichment by the coral feeding on zooplankters artificially attracted into

517

the area by underwater flashlights. Gut contents are then extracted from the polyps randomly or from specific localities on the head (up-current polyps may receive more plankton than those on the down current side of the head). The syringe needle is inserted into the gastrovascular cavity of each polyp through its mouth and the contents of the stomach slowly extracted until the column wall and the oral disc collapse over the skeleton. These gut samples are then injected into the Vacutainers. At the same time, an equal number of water samples can be syringed from the surrounding water one to two centimetres from the head. These serve as controls to detect plankton which might be accidentally sucked into the gut sample during extraction. Since the controls in the *M. cavernosa* study showed virtually no plankton in them, and since the two or three plankters found in the 1000 or so controls showed no digestion and were therefore readily distinguishable from all of the gut plankters, this 'control' system was unnecessary.

Counting

The samples in the Vacutainers are stained by injecting solutions of 1 per cent aqueous Eosin-Y (a nonspecific strain for animal tissue) and Alcian Blue (a stain for mucus). At least 24 hours later, the samples are individually filtered on to gridded 1.2 micron pore Millipore filters under a five mm Hg vacuum pressure and, without rinsing or drying, transferred to glass slides. The gridded, 25 mm diameter filters (there is room for two per 2 in $\times$ 3 in slide) are aligned on a drop of polyvinyl lactophenol, an embedding resin that does not require dehydrated specimens, two more drops pipetted on top, and a thin glass cover slip of similar diameter added. It was found that any sort of drying or dehydrating destroyed the already partially digested zooplankters beyond recognition. The edges of the mount are sealed with clear nail polish. The prepared filters usually clear within 48 hours. Where large amounts of mucus are present, the samples are filtered a drop at a time, often with a change of filters if clogging occurs.

The filters are scanned at $\times 35$ magnification, and most organized structures, remnants of coral polyps, zooplankton, and blobs of mucus, examined at higher power ($\times 100$ to $\times 200$), with a few squares examined under oil immersion. Everything that has been ingested by a polyp is measured and identified as accurately as possible with a note made on its state of digestion. The dimensions are used to approximate the plankter's volume, and by further extrapolation (American Public Health Association, 1965; Johannes *et al.*, 1970; Cummis and Wuycheck, 1971; Porter, 1974) its caloric content determined.

Plankter identification can be difficult. Several works are excellent introductions. For Caribbean species, see Trégouboff and Rose (1957) for a general description; Owre and Foyo (1967) and González and Bowman (1965) for copepods; Deevey (1968) for ostracods; and Hedgpeth (1948) for pycnogonids. Unfortunately, widely separated publications, individuals, and museum collections must be consulted for detailed plankton identification.

INTERPRETATION, EXTRAPOLATION, LIMITATION

Extensive presentation of the data has appeared elsewhere (Porter, 1973; Porter, 1974) and will not be presented here. An analysis of the plankton contained in the guts of *M. cavernosa* two hours after sunset indicated that it contributes an average of between 1 μg dry weight and 75 μg dry weight per polyp per night. Assuming published respiration rates for *M. cavernosa* (Johannes *et al.,* 1970) this could account for between 1 and 11 per cent of the daily energy requirement. Further, most of this plankton both by number of individuals and by total weight were demersal plankton coming up from the reef at sunset and being heavily preyed upon at this time (based on the determined digestion rates and the degree of digestion of the plankters removed from the gut, most of the plankters had been there for approximately two hours, i.e. since sunset). These results are indicative of tight recycling of nutrients on these coral reefs off the Atlantic coast of Panamá.

The more one knows about the biology of the animal being studied, its physiology, feeding behaviour, distribution and position on the reef, etc., the more fully interpretable these gut samples will be, in the context of both the species under examination and the reef ecosystem in general.

ALTERNATIVE TECHNIQUES

In vitro

Several successful experimental approaches have been developed which show great potential. These will be mentioned briefly in the context of feeding activity although all have implications for ecological and biochemical studies. In a series of experiments, Franzisket (1969 and 1970) held reef corals in tanks under differing conditions of illumination and zooplankton availability to test some of the field experiments of Yonge (1930) and others. His results for four Hawaiian hermatypic species tested for 60 days (1970) indicate survival, but without growth, for three of the four in the dark tank and death for the other under these conditions, regardless of whether or not the water was filtered. All four, however, grew under lighted conditions in tanks receiving either filtered or unfiltered sea water. Before these results can be interpreted, the definition of filtered and unfiltered must be worked out carefully. The results presented above (see also Porter, 1974) indicate that the plankton that is actually serving as coral food is not coming from open water but from very close to the reef. Whether or not intake water in a salt water system represents a normal plankton supply will depend on the animal under study. Also, as Franziskt points out, long term experiments are desirable when testing delicate nutrient balances.

In another tank study, Coles (1969) was able to show that three species of Caribbean corals, including *M. cavernosa,* were capable of more than meeting their daily energy requirements when fed *Artemia* nauplii *ad libitum* in closed containers. Leversee (1976), working with a round trough of circulating

519

water also tested the abilities of certain Caribbean gorgonian species to remove plankton from the water. Extrapolation back to the natural situation is desirable for both of these studies, but they allow the investigator a high degree of control over the questions asked which would be very difficult, if not impossible, for the field experimentalist.

In situ

Johannes and Tepley (1974) have designed a means of estimating zooplankton feeding in corals using close-up time-lapse cinematography. The camera is positioned in front of a coral head and at regular intervals takes a photograph. By observing the film and the feeding behaviour of the coral species under study, an estimate can be made of the feeding activity and success of the coral. They show that for the stubby-tentacled Hawaiian star coral, *Porites lobata,* feeding on zooplankton did not appear to account for more than ten per cent of the energy requirements of the coral, despite its 24 hour per day feeding activity.

Scientists are beginning to appreciate the frustrating complexity of the energetics of survival of reef organisms in the nutrient poor waters of tropical oceans. It is hoped that the techniques described and mentioned above will allow them to understand the diverse mechanisms by which this survival is achieved.

ACKNOWLEDGEMENTS

The author thanks K. G. Porter, J. T. Lehman, and S. Rachootin for help in the field and in the laboratory. W. D. Hartman, R. K. Trench, N. I. Goreau and R. E. Johannes have given advice on this research. The research was supported by NSF Grant GA-30979 and a Pre-Doctoral Fellowship from the Smithsonian Institution.

References

AMERICAN PUBLIC HEALTH ASSOCIATION. 1965. *Standard methods for the examination of water and waste water including bottom sediments and sludges.* New York, Am. Publ. Health Assoc., (xxxi + 769 p.).

BOSCHMA, H. 1925. On the feeding reactions and digestion in the coral polyp *Astrangia danae,* with notes on its symbiosis with zooxanthellae. *Biol. Bull. Mar. Biol. Lab. Woods Hole, Mass.,* vol. 49, p. 407–39.

COLES, S. L. 1969. Quantitative estimates of feeding and respiration for three scleractinian corals. *Limnol. Oceanogr.,* vol. 14, p. 949–53.

CUMMINS, K. W.; WUYCHECK, J. C. 1971. Caloric equivalents for investigations in ecological energetics. *Mitt. Int. ver. theor. angew Limnol,* vol. 18, p. 1–158.

DEEVEY, G. B. 1968. Pelagic ostracods of the Sargasso Sea off Bermuda. *Bull. Peabody Mus. Nat. Hist.* Yale Univ., vol. 26, p. 1–125.

FRANZISKET, L. 1969. Riffkorallen können autotroph leben. *Naturwissenschafften*, vol. 56, p. 144.
——. 1970. The atrophy of hermatypic reef corals maintained in darkness and their subsequent regeneration in light. *Int. Rev. gesamt. Hydrobiol.*, vol. 55, p. 1–12.
GONZÁLEZ, J. G.; BOWMAN, T. E. 1965. Planktonic copepods from Bahía Fosforescente, Puerto Rico, and adjacent waters. *Proc. U.S. Nat. Mus.*, vol. 117, p. 241–303.
GOREAU, T. F.; GOREAU, N. I.; YONGE, C. M. 1971. Reef corals: Autotrophs or heterotrophs? *Biol. Bull. Mar. Biol. Lab. Woods Hole, Mass.*, vol. 141, p. 247–60.
HEDGPETH, J. W. 1948. The Pycnogonidae of the western North Atlantic and the Caribbean. *Proc. U.S. Nat. Mus.*, vol. 97, p. 157–342.
JOHANNES, R. E.; COLES, S. L.; KUENZEL, N. T. 1970. The role of zooplankton in the nutrition of some scleractinian corals. *Limnol. Oceanogr.*, vol. 15, p. 579–86.
——; TEPLEY, L. 1974. Examination of feeding of the reef coral *Porites lobata in situ* using time-lapse photography. In: *Proc. Second Int. Coral Reef Symp.* Bisbane, Great Barrier Reef Committee, vol. 1, p. 127–31.
LEHMAN, J. T.; PORTER, J. W. 1973. Chemical activation of feeding in the Caribbean reef-building coral *Montastrea cavernosa*. *Biol. Bull. Mar. Biol. Lab. Woods Hole, Mass.*, vol. 145, p. 140–9.
LENHOFF, H. M. 1968. Chemical perspectives on the feeding response, digestion, and nutrition of selected coelenterates. In: M. Florkin and B. T. Sheer (eds). *Chemical zoology*, vol. 2: Porifera, Coelenterata, and Platyhelminthes. Academic Press, New York, p. 157–221. (xx + 639 p.).
LEVERSEE, G. J. 1976. Flow and feeding in fan-shaped colonies of the gorgonian coral, *Leptogorgia*. *Biol. Bull. mar. Biol. Lab. Woods Hole, Mass.* vol. 151, p. 244–56.
MARISCAL, R. N.; LENHOFF, H. M. 1968. The chemical control of feeding behaviour in *Cyphastrea ocellina* and in some other Hawaiian corals. *J. exp. Biol.*, vol. 49, p. 689–99.
OWRE, H. B.; FOYO, M. 1967. Copepods of the Florida Current. Crustacea, Part 1: Copepoda. *Fauna Caribeae*, vol. 1, p. 1–137.
PORTER, J. W. 1973. Biological, physical, and historical forces structuring coral reef communities on opposite sides of the Isthmus of Panama. Ph.D. Dissertation, Yale University, New Haven, Connecticut (xiii + 146 p.).
——. 1974. Zooplankton feeding by the Caribbean reef-building coral *Monastrea cavernosa*. In: *Proc. Second Int. Coral Reef Symp.*, Brisbane, Great Barrier Reef Committee, vol. 1, p. 111–25.
REISWIG, H. M. 1971. Particle feeding in natural populations of three marine demosponges. *Biol. Bull. Mar. Biol. Lab. Woods Hole, Mass.*, vol. 141, p. 568–91.
——. 1972. The spectrum of particulate organic matter of shallow-bottom boundary waters of Jamaica. *Limnol. Oceanogr.*, vol. 17, p. 341–8.
TRÉGOUBOFF, G.; ROSE, M. 1957. *Manuel de Planctonologie Méditerranéenne*. Paris, Centre National de la Recherche Scientifique, Tome I et II (587 p. + 207 pls.).
TREMBLEY, A. 1744. *Memoires pour servir a l'histoire d'un genre de polypes d'eau douce, a bras en forme de cornes*. Leide, Verbeek.
VAUGHAN, T. W. 1919. Corals and the formation of coral reefs. *Ann. Rept. Smith. Inst. for 1917*, p. 189–276.
YONGE, C. M. 1930a. Studies on the physiology of corals. I. Feeding mechanisms and food. *Sci. Repts Gt Barrier Reef Exped. 1928–29*, vol. 1, p. 15–57.
——. 1930b. Studies on the physiology of corals. II. Digestive enzymes with notes on the speed of digestion. *Sci. Repts Gt Barrier Reef Exped. 1928–29*, vol. 1, p. 59–82.

521

40

Coral growth: alizarin method

A. E. Lamberts[1]

Living reef corals subjected to Alizarin Red S dissolved in sea water incorporate this magenta dye into their newly forming skeletons. The colour remains as a permanent implant indicating where calcification occurred during the experiment. The brightness of the colour, however, depends on many factors including the purity of the dye used, the concentration of the dye in solution, length of exposure to the dye, and the biological activeness of the calcifying tissues being studied.

Alizarin has a long and illustrious history as a textile dye. Cameron (1930) considered it to be unsurpassed as a histological stain for calcium and he gave a good bibliography of its early use in staining bones and calcifying tissues. It was first used in marine science by Kendall (1961) who fed it to sharks to stain growing teeth, scales and calcifying tissues. Swan (1961) focused attention on Alizarin Red S but also mentioned Alizarin Blue purpurins and the tetracyclines as colouring substances to be considered in marine biological research. Barnes (1972) used Alizarin Red S on growing corals and alternated it with Alizarin Blue to give discrete lines from which growth could be measured. He found that the red marks persisted but that the blue lines so formed faded away within hours.

The author has used Alizarin Red S, usually referred to simply as alizarin, to visualize sites of calcification in reef corals under controlled laboratory and aquarium conditions (Lamberts, 1973). The studies were carried out primarily with the common Pacific reef coral *Pocillopora damicornis* (L.) although many other genera of coral, serpulid worms, echinoderms, molluscs, and calcareous algae were also marked in the same way. The dye was readily incorporated into the corallum but only through biological activity and reflected the degree of calcification that had occurred. Simultaneous studies employing alizarin and calcium in the form of $^{45}CaCl_2$ indicated a high correlation between these two markers. Both are accurate measures of sites and rates of calcification in reef corals. Alizarin is simpler to use and does not require the sophisticated apparatus necessary when working with radio-isotopes.

1. 1520 Leffingwell, N.E., Grand Rapids, Mississippi, 49505, U.S.A.

For maximal usefulness, a calcium marker for marine organisms should have the following properties, it should be easy to obtain, simple to use and it should make a discreet junction mark in the skeleton which will permit accurate linear measurements. Application of the substance should cause minimal disturbance to the organisms being studied and should be relatively non toxic. The marker should give a permanent stain which can be measured quantitatively and photographed. The various experiments should be reproducible. The substance should be inexpensive and have a long laboratory shelf life. The excess should be relatively non-polluting to the environment.

Alizarin Red S suitable for staining bone (Colour index—59005) comes close to meeting these requirements; however, it is mildly toxic to marine and other organisms. The author found that in small but useful amounts it produced enough stress to cause mature corals to release their planulae but did not alter the rhythmical contractions which time-lapse cine-photomicrographic sequences revealed in *P. damicornis* polyps. Serpulid worms of the genus *Spirorbis* constructed a shorter length of coloured tube when in alizarin solution than that formed during an equal control period when no dye was present. Presumably it does decrease the calcium carbonate deposited by coral tissues. Paff and Bennett (1951) found that the calcification in new bone stopped entirely when an excessive amount of the dye was used. The author's studies showed that coral skeletons became coloured when the alizarin content of the sea water was one part per million but the most effective level was 10 ppm. This gave a high colour to *P. damicornis* skeletons but greater concentrations gave increasingly diminished deposition of the dye. Alizarin can be used to give a qualitative measure and a comparative quantitative measure of calcium deposition even though it cannot be considered to give absolute values.

Alizarin is a hydroquinone dye and precipitates as red–orange needle-like crystals that are very slightly soluble in distilled water and slightly more so in alcohol. Sodium–sulphalizarinate (Alizarin Red S) has a solubility of 7.69 per cent in distilled water and much less so in sea water. This varies with the water sample but approximates 15 ppm (0.0015 per cent). For laboratory use, then, it is convenient to make a stock solution of 4 to 5 mg dye per ml. of distilled water. When a range of dye concentrations is needed, various amounts of this solution can be added to the sea water. In experiments with organisms maintained in tanks supplied with running sea water, alizarin can be added to the intake by continuous drip, or with a suitable pump, to give any desired ambient concentration.

In experiments with marine organisms in either closed aquaria or those supplied with running water, it is essential to have a large volume of water compared to the weight of living tissue to avoid any container effect. Supplemental aeration with airstones or other means is imperative. Also, living organisms placed in such tanks should be allowed to become acclimated to the changed environment for a day or two.

When alizarin is added to such tanks deposition of the dye begins immediately. Using cine-photomicrography, well-stained septa were found in the newly settled polyps of *P. damicornis* in less than two hours from the time the planulae began to settle. The author found that it was advisable to prolong most of the experiments for 24 hours to ensure a well-stained corallum although in some species of slow-growing scleractinians, no change in colour was demonstrable even after 48 hours exposure. Hidu & Hawks (1968) when marking bivalve molluscs recommended leaving the organisms in the alizarin solution for a week. Time of exposure, then, can be varied considerably depending on the organisms used and the depth of colour desired.

In a closed system alizarin is often oxidized to a colourless by-product within 24 hr. This phenomenon is not entirely predictable. The decoloration is influenced by the total amount of living tissue depositing the dye, the amount of available light, foreign material suspended in the test tanks, vigorousness of aeration and probably other factors. Enough of the dye may have been deposited during the test time for comparative studies to be completed but in prolonged studies it may be expedient to add more alizarin from time to time to keep the concentration near optimum levels. Coral skeletons uncovered by living tissues also become coloured by passively adherent dye. This has a different hue from that actively deposited and can be eliminated at once by dipping the specimen in dilute hypochlorite (Clorox) which has no effect on the alizarin incorporated into the skeleton itself.

Corals and other marine organisms may be marked with alizarin for growth studies and at the same time observations can be made on patterns of calcification or changes in calcification rates. It may be used to measure physiological activity of the organisms when various environmental parameters are altered. These can include changes in salinity, nutrients, pH., incident light, temperature, or various changes in the chemical constituents of sea water. Various additives or pollutants can be evaluated by their effects on alizarin deposition.

Some of the test substances may not be compatible with alizarin in stock solution and may cause it to precipitate. The alizarin may be added to the sea-water intake of the system by slow calibrated drip and at times, other additives can be added to the same reservoir. Individual tests for compatibility should be done before any attempt is made to mix the various substances. Even if they are incompatible in concentrated form they may still be used if they are added separately to the sea water in the test tanks.

An alternative method of *in situ* coral marking has been used by a number of workers for long term coral studies. Dustan (pers. comm., 1973) described a pyramidal tent for this purpose made from 5 mil plastic sheeting. The tent volume varied from $\frac{1}{2}$m^3 to 4m^3 and each tent was weighted around its base with $\frac{3}{8}$-in. galvanized chain which held the bag down and provided a reasonable seal. When the bag was anchored over a coral head it still allowed some water movement with a slow exchange of gas and water so that corals calcified despite the imposed stress. Sufficient alizarin was introduced through a small slit in the bag or by simply lifting a corner. Each coral head was stained for three consecutive days to insure good marking and in this way 97 per cent of the corals took the dye.

Alizarin deposited by corals can be measured quantitatively in controlled experiments (Lamberts, 1974). The dye is deposited by the living coral tissues upon the existing corallum as a very thin layer intimately mixed with calcium carbonate. Any convenient acid can be used to remove this layer; however, alizarin is an indicator dye and becomes virtually colourless at Ph 5 or less. To preserve the magenta colour the author used EDTA (ethylenediaminetetra-acetic acid) to dissolve away the superficial layers. A 10 per cent solution of EDTA in distilled water (w/v) was brought to pH 8.2 (sea water) with pellets of sodium hydroxide and, after standardization, this solution was found to be stable for an entire season. Five ml of this preparation were added to 1 gm of crushed coral fragments with incorporated alizarin and allowed to stand with occasional swirling for one hour. By that time 99 per cent of the dye was in solution. The coloured liquid was decanted, centrifuged and samples were compared in a spectrophotometer at a setting of 548 μm. This had been found to be the spectroscopic maximum for solutions of EDTA and alizarin dissolved from coral skeletons by this method. In this way, comparable coral heads were subjected to reproducible stresses, and changes in the amount of alizarin deposited was demonstrated. Comparable samples were then taken and the alizarin content was measured by an objective means that was satisfactory. It should be mentioned that attempts were made to quantify newly deposited alizarin by split-field photometry. The irregular deposition patterns of the dye made this method impractical and it was abandoned.

Various brands or manufacturers lots of Alizarin Red S acted differently when compared under standardized conditions. Most brands tested produced satisfactory colour patterns through biological action but some seemed almost totally inactive. Superior results were obtained with only one sample. This was Alizarin Red S, suitable for staining bone, Lot 6, distributed by Matheson Colman & Bell.

In conclusion: Alizarin Red S has been found to be a useful means of marking coral in a laboratory or *in situ* for growth studies. It can also be used to assess calcification processes qualitatively and quantitatively under many conditions. Its use will broaden the scope of many aspects of coral reef biology.

References

BARNES, D. J. 1972. The structure and formation of growth ridges in scleractinian coral skeletons. *Proc. R. Soc. Lond.* (B: *Biol. Sci.*), vol. 182 (no. 1068), p. 331–50.

CAMERON, G. R. 1930. The staining of calcium. *J. Path. Bact.*, vol. 33, p. 929–55.

HIDU, H.; HAWKS, J. E. 1968. Vital staining of bivalve mollusc shells with alizarin monosulfate. *Nat. Shellfish. Assoc.*, vol. 58, p. 37–41.

KENDALL, J. I. 1961. *In vivo* staining of calcified tissues of sharks. *Turtox News,* vol. 39, p. 77.

LAMBERTS, A. E. 1973. Alizarin deposition by corals. Ph.D. dissertation, University of Hawaii, Honolulu. (163 p.).

——. 1974. Measurement of alizarin deposited by corals. In: *Proc. Second Int. Coral Reef Symp.* Brisbane, Great Barrier Reef Committee, vol. 2, p. 241–4.

PAFF, G. H.; BENNETT, S. 1951. Probable mechanism of alizarin inhibition of calcification. *Proc. Soc. exp. Biol. Med.,* vol. 77, no. 3, p. 385–8.

SWAN, E. F. 1961. Some uses of coloured materials in marine biological research. *Turtox News,* vol. 39, p. 290–3.

41

Coral growth: buoyant weight technique

P. L. Jokiel[1], J. E. Maragos[2]
and L. Franzisket[3]

INTRODUCTION

This technique involves weighing the living coral while it is suspended in a buoyant medium of sea water. The authors have found this to be an attractive technique for the measurement of coral skeletal growth for the following reasons:

1. The technique is a direct physical measurement of aragonite. It is insensitive to factors such as the amount of water contained in the porous skeleton, amount of tissue and mucus present and biomass of commensal organisms on and within the skeleton.
2. Specimens are not removed from the water or damaged in any way by the procedure, allowing repeated growth determinations on the same specimen.
3. Sensitivity of the method can be refined to detect changes in mass over short time intervals (as little as 12 hours).
4. The method is inexpensive, rapid and easy to use; applicable to laboratory and remote field situations alike; and suitable for any size or shape of coral.

Although this technique has been applied to the measurement of coral skeletal growth by the authors of this paper (Franzisket, 1964; Maragos, 1972; Jokiel and Coles, in the press) and by Bak (1973), it has not been widely used, probably due to the difficulty involved in understanding and accounting for the major assumptions involved. Therefore in the following discussion we present: the theory behind the method, an empirical test of the theoretical relationship, various applications of the method, and comparisons with the classic weighing and geometric techniques commonly employed as indices of coral growth.

1. Hawaii Institute of Marine Biology, University of Hawaii, P.O. Box 1346, Kaneohe, Hawaii, 96744, U.S.A.
2. Environmental Resources Section, U.S. Army Corps of Engineers, Pacific Ocean Division, Bldg. 230, Fort Shafter, Honolulu, A.P.O., 96558, U.S.A.
3. Westfälisches Landesmuseum für Naturkunde, D-44 Muenster, Federal Republic of Germany.

2L

BUOYANT WEIGHT METHOD

Derivation of theoretical model

It follows from Archimedes' Principle that the weight of an object in air is equal to the object's weight in a liquid medium plus the weight of the liquid displaced by the object. This principle allows objects to be weighed while they are submerged, including *in situ* weight determination for corals. Considering only the aragonite skeleton, a simple testable relationship between its buoyant weight and dry weight can be derived.

The following definitions will be used:

D_w = density of the buoyant fluid used in weighing (sea water).
D_a = density of the skeletal material (aragonite).
W_a = total dry weight of skeletal material (aragonite).
W_w = measured buoyant weight of specimen
V_a = volume of skeletal material (aragonite) in specimen
    = volume of liquid (sea water) displaced by aragonite.

Archimedes' Principle can be rearranged in the from of the following equation:

$$W_a = W_w + (V_a \cdot D_w) \tag{1}$$

where $V_a \cdot D_w$ is equal to the weight of the liquid (sea water) displaced. Since $V_a = W_a \cdot D_a^{-1}$, substituting for V_a in equation (1) yields:

$$W_a = W_w + (D_w \cdot W_a \cdot D_a^{-1}) \tag{2}$$

or

$$W_a = \frac{W_w}{1 - (D_w \cdot D_a^{-1})} \tag{3}$$

Substituting the density of aragonite ($D_a = 2.93$ g/cc) and an approximate value for sea water ($D_w = 1.03$) into equation (3) yields:

$$W_w = W_a(1 - 1.03/2.93) \tag{2}$$

$$W_w = 0.649 W_a$$

$$\boxed{W_a = 1.54 W_w}$$

The density of sea water can vary considerably with changes in salinity and temperature. Therefore, accurate density measurements must be made on the water used in the buoyant weight determinations.

It is apparent from equation (3) that as the density of the object being weighed (D_a) approaches the density of the buoyant medium (D_w), the buoyant weight will approach zero, and the object becomes neutrally buoyant. Coral tissue and mucus, being composed largely of water, will have a density that is very close to that of sea water. Therefore the method is insensitive to tissue, mucus, and water located in skeletal voids, but is quite sensitive to skeletal aragonite, which has a density of almost three times that of sea water.

Four basic testable assumptions are involved in using this method:

(1) The skeletal material of coral (dry weight of clean skeleton) consists entirely of aragonite. This is a safe assumption since the composition of coral skeletal material (*Pocillopora damicornis*) has been determined by Wainwright (1963) to consist of 99.9 per cent aragonite.

(2) The buoyant weight contributed by cryptic fauna which consists largely of neutrally buoyant tissue does not affect the buoyant weight of the coral skeleton. This assumption will not be equally important for all coral taxa. For example, the solitary coral *Fungia* offers no places of concealment for cryptic macro-organisms. Specimens of most colonial corals can be found that are relatively free of habitable crevices. Large highly branched corals, on the other hand, often contain an assemblage of associated crabs and shrimps which cannot be removed without damage to the coral.

In order to test the second assumption a large tightly branched *Montipora* fragment containing many cryptic organisms was weighed using the buoyant weighing method. The cryptic macrofauna were then removed by carefully breaking apart the coral head. Twenty-two ophiuroids, three polychaetes, one alpheid shrimp, one stomatopod, and one small hermit crab in a *Trochus* shell were removed from the specimen. The combined weight of the cryptic macro-fauna accounted for only 0.16 per cent (0.30 g) of the gross buoyant weight (196.8 g) of the whole specimen.

(3) Voids and spaces within the porous skeletal material are filled with liquid of the same density of the buoyant medium. This assumption can introduce errors if air bubbles are allowed to form on the underside of the coral during periods when the water is supersaturated with air.

(4) The densities of both living coral tissue and mucus are of the same density as sea water. This assumption is reasonable since mucus and tissue removed from coral skeletons can be observed to be nearly neutrally buoyant in sea water, although eventually this material will settle out.

Empirical test of model; comparison with other classic measurement techniques

The relationship between buoyant weight, dry skeletal weight, and various other classic growth parameters was established empirically on three dissimilar species of scleractinian corals representing three different families. *Fungia scutaria* Lamarck was chosen because of its dense skeleton, massive shape, and fleshy organic parts. *Pocillopora damicornis* (Linnaeus) was selected as a representative branching form. *Montipora verrucosa* (Lamarck) is typical of species with highly perforate skeletons.

The following data were recorded for each of 31 corals (three species): buoyant weight, wet weight, width (mean of four measurements), and height. Displacement (mean of three measurements) was determined by measuring the

531

overflow from a container full of sea water when the specimen was slowly lowered into the water on a string. The apparatus used in the buoyant weighing is described later in this paper. Afterwards each specimen was thoroughly cleaned, dried for several days at 90°C and weighed.

Correlation coefficients between the measurement of dry skeletal weight and each of the other measurements were calculated for each species (see Table 1).

TABLE 1. Dry weight (y) as a function of various other measurements (x) and percentage variance explained ($100\ r^2$).

Species	P..damicornis	M. verrucosa	F. scutaria
Number of specimens	12	9	10
Buoyant wt (g)	$y = 1.56x{-}0.42$ $100\ r^2 = 100$	$y = 1.55x{-}0.42$ $100\ r^2 = 100$	$y = 1.55x{-}0.12$ $100\ r^2 = 100$
Wet wt (g)	$y = 0.739x{-}4.24$ $100\ r^2 = 99.6$	$y = 0.591x{-}9.94$ $100\ r^2 = 99.3$	$y = 0.850x{-}10.76$ $100\ r^2 = 99.8$
Displacement (cc, mean of 3 measurements)	$y = 1.49x{-}1.28$ $100\ r^2 = 98.3$	$y = 0.943x{-}3.41$ $100\ r^2 = 98.8$	$y = 1.77x{-}2.65$ $100\ r^2 = 99.2$
Width (mm, mean of 4 measurements)	$y = 4.48x{-}248.36$ $100\ r^2 = 94.6$	$y = 4.54x{-}261.48$ $100\ r^2 = 88.2$	$y = 3.61x{-}186.53$ $100\ r^2 = 81.7$
Height (mm)	$y = 4.01x{-}139.35$ $100\ r^2 = 77.9$	$y = 3.89x{-}193.12$ $100\ r^2 = 78.2$	$y = 10.77x{-}133.84$ $100\ r^2 = 36.0$

The results demonstrate the validity of the assumptions used in the buoyant weighing technique as well as the accuracy of the method. A perfect correlation ($r^2 = 1.000$) existed between buoyant weight and dry skeletal weight. The derived slopes (1.55–1.56) are within 1–2 per cent of the value predicted by the model. Much of this difference can be attributed to the slight negative buoyancy of organic material on and within the skeleton. The y-intercept is nearly zero, as predicted.

It is apparent that the buoyant weight measurements showed the highest correlation with dry skeletal weight. The other methods based on weight or volume showed good correlations, while the linear measurement methods were the poorest indexes of dry skeletal weight (Table 1). Since a great deal of variation existed between successive determinations of displacement and width the correlations would be much lower if based on single measurements as was done for buoyant weight, wet weight and height rather than means of 3–4 measures. This analysis supports the belief of previous workers that changes in linear dimensions, volume, and wet weight correlate well with changes in skeletal weight. Also, the analysis shows that the slope and intercepts can be empirically derived for each of the various species, and that much diverse data existent in the literature can eventually be expressed in the common denominator of skeletal weight change.

The authors conclude that the buoyant weight method is a superior measurement technique because of, (a) a high correlation with dry skeletal weight, (b) the slope and x-intercepts of the regression line are nearly the same for all species, (c) the relationship between dry weight and buoyant weight can be determined with a high degree of accuracy from the theoretical model or can be established empirically, and (d) repeated measurements can be made on the same specimen.

Applications

The authors have used this method in a variety of experimental situations involving field and laboratory growth measurements of both long- and short-term duration. Selection of the proper weighing device and associated apparatus for a given experiment will depend upon a number of factors including degree of accuracy required, size range of corals to be studied, cost, portability, availability and time allowable per weight determination. Selection of the proper weighing technique should be considered to be an integral part of the experimental design, and the individual investigator must test the accuracy and reproducibility of measurements made with his apparatus. The three examples that follow were chosen as a guide to demonstrate weighing configurations and experimental procedures in a variety of sensitivities, and to demonstrate how several aspects of coral skeletal growth can be investigated using this technique.

Analytic balance method
Sensitivity 0.1–1.0 mg
Specimen size ~10 grams buoyant weight
Weighing interval 12 hours
This variation was employed by L. Franzisket on the 1957/1958 Xarifa Expedition to the Maldive Islands, and represents the ultimate in the refinement of its sensitivity (0.1 mg). The basic configuration involves an analytic balance and beaker (see Fig. 1). The analytic balance requires a very stable platform and still air. Since the density of the water must be measured to as many significant figures as weight in air (see equation (1)) we must measure to five significant figures. Salinity and temperature of the water can be accurately measured and the density calculated using standard hydrographic tables. Sea-water hydrometers accurate to five significant figures are available and provide a faster and more direct measure. A monofilament (non absorbent) line to support the coral eliminates the error caused by wetting of the line. A similar technique has been used to measure daily oyster growth (Havinga, 1928).

During the period of 23 February 1958 to 20 March 1958, specimens of the corals *Fungia scutaria* Lamarck and *Porites maledivium tertium* (Bernard) were maintained on the reef at Ras-Du Atoll, being brought into the laboratory at 12-hour intervals (day/night) for weighing to the nearest 0.1 mg. These data (unpublished) are presented in Figure 2 and demonstrate the reproducibility of

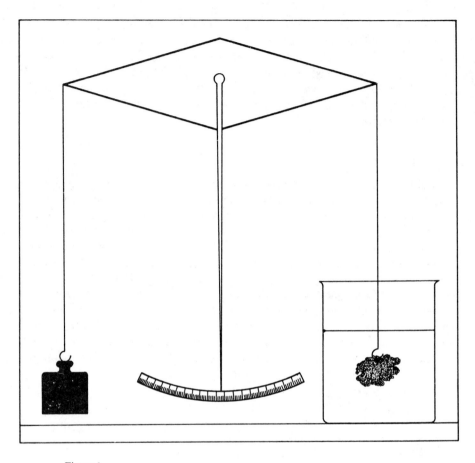

Figure 1
Schematic drawing of apparatus used in analytical balance method.

the results. The method was sensitive enough to detect differences between day and night incremental growths. The observed diurnal rhythm in calcification probably can be attributed to light, which is known to accelerate calcification in hermatypic corals (Goreau, 1959; Goreau and Goreau, 1959).

During a nine-day interval within the 25-day period (break in abscissa on Fig. 2) the ship visited another atoll and no measurements could be made. This event provided some interesting data. Table 2 compares daily growth increases over the 17-day period of frequent weighings with the daily growth increase during the 8-day period when the coral was undisturbed. It is apparent that coral growth was much slower during the period of frequent handling. This implies that manipulation of the experimental specimen which is often necessary during short-term measurements might yield calcification rate values that are lower than those occurring in nature.

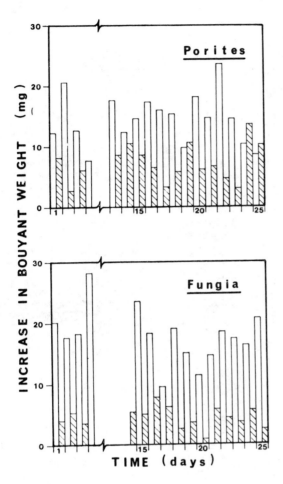

Figure 2
Growth data taken at twelve-hour intervals with apparatus shown in Figure 1
Unshaded bars represent daylight growth increments: shaded bars night
growth increments.

TABLE 2. Comparison of growth during periods of daily weighing and period of no weighing.

	Porites	Fungia
Initial buoyant wt (gm)	7.1391	8.7003
Final buoyant wt (gm)	7.7440	9.2996
Days	25	25
Daily increase (mg/day) entire 25-day period	24.2	23.0
Daily increase (mg/day) for 17-day period of twice daily weighings	22.2	22.8
Daily increase (mg/day) for 8-day period of no weighings	30.0	29.2

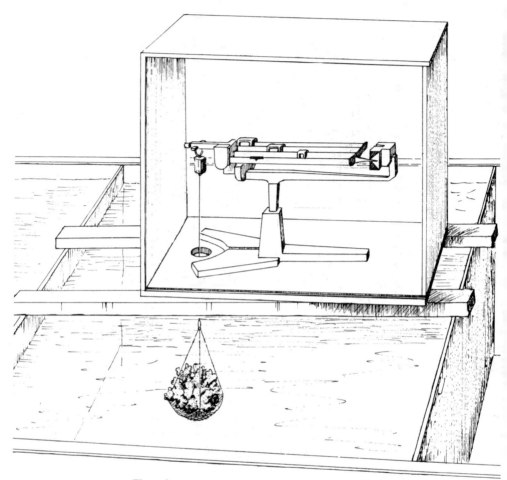

Figure 3
Apparatus used in utility balance method.

Utility balance method (*triple beam or platform balance*)
    Sensitivity 0.01–0.50 g
    Specimen size ~10–1000 g buoyant wt.
    Weighing interval 30 days.

In this method two orders of magnitude in accuracy over the previously described method have been sacrificed in order to gain the advantages of lowered cost, reduced time involved in weighing, and use of larger corals. Water density needs to be known only to three significant figures, in normal sea water 1.03. Utility triple beam or pan balances are available with an accuracy of from 0.01 to 0.3 grams at only several per cent of the cost of analytic balances. These units are much less prone to damage, an important consideration in remote locations where quick repair or replacement is not feasible. Because of the lower sensitivity the weighing interval was increased from 12 hours to at least several weeks in order to obtain a growth increment that is large in comparison with the absolute weighing error.

A typical laboratory configuration is presented in Figure 3. An inexpensive triple beam or torsion balance enclosed in a protective plywood case with sliding plastic door is shown supported over an experimental tank containing growing corals. The weighing pan has been replaced with counterweights and a weighing basket formed from plastic mesh and supported with plastic monofilament line. In the case of platform balances, the weighing basket can be suspended directly from a hook on the bottom of the pan support. Once the device is balanced, a coral can be gently moved into the weighing pan, weighed and replaced in the tank in a matter of one to two minutes. A Mettler-type balance which increases accuracy and speeds the process considerably, has been used in the buoyant weighing of oysters (Andrews, 1961).

An example of the use of such configuration is the study of the effect of initial size on percentage increase in skeletal weight in the coral *Fungia scutaria*. The increase in buoyant weight of 54 specimens of this species ranging from 1 gm to 190 gm buoyant weight was measured over a 30-day growth period. Percentage increase has been plotted against initial buoyant weight in Figure 4 (P. Jokiel, unpublished data). A clear effect of initial size on this growth parameter is apparent. This provides a warning to the investigator planning to design a growth experiment. Coral growth is size dependent if measured by a percentage increase method, even in highly symmetrical forms such as *Fungia*.

A great deal of additional scatter in growth data is encountered with the

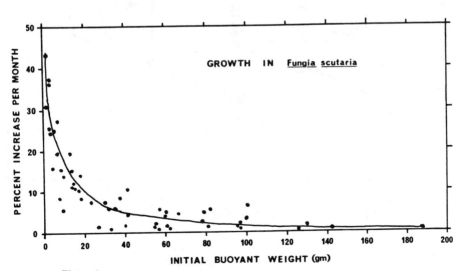

Figure 4
Per cent increase in skeletal weight for the solitary coral *Fungia scutaria* plotted against initial weight, data taken using apparatus shown in Figure 3.

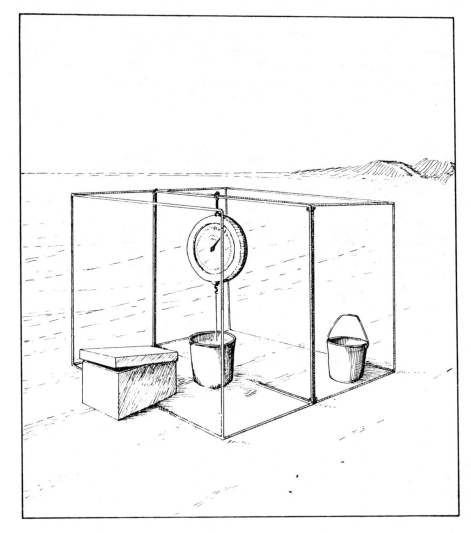

Figure 5
Weighing apparatus used in field method.

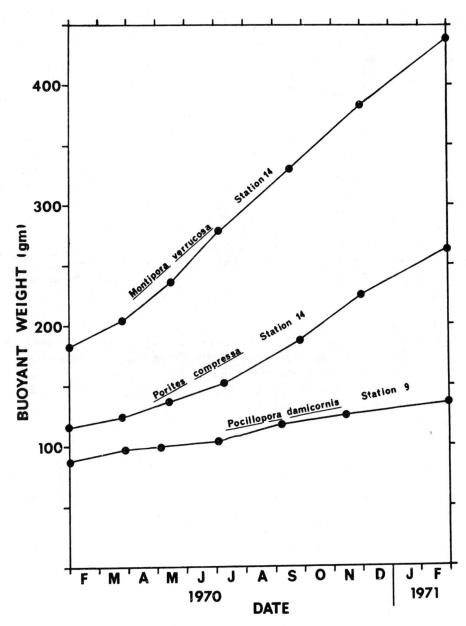

Figure 6
Sample growth data on three specimens (Maragos, 1972 and unpublished)
taken with apparatus shown in Fig. 5.

use of complex asymmetrical forms such as *Montipora*. This scatter is not a measurement error but rather a basic characteristic of some species and can make comparison of growth between treatments quite difficult.

Field method

    Sensitivity 1–2 g

    Specimen size 1–5 kg buoyant weight

    Weighing interval 1 month to 1 year

Use of a portable weighing device and associated apparatus allows buoyant weight measurements to be carried out on the reef. Maragos (1972) transported a spring balance to reef areas by small skiff. The spring scale was a Chatillon 6.8 kg capacity temperature compensated device having a precision and accuracy of ± 1.5 grams. The spring scale was suspended across a metal frame set up on a shallow patchreef or flat portion of the beach above sea level (Fig. 5). Corals were removed from their growing places and placed in buckets. The buckets with corals submerged in sea water were quickly transported to shore and placed under the scale and weighed while submerged. After weighing, the corals were promptly returned to their original locations. Data taken by this method is presented in Figure 6. It is unlikely that corals larger than 5 kg buoyant weight (> 10 kg wet weight) can be transported to shore without damage. A device for measuring corals *in situ* on the reef has been described by Bak (1973). This device can be used to weigh quite large corals. Although less portable, this approach enables the investigator to avoid the necessity for transporting corals to shore and can be reduce handling of the corals and time spent in weighing. In studies involving measures of growth at depths greater than 10 m, Bak's technique is far more practical.

CONCLUSIONS

Buoyant weighing is a simple, inexpensive, flexible, and highly accurate technique for the determination of aragonite mass or mass increase in living corals. If the corals are not handled excessively, the method does not harm the coral in any way, allowing repeated measurements on the same specimen.

ACKNOWLEDGEMENTS

The research work carried out by P. L. Jokiel was partially supported by Environmental Protection Agency Grants 18050 DDN and R800906. The research work by L. Franzisket was supported by Deutsche Forschungsgemeinschaft. This paper is Hawaii Institute of Marine Biology Contribution No. 506.

References

ANDREWS, J. D. 1961. Measurement of shell growth in oysters by weighing in water. *Proc. Nat. Shellfish Assoc.*, vol. 52, p. 1–11.

BAK, R. P. M. 1973. Coral weight increment *in situ*. A new method to determine coral growth. *Mar. Biol.*, vol. 20, p. 45–9.

FRANZISKET, L. 1964. Die Stoffwechselintensität der Riffkorallen und ihre ökologische, phylogentische und soziologische Bedeutung. *Z. Vergleich. Phys.*, vol. 49, p. 91–113.

GOREAU, T. F. 1959. The physiology of skeleton formation in corals. I. A method for measuring the rate of calcium deposition under different conditions. *Biol. Bull. Mar. Biol. Lab. Woods Hole, Mass.*, vol. 116, p. 59–75.

——; GOREAU, N. I. 1959. The physiology of skeleton formation in corals II. Calcium deposition by hermatypic corals under various conditions in the reef. *Biol. Bull. Mar. Biol. Lab. Woods Hole, Mass.*, vol. 117, p. 239–47.

HAVINGA, B. 1928. The daily rate of growth of oysters during summer. *J. Con. CIEM*, vol. 3, p. 231–45.

JOKIEL, P. L.; COLES, S. L. The effects of temperature on the mortality and growth of Hawaiian reef corals. *Mar. Biol.* (in the press).

MARAGOS, J. E. 1972. A study of the ecology of Hawaiian reef corals. Ph.D. Thesis, University of Hawaii, Honolulu (292 p.).

WAINWRIGHT, S. A. 1963. Skeletal organization in the coral *Pocillopora damicornis*. *Quart. J. Micros. Sci.*, vol. 104, p. 169–83.

42

Coral growth: geometrical relationships

J. E. Maragos[1]

INTRODUCTION

Growth studies on individual reef coral specimens have provided much information on the biology and physiology of reef corals. Serious methodological problems arise, however, in investigations where the growth of a number of different corals are compared. While many organisms exhibit some geometrical consistency of shape and structural organization, allowing the application of widely accepted and standardized growth techniques, reef corals possess no common geometrical denominator other than the presence of a thin layer of live tissues and polyps which covers an inert skeleton of carbonate.

The skeleton may vary greatly in size, shape, and bulk density even for specimens of the same species. The polyps themselves may vary in size, form, and spatial density, even among different regions of the same corals. As a result many different techniques have been developed to acquire estimates of coral growth; some have little or no apparent relationship to one another. The resulting lack of standardization of methods has confused objective comparisons between different growth studies and has retarded progress in acquiring fundamental information on the biology and geology of corals.

A recent review of the relationships among a large number of coral growth methods (Maragos, in preparation) indicated that no one technique could satisfy all important criteria needed for application in comparative studies. However, it was determined that the only deficiency of weight growth methods was the pronounced effect of size on growth rate. This deficiency is easily removed using a cube root transformation of weight data. Here the new method is described and applied to some real data on coral growth.

1. Hawaii Institute of Marine Biology, University of Hawaii, P.O. Box 1346, Kaneohe, Hawaii, 96744, U.S.A. Present address: Environmental Resources Section, U.S. Army Corps of Engineers, Pacific Ocean Division, Bldg. 230, Fort Shafter, Honolulu, Hawaii, A.P.O., 96558, U.S.A.

THEORY AND DERIVATION OF THE METHOD

In a recent study (Maragos, in preparation) a number of coral growth techniques were classified into one or other of three categories based upon dimension of measurement. One-dimension techniques involve growth measured along a line or axis and include such methods as colony height, width, length, radius, etc. Two-dimension techniques involve growth measured along a plane or surface area and include such methods as tissue area, polyp number, projected area, etc. Three-dimension techniques involve growth measured within a volume or space and include such methods as displacement volume, dry weight, buoyant weight, etc.

In the same study the techniques were then evaluated with respect to precision, accuracy, effect of size on growth rate, and convenience. It was concluded that one-dimension methods (linear) were convenient and frequently inexpensive. Furthermore, the growth rate of the radius of many colonial corals appears to remain constant with respect to time or size according to the studies of Buddemeier and collaborators (Knutson *et al.*, 1972; Buddemeier, 1974; Buddemeier *et al.*, 1974). However the application of one-dimension methods is seriously limited in comparative studies by problems of imprecision and inaccuracy resulting from the asymmetry and variable form of practically all species of reef corals. These problems appear to be difficult or nearly impossible to resolve.

In the review study (Maragos, in preparation) it was concluded that two-dimension (area) techniques have not been utilized much because of the technical problems and time involved in the acquisition of accurate surface area data from corals having complex forms such as branching and cespitose corals.

Three-dimension techniques (volume or weight) appear to be precise and accurate because all corals, no matter what their form, can have only a single weight value or volume value at any given time. Recent advances also show that growth in weight techniques are also convenient and inexpensive (Jokiel, *et al.*, Chapter 41).

The principal limitation of weight growth methods stems from the pronounced effect of size on the rate of weight accumulation. Recalling that many colonial corals increase their linear dimension (radius) at a constant rate with time, it necessarily follows that the corresponding weight accumulation rate for the same corals will proceed at a cube of the rate of the linear increase, or that weight accumulation will accelerate with time or size. This is based upon the geometric axiom that the third dimension of a solid of constant form and variable size is proportional to the cube of the first dimension (length) of that solid. A numerical example based upon the axiom is presented in Table 1 where the form of the solid is a hemisphere. Thus, based merely on geometrical principles, the weight and linear growth rates within the same corals will be proceeding at different rates (Table 1).

This simple hypothesis is supported by the studies of Maragos (1972, p. 84–93, Tables 2–3) who demonstrated that larger corals accumulate more

TABLE 1. The relationships between length (radius), surface area and weight of different sized solids (of corals) of hemispherical shape. The length of the radius is shown to be increasing at a constant rate with respect to time as available evidence on corals seems to indicate. Data on surface area were computed from radius data using the formula for the surface area of a hemisphere: $A = 2\pi R^2$. Data on weight were computed from radius and a bulk density value of 2.0 gm/cm^3 using equation (1.3) of the text derived from the equation of the volume of a hemisphere $V = \frac{2}{3}\pi R^3$. Note the non-linear relationship of surface area or weight to both time or radius.

Time	Radius (cm)	Surface area (cm^2)	Weight (gm)
0	0	0	0
n	1	6.28	4.19
$2n$	2	25.12	33.51
$3n$	3	56.52	113.10

weight per unit time than smaller corals, of the same species and form, growing in the same environments; when growth in the same group of corals was expressed as a linear dimension, statistical analysis revealed that the larger corals no longer 'grew' at a faster rate than their smaller counterparts. Unless the size effect on weight growth is eliminated, most comparisons involving different corals will be restricted to those of similar initial size.

The effect of size on the growth of weight of corals can be simply eliminated because of the known geometrical relationship between weight and length. Transforming weight data into a cube-root approximation essentially results in the conversion of three-dimension data into computed one-dimension estimates.

The transformation is achieved using the equation for the volume (V) of a hemisphere where:

$$V = \tfrac{2}{3}\pi R^3. \tag{1.1}$$

The weight (W) of any solid of constant bulk density can be related to its volume and bulk density (d) by:

$$V = W/d. \tag{1.2}$$

Combining equations (1.1) and (1.2):

$$W = (\tfrac{2}{3}\pi R^3)d \tag{1.3}$$

and solving for the radius (R), we find that:

$$R^3 = (W/d)(\tfrac{2}{3})(1/\pi) \tag{1.4}$$

and:

$$R = \sqrt[3]{\frac{3W}{2\pi d}} \tag{1.5}$$

Using expression (1.5) the weight dimension of any coral can be converted into a computed linear dimension R, the radius of a hemisphere having the same weight and bulk density characteristics as the coral.

545

2M

The hemisphere rather than some other form was selected as the standard reference shape for the transformation since the hemisphere, perhaps more than any other form, most typifies the many forms assumed by corals. The predominant growth of corals is frequently both upward and outward in a hemispherical fashion but is seldom downward due to the presence of a usually level substratum.

In brief, R can be used to represent coral growth expressed as the change in length of the radius of a standard solid hemisphere rather than in terms of weight change. The size of the hemisphere and the length of the radius are dependent only upon the weight and bulk density of the coral. The relationship between R and r, the measured or maximum radius is illustrated in Figure 1 for

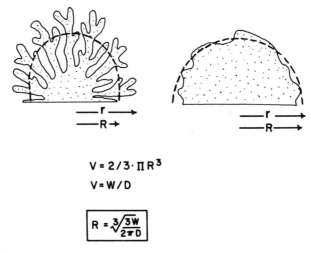

$$V = 2/3 \cdot \Pi R^3$$

$$V = W/D$$

$$R = \sqrt[3]{\frac{3W}{2\pi D}}$$

Figure 1
Diagrammatic sketch illustrating the association between R (solid radius) and r (maximum measured radius) in two forms of corals having approximately hemispherical shapes. Equations are shown illustrating how R can be computed from weight and density data (after Maragos, 1972).

two common coral forms. The two expressions of radius are the same only in the unique situation where the coral being examined is a perfect solid hemisphere shape. Otherwise the two approximations will differ more from one another as the form of the coral itself deviates more from that of a solid hemisphere.

The expression R can be computed for any coral that can be weighed, even for those that do not actually show a hemispherical shape. Thus the computed mean solid radius can allow growth comparisons to be made between corals of varying form, size, species, and bulk density.

ALTERNATIVE EXPRESSIONS

The computed mean weight increase

The bulk density of coral skeletons has been found to vary considerably among different species, different forms of the same species, and different regions of the same specimens (Buddemeier *et al.*, 1974). Some corals showing large linear growth rates but having porous skeletons may actually accrete less carbonate than other corals having compact skeletons showing smaller linear growth rates. The computed increase in mean weight offers an alternative for investigators, especially geologists, who wish to account for discrepancies in growth of corals due to variations in bulk density.

The increase in the computed mean solid radius R over known time intervals is converted to a weight index of growth by multiplying the value of the change in R by a standard surface area (such as one cm^2) and then determining the weight of the coral contained within the volume using data on bulk density. For example, assume a certain coral grows upward at an R value of 1.0 cm/yr and shows a bulk density of 2.0 gm/cm^3. The weight accumulated within a one cm^2 surface area on the coral is calculated to be

$$(1.0)(1.0)(2.0) = 2.0 \text{ gm cm}^{-2} \text{yr}^{-1}.$$

If one always uses one cm^2 as the standard area section then the computed mean weight increase (C) is determined simply from the product of the bulk density (d) and the change in R or:

$$C = d(R_1 - R_0) \qquad (1.6)$$

where R_1 equals the radius value at time 1 and R_0 equals the radius value at time 0.

The computed mean aragonite radius

Some investigators may find it inconvenient or impossible to acquire accurate bulk density data but still want to account for variations in density in the comparisons of growth between different corals. One valid solution involves the use of a standard bulk density value for all R computations regardless of the actual density values. A natural choice for a standard or reference density would be that of pure aragonite, the form of carbonate found in coral skeletons.

According to Palachi *et al.* (1951) pure aragonite has a bulk density of 2.95 gm/cm^3. Linear growth computed using a density value of 2.95 would represent the change in the length of the radius of a hemisphere of pure aragonite. The size of the hemisphere would be dependent only upon the weight of the coral. Hence the computed mean aragonite radius R_a could allow comparisons between corals of different bulk densities without the need to acquire

547

density data. Substituting 2.95 for d in equation (1.5), we find that:

$$R_a = \sqrt[3]{\frac{W}{6.174}} \qquad (1.7)$$

The principal difference between R and R_a is that the void space in the coral skeleton is removed when computing R_a. Actually R_a represents the minimum radius value and will always be smaller in length than the corresponding value of R.

APPLICATION OF THE NEW EXPRESSIONS TO REAL GROWTH DATA ON CORALS

Examples of weight data acquired during growth studies on corals in Kaneohe Bay (Oahu, Hawaii) during 1969–1970 are presented in Table 2. The specific specimen monitored was a small colony of *Pocillopora damicornis* (L) weighed on 8 different occasions over a 469 day period. The step-by-step conversion of the raw data into the new expressions is outlined. The bottom half of Table 2 offers comparisons of growth rate expressed both in the original weight data and in the new form.

TABLE 2. Change in size of a coral *Pocillopora damicornis* (L) weighed on 8 occasions during a 15-month interval in 1969–1970. The specimen was weighed underwater, and buoyant weight was multiplied by a factor of 2.6 to convert to dry weight. The mean solid radius (R) and aragonite radius (R_a) were computed using dry weight data and equations (1.5) and (1.7) respectively. Computed mean weight increase (C) was determined from equation (1.6). Bulk density of the coral was 1.6 gm/cm^3. The bottom group of columns shows the growth rates for each time interval both in terms of the original weight data and the new expressions.

SIZE

No of days	Buoyant wt. (gm)	Dry wt. (gm)	Computed R (cm)	Computed R_a (cm)
0	74	192	3.86	3.16
78	80	207	3.95	3.23
171	102	266	4.30	3.52
231	114	295	4.46	3.65
277	133	347	4.70	3.85
324	153	399	4.92	4.03
396	185	480	5.24	4.29
469	224	583	5.59	4.57

GROWTH RATE

Time interval (days)	Wt. growth (gm/yr)	R growth (cm/yr)	C growth (gm/cm^2/yr)	R_a growth (cm/yr)
0–78	70	0·42	0.67	0·34
78–171	232	1.37	2.19	1.12
171–231	176	0.97	1.55	0.80
231–277	413	1.90	3.04	1.56
277–324	404	1.71	2.74	1.40
324–396	411	1.62	2.59	1.33
396–469	515	1.75	2.80	1.44

FUTURE APPLICATION AND CONSTRAINTS

The new expressions can be used to compare the growth of any set of corals that can be weighed. Recent advances in weighing procedures may expand the potential of the new computed expressions (Jokiel *et al.,* Chapter 41). The new techniques may be chosen for some field studies where other sophisticated or expensive methods such as radiography are not warranted. The new expressions also seem useful in studies involving repetitive measurements since specimens need not be exposed or damaged during the weighing process. The new methods may allow comparisons of coral and reef growth to be made between different regions of coral seas and lead to a better understanding of the factors controlling the unusual geography of reef corals.

The mean radius expressions not only may have wide application in growth studies but may also serve as universal numerical indices of size for all corals regardless of form. Also the ratios between the maximum linear dimension (r) and the computed linear dimension (R) may serve as numerical indices for the many types of growth forms of corals which at present are best described qualitatively. For example, ratios might be close to one for massive and hemispherical corals and far greater than one for foliaceous, cespitose, vasiform, encrusting, columniform and other forms of coral.

The new expressions cannot be used without reservation. The growth of solitary and specialized corals as *Fungia* and *Manicina* appears to be determinate which may restrict growth comparisons to specimens of similar initial size. Evidence of determinate growth in other colonial corals may eventually be forthcoming and this may further limit some of the application of the new methods.

The investigator should also proceed cautiously in comparing different corals. It seems valid to compare growth rates of corals to determine which types are important carbonate producers on a particular reef, but it may not be valid to compare the growth rates among a variety of corals to determine which are most successful in certain reef habitats. Such studies, for example, may show branching forms to grow rapidly but such forms may not survive catastrophic storms and waves to which the slower growing encrusting forms may be better adapted. This serves to emphasize that corals adjust to different ecological situations by varying growth rate, growth form, and other characters.

ACKNOWLEDGEMENTS

Much of this study was taken from the author's Ph.D. dissertation (University of Hawaii, 1972). The author thanks thesis chairman Keith Chave and advisors Richard Grigg and Sidney Townsley for useful discussions and encouragement. Paul Jokiel provided useful suggestions and criticisms. Robert Johannes is also thanked for his interest in this study. The Hawaii Institute of Marine Biology provided laboratory space, boats, equipment, computer time, and typing assist-

549

ance. This study was supported by National Science Foundation Sea Grant contract No. 04-3-158-29.

References

BUDDEMEIER, R. W. 1974. Environmental controls over annual and lunar cycles in hermatypic corals. In: *Proc. Second Int. Coral Reef Symp.*, Brisbane, Great Barrier Reef Committee, vol. 2, p. 259–67.

——; MARAGOS, J. E.; KNUTSON, D. W. 1974. Radiographic studies of reef coral exoskeletons: Rates and patterns of coral growth, *J. exp. mar. Biol. Ecol.*, vol. 14, no. 2, p. 179–200.

KNUTSON, D. W.; BUDDEMEIER, R. W.; SMITH, S. V. 1972. Coral chronometers: Seasonal growth bands in reef corals. *Science,* vol. 177, p. 270–2.

MARAGOS, J. E. 1972. A study of the ecology of Hawaiian reef corals. Ph:D. dissertation. Univ. Hawaii, Honolulu (290 p.).

——. 1974. A geometric approach to the measurement of reef coral growth. (In preparation).

PALACHI, C.; BERMAN, H.; FRONDEL, C. 1951. *The system of mineralogy*, 7th edit., vol. II. New York, John Wiley (1124 p.).

43

Coral growth: retrospective analysis

R. W. Buddemeier[1]

INTRODUCTION

Scope, content and organization

The basic goal of this paper is to introduce the reader to the uses of, and techniques for use of, growth patterns in reef organisms. Since most of the examples involve organisms or environments other than those found on tropical coral reefs, the discussion is developed with rather more breadth than depth.

Applications of retrospective growth studies are outlined, and some of the problems involving terminology and concepts are considered. A summary of growth pattern-producing organisms is provided (with emphasis on relevant marine organisms). The bulk of the discussion is devoted to methods of sample preparation and pattern observation or measurements, with specific attention to the problems of this type of work and to methods for validating proposed chronologies or periodicities.

Although other organisms and methods are covered, the major subject of this discussion is the use of growth patterns found in the exoskeletons of invertebrates—a class of studies collectively designated sclerochronology.

Since this is intended as a methodological overview, standard techniques and recipes are handled by literature citation; method descriptions are reserved for techniques not elsewhere summarized (in particular, preparation of corals and other specimens for radiographic examination). With the exception of technique references, the literature references are intended to provide basic information and access to, rather than a complete list of, the literature. Recent papers, comprehensive reviews, methodological studies, and publications with good and extensive bibliographies are preferentially cited. As in any rapidly developing field, informal communication with those already active in growth pattern studies is important for avoiding duplication of effort and keeping abreast of recent developments.

1. Department of Oceanography, University of Hawaii, Honolulu, Hawaii, 96822, U.S.A.

Applications

For the purposes of this chapter, 'retrospective growth analysis' refers to inferences about the past rate or form of growth of an organism in the absence of any previous direct observations. Such inferences are normally based on a durable physical or chemical record produced by the organism in the course of its skeletal deposition.

If the time periodicity of structural variation is known (and constant), growth patterns can provide detailed information on growth rates and their variations over known intervals of time. This in turn may permit the use of the organisms as environmental sensors, or provide important clues to the external controls over growth. Two examples of highly developed studies of environmental history through preserved growth patterns are the fields of dendrochronology (Fritts, 1971; Stokes and Smiley, 1968; Ferguson, 1970) and paleogeophysics (see, for example, the various reviews cited below in discussion of fossil organisms).

Even without the ability to construct a precise relationship between calendar time, or environmental variables, and growth pattern, structural variations can often be used to provide general information on overall age or growth rate. Finally, even completely uncalibrated patterns may be used to study morphological development, since all portions of a physically continuous growth pattern element may normally be considered to have been deposited approximately concurrently. A recent example of such a morphogenesis study is the work of Glynn (1974).

Terminology and concepts

Studies of growth periodicities suffer from the need to use terms which have colloquial or intuitive meanings for most people. This leads to inadequate attention to definitions and significance on the parts of both writers and readers. For example, 'day' may mean one thing to a researcher armed with calendar and clock, but something rather different to a photosensitive organism with both light intensity and photoperiod duration response thresholds. A 'line' in an organism's structure will almost invariably turn into a 'band' if sufficient magnification is employed. Most scientists preserve the temperate zone terrestrial bias of associating 'winter' with lowered temperature and light levels, but tropical marine organisms often experience warmer ambient temperatures during the low-light (rainy) season; 'winter' is therefore ambiguous, but substitution of 'warm' or 'cloudy' may imply a causality or control that does not exist.

In the interests of communication, three rules for the handling of terminology problems may be suggested: (a) Scrupulously define all terms used; the more obvious the meaning, the more critical the definition; (b) if someone else has developed a self-consistent and appropriate terminology for your work, use it gladly and acknowledge it; (c) although propagation of unnecessary jargon is a heinous crime, it may be better to invent (and thoroughly define!)

new terms than to subvert existing popular or technical words to different usages—especially if the intended difference is subtle.

The concept of growth is a critical one, and use of the term is subject to the problem mentioned above. Growth may be measured as change in mass per unit time, change in volume per unit time, change in surface area per unit time, or change in some linear dimension per unit time. A further refinement is the use of specific mass accretion rates—change in mass per unit area per unit time. Many of these require careful definition. Does the organism follow an indeterminate growth pattern, as appears to be the case with some massive corals and algal masses? If not, have the growth patterns or rates been corrected for the determinate growth curve, and how does that affect the data? If a linear growth rate can legitimately be used, is it representative of the maximum dimension of the organism or of a weighted average rate? If the latter is the case, it should be proportional to the cube root of the volume or (assuming constant density) mass increase, at least for reasonably symmetric organisms. Surface area may refer to projected surface area or to 'actual' surface area as measured by one of a variety of techniques. Finally, the time base is critical; average daily or annual growth rates, even with assessment of variance, do not hint at, or evaluate, potentially large diurnal or seasonal variations in growth rate.

Measurements of mass, volume or average dimensional change should be interconvertible, given basic information or organism geometry and density (see Maragos, Chapter 42, for a discussion of the use of normalized or projected equivalent volumes). The importance of making and reporting the additional measurements necessary for conversion between the various units of growth assessment cannot be overstressed; not only does it make the data useful to a much wider spectrum of the scientific community, but it also provides the researcher with insurance against having chosen an inappropriate primary variable.

Another caveat concerns the equation of skeletal growth with tissue growth or organic metabolic rates. Although this is a convenient (and in some cases an apparently reasonable) assumption, it is only recently that concurrent measurements of the organic and calcification metabolisms of the same organism have been carried out (Smith and Kinsey, Chapter 36). For most organisms, situations and time scales, the relationship between exoskeletal deposition and tissue metabolism, quantity or composition is not firmly established; researchers should keep this in mind and take pains to formulate carefully and state clearly the assumptions they use in relating skeletal accretion to other aspects of organism 'growth'.

Finally, it should be kept in mind that a variety of disciplines have evolved content or techniques relevant to growth-pattern studies, with only imperfect overlap in their scientific literatures. One such field is that of biorhythm research and chronobiology. The review monograph by Luce (1971), although oriented toward human medical aspects of the field, provides a readable introduction to terms and concepts and an extensive general bibliography.

553

Familiarity with the field of dendrochronology (see citations above) is essential for any serious worker in growth-pattern studies, as tree-ring research represents by far the most extensive compilation of experimental, retrospective and environmental studies of growth-pattern significance and application. From geology and geophysics stem two relevant subdisciplines; the paleontological study of fossil growth records (Termier and Termier, 1975; see also other citations throughout this discussion), and the study of cyclic sedimentation processes (Duff *et al.*, 1967). This latter field has developed not only environmentally sensitive chronologies analogous to growth patterns, but also conceptual and mathematical tools for dealing with time-series analysis, pattern matching, etc.

PATTERN PRODUCING ORGANISMS

Terrestrial organisms

Although the primary focus of this paper is marine reef organisms, the terrestrial biota on atoll motus and continents or high islands adjacent to reef systems are certainly part of the large-scale reef system, and their growth patterns may conceivably contribute environmental information complementary to that available from marine organisms.

Dendrochronology has not yet been extended to tropical regions; trees with apparently seasonal growth patterns occur, but the lack of a dormant season produces continuous bands rather than discrete line growth patterns, complicating analysis. In this respect the tropical trees are more similar in growth pattern to some of the marine species, especially corals, than they are to temperate zone trees. Densitometry (see below) may be a fruitful approach to tropical dendrochronology, and it seems reasonable that the development of this field should follow rather closely the development of tropical sclerochronology.

Neville (1967) has reviewed the occurrence of daily growth lines in a number of terrestrial organisms, and cites reviews of annual growth patterns as well.

In both the terrestrial and the marine environments, tropical organisms have not been the subject of much growth pattern research; but among possible candidates must be considered the terrestrial snails and crabs, especially since various crabs have been shown to have photosensitive biorhthyms (Palmer, 1973).

Marine organisms

The following discussion attempts to touch upon all of the classes of organisms known to possess growth patterns of potential utility. This includes both those with apparently regular growth patterns of unknown period or consistency and those whose responses have been calibrated to specific periods. Because of the

554

paucity of contemporary tropical organism studies, references to the literature on fossil and temperate zone growth pattern studies are also included.

Fish. The otoliths and scales of some fish possess seasonal and/or daily growth patterns. As usual, the use of seasonal growth lines has been most extensive and most successful with temperate zone fish, and research on reef fish patterns is currently emphasizing daily patterns. Because of fish mobility, their growth patterns will presumably be much less sensitive to environmental variation than those of more sessile organisms and therefore useful primarily for ageing specimens. The current state of the art is well covered in the proceedings of a recent symposium on the subject (Bagenal, 1974).

Algae. Coralline algae and related species are well known for the deposition of laminated carbonates. Chave and Wheeler (1965) have demonstrated seasonal mineralogical and chemical variations in the skeletal calcite of a red alga, and their growth rate estimates have received qualitative confirmation from the work of Bosellini and Ginsburg (1971) on laminated rhodolites. It should be emphasized that there is virtually no information on the depositional periodicity (if any) or long-term reliability of tropical algal patterns, and much ground work would be required for algal chronometry.

Fossil stromatolites, on the other hand, clearly possess environmentally sensitive paleontological growth records (Panella, 1972, 1975; Scrutton and Hipkin, 1973), leaving us with the hope that some of their presumed contemporary relatives may prove as useful.

Invertebrates. This is by far the largest class of organisms with potentially useful growth patterns, and the one for which the largest data base exists.

The only important reef organisms with demonstrated potential for sclerochronology are the hermatypic corals. The existence of diurnal growth patterns has been demonstrated by scanning electron microscopy in combination with *in vivo* experiments (Barnes, 1970, 1972). Seasonal (i.e. normally annual) cycles in skeletal density have been verified and are best studied by x-radiography (Knutson *et al.*, 1972; Buddemeier *et al.*, 1974; Buddemeier, 1974; Macintyre and Smith, 1974; Dodge and Thomson, 1974; Buddemeier and Kinzie, 1975). In addition, lunar monthly cycles in skeletal density appear probable, but await further confirmation (Buddemeier, 1974; Buddemeier and Kinzie, 1975).

In addition to the hermatypes, gorgonian corals have been shown to possess annual growth bands (Grigg, 1974), and it appears probable that skeletal layers in black and bamboo corals and colour rings in pink corals have annual periodicity (R. W. Grigg, pers. comm.).

The other major class of invertebrates for which large amounts of data on growth periodicities are available are the molluscs (Clark, 1974, 1975; Hall *et al.*, 1974; Pannella, 1972; Whyte, 1975). Although much of the experimental work has been on clams, other species are represented. As usual, however, temperate and sub-tropical organisms dominate the literature, although *Tridacna* has been shown to possess approximately annual (Bonham, 1965) as well as probable daily and tidal patterns (Pannella, 1972). Tidal and daily patterns have received the most attention in the molluscs, and the usual methods of measurement are by direct microscopy or peel studies (see below).

Echinoids have readily observable growth-related structures in both plates and spines, but pattern significance and periodicities are not unequivocally determined (Jensen, 1969; Sumich and McCauley, 1973). Direct or microscopic observation of the patterns has been the usual approach, but Pearse and Pearse, in conjunction with the author (1975), have shown that x-radiography of both plates and spines yields strikingly clear density patterns which correlate with the visually observable patterns.

Other contemporary reef organisms which are likely candidates for growth pattern analysis include the brachiopods, the barnacles, arthropods, and sclerosponges. The sclerosponges have been shown to possess regular density variations analogous to those in corals (Buddemeier and Kinzie, unpublished data).

Among the fossil invertebrates numerous examples of growth patterns and pattern studies are available. These have been reviewed by Pannella (1972, 1975), Scrutton and Hipkin (1973) and Clark (1974), among others. Corals, molluscs, brachiopods and others have all been studied, and much ingenuity applied to the acquisition and interpretation of data.

EXPERIMENTAL METHODS

Sample preparation

Although growth structures are visible on the surfaces of a few organisms (e.g. the shells of some molluscs and the epithecae of a few corals), it will generally be necessary to section a specimen in order to examine internal variations in structure. Accordingly, procedures for various cutting, grinding and mounting techniques are discussed below.

Cutting. Fortunately, the minerals of most skeletal structures are soft by geological standards, and any geological cutting or grinding equipment will handle reef organism exoskeletons with ease. Both water- and oil-lubricated rock saws are effective; the type with an adjustable sample vice and worm-gear feed is particularly convenient for x-ray sample preparation, where a slice of uniform thickness is desired. For samples small enough to be mounted on a slide, a thin-section cut-off saw may be used as a mini-rock saw.

However, the more usual situation involves samples which are too large, too small, or the wrong shape for use of standard rock saws, or rock saws may not be available. Masonry blades (carborundum chips bonded into a composite disk) are commercially available in a variety of sizes for table, radial and hand-held circular saws. The permanently-mounted saws can be adequate

556

substitutes for a 'real' rock saw, and the hand-held saws are very useful for shaping samples to fit a rock-saw vice or for trimming the centres out of coral heads sampled at remote locations in order to minimize the excess weight shipped home. It also is possible to use these saws to make a reasonably clean cut through a coral head much too large for the blade to penetrate completely. The saw is used to cut a groove to the maximum possible depth all the way around the piece to be removed, and then a series of chisels or thin wedges (wide blade, narrow handle wood chisels are ideal, but screwdrivers and even large spikes can be pressed into service) is driven into the slot all around its perimeter. It is desirable to use a number (e.g. six or more) or evenly-spaced wedges and to drive them in alternately and in small increments; otherwise, an uneven fracture will result, and invariably any inequity is at the expense of the piece you wanted to save.

If, after all possible trimming and shaping, you still have a single piece of coral or reef rock which you wish to cut as a single unit and which is too large for any of your cutting equipment, the logical person to turn to is your local tombstone supplier. He will almost certainly be equipped to make extremely smooth and regular cuts on rocks several feet on a side, and although he probably will charge for this work it should not cost very much for a few quick limestone slices.

In the absence of geological equipment, a number of standard shop tools in addition to the above-mentioned saws may be pressed into service. Band saws will cut coral, but the blade is likely to be ruined for more conventional applications, and blade flexibility makes a really uniform cut difficult to achieve. Power hacksaws are much more effective and can rival rock saws for quality of cut. Disk and belt sanders can produce a reasonably good flat surface, and can even be used to produce slices by grinding one side of a sample, gluing it to a handle of some sort, and then grinding the other side. Surface grinding machines can do an even more elegant job. However, from the public relations standpoint it is wise to remember that most machinists are loathe to cut even soft rocks on their equipment, and that even dry marine samples have enough salt content to make their residues quite corrosive. Good housekeeping and forethought in the use of shared equipment are essential for the would-be coral or reef-rock cutter.

Most of the foregoing discussion has related to large samples. If small samples are to be examined they will normally be prepared by somewhat the same methods (although not necessarily to the same standards) as petrographic thin sections (Ireland, 1971). If thin-section saws, grinders and polishing tables are not available then there may be no alternative to grinding one's sections by hand after rough cutting or grinding them as outlined above. However, it is worth remembering that glassblowing and optical equipment shops often have cutting and grinding equipment and materials which will work nicely on small rocks, as do many lapidary and hobby shops.

For freehand cutting or grinding operations, and for cutting irregular samples in a vice-type rock saw, it is desirable to have the sample attached to a firm and convenient mount. If the size and shape of the sample mount is more or less standardized, then it is possible to improvise jigs, mounts or carriages for feeding the sample into saws or grinders, thus improving the quality of the final surface.

Mounting and impregnation. Impregnation of porous samples with any of a variety of resins, etc., is described by Stanley (1971), as is the cutting and mounting of such samples. These methods are of particular use in dealing with fragile or small samples which cannot be safely or simply manipulated.

However, these methods are likely to be peripheral to the needs of.most growth-structure workers, who will be primarily concerned with preparing a clean, representative surface or slice. In order to do so, it is frequently necessary to fasten a sample to something to facilitate cutting or grinding.

It is possible to turn a coral head into a semi-rectangular block by propping it up in a cardboard box and setting plaster of Paris around it. Aside from the fact that it makes a very heavy sample, the major drawback to this method is the chemical and mineralogical contamination of the sample; after such treatment most analyses would be untrustworthy. When a surface grinder is used, the problem is one of mounting the sample in a completely flat orientation for grinding its second side. Fastening it to a flat plate or block of metal or hardwood by pouring melted paraffin all around the edges has worked well in these cases, and does not coat the sample as irretrievably as plaster of Paris or the resin glues.

Resin-type materials (epoxy glues, fibreglass, etc.) have both the advantage and disadvantage of being durable and permanent, and are consequently the materials of choice for impregnation. For temporary mounting as an aid to cutting or grinding they are not particularly suitable; in addition to being permanent, they are relatively expensive and must be mixed before each use.

For simple temporary mounting ordinary household adhesives may well be adequate. The author has been quite successful in sticking coral slices to wooden blocks with Duco Rubber Cement, liberally applied and allowed to cure overnight. Naturally, a water-soluble glue should not be used if you are cutting with water-lubricated equipment, but ready release and clean-up with solvents is one of the advantages of the simple glues. The appropriate solvent for each glue can usually be deduced from the instructions or contents listed on the label. If not, then experimentation with acetone, toluene and trichloro-ethylene should determine which general class of solvent types is most suitable.

For attaching small pieces to glass slides, even on a temporary basis, the traditional thermoplastic thin-section resins such as Lakeside-70 and Canada balsam remain the obvious choices. They are easily applied and released by heating, making transfer from slide to slide reasonably simple (e.g. where it is desired to hand grind a flat surface for slide attachment, finish-grind the opposite face, and then reverse to finish-grind the original face for smoothness and final dimension). If loose specimens are required, the resins can be cleaned off reasonably well with solvents after release from the slide, provided that the resin is sparingly applied in the first place to avoid deep penetration into the sample.

When removing the thermoplastic resins there will almost inevitably be heat sources around, and it is readily observed that some other adhesives will also dissolve faster if they are warm when attacked with solvent. Two potentially serious hazards should be kept in mind. One stems from the toxicity of most organic solvents; when warmed, their increased vapour pressure may lead to dangerous concentration levels. The other is their fire hazard. While most scientists know enough not to use open flames around organic solvents, it is not so generally appreciated that the motors in heat guns and the thermostat contacts in many hot plates produce sparks which are quite capable of igniting organic vapours. Any use of solvent should be carried out in a well-ventilated, flame-free room, and if both heating and solvent washing are being done simultaneously the operations should be in a protected fume hood with solvent use separated from the heating by as great a distance as is feasible.

Surface preparation. The extent to which a sample must be cleaned, polished, stained, etc., will be determined by the method of examination and the desired result. Inevitably a certain amount of experimentation will be required, especially if new techniques are being employed or previously uninvestigated organisms studied. For x-radiography of sections a millimetre or more thick, the surfaces cut on a firmly mounted sample by a rock-saw blade in good condition are completely satisfactory. For thinner sections, standard thin-section cut-off saws and grinders usually provide an adequate surface. For example, the author prepares 100–200 micron thick sections of sea urchin plates and spines for x-radiography by mounting the specimen (after preliminary hand grinding, if necessary) on a slide and grinding one surface with a micrometer-feed thin section grinding wheel. The sample is then reversed onto another slide, using a minimum amount of resin and ground down to the desired dimension. The sample is then freed from the slide with gentle heating and a razor blade, and cleared of resin by flooding with solvent while warm. In addition to urchin skeletons, this technique has also been used to prepare precious coral sections for radiography, and produces surfaces amply good enough for all macro- and semimicroradiography (see below).

For applications other than radiography, cut surfaces may or may not be adequate. This will depend on the size, scale and clarity of the patterns being observed, whether they are surface or bulk properties, and the requirements of the specific technique. If a pattern exists but shows up with poor contrast or indistinct boundaries, then differentiating techniques such as etching or staining may be in order; on the other hand, if patterns are obscured by scratch marks, striations, etc., then further polishing is indicated. No precise rules can be formulated, but the following guidelines may be of assistance.

(a) Grinding with successively finer grit abrasive powders or papers produces an extremely smooth surface on low porosity (e.g. many shells) or impregnated samples, but is likely to fill the open pores of unimpregnated coral and urchin skeletons with bits of abrasive and grinding detritus.

(b) Detrital material, both natural and that introduced by grinding, may be removed from robust samples by water jets or ultrasonic agitation. These techniques are also useful in removing tissue from the skeleton, but for complete cleaning must be combined with tissue solubilizer solutions, pyrolysis, or oxidation with H_2O_2, bleach or low temperature RF plasma reactors.

(c) Fractured surfaces are often much more effective at revealing growth or structural patterns than are cut or polished surfaces.

(d) Etching may be used to restore structure to a surface polished to a featureless plane. The rate of acid attack on most minerals varies with the chemical, physical and mineralogical composition of the solid. A slow etch with a very weak acid (dilute acetic acid or very dilute HCl) is most effective at bringing out delicate structural variations, and is often used to prepare a surface for electron microscopy (Krinsley and Margolis, 1971) or acetate peel preparation (Klein, 1971). However, when gross structural differences exist a vigorous etch may produce dramatic enhancement. For example, when sections of certain coral skeletons (massive *Porites* and *Hydnophora* species) are etched with ordinary dilute HCl, the low density growth bands are selectively attacked, resulting in pronounced ridges on the surface (J. E. Houck, unpublished data). This is analogous to the selective weathering observable in subaerially exposed fractured coral heads, and may prove useful either as a growth-band enhancement technique or as a measure of relative specific surface areas.

(c) Tissue stains are familiar to most biologists, and mineral stains (Friedman, 1971) are used by petrologists to differentiate mineral components of a sediment. Most structural growth patterns do not have dramatic mineralogical variations, but staining may be useful to differentiate various degrees of porosity, to enhance contrast between alternating mineral and organic layers, or simply to make the skeleton visually easier to view than the stark white of pure $CaCO_3$, especially when viewed with transmitted light.

All of these sample preparation techniques need to be developed empirically to fit the case at hand. Variations in sample thickness, the duration and strength of acid etch, surface polish, etc., can all make substantial differences in the final appearance of the sample. It is essential to cultivate a curiosity about whether apparently nonexistent structural patterns would show up, or visible ones appear qualitatively different, if different methods of sample preparation were used. It is also essential, having experimented with various techniques, to adopt a rule of parsimony and settle on the method that yields satisfactory results with the minimum possible sample manipulation. This is particularly critical where chemical, physical or mineralogical analyses are to be made on the sample following pattern analysis.

Sample examination

The obvious way to examine a specimen is to look at it from various angles, under various lighting conditions, and if appropriate, with various magnifications and a variety of the sample preparation or surface treatment techniques discussed above. In a surprisingly large number of cases, the impressions or data thus obtained will be difficult to improve upon. However, instrumental or indirect methods of observation and measurement are frequently required; the most common and useful of these are summarized below.

Microscopy. A variety of standard microscopical examination techniques (transmitted or reflected light, polarized light, phase contrast, etc.) are readily available and adequately described in the methodological literature of both biology and geology, and will not be described here. However, in studying growth patterns it is wise to remember that the human eye and mind are very effective pattern-recognition devices. Patterns, especially indistinct ones, are often easiest to recognize when viewed in their totality, and magnification of limited portions may result in a 'cannot see the forest for the trees' situation.

Photography. In many cases, especially where permanent records or verifiable quantitative data are desired, indirect means of examination are appropriate. One obvious method is photography, which has several advantages. An enlarged macrophotograph, or a composite microphotograph series, can provide substantial magnification without the disadvantage of losing sight of the overall pattern. These also provide a means by which band counts or measurements can be independently crosschecked, and the negatives can be used in various densitometric applications (discussed below).

Acetate peels. Another indirect technique which is both simple and very effective for some samples is the acetate peel procedure (Klein, 1971). It has been widely and effectively used in studies of molluscan growth patterns (see, for example, Hall *et al.* (1974) and Pannella (1975)). The exact recipe for peel preparation will vary according to the organism studied and the investigator's microscope technique and personal preference, but peel studies in general have the advantage of producing a much clearer picture of structural variations than can be seen by direct examination.

x-Radiography. Radiography has long been an established technique in geological studies, but its extensive application to studies of biological growth patterns is a recent development and is still rapidly expanding. Adequate explanations of theory, practice and some (non-biological) applications are given by Hamblin (1971), Krinitzsky (1970), and applications manuals published by Eastman Kodak (1969) and other x-ray equipment or product suppliers. However, in view of the recent developments in the field, some basic methodological observations seem called for.

As was mentioned earlier in this paper, reef organisms possessing growth patterns in the form of density variations susceptible to radiographic detection include the hermatypic corals, echinoids, sclerosponges, some precious corals,

561

and probably algal concretions. This list is by no means all-embracing; many calcifying organisms have not yet been tested for systematic skeletal structure variations.

For macroscopic radiography (e.g. inspection of annual patterns in hermatypic corals) almost any type of equipment and film can be made to serve; however, to cover the widest range of possible applications, certain specific characteristics are needed. To improve resolution by avoiding beam dispersion and parallax effects, the x-ray unit should have a small focal spot (commercial units with 0.5 mm focal spot tubes are available from stock) and should permit source–sample separations of at least a metre. Since softer (low energy) x-rays produce more contrast when samples have only small internal density differences, the unit should be capable of operation at least as low as 30 kVp (peak kilovolts), and preferably down to 10 or 15 kVp. Although not essential, an automatic exposure control is extremely desirable and results in great savings in time and film. For certain types of work a beam locator light is also a desirable accessory. Finally, adequate shielding for the operator and others in the vicinity must be ensured; radiation exposure can be a significant hazard, particularly if equipment is modified or used for other than its designed purpose.

The author uses a Faxitron 8050 x-ray unit (marketed by Hewlett-Packard) which has proved quite satisfactory; Picker X-Ray produces a unit with similar performance specifications which should be comparable. However, serviceable radiographs may be obtained without possessing optimal instrumentation. The researcher who wants to try radiography would do well to check with any local geological or oceanographic research centres which may have equipment for sample or sediment core radiography. Failing that, a standard x-ray diffraction unit is an eminently suitable source of x-rays, provided that suitable sample mounting or traversing gear can be devised and beam collimation reduced to provide adequate areal coverage. Many cities have industrial x-ray service companies who will do very competent work for a price. Finally, medical x-ray clinics or radiologists are often willing to undertake side projects on a time-available basis. Medical x-ray techniques can produce adequate radiographs of reasonably large structures, but are oriented toward rapid exposures and low patient doses rather than contrast and resolution. Consequently, voltages are higher, focal spots are larger and films are faster and grainier than is desirable for research work. The diagnostic technique which comes closest to industrial or research techniques is probably mammography.

For most purposes the film of choice will be Kodak AA or equivalent. It is much finer grained than medical film, but offers high speed and contrast. For the ultimate in high resolution work or x-ray microscopy, it will be necessary to use a very fine grain, single emulsion film (e.g. Kodak type R single coat or equivalent); however, most researchers will run into resolution limits imposed by their equipment or sample preparation techniques before the film itself becomes the limiting factor.

High resolution x-ray microscopy (Cosslett, 1956) requires specialized techniques and equipment, and has not yet been routinely applied to growth pattern studies. It is therefore not included in this discussion, except to note that it represents a potentially interesting methodological frontier in research on reef organisms.

It should also be noted that reference to specific manufacturer's products in the foregoing discussion does not imply any sort of exclusive endorsement, but is intended only to provide examples of a type or class of product.

The other major area of radiographic technique consideration is that of sample preparation. This will depend on the equipment, the organism and the goal of the study, so specific detailed recipes are not possible. However, some general considerations can be summarized. Sample thickness represents a compromise between the desirability of averaging out irrelevant structural details and enhancing density contrast by having adequate path lengths through the sample, and the desirability of having the sample thin enough to yield good resolution of the smallest structural variation of interest (normally, this means having dimensions of the same order of magnitude). The conflict is somewhat relieved if the sample can be prepared and oriented so that the structures of interest are uniformly parallel to the beam direction. This, in combination with a small focal spot and adequate source-to-sample distance, minimizes the degradation of resolution caused by use of a thick sample. Other problems of radiographic geometry and sample preparation are adequately covered in the references cited or the foregoing discussion.

Densitometry. The use of scanning optical densitometers to obtain quantitative data on sample density variations by calibrating x-ray negative emulsion density in terms of sample density has been described by Buddemeier (1974) and by Dodge and Thomson (1974). This technique cannot as yet be considered a standard laboratory method, as it requires a good deal of effort to set up, and access to a fairly specialized piece of equipment. However, the concurrent production of linear dimension and density data permits direct calculation of calcification rates as well as linear growth rates. Further, the output is in an analogue and/or digitized form which facilitates pattern matching, pattern averaging, and the choice of objective criterion for identification and measurement of structural features. These latter characteristics make it applicable to characterization of macro-, micro-, and scanning electron microscope photographs as well as x-radiographs.

Other techniques. Sophisticated instrumental techniques for growth pattern examination do not constitute the primary focus of this chapter. However, their historic importance and continued utility make it essential to summarize some of the more significant techniques.

Scanning electron microscopy represents an obvious and powerful extension of optical microscopic techniques, offering higher magifications, better resolution, and (in some instruments) more flexible sample manipulation capability. The SEM has been applied to a wide variety of problems; two recent and important studies in growth pattern investigation are those of Barnes (1972) and Jell (1974). Because of the detail and magnification provided, SEM studies are most effective for identification of very small growth structures or for investigation of the internal structure of larger patterns; use of the technique for large-scale band counting or measurement usually lands one squarely in the 'trees versus forest' problem. SEM operation and sample preparation is complex enough so that it is normally left to professional techniques, and will therefore not be discussed here.

Since growth patterns are almost by definition a physical variation in structure, it follows that chemical and/or mineralogical variations may also occur. Although such chemical variations associated with growth patterns have been found through incremental analysis of samples (Houck and Buddemeier, unpublished data), this approach is tedious and not well-suited to the original identification or measurement of growth patterns. Certain instrumental techniques provide the ability to scan or map a sample surface in terms of some compositional parameter, and these may be useful both in identifying patterns and in studying the underlying mechanism of formation (Rosenberg and Jones, 1975).

The most obvious instrument is the electron microprobe, or the small 'mini-probe' attachments which are accessories to scanning electron microscopes. The latter are much less sensitive, but have the advantage of a smaller and more controllable beam spot for precise analysis. In addition to these 'stock' instruments, a new generation of chemico-physical instruments is being developed for surface or near-surface analysis; the principles applied include low-energy electron diffraction, Auger spectroscopy, soft x-ray and low-energy electron spectroscopy, and others. Most of these techniques have not yet found wide application in geological or biological studies, but seem to have great promise for the future.

A final methodological approach to growth-pattern variations is through variations in stable or radioisotope content. Although these are systematic oxygen and carbon isotope ratio variations as a function of the density bands in corals (Weber et al., 1975), the analyses are tedious and the exact significance is not yet understood. Radiometric techniques are primarily useful for calibrating or confirming ages or growth pattern periods, and are discussed in the following section.

VALIDATION AND INTERPRETATION

Numerous problems

It is normally good judgement to consider in advance what a series of measurements may tell you and whether or not the information will be worth having. In growth-pattern research it is important to consider the same questions after the results are in hand, since few other fields of study evoke so strongly the natural human tendency to assume that you have found what you expected to find.

To be of utility for rate measurements or comparisons, dating or environmental reconstruction, growth patterns must have a reasonably constant and known or knowable periodicity. Such patterns may be the result of endogenous rhythms entrained by environmental signals, or of direct organism response to cyclic environmental changes. Unfortunately the utility or comprehensibility of the pattern are not guaranteed even when one of these conditions obtains. Clark (1974) has recently reviewed the problems and utility of invertebrate growth lines in some detail. What follows is a pessimistic summary of potential problems and errors.

Lack of pattern periodity. Organisms may deposit growth structures with periodicities so weak or irregular as to be virtually useless as a time base (Evans, 1975).

Inexact records. Perfect fidelity in biological recorders is the rare exception rather than the rule; a 'good' record is one which reliably comes within a few per cent of the number of days, tides, months or years of which it normally produces a record. More extensive errors are common, for reasons discussed below.

Sensitivity to more than one environmental parameter. Growth pattern elements may be produced or suppressed by either random or regular environmental stimuli other than the one controlling their basic periodicity. For example, numerous authors have noted the potential for storms to mimic or suppress daily and tidal growth lines in shallow-water organisms. Also, retardation of growth under suboptimal conditions such as lowered water temperature may cause failure to produce normal patterns during that season; this has been shown to be the cause of incomplete daily growth records in bivalve molluscs (Hall *et al.*, 1974) and suggested as the reason for incomplete monthly patterns in hermatypic corals (Buddemeier and Kinzie, 1975).

Another consideration relevant to multiple sensitivities is their significance for the use of organisms as environmental recorders; the data being 'recorded' by the organism may be different in different localities. The evidence to date suggests, for instance, that the seasonal density bands in corals are entrained by light variations where the water temperature does not range too far from optimal values, but that lowered temperature becomes the control over high density calcification in more marginal environments (Buddemeier, 1974; Dodge and Thomson, 1974; Buddemeier and Kinzie, 1975).

Misidentification of pattern frequency. It is by no means impossible to confuse days with tides, months with years, etc., when working with unfamiliar organisms or locations; this is particularly true when up to two-thirds of the expected structures may be missing or suppressed (see references listed under preceding item).

565

Miscounting a valid pattern. Errors introduced in this fashion are usually at about the same level as the recording reliability of the organism, but can be critical if precise dating is attempted. Visual counting combines the advantages of human pattern recognition and judgement with the disadvantages of unconscious bias. Instrumental methods (Buddemeier, 1974; Dodge and Thomson, 1974; Rosenberg and Jones, 1975; Dolman, 1975) ostensibly increase objectivity but in fact usually just transform the subjective elements into a less discernable and criticizable form. Persistent scepticism, honest evaluation of uncertainties, and regular cross-checks remain the best defences.

Mismeasurement may be treated as another aspect of miscounting, and usually reflects a poor choice on the part of the researcher rather than actual mechanical error. Improper boundary identification, inadequate correction for an overall determinate growth curve, measurement at an angle to the growth surface or direction, selection of an inappropriate parameter (e.g. maximum linear growth instead of average linear growth or mass deposition rate), and other judgmental errors can all result in distortion of results and conclusions.

Over enthusiasm and/or poor statistics. In view of the multiple possibilities for errors and uncertainties, and the general lack of knowledge about growth pattern reliability, it requires large amounts of data carefully collected and processed to validate detailed or precise chronologies, or conclusions based on previously unstudied organisms. If a limited number of specimens or pattern counts per specimen are used, then an honest and pessimistic assessment of the inherent uncertainties in the study is particularly critical. As an example, the reader's attention is directed to the data and effort which go into the development of detailed tree-ring master chronologies—and trees and their environments are well understood and easily accessible in comparison with marine organisms (Stokes and Smiley, 1968).

A few solutions

In view of the formidable and persistent problems involved in their use, how may growth patterns be validated and calibrated? All of the possible methods involve cross-checking the known or proposed growth chronology against other, independent chronologies.

Experimental validation. For investigation of daily and tidal periodicities, introduction of known markers or tracer into the organism provide time marks against which to measure subsequently deposited growth patterns (see, for example, Barnes, 1970, 1972). The use of such labels as Alizarin Red and radioisotopes is discussed elsewhere in this Monograph. This method is direct and positive, but it involves manipulation—and hence possible perturbation—of the specimen, and real-time experiments are frequently not feasible for study of monthly and annual structures.

566

Internally consistent chronologies. When a single organism has more than one level of growth-pattern structures, the assignment of periodicities gains a good deal of confidence if an appropriate number of finer structures (daily, tidal or monthly) are grouped to form a higher order series (monthly or annual). This internal cross check is generally the only type available for fossil organisms, as reviewed by Scrutton and Hipkin (1973).

Radiometric techniques. Radioactivity, both natural and anthropogenic, can provide valuable clocks for dating samples. Most of these techniques require rather specialized low-background counting techniques and are not normally suitable for use by non-specialists, but they have been critically useful in providing independent verification of growth pattern periodicities and are widely enough used to be accessible if needed.

Naturally occurring radionuclides with convenient half-lives and marine geochemistries are Pb^{210} an Ra^{228}, which have been used by Dodge and Thomson (1974) and Moore and Krishnaswami (1974) to validate coral growth bands.

Globally distributed fallout radionuclides from atmospheric nuclear testing in the 1950's and 1960's have geographical and temporal distributions which are well enough characterized to serve as environmental time markers. Excess C^{14} and Sr^{90} are particularly useful, and have been used by Knutson and Buddemeier (1973) and Moore and Krishnaswami (1974) in coral studies.

Local excesses of artificial radionuclides may be found in the vicinities of nuclear facilities and test sites. Activities may be relatively high, and if their input histories are known they can serve as readily detectable time markers. Examples of applications are the works of Bonham (1965), Knutson *et al.* (1972), Knutson and Buddemeier (1973), Buddemeier *et al.* (1974), and Noshkin *et al.* (1975).

Several further points about the radionuclide studies should be mentioned. They are particularly suitable for validation of long-period (e.g. annual) patterns which are difficult to study on a real-time basis. The methods are retrospective and radiation levels involved are far below those observed to produce biological effects, so possible pattern perturbation is not an issue. Finally, the studies cited have demonstrated that corals are representative samplers for marine radioactivity, and from an initial effort to calibrate growth bands with radioactivity we have reached a point where we can use band-dated corals to reconstruct a more detailed history of marine radioactivity.

Other environmental event markers. Datable alterations in growth substratum or environment (catastrophic storms, pollution, dredging, etc.) may be used in a manner similar to, but less convenient than, radioactivity changes. Examples of this approach include the work of Shinn (1972), Barnard *et al.* (1974), Macintyre and Smith (1974) and Moore and Krishnaswami (1974). These are not particularly general or powerful techniques, and it is probably more appropriate to use growth patterns to study environmental history than vice versa.

Comparison with other data. Often the organism of interest will have been the subject of growth rate or age–size observations, or may be related to species with validated growth patterns. These data will provide the basis for argument by analogy or general comparison of magnitudes. This is a very weak form of corroboration, and is primarily useful for avoiding misassignment of basic periodicities.

Statistical agreement. Obtaining similar growth rates and similar variations with time for different specimens of the same organism in comparable environments constitutes confirmation that the growth pattern is an environmentally sensitive characteristic of the organism, and hence potentially useful. If oceanographic or climatological records are available and correlate with growth-pattern dimensions it is particularly convincing, but also rather unusual.

Some form of one of the above validation techniques is used implicitly or explicitly in any extension of growth pattern studies to a previously uninvestigated species or environment. The researcher owes it to himself and his audience to formulate and state his assumptions clearly, and to assess realistically their probable validity or uncertainty.

Data handling

The diversity of organisms, methods and potential applications covered in this discussion makes it virtually impossible to specify any preferred data processing or presentation techniques. As with terminology, this diversity and lack of standardization increases the importance of fully and clearly specifying one's methods. Examples of individual approaches may be found in the literature citations, and most workers in the field are quite willing to advise the newcomer. In addition to various individuals, at least two institutional research groups are repositories of substantial amounts of relevant experience and technique: these are the Laboratory of Tree Ring Research at the University of Arizona, Tucson, Arizona, USA, and the group of Professor S. K. Runcorn in the School of Physics, University of Newcastle upon Tyne, England.

CONCLUSIONS

The application of growth pattern and chronological studies to contemporary coral reef organisms and systems is a young, diverse and rapidly growing field. Although many organisms have potential for growth-pattern-study applications, corals and molluscs are the only general groups for which a substantial amount of initial work has been done.

Uncertainties in growth chronologies and environmental correlations remain high, and a careful, conservative approach is essential. However, growth patterns can be used to establish general growth rates, age-size population classifications, to study morphological development, and to look for

568

evidence of environmental growth controls. For those few environments and classes of organisms with adequately validated data bases it is becoming possible to establish detailed chronologies and mechanistic links between environment and organism response.

Coral reef growth-pattern studies represent a relatively new offshoot of several interdisciplinary fields; those who enter the field should keep in mind the obligation and opportunity to interact with and to make their work available and useful to the widest possible range of relevant disciplines.

ACKNOWLEDGEMENT

This paper is Hawaii Institute of Geophysics contribution No. 799.

References

BAGENAL, T. B. (ed.). 1974. *The aging of fish*. Old Woking, Surrey, England, Unwin (234 p.).

BARNARD, L. A.; MACINTYRE, I. G.; PIERCE, J. W. 1974. Possible environmental index in tropical reef corals. *Nature* Lond., vol. 252, p. 219–20.

BARNES, D. J. 1970. Coral skeletons: an explanation of their growth and structure. *Science*, vol. 170, p. 1305–08.

——. 1972. The structure and formation of growth ridges in Scleractinian coral skeletons. *Proc. R. Soc. Lond.* (*B: Biol. Soc.*), vol. 182, p. 331–50.

BONHAM, K. 1965. Growth rate of giant clam *Tridacna gigas* at Bikini Atoll as revealed by radio-autography. *Science*, vol. 149, p. 300–2.

BOSELLINI, A.; GINSBURG, R. N. 1971. Form and internal structure of recent algal nodules (Rhodo-lites) from Bermuda. *J. Geol.*, vol. 79, p. 669–82.

BUDDEMEIER, R. W. 1974. Environmental controls over annual and lunar monthly cycles in herma-typic coral calcification. In: *Proc. Second Int. Coral Reef Symp.*, Brisbane, Great Barrier Reef Committee, vol. 2, p. 259–67.

——; MARAGOS, J. E.; KNUTSON, D. W. 1974. Radiographic studies of reef coral exoskeletons: rates and patterns of coral growth. *J. exp. mar. Biol. and Ecol.*, vol. 14, p. 179–200.

——; KINZIE, R. A., III. 1975. The chronometric reliability of contemporary corals. In: G. D. Rosenberg and S. K. Runcorn (eds). *Growth rhythms and history of the earth's rotation*. London, John Wiley, p. 135–48.

CHAVE, K. E.; WHEELER, B. D., JR. 1965. Mineralogic changes during growth in the red alga, *Clathomorphum compactum*. *Science*, vol. 147, no. 3658, p. 621.

CLARK, G. R., II. 1974. Growth lines in invertebrate skeletons. *Ann. Rev. earth Plan. Sci.*, vol. 2, p. 77–99.

——. 1975. Periodic growth and biological rhythms in experimentally grown bivalves. In: G. D. Rosenberg and S. K. Runcorn (eds). *Growth rhythms and history of the earth's rotation*. London, John Wiley, p. 103–18.

COSSLETT, V. E. 1956. Comparison of the practical limits of x-ray and electron microscopy. In: *Proc. 3rd Int. Conf. on Electron Microscopy*. London, Roy. Microscop. Soc., p. 311–7.

DODGE, R. E.; THOMSON, J. 1974. The natural radiochemical and growth records in contemporary hermatypic corals from the Atlantic and Caribbean. *Earth Plan. Sci. Lett.*, vol. 23, p. 313–22.

DOLMAN, J. 1975. A technique for the extraction of environmental and geophysical information from growth records in invertebrates and stromatolites. In: G. D. Rosenberg and S. K. Runcorn (eds). *Growth rhythms and history of the earth's rotation*. London, John Wiley, p. 191–222.

DUFF, P. McL. D.; HALLAM, A.; WALTON, E. K. 1967. *Cyclic Sedimentation*. New York, Elsevier.

EASTMAN KODAK CO. 1969. *Radiography in Modern Industry*, 3rd edit. Rochester, N.Y. (166 p. and supplements).

569

EVANS, J. W. 1975. Growth and micromorphology of two bivalves exhibiting non-daily growth lines. In: G. D. Rosenberg and S. K. Runcorn (eds). *Growth rhythms and history of the earth's rotation.* London, John Wiley, p. 119–34.

FERGUSON, C. W. 1970. Concepts and techniques of dendrochronology. In: R. Berger (ed.). *Scientific methods in medieval archaeology.* Los Angeles, University of California Press, p. 183–200.

FRIEDMAN, G. M. 1971. Staining. In: R. E. Carver (ed.). *Procedures in sedimentary petrology.* New York, Wiley-Interscience, Chap. 22.

FRITTS, H. C. 1971. Dendroclimatology and dendroecology. *Quaternary Research,* vol. 1, p. 419–49.

GLYNN, P. W. 1974. Rolling stones among the Scleractinia: mobile corallith communities in the Gulf of Panama. In: *Proc. Second Int. Coral Reef Symp.,* Brisbane, Great Barrier Reef Committee, vol. 2, p. 183–98.

GRIGG, R. W. 1974. Growth rings: annual periodicity in two Gorgonian corals. *Ecology,* vol. 55, no. 4, p 876–81.

HALL, C. A., JR.; DOLLASE, W. A.; CORBATO, C. E. 1974. Shell growth in *Tivela stultorum* (Mawe, 1823) and *Callista chione* (Linnaeus, 1758) (Bivalvia): annual periodicity, latitudinal differences, and diminution with age. *Palaeogeography, Palaeoclimatology, Palaeoecology,* vol. 15, p. 33–61.

HAMBLIN, W. K. 1971. X-ray photography. In: R. E. Carver (ed.). *Procedures in sedimentary petrology.* New York, Wiley-Interscience, Chap. 11.

IRELAND, H. A. 1971. Preparation of thin-sections. In: R. E. Carver (ed.). *Procedures in sedimentary petrology.* New York, Wiley-Interscience, Chap. 15.

JELL, J. S. 1974. The microstructure of some scleractinian corals. In: *Proc. Second Int. Coral Reef Symp.,* Brisbane, Great Barrier Reef Committee, vol. 2, p. 301–20.

JENSEN, M. 1969. Age determination of echinoids. *Sarsia,* vol. 37, p. 41–4.

KLEIN, G. DE V. 1971. Peels and impressions. In: R. E. Carver (ed.). *Procedures in sedimentary petrology.* New York, Wiley-Interscience, Chap. 10.

KNUTSON, D. W.; BUDDEMEIER, R. W.; SMITH, S. V. 1972. Coral chronometers: seasonal growth bands in reef corals. *Science,* vol. 177, p. 270–2.

——; BUDDEMEIER, R. W. 1973. Distribution of radionuclides in reef corals: opportunity for data retrieval and study of effects. In: *Radioactive contamination of the marine environment.* Vienna, International Atomic Energy Agency, p. 735–46.

KRINITZSKY, E. L. 1970. *Radiography in the earth sciences and soil mechanics.* New York, Plenum Press (163 p.).

KRINSLEY, D. H.; MARGOLIS, S. V. 1971. Grain surface texture. In: R. E. Carver (ed.). *Procedures in sedimentary petrology.* New York, Wiley-Interscience, Chap. 8.

LUCE, G. G. 1971. *Biological rhythms in human animal physiology.* New York, Dover Publications. (183 p.).

MACINTYRE, I. G.; SMITH, S. V. 1974. X-radiographic studies of skeletal development in coral colonies. In: *Proc. Second Int. Coral Reef Symp.* Brisbane, Great Barrier Reef Committee, vol. 2, p. 277–87.

MOORE, W. S.; KRISHNASWAMI, S. 1974. Correlation of x-radiography revealed banding in corals with radiometric growth rates. In: *Proc. Second Int. Coral Reef Symp.* Brisbane, Great Barrier Reef Committee, vol. 2, p. 269–76.

NEVILLE, A. C. 1967. Daily growth layers in animals and plants. *Biol. Rev.,* vol. 42, p. 421–41.

NOSHKIN, V. E.; WONG, K. M.; EAGLE, R. J.; GATROUSIS, C. 1975. Transuranics and other radionuclides in Bikini Lagoon: concentration data retrieved from aged coral sections: *Limnol. Oceanogr.,* vol. 20, p. 729–72.

PALMER, J. D. 1973. Tidal rhythms: the clock control of the rhythmic physiology of marine organisms. *Biol. Rev.,* vol. 48, p. 377–418.

PANNELLA, G. 1972. Paleontological evidence of the Earth's rotational history since early Precambrian. *Astrophysics and Space Science,* vol. 16, p. 212–37.

——. 1975. Palaeontological clocks and the history of the Earth's rotation. In: G. D. Rosenberg and S. K. Runcorn (eds). *Growth rhythms and history of the earth's rotation.* London, John Wiley, p. 253–84.

PEARSE, J. S.; PEARSE, V. B. 1975. Growth zones in the echinoid skeleton. *Am. Zool.,* vol. 15, p. 731–53.

ROSENBERG, G. D.; JONES, C. B. 1975. Approaches to chemical periodicities in molluscs and stromatolites. In: G. D. Rosenberg and S. K. Runcorn (eds). *Growth rhythms and history of the earth's rotation.* London, John Wiley, p. 223–42.

SCRUTTON, C. T.; HIPKIN, R. G. 1973. Long-term changes in the rotation of the Earth. *Earth-Science Rev.,* vol. 9, p. 259–74.

SHINN, E. A. 1972. *Coral reef recovery in Florida and the Persian Gulf.* Houston, Shell Oil Company.

STANLEY, D. J. 1971. Sample impregnation. In: R. E. Carver (ed.). *Procedures in sedimentary petrology.* New York, Wiley-Interscience, Chap. 9.

STOKES, M. A.; SMILEY, T. L. 1968. *An introduction to tree-ring dating.* Univ. Chicago Press (73 p.).

SUMICH, J. L.; MCCAULEY, J. E. 1973. Growth of a sea urchin, *Allocentrotus fragilis,* off the Oregon coast. *Pac. Sci.,* vol. 27, p. 156–67.

TERMIER, H.; TERMIER, G. 1975. Sedimentary behaviour and skeletal textures available in growth cycles analysis. In: G. D. Rosenberg and S. K. Runcorn (eds). *Growth rhythms and history of the earth's rotation.* London, John Wiley, p. 89–102.

WEBER, J. N.; DEINES, P.; WHITE, E. W.; WEBER, P. H. 1975. Seasonal high and low density bands in reef coral skeletons. *Nature,* Lond. vol. 255, p. 697.

WHYTE, M. A. 1975. Time, tide and the cockle. In: G. D. Rosenberg and S. K. Runcorn (eds). *Growth rhythms and history of the earth's rotation.* London, John Wiley, p. 177–90.

Author citation index

Page numbers relate to the lists of references at the end of each chapter; italic numbers refer to authors or editors not printed first in the citation.

Aaronson, S. 437
Abe, N. 228
Abel, E. F. 342
Aberdeen, J. E. C. 215
Adams, W. 42
Adey, W. H. 52
Afghan, B. K. 419
Agassiz, A. 13
Ahlstrom, E. H. 512
Alberts, J. *xiv*, *360*, *419*, *430*, *468*, *495*
Aldridge, A. L. 512
Alevizon, W. S. 342, *342*
Allen, J. C. *294*
American Public Health Association, 376, 520
American Society of Photogrammetry, 42
Amouroux, J. M. 293
Anderson, D. H. 483
Anderson, D. T. *514*
Anderson, G. C. *513*
Anderson, K. L. 215
Andrews, J. D. 541
Anson, A. *52*
Aplin, J. A. 342
Armstrong, A. J. *419*
Armstrong, F. A. J. 419
Arnold, R. *43*
Ashby, W. C. 215
Atlas, E. L. 419
Austin, T. S. *360*, *376*, *395*, *468*
Avidor, A. *342*
Avron, M. 495

Badgeley, P. C. 42
Bagenal, T. B. 569
Bailey, A. *148*
Baissac, J. de B. 146
Bak, R. P. M. 541
Baker, J. R. 228
Bakus, G. J. 146

Ballantine, W. J. 146
Bancroft, K. 437, *437*
Bannert, D. 42
Banoub, M. W. 410
Bardach, J. E. 342
Barlow, G. W. 342
Barnard, L. A. 569
Barnes, D. J. 526, 569
Barnes, H. 512
Barnes, J. 13, 215
Barnett, P. R. 293
Bates, R. G. 483
Bathen, K. W. 360
Bathurst, R. G. C. 65
Battistini, R. 13, *295*
Bauer, H. L. 215
Beard, D. C. 293
Beardsley, A. J. 343
Beers, J. R. 513
Bell, G. R. 342
Bellamy, D. J. *13*, 215
Bennett, I. *148*, *229*, *297*
Bennett, S. *527*
Benson, A. A. 495
Ben-Tuvia, A. *342*
Ben Yaakov, S. 483
Berger, R. *570*
Berman, H. *550*
Berthois, L. *43*, *295*
Betzer, S. *xiv*, *360*, *419*, *468*, *496*
Betzer, S. B. *423*, *496*
Beyers, R. J. 393, 483
Bien, G. 90
Bilham, R. G. 107
Biological Methods Panel Committee on Oceanography, 512
Birkett, L. 260
Bishop, D. W. *512*
Black, S. A. 80
Blackith, R. E. 215
Blanc, F. 293

Blanchard, R. L. *91*
Blasco, F. *495*
Bliss, C. I. 393
Bloom, A. L. 90
Boardman, R. S. *312*
Bodechtel, J. 42
Boden, B. P. 512
Böhlke, J. E. *313*
Böhlen, P. *419*
Böhm, E. L. 483
Bond, G. 13
Bonham, K. 569
Boon, J. D. III. 65
Booth, C. R. *437*
Borojević R. 312
Boschma, H. 520
Bossellini, A. 569
Bossy, C. *297*
Boudouresque, C. F. 293
Bourrouilh, F. *13*
Bowman, T. E. *512*, *521*
Bradley, J. S. *229*
Braithwaite, C. J. R. 13, 65
Brakel, W. 393
Brand, R. H. *215*
Brander, K. M. *107*, 260, 326
Brandt, K. 393
Braun Blanquet, J. 137, 173, 195, 215, 293
Breed, R. S. 437
Brett, C. F. 293
Brien, P. 312
Brock, V. E. 342
Broecker, W. S. 90, *90*, *91*, 404, 467
Brooks, M. G. *342*
Buckman, N. S. 342, *344*
Buddemeier, R. W. 550, *550*, 569, *570*
Buhaut, J. *52*
Burger, H. 65
Burke, K. *14*

573

[B80] SC.76/XVIII–5/A